STRATEGIC NEWSPAPER MANAGEMENT

Conrad C. Fink
University of Georgia

Allyn and Bacon
Boston • London • Toronto • Sydney • Tokyo • Singapore

Vice President: Joseph Opiela
Editorial Assistant: Susannah Davidson
Marketing Manager: Karon Bowers
Production Administrator: Susan McIntyre
Editorial-Production Service: Ruttle, Shaw & Wetherill Inc.
Cover Administrator: Suzanne Harbison
Composition Buyer: Linda Cox

Copyright © 1996 by Allyn & Bacon
A Simon & Schuster Company
Needham Heights, Mass. 02194

Library of Congress Cataloging-in-Publication Data

Fink, Conrad C.
    Strategic newspaper management / Conrad Fink.
        p.   cm.
    Includes bibliographical references and index.
    ISBN 0-02-337731-3
    1. Newspaper publishing—Management.   I. Title.
PN4734.F54   1996
070.5'068—dc20   95-7144
                                                                              CIP

⟡ Printed in the United States of America

10   9   8   7   6   5   4   3   2   1   00   99   98   97   96   95

*This book is dedicated to
William S. Morris III and his family team,
great supporters of journalism education
at the University of Georgia.*

CONTENTS

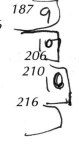

PREFACE

Let's tackle, right away, questions probably troubling you as you begin study of "Strategic Newspaper Management":

- Is the newspaper a dinosaur, a giant—but doomed—relic of the past?
- Can the newspaper, still putting ink on paper, as Gutenberg did in the 1400s, offer you an exciting and meaningful career, or is the future in razzle-dazzle space-age communications technology?
- And, anyway, isn't management something for accounting students and people in $800 suits, not for journalists?

Believe it: The newspaper industry is enormously strong, innovative in many ways and a proven survivor of many competitive fights. Newspapers today fulfill (better than any other single medium) an extremely important societal role—providing the news and information each day, in detail and within a context of analysis and interpretation, that our decision-making public must have if democracy is to function properly. And, through the advertising they carry, newspapers create a commercial marketplace that's vital to buyers and sellers driving America's free-enterprise economy.

However, newspapers confront hugely complex problems. If they aren't solved, chances are newspapers won't prosper in a rapidly changing media world that's attracting a growing list of powerful competitors. Of course, therein lies your career opportunity.

PLANNING A NEWSPAPER CAREER

You can become a hot career prospect in this multibillion-dollar industry if (a) you develop a strategic overview of how the newspaper should be managed in years ahead and if (b) you start building an effective managerial style now that you can use one day as an executive in the newsroom or other departments of a newspaper. Basic understanding of newspaper strategy and management, combined with a sound general education *and* strong journalistic training, will position you not only to compete against accountants in $800 suits, but to enter the career competition with distinct advantages.

The newspaper industry deals principally, of course, in news, information and advertising. But it is a multifaceted industry needing talented young people who understand research methods, manufacturing (we print about 60 million copies daily), distribution (circulation and marketing careers are booming), technology and more.

But, are journalism students candidates for management? Yes. In fact, I think many are strong long-term candidates for major roles in management because they generally are attracted initially to newspapers by respect for—love for—news, and news is the soul of a newspaper. But understanding news isn't enough. Your generation of business and newsroom managers will need to juggle technological and financial complexities amid rapid shifts in the marketplace and changes among media competitors—all while serving readers, advertisers and society efficiently, profitably and responsibly.

Whether you aim for management in news, circulation, advertising or the publisher's office, you'll need a wide "horizontal" view—a vision of the total newspaper, its marketplace, its competitors and its societal responsibilities. You'll also need deep "vertical" skills—intimate understanding of a specialty such as newsroom management or marketing.

FIVE THINGS TO REMEMBER

This book will help you move forward in both horizontal and vertical dimensions, if you keep the following points in mind.

First, remember the old wisecrack about why railroads failed: Their managers thought they were in the railroad business, not transportation. This book introduces you to the news and information business and the advertising business. Whether those businesses are conducted in the future solely on newsprint or, in part, via interactive electronic systems linking homes or through some other still undreamed of marvel should be irrelevant. Your generation of managers likely *will* use newsprint and the newspaper likely *will* be the core business of many diversified media companies. But don't get wedded to newsprint (as those railroad people got wedded to trains). As the wags put it, our business isn't to kill trees. Principles you'll study in this book are applicable to *any* technology for serving readers, advertisers and community.

Second, newspapers must have higher ideals than making money, responsibilities beyond keeping shareholders happy. But newspapers *are* businesses. Profit is *not* a dirty word. Out-of-business newspapers can't defend the people's right to know. Just ask journalists who worked for the *Washington Star, Philadelphia Bulletin,*

New York Herald Tribune and other once-great (but now dead) newspapers. Those newspapers failed not for lack of strong news content or readers but, rather, for lack of advertising revenue and sound business strategies.

Third, a manager's task is to build, inspire and lead an integrated management team drawn from *all* departments, including news. The business as well as journalistic success of a newspaper is the responsibility of all who work for it, not just its publisher or business manager. Some of your predecessors in the newsrooms of the *Star, Bulletin* and *Herald Tribune* didn't believe it: The news and business departments of a newspaper are inseparable. They're also too complex for one individual to manage alone. To succeed in newspaper management you must build an effective management team and delegate responsibility.

Fourth, this book won't make you into a publisher or executive editor overnight. No book can. So, treat *Strategic Newspaper Management* as a friendly helping hand for your first step—the first of many you must make—toward understanding the totality of newspaper management.

Fifth, don't let "management" frighten you. There's no mystery about it—or about what you will study in this book: effective long-range planning techniques you can use to identify opportunities and avoid problems, and daily procedures necessary for efficient operations. Don't search pages ahead for insights into accounting, financial planning or other "countinghouse" esoterica. Business school texts give you that. But what's ahead *will* let you taste the adventure and rewards of newspaper strategy—and help you prepare for an entry-level job, in the newsroom or elsewhere, while opening the option of one day becoming a manager.

ORGANIZATION OF THIS BOOK

This text provides a detailed look at the necessary foundations for studying newspaper management—where the industry is today and what makes a newspaper's market.

Throughout, I have included case studies illustrating principal concepts that must be mastered in each chapter. Some cases continue from chapter to chapter, illustrating how newspaper managers wrestle with strategic challenges that span all operational sectors discussed in this book. Also included are "Standards to Plan By," reflecting industry norms for most newspaper departments.

The text provides a broad view of newspapers' competitors, including the new electronic media. The view is primarily of *concepts* behind experiments in electronic newspapers and by-pass technology, rather than a detailed discussion of operational methods. It's much too early to say which technology or company will emerge strongest, so there is no "scorecard" on who is ahead as of this writing. Some futurists are beginning to doubt newsprint will be shoved aside soon, if ever, as a medium of news and information, but all major newspaper companies have elaborate experiments under way in electronic newspapers. You can find the *New York Times* on America Online, the *Washington Post* on AT&T's Interchange on-line service and the *Los Angeles Times* (under the name TimesLink) on Prodigy. *The Wall*

Street Journal offers a limited edition called Personal Journal via a search-and-retrieval system marketed by its parent company, Dow Jones.

With the electronic future so unsettled, *Strategic Newspaper Management* strives to equip prospective newspaper managers to exploit the new technology as a companion medium to newsprint. Based on current evidence, I believe the newspaper will be the core business of many companies that also use electronic and other media to distribute news and information and advertising. If that doesn't happen, future managers of newspapers must be positioned to compete against the electronic media in the commercial marketplace, and helping readers prepare for this is another goal of *Strategic Newspaper Management.*

Whatever the precise shape of the technological future, it appears that putting ink on newsprint—yes, much as Gutenberg did in the 1400s—will continue to be a major part of that future. The nearly 60 million Americans who buy daily newspapers and the 56 million who buy weeklies seem to agree.

Conrad C. Fink
Athens, Georgia

PART I

THE FOUNDATION

To succeed in newspaper strategy, as in love or war, you must understand three things before the contest begins:

1. Understand yourself, your strengths, your weaknesses.
2. Understand the battleground where the struggle will take place.
3. Understand your competitors and their strengths and weaknesses.

Those three factors are at the core of a preplanning process that should precede any decision you make in newspaper strategy or operations. When you meet challenge or opportunity in the future, silently repeat it as a "manager's mantra": Do I thoroughly understand my own newspaper, my market, my competitors?

Your study of newspaper strategy begins by laying the foundations with three chapters on the newspaper industry, its marketplace battleground and its competitors.

Chapter 1, "Understanding Your Industry," outlines the industry's strengths and weaknesses and its current status. On balance and despite severe problems, the industry is strong.

Chapter 2, "Understanding Your Market," describes the free-enterprise marketplace where you'll struggle for your newspaper's lifeblood—reader time and advertiser dollars. Understanding what the marketplace wants and needs is key to your success.

Chapter 3, "Understanding Your Competitors," covers the strengths and weaknesses of those who will fight you for reader time and advertiser dollars. Your competitors are many; their numbers—and strengths—will increase.

1

UNDERSTANDING YOUR INDUSTRY

The U.S. newspaper industry stands strongly positioned for the 21st century. Witness: Despite dramatic (at times, *traumatic*) changes in societal attitudes and the competitive marketplace, the newspaper is the leading medium of news, information and advertising in the country. Nearly 60 million copies of newspapers are sold daily. Circulation of weekly newspapers tops 55 million. Newspaper ad revenue is the largest single slice of the advertising pie. To emerge that strong in both the news and commercial marketplaces after decades of challenge shows that the newspaper industry has tremendous resilience and ability to adjust to change.

To put that in proper perspective, reflect on how poorly some other U.S. industries weathered socioeconomic change since 1950: steel, autos, shipbuilding—all are virtually dominated by foreign firms or scrambling in fundamental (and agonizing) reorganization simply to survive. Of course, newspaper success yesterday doesn't ensure success tomorrow. And there is much bad news mixed with the good news as the industry—and you and I—look ahead. This chapter will take a balanced view of all that.

THE NUMBERS: GOOD AND BAD

The newspaper industry's numbers look extremely strong if you quickly—superficially—view what's happened since 1950, a benchmark year when television emerged as a viable competitor (and about the time I first heard newspapers were doomed dinosaurs).

High points:

- Despite wrenching change in marketplace and competition since 1950, the total number of daily newspapers published in the United States is down just a couple hundred.

- Total daily circulation is up handsomely, from 53.8 million in 1950 to nearly 60 million. On Sunday, the single most profitable day for many newspapers, circulation is well over 62 million, up from 46.5 million.
- Advertising revenue, which is 75 to 80 percent of most newspapers' total revenue, is up enormously—from $2 billion in 1950 to well over $31 billion.

However, behind the glowing numbers are serious problems:

- Despite circulation increases, the percentage of Americans reading newspapers is dropping and the percentage of American households subscribing to newspapers is the lowest in history. This is the "silent crisis" of the U.S. newspaper: Advertisers demand deeper "penetration" of households than many newspapers deliver.
- Though newspapers are—and always were—the largest single advertising medium, the ad dollar is increasingly being fragmented by a host of competitors. Ad revenue is growing at a faster rate for television and other serious competitors, and dollars newspapers once counted on almost automatically are being divided among a large number of advertising media.
- Competing media are developing target marketing capabilities desired by advertisers. Direct mail, the nation's fastest-growing ad medium, can deliver advertiser messages to narrowly focused audiences—all physicians (but not dentists) in a county, wine (not beer) drinkers. Magazines tailor content to target niche audiences; radio targets through programming (Cadillac dealers advertise on "golden oldies" music programs; retailers reach teenagers through rock music programs). Newspapers, broadly based in content, have difficulty meeting advertisers' demand for target marketing.
- Many well-financed competitors, including telephone companies, are working on "bypass technology"—what they hope will be attractive, low-cost electronic methods of end running newspapers. The goal is to deliver at least some news (and lots of advertising), as well as entertainment and other services, directly to homes, not through newspapers.

In those four concepts—penetration, market fragmentation, target marketing and bypass technology—lie the principal dangers facing newspapers.

So you have arrived on the scene, with your interest in newspaper management strategy, as a fascinating new era opens. To understand what's ahead, let's look more closely at the numbers.

Number of Papers: Down Slightly

The total number of morning and evening (or afternoon) newspapers has dropped just a couple hundred since 1950. The number of Sunday papers has increased enormously.

On the surface, the stability reflected in the numbers in Table 1.1 looks good.[1] After all, the period since 1950 has been one of dramatic change in the media world, but the numbers require closer examination.

TABLE 1.1   Number of Daily Newspapers

Year	Morning	Evening	Total M&E	Sunday
1950	322	1,450	1,772	549
1960	312	1,459	1,763	563
1970	334	1,429	1,748	586
1980	387	1,388	1,745	735
1985	482	1,220	1,676	798
1986	499	1,188	1,657	802
1987	511	1,166	1,645	820
1988	529	1,141	1,642	840
1989	530	1,125	1,626	847
1990	559	1,084	1,611	863
1991	571	1,042	1,586	874
1992	596	994	1,570	893
1993	621	956	1,556	889

Note, for example, that Table 1.1 shows the number of morning and Sunday papers is up substantially but there are fewer evening papers. A few things about this are crucial to your understanding of newspaper strategy.

IMPACT OF LIFESTYLE

Lifestyles—how people think, eat, dress, work and amuse themselves—have enormous impact on newspapers (and how you should manage one). An example is how changing lifestyles contributed to a weakening of afternoon papers relative to morning and Sunday papers.

In times bygone, when the U.S. economy was based on "smokestack" industries, such as steel and autos, there was little time for reading newspapers at breakfast. "Blue-collar" workers were in factories, farm fields and mines early each day, sometimes before dawn. However, day shifts ended at about 3 to 4 P.M., and afternoon papers became fixtures in many households throughout America, providing relaxation and entertainment, as well as news.

Today, the U.S. economy is principally "white collar," and sons and daughters of yesteryear's factory workers are computer programmers or perhaps work in sales or administration. Many work for multinational corporations with global operations. To keep pace in today's highly competitive global marketplace, white-collar workers must know, at the *start* of each workday, by about 9 A.M., what happened during the night that might affect their job performance over the next eight hours. And, what happened can be important regardless of where it happened—down the street, in Washington, or in London, Tokyo or other faraway places.

The morning newspaper, then, is important as a "news fix" full of "hard" information—what Japan's prime minister said about foreign trade, how the Zurich stock market performed, where the newest war broke out (and, importantly, how the reader's favorite sports team made out in last night's game). Morning papers have the first opportunity to print most news stories that break during the day and evening, because they go to press at midnight or later. Distribution is over relatively empty predawn streets for an optimum delivery time of about 6 A.M. in driveways and roadside tubes—in plenty of time to give readers a fresh update over breakfast.

For afternoon papers, optimum delivery time is about 4 P.M. That means delivery trucks must struggle through streets clogged with traffic. That, in turn, requires press times of noon or so—and copy deadlines of 10:30 A.M. or earlier. Because not much fresh news breaks in many communities by midmorning, afternoon papers tend to be "soft" and featurish, heavy with columns, analysis and updates of stories that first appeared in morning papers.

But, why must afternoon papers be delivered by 4 P.M. and thus squeezed for time to develop hard news stories during the day?

IMPACT OF TELEVISION

Picture a white-collar IBM programmer or General Motors marketing executive at day's end: home by 5 to 6 P.M., dinner at 6:30 to 7 P.M., or thereabouts. Then what? *Television.*

Television's entertainment draw is phenomenal. Tens of millions of people tune in sitcoms and comedy shows. For afternoon papers, therefore, the "window of opportunity" for catching readers is somewhere between 4 P.M., for the first to arrive home, and perhaps 7 P.M., when television is turned on. For afternoon papers, analysis and commentary on serious news events can be a hard sell with "couch potatoes" drawn to the glitzy color and motion of TV entertainment.

And, of course, for those TV viewers who *are* interested in news, television's nightly news shows at least briefly update or advance afternoon newspapers' stories (which, remember, were written hours earlier, by about 10:30 A.M.). Even some long-time newspaper readers, feeling "time-starved" by their hectic lifestyles, drop the seven-day paper, watch TV news sporadically and "catch up" on the world by reading Sunday papers. This explains the growth of Sunday papers—and their increasing importance to advertisers anxious to catch modern fast-track consumers on the one day they settle back to read. Millions of Sunday-only readers and other millions of Americans who don't read newspapers at all (or much of anything else) perceive themselves as "informed" if they catch a bit of TV news now and then.

You may scoff that people cannot trust the scant offerings of TV news to keep them atop today's fast-changing world. Nevertheless, this is a widely held perception, and your newspaper strategies must deal with audience perceptions as well as realities, as you and other professional newspaper journalists define them. Plain fact: Even journalistically outstanding newspapers suffer from marketplace perceptions that they aren't crucial, that a few effortless minutes of watching television will suffice.

But why, then, didn't the newspaper simply vanish? Why, as Table 1.1 illustrates, did the number of newspapers drop just a few hundred after 1950, during the decades of most intense competition from television? It's because newspaper editors generally adjusted quite well to television: Newspapers learned to concentrate heavily on local news, important to millions of Americans and not covered nearly as well by television or any other medium. Newspapers switched reporting and writing styles to explain the news, to reveal not simply what happened but also why and how and its meaning. No other daily medium, including television, can do this as well. And, to their surprise, editors found readers hungry for newspaper analysis and commentaries on sports and other news stories already shown on television.

Still, the U.S. population grew from 151 million in 1950 to over 240 million today. If editors adapted so well to television, why, then, didn't the number of newspapers also grow?

IMPACT OF NEWSPAPER ECONOMICS

Complexities of newspaper economics help explain the seeming contradiction—U.S. population is up but the number of newspapers is down. These complexities will be discussed later in detail. For now, note these factors:

- Newspapers are high-cost enterprises. They are people-intensive—and people are expensive, accounting for 45 to 50 percent or more of most newspapers' total costs. Also, newspapers use an extraordinarily expensive raw material, newsprint. Television, radio and direct mail have lower costs and therefore often can undercut newspaper advertising rates. And, advertising, again, provides 75 to 80 percent of total newspaper revenue.
- The U.S. retail industry, on which all advertising-supported media depend heavily, is undergoing radical change. Upscale department stores, long a major source of newspaper ad revenue, are giving way to Wal-Mart, Sam's Club and other discount stores that prefer to advertise through direct mail or free circulars—or, indeed, that don't advertise at all.
- Socioeconomic deterioration in the core of many cities drives affluent residents to the suburbs and beyond. In cities large or small, many residents who stay behind are less affluent and thus less attractive to advertisers.

In sum, many newspapers face (a) soaring costs, (b) increased competition for ad revenue from a changing retail industry and (c) weakening economic base in their home cities. As a result, only a handful of cities today have two or more competing dailies of like size and characteristics; in recent memory, some cities lost three or more once-vigorous newspapers.

Another economic reality contributed to the death of newspapers in cities that once supported many: Because of soaring costs, newspapers must broaden their news and editorial positions to gain wide market support. Newspapers can no longer find sufficient reader or advertiser support if they identify themselves—as many once did—as special-interest niche publications, serving labor, perhaps, or appealing to conservative groups. Today, it's move toward broadly based centrist positions appealing to readers and advertisers of all persuasions or die. And, there is room at the center for only one newspaper. Advertisers simply won't support more.

The *Chicago Tribune,* once a fortress of Midwestern right-wing conservatism, successfully moved toward the center and today enjoys widespread support from many types of readers, not only conservatives. *USA Today,* launched in 1982, promotes itself as a centrist "world of different voices" and is noted for its "on-the-one-hand-but-also-on-the-other" editorials. The *Cleveland Press,* once a famed "blue-collar" labor paper, went out of business, as did many papers whose managers would not—or could not—shift them out of their narrowly focused partisan stances. Let's look for further clues about the newspaper industry's structure in Table 1.2.[2]

As Table 1.2 illustrates, most daily newspapers have a circulation of less than 50,000. These papers are published primarily in relatively small cities and stress local news. However, note that the under-50,000 category is shrinking, and larger dailies are showing significant growth. In 1950, 11.3 percent of all dailies were over 50,000; by 1992, 15.6 percent were. Most of the larger papers are not newly established but are former weeklies or small dailies that grew rapidly when their suburban or small-town markets increased with an influx of affluent residents fleeing nearby cities.

Newspaper economics, therefore, create a competitive picture of roughly two dimensions: First, only rarely do newspapers of like size compete head-on with each other. Direct newspaper-to-newspaper competition is mainly metro daily vs.

TABLE 1.2   Circulation Size of Dailies

Year	Total	Under 50,000	50,001–100,000	100,001–250,000	Over 250,000
1950	1,772	1,571	82	84	35
1960	1,763	1,540	96	83	44
1970	1,748	1,491	127	92	38
1980	1,745	1,479	145	86	35
1985	1,676	1,418	141	82	35
1987	1,645	1,394	137	75	39
1988	1,642	1,377	143	79	43
1989	1,626	1,362	139	81	44
1990	1,611	1,343	143	82	43
1991	1,586	1,336	129	78	43
1992	1,570	1,323	132	72	43
1993	1,556	1,302	131	74	49

TABLE 1.3   Circulation: Past to Present

Year	Morning	Evening	Total M&E	Sunday
1950	21,266,126	32,562,946	53,829,072	46,582,348
1960	24,028,788	34,852,958	58,881,746	47,698,651
1970	25,933,783	36,173,744	62,107,527	49,216,602
1980	29,414,036	32,787,804	62,201,840	54,671,755
1990	41,308,361	21,015,795	62,324,156	62,634,512
1991	41,469,756	19,217,369	60,687,125	62,067,820
1992	42,306,579	17,776,686	60,083,265	62,542,031
1993	43,053,747	16,761,294	59,815,032	62,643,379

suburban daily. Second, the most crucial competitive fight is between the newspaper, large or small, and all other media in sight—television, radio, direct mail, magazines, you name it. More on competition in Chapter 3.

Circulation Up, Penetration Down

Of all the numbers you must understand about the newspaper industry, circulation numbers are among the trickiest. Let's start by examining what the numbers in Table 1.3 show, at least on the surface.[3]

First, note Table 1.3 shows total morning and evening circulation is up strongly from 53.8 million in 1950 to nearly 60 million in 1993. Sunday circulation growth is even better. Second, evening circulation is down greatly since 1950, reflecting the lifestyle changes, TV competition and newspaper economics we've discussed. Third, morning circulation more than doubled since 1950, also a direct reflection of lifestyle changes. Other factors: Since 1950, many metropolitan papers have developed extensive circulation in suburbs and nearby small towns. Morning metros can reach outlying areas more easily than can afternoon papers. Also, three national morning newspapers have developed since 1950—*USA Today, The Wall Street Journal,* and *The New York Times.* These three alone add over 4 million to morning totals. Table 1.4 on page 10 lists the circulation leaders.[4]

Note in Table 1.4 that all top 20 U.S. papers, as measured by circulation, are morning papers, except for two: *Newsday* and the *Houston Chronicle,* which are "all day"—meaning they publish editions in both the morning and evening "cycles" or "fields."

The papers in Table 1.4 have truly huge circulations—but even greater "reach" and influence because 2.2 persons on average read each copy of a daily sold. The average is higher for Sunday papers, which have high "pass-along" readership (and for weeklies, which have a five- or six-day "shelf life"—meaning they are kept in homes generally until next week's paper arrives and thus are exposed to more readers). However, the numbers in Tables 1.3 and 1.4 hide some harsh realities. The

TABLE 1.4   Average Daily Circulation

The Wall Street Journal	1,780,422 (m)
USA Today	1,465,936 (m)
The New York Times	1,114,905 (m)
Los Angeles Times	1,089,690 (m)
The Washington Post	810,675 (m)
New York Daily News	753,024 (m)
Newsday	693,556 (all day)
Chicago Tribune	678,081 (m)
Detroit Free Press	544,606 (m)
Chicago Sun-Times	518,094 (m)
San Francisco Chronicle	509,548 (m)
The Boston Globe	506,545 (m)
The Dallas Morning News	491,480 (m)
The Philadelphia Inquirer	478,999 (m)
Newark Star-Ledger	455,919 (m)
Houston Chronicle	409,340 (all day)
The Minneapolis Star Tribune	407,504 (m)
New York Post	405,318 (m)
The Cleveland Plain Dealer	394,692 (m)
Miami Herald	380,328 (m)

harshest, simply put, is that newspapers reach lower proportions of total national population and households than in half a century or more. Note:

- In 1950, 124 newspapers were sold per 100 households; today, about 64 papers are sold per 100.
- In 1950, 382 newspapers were sold per 1,000 people in the United States; today, about 250 are sold per 1,000.
- The habit of reading a newspaper every day is weakening among Americans under 20 years of age and in age categories 20 to 29 and 30 to 39.[5]
- Finally, look closely at total daily circulation in Table 1.3. The high point was in 1990 and total morning and evening circulation has slipped considerably since then. The economic recession of the early 1990s caused some slippage, but the question is raised: Is newspaper circulation going to tread water—or drop—while population and number of households increase?

Deep household penetration is demanded by advertisers because they want to reach more than one consumer, the person who bought the newspaper. But, also, advertisers know important "buy" decisions are made in households, not on a street, at coin machines, or in airports or hotels, where many "single-copy" purchases of newspapers are made. Often, the woman of the household makes most buy decisions—and she is reached, either during the day or after her workday, in the home.

The industry's shallow household penetration is reflected in dismal figures for many individual newspapers. For example, the *Los Angeles Times* penetrates only 25.4 percent of households in Los Angeles County with its daily paper, just 31.2 percent on Sundays. The *Chicago Tribune*'s daily penetration is just 23.1 percent in Cook County, its home turf, and 35 percent on Sundays.[6]

All this creates enormous dangers. First, American newspapers overall never have been stronger journalistically than they are today. The *Los Angeles Times* and *Chicago Tribune* are truly great newspapers. Unfortunately superior news content alone won't guarantee circulation and penetration success and, thus, advertising success.

Second, advertisers cannot regard newspapers as truly mass communications media. Discount stores, increasingly important in the overall retail scheme, seek an extremely wide consumer base and try to sell something to virtually all households—not just the 25 percent of homes that newspapers reach in some counties or the 64 percent nationwide. And, advertisers demand deeper penetration than many newspapers achieve among young persons—those who still must buy "big-ticket" items, such as cars, homes and appliances, and whose brand loyalties are yet to be established.

Third, shallow penetration carries sobering societal implications for newspapers. Those reaching only 25 percent of their households—and thus obviously having no relevance for 75 percent—cannot possibly perform their traditional role of education and social uplift. Since Colonial days, our society has granted newspapers preferential treatment—low postal rates, for example—in the assumption that dissemination of news and ideas is essential in a democracy and that newspapers, then the only mass-circulation medium, should be encouraged. Is the newspaper's special niche in society now at risk? Very possibly. But there is more immediate danger.

Advertising: Dollars Up, Confidence Down

Newspapers always have enjoyed the largest single slice of the advertising revenue pie, and that slice is huge—over $31 *billion* annually. But, other media are gaining ground rapidly, and new competitive threats are just over the technological horizon. All that, plus the lifestyle and other changes discussed earlier, makes some newspaper executives worry whether their future will be as prosperous as their past. First, the numbers as shown in Table 1.5 on page 12.[7]

Now the explanation:

- Total spending for all media advertising is enormous—well over $130 billion. But competition is varied and fierce. You'll find newspaper strategists jittery about increasing, in industry lingo, share of market.
- The revenue growth rate for some competing media surpasses that of newspapers. Note particularly the growth enjoyed by television and direct mail. Television, the newspaper industry's largest single competitor, courts advertisers with huge numbers of viewers—tens of millions for some programs. Direct

TABLE 1.5   How Ad Dollars Are Shared

	1992 (millions)	% of Total	1993 (millions)	% of Total	% of Change
Daily Newspapers	$30,639	23.4	$31,906	23.1	4.1
Magazines	7,000	5.3	7,420	5.4	6.0
Television	29,409	22.4	30,600	22.2	4.0
Radio	8,654	6.6	9,390	6.8	8.5
Farm Publications	231	0.2	245	0.2	6.1
Direct Mail	25,391	19.4	27,425	19.9	8.0
Business Publications	3,090	2.4	3,200	2.3	3.6
Outdoor	1,031	0.8	1,020	0.7	−1.1
Yellow Pages	9,320	7.1	9,515	6.9	2.1
Miscellaneous	16,427	12.5	17,125	12.4	4.2
TOTAL—ALL MEDIA	$131,192	100.0	$137,846	100.0	5.1[7]

mail, growing more rapidly than any other medium, appeals with its riflelike ability to target tightly focused groups of consumers desired by advertisers, contrasting with the shotgun pattern of hits scored by newspapers and, certainly, television.

- Classified advertising, well over $11 billion of the newspaper industry's total $31 billion, lends itself nicely to computerized electronic systems envisaged for home delivery as does Yellow Page advertising. That is, the new systems probably challenge newspapers more seriously in advertising than in news, and newspapers that don't alertly participate in the coming technological revolution could well become victims of it.

The Newspaper Counterattack

The newspaper industry's effort to improve its share of reader time and advertiser dollars revolves around four principal tactics. Pending full discussion later, here is a quick look at each.

Improved Product and Service

Newspaper managers got the scare of a lifetime in the 1980s and early 1990s: Once-loyal readers were giving up newspapers; circulation and penetration were leveling off, then dropping. Advertisers were bucking at ever-increasing ad rates (necessary because circulation rates were kept low) and media competitors were showing new strength.

To learn what was going wrong and how to fix it, newspapers launched expensive research into reader needs and wants. Two innovations are striking: First, editors now produce "zoned editions" that break their newspapers' total circulation into smaller editions featuring news tailored for individual segments of readers. For example, if an affluent new suburb develops, editors open a bureau there and present in-depth local news daily or weekly for readers who live there. For advertisers, this targets extremely attractive audience segments *and* permits lower ad rates because advertisers pay for only zoned circulation rather than a newspaper's total circulation. This puts newspaper advertising within reach of a whole new group of advertisers—those who can afford rates based on a circulation of, say, 25,000, but who can't pay for (and don't need) the total circulation scattered across a large metropolitan area. In newspaper parlance, this produces a "lower CPM"— lower cost for reaching 1,000 persons desired by an advertiser.

Second, editors push for overall improvement of the entire newspaper— stressing better reporting and writing, more inviting photos and graphics, and more attractive design and page layout. Most use extensive color (which is expensive and technically difficult to reproduce properly). Strong newspapers today are integrated packages of news, informative graphics and sometimes superb photography.

Editors also strive to make their increasingly bulky newspapers easier to manage, easier to read. Most "internally zone" their newspapers—collecting important news in special sections or "anchoring" specialized news by placing it in the same easy-to-find location each day. Newspapers blossom with "Business Monday" sections or "Science Tuesday." "Weekend" sections cover entertainment news and where to go and how to enjoy yourself. Newspapers thus become a tool for use in daily life.

Alert editors today, then, undertake two broad missions: strengthen the all-encompassing, general news content of the newspaper *and* introduce expertly written specialized news for upscale business executives, professional women, sports buffs and other special-interest groups. Each day's paper must be crucial to readers, not merely nice to have.

Dramatic shifts are under way in newspaper attitudes toward serving advertisers. Most striking: In days bygone, when newspapers nearly monopolized local retail advertising, a common attitude toward advertisers was, "C'mon into our office and we'll sell you space—on our terms, of course." Today, well-run newspapers aggressively court advertisers, presenting themselves as marketing partners and jointly planning campaigns to help sell products and services. Newspapers take impressive consumer research and competitive rates and terms into the fight for ad dollars.

Volume versus Profit Pricing

Newspaper circulation executives practice volume pricing. That is, single copies and subscriptions are priced low in the hopes that that will maintain high circulation numbers. Many magazines employ profit-oriented pricing—raising cover prices to $4, $5 or more, which inhibits circulation growth but guarantees readers will contribute a greater share of total revenue. Readers contribute about 53 percent of the magazine industry's total revenue, compared with 20 to 25 percent to

TABLE 1.6   Single-Copy Prices

Year	5¢	10¢	15¢	20¢	25¢	30¢	35¢	40¢	45¢	50¢	75¢
1965	456	892	3	2	—	—	—	—	—	—	—
1970	46	1,507	139	5	1	—	—	—	—	—	—
1975	4	428	1,153	137	10	1	—	—	—	—	—
1980	—	41	497	644	555	9	7	1	—	—	—
1985	—	5	31	84	1,245	130	169	3	—	4	—
1990	—	2	8	8	656	64	742	17	—	111	1
1991	—	2	4	6	448	34	809	23	4	243	3
1992	—	1	4	6	348	32	779	25	5	352	3
1993	—	—	4	3	267	17	703	28	5	522	2

Source: Newspaper Association of America

newspapers.[8] Note in Table 1.6 that virtually every daily newspaper in the United States will sell you a daily copy for less than the cost of a cup of restaurant coffee over which you read it.

Table 1.6 reveals what can only be called pricing timidity in single-copy prices. Which supermarket item of comparable size, quality and usefulness is priced as low as newspapers? What other industry has held down price increases as the newspaper industry has held down circulation prices? Sunday newspapers are a bit more aggressive in pricing. But, in 1992, 19 still charged only 25 cents; just two boldly charged $1.75.

Bottom line: Pricing timidity reveals lack of confidence that readers consider news and editorial content valuable enough to justify higher prices. By charging $5 per copy, *Forbes* magazine displays confidence that it is crucial to its readers and worth the higher prices. One of the most important challenges for the next generation of newspaper newsroom managers is to get that element of cruciality into the daily newspaper and justify higher prices.

Quality versus Quantity

As circulation and penetration slow, relative to growth in population and households, the "mass circulation" newspaper is losing the "mass" in its appeal to advertisers. Therefore, publishers are shifting to new tactics with advertisers, emphasizing quality of circulation, not quantity. In sum, newspapers sell themselves to advertisers as an upscale, elitist medium that reaches households with demographics (income, education and so forth) and psychographics (lifestyle, spending habits, way of thinking) that make them most attractive to sellers of goods and services.

Says the *Los Angeles Times:* Yes, we reach only 25 percent of the households in Los Angeles County but you can bet they include virtually all those with $50,000 or more annual household income. If you want to sell Cadillacs and diamond rings, goes the sales pitch, use newspapers; sell your razor blades, beer and other

TABLE 1.7   The Affluent Read More

Household Income	Readership	
	Percent Daily	**Percent Sunday**
$60,000 or more	75	81
$50,000 or more	74	81
$40,000 or more	72	79
Less than $40,000	56	61

Readership Increases with Education

	Percent Daily	**Percent Sunday**
College graduate or beyond	74	81
Non-college graduate	60	65

Big Job Equals High Readership

	Percent Daily	**Percent Sunday**
Professional	73	80
Managerial, administrative	72	79
Technical, clerical, sales	67	74
All other employed	58	63

Source: Newspaper Association of America

mass consumption products on television, whose viewers, by contrast, are less affluent and less well educated on average.

Research (such as that in Table 1.7) shows that Americans who are affluent and better educated are readers—of newspapers (and magazines.) Television is the medium choice for less-affluent, less-educated audiences and, therefore, television offers less attractive audience demographics to advertisers.

For students of newspaper management, the meaning behind the figures in Table 1.7 is of compelling importance: First, editors increasingly are constructing "upscale" newspapers with content that attracts the educated affluent. Second, advertising executives sell—successfully—the idea that they can put advertiser messages in the hands of educated, high-income professionals and managers who, simply put, have more to spend and who spend it more willingly than do lower-income, television-watching households.

Is the newspaper becoming an elitist document? Yes.

Lick 'Em or Join 'Em?

U.S. newspaper owners historically misjudged the strengths of new competitors and adopted faulty strategies to fight them. For example, the initial reaction to radio was (believe it or not) to laugh it off as a potential rival for reader time and advertiser dollars. Then, when radio demonstrated strength in the 1930s, the newspaper industry tried to keep it out of the news business. The industry's newspaper-owned news cooperative, The Associated Press, was instructed to deny news services to radio stations, then grudgingly was permitted to provide skeleton service only. (AP today is the leading news service for radio.)

Some smart newspaper owners recognized early that they couldn't wish—or drive—radio away and, further, that buying stations would complement nicely their print offerings for readers and advertisers. Thus were created the first "diversified media conglomerates." However, many in the very next generation of newspaper managers missed the lesson in all that, and tried to fight, rather than join, television, free-circulation or "shopper" publications, and direct-mail services. Today, long after those three forms of competing advertising media are well established, many newspaper companies own TV stations, publish shoppers and offer direct-mail services.

Incredibly, the newspaper industry blindly closed ranks when telephone companies and other firms strong in cable TV or electronic technology signaled in the 1970s and 1980s their interest in offering news and advertising services. The industry's trade association, the American Newspaper Publishers Association (now Newspaper Association of America), lobbied Congress and the public to keep telephone companies out of the information business. The publishers argued that telephone companies were so strong financially that they eventually could force newspapers out of business. Newspapers, which since Colonial times demanded the right to free expression, positioned themselves in public perception as arguing that telephone companies should be denied that right.

No industry in modern times has made a worse strategic error: Newspaper executives somehow decided they could lobby away new competitors and, with them, a new, exciting technology. It was as if horse ranchers and carriage makers had lobbied Congress to keep Henry Ford from building automobiles. For more than a decade, the newspaper industry stuck to its position. Today, embarrassed at appearing to be self-serving, 20th-century Luddites and sensing possibilities in the new technology, many newspaper companies are breaking ranks and making their own deals with telephone and other high-tech companies.

Clearly, the newspaper counterattack will involve your generation of managers in two broad strategies: (a) diversify newspaper-based companies into other (but related) businesses that will reduce dependence on advertising revenue and (b) use the new electronic technology. The exact shape of all that and, particularly, the marketplace demand for the new technology is yet to be determined.

Profits: Down But Still Rewarding

It was a curious contradiction: Once-famous newspapers were going bankrupt in large cities, creating widespread public perception in the 1960s and 1970s that the newspaper was doomed. Meanwhile, quietly and mostly out of public view, many newspapers were enjoying extraordinarily high profit margins.

How high? Newspaper managers, except for a few in competitive metropolitan markets, grew accustomed to operating—or pretax—profits of 20 to 40 percent of revenue. That is, of every $1 in advertising and circulation revenue, 20 cents to 40 cents was cleared after salaries, newsprint costs and other expenses of operating the paper were paid.

Newspaper profit margins often were three or four times those enjoyed by other industries. Even in the early 1990s, when newspapers were hard hit by recession because of a slump in retail advertising, newspaper operating profit margins stayed high—12 to 15 percent for many, and still in the 25 to 30 percent range for some. For comparison: General Motors' was 4.3 to 4.4 percent at that time, Exxon's 5.8 to 9.4 percent.

Though the public wasn't generally aware newspapers could be gold mines, industry insiders were. And quietly, but very quickly, acquisition executives fanned out across the United States in the 1960s and 1970s, buying up independently owned newspapers. In a short time, the family-run newspaper, a tradition in American journalism, virtually disappeared into huge media conglomerates. Today, nearly all daily newspapers of significance are owned by conglomerates. Most conglomerates, in turn, are publicly owned by thousands of shareholders and investment institutions. In total circulation, the largest newspaper owners in the country are shown in Table 1.8 on page 18.

Why the Expansion?

Two principal factors drove expansion of newspaper groups: First, aggressive group managers (some were egocentric empire builders) bought newspapers as a way to improve profits quickly. And, they built strength into their companies by diversifying into different regions of the country, into newspapers of different sizes and into cities with different economic bases.

For example, *New York Times* owners, increasingly concerned about New York City's economic future, bought newspapers in the booming Sun Belt. *Wall Street Journal* owners, vulnerable in their dependence on financial news and business advertising, acquired an entire family-owned group (Ottaway Newspapers) of medium-size community newspapers scattered throughout the country.

Tax laws made it irresponsible to not expand. If newspapers retained—banked—the extraordinary high profits they were generating, special additional, almost punitive, "retained earnings" taxes were levied. However, enormously at-

---

Newspaper Profits Are Down?

"All that is really happening is that instead of being two or three times more profitable than most businesses, newspapers this year are reduced to being only one or two times more profitable."

Newspaper analyst John Morton, revealing that operating profits for 13 publicly owned newspaper companies dropped to an average of 16.5 percent during the recession year 1990.

TABLE 1.8   Who Owns America's Dailies?

	Daily Circulation	Number of Dailies	Sunday Circulation	Number of Sunday Editions
Gannett Co. Inc.	5,843,238	83	6,094,266	67
Knight-Ridder Inc.	3,678,200	28	5,183,032	24
Newhouse Newspapers	2,983,429	26	3,847,953	21
Times Mirror Co.	2,713,742	11	3,427,089	8
The New York Times Co.	2,471,587	25	3,394,598	17
Dow Jones & Co. Inc.	2,377,538	22	528,786	13
Thomson Newspapers Inc.	2,072,649	109	1,910,958	78
Tribune Co.	1,355,630	6	1,995,680	6
Cox Enterprises Inc.	1,312,239	19	1,757,110	17
Scripps Howard	1,300,391	19	1,334,788	12
Hearst Newspapers	1,256,202	12	2,534,492	10
MediaNews Group	1,045,406	17	1,269,523	15
Freedom Newspapers Inc.	943,227	26	1,007,168	19
The Washington Post Co.	865,781	2	1,202,419	2
Central Newspapers	817,853	9	1,011,395	4
McClatchy Newspapers	809,578	12	955,089	9
Stephens Group Inc.	750,945	54	790,726	46
Capital Cities/ABC Inc.	744,291	8	1,002,330	6
Copley Newspapers	738,996	10	774,921	6
The Chronicle Publishing Co.	711,682	4	897,634	3

Circulations for six months ended Sept. 30, 1993. Source: Newspaper Association of America. (Publicly owned groups appear in italics.)

tractive tax breaks were granted any company that reinvested in new businesses and thus presumably created new jobs and business activity. In the heyday of group expansion, some companies could generate 25 cents to 45 cents in tax savings for every $1 spent acquiring newspapers. That explains why companies *bought* newspapers. But why did families *sell* their privately owned newspapers? The second factor driving group expansion was, again, tax law.

In sum, inheritance (estate) taxes in the era of most rapid group expansion often prevented newspaper families from passing their papers to succeeding generations. Inheritance taxes for any type property are levied on fair market value (what a willing buyer will pay a willing seller). This hit newspaper families much harder than families owning farms or gas stations because so many cash-rich media conglomerates were bidding for a limited number of available papers.

The law of (limited) supply and (unlimited) demand sent newspaper fair market values soaring, and with inheritance taxes as high as 63 percent of value, many—indeed most—family newspaper heirs couldn't raise the cash to pay off the Internal Revenue Service. Hundreds of papers were sold to groups for this reason.

(Maximum inheritance tax is now 50 percent, still prohibitively high for families lucky enough to own independent newspapers.)

All this caused a significant turn in U.S. media ownership: Families that owned large newspapers or several media properties saw they could "go public"—sell shares on the open market—and (a) raise money for new equipment, buildings and expansion, or (b) pocket millions of dollars and still retain control of their newspapers.

Thus were born the "publicly owned" media companies that today own nearly all important newspapers. These companies, whose stock is bought and sold on the New York Stock Exchange or other exchanges, generally are staffed heavily by professional, nonfamily managers. But many owning families, including those at *The New York Times* and *The Washington Post,* managed to retain control by issuing two types of stock. Family members held the type that carried major voting rights and the public could buy stock with lesser voting rights.

Should you be concerned over whether the newspaper you work for is privately owned or group owned? Read on.

Profits, Owners and You

As a newspaper manager you occupy a position of trust. You are paid to guard assets owned by others and improve their return on investment (ROI). This is called fiduciary responsibility. You also have a journalistic responsibility to publish accurate, high-quality, ethical journalism, and to serve—fairly and well—your readers, your community. Can these two responsibilities—fiduciary and journalistic—conflict? You bet, because high-quality journalism is expensive and is regarded by some owners as inconsistent with profitability.

All managers are under strong pressure to increase profits. I call it the "rising tide of shareholder expectation"—a demand for ever-improved return on investment that's relentless whether a newspaper is publicly owned or privately held. However, a family that owns a privately held newspaper often has lived for generations in its town and feels a responsibility to ensure the newspaper serves its town well. Shareholders of publicly owned companies usually have no more commitment to newspapers than to any other investment, and often they live far from towns where their company's newspapers are published.

Shareholders of publicly owned companies are *investors*—a widow in Keokuk, Iowa, who invested in newspapers on advice of her broker; a retiree in Boston who hopes to supplement his pension; a mutual fund manager in New York City driven to show his fund's investors greater return. If they own stock in Gannett Co. (traded on the New York Stock Exchange), these investors aren't interested in what's good for far-off Gainesville, Georgia, where Gannett publishes *The Times*. Profit-oriented investors in Michigan or New Mexico who buy New York Times Co. stock (traded on the American Stock Exchange) don't care whether that company produces high-quality journalism for New York City or for Floridians who read small newspapers Times Co. publishes in Florida.

The shareholder desire for profit holds a major challenge for you if you are interested (and I hope you are) in a career in high-quality, responsible journalism. Trying to simultaneously meet your fiduciary and journalistic responsibilities is not easy.

Bluntly, some of the highest profit margins in American journalism are produced by inferior papers whose low-quality content cheats readers and community alike. Conversely, some journalistically great newspapers are only marginally profitable. Indeed, some have folded.

One theme of this book is that long-range profitability depends on journalistic quality, and that methodical research and planning, if linked to intelligent daily operating procedures, can deliver both profit and quality.[9] If you can learn to deliver both you have an exciting, rewarding career ahead.

You and a Newspaper Career

The newspaper industry is one of the nation's largest employers (see Table 1.9).[10]

Two factors are particularly important in Table 1.9: First, total employment peaked in 1990. Reductions since then are due principally to (a) implementation of new technology, such as electronic editing and layout systems, which eliminate jobs, and (b) planned force reduction to reduce costs during the economic recession of the early 1990s. Second, the number of women employed by newspapers has grown dramatically since 1960, and, the number of women in top jobs, in both news and business management, is increasing rapidly.

Entry-level jobs in newspapers involve hard work and, often, low salaries; however, attractive salaries await those who are successful. Note the average salaries in Table 1.10.

Table 1.10 illustrates that rewarding careers are available in departments other than news. Only about 15 percent of a typical newspaper's work force is assigned to news. Production, circulation, advertising and other departments hire the bulk of any newspaper's workforce.

TABLE 1.9   Newspaper Employment (Thousands)

Year	Total Employment	Male	Female
1960	325.2	260.0	65.2
1970	373.0	275.3	97.7
1980	419.9	262.3	157.6
1990	475.2	266.2	209.0
1991	459.4	255.8	203.6
1992	453.0	250.9	202.1
1993	451.7	246.9	204.0

TABLE 1.10   Average Salaries (1993 Survey)

Newspaper Circulation	Average Base Pay	Total Compensation (Incl. Bonus, etc.)
Publisher		
5,001 or less	$38,857	$45,539
10,001–15,000	73,649	86,512
50,001–75,000	140,510	168,655
100,001–150,000	179,580	210,578
500,001 and over	365,809	521,813
Editor		
5,000 or less	$20,697	$20,810
10,001–15,000	41,995	43,612
50,001–75,000	75,937	82,710
100,001–150,000	111,558	123,244
500,001 and over	200,745	270,930
Top Circulation Executive		
5,000 or less	$14,428	$14,428
10,001–15,000	31,879	34,116
50,001–75,000	61,730	68,711
100,001–150,000	80,919	91,589
500,001 and over	156,070	203,831
Top Advertising Executive		
5,000 or less	$23,634	$24,590
10,001–15,000	36,697	40,578
50,001–75,000	68,150	78,653
100,001–150,000	89,635	101,308
500,001 and over	152,045	193,339
Top Production Executive		
5,000 or less	NA	NA
10,001–15,000	$36,358	$39,639
50,001–75,000	63,659	68,632
100,001–150,000	85,219	95,039
500,001 and over	148,223	182,235

Source: Newspaper Association of America. The Top Production or "Operating" Executive is in charge of printing and other manufacturing functions.

Learn Newspaper Language

Newspaper insiders have their own language, and learning it will help you achieve the professionalism essential in a newspaper career. Learning these terms also will help you study the early chapters of this book.

❋ **Adversarial journalism**—aggressive, sometimes combative investigative reporting.

Agenda setting—media influence over public perception of issues and their importance; some media (e.g., *The New York Times, Washington Post*) are agenda setters for other media.

Alternative press—nontraditional publications such as "underground" newspapers, radical magazines.

A.M. newspaper—paper edited in late evening or early morning for optimum delivery around 6 A.M.

Analog transmission—sends sound waves, usually on copper wires; system is slow, limited in amount of information that can be sent and is susceptible to interference.

Audiotext (also called "voice services")—system permitting callers to use telephones to access a computer and prerecorded information.

✳ **Audit Bureau of Circulations** (ABC)—nonprofit organization established in 1914 by newspapers, magazines and advertisers to verify circulation data.

Bulk sales—quantity sales of publications or subscriptions to one purchaser such as a hotel or an airline at a reduced rate; whether these should be counted as valid paid circulation is controversial.

Business press—publications dealing in specialized information covering business, finance, economics or a specific industry.

Bypass technology—linking ultimate consumers of news and advertising directly to distant databases, usually by two-way interactive computerized circuits, rather than through traditional media, such as newspapers, magazines, television.

Carrier—individual or organization distributing newspapers or magazines.

CD-ROM (Compact Disk Read-Only Memory)—a compact disk that stores digital information, including text, and audio and visual images.

✳ **Churn**—the effect of subscribers who take, then drop a publication; a major problem for newspapers and magazines that must continually replace a high percentage of their subscribers.

Circulation—total number of copies *sold* (not distributed free) through home delivery and on newsstands.

✳ **Cold type**—process for pasting news and advertising copy on page layouts, which then are photographed to create plates for the printing press.

Combination ("combo") sale—selling subscriptions to, or advertising in, two different publications at special reduced price.

Commercial speech—expression of views through advertising; does not have full First Amendment protection.

Computer bulletin boards—systems built on use of personal computers and telephone circuits to access databanks, exchange information and so forth.

Controlled circulation—free distribution to every household in an area ("total market coverage") or to a selected audience ("selective market coverage").

Cost per thousand (CPM)—advertiser's cost to reach 1,000 persons with commercial message; an important measurement cost-conscious advertisers use in judging which medium is most "efficient."

Cross-media ownership—individual or company owning both print and broadcast media in the same city; limited by law.

Cycle—for newspapers, either the A.M. (morning) or P.M. (afternoon) publication period.

Database—information storage system, usually computerized.

Database marketing—compiling detailed computerized files on consumers or households in a market, which permits targeting them with special news products and circulation techniques.

Demographics—identifying households, readers or viewers by age, income, educational level.

Desktop publishing—using personal computers to design and print documents of a quality normally requiring a much more expensive process.

Digital transmission—translating information from sound into numbers (binary digits) and transmitting them to a receiver that decodes them and turns them back into sound; system is fast, often interference-free and permits movement of large amounts of information.

Electronic carbon—copy transmitted from one computer to another.

Electronic darkroom—computerized, nonchemical processing and, often, transmission of photographs.

Electronic magazines—making editorial and advertising content available for personal computer use through disks or computer bulletin boards.

Electronic mail—computer-to-computer exchange of messages, often via telephone circuits.

Electronic publishing—computerized production of news content for display on a computer monitor or TV screen.

Fiber optics—uses thin strands of glass as high-speed communications circuits that carry enormous quantities of information coded in digital form.

Flat-panel newspaper—hand-held computer appliance that looks like a large notepad, permitting user to electronically order up a "personal newspaper."

Flexographic printing—cheaper, less complicated process than several in use (see *Offset*).

Franchise—in publishing, a strong position in serving readers or advertisers in a given territory.

Freedom of Information Act (FOI)—a 1966 law giving the public the right to access to many government files; frequently used by investigative reporters.

Gatekeeper—individual, such as an editor, in position to select or influence information that reaches the public.

High-definition television (HDTV)—technology enhancing picture and sound quality by transmitting more "information" per screenful.

Household penetration—ratio of circulation to number of households in a given area; an extremely significant measurement of a publication's success with readers.

Information center concept—in a media sense, employing reporters and editors in their traditional roles of sifting the world of news and transmitting, electronically or on paper, a finished product to the ultimate user.

Interactive—two-way technology permitting viewers to select information and entertainment programming and shop and bank from home.

Interpretive reporting—analytical (rather than straight news) coverage of complex subjects.

Investigative reporting—reporting that emphasizes long-term, deep digging for information (as contrasted with "spot" news, written quickly).

Linotype—now generally obsolete typecasting that uses hot lead and is manually operated.

Marketing—producing a journalistic product that responds to consumer needs and wants as revealed through research.

Marketing segmentation—creating publications for narrowly focused audiences (magazines for joggers or business people, for example) rather than mass or unsegmented audiences.

Marriage mail—several advertising pieces distributed in a single cover via third-class mail.

Motor route—delivery of publications via car or truck by adult carriers.

Newshole—portion of total newspaper space dedicated to news and not advertising.

Niche publishing—producing publications or other services tightly tailored in news content and advertising for narrowly defined reader groups.

Nomadic devices—mobile telephone and other portable technology permitting two-way communication at times and places of users' choosing.

Offset—printing process of transferring images from photosensitive plates to rubberized "blankets," then to paper; used by most newspapers.

Ombudsperson—publication employee assigned to represent the public's interests with reporters and editors and to critique journalistic performance.

On-line services—computerized services available via electronic circuit; Prodigy and CompuServe are examples.

Op-ed page—page facing the editorial page normally dedicated to guest columnists and opinion pieces.

Pagination—computerized layout of pages on a video screen; extremely important breakthrough in publishing technology.

Paid circulation—copies of a publication sold through a single-copy vendor or by subscription; an important yardstick of a publication's success with readers.

Pass-along audience—individuals who read a publication they didn't purchase; important measurement of a publication's reader attraction.

Penetration—see *Household Penetration.*

P.M. newspaper—newspaper produced in the late morning or early afternoon for delivery around 4 P.M.

Positioning—in journalism, creating a product for a special market and differentiating it from competing publications.

Precision journalism—use of scientific research, often computerized, in reporting complex, technical stories.

Psychographics—identifying households, readers or viewers by attitudes, spending habits, lifestyle.

Shopper—free newspaper carrying mostly advertising and little or no news copy.

Smart telephone—phones enabling access to wide array of computerized services, in addition to normal conversations.

Split run—breaking total circulation into limited editions (or press runs), often with news and advertising focused on special audiences.

Target marketing—using research to locate potential consumers desired by advertisers, then refining news products and distribution techniques necessary to "deliver" them to advertisers.

Teletext—transmitting information to TV screens and equipping viewer with the capability of holding or "freezing" portions for perusal.

Video display terminal (VDT)—writing and editing device that permits users to recall information from a distant computerized database.

Zoning—breaking a newspaper's total circulation into smaller segments, then focusing content narrowly on specific news and advertising needs of a limited audience, defined either geographically or demographically.

SUMMARY

The U.S. newspaper industry is strong—dailies have a circulation of nearly 60 million, weeklies over 55 million. Advertising revenue is over $31 billion annually. And the newspaper is better than other media at providing news in a context of analysis and understanding needed in a democracy.

However, the percentage of Americans reading newspapers is dropping and the percentage of households subscribing is the lowest in decades. Thus the "silent crisis" of U.S. newspapers: Advertisers, who provide 75 to 80 percent of total newspaper revenue, demand deeper household penetration.

Competition is growing stronger. TV and direct mail ad revenue is growing faster than newspapers'. Strongly financed telephone companies and other high-tech firms are entering the news and advertising businesses. Since 1950, when television became a competitor, the number of newspapers has dropped just a few hundred. Meanwhile, U.S. population and number of households increased dramatically. Reacting to television, newspaper editors shifted emphasis to local news, generally covering it better than any other medium. They stressed interpretive coverage—the "why" and "how" that go beyond TV's "what" happened.

Newspapers are high-cost enterprises. Many are published in cities suffering socioeconomic deterioration. Consequently, only a few cities have two newspapers competing head-on. Newspaper-to-newspaper competition is mainly metro versus suburban. Most large newspapers publish in the morning. However, afternoon papers, published mostly in small cities, outnumber morning papers.

The newspaper "counterattack" against weak market conditions and strong competitors includes: (a) improving product quality and service for readers and advertisers, (b) pricing newspapers low to ensure circulation stays high, (c) stressing solid research that shows upper-income, well-educated Americans, the type sought by many advertisers, generally are newspaper readers, and (d) joining high-tech companies in jointly producing interactive electronic services or in other ways using new technology. Despite problems, the newspaper industry is highly profitable, with operating profit margins surpassing those of many other industries.

Media conglomerates in the 1970s and 1980s swept up privately owned newspapers by the hundreds. Inheritance taxes made it impossible for many families to pass newspapers to succeeding generations and tax laws made it highly advantageous for profitable groups to buy them. Result: Most significant dailies today are owned by profit-oriented groups.

This created a challenge for newspaper managers: How to meet the fiduciary responsibility of delivering ever-improved profits and simultaneously meet the journalistic responsibility of providing high-quality (and thus expensive) news coverage.

RECOMMENDED READING

An extremely valuable overview of the U.S. newspaper industry is available through trade journals: *presstime* (published by the Newspaper Association of America), *American Journalism Review, Columbia Journalism Review, Editor & Publisher, Advertising Age, Quill* (journal of the Society of Professional Journalists).

Journalism Quarterly, Newspaper Research Journal, and *Neiman Reports* are strong scholarly publications.

For news coverage, note particularly *The New York Times, The Wall Street Journal, Los Angeles Times, Forbes.*

Excellent industry research is published by The Newspaper Association of America,

The Newspaper Center, 11600 Sunrise Valley Drive, Reston, Va. 22091–1412; American Society of Newspaper Editors, same address; and The Associated Press Managing Editors, 50 Rockefeller Plaza, New York, N.Y. 10020.

Superb reporting and analysis of publicly owned newspaper groups are done by John Morton, Lynch, Jones & Ryan, 1037 Thirtieth St. N.W., Washington, D.C. 20007.

NOTES

1. *Facts About Newspapers '94,* published by Newspaper Association of America, The Newspaper Center, 11600 Sunrise Valley Drive, Reston, Va. 22901-1412, quoting Editor & Publisher Magazine.

2. Ibid.

3. Ibid.

4. Except for *The Los Angeles Times,* all figures are from *ABC FAS-FAX,* Sept. 30, 1994, published by Audit Bureau of Circulations, Schaumburg, Ill. *The Los Angeles Times* circulation is as of Sept. 30, 1993.

5. Household penetration was examined by Simmons Market Research Bureau for the Newspaper Association of America and reported in "Weekday Newspaper Readership Rises Slightly," *Editor & Publisher,* Sept. 12, 1992, p. 45. Sales per 1,000 population are discussed in, "The Disappearing Newspaper Reader," a speech by Professor Robert L. Stevenson, School of Journalism, University of North Carolina, at the Association for Education in Journalism and Mass Communication annual convention, Minneapolis, August 1990.

6. *Circulation '93,* published by Standard Rate and Data Service, Wilmett, Ill.

7. McCann-Erickson, quoted in *Facts About Newspapers '94,* op. cit.

8. Magazine figures, for 1991, are from Magazine Publishers of America. For detailed discussion of magazine economics see Conrad C. Fink and Donald E. Fink, *Introduction to Magazine Writing* (New York: Macmillan Publishing Co., 1994).

9. I discuss the profit and social responsibilities of managers in Conrad C. Fink, Media Ethics (Needham Heights, MA: Allyn & Bacon, 1995).

10. *Facts About Newspapers '94,* op. cit.

2

UNDERSTANDING YOUR MARKET

We turn now to the single most important factor in newspaper strategy—your market.

Most important? Yes. Consider two factors:

- Your newspaper will live, or die, on the basic economic strength of your market. Your newspaper needs literate, affluent residents as readers and prosperous local retail merchants as advertisers. A market without them will not support a newspaper. And, bluntly, you will fail in newspaper management if you cannot locate, serve and extract revenue from those two market constituencies.
- You'll juggle many variables as a newspaper manager but none as volatile, or as important, as changes in your market. Populations shift rapidly, retailing has its unexpected ups and downs, industries can come and go overnight—and monitoring such changes, then revising your newspaper's strategies accordingly, will be crucial to your success. Examine the failure of long-established major dailies in recent decades and you'll find managers who didn't adjust to changes in their markets. Find newspapers that flourished even under adverse conditions and you'll discover managers who saw change coming and adjusted their strategies to turn change into opportunities.

The key is anticipatory management—anticipating change and adjusting strategies before it hits. Don't get trapped in reactive management, making adjustments only after change hits.

We'll examine, here in Chapter 2, the role of anticipatory management in the second element of your manager's preplanning mantra—know your newspaper, *know your market*, know your competition.

WHAT MAKES A MARKET?

Think of a newspaper market in roughly two dimensions: First, it can be a slice of geography—a city and five surrounding counties, for example. Second, a newspaper market can be a group of persons with shared interests or characteristics—potential readers interested in, say, business news and who enjoy annual incomes of $50,000 or more. Frequently, a newspaper seeks to carve out a combination market: for example, high-income persons with shared news interests who live in a geographic area that the newspaper can reach and serve.

A market, then, has geographic characteristics. Readers who live in that market have demographic characteristics (age, education, income) and psychographic characteristics (lifestyle patterns, buying habits). Always, the geography served and readers sought must be defined by their appeal to advertisers. For any newspaper, reaching an area or readers *un*attractive to advertisers is a costly, futile exercise. Readers who cannot be "sold" to advertisers generate only costs, not revenue. Targeting attractive readers draws advertisers—and they provide 75 to 80 percent of our revenue.

Lesson: Money, journalistic genius and idealism can be poured into a newspaper—all to no avail unless the newspaper is "tuned" to provide what the market wants and needs. (Note the distinction: Financial success lies in providing what the market says it wants; journalistic success requires providing, additionally, what we, as trained and responsible journalists, think the market needs. More later on the social responsibility in that.)

Establishing a Franchise

To succeed, a newspaper must identify a market that is geographically coherent and whose "lay of the land" permits establishing a "franchise." Three things must be done: First, serve readers and advertisers to attract and hold their support. Second, hold the franchise against competitors clamoring for readers' time and advertisers' dollars. Third, the newspaper must be managed, internally and externally, in a manner certain to achieve maximum economic reward from the market.

The franchise for most newspapers is a city plus surrounding counties with a sense of community. Such a market has a commonality of news interests, enabling the newspaper to fashion a news and feature product of wide appeal. Common economic interests—employment, shopping—give the newspaper another frame of reference for news and business operations. Unlike many industrial companies, a newspaper must conduct operations within its geographic market. A manufacturer of hair driers can move to Mexico in search of cheap labor and still sell its product in California. Not so a newspaper. Its product—news and advertising—is perishable and must be collected, manufactured and sold in its primary market.

The market must be economically appealing, offering a fundamental business strength that's attractive to advertisers. Just as the newspaper is tied to market geography, so is it inextricably linked with the size, location and economic quality of its readership and the general strength of its market. Residents in the market—readers and potential readers—must be demographically appealing, offering educational and income levels and other characteristics sought by advertisers. The population's psychographic qualities—attitudes, spending habits—must be attractive to advertisers.

National newspapers, of course, pursue demographic and psychographic targets regardless of where they are located geographically. *USA Today*, the *Wall Street Journal* and *The New York Times* seek high-income, heavy-spending readers anywhere in the United States and in many countries overseas.

Standard Market Designations

Basic geographic delineations commonly used throughout the industry are charted by the Audit Bureau of Circulations. ABC is a nonprofit organization created by newspapers in 1914 to offer independent audit of circulation figures and thus inject some order (and objective reliability) into what historically was a chaotic jumble of circulation claims and counterclaims aimed at bewildered and suspicious advertisers. Under ABC rules, publishers may record circulation in these areas:

City Zone (CZ). Normally the area within a city's corporate limits but it sometimes includes more when the term is used to describe the target area for circulation efforts.

Primary Market Area (PMA). The area in which the newspaper is judged to provide primary journalistic and advertising service.

Retail Trading Zone (RTZ). That area beyond the CZ whose residents regularly trade to an important degree with retail merchants in the CZ.

Newspaper Designated Market (NDM). The geographic area that the newspaper itself regards as its market.

U.S. Census Bureau designations also are used:

Metropolitan Statistical Area (MSA). A geographic area around a city of at least 50,000 population, with 100,000 or more total metro-area population. The MSA can include nearby communities whose populations have a high degree of "economic and social integration" with the principal city. That is, they shop or seek entertainment here.

Primary Metropolitan Statistical Area (PMSA). An MSA with 1 million or more population.

Consolidated Metropolitan Statistical Area (CMSA). Formed of two or more contiguous PMSAs, one having at least 1 million population or being 75 percent urban.

A TV market designation, *Area of Dominant Influence (ADI)*, often is used to compare a newspaper's circulation and influence with what a TV station can offer advertisers. An ADI consists of all counties in which home-market TV stations receive a preponderance of viewing. Each county in the country is assigned to just one ADI.

You can visualize how newspapers chart their markets if you study Figure 2.1 on page 32, an ABC presentation of the RTZ and PMA for fictional "Anytown, Ill."[1]

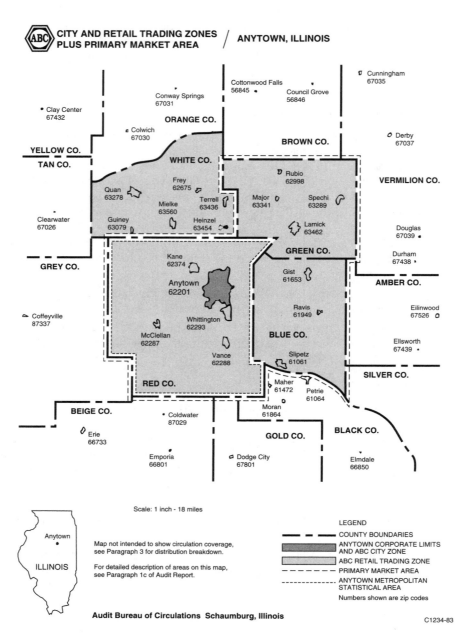

FIGURE 2.1 **The Audit Bureau of Circulations illustrates here how it delineates newspaper markets. The Retail Trading Zone for "Anytown, Ill.," is composed of White, Green, Blue and Red counties. The Primary Market Area is made up of only Green, Blue and Red counties.**

Reprinted with permission from the Audit Bureau of Circulations.

Most importantly, regardless of which market designation is used, the newspaper's mission for advertisers is to reach the types of readers they want, in the areas they want covered. You make advertisers happy by pulling in customers who buy their goods and services.

RESEARCHING THE MARKET

Advertisers—and newspaper managers—assess a market's appeal by studying its basic economic underpinnings. In bygone days, advertisers and newspaper managers alike had intimate personal understanding of their market. They lived in the market, walked Main Street daily, and personally knew retailers, bankers, government officials and others who understood the market's strengths and weaknesses.

Today, markets are complex. Many are sprawling metropolitan areas tugged and pulled by fast, almost bewildering socioeconomic changes. It's not easy to understand what people are thinking "out there." People move from job to job, town to town. Public opinion—the mood of the market—can shift rapidly. Modern management technique, therefore, must be research-driven and skilled researchers must have influential voices in top-level strategy sessions.

Broadly, market research is used two ways: Externally, research illustrates for advertisers the geographic, demographic and psychographic strengths of the market and the newspaper's ability to perform its role. Internally, research enables editors and other department heads to adjust to market changes and needs.

Some market feedback is audience-generated and qualitative. This includes letters to the editors, telephoned complaints or (occasionally) compliments and reader or advertiser sentiment that newspaper staff members pick up every day. However, such feedback is random, nonscientific and unreliable. So, highly precise quantitative research is required. This involves, for example, scientific selection of a representative sample of the relevant population to be measured and careful analysis of respondents' thinking. This is accomplished through telephone polls, mailed questionnaires or, increasingly, focus groups of people who are questioned in depth.

Market research is something of an art form, requiring persons with strong academic background in research methodology. Increasingly, newspapers employ outside research firms, which, for a fee, design and implement market studies. Research objectives must be stated in detail by the newspaper executives who implement the findings—the publisher, editor, advertising director and circulation manager (see Figure 2.2 on page 34).

What Advertisers Want

Advertiser-oriented market research must cover four fundamental themes: First, that a geographic market exists for advertisers' goods and services and that residents in the market have demographic and psychographic characteristics making them attractive sales targets. Second, research must emphasize overall economic strength in the market, as revealed in retail sales figures, household incomes and

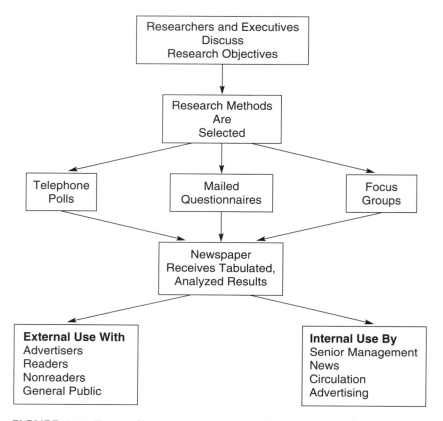

FIGURE 2.2   **Rewarding careers are open for researchers who can develop marketing data used to "drive" internal decision making by newspaper managers and, externally, by advertisers and others.**

general business activity. Third, the newspaper must prove it can "deliver" the market—that its circulation and household penetration are sufficient to reach the advertisers' targets. Fourth, the newspaper must show it can generate response— that it can "pull" customers into buying the advertisers' goods and services. This generally is demonstrated two ways: broad, industry-based research is used to show that print ads "sell" better than TV commercials, for example, and locally originated research is used to show that, for example, a series of four ads will reach a high percentage of educated adults in the market and produce "store traffic."

Here are principal economic indicators of interest to advertisers:

Population Size

Advertisers want to reach an audience of sufficient size, of course. U.S. Census Bureau figures, updated annually with ABC estimates, are available in *Editor & Publisher International Year Book* and *Circulation* for newspaper markets.[2] Current figures are available from local authorities, such as planning commissions or chambers of commerce.

Households

Most U.S. newspapers are delivered to households, not sold singly to individuals. That's because household delivery—*penetrating* households with the advertising message—most attracts advertisers.

"Household" covers all individuals living in a housing unit and should not be confused with "family." Household counts do *not* include persons living in institutions, such as college dormitories or military barracks. Household estimates from ABC are available in *Editor & Publisher International Year Book, Circulation* or local authorities.

Note in Figure 2.3 on page 36 how newspapers use ABC reports to show advertisers their circulation figures in cities and retail trading zones. Most retailers, however, want more refined circulation figures for use in "target marketing"— reaching only persons most likely to be potential customers—in a market area smaller than an RTZ or CZ. Note in Figure 2.4 on page 37 how newspapers break down circulation by U.S. Postal Service ZIP code areas. Depending on where their customers—or potential customers—live, advertisers often want their message carried in only those copies reaching a few ZIP code areas.

Income

This is *crucial* in analyzing the appeal of households to advertisers and, thus, to the newspaper itself. Measurements used most are Effective Buying Income (EBI), sometimes called "after-tax" or "disposable income," and Average Household Income (AHI). County totals are available in *Editor & Publisher Market Guide* and *Circulation*. Because advertisers are household-oriented, personal income figures are used less commonly in market analysis. But per capita income is listed by counties in both *Market Guide* and *Circulation*.

Retail Sales

Retail sales, an extremely valuable indicator of a market's demographic attractiveness, measure business activity in retail stores, that sector of the economy yielding the most newspaper advertising revenue. To get a true fix on spending habits in a market, break down total retail sales into food sales (single most important source of ad revenue for many newspapers), eating/drinking, general merchandise, furniture/appliances, automotive, drug sales. U.S. Census findings and updated estimates, including retail sales breakdowns, are available in *Market Guide.*

Other indicators of a market's economic activity and potential include:

- Character of local industry and business, particularly whether stable or cyclical. Note any educational or governmental institutions that promise payroll stability even in economic bad times.
- Construction permits for new commercial or residential buildings. Also watch installations by telephone, gas, water and electric companies as signs of new construction and, thus, economic growth.

AUDIT REPORT: Newspaper

Audit Bureau of Circulations

THE TRIBUNE (Evening)
Anytown (Red County), Illinois

TOTAL AVERAGE PAID CIRCULATION FOR 12 MONTHS ENDED SEPTEMBER 30, 19–:

		Evening
1A. TOTAL AVERAGE PAID CIRCULATION (BY INDIVIDUALS AND FOR DESIGNATED RECIPIENTS:		41,315

1B. TOTAL AVERAGE PAID CIRCULATION (BY INDIVIDUALS AND FOR DESIGNATED RECIPIENTS) BY ZONES:
(See Par. 1E for description of area)

CITY ZONE

	Population	Occupied Households	
1980 Census:	80,109	29,143	
# 12-31-87 Estimate:	80,500	30,000	

Carrier Delivery office collect system, See Pars 11(b) & (c)............................	1,875
Carriers not filing lists with publisher	18,649
Single Copy Sales	2,168
Mail Subscriptions	47
School-Single Copy/Subscriptions, See Par. 11(d)	50
Employee Copies, See Par. 11(c)	100
Group (Subscriptions by Businesses for Designated Employees), See Par. 11(f)	50
TOTAL CITY ZONE............................	22,939

RETAIL TRADING ZONE

	Population	Occupied Households
1980 Census:	268,491	75,140
# 12-31-87 Estimate:	272,000	79,000

Carriers not filing lists with publisher	15,138
Single Copy Sales	1,549
Mail Subscriptions............................	908
School-Single Copy/Subscriptions, See Par. 11(d)	25
Employee Copies, See Par. 11(c)	25
Group (Subscriptions by Businesses for Designated Employees), See Par. 11(f)	50
TOTAL RETAIL TRADiNG ZONE............................	17,695
TOTAL CITY AND RETAIL TRADING ZONES............................	40,634

	Population	Occupied Households
1980 Census:	348,600	104,283
# 12-31-87 Estimate:	352,500	109,000

ALL OTHER

Single Copy Sales & Carrier not filing lists with publisher	256
Mail Subscriptions............................	375
School-Single Copy/Subscriptions, See Par. 11(d)	20
Employee Copies, See Par. 11(c)	20
Group (Subscriptions by Businesses for Designated Employees), See Par. 11(f)............................	10
TOTAL ALL OTHER............................	681
TOTAL PAID CIRCULATION (BY INDIVIDUALS AND FOR DESIGNATED RECIPIENTS)............................	41,315

1C. THIRD PARTY (BULK) SALES:

Airlines—Available for passengers............................	1,000
Hotels, Motels—Available for guests............................	500
Restaurants—Available for patrons............................	500
Business—Available for employees............................	50
Other	600
TOTAL THIRD PARTY (BULK) SALES	2,650

#S&MM Estimate. See Par. 11(a).

FIGURE 2.3   In this ABC report, the *Anytown (Ill.) Tribune* lists total city zone circulation of 22,939. Divided by the estimated number of occupied households (30,000), that yields a healthy 76.5 percent household penetration—enough to keep most advertisers happy.

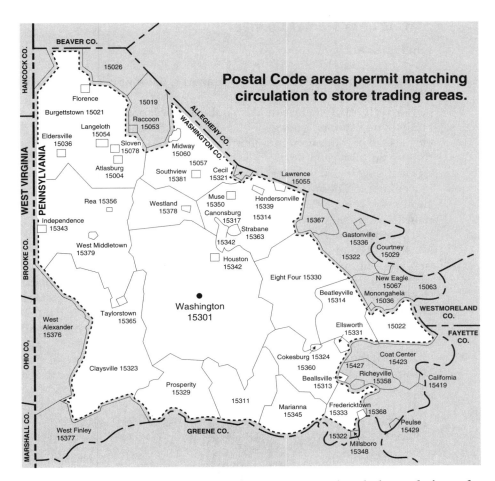

FIGURE 2.4 **ABC illustrates here how newspapers break down their total circulation into segments targeted on individual U.S. Postal Service ZIP code areas. This permits advertisers to use only portions of a newspaper's circulation and reach, for example, just a few pockets of particularly affluent households.**

Reprinted with permission from the Audit Bureau of Circulations.

- Asset levels (sometimes called "footings") of local banks and savings and loan associations, reported in *Editor & Publisher Market Guide*. Updates are available from chambers of commerce and, of course, banks. Asset levels indicate money available locally to finance business expansion.
- Opinions of bankers, realtors, retailers and, of course, local government and chamber of commerce officials. Probing interviews with well-placed business and government officials are crucial to understanding a market.

Staying atop Market Changes

Fundamental changes are under way in how and where Americans live and, indeed, in who and what Americans perceive themselves to be. To remain valid in such a changing environment, newspapers must conduct alert, never-ending market research.

Broadly, three socioeconomic changes are of major interest at this point in your study of newspaper strategy: First, cities that once were well-defined, stand-alone entities are becoming metropolitan sprawls of end-to-end suburbs. Population, affluence and the economic center of many cities are on the move. Even in smaller cities of, say, 30,000 to 50,000 population, affluent residents are moving to suburbs, loosening their ties to the city core. This creates enormous difficulty for newspaper strategists trying to identify commonalities of news and advertising interests in a market where they can establish a franchise.

Second, American readers, target of advertisers and newspaper strategists alike, are becoming increasingly difficult to identify, reach and "capture" (note Figure 2.5). The image of a "typical" household of white, middle-class male wage earner, homemaker wife and, on average, two neatly dressed, well-educated children drove newspaper strategy for decades. No more. Households increasingly are "nontraditional," often headed by single parents with outside jobs. Racial, ethnic and social influences are blurring once-clear definitions of who readers are and how editors can attract them (note Figure 2.5).

Third, the fundamental nature of retailing, long the principal source of major newspaper revenue, is changing dramatically. "Upscale" department stores are

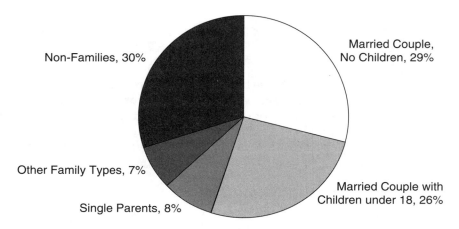

FIGURE 2.5 **The American household, target of advertisers and newspapers alike, is changing character rapidly. Of 94.3 million households counted in the 1990 U.S. Census, only 26 percent were the traditional "nuclear" families of working husbands, housewives and two children.**

Source: U.S. Census Bureau.

waning; discount stores offering low-priced goods are booming. Advertisers are becoming increasingly discriminating in how they identify—and reach—potential customers. Upscale stores today often use direct mail to deliver glossy, high-cost catalogs to a finely tuned list of households whose past spending patterns and credit card use identify them as likely purchasers of high-priced goods. Other types of retailers have different advertising needs—and they have many alternatives to newspapers for meeting those needs. Let's look more closely at these changes.

CITIES AS A MARKET

Item: Charlotte, North Carolina, a city of 30 square miles in 1950, today sprawls, thanks to annexation of surrounding areas, over more than 174 square miles. Houston, Texas, has exploded over 540 square miles, compared with 160 in 1950.[3]

Item: Eighty-six percent of metropolitan Atlanta's residents live outside the city limits.[4] New "edge cities" are flourishing well beyond the first ring of suburbs around Los Angeles, Chicago, New York and other major cities. Whereas suburbs historically were bedroom communities for commuters who worked in nearby core cities, "edge cities" often are self-contained units, offering jobs as well as overnight and weekend lodging.

Item: In the Atlanta metropolitan area, 26 percent of all residents are black; within Atlanta's city limits, 67 percent are black. In metro Atlanta, 10 percent of the population is officially termed "poor." Within the city limits, 27.4 percent are "poor."[5] (The U.S. Census Bureau defines "poverty" as a family of four living on an income of $14,335 annually or less.)

The meaning of all this? Dramatic change: Cities are expanding into geographically contiguous areas in an attempt to annex population—particularly affluent population—and thus maintain an economic coherency and a tax base that will keep the core city vital and prosperous. However, affluent residents are fleeing farther from the cities, their violence, their crowding and their noise, and seeking better schools and more enjoyable lifestyles in the suburbs.

This once was called "white flight," but today should be called "the flight of the affluent" because many prosperous blacks, Hispanics, Asian-Americans and other minorities also are moving to the suburbs. Nevertheless, those left behind in the socioeconomic deterioration of many core cities are primarily blacks and Hispanics. Almost by definition, minorities have low incomes relative to whites: The median household income nationwide for whites was $32,368 in 1992; for Hispanics, it was $22,848; for blacks, $18,660.[6]

Roughly two options are open for a newspaper that's anchored downtown in a city ravaged by socioeconomic core deterioration and the flight of the affluent: One, adjust to market change and follow the affluent, recapturing them in the suburbs, or, two, wither and die. Too few newspaper strategists were market research–oriented when these socioeconomic changes picked up speed in the 1950s

TABLE 2.1   **Newspapers in and around New York City**

Newspapers in New York City

Paper	Circulation 1949	Circulation present[a]
The Sun	294,195	Ceased publication, 1950
The Brooklyn Eagle	130,479	Ceased publication, 1955
The Mirror	1,020,879	Ceased publication, 1963
The Journal-American	707,195	Merged in 1966 into *The World Journal Tribune,* which ceased publication in 1967
The World-Telegram	373,034	
The New York Herald-Tribune	340,430	
The Long Island Star-Journal	79,709	Ceased publication, 1968
The Long Island Press	151,602	Ceased publication, 1977
The New York Times	543,943	1,187,950
The Daily News	2,254,644	764,230
The New York Post	366,286	381,254
Staten Island Advance	38,911	77,529

Suburban Newspapers around New York City

Paper	Circulation 1949	Circulation present[a]
Newsday (Long Island)	96,421	720,352
The Star-Ledger (Newark, N.J.)	163,658	463,412
Asbury Park Press (Asbury Park, N.J.)	22,088	162,790
The Record (Hackensack, N.J.)	43,896	160,229
The North Jersey Herald and News (Morristown, N.J.)	50,235	56,791
The Times Herald-Record (Middletown, N.Y.)	10,155	86,070
Daily Record (Parsippany, N.J.)	9,123	58,210
Central New Jersey Home News (New Brunswick, N.J.)	27,212	51,248
Jersey Journal (Jersey City, N.J.)	49,998	56,847
News Tribune (Woodbridge, N.J.)	24,952	54,716

[a]Current circulations as of ABC's Sept. 30, 1994, audit reports.

and truly began transforming America in the 1960s and 1970s. Although editors front-paged news stories on what was happening to their cities, many strategists failed to incorporate the news into their planning.

You virtually can chart the relationship between market change and newspaper fortunes by looking at what happened to newspapers in New York City and around it. From 1950 to the present was a period of socioeconomic upheaval in metropolitan New York City. The core city's economy and lifestyle deteriorated, relative to fast growth and comfortable lifestyles in commuter suburbs. Though they continued to work in New York City and draw their salaries there, tens of thousands of high-paid executives moved households and families (and their retail spending) to suburbs in New York state and New Jersey. Note in Table 2.1 the impact on newspapers in and around New York City as the economic base of the city moved outward, to the suburbs.

As Table 2.1 illustrates, the single major success story in New York City newspapering, 1950 to the present, was *The New York Times.* Why did the *Times* alone flourish? Because *Times* market researchers properly interpreted change (somewhat belatedly but accurately) and *Times* news strategists reacted by (a) creating a paper whose high quality today is deemed essential by thousands of affluent suburban residents, and (b) by launching a national edition that scoops up demographically desirable readers from coast to coast. Note also in Table 2.1 how newspapers in New York's suburbs prospered with the growth that followed the arrival of the affluent who fled from downtown.

Clearly, a core city as a newspaper market is a tricky, changing proposition. Stay atop changes in your city market or you'll fail to avoid problems those changes bring, or to exploit the opportunities they offer.

READERS AS A MARKET

If forced to describe, in a single sentence, how the American newspaper reader market is changing, you might say something like this: Readers increasingly are in a rush ("time-deprived," we call it); they're ever more difficult to please, and relative to our population as a whole, they're getting older—and there are fewer of them. Note, first, in Table 2.2 how American newspaper readership stacks up against readership in other countries.[7]

TABLE 2.2   Daily Newspapers Sold per 1,000 Inhabitants

	1988	1991	1992
1. Norway	550	600	619
2. Japan	580	591	584
3. Sweden	519	518	522
4. Finland	550	539	521
5. Germany	336[a]	311	335
6. Switzerland	432	416	415
7. Austria	357	337	409
8. Czech Republic	—	—	396
9. United Kingdom	391	367	362
10. Singapore	281	329	348
11. Denmark	355	327	340
12. Luxemburg	—	320	333
13. Netherlands	313	317	317
14. New Zealand	—	301	264
15. USA	255	251	244

[a]West Germany only

TABLE 2.3   Weekday Newspaper Readers

Year	% of Total Adult Population	Adult Readers (thousands)	Male (thousands)	Female (thousands)
1970	78	98,183	46,659	51,524
1980	67	106,043	52,559	53,484
1985	64	108,812	53,718	55,094
1986	63	107,753	52,597	55,156
1989	63.6	113,337	56,018	57,319
1990	62.4	113,090	55,798	57,292
1991	62.1	113,322	56,114	57,207
1992	62.6	115,296	57,499	57,797
1993	61.7	114,669	57,091	57,578

Source: Newspaper Association of America, quoting Simmons Market Research Bureau. Adults are 18 or older.

Illiteracy helps explain declining readership in America (23 to 27 million Americans cannot read well, and an estimated 2 million illiterates are added to our society annually).[8] But, clearly, other factors are at play. Let's try to pin down who the readers are, and why the newspaper reader market is changing so rapidly.

Note in Table 2.3 the steep decline since 1970 in the percentage of adult Americans who read a newspaper Monday through Saturday.

Some of the fall in weekday readership can be attributed to "time-starved" Americans dropping seven-day subscriptions and reading newspapers only on Sundays to "catch up." Note in Table 2.4 that the decline in Sunday readership is less precipitous.

A very sobering message is hidden in the argument, "I don't have enough time to read newspapers." The real message is, "I don't have enough time relative to the value I receive from reading newspapers."

It's irrelevant to argue that Americans who thus undervalue newspaper content are wrong. It's their *perception* of value received that counts, and we'll discuss later how newsrooms must bolster content and promotion departments must change public perceptions of its value. But, what is it that Americans who do read are after in newspapers? They spend, on average, 28 minutes daily with a newspaper, and you'll note in Table 2.5 some clues about what they read.

First, note readers have wide-ranging interests. Just a little more than half glance at every page; for most readers, the newspaper is a broad-based compilation of news and information available for sampling as desired. Note the high

TABLE 2.4   Sunday/Weekend Readers

	% of Total Adult Population	Adult Readers (thousands)
1970	72	91,642
1980	67	106,740
1985	65	110,255
1986	64	109,775
1989	67	119,349
1990	67	121,622
1991	66.9	122,045
1992	68.4	125,940
1993	69	128,227

Source: Newspaper Association of America, quoting Simmons Market Research Bureau. Adults are 18 or older.

readership scores for some specialized news, such as entertainment, sports, business. However 95 percent of all adults read general news.

The dilemma: We must sharpen the newspaper's coverage of specialized news, such as business and science, to compete against "niche" magazines and other media that focus on those specialties. Yet, we cannot relax our coverage of the entire world of general news, still the single strongest attraction newspapers have for readers.

TABLE 2.5   What Readers Read (Percentage of Weekday Audience)

	Adults	Men	Women
Read every page	57	58	55
Read certain pages/sections	43	42	45
General news	95	94	95
Entertainment (movies, theater)	78	74	82
Editorial page	79	79	80
Sports	75	84	65
Comics	74	74	74
TV, radio listings	73	72	74
Business, finance	74	77	72
Home	72	68	77
Food, cooking	73	66	81
Classified ads	73	75	72

Source: Newspaper Association of America

TABLE 2.6   Newspaper Readership by Age Categories

Age	Percentage Daily	Percentage Sunday
18–24	51	61
25–34	56	67
35–44	64	70
45–54	66	74
55–64	70	74
65+	66	68

Source: Newspaper Association of America

Research into readers as a market reveals another problem: Newspapers aren't attracting enough young readers (see Table 2.6).

First, newspaper readership will die off—literally—unless we start attracting more readers 18 to 24 years old. Those age categories 55–64 and 65+ in Table 2.6 won't provide the readership support newspapers need for much longer. There must be constant renewal of readers among younger people.

Second, simply put, advertisers demand younger readers. The affluence of older newspaper readers, compared to TV viewers, attracts advertisers. But advertisers want to build brand loyalty among younger people who have a lifetime of buying still ahead.[9]

No examination of readers as a market is complete without pondering why more young people don't read newspapers. (And, incidentally, you college students *know* that readership in the 18 to 21 college-age category is much lower than the 51 percent listed in Table 2.6 for readership among adults 18 to 24. College students generally are not avid newspaper readers.)

Pending later discussion of news strategy, two factors clearly influence newspapers' poor showing among young persons: Young Americans grow up watching TV entertainment, and reading—newspapers or anything else—is not a family habit for many. And, frankly, many newspapers don't offer content appealing to young people. Newspapers generally are structured for householders and parents, who need information on house buying, schools, taxes and so forth. Yet, many Americans today delay until their late 20s or 30s formally establishing households and becoming parents, so information on how to negotiate a mortgage or select a good school is irrelevant. What *is* relevant for young singles—entertainment news or music information, for example—is not found in many newspapers.

And, Looking Ahead . . .

Meeting the challenge of the reader market won't get easier for newspapers. The U.S. Census Bureau and demographers project dramatic change in these areas of crucial interest to newspaper strategists:

Ethnic Diversity

By the year 2050, U.S. population will increase to 383 million from 252 million in 1991, and ethnic diversity will increase. Whites, 76 percent of total population in 1990, will be a projected 53 percent in 2050. The percentage of blacks will increase to 15 percent from 12 percent, Hispanics to 21 percent from 9 percent, Asian- and Pacific-Americans to 10 percent from 3 percent in 1990. (American Indians will remain at 1 percent, the Census Bureau projects.)[10] Editing newspapers to appeal across ethnic lines, already a major problem, will get more difficult.

The Graying of America

About 13 percent of Americans were 65 or older in 1990. That will rise to 21 percent in 2050, according to the Census Bureau.[11] Older Americans are the heaviest newspaper readers, so you can see how the projected "graying of America" will further tip the readership statistics in Table 2.6 toward older age categories—the ones of lesser interest to advertisers. And, of course, editors will face an even more difficult straddle in the future—reaching down for younger readers with appropriate content while simultaneously serving interests of the burgeoning ranks of older readers.

THE NEW TECHNOLOGY

If you think young Americans today are oriented toward electronic media, the futurists say, just wait a decade or so. Today's youthful TV watchers could ease smoothly into a new era of portable satellite telephones, interactive home computer centers, 3-D television and all the other technological tools being put forth as alternatives to newspapers. Clearly, your generation of newspaper managers will find it increasingly difficult to define, reach and hold the reader market.

ADVERTISERS AS A MARKET

Four principal areas of the advertising market concern us at this point in our study:

Local Retail (or Display)—Advertising by, of course, local retail merchants who sell directly to consumers. Local retail ads prominently list retailers' store names and addresses.

National (or General)—Advertising by firms offering mass-produced goods and services for multi-outlet sale. Ad themes often are institutional—"Coke Is It," "Diamonds Are Forever." National ads don't list local merchants' names or addresses.

Classified—Enormously popular with advertisers and readers, and highly profitable for most newspapers. Recall from Table 2.5 that 70 percent of adult readers regularly check "Help Wanted," "Cars for Sale" and other classified columns, as well as news columns.

CASE STUDY 2.1   Regional Markets Redefined

For generations, many metropolitan daily newspapers transformed themselves into regional powerhouses by extending circulation hundreds of miles from home base.

The goal: sell more newspapers, regardless of who bought them or where. Marketing success was defined as increasing circulation every year.

The Boston Globe considered all New England its turf. The *Atlanta Journal* boasted it "Covers Dixie Like the Dew." The *Minneapolis Star and Tribune* created its own regional concept, "The Upper Midwest," and sold home-delivered subscriptions throughout Minnesota and in the far-off Dakotas. The *Los Angeles Times* pushed throughout southern California and more.

Then, two things happened: First, newsprint costs skyrocketed, from $179 per metric ton in 1970 to $440 in 1980 and well over $700 by 1995. Production and distribution costs exploded. *And,* subscriber contributions to total newspaper revenue settled down at about 20 percent—not enough to cover even newsprint costs. Clearly, newspapers no longer could afford to sell a single copy to anyone who, in turn, couldn't be "sold" to advertisers. Indiscriminately pushing circulation everywhere, at any cost, was the path to bankruptcy.

Advertisers became increasingly sophisticated in redefining what, for them, was efficient circulation: It was home delivery in, roughly, an area about 50 miles distant from their stores. Why should Minneapolis retailers pay for circulation reaching readers 400 miles distant, in North Dakota? Would those readers drive to Minneapolis to buy groceries or furniture?

All this was traumatic for regional dailies. The *Atlanta Journal* and *Constitution,* for example, had circulation throughout Georgia, a state of 58,910 square miles, the largest land mass of any state east of the Mississippi. In 1964, the papers had 5 percent or more household penetration in 142 of the state's 159 counties. The papers had 30 percent or more in 43 counties, some 170 miles from Atlanta. Much of the *Jour-*

nal and *Constitution* distant circulation couldn't be "sold" to any discerning advertiser: It was too far away for Atlanta-area retailers; it was too shallow for local advertisers in communities scattered across the state and served by their own dailies and weeklies.

By the 1970s, the retreat toward home base was under way at most regional newspapers. The *Journal* and *Constitution* trimmed much distant circulation (over the strenuous objections of reporters and editors who fought hard for years to extend their domain). By 1979, the papers had 5 percent penetration in only 103 counties, down from 142 in 1964. In 1979, the papers had 30 percent or more penetration in just 11 counties, down from 43. All 11 counties were within 40 miles of the city.

From 1964 to 1979, *Atlanta Journal* and *Constitution* combined penetration declined in 154 counties. The average decline per county was 68 percent. However, it was a vibrant, expanding market that awaited the papers at home. Between 1964 and 1979, the population growth in metro Atlanta was *twice* that of the rest of the state.

There was concurrent demographic improvement in the Atlanta metro market, compared with the far-flung regions being vacated. Among the nation's top 20 markets, metro Atlanta by 1979 was 17th in total retail sales and 19th in total effective buying income (EBI). The metro area was in the top 10 for projected growth in population, retail sales, EBI and other market indicators.

Bottom line: The *Atlanta Journal* and *Constitution* trimmed circulation from 460,096 in 1964 to 435,648 in 1979. But, the shift to home base guaranteed circulation was mostly in the basic advertising market and thus highly saleable.

In 1964, 70 percent of total subscriptions were in the 15 counties later designated as Atlanta's Standard Metropolitan Statistical Area (SMSA). By 1979, 80 percent were within the SMSA. Just 20 percent were outside the metro area and, thus, of less interest to Atlanta advertisers.

CASE STUDY 2.1 *Continued*

By 1995, *Journal* and *Constitution* combined circulation had soared over 500,000 daily and 680,000 Sunday—mostly smack in areas of vital interest to Atlanta metro advertisers.

The "Retreat to Atlanta"—as the wags put it, only the second since the Civil War—was replicated by metropolitan papers pulling back on home base throughout the country. So ended a glorious period of far-flung regional newspapers in the United States.

Source: Conrad C. Fink, *The Atlanta Journal and Constitution, a Case Study,* (St. Petersburg, Florida: The Poynter Institute for Media Studies, 1989).

Preprints (or Inserts)—Literally *billions* are delivered in newspapers annually. They are produced in bulk by national or local retail advertisers, who then use the newspaper solely as a distribution vehicle.

Note in Table 2.7 the growth in newspaper advertising since 1950, compared to growth in Gross Domestic Product (the dollar value of all goods and services produced in the United States).

Though total newspaper ad dollars are impressive—nearly $31 *billion*—careful analysis reveals two problems: First, newspaper advertising growth is lagging behind GDP growth after 40 years of keeping pace step by step, and, second, competing media are taking an ever-increasing share of total U.S. ad dollars. Note in Figure 2.6 how newspaper ad revenue failed to increase in 1989 and 1990, relative to GDP growth, then fell behind.

TABLE 2.7   Newspaper Ad Revenue

	National (millions)	Retail (millions)	Classified (millions)	Total (millions)	Gross Domestic Product (billions)
1950	$518	$1,175	$377	$2,070	$286.4
1960	778	2,100	803	3,681	513.4
1970	891	3,292	1,521	5,704	1,010.7
1980	1,963	8,609	4,222	14,794	2,708.0
1985	3,352	13,443	8,375	25,170	4,038.7
1986	3,376	14,311	9,303	26,990	4,268.6
1987	3,494	15,227	10,691	29,412	4,539.9
1988	3,821	15,790	11,586	31,197	4,900.4
1989	3,948	16,504	11,916	32,368	5,250.8
1990	4,122	16,652	11,506	32,280	5,546.1
1991	3,924	15,839	10,587	30,349	5,722.9
1992	3,834	16,041	10,764	30,639	6,038.5
1993	3,853	16,874	11,179	31,906	6,377.9

Source: U.S. Department of Commerce figures quoted by Newspaper Association of America. Figures for 1988 are not directly comparable to prior years due to change in methodology.

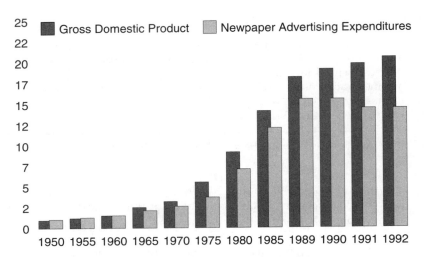

FIGURE 2.6 Newspaper advertising spending and Gross Domestic Product. Growth index beginning in 1950 with 100 as base.

Source: Newspaper Association of America, using U.S. Department of Commerce Statistics.

The leveling off of ad revenue growth, relative to GDP, is explained in part by the economic recession—and subsequent advertising slump—of the late 1980s and early 1990s. However, Figure 2.7 illustrates a more fundamental problem: Newspapers, the dominant advertising medium 40 years ago, today share ad dollars with vigorous competitors, particularly television and direct mail.

In addition to losing revenue to competing media, newspapers suffer heavily from economic recession and another factor beyond their control—fundamental change in the nature of U.S. retailing.

The change involves primarily (a) the switch of American consumers to discount houses, such as Wal-Mart, offering low prices and (b) the bankruptcy of some of the nation's most famous upscale retailers, traditionally big newspaper advertisers.

Wal-Mart, a discounter that's *not* a large user of newspaper advertising, flourishes in many towns at the expense of local retailers who *do* use newspapers. An Iowa State University economist, Kenneth Stone, studied Wal-Mart operations in Iowa and concluded, "About three years after a Wal-Mart opens, stores near it begin to close." Stone said that of 43 Wal-Marts in Iowa, one-fourth of the towns near them now have smaller commercial areas.[12]

Discount retailing growth is extraordinary. In 1993, Wal-Mart had 1,967 stores; Kmart, 2,438; and Target, 526. Almost without exception, discounters locate in suburban malls. Core-city retailers must move out there also, or die. Woolworth Corp., a Main Street retailer for generations, closed 100 downtown stores in 1992, and announced in 1993 it would close 970 more (and eliminate 13,000 jobs), in the biggest and most costly reorganization in its 114 years.[13]

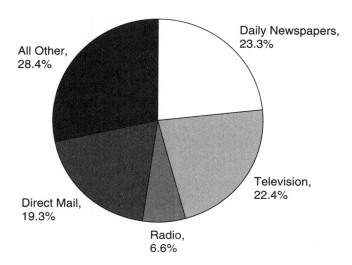

FIGURE 2.7 How advertising dollars are shared.
Daily newspapers take the largest single
slice of the advertising revenue pie. But
television is a close second—and direct
mail is growing rapidly. The figures are
for 1993.

Source: Newspaper Association of America

Clearly, *both* the character and location of the newspaper advertising market are changing.

ANALYZING A NEWSPAPER'S ADVERTISING MARKET

So, how does a budding strategist analyze a newspaper's advertising market? First, familiarize yourself with the principal sources of revenue. Ranked by dollar spending, Table 2.8 lists the leaders.

Second, determine which advertisers are in the market. *Editor & Publisher Market Guide* lists shopping centers and malls and, by name, leading stores. But consult a local authority, such as the chamber of commerce, for updated figures and drive the market. Driving around town and studying retailing patterns firsthand is the best way to get the "feel" of a newspaper's advertising market.

Third, study the newspaper carefully to note which advertisers are (or aren't) using the paper. How often are advertisers in the paper? What size ads do they use? This qualitative analysis, done over several weeks, yields valuable clues about how well the newspaper serves its advertising market.

Fourth, do a quantitative study by calculating the ad-to-news ratio in the newspaper. Measure a column length and multiply that by the number of columns on a page to obtain the number of column inches per page. Multiply that by the

TABLE 2.8   Principal Sources of Newspapers' Ad Revenue

Rank	Category	Total Ad Spending (millions)
1.	automotive	$7,754.5
2.	business, consumer services	5,259.4
3.	entertainment	3,749.9
4.	food	3,442.8
5.	toiletries, cosmetics	2,608.4
6.	drugs, remedies	2,294.7
7.	travel, hotels, resorts	2,240.7
8.	direct response companies	1,404.8
9.	candy, snacks, soft drinks	1,286.7
10.	insurance, real estate	1,242.3
11.	apparel	1,090.5
12.	sporting goods, toys	990.9
13.	publishing, media	806.6
14.	computers, office equipment	799.8
15.	beer, wine	779.0

Figures for 1993. Source: *Advertising Age,* quoting Competitive Media Reporting

number of pages in the entire paper and you'll have the total amount of space available for news and advertising. You then measure the amount of advertising (or news) to arrive at the ad-to-news ratio. Note in Table 2.9 the percentage of ad content in U.S. daily and Sunday papers.

TABLE 2.9   Advertising Content of U.S. Daily and Sunday Newspapers

	Percentage Morning	Percentage Evening	Percentage Sunday	Percentage Total
1950	57.5	60.4	54.6	58.3
1960	60.2	60.3	56.4	59.4
1970	61.6	61.4	61.5	61.5
1980	62.1	59.9	66.8	62.6
1985	60.4	59.7	69.4	62.8
1986	59.6	58.4	69.6	62.2
1987	59.4	57.6	69.6	62.0
1988	59.8	58.2	70.6	62.7
1989	58.4	56.2	69.9	61.6
1990	60.8	59.8	69.9	63.4
1991	57.3	56.6	67.0	60.0
1992	55.3	54.8	66.3	58.8

Source: Newspaper Association of America

Many newspaper analysts regard the correct ratio to be 60 percent advertising content and 40 percent news. Ad content substantially under 60 percent can mean a newspaper is starving for advertiser support. Ad content appreciably over 60 percent can so reduce the "newshole"—space allocated nonadvertising material—that readers feel cheated. The long-term result: Disaffected readers complaining, "There's no news in this newspaper."

In sum, analysis of advertising content revolves around whether there is sufficient advertising content from enough of the market's quality advertisers at ad rates consistent with profitable operation. More on rates later.

SUMMARY

In newspaper strategy, the single most important factor to consider is the market. Your newspaper will live, or die, on the basic economic strength of your market. You need literate, affluent readers and prosperous local retail merchants, the underpinnings of any newspaper market.

Markets can change rapidly, and some newspaper strategists who didn't adjust for changes in theirs were trapped in reactive management, attempting to make adjustments only after change hit them. Such managers—and their newspapers—often failed. The key to success is anticipatory management—anticipating change and adjusting strategies before it hits.

Think of a market as a slice of geography or a group of persons with shared interests or characteristics. Newspapers often create combination markets of, for example, persons with shared interests in a geographic area that can be reached and served. Markets, then, have *geographic* characteristics. Readers who live there have *demographic* characteristics (age, income) and *psychographic* characteristics (lifestyle, buying habits). Always, the geography served and readers sought must be defined by their appeal to advertisers. Commonly used market definitions are City Zone, Primary Market Area, Retail Trading Zone, and Newspaper Designated Market.

Researching a market, advertisers *and* newspaper strategists study population size, households, income, the character of local industry, and business and construction growth. Broadly, newspaper strategists are concerned about socioeconomic change in three areas:

- Many cities, once well-defined, stand-alone entities, are becoming sprawling metropolitan markets. Newspapers anchored in deteriorating downtowns have difficulty following affluent residents, many of whom flee to distant suburbs.
- The "typical" white, middle-class household no longer drives newspaper strategy. Minority Americans are increasing in numbers, complicating editors' tasks of creating newspapers that appeal across ethnic lines.
- The fundamental nature of U.S. retailing is changing. Many top-of-the-line department stores, always strong users of newspaper advertising, are giving way to discount houses that do little or no advertising in newspapers.

Readers as a market increasingly are "time-deprived" and ever more difficult to please. Relative to our population as a whole, they're getting older—and there are fewer of them. When readers say, "I don't have time to read newspapers," they *really* are saying, "I don't have enough time relative to the value I receive from reading newspapers."

Advertisers as a market present newspaper strategists with crucial challenges. Ad revenue growth is leveling off, relative to growth in the gross domestic product, and media competitors are fighting for increasing shares of the U.S. ad dollar.

RECOMMENDED READING

Staying atop relevant changes in market dynamics, reader demographics and advertiser attitudes is a challenge. Significant national developments are reported extremely well by *The New York Times, The Wall Street Journal* and *U.S. News & World Report*, among easily accessible publications, and the magazine *American Demographics.*

Important research is published by the Audit Bureau of Circulations, 900 N. Meacham Road, Schaumburg, Ill. 60195; and Newspaper Association of America, The Newspaper Center, 11600 Sunrise Valley Drive, Reston, Va. 22091-1412.

For students, a newspaper's own research is extremely valuable. Ask the advertising or promotion department for the "standard marketing kit" or "market research." Often, at least partial results of proprietary market analysis can be obtained.

NOTES

1. With thanks to the Audit Bureau of Circulations staff for its continued assistance in my teaching and writing efforts.

2. Other standard reference works include the annual *Statistical Abstract of the United States,* available from the Bureau of Census, U.S. Department of Commerce, Washington, D.C.; and, from the Bureau of Census, the *Census of Population* and *Census of Housing,* revised every 10 years. Monthly publications include the *Monthly Catalog of U.S. Government Publications,* the *Monthly Checklist of State Publications* and *Economic Indicators,* all available from the Superintendent of Documents, U.S. Government Printing Office, Washington, D.C.

3. Chet Fuller, "Cities Becoming Poor Cousins of the Suburbs," *Atlanta Constitution,* Oct. 19, 1993, quoting U.S. Census Bureau figures.

4. Ibid.

5. Ibid.

6. U.S. Census Bureau figures in "Outlook," *U.S. News & World Report,* Oct. 18, 1993, p. 16.

7. "Newspaper Sales Around the World," *presstime,* July 1993, p. 66.

8. Donald E. Newhouse, Newspaper Association of America chairman, "Spread the Word," *presstime,* August 1993, p. 5. The term "cannot read well" is defined by the U.S. Department of Education. The 2 million additional illiterates annually are immigrants, high-school dropouts and school graduates who cannot read well.

9. "Newspaper Numbers," *presstime,* October 1992, p. 48.

10. These projections were released on Dec. 3, 1992. For a quick, accessible reference, see Robert Pear, "New Look at the U.S. in 2050; Bigger, Older and Less White," *The New York Times,* national edition, Dec. 4, 1992, p. 1.

11. Ibid.

12. "Do Chains Cost Jobs?" *The New York Times,* national edition, Oct. 3, 1993, p. 6-F.

13. Andrea Adelson, "Woolworth to Shutter 970 Stores," *The New York Times,* national edition, Oct. 14, 1993, p. C-1.

3

UNDERSTANDING YOUR COMPETITORS

You now are at a crucial point in the preplanning process: competitive analysis. You've studied the newspaper's strengths and weaknesses. You've studied—carefully—your market. Now, which competitors will fight you, with skill and tenacity, in that market for your readers' time and your advertisers' dollars?

Many competitors are scrambling for any advantage they can gain in your market and, if you let them, they will take it at the expense of your newspaper (and, thus, your career). Is that too melodramatic? No. What we're talking about here is marketplace war.

The history of U.S. media in our free-enterprise system is one of unending conflict. Down through the years, new contenders for readers and advertisers have edged out—sometimes literally killed off—long-established media that once enjoyed marketplace domination. Note the once-great, now-dead *Washington Star, Philadelphia Bulletin, Cleveland Press, Chicago Daily News, Los Angeles Herald-Examiner*—many are the broken mastheads littering the U.S. media landscape. And note what happened to once-famous magazines: *Look* and *Collier's* are long gone; *Life* and *Saturday Evening Post,* once literally American institutions, are mere shadows of their former selves.

Television forced radio to move over and make room in the marketplace. Now, cable TV is threatening broadcast TV. And coming soon to neighborhoods near you are new electronic systems likely to force yet another reshuffling in the media marketplace.

Clearly, your job as a newspaper strategist will be complicated. In fighting for readers you must position your newspaper carefully to emphasize its news and information strengths and to play against the weaknesses of competitors who are after the same readers. In fighting for advertisers you must understand thoroughly the strengths your competitors will be boasting about as they sell up and down Main Street. In that battle, you'll need to locate—and exploit—your competitors' weaknesses. Let's turn, then, to competitive analysis, the final step in the preplanning process that leads us to devising newspaper strategy.

WHO OR WHAT IS A COMPETITOR?

For years, your predecessors in newspaper strategy enjoyed a single-minded approach to competition: Beat that rag on the other side of town and we win. Today, you don't have the luxury—the simplicity—of competing merely against another cross-town newspaper of like size and characteristics. The competition is varied and fierce—anything or anybody who steals your readers' time or your advertisers' dollars.[1] Few of even our largest cities have two or more competing newspapers. Yet, all cities, large or small, are "media intensive," with print, broadcast, electronic and other forms of competitors struggling for a market niche (see Figure 3.1).

An important point about Figure 3.1: Seldom do media competitors find an exclusive step in the competitive staircase and stay there. Inevitably, media competitors attack up and down the staircase, seeking new marketplace opportunities and, also inevitably, treading on another medium's turf.

So, the first lesson in competitive analysis: A donnybrook is under way in virtually every city as a snarling pack of media competitors fight head-on against each other over the same reader time and advertiser dollar. The second lesson: It is not you who will define who or what are your newspaper's competitors. That is done by the marketplace—your readers' perceptions of whether other media return greater value for their time, your advertisers' perceptions of whether other media are more cost efficient than your newspaper in delivering consumers. Many

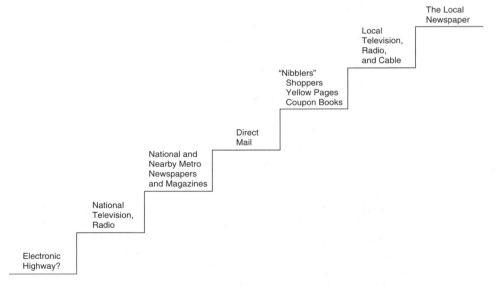

FIGURE 3.1   The competitive staircase. U.S. cities are "media intensive," with many competitors fighting for a marketplace niche. You can visualize this as a struggle for a step on the competitive "staircase."

of your newspaper predecessors were so busy fighting other newspapers that they failed to see many competitors springing up all around them, offering readers alternative sources of information and courting advertisers with new ways of getting their messages out. Compared to what you face, your predecessors had a simple task—analyzing the strengths and weaknesses of a single newspaper competitor across town, then devising a strategy to combat it. You'll need a panoramic view of your marketplace and a wide variety of strategies to defeat attackers coming at you from all directions.

But how can you assess the severity of threats posed by competitors and assign priorities to fighting each of them? You first analyze each competitor in terms of how you define your market.

First, Guard Your Geographic Market

Turn first in competitive analysis to who or what threatens you on the ground, in your newspaper's geographic market. Recall from Chapter 2 that a newspaper can define its market as a city and surrounding counties. Note again how the concept is represented by the Audit Bureau of Circulations' map of the market for "Anytown, Ill." (see Figure 3.2 on page 56).

Now, visualize yourself managing the *Anytown Daily:* You should analyze each competitor within two time dimensions, as part of devising two separate competitive strategies.

First, you must understand who currently competes in Anytown's existing four-county Primary Market Area. Your newspaper's own sales force will provide the earliest—and best—input. Advertising sales people are quick to report competitor attempts to win away their accounts (and, thus, their sales commissions). Listen to your sales staff. You and your staff also should keep in close touch with sales racks and newsstands in the PMA, to note the appearance of any new print competitors. Watch your own mailbox for direct mail activity. For a broader view, check media listings in these standard reference works: *Gale Directory of Publications and Broadcast Media, Editor & Publisher International Yearbook, Circulation, Bacon's Newspaper Directory, Broadcasting & Cable Yearbook.*

When you and your *Anytown Daily* staff understand thoroughly your current competitors, you must shift your thinking into a second time dimension: Who or what will compete against you in the geographic market as it likely will be in, say, five years. Recall from Chapter 2 how population and business activity are shifting rapidly in and around cities across the United States. Even small towns are losing affluent residents to newly established suburbs outside city limits. Now, look again at Figure 3.2 and envisage the flight of affluent residents from the Anytown City Zone in a southeasterly direction, into the panhandle of Black County. That could mean the economic core of your market is shifting toward the towns of Maher, Petrie and Moran. You'll have to start planning, now, for increased news coverage of that developing area and for energized circulation and advertising sales there. You can bet your competitors see the same economic shift and that they, too, will be planning to exploit the opportunity opening in Black County.

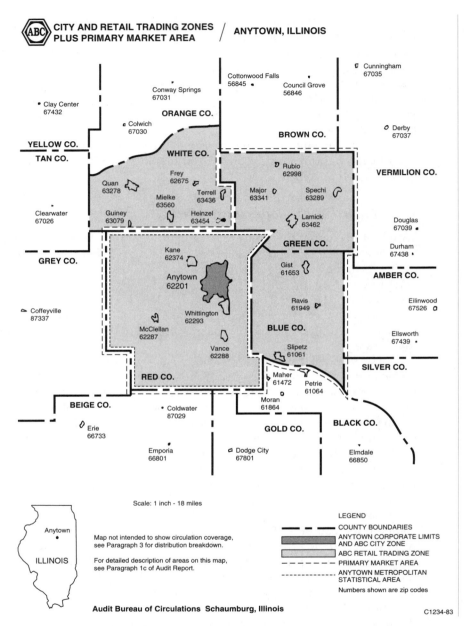

ABC CITY AND RETAIL TRADING ZONES
PLUS PRIMARY MARKET AREA / ANYTOWN, ILLINOIS

Scale: 1 inch - 18 miles

Anytown
ILLINOIS

Map not intended to show circulation coverage,
see Paragraph 3 for distribution breakdown.

For detailed description of areas on this map,
see Paragraph 1c of Audit Report.

LEGEND

COUNTY BOUNDARIES
ANYTOWN CORPORATE LIMITS
AND ABC CITY ZONE
ABC RETAIL TRADING ZONE
PRIMARY MARKET AREA
ANYTOWN METROPOLITAN
STATISTICAL AREA
Numbers shown are zip codes

Audit Bureau of Circulations Schaumburg, Illinois

C1234-83

**FIGURE 3.2 In competitive analysis, a newspaper strategist's first concern
must be to understand who or what competes for reader time
and advertiser dollars in the geographic market. For a
newspaper in "Anytown, Ill.," the most dangerous
competitors operate in the City Zone and White, Green, Blue
and Red counties.**

So, your competitive analysis must go beyond who or what can do you damage in your geographic market as it is defined today. You also must assess which competitors you'll likely face in the years ahead on Black County turf, which by then will be extremely important to you. But defending geography is only part of your battle.

CASE STUDY 3.1   The Second Battle of Atlanta or
In War, It's Fatal to Misjudge the Enemy

It was a hot topic on the newspaper industry gossip circuit: The Atlanta metropolitan market is exploding in growth. New industry is flocking there, along with thousands of well-educated, prosperous people. America's Sun Belt is booming, and Atlanta is the place to be.

Why, it's another Orange County!

For years, acquisition-minded media executives nationwide watched Orange County, Calif., which was catching spill-over growth—and the fleeing affluent—from neighboring Los Angeles County and becoming one of the wealthiest counties in the country. (By 1993, the average household income in Orange County was an impressive $47,735.)

Riding that growth, a small daily, the *Orange County Register,* became one of the greatest newspaper success stories of all time. It soared over 300,000 circulation and was enormously profitable—right under the nose of the giant next door, the *Los Angeles Times.* The gossip was that New York Times Co. was among powerful, well-financed companies trying to find a way to share in the "action" in metro Atlanta, just as the *Register's* owners shared in Orange County's growth.

In June 1987, Times Co. broke the news that it was acquiring the *Gwinnett Daily News,* a 27,500-circulation daily in Gwinnett County, a contiguous suburb northeast of Atlanta. Gwinnett County was at the time the fastest-growing county in the United States. Affluent Atlantans fleeing the city's deteriorating socioeconomic core were resettling in Gwinnett, along with thousands from out of state. It was clear to all that the economic focus of the Atlanta market was shifting toward Gwinnett and other suburbs northeast of the city.

Nothing was wrong with the market research conducted by Times Co. executives. They understood completely the Atlanta growth patterns outlined in Case Study 2.1, in Chapter 2. But, in competitive analysis, Times Co. erred. Here's the story: At the time, the *Atlanta Journal* and *Constitution* were known widely as good but rather sleepy, comfortable newspapers. They were filled with nostalgia for the Old South and were on nobody's list of the best ten newspapers. Their parent, privately owned Cox Enterprises, was heavily in debt, and had slipped from number 13 among the nation's largest media firms to number 14. Cox was diversifying, especially into cable, and having trouble with some of its newspapers. Its *Miami Herald* was known to be shaky (it closed in 1988). Times Co., publisher, after all, of *everybody's* number 1 paper, *The New York Times,* obviously saw the *Atlanta Journal* and *Constitution* as pushovers.

To the industry's astonishment, Times Co. revealed it paid $88.2 million for the *Gwinnett Daily News*—equivalent to $3,207.27 per *Daily News* subscriber. Why, Gannett Co. got the famous old *Des Moines Register* in 1985 for only $688 per subscriber, and the *Louisville Courier Journal* in 1986 for $1,022 per subscriber. Then, Times Co. announced it was upping the ante: It would spend $40 million for a new *Daily News* headquarters and production facility. Soon, word got out that Times Co. executives were boasting, "We're going to kick the *Constitution* and *Journal* back across 285." That was a refer-

Continued

CASE STUDY 3.1   *Continued*

ence to Highway 285, a beltway circling Atlanta and separating the city from Gwinnett County and other rich northeast suburbs. *Constitution* and *Journal* executives drew three conclusions.

First, the enormous Times Co. capital investment meant the *Gwinnett Daily News* would not be operated as a small county daily but, rather, would be positioned head-on against the *Constitution* and *Journal* in affluent suburbs, the core of their future market. Only by dominating a much wider market than Gwinnett County could Times Co. hope for appropriate return on its initial investment of $128 million. Second, therefore, no cost was too great to beat off Times Co. The very future of the *Journal* and *Constitution*, Cox Enterprises' flagships, was at stake. This was no mere suburban fight; it was a fight for an entire metro market of the future. Third, it was damned annoying for those New Yorkers to come down south and talk about kicking around two grand old Southern newspapers. Whether Times Co. executives actually set up Highway 285 as the battle line is irrelevant; what's relevant is that *Constitution* and *Journal* executives *believe* they did. There was an incredibly emotional response to Times Co.'s threat. The *Constitution* and *Journal* launched an old-fashioned, knock-down counterattack. It was newspaper war.

In sum, Times Co. poured in impressive journalistic and managerial talent, and *millions* of dollars in operating funds. The *Gwinnett Dai-*

ly News doubled its circulation and became perhaps the country's best journalistic product in the 50,000 circulation category. But, the *Daily News* never had a single profitable year.

For, the *Constitution* and *Journal*, the sleeping journalistic giants of the South, had awakened. Cox changed publishers and editors and poured in its own millions of dollars. For five years the battle raged. Then, Times Co. tried to sell out. There were no takers (who wants to buy into a street brawl?) and Times Co. shut down the *Daily News*. The total loss is thought to have exceeded $200 million.

Lessons:

- In your competitive analysis, seek to understand your foe's capabilities as well as intentions. Cox, after all, was a $1.8 billion company when Times Co. arrived on the scene and could afford a long fight.
- When you threaten a competitor's very existence, as Times Co. threatened the future of the *Constitution* and *Journal*, you can expect a vigorous fight.
- Never underestimate the emotional response from a competitor. The marketplace realities awakened the sleepy *Constitution* and *Journal*. But to this day, it's the "arrogance" of that statement about Highway 285 that *Constitution* and *Journal* executives mention as they look back on the fight they won.

Second, Guard Your Demographic Market

Defending your newspaper's market against competitors is akin to defending your home against burglars: Pay closest attention to protecting your most valuable possessions. In newspapering, your most valuable possessions are your market's demographically attractive households—those advertisers seek for their high incomes and free-spending lifestyles. Just as your newspaper must try to scoop up demographically attractive readers, so must raiding competitors attempt to ensnare households they easily can "sell" to advertisers.

Figure 3.3 will help you visualize a market structure of demographic niches and understand how each will be under attack by competitors. Let's examine, from

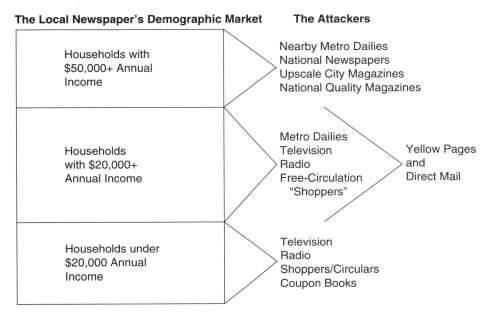

FIGURE 3.3   Competitors will use a variety of media to attack your market. Above are media frequently used to attack demographic niches in a market.

a newspaper strategist's viewpoint, the strengths and weaknesses of competitors listed in Figure 3.3. We'll prioritize our examination in accordance with each competitor's rank in advertising revenue behind the number 1 ad medium, newspapers.

Television

In the battle for readers' time, television's entertainment programming has enormous pull. Take your pick of whose research to believe, but a television set is at least on and playing (if not watched) for hours—perhaps seven or eight daily—in the average household.

Television's appeal to advertisers is clear: The huge audiences for entertainment programming and the sight-and-sound drama of well-done commercials appeal mightily to sellers of goods and services. Consequently, television attracts more than 22 percent of all ad dollars spent in the United States. And, in recent years, television's revenue growth rate has outstripped all media, including newspapers.[2]

However, newspapers successfully counterattack television on several fronts: To advertisers, newspapers point out that TV advertising is intrusive, inserted in entertainment programming against the wishes of viewers. This doesn't create the

TABLE 3.1   Where Does Time Go?

Medium	Time Spent
Television (including cable)	Four hours, nine minutes
Radio	Three hours
Recorded music	36 minutes
Daily newspapers	28 minutes
Consumer books (not textbooks)	16 minutes
Consumer magazines	14 minutes
Home video	7 minutes
Theater movies	2 minutes

Average time Americans spend daily on various media.

Source: *Atlanta Constitution*, Sept. 9, 1992, p. A-13, quoting Veronis, Suhler & Associates' 1992 survey.

best consumer mindset for a sales message. Indeed, many viewers "zap" commercials by flipping to other channels. Many talk or read—or simply leave the room until programming resumes.

Clearly, television's research showing phenomenally large audiences doesn't make clear the reality that it is entertainment programming, not commercials, that Americans watch most. Ratings measure viewership of programming, not commercials. Newspaper strategists also compete fiercely by claiming TV viewers simply don't retain much of the operative information in commercials—company name, product specifications, prices and so forth. (Try this game on a friend next time you watch television together: About 15 minutes after you've watched three or four commercials squeezed into a break in your favorite program, ask your friend to jot down names of companies that sponsored the commercials, the goods or services being sold, and product specifications for each.)

In fighting TV advertising, newspaper strategists say that their readers (unlike TV viewers) pay for their product, the newspaper, because they find it a valuable source of information and, therefore, readers are in an information-seeking mode. Newspapers point out their readers are searching for facts and figures and thus are in a perfect mindset to be wooed by advertising pitches in adjacent columns.

In the battle for reader's time, TV news advocates boast these advantages:

- TV news is easy to watch: You just settle back and let somebody else do the thinking. Newspaper reading requires effort and concentration.
- Television is fast—26 minutes or less is actual time devoted to news during a standard 30-minute network show. Yet, TV news gives the impression of covering the world's most important stories.
- TV news has a personalized warmth. TV anchors are real, live humans invited into millions of homes as guests each evening. Viewers know them, their moods, their personalities—and viewers trust these friends of theirs.

The newspaper counterattack takes two forms: First, reorientation of news content to emphasize interpretive, analytical writing, which contrasts sharply with the superficial parade of bits and pieces on the evening TV news. That is, the best way for newspapers to combat TV news is to be demonstrably superior every day in story selection, fullness of reporting and writing, and keenness of analysis. Second, newspapers must better promote themselves, explaining to the public why TV news, as excellent as some is, simply isn't deep enough to serve as a sole source of information for anyone in our modern society. As we'll discuss in a later chapter, such promotion must use competing media—including, yes, television—to tell the newspaper story.

Direct Mail

In the fight for advertisers' dollars, direct mail is an enormous threat because it does—extraordinary well—two things newspapers and other media must struggle to achieve: First, direct mail can achieve total market coverage—reach 90 to 95 percent or more of the households (or, at least, the mailboxes) in a market. (*No* medium reaches 100 percent, due to household vacancies, address changes and so forth.) Second, direct mail can achieve unrivaled accuracy in finely tuned target marketing—reaching just those households whose demographics, lifestyles or consumer habits are attractive to advertisers. Because unwanted—unattractive— households are *not* reached, advertisers get efficient circulation and a low cost per thousand ("CPM," in industry parlance). CPM is the cost of delivering an advertising message to 1,000 selected recipients.

Direct mail exploded in growth in the past decade. In 1992, revenue surpassed $25 billion, or more than 19 percent of all ad dollars spent in the United States. Importantly, direct mail revenue that year grew 4 percent over the previous year's revenue, compared with 1 percent growth for newspapers.[3]

Three factors most influence direct mail's growth: First, the retail industry increasingly is turning to identifying the demographics and psychographics of the most attractive potential customers, then demanding advertising media target them. Of all media, direct mail has the strongest capability for that. Second, in an example of how new technology can influence the media, computers are coming into widespread use in marketing. Without them, it would be impossible to maintain databases on household demographics, addresses and the other marketing information retailers demand today. Third, the U.S. Postal Service has rate structures conducive to direct mail. Newspaper strategists argue that first-class postal rates subsidize and thus lower direct mail rates, putting newspapers and other media at a disadvantage. Postal officials and direct mail executives argue that's not true, of course.

The newspaper counterattack against direct mail generally takes three forms: First, some newspaper strategists denigrate direct mail as "junk mail" that is ineffective for advertisers. The connotation of "junk mail" indeed does hang over this medium, and consumer response to a mailing sometimes is muted (a campaign can be deemed successful if only 1 or 2 percent of recipients respond). Nevertheless, direct mail campaigns, particularly those directed at affluent households, often are successful—and advertisers know it. So, the "junk mail" counterattack is the least successful response the newspaper industry makes to this competitive threat.

Second, in their most successful response, newspapers (a) improve their own journalistic quality and subscription sales efforts, to penetrate their markets more deeply and (b) use free-circulation, total market coverage papers to reach nonsubscriber households. The combination of paid and free circulation thus offers advertisers something akin to the 90 to 95 percent penetration promised by direct mail.

Third, many newspapers create their own direct mail subsidiaries, thus offering advertisers paid and free newspapers, direct mail and other media services—alone or in combination with others. Colorful circulars and slick catalogs are delivered to some households as inserts in paid-circulation newspapers and to others in total market coverage papers or via direct mail. Regardless of which medium you use to achieve it, your generation of newspaper strategists must offer precise targeting of market niches that advertisers seek to reach.

Yellow Pages

With ad revenue around $10 billion annually, Yellow Pages are formidable competitors—and they, or their electronic successors, threaten to be even more formidable in the future.[4] The basic strength of Yellow Pages, of course, is their direct tie to the telephone in the consumer's household or office, where most purchasing decisions are made. Whatever the need—airline reservations for next week, a plumber right now— the consumer can act immediately, efficiently and economically through the Yellow Pages and the telephone. Importantly, about 88 percent of Yellow Pages advertising is from local advertisers—the single most important source of newspaper advertising.[5]

The great weakness of Yellow Pages is that their information is static for more than a year: Airline telephone numbers, the plumber's address and, particularly, what the plumber charges—all are fixed in print for the life of the telephone book. An error in Yellow Pages advertising also stands uncorrected for a year. Some very big players in the telephone and information businesses plan to fix that weakness. Regional Bell operating companies, all multibillion dollar organizations, are devoting huge sums to research and development of *electronic* Yellow Pages.

A vision of the future includes a desktop "communications center" in homes and businesses. The center would include telephone service but also offer computerized, interactive access to distant databases—including a service that, for example, would summon up automatically the names, current addresses, telephone numbers and hourly rates for all plumbers near your home who could react quickly in an emergency.

The concept of electronic Yellow Pages is drawing telephone companies into the competitive arena and confronting newspapers with, basically, two choices: (a) somehow develop competitive services that will fight off the telephone companies, or (b) join forces with telephone companies. Many major newspaper-based companies hope to join, rather than fight, telephone companies.

Many newspapers, for example, offer low-cost audiotext service via telephone. *The Los Angeles Times'* TimesLink provides 75 different information lines. The company reported in 1994 this service was generating close to 100,000 calls per week from readers who wanted information on everything from a stock price to the weather in Stockholm.

But telephone information services are only the beginning. Knight-Ridder Inc., for example, created an electronic version of a newpaper—advertising and all—at its *San José Mercury News*. Using computer access, subscribers keyboard the specifications of, for example, a used car they want to buy. Instantly, a Knight-Ridder computer scans a classified database and flashes to the user the three or four ads that precisely meet the caller's specifications. Users also can summon up classified display ads—for example, an advertisement of a home for sale, complete with color photo, description, price and name and telephone number of the owner or realtor.

To understand the threat that poses newspapers you must realize that some newspapers—the *Los Angeles Times*, for example—get *50 percent or more of their total revenue from classified advertising.* You must also realize that although the largest U.S. media company, Time Warner, had a whopping $5.5 billion total media revenue in 1992, eight Yellow Pages publishers were twice that large. They include GTE Corp. ($19.9 billion total revenue 1992), BellSouth ($15.2 billion), Bell Atlantic ($12.6 billion), Nynex Corp. ($13.1 billion), and U.S. West and Southwestern Bell Corp. (each over $10 billion).

Linking forces makes sense for both newspapers and telephone companies. Envisage consumer services based on the newspaper's unrivaled ability to gather, edit and format information, combined with the telephone companies' technology, communications circuits already into nearly all homes, and established administrative and billing procedures. Then, add to that the newspaper's link with Main Street retailers and its record of efficiently conducting advertising services of all kinds. Such a combined service would do powerful things for readers and advertisers alike.

Radio

Radio is a survivor in the media wars. Well into the late 1940s, radio was the dominant electronic medium of news and entertainment. Then came television, improved newspapers, thousands of new magazines—and still radio survives. Radio's tenacity (its annual revenue is substantially over $9 billion) is based primarily on three factors:

- *Technology.*   FM radio, with its superior sound quality, arrived just as AM radio's future began to dim. In 1950, 733 FM stations were on the air; today more than 6,300 are broadcasting (compared to 4,900 AM stations.)
- *Programming shrewdness.*   Whatever the marketplace demands, wherever a marketing niche opens, radio has an offering: music, talk, ethnic slant, all-news formats and so forth. Huge audiences are pulled in. Conservative talk show star Rush Limbaugh had 3.8 million listeners on 571 stations nationwide in 1993.[6] But it is local *narrowcast* programming, contrasting with national *broad*casting, that gives radio unique strengths. Want to reach a "mature," affluent audience? Play golden oldies tunes. Want to reach young listeners? Play their

music. Radio is very successful, especially with local retailers, in selling its ability to reach targeted audiences.

• *Low cost.*   Relative to other media, radio has low costs—and that permits offering low ad rates to advertisers. In small towns, $100 will buy many commercial "spots" on local radio, very appealing to "mom and pop" stores that cannot afford newspaper advertising.

Radio isn't a strong competitor in news, with two exceptions: First, all-news formats are popular in some large cities (although they still offer little more than "headline" service). Second, for some ethnic groups, especially inner-city blacks and Hispanics, talk radio is extremely popular and in some cities, supplants newspapers as the leading forum for minorities.

In the battle for ad dollars, few individual radio stations are major threats. But in their totality, radio stations take a great deal of ad revenue out of virtually every medium-size and large city—and many small towns, too.

The newspaper counterattack against radio in advertising sales takes two forms: First, newspaper strategists say, everybody listens to radio while doing something else—driving, doing housework, (allegedly) studying and so forth. So, it's impossible for radio commercials to grasp listener attention and communicate operative information about products or services. (Radio jingles—"Coke is It!"— do work their way into consumer awareness with repetition, of course.)

Second, newspapers develop alternate means, other than the mainframe newspaper, of serving small "mom and pop" retailers who are attracted to low-cost advertising on radio. Newspapers produce "zoned" editions of relatively low circulations, thus offering small retailers lower ad rates. Or, newspapers produce alternative media—coupon books, neighborhood shoppers and so forth—which offer rates low enough to lure advertisers away from radio.

Magazines

Despite being one of the world's oldest media, magazines show youthful agility in adjusting to new marketplace realities and traumatic change. Today, this "old" industry is a fierce competitor.

Broadly, three things happened: First, major national, general-interest magazines withered, then died. Even the weekly *Life, Look,* and *Collier's* with their tens of millions of readers, couldn't deliver the mass audiences easily scooped up by television. And, importantly, such mass-circulation magazines were collecting readers of all demographic descriptions, in all parts of the country—just as U.S. retailers began demanding highly targeted access to narrowly defined demographic groups.

Second, the cost of magazine production soared. Magazine historians remember wistfully the weekly version of *Life,* with its glossy (high-cost) paper and beautiful full-color (and extremely expensive) photographs. Printing and shipping millions of such high-quality magazines drove costs so high that advertiser cost per thousand reached astronomical—and noncompetitive—heights.

Third, genius prevailed in magazine editing and publishing: Magazines switched to *niche audiences,* producing highly refined editorial content for narrow groups of readers who depended on tailored information to perform better on the job and live better at home. For example, *Adhesive Age,* a trade magazine (slogan: "All the News About Glue"), reaches executives in the packaging industry and attracts impressive advertising support. Another trade magazine, *Aviation Week & Space Technology,* flourishes as the principal medium of industry information *and advertising* for demographically attractive executives in aviation and space industries. Even consumer magazines focus their content for targeted audiences—*Forbes* for rich corporate executives, *Money* for high-income personal investors, *Better Homes & Gardens* for the wealthy grass and flowers crowd. Today, most of the nation's 11,000+ magazines are trade publications serving niche audiences and attracting advertisers who have no other medium quite so efficient for reaching those narrow audiences.

The magazine industry's evolution into niche publishing has another enormously important impact: If written by experts, narrowly focused editorial content—"news you can use"—is deemed more important by readers than general news and they'll pay more for it. Some magazines have single-copy prices of $5 or more, and the industry as a whole today gets about 51 percent of its total revenue from readers and 49 percent from advertisers (newspapers, as you know, get about 80 percent from advertisers and 20 percent from readers.)[7]

Because so much of their content is deemed crucial and because of the nature of magazine reading—a bit today, maybe a bit again tomorrow—magazines generally have a longer "shelf life" than newspapers do. Most magazines are kept in homes and offices for months (just check, next time you visit your dentist). Advertisers value that repeated "shelf-life" exposure to readers.

The newspaper counterattack against magazines generally takes two forms: First, newspaper content is changing. Much newspaper writing is similar to magazine style—broad survey articles, personality profiles and interpretive writing all designed to match consumer magazine appeal to readers. More importantly, however, through "internal zoning"—production of special sections—newspapers try to develop highly specialized news content to rival the precision and in-depth coverage that magazines offer niche audiences. For example, newspaper business news sections are booming, with special emphasis on personal finance and investing—a direct shot at *Money* and similar magazines. Nevertheless, newspapers by their nature are broad-based consensus documents, and their editors often have difficulty, even in special sections, of achieving the tight focus and in-depth coverage that magazine editors offer in trade publications.

Second, some newspapers, even in small towns, launch their own magazines, either in their Sunday issues or as stand-alone publications, and try to corral readers and advertisers they otherwise would lose. For example, the *Athens (Ga.) Banner-Herald* and *The Daily News,* with combined morning and evening circulation of only 28,000, publish the stand-alone *Athens Magazine,* a slick, high-cost publication that reaches high-income households and thus attracts top-drawer advertisers.

The publisher maintains the magazine opens new sources of revenue and doesn't draw down newspaper subscriber or ad revenues.[8]

The "Nibblers"

You see them everywhere: billboards along Main Street, touting everything from extra-juicy hamburgers to new cars; business periodicals in homes and offices; farm publications in implement stores and farm and ranch homes. Do they compete against newspapers? You bet—in a big way. Those three forms of media alone—outdoor advertising, business periodicals and farm publications—approach $4.5 billion in annual revenue.[9] Now, add to them the other "nibbler" competitors you see all over town—the real estate booklets in racks outside food stores, the "dining out" publications scattered about restaurants, the entertainment magazines, the "pennysavers," coupon books, shoppers...

For newspapers, the impact of these many competitors is threefold: First, of course, in their totality, the "nibblers" take billions of dollars out of the advertising market—and every dollar they get is a dollar newspapers cannot get. Second, the "nibblers" clutter the advertising environment. They distract advertiser and consumer alike—and dilute considerably the strength of the newspaper as the single dominant advertising medium in a market. Third, for newspapers, "nibblers" are a competitive threat almost impossible to defend against. Devising strategies against another newspaper or a single TV station is relatively easy; figuring out what to do against competing magazines is simple. But how does a newspaper strategist devise an attack plan against a pack of media competitors as diverse as billboards on Main Street and free real estate booklets outside supermarkets? We'll later discuss two broad strategies: (a) improve the mainframe newspaper to simply do a better job of catching more readers and advertisers, and (b) launch your own "nibblers" to protect your newspaper's flanks.

WHO CAN HURT YOU THE MOST?

Somewhere in the Pentagon, birthplace of U.S. military strategy, there undoubtedly is a rather lonely colonel in charge of war plans to be executed in the highly unlikely event that Canada or Peru attacks the United States. Elsewhere in the Pentagon are colonels—lots of them, and generals and admirals, too—looking after plans to use if a large and powerful nuclear-armed nation tries the same thing. Military strategists, obviously, spend most of their time guarding against foes who can do the most damage.

So, too, must you, as a newspaper strategist, turn quickly and fully to those competitors most dangerous in the fight for readers and ad dollars in your market. That is, think back over this chapter's discussion of how to defend your geographic market and your demographic market, then assign top priority to the most powerful competitors you face in both of those market dimensions. Don't get tied up worrying about mom and pop nibblers.

You'll find the most dangerous competitors have these characteristics: First, financial strength. Launching successful raids against established newspapers is expensive, requiring high-quality efforts in news, circulation and advertising sales. If you're managing a suburban or small-town daily, watch carefully any neighboring metropolitan dailies. They likely have the financial guns to damage you. Watch particularly for any publicly owned media companies. They're under constant pressure—the "rising tide of shareholder expectation"—to improve profits, and that often requires expansion into new markets and diversifying by launching new reader and advertiser products.

Second, they have a record of marketplace aggression. Recall Case Study 3.1: Why did New York Times Co. shut down the *Gwinnett Daily News* rather than sell it after losing the competitive battle against the *Atlanta Journal* and *Constitution?* Because the entire media world watched that battle and no other company wanted to buy into a market where it would face the aggressive news, circulation and advertising strategies the Atlanta papers used to drive out New York Times Co. Every other medium-size daily within reach of the Atlanta giants noted that aggressive reaction, too, and today constructs its competitive strategies around the need to avoid a similar confrontation.

Never forget: You may not be able to guess a foe's intentions. But you can analyze the foe's current financial capabilities and past actions in the marketplace.

Third, they are an example of quality. Even if it doesn't threaten a suburban newspaper directly, a metropolitan daily can exert strong competitive pressure merely by representing to readers an example of outstanding journalistic quality. New York City, Chicago, Dallas, Atlanta, Los Angeles—all have outstanding papers that simply overshadow the comparatively weak coverage of smaller neighboring papers. Metros consequently often achieve deep household penetration in suburbs without zoned editions or other special efforts. And, the metros by definition penetrate the most affluent households— the top of the market that suburban papers must corral for their advertisers.

Direct mail also competes through an example of quality: It gives advertisers 90 to 95 percent household penetration, a "quality" performance newspapers are hard pressed to match. In other words, assess all competitors' quality of performance—in news, information, penetration, service to advertisers or whatever—and adjust your strategic priorities accordingly.

Finally, put yourself in their shoes. Each time you plan a move in your marketplace, sit back and analyze the likely effect it will have on your competitors—then try to calculate what their reactions will be. As Case Study 3.1 makes clear, the New York Times Co. should have spent more time on that type of competitive analysis. Times Co. then might have guessed that by threatening the *Atlanta Constitution* and *Journal* in the very core of their future market, a vicious reaction would be forthcoming.

Remember: Whatever you do to expand or improve your newspaper's hold on the marketplace, you'll likely be trodding turf that's very important to a competitor. Note who that competitor is, then analyze the likely reaction before you judge whether you want to get into a fight.

FUTURE ELECTRONIC COMPETITORS

We all know it's coming: a new "electronic highway" featuring astounding technological innovations likely to change dramatically how entertainment, information and advertising are distributed. No one, however, is certain of what shape all this will take or, indeed, the competitive implications it will hold for newspapers.

Whatever the eventual outcome, you can manage your newspaper to resist the technology or use it. I recommend—strongly—that you use it as one tool among many, including newsprint, that you'll employ as manager of a newspaper-based "profit center" offering many media services. Plan around the following competitive realities.

CONSUMERS WANT GREATER CONTROL

Whether "consuming" news, entertainment or advertising, Americans are demanding greater control over what they get, when and in what shape or format. Why did households taking cable soar from 29 million in 1982 to 58 million in 1993? Because those households wanted more variety of entertainment than the offerings of the three traditional networks, ABC, NBC and CBS.

Why is Cable News Network (CNN) so successful with 24-hour news? Because TV watchers want news on *their* timetable, not only when CBS, ABC and NBC say it's time for the evening news. Why are trade magazines so successful with niche publishing? Because millions of readers want job-related, fact-filled specifics on developments crucial to their careers. And, they want it delivered in authoritative, no-nonsense reporting and precision writing quite unlike the broader, more general style of newspapers. Why are advertisers making direct mail the fastest-growing medium in America? Because direct mail gives them the control they want over households reached.

Clearly, *all* news and advertising media must plan to respond more alertly than in the past to precisely what audiences want. Newspapers, first, must be research-driven, ensuring the mainframe product itself meets, as closely as possible, reader and advertiser demands. Second, newspapers will need to use other tools—including the "electronic highway"—to offer diversified services, each structured to meet what competitors are offering readers and advertisers.

TECHNOLOGY OPENS UNDREAMED CHOICES

New technology clearly offers your competitors—and your newspaper, if you're smart—incredible opportunities to serve readers and advertisers in new ways. For example, one innovation alone—fiber optics—changes completely the dynamics of information distribution. To explain: Until now, we've relied mostly on *analog* transmission, in essence the broadcasting of sound, along copper wires. This technique is "slow," in a technical sense, and copper wires are badly limited in the amount of "information" they can carry.

However, telephone companies are replacing the copper wire with a fiber-optics circuit—a thin strand of glass. Information is converted to *digital* form and "broadcast" as light through the circuit. Result: A circuit that once carried only a single telephone connection now can carry—simultaneously—hundreds of telephone conversations, hundreds of cable TV circuits, plus burglar and fire alarm systems *and* give you interactive (two-way) computerized capability for banking or shopping from home. That is, there will be hardly any limitation on the amount of information that can be dumped in American households or made available through computerized recall from distant databases. There won't be limitations, either, on the speed of transmitting information or providing it in any format the householder chooses. The electronically delivered information is portable, too. Roger Fidler of Knight-Ridder developed an electronic tablet about the size of a newsmagazine that can be loaded with news and photos and carried anywhere for use. Images are stored in the tablet, which he calls a "personal information appliance," and presented to viewers with all the high-definition color and typographic techniques of a newspaper. By touching the tablet's screen, the user summons up the desired "page."

AMERICANS ARE "COMPUTER COMFORTABLE"

Don't base your newspaper strategy on the assumption that Americans won't take to the "Star Wars" technology envisaged for the new "electronic highway." First, Americans have a history of adapting quickly to new technology the moment the price is right. For example, witness how quickly hand-held calculators became part of the landscape when the price descended from hundreds of dollars each to $1.98 or so.

Second, we already are using the new technology needed for the information revolution. Note these numbers for 1993:

- Personal computers used in business average 41.7 per 100 workers. (These are the same Americans, incidentally, who are showing increasing reluctance to read newspapers or anything else.)
- There are 3,900 commercial databases making information available to computer users. One service, Prodigy, has more than 2 million subscribers and $230 million annual revenue.
- There are 1.8 million computers directly connected to Internet, the international computer linkup.
- Cellular telephone subscribers surpass 10 million and usage averages 4.4 per 100 persons.[10]

The increasing acceptance of new technology speeds the growth, of course, of such online computer services as Prodigy, Compuserve, America Online and Internet. Additionally, millions of users worldwide tap into Internet.

BOX 3.1   The Interactive, Multi–Media, Digital Era

"What are the characteristics of this era? Information will be interactive. This means that customers will be able to significantly control the information they receive, where they receive it, how they receive it, the timing, the form and the content.

"Information will be multi-media, that is presented via some combination of text, sound, graphics, animation and video. The results will often be much more compelling and powerful than if just one form were used. Information will be digital. It will be developed, stored, edited and transmitted electronically.

"In the future, information will be presented in new ways over interactive or 2-way television, where the remote control will allow a variety of actions by the consumer; over multimedia personal computers, which will offer video, sound, graphics and text; over portable, often hand-held devices, sometimes called Personal Digital Assistants (PDAs), which recognize handwriting or speech and work with pens; and over smart phones, which look much like familiar telephones, but which can deliver information and transactions over a touch sensitive screen.

"All of these devices will be easy to use and may incorporate compact disks, laser disks and receive real-time information from cable, telephone lines and wireless communications networks.

"Certainly, information will be presented differently in this new era, but, more importantly, *new value will be added to the information* (author's emphasis). The result will be information which is more compelling, more useful, more entertaining and very convenient. It will change the way people learn, work, enjoy themselves and do routine transactions."

Cecilia McRoskey, vice president, information systems, Times Mirror Co., publisher of the *Los Angeles Times* and other newspapers, in the company's first quarter 1993 report to shareholders.

ELECTRONIC NEWS MAY BE INEXPENSIVE

Past efforts to link households with electronic information systems failed badly. Knight-Ridder Inc. lost more than $50 million in the 1980s with an experimental Viewtron service to southern Florida homes and Times Mirror Co., publisher of the *Los Angeles Times,* lost massively with its Gateway service in southern California. Both experiments had a common failing: News and information services had to bear the total cost of communications circuits and technology for householder use.

Householders demonstrated quickly they wouldn't pay high rates to receive electronically, right now, information available free on television tonight or for 35 cents in the newspaper tomorrow morning. Simply put, the American householder prefers to read baseball scores in tomorrow's paper rather than pay $30 to $40 or more monthly to get them and similar information immediately on a personal computer. However, the "electronic highway" of the future is certain to be entertainment-driven—offering hundreds of cable TV channels and movies on demand. For entertainment, American householders *will* pay—and plenty. The average monthly bill for basic cable TV service in 1992 was $18.85 (up from $8.46 in 1982). Hundreds of millions of dollars extra are paid for additional services, movies and pay-per-view events. Also, the new system will have additional revenue from banking, shopping and other services plus advertising. In 1992, cable TV ad revenue hit \$3.4 billion, up from a paltry \$230 million in 1982.[11]

In the future, news will be transmitted on only one or, at most, several circuits in a huge fiber-optics "bundle" of circuits reaching households. So, it's quite possible that costs allocated to news (as contrasted with entertainment) therefore will be relatively low. That, in turn, could permit appropriately low charges to householders for the information component of the electronic highway. That is, don't base your newspaper's competitive strategy on the assumption that cost-conscious householders automatically will favor your 50-cent newspaper over extravagantly priced electronic services. You may be up against a modern version of the \$1.98 calculator.

THE SPECTRE OF BYPASS TECHNOLOGY

Since Gutenberg's day, the media have collected information and relayed it, at a time and in a manner of their choosing, to news "consumers." Trained journalists—and their news values, their decision-making instincts—have been the essential core of that system. But, if the future is one of computer-equipped households having instantaneous, electronic access to the libraries of the world and mountainous databases, will the media—the journalist— always be at the core?

Some futurists say no. See Figure 3.4 for a view of the traditional news collection and distribution system and the "bypass" technology futurists envisage. De-

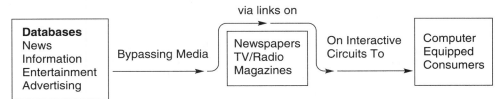

FIGURE 3.4   Some futurists predict the new "electronic highway" will permit "consumers" of news, entertainment and advertising to use computers to interrogate distant databases and thus bypass traditional media.

spite the superficial logic of the bypass concept (and the certainty of bypass proponents), it appears clear the media in some form—and the trained journalist—will remain the core of future information systems. The bypass concept simply demands too much of users, no matter how "computer-comfortable" they are: It presumes news and information consumers—average householders—will have the time, reportorial training *and inclination* to sit before a computer screen, searching those libraries of the world and those mountainous databases.

A more reasonable basis for your competitive strategy of the future is to position your newspaper to use any technology available to meet any possible consumer need or desire—and to assume that you, the trained journalist and manager, will be crucial to that process. Chapter 4 will help you plan for that future.

SUMMARY

Newspapers are engaged in marketplace war and each newspaper strategist must study carefully which competitors are in the fight for reader time and advertiser dollar. Although few cities have two dailies of like size and characteristics fighting head-on, all cities—even small towns— are "media intensive." Many competitors of all types fight for niches on the "competitive staircase."

Who or what are your competitors is defined by readers, who decide whether competing media return greater value for time invested, and by advertisers, who decide whether other media are more cost-efficient in delivering their messages to consumers.

Guard, first, your *geographic market,* analyzing carefully who or what competes against you on your newspaper's turf. Decide who competes most strongly now—and who likely will in the market as it will be defined in five or 10 years. Second, guard your *demographic market,* particularly the affluent households so desired by advertisers. The most attractive households, those with $50,000 or more annual income, will draw competition from nearby metro dailies, national newspapers, upscale city magazines, and national quality magazines.

Households under $20,000 annual income will attract metro dailies, television, radio, free-circulation shoppers and other marketplace "nibblers" seeking ad revenue. Prioritize your competitive strategies in accord with which media attract the most ad revenue.

Television is number 2 (after number 1 newspapers) in total ad revenue, because it draws huge audiences for entertainment programming. Newspaper strategists counterattack in part on grounds the intrusive nature of TV advertising angers viewers and that commercials are avoided. Direct mail is number 3 in the ad dollar sweepstakes, primarily because it can deliver 90 to 95 percent household penetration and, conversely, can target selected (and attractive) households with accuracy. Newspapers must offer the same total market coverage and targeting ability.

Yellow Pages, number 4, are strong because they are tied to the telephone, in the home and office, and can be used quickly and economically by the consumer. This medium's greatest weakness is that its information is static for the life of the printed directory. Electronic Yellow Pages are a threat for the future because they could be updated constantly.

Radio, number 5, and magazines, number 6, take billions of ad revenue from the marketplace and are serious contenders for the reading time of newspaper subscribers. Number 7, the "nibblers," are outdoor advertising, coupon books, farm publications—a host of advertising media that in their totality are formidable competitors for advertiser dollars.

In devising competitive strategies, pay close attention to which media have the financial strength to hurt your newspaper the most. In positioning your newspaper against electronic competitors, plan for these realities: Consumers want more control over what information they get and when; technology is opening undreamed choices for delivering what consumers want; Americans (the same ones who are reading fewer newspapers) generally are "computer comfortable"; and electronic news services may be relatively inexpensive.

Finally, whatever the future holds, the media—and the journalist—likely will be at the core of future systems, using their training and news judgments to collect, format and distribute information.

RECOMMENDED READING

Any newspaper strategist must stay in close touch with competing media. For an overview, *Advertising Age* does an outstanding job of monitoring all media competing for ad dollars. It frequently publishes special supplements on direct mail, outdoor advertising and Yellow Pages, in addition to covering traditional media. *Broadcasting & Cable* is an excellent source for developments in radio, television and cable that are of interest to newspaper strategists. *Folio* is an excellent source for news coverage of editorial *and* business developments in the magazine industry. The Direct Marketing Educational Foundation, Inc., 6 East 43rd St., New York, N.Y. 10017-4646, issues regular reports on developments in direct mail marketing.

Watch *Forbes* for its occasional, but superb, profiles of media companies. The *Economist* is strong on multinational media companies. The media sections of *The New York Times* and *The Wall Street Journal* are important sources of spot news coverage on newspaper competitors.

For a broader look at competing media, see Conrad C. Fink, *Inside the Media* (White Plains, N.Y.: Longman, 1990), and a two-chapter discussion of magazine publishing in Conrad C. Fink and Donald E. Fink, *Introduction to Magazine Writing* (New York: Macmillan Publishing Co., 1994).

NOTES

1. I discuss all media and provide case studies on the major ones in Conrad C. Fink, *Inside the Media* (White Plains, N.Y.: Longman, 1990).

2. *Facts About Newspapers '94*, published by Newspaper Association of America, p. 11.

3. Ibid.

4. Ibid.

5. For a discussion of this and Yellow Pages in general, see Jaime Trapp, "Small-business Aftershock Felt," in a special supplement on Yellow Pages in *Advertising Age*, Sept. 27, 1993, p. 28.

6. Arbitron survey quoted in "For Limbaugh, Yet Another Ratings Rush," *Broadcasting & Cable*, March 8, 1993, p. 33.

7. The economics of the magazine industry and niche publishing are discussed in Conrad C. Fink and Donald E. Fink, *Introduction to Magazine Writing* (New York: Macmillan Publishing Co., 1994).

8. Personal conversation with Publisher Will Morris, Nov. 12, 1993, Athens, Ga.

9. *Facts About Newspapers '94*, op. cit.

10. Andrew Pollack, "Now It's Japan's Turn to Play Catch-Up," *The New York Times*, national edition, Nov. 21, 1993, F-1.

11. "Database," *U.S. News & World Report*, March 29, 1993, p. 8.

PART II

YOU, LEADERSHIP AND PLANNING

So, you've analyzed the newspaper industry, the media marketplace and all who compete there against us. What now? Now, you *lead.* You lead your staff and your newspaper. You lead them toward successfully exploiting the journalistic and business opportunities your market analysis uncovered. You lead them toward defeating whatever—whomever—your competitive analysis identified as a threat.

And, what's the first function of leadership? *Planning.* Here in Part II, we turn to the skills you'll need in both leadership and planning. Those skills are crucial to your career success at any level in newspaper management.

Chapter 4 is "Leadership: Influencing Others to Achieve." That title is meant to emphasize that whatever else you do in newspaper management, you will fail unless you can influence others to perform as you wish and to help your newspaper reach the corporate goals you lay down.

Chapter 5, "The Plan," is a detailed discussion of the planning function. Bottom line: Know precisely where you want your newspaper to go, be certain everybody on your staff knows—and ensure each staffer knows what he or she must do to make it all happen.

4

LEADERSHIP: INFLUENCING OTHERS TO ACHIEVE

Let me guess what you're thinking. Perhaps it's something like this: Leaders are publishers. Editors, too. Maybe, department heads, as well. But, what does the subject of leadership have to do with me?

Well, envision these scenarios: It's been 13 months or so since your graduation and you're happily covering cops for a small daily. Then, your editor asks you to coordinate efforts by two fellow reporters on a team investigating a scandal at City Hall. Or, you're selling advertising for the daily and you're asked to direct the two-person classified ads staff.

Congratulations. *You have become a manager.* The moment you start supervising the performance of one other person, you are a manager. But you don't become a *leader* until you prove it. Where to turn? Where to start?

We start, here in Chapter 4, by considering the theory of newspaper management and the skill—call it the "art"—of leadership. The principles are applicable to the challenge ahead of you, whether on a metro daily or country weekly, whether you supervise one person or 1,000, in news or on the business side. Effective newspaper management is efficient use of all resources at every level to move the newspaper toward planned organizational goals. Resources include people, money, time, the goodwill of readers and advertisers and—increasingly these days—the new technology revolutionizing the industry.

To succeed as a manager, you must coordinate efforts of individual employees and groups of employees primarily in two time frames: in short-range or day-to-day operations and over the long range, to achieve strategic goals. This must be done in continually changing environments. A state of flux exists in any newspaper's external environment, in the socioeconomic dimensions of its marketplace, among its competitors and customers, and in the law and society's values and expectations. Change also is constant in a newspaper's internal environment, in human relationships, cost/revenue patterns and many operational areas. Making correct decisions in such shifting sand is each manager's responsibility. At every level, the challenge is to ensure that, despite unforeseen trials and tribulations along the way, the newspaper ultimately reaches planned goals.

And that is what it means to be a leader—getting it done and done properly, no matter what. To accomplish this, each manager at every level engages in continual planning, decision making, goal setting, organizing and motivating employees, disseminating information, monitoring and controlling employee performance, and then adjusting operations as necessary to make sure goals are met.

MANAGEMENT THEORY: THE BEGINNINGS

Early management theories may seem to you too narrow philosophically and too dependent on harsh regimentation of both managers and employees. Yet, those early theories influence, for better or worse, many of today's management practices. To understand what newspaper leaders do today, let's look briefly at yesteryear.

In the beginning, there was Adam Smith (1723–1790), who originated the theory that human work performance is motivated almost exclusively by monetary reward. Smith paid scant attention to the whole human being—to workers' real needs, beyond pay, for fulfillment and recognition. Today, such a one-dimensional approach to motivating newspaper employees can be disastrous. A wide range of human needs must be satisfied if employees are to be motivated effectively. Yet some newspaper managers still try to motivate employees in the erroneous belief that money alone answers all personnel problems.

Frederick W. Taylor (1856–1915) and colleagues of his era, notably Henry Gantt and Frank and Lillian Gilbreth, advanced a theory known as *scientific management.* Though widely discredited, that theory today persists in some newspaper departments. Taylor, working at U.S. Steel and Ford Motor Co., attacked production inefficiency with a scientific approach featuring incentive pay for workers in what amounted to piecework assignments. This advanced the assembly-line approach to mass production. Taylor, however, like Smith, saw economic reward as the primary motivation for work performance; he underestimated a manager's obligation to help employees fulfill other, psychological needs. Today, the impersonal treatment of employees as assembly-line automatons is ineffective in the newspaper business.

Max Weber (1864–1920) saw greater efficiency flowing from an organizational structure that clearly communicates work procedures, clearly outlining the flow—the "hierarchy"—of authority mandating highly specialized work roles for all employees. Weber and other theorists of his time created the *administrative* or *bureaucratic school of management thought,* expecting that a corporate bureaucracy operating under firmly established rules would be evenhanded—even impersonal—in selecting, promoting and disciplining employees. Meritorious performance, nothing else, is what counts.

Today, Weber's concept influences the tables of organization drawn by many newspapers. The assignment of employees to narrowly specialized work in circulation or production smacks of Weber's theory that specialized work roles lead to efficiency. However, today's managers must not let Weber's approach become distorted in practice, creating an inflexible organization whose employees are coldly, impersonally fitted into slots. Rigid tables of organization can lead to barriers between departments, an obstacle to the totally integrated management thrust so necessary in an effectively run newspaper.

Breakthroughs toward modern management technique occurred in the 1920s. Theorists became aware that human relationships in a work force are as important to efficiency as are, for example, physical surrounding and that those relationships are not restricted to the connecting lines on a table of organization. It became clear that numerous unofficial groups and subgroups form in any company and that a manager must understand them. Perhaps most important, it became obvious that more than money is needed to motivate employees. Thus was born the *human relations* theory of management.

Seminal research was done by George Mayo (1880–1949) and others at Western Electric Co. in Hawthornes, New Jersey; this became known as the "Hawthorne Study." Mayo and fellow theorists, including Abraham Maslow (1908–1970) and Chester Barnard (1886–1961), contributed heavily to the philosophy that each employee is unique in personality and attitudes and that no single motivational program, particularly one relying solely on economic reward, will be uniformly successful with large numbers of employees. Successful management flows from understanding each worker as an individual—truly a key concept for the manager of highly imaginative and creative writers in a newsroom.[1]

The Modern Way

New influences were felt in management theory in the 1940s that remain central to progressive thinking today. Behavioral scientists studied worker attitudes and how to motivate better performance. As a result, many leading newspapers today employ psychologists to help design their internal organization and personnel policies. A scientific approach to motivating employees—whether 10 or 1,000—helps create a work environment free of rigid guidelines, encouraging each worker to develop personal responsibility and to participate in decision making.

In contrast with the absolutism of early management theories, the *contingency theory* came into vogue in later times and is used today by many newspapers to create flexibility in management practice. The key is taking a situational approach, with managers adjusting their methods as the newspaper's external and internal situation changes. For example, the newspaper's market or competition may change, as we saw in Chapters 2 and 3, and so must its journalistic and business responses.

The *systems theory* holds that managers must ensure an integrated effort by all departments. Neither a problem nor an opportunity arises from a single cause, this theory holds, and neither does a solution. This approach is applicable particularly to newspapers because managers must overcome a tradition of permitting barriers between departments to stand. This prevents many newspapers from instituting the integrated-management team effort so necessary in today's marketplace. Applied to newspapers, the systems theory holds that managers must be alert to any internal development in one department that will affect the paper's overall performance— and to ensure appropriate responses by all departments concerned.

WHERE THE MANAGER'S ROLE STARTS

Entry-level jobs in advertising and news traditionally led to the top in newspapers. However, marketing, circulation and—to a lesser degree—production now contribute men and women who work up through the ranks. Whatever the route upward, top executives must be experienced in both of the broad dimensions of newspaper management—operations and strategy. And, you'll need particular skills in two managerial tasks:

> *Problem solving,* which involves spotting difficulties (hopefully before they erupt) and quickly finding solutions.
> *Decision making,* the process of collecting the required information, consulting others for their views, then settling on a course of action.

You'll be exposed to all this on three levels of managerial responsibility.

THE FIRST LEVEL

First, the management role starts far down the line, when you become responsible for supervising the performance of even one other employee. That is at the operating level, where supervisors are first-level managers, working face-to-face with employees everyday. First-level supervisors must motivate individuals and groups of employees, providing leadership and using strong communication skills to pass down management's policies and elicit feedback, to be sent back up the ladder, from subordinates. Key here is the ability to build the teamwork needed to get the job done.

Higher management will ignore at its peril the importance of first-level supervisory functions performed, for example, by a desk editor or a carrier supervisor in circulation. Final implementation of policy is in the hands of these first-line supervisors, yet they often are the youngest, most inexperienced and least trained of all managers.

At the Middle

Middle managers—heads of news, advertising and circulation departments, for example—communicate top management's policies to supervisors and coordinate between departments to solve conflicts that arise. At this level, the significant power and authority of management truly come into play.

At the Top

Top management includes the president, the publisher and the executive staff responsible for overall direction of the newspaper. The individual alone responsible for the total management function and for planning the newspaper's basic direction is the chief executive officer (CEO). Top management must ensure that the newspaper makes effective use of all internal resources so as to adjust to its changing external environment—answering both the needs of the marketplace and threats from the competition.

Peter Drucker, one of America's foremost management commentators, describes top management's functions as constructing master strategy, setting standards for the organization; building and maintaining the "human organization"; conducting relations with outside groups such as banks, government bodies and so on; serving at "ceremonial" functions; and, simply put, pitching in with leadership when things go wrong.

WHO DIRECTS TOP MANAGEMENT?

Owners direct top management. A single individual can hold 100 percent of the newspaper company's stock and run it as a private enterprise. Or there can be a partnership or small group of individuals holding stock in the company. Many small newspapers owned by individuals or families have been acquired by large communication conglomerates. Of the 15 largest (in media revenue) companies in the country, 12 are publicly owned—their stock traded on exchanges across the country.

The three exceptions are Advance Publications, controlled by the Newhouse family and owner of large papers such as the *Cleveland Plain Dealer;* Hearst Corp. (*San Francisco Examiner,* and many other media properties); and Cox Enterprises (*Atlanta Journal* and *Constitution* and many others). A few newspapers, such as the *St. Petersburg (Fla.) Times,* are owned by trusts. (The *Times'* late owner, Nelson Poynter, gave his stock to a nonprofit trust charged with keeping the paper independent of group control.)

But most newspapers are run as businesses charged not only with covering the news and serving their community but also with making a profit for their owners. Often, owners serve in management.

Katherine Graham is chairman of the executive committee of Washington Post Co., and her son, Donald, is chairman of the board and publisher of the company's flagship, *The Washington Post.* Their family owns enough stock to control the publicly owned company. The New York Times Co., also publicly owned, is controlled by members of the Sulzberger family, which owned *The New York Times* privately for generations.

Owning families can sell stock to raise capital for improving their companies, or, simply, to pocket millions of dollars. They can retain control of their companies, however, by selling less than a majority of stock or, more commonly, by establishing two tiers of stock—retaining voting stock and selling to the public only that type of stock with limited or no voting power.

ROLE OF THE BOARD OF DIRECTORS

Most publicly owned companies are managed by professionals hired from outside. Policy is set by a board of directors whose members ostensibly are selected to bring to the company outside skills needed in newspapering—the law, finance, accounting and so forth. For publicly owned companies, boards are, in theory, composed of individuals selected not only to guide management but also to represent the interests of each shareholder. And, again in theory, even a shareholder owning just one share can rise on the floor of the company's annual meeting to ask a question, make a speech or nominate someone to the board and thus influence the conduct of company affairs.

In fact, however, boards most often are composed of—or controlled by—a relatively few individuals who own large numbers of shares or of people selected by these individuals. In corporate affairs, if you have large shareholdings, you have the votes. However, if a professional manager is a strong personality with a solid track record, he or she can influence strongly the makeup of the board and policy it lays down.

Indeed, boards at most major media companies are chaired by "hired guns" who became reporters in their youth or took other entry-level jobs and worked their way to the top. Such companies include Gannett, Knight-Ridder, Tribune Co., Hearst and Times Mirror, all among the nation's most influential media companies. At Gannett, John Curley, a former reporter, is both chairman of the board and CEO. At many companies, board members and professional managers similarly mesh in a hierarchy of command. Those most important on the board control the board's inner circle, sometimes designated as the "executive committee."[2]

Policy, then, is transmitted to the CEO, who must translate policy directives into results; this frequently is done through yet another inner circle in the hierarchy of the newspaper itself, often called the "management committee." This inner circle is made up of executives who exercise leadership within the individual departments. Without effective leadership down the ladder, the newspaper will fail to perform well.

BUILDING YOUR PERSONAL LEADERSHIP STYLE

As chairman and CEO of Gannett, former reporter John Curley is a quiet, at times almost self-effacing leader. His style: Follow me. I was a reporter, editor and publisher, and I know what you must do to succeed in those roles.

Curley's predecessor, Al Neuharth, was a showman, always impeccably groomed, always expensively dressed in specially tailored clothing (only in black, white or gray). He restlessly darted about the Gannett communications empire by private jet, pushing subordinates, prodding, punishing, rewarding. Neuharth was a *personality* people talked about.[3]

Some leaders stay behind the scenes and take the business school approach: a heavily staffed solution for each problem, a form to fill out, a computer to monitor progress. People talk about their management *systems*. Other leaders are team builders—carefully selecting and motivating a cadre of expert professionals. As chairman and CEO of Knight-Ridder Inc., Jim Batten leads a team few companies can match for depth. People talk about the Knight-Ridder management *team*.

Lesson for aspiring managers: A variety of personal styles and egos drive the overachievers who lead America's influential newspapers and multibillion-dollar communications conglomerates. Lesson number 2: Some industries flirt with management fads, Japanese-style consensus management or leadership by committee. But in newspapering there is a tradition of strong-willed individuals being firmly in charge, either directly and hands-on, as with Neuharth, or more indirectly, through a strong staff, as with Knight-Ridder's Batten.

In selecting your personal style, however, note one commonality among today's newspaper managers: They show deep commitment to making a difference, to putting a personal stamp on the way things are done each day.

And, it may be that of all business institutions, the newspaper perhaps lends itself to that type of leadership. Tom Vail, for many years publisher and editor of the *Cleveland (Ohio) Plain Dealer,* saw it like this: "I would say that no institution in our society so reflects the personalities of the people who run them as do the nation's newspapers. If a newspaper management team is interesting or boring or aggressive, or really doesn't care at all, it shows up immediately in the newspaper. If there is just a formula established to make money and little else it is all too obvious to the people who are reading your newspaper. There is just no way out. If you do a good or bad job everybody knows about it."[4]

ARE LEADERS BORN?

It is said some leaders are born to the task. And certainly there have arisen, from time to time, individuals who, despite lack of training and experience, somehow prove able to step into a leadership role. But that's no answer for you, the student, who is aiming for a management career in newspapering.

Where, then, are leadership qualities found? Can their origin be traced? Is their appearance in some individuals, but not in others, predictable? Nobody can be completely sure.

Until the 1950s, the *traitist school* dominated general research in this area. Some suggested, for example, that a man's height was a determinant; a man who was less than 5 feet 8 inches tall had reduced prospects, it was said. Many researchers, notably Ralph M. Stogdill (1904–1978), took the broader view that successful leaders have certain behavioral traits in common:

- Clarity of purpose, the ability to act decisively, persistence
- A strong need to succeed, to achieve on the job
- A desire for responsibility and the wish to supervise others
- Confidence in oneself, a high regard for own's own abilities
- Sound judgment and verbal intelligence, flexibility in thinking, a willingness to try new ideas and methods

Ranked as less important were traits such as the need for job security and financial reward—also masculinity or femininity.

The situational theory holds that there is no universally applicable list of traits predicting success in leadership and that, in fact, the situation in which leadership is exercised can be a determinant of success. For example, this theory holds that leadership traits leading to success in one situation may be no help in another. In other words, to be effective, leadership must vary in style and approach to the situation at hand.[5]

Leadership is a complex subject, obviously, and no single theory explains its origins or how to exercise it. In any newspaper, however, it takes two broad forms:

- Formal or legitimate leadership, flowing from position or rank in the company's management hierarchy. The president of a communications company exercises legitimate leadership.
- Informal leadership, which develops spontaneously in work groups that form outside the newspaper's table of organization or formal work structure. Thus a reporter may *assume* (even if not given) a leadership role among a group of colleagues assigned to investigate a given story.

Gaining the "right" to lead through promotion to rank or title does not guarantee effective leadership. In addition, each manager must learn to recognize—and harness—the often invaluable leadership support that can come informally from below. Well, then, how should you, as a beginning leader, behave?

Developing Leadership Values

A starting point is how a leader (or manager) views followers (or employees). One theory, enunciated by Douglas McGregor, is that leaders traditionally take one of two basic attitudes: that people are lazy, dislike work and responsibility and are effective only if they are tightly controlled and punished when necessary. This essentially pessimistic view is known as Theory X. The second attitude is that people who are properly motivated, encouraged and rewarded will perform well because they are eager to express themselves at work in a creative manner and to assume responsibility—that work is natural and can be enjoyed. This optimistic view is called Theory Y.

As a leader, you seldom will find well-defined situations covered entirely by either Theory X or Theory Y. This is certainly true on a newspaper, where a widely diverse work force under a single roof ranges from highly creative reporters and writers to the lowest-paid manual laborers, and where jobs range from the daily production of a news and advertising package to making newspaper deliveries.

Before attempting to assume your own leadership style, consider your personal strengths and weaknesses, the overall managerial situation at hand and the type of employee to be dealt with. Research at the University of Michigan, led by Rensis Likert, found leaders taking two broad views: The job-centered or task-oriented view that personal interest in workers should be avoided and that demanding attitudes and goals, all tightly controlled and with performance closely monitored, are necessary. Decisions are made only by managers, and leaders get intimately involved in worker performance. The employee-centered view that leaders must take a personal interest in workers and be supportive, not punitive.

The "Ohio State Leadership Studies" probed employee perceptions of leaders; this research uncovered two general views of leader values and behavior: initiating structure, or leadership perceived by employees as reliant on highly structured organizational lines and methods; and the consideration approach, perceived from below as relying on friendship with employees, with support and recognition for their contributions in the form of respect and warmth.

Such neatly defined approaches to leadership presume the ideal leader in the ideal situation—and that does not often happen. So each leader must affect a style to fit each situation, keeping in mind both the employees' interests and the corporation's goals. The type of individuals or group to be led, along with nature of the task to be performed, must be considered. The contingency theory holds that leadership success depends on achieving the proper mix of leader behavior and style plus organizational or environmental factors. In other words, adapt to the situation.

The nature of newspaper work and the creative, independent people it attracts make it imperative that the aspiring manager use a leadership style featuring the employee-centered and consideration approach. But, you might rightly ask, how does the leader make it all happen? How do I make sure my direction and commands will be accepted? Where does the power come from?

BOX 4.1   Effective Leadership: Two Views

In years of searching for effective leaders, staff psychologists at Knight-Ridder Inc. identified these characteristics essential to manager's success:

General intelligence	Social aggressiveness
Verbal reasoning	(a willingness to
Quantitative reasoning	stand for what is
Analytical thinking	right)
Supervisory knowledge	Sociability
Practical judgment	Objectivity
Energy	Friendliness
Seriousness	Thoughtfulness

Asked for their views, 28 Knight-Ridder editors and 40 reporters said these characteristics are essential to a manager's success:

Leadership	Flexibility
Problem solving and	Delegation/control
judgment	Personal motivation
Planning and	Tenacity
organizing	Stress tolerance
Decisiveness	Energy
Creativity	Oral/written
Sensitivity	communications skills

Source: Douglas C. Harris, vice president and corporate secretary, Knight-Ridder

CASE STUDY 4.1   Leadership Makes the Difference

Winning on any battlefield depends on team effort. But, just as military historians point to individual leaders who turn defeat into victory, so can we find individuals who turn the tide in newspaper wars.

Case studies in Chapters 2 and 3 show that many market and competitive factors figured in the victory by Cox Enterprises' *Atlanta Journal* and *Constitution* over the New York Times Co.'s *Gwinnett Daily News* in suburban Atlanta. However, a handful of alert, tough Cox executives clearly were instrumental in routing the New Yorkers, forcing them to close the *Daily News* and swallow losses of $200 million or so.

Detailed study of that fight identifies these key executives and important managerial concepts they represent:[a]

1. James Cox Kennedy, heir to a major share of the Cox fortune, became chairman of the huge communications conglomerate at age 39, and immediately displayed abilities crucial in top management: He took a broad strategic view, expanding and diversifying the company in traditional print operations but also in new electronic journalism and other areas. Kennedy, however, didn't float blissfully above the battlefield. He personally focused on the threat to his company's flagship papers in Atlanta. It's essential to commit your personal resources—your time, your energy—to major threats (and opportunities.) Kennedy shook up his company's moribund management. He inserted aggressive, intelligent men and women in key spots. Like any battlefield commander, commit your best talent to the most important tasks.

2. David Easterly, publisher of the *Journal* and *Constitution*, and credited by Kennedy with reversing their circulation slide, was named president of Cox Enterprises' newspaper division. Lesson: Promote on the basis of proven accomplishment. Identify winners at all levels in your organization; groom them, train them, promote them.

3. Jay Smith, longtime Cox employee, former reporter, editor and publisher *(Austin (Tex.) American-Statesman)*, was appointed *Journal* and *Constitution* publisher. His managerial strengths are many; two impress an outsider: First, Smith kept communications open, both up and down the corporate ladder: He met informally almost daily with subordinates, twice weekly in formal planning conferences. Nearly every day, he talked with his boss, Easterly. Says Smith: "The rule—no surprises...I keep him informed...*it's a mortal sin to lay unpleasant surprises on your boss* (author's emphasis)." Second, Smith displayed guts. He decided Editor Bill Kovach, a newsroom hero, wasn't moving the papers ahead, and replaced him with Ron Martin, a founding editor of *USA Today,* initially an unpopular choice in the newsroom. Lesson: Diagnose your newspaper's problems, then act—and take the heat. (Postscript: In 1992, Smith was named executive vice president of the Cox Newspapers division. Another lesson for aspiring managers: Reward the victors.)

4. Ron Martin, appointed editor in 1989, put his imprint on the *Journal* and *Constitution.* They blossomed with new color, graphics, exciting layout and, simultaneously, in-depth reporting of major stories. Lesson: Hire the best editor you can afford. As at the *Constitution* and *Journal,* improved circulation and journalistic service to the community will follow, to be followed, in turn, by improved advertising revenue.

Now, how about the losers? There were plenty at New York Times Co., and some paid for the Gwinnett debacle with their careers. A few, however, showed the realism—and grace—of Seymour Topping, a Times Co. executive involved in desperate attempts to save the *Daily News.* In 1992, Topping described how Times Co. underestimated the competitive reaction from Cox and thus was forced to spend more heavily than anticipated. He concluded:

> As a consequence, the Times Co. suffered losses in each year of its ownership. The Times Co., publicly owned, projecting unending losses, decided to retreat. Looking to their fiduciary re-

CASE STUDY 4.1 *Continued*

sponsibilities to stockholders, its executives accepted failure, a blow to professional pride and deep pain, knowing what their loyal employees would suffer.

The company entered into the Justice Department ritual, offering the paper to more than 40 possible buyers, although chances obviously were slight that anyone would be willing to take on Cox. With no takers, the paper's assets were then sold to Cox preparatory to a shutdown.

It would not be fair simply to fault Cox for the shutdown. Similar turf wars involving newspaper fatalities are common, increasingly so. If positions were reversed, the Times Co. might have employed the same

aggressive pricing strategy. Whatever the rationale, the *Journal* and *Constitution,* a good newspaper, is now to reign unchallenged in the Atlanta metro region.

Yet still there were the questions. What about those readers who had lost their "other voice," the advertisers without a local alternative and the 276 people who had lost their jobs and a dream? "What shall we say?" Several of the staffers facing me in the semicircle cried out. By the book I should have replied: "Nobody is at fault, of course, because newspapers in our country live and die by the bottom line." But I didn't. I put my arms around the reporter who had been a Pulitzer finalist and wept with her.[b]

[a]See Conrad C. Fink, *The Atlanta Journal and Constitution, A Case Study* (St. Petersburg, Fla.: Poynter Institute for Media Studies, 1989).
[b]Seymour Topping, "Staff, Readers Mourn Another Daily Closure," *ASNE Bulletin,* Oct. 1992, p. 2.

THE SOURCE OF POWER

At every level in a newspaper, leadership power flows from various sources, under a variety of labels:

- Legitimate power is granted by owners who appoint a leader. Appointment as, say, a special project leader in the newsroom gives you a certain amount of power in the hierarchy.
- Expert power flows from the leader's own special skills or experience, as in the case of an editor who has a track record as a great reporter.
- Referent power is granted by followers who admire the leader or want to identify with his or her charismatic personality or style. Ben Bradlee, executive editor of *The Washington Post,* displayed such charisma (captured perfectly, incidentally, by actor Jason Robards in the movie "All the President's Men").
- Coercive power flows from the leader's ability to punish and thus is based essentially on fear.
- Reward power comes with the power to recognize good performance and give something—a raise, public praise, a choice assignment—in return.[6]

Of course, a newspaper manager can possess power flowing from all five factors. The key is when and how to use each type of power or in what mix—and that requires careful situational analyses of the individuals or groups involved and the tasks to be performed.

Note a basic theme: the need for flexibility and careful adaptation to the challenge at hand. It is nowhere more important than in the effort to make effective use of power. One noted researcher, Fred E. Fiedler, suggests that a leader's effectiveness depends primarily on three factors:[7]

- Leader-group relations, or the leader's ability to engender support and respect from subordinates, to build confidence and loyalty in the work group.
- Task structure, or whether or not jobs are simple and routine.
- Position power, or the leader's ability, granted by the organization, to reward and punish.

The *path-goal theory* of leadership seeks predictors of success in a leader's behavior (not traits or characteristics) and ability to motivate subordinates. As a leader, you must determine what rewards will motivate employees and set a motivational example through your own activities; then, you are likely to be perceived by subordinates as charting a course that will satisfy their needs.

The path-goal approach—how the leader affects the subordinates' paths to their goals—requires the leader to communicate clearly that ambitious goals are being set and then, using rewards, to stimulate performance required to meet them. It is crucial to carefully match employees and their skills to the tasks and then provide strong, considerate support to eliminate barriers to their success. A key is making each subordinate's assignment as meaningful and personally satisfying as possible.

WHAT TODAY'S LEADER'S SAY

Against this theoretical backdrop, what lessons can students of leadership draw from leaders in the newspaper industry? These ideas come from interviews and correspondence with corporate leaders and publishers:

1. *Be well informed.* Know what is happening inside *and* outside the company. An ill-informed leader is a poor leader. Warning: Avoid being swamped by information. Create a communications system that brings you the right information at the right time in clear, concise and manageable form. This requires building a favorable environment for the exchange of information. Deal openly with subordinates; be receptive to their to their ideas—LISTEN.

2. *Know your purpose.* The successful leader sees the goal, understands how to get there and builds effective communications to transmit the vision to subordinates. Warren Phillips, who as chairman of Dow Jones Co., Inc. expanded his company internationally, puts it this way: "I have worked consciously on this, through repeated conversations with our executives and staff members, through increased communications via such devices as the employees newsletter and by other means . . . and of

course standards also are set via example." The vision, he says, is primarily one of "maintaining and raising standards—standards of editorial excellence, of efficient service to readers, of ethics, of independence in news coverage...."[8]

3. *Delegate and share.* To clear time for top-priority tasks, a leader must delegate duties to subordinates. That requires training subordinates to accept more work, giving them responsibility to act, then motivating them to do well. Be honest and fair with subordinates. Give them public credit and reward for success; consistent unsatisfactory performance—or failure—must be dealt with decisively and privately. Successful leaders demonstrate a knack for selecting and motivating subordinates. Alvah Chapman, an extremely successful chairman of Knight-Ridder (1982–1989), says, "... the most important part of my job (was) insuring we have the best possible people in our key jobs.... I think that must be a prime responsibility of any CEO."[9]

4. *Work hard.* There is no substitute for disciplined, effectively organized hard work. Organize your workday (and evening) for maximum efficiency. Waste no time, yours or others'. Meet deadlines and carry your share (and more) of the work load. Set this example for subordinates and insist that they follow it.

5. *Study the options.* "Instinct" may help spot a problem or opportunity, but it is not operative in the decision-making process used by effective managers. Repeatedly, today's leaders demonstrate that they favor, instead, the solid, methodical research we discussed in Chapters 2 and 3 plus careful study of possible risks and benefits in any important move. Today, even for relatively small papers, a single decision can put a great deal of money at risk, and no manager should approach significant risk without carefully calculating the odds for success.

6. *Seek opportunity.* Only in fairy tales does opportunity arrive unsummoned, in the nick of time, on your doorstep. Successful leaders *make* their luck and search out opportunity in its many guises. Learn to recognize it, then boldly commit the necessary resources—money, time and people—to exploit it.

Examples: Dow Jones and Co. deliberately set out in the early 1970s to diversify from its narrow base—essentially *The Wall Street Journal, Barron's* and "Ticker" services for business clients. At that time, activities other than the *Journal* accounted for 6 percent of the company's net income; by 1980, they contributed over 40 percent. Company leaders sought out acquisitions such as Ottaway Newspapers, a group of small community papers that fit nicely—and profitably—into today's expanded Dow Jones. In 1992, all Dow Jones print publications contributed less than 50 percent of the company's total revenue. Gannett leaders sought out opportunities to diversify their company and built it into a global conglomerate that by 1993 had well over $3 billion annual revenue.

7. *Lead with integrity.* Acting with courage and integrity is essential to successful leadership. It can bring great pain and expose you to risks. But beware the expedient solution to matters of professional conscience. Leaders set the "tone" for subordinates and a failure of courage or integrity can hurt morale internally and damage a newspaper's public image.

In decades of high-caliber reporting of public affairs, *The New York Times* resisted heavy pressure from presidents and kings many times. Katharine Graham, then chairman of Washington Post Co., withstood the Nixon administration's ire and, at great risk to her company, refused to halt *The Post's* Watergate investigation. *The Wall Street Journal* has risked millions of dollars in revenue by spurning advertiser efforts to influence news coverage.

For all three newspapers, courageous stands on matters of integrity inspired staff members as little else could, won public acclaim—and were translated into long-term business strength. For the young manager, a display of integrity can, like few other techniques, win the support of subordinates.

8. *Develop command presence.* It's a learned skill. Work at it. Exclude success, be affirmative and positive. Be visible. Act like a leader. Sell yourself. Use imagination, flair and, yes, showmanship. Dramatize what you do (but don't get too far out of character; that won't work). Successful leaders develop a sense of when to intervene and when not to; a sense of when to praise and when to punish. And, smile. It's hard work, leading others. At times, it is a crisis minute in management. Don't get too gloomy; don't forget to be human through it all. People perform better for leaders with a streak of humor, a glimmer of sensitivity. Relax once in a while, have fun. If you can't do that, you can't be effective—and maybe you belong in another line of work.

BOX 4.2   Do Journalists Make Good Publishers?

Often discussed in the newspaper industry is which kind of operational training yields the best publishers. Frequently, the top jobs go to men and women with background in advertising, marketing or other "business-side" departments. Some companies, however, prefer cross-trained candidates with experience in both news and business. One such company is Knight-Ridder, whose chairman, Jim Batten, is a former editor. Many Knight-Ridder publishers have extensive news experience.

One editor-turned-publisher is Billy Watson, publisher of Knight-Ridder's *Columbus (Ga.) Ledger-Enquirer,* with 53,000 circulation daily, 67,000 on Sundays. Watson previously was editor of Knight-Ridder's *Macon (Ga.) Telegraph.* His views:

I have found the 20 years I spent in the news and editorial area to be extremely valuable since becoming publisher. I have always thought that the job of

editor was the most difficult of any in newspapering. That's because there are no firm guidelines to follow, no absolute rights and wrongs. Most news and editorial decisions are subjective, based in part on experience, in part on a sense of what the newspaper's role in the community ought to be, in part on common sense.

A publisher has to make or defend many of those same kinds of judgments. The reputation and community standing of the paper and its image among other newspaper professionals depend heavily on those day-to-day decisions.

I would feel far less comfortable with our news and editorial decisions if I did not have the experience to participate in them in what I think is a positive way.

Source: Billy Watson in a letter to the author.

9. *Act.* Nothing happens until you act. If you've done your homework, consulted your subordinates, carefully calculated the odds, you have a high probability of deciding correctly. But you must make a move; you must take action. Committees pass resolutions; strong leaders act.

DESIGNING YOUR ORGANIZATION

By now, two realities probably are clear to you: First, being a newspaper manager—at virtually any level—can be overwhelming in the demands on your time and energy. So, second, you'll need help.

Let's turn, then, to designing an organization that will help you move your newspaper toward its goals. Remember throughout that you're after efficiency, systematic management and coordination of effort. And, as publisher, design a support system that will free you for critical functions: conceptualizing and planning strategy, representing the newspaper in its external environment and organizing the newspaper internally.

Delegate Responsibility, Grant Authority

No matter what your management title may be, you never can delegate complete responsibility to subordinates. Indeed, their very performance is your responsibility, along with everything else that's on your plate. If you are publisher, the total fiduciary and journalistic responsibility for the newspaper remains with you—day and night. If you are editor, what individual reporters are doing remains your responsibility. As advertising director, you are responsible for what happens in the retail ad department, in classifieds and so on.

Nevertheless, managers must be free to balance the competing goals and needs of departments; to motivate individuals and lead the entire group toward planned objectives; to establish performance standards; to control, measure and evaluate performance; and to make adjustments when performance is unsatisfactory.

Importantly, when tasks are delegated, authority also must be handed down. No first-level editor should be asked to improve journalistic quality, for example, without being given authority to hire and fire in order to build a staff capable of producing quality. Of course, significant responsibility for success goes to any subordinate who is delegated both task and authority.

Unity of command is another objective in organizational design. It means making sure each employee receives orders from only one supervisor at a time and reports to that supervisor. This is elusive in newspaper organizational design because of the interdependence of news, circulation, advertising and other departments. But unless straight-line flow in authority and reporting relationships is achieved, conflict and confusion will result.

Span of control (or span of management) is the concept of assigning each supervisor the ideal number of subordinates to achieve optimum performance and efficiency. Many variables exist, including the abilities of the leader, the complexity of the task and the skills of the individuals being supervised. Careful experimentation can determine the optimum number of employees each supervisor can handle effectively.

Division of labor or specialization is a concept developed in U.S. manufacturing firms seeking maximum efficiency by assigning workers exclusively to certain tasks, as on an assembly line, and thus obtaining full benefit of their skills. But the concept calls for the uninterrupted concentration of employees' efforts on a narrowly defined task, and this can create boredom and low morale. Newspaper managers should approach the concept warily, particularly in newsrooms where highly individualistic, self-motivated people are required. Rotating employees to other jobs or enriching their jobs with new responsibility can help avoid boredom.

Decentralization in design—giving more authority to subordinate managers—frees you to do more things or, in effect, be in more places at once. But many managers find decentralization difficult, for it relaxes their control and increases chance for error at lower levels. And although a manager may delegate authority, he or she never can delegate responsibility—thus the very human tendency to resist decentralization.

The profit-center concept in organizational design gives a subordinate, department, or subsidiary unit a degree of independent authority. It is a goal sought by many newspapers today. Individual newspapers and communications conglomerates try to create autonomy, which carries with it decision-making authority (and also, of course, responsibility for success).

The Executive Staff

The design of the executive staff is particularly important in newspapers, where strong personalities often serve as semiautonomous department heads. They often are at odds with each other, a condition that certainly does not contribute to a team effort or move the newspaper toward corporate goals.

Manager disunity—at any level—is inefficient, cumbersome and costly, a form of management neglect that cannot be tolerated in this era of intense competition, rising costs and rapidly evolving new technology. An executive staff must organize cooperation between departments. The staff must focus all its energies toward common goals through action-oriented planning and supervision.

Publisher and executive staff together will set the tone for a newspaper's operation. If they are alert, aggressive managers, the newspaper will be alert and aggressive. Conversely, no newspaper will rise above the limitations of its managers for long.

The Formal and Informal Structures

The newspaper's basic structure is represented in the organizational chart, whose purpose is to schematically outline, usually vertically, the formal relationships between the organization's people and their tasks.

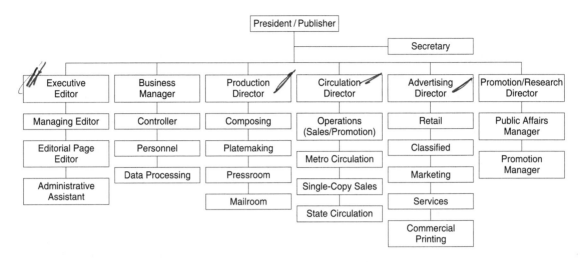

FIGURE 4.1 Table of organization for the *Columbus (Ga.) Ledger-Enquirer.*

Theoretically, the chart shows lines along which flow authority (the "chain of command"), internal communications and reporting responsibility. But the word "theoretically" is important here, since newspaper work also includes informal relationships—sometimes horizontal, not vertical—and enormous amounts of information may flow outside official channels. An aspiring manager must pick up on these informal arrangements quickly—particularly on the "grapevine," along which much information, both accurate and inaccurate, is liable to travel.

Tables of organization vary widely. Each must reflect the newspaper's size, its own unique organizational needs and, importantly, the availability of talented executives. For example, see Figure 4.1, the "TO" of the *Columbus (Ga.) Ledger-Enquirer,* a Knight-Ridder paper of 53,000 circulation daily, 67,000 on Sundays. Note the paper has a president who serves also as a publisher.

Danger: The executive staff can become an end in itself, swelling in numbers and simply grinding out more studies, exchanging more paper. Another danger is that conflicts can arise between staff executives and line supervisors.

Line supervisors meet their primary organizational mission through direct supervision of employees and discharge of daily activities. One example is a desk editor with responsibility for the performance of copy editors.

Staff executives should make expert knowledge available and serve in advisory capacities, but they should *not* directly supervise line activities. A vice president in charge of marketing, an important staff executive, would not directly supervise a clerk taking classified advertisements by telephone. Beware: Conflict often arises if staff executives maneuver in ways likely to reduce the authority of line supervisors.

ASPIRE TO THE TOP JOBS

At each newspaper, an aspiring manager can aim for the following slots.

Publisher and CEO

This single individual is responsible for overall performance of the newspaper, having primary responsibility for the newspaper's relations with its community, advertisers and readers. Internally, the publisher must coordinate the efforts of all departments and oversee the allocation of resources to each. In most newspapers, this is a position of great responsibility, prestige and potential reward.

General Manager

The GM runs daily *business* (as contrasted with *news*) operations, supervising at most newspapers the advertising, circulation, promotion, production and personnel departments. The GM reports to the CEO (who should avoid daily operational control, so that his or her time and energy are reserved for broader questions of strategy and relations with the external environment). At smaller papers, where the CEO takes a more active role in daily operations, there may be no GM or perhaps one with authority in only some aspects of operations. Then, the title is often business manager. Whatever the title, the job calls for the ability to coordinate interdepartmental efforts.

Chief Financial Officer

The CFO maintains outside relations with bankers and the financial public—important for any newspaper that borrows, as most do, for acquisition and expansion or capital improvements. Internally, the CFO is responsible for financial planning and projections, cost control, and providing each department with the detailed financial information necessary for efficient management.

Editor

Depending on the newspaper's size and tradition, the chief news executive carries the title of editor, executive editor or managing editor. On some papers, the editor writes editorials; the executive editor or managing editor supervises the daily production of news. Whatever the title, the individual in daily control of news coverage must be highly competent, capable of independent action and closely attuned to the market's news needs and desires.

Marketing Director

At larger newspapers, this executive coordinates efforts to analyze the market and its changing needs, to design new products, and then to price, promote, sell and distribute them. The advertising, promotion and circulation departments report to the marketing director, who reports, in turn, to the publisher. The marketing director is often active in supervising shoppers, direct mail efforts and commercial printing facilities—all within a comprehensive marketing plan. On smaller papers, the publisher or ad director serves as marketing director.

Advertising Director

With 75 to 80 percent or so of most newspapers' total revenue coming from advertising, this executive must be a strong administrator who can coordinate sale of local/retail, national and classified advertising. He or she is often among the highest paid executives.

Personnel or Human Resources Director

Few individuals have greater impact on a newspaper's character than the executive in charge of hiring, firing and motivating employees, for quality of staff determines quality of newspaper. This executive must build a staff whose quality and productivity continually improve and do it within increasingly restrictive legal and societal guidelines. A danger is that this position will be ignored by top management or will go to an individual able and willing to fight unions and hold down wages when the true need is for creative, sensitive personnel techniques.

Circulation Director

This executive's responsibility involves everything from marketing and sales strategy at the highest level to making sure that the newspaper has enough 13-year-olds on bicycles to make the day's deliveries. This job's importance is shown by the fact that, of frequent newspaper readers responding to one national survey, 35 percent said they had problems getting their papers delivered and 22 percent of nonsubscribers cited service problems as one reason for not taking a newspaper.[10]

Production Chief

In another industry, this executive might be called the director of manufacturing. Taking news and advertising copy on the one hand and raw materials—newsprint and ink—on the other, the production chief manufactures the daily newspaper. Extraordinary capital investments are necessary to give this person the tools: The *Los Angeles Times* spent $215 million on press expansion, and even small papers spend hundreds of thousands of dollars on presses. Profound technical skills are needed by the production chief. Computers and technically complex editing terminals are used widely; operating costs are high. It takes a talented executive to keep it all running—and running on time.

CORPORATE STAFF JOBS

With growth of publicly owned communications conglomerates and their large staffs, the student of newspaper organization must become familiar with the corporate-level executive staff. This staff deals with all aspects of the conglomerate's business activity, which often includes managing television and radio stations, cable TV, direct mail efforts, or magazines and other business activities as well as newspapers.

For example, corporate executives at Knight-Ridder headquarters in Miami have nationwide responsibilities for managing newspapers as well as business information services, such as commodity news wires for brokers and traders. If Knight-Ridder's chairman wants to pass instructions to the publisher of the group's *Lexington (Ky.) Herald-Leader,* he could contact Lexington directly, of course. But that would bypass his own immediate subordinates in Miami, so instructions more likely would follow the table of organization through the president of the newspaper division, Anthony Ridder, and onward to Lexington.

BOX 4.3   "Management by Walking Around"

While newspapers around him draw formal tables of organization, an elaborately unstructured approach to management is taken by Bob Haring, executive editor of the *Tulsa (Okla.) World,* a paper of 127,000 morning and 224,000 Sunday circulation:

Most observers would probably think this newsroom is not managed at all. Which is exactly the style of management we seek. We're very low key, informal. We let organization evolve out of people in it, rather than build an organization chart and try to cram the folks into those little boxes.

Our formal flow chart is non-existent. Much of our organization is horizontal, relying on interdepartmental communications below the supervisor level. The current buzzword for this approach, I believe, is "networking."

We also strive for lots of communication. My office door is never closed. We take three to five staffers from various areas to lunch each week. Senior executives meet outside the office every few weeks. And all department heads, etc., meet several times a year, both in the office and outside. We also have periodic group meetings (not full formal staff meetings) to present ideas, exchange thoughts, introduce new technology, etc. Sometimes top management (i.e., me) sits in, sometimes staffers are left to talk among themselves.

We also practice a lot of what some "experts" call "management by walking around"—that is, by having me and other senior managers out in the newsroom, sitting at the copy desk, etc. And, of course, we do the routine stuff of sponsoring softball and basketball games, buying drinks at Press Club parties, etc. Anybody in this place who feels he can't communicate with the management is not trying very hard.

Source: Bob Haring in a letter to the author.

The two-tier approach leads to inefficient proliferation to staff jobs at many companies. Peter Drucker, widely recognized expert on management systems, estimates that staff employment grew 5 to 10 times faster than the number of operating people in production, engineering, accounting, research, sales and customer service in major U.S. manufacturing after 1950. Drucker quotes foreign critics, including some Japanese, as blaming bloated staffs for many of corporate America's ills.[11]

ARGUMENTS FOR FLEXIBILITY

Some executives reject formal tables of organization, rigid staff assignments and stylized executive conferences. Like their more tightly organized brethren, however, they fashion, perhaps unwittingly, a management style featuring many characteristics of the formal approach. Among those are goal setting—if only scribbled on the back of an envelope—and a well-developed internal communications system that makes sure each manager understands corporate goals and what other managers are doing to help reach them.

Thomas Vail, who as publisher of the *Cleveland (Ohio) Plain Dealer*, engineered that paper's victory over the *Cleveland Press* (which folded in 1982), put his philosophy this way:

> *I used to make up notes for myself about objectives for the coming year and had consultations with all of our management team at the end of the year to see how we did. The overall goal was always to maintain editorial leadership followed by circulation leadership, to be followed by advertising leadership and, of course, we participated aggressively with the unions to fully automate the* Plain Dealer *and take part in the technological revolution in the printing industry.*
>
> *In the day-to-day operation of the paper there was no formal long-range strategy except the ones I have stated above. I never passed around any written statements or memos on the subject, although I often made speeches inside and outside the office about what we were trying to achieve. I do not have any committees and I seldom have a lot of meetings, although some department heads do meet daily or weekly just to see how reporters, salesmen and others are getting along.*
>
> *We do not have any budgets although we keep a very close tab on all cost increases. We will do special studies of individual departments of the paper to see if over a period of time we need more or less of certain activities or certain personnel.*

Despite his informal approach, Vail clearly managed to engender interdepartmental cooperation, a prime mission of any executive staff.

> *I should state that when you establish an aggressive series of goals for a newspaper that it must involve all of the departments of the paper.... I do not subscribe at all to the notion that editorial, advertising and other departments should not cooperate with each other. Each department should have the final authority in [its] field*

of responsibility, but I have tried to create both an understanding and cooperation between all areas of the newspaper and I have encouraged department heads to make comments about other departments. Circulation, for example, is very sensitive to sports coverage, and we have 5,000 carriers and four or five hundred other people in the circulation department. I see no reason why this vast source of information cannot be passed on to our editorial and sports departments. In addition, advertising (salespersons) get all kinds of interesting information, and this can be useful.[12]

Many newspapers promote to staff duty only those men and women who have proven themselves in operating roles. Exceptions might be, say, outside legal or accounting experts whose skills can be inserted into an organization at the staff level.

Whether drawn from inside or outside, executives considered for staff duty should be of proven competence, having demonstrated that they are leaders with general management abilities. Care should be taken to select executives of varying backgrounds and opinions. Staff diversity is essential to effective attack on the high-priority tasks of running a newspaper.

SUMMARY

Newspaper management at any level must make efficient use of people, money, time and other resources to make sure that the newspaper, large or small, reaches planned organizational goals. The manager—of no matter how many or few employees—must coordinate efforts over both the short and long term, adjusting to continual change in the newspaper's external environment (marketplace, law, society's values and so on) and change in the internal environment (relations between employees, costs, revenue and so forth). Getting the job done properly, regardless of obstacles, is the manager's responsibility. It requires continual decision making, planning, goal setting, the organization of resources, leading and motivating, the monitoring and controlling of performance. Management at the *first level* directly supervises employees; *middle managers* communicate policy to supervisors and coordinate between departments; *top management* (which includes the chief executive officer) is responsible for the entire management function.

Leadership is a complex function that can be exercised in many ways to meet many situations. The nature of newspaper work is that leaders who take a personal interest in employees and who are supportive often get best results. At every level, the newspaper organization must be designed for efficiency, systematic management and coordination of efforts. A traditional vertical organizational chart presents such organization schematically, but an informal flow of authority and information often exists outside the chart. The executive staff must be constructed carefully, for no publisher can manage even a small paper single-handedly. And along with the publisher, the executive staff will set the tone for the newspaper organization and its effectiveness.

NOTES

1. Books on management theory abound, of course, but I found these particularly helpful: James H. Donnelly Jr., James L. Gibson and John M. Ivancevich, *Fundamentals of Management* (Dallas: Business Publications, 1978); James A. F. Stoner, *Management* (Englewood Cliffs, N.J.: Prentice-Hall, 1978); W. Jack Duncan, *Management* (New York: Random House, 1983); Michael Hitt, R. Dennis Middlemist and Robert L. Mathis, *Effective Management* (St. Paul, Minn.: West, 1979).

2. For details on ownership and boards of directors see annual reports published by publicly owned companies and their "annual letter to shareholders." Both are available in most major libraries and from secretaries of the respective corporations. Ask as well for the 10-K report, a more detailed financial document, also filed with the Securities and Exchange Commission.

3. For entertaining insights into Neuharth's personality and managerial style, see his *Confessions of an S. O. B.* (New York: Doubleday, 1989).

4. Tom Vail, letter to author.

5. See Fred E. Fiedler, *A Story of Leadership Effectiveness* (New York: McGraw-Hill, 1967); and J. W. Reddin, *Managerial Effectiveness* (New York: McGraw-Hill, 1970).

6. Note John R. P. French and Bertram Roven, "The Babes of Social Power," in Darwin Cartwright and A. F. Zander, eds., *Group Dynamics*, 2nd ed. (Evanston, Ill.: Row, Peterson, 1960).

7. Fiedler, op. cit.

8. Warren Phillips, letter to author.

9. Alvah Chapman, letter to author.

10. These complaints show up in most reader surveys. This particular research is reported by Celeste Huenergard, "Newspapers Must Hustle For More Readers: Bogart," quoting Leo Bogart, then executive vice president, Newspaper Advertising Bureau, in *Editor & Publisher,* June 25, 1983, p. 8a.

11. Drucker warns repeatedly against bloated staffs. He is particularly pointed in, "Getting Control of Corporate Staff Work," *The Wall Street Journal,* April 28, 1982, p. 19.

12. Tom Vail, letter to author.

5

THE PLAN

By now, you've probably tumbled to a reality and a danger facing all newspaper managers: Reality—we live in a busy, hotly competitive marketplace and manage in constantly changing environments. Danger—you can get overwhelmed by the frantic daily pace in all that and lose sight of a manager's single most important function: planning.

Planning? Yes, at any level of management, planning is your first function. In top management, you must keep free of unnecessary encumbering detail so you can plan long-range strategy to achieve, in years ahead, the newspaper's overall mission. As a junior manager, your planning involves primarily detailed *short-term operating plans* for, say, the next 12 months. At all levels, you must map coming events as best possible so that—whether you're working for the smallest country weekly or largest metro daily—you can get the best possible fix on the future, plan for it and adjust along the way so goals are met.

You're already taken the first step: To ensure planning validity, you must audit those factors in the newspaper's external and internal environments that will influence your planning and, eventually, your chances of success. You learned this in earlier chapters dealing with the marketplace and competition.

Now, in Chapter 5, we'll deal with planning in two sections. First, we'll discuss marketing the newspaper, which means, simply, managing through a concept whose time has arrived: Plan your newspaper operations as an integrated whole, which creates a product (or products) in response to consumer desires and needs. Second, we'll look at specific goals of planning and tools you'll use.

THE THEORY OF MARKETING

Once upon a time, newspaper editors surveyed each day's news, then published what they thought was important or interesting, and that was that. This is no fairy tale. It happened that way.

Advertising sales forces made themselves available to sell space in the newspaper, take it or leave it. Circulation employees sold as many papers as possible—where and to whom didn't really matter; only total numbers counted. Newspaper production was so cumbersome, costly and time-consuming that newspaper operations were production-dominated. Weekly editors weren't really editors; most spent their time in the back shop, just getting the paper out. Promotion? Did newspapers actively promote themselves with customers and society at large, as must any consumer-oriented business? Mostly, that simply wasn't done.

Well, times changed.

Today, the *marketing concept* is upon us and you must become a marketing expert, skilled in discovering scientifically what customers want and need, then focusing the newspaper's resources on satisfying those wants and needs. Operating departments—news, advertising, circulation, production—must be integrated into an organizational whole. The marketing concept requires you to harness each department in a *customer-oriented team* which must identify and satisfy customer needs.

Now, two points: First, "marketing" newspapers isn't totally popular in our industry. Particularly in newsrooms, some journalists say newsrooms should be kept clear of the mud wrestling for economic survival in the crassly commercial marketplace. And, to some, news isn't a commodity to be collected, packaged and sold; rather, it's some sort of sacred thing, handed down from on high. However, second, today's successful publishers and other industry leaders—whether they rose through advertising, circulation, production or news—all arrived eventually at the same point: They managed under a plan that positioned their newspapers as customer-oriented, truly integrated organizations with all resources, human and other, coordinated in a focused marketing thrust. Their experience demonstrates marketing is a concept you must learn to employ effectively, whether your primary career interest is news or the business side.

If you think about it, the marketing concept seems ideal for a newspaper. Its business, after all, is to sell news to readers, then sell those readers to advertisers. In pursuit of that goal, daily newspapers sell about 60 million units of their product each weekday; weeklies, 55 million each week. The dailies alone sell over $32 billion in advertising annually.

Surely, any industry with such sales volume and which serves two consumer constituencies—readers and advertisers—naturally would be consumer-oriented in the true sense of marketing. Not so. Newspapers traditionally were production-oriented, burdened with the complex manufacturing process that led to business strategies revolving around the newspaper and its problems, not around consumers and their needs.

In other industries, many companies switched to full marketing orientation decades ago. But only now are newspapers switching to the marketing concept, tailoring their products to satisfy customer needs and selling them in a competitive marketplace, just like any other product. Only recently have tables of organization been redrawn to insert "marketing director."

WHY MARKETING IS NECESSARY

Three basic factors force newspaper managers to plan around the marketing concept:

Competition

It's forcing newspapers to anticipate, to change, to build creatively as never before. We're being challenged fiercely for advertisers and readers. Obviously, relying blindly on techniques of the past won't work anymore.

Weakness in Newspaper Performance

Frankly, neither reader nor advertiser is being served well by many newspapers. For advertisers, we're failing to deliver deep enough penetration of households or provide selective targeting. For readers, too many newspapers are failing to meet changing societal needs and attitudes. Reader (or, more properly, *non*reader) apathy grows because many of us are putting out unattractive, old-fashioned news products.

Failure to Exploit Our Strengths

Old-fashioned managerial techniques won't properly exploit newspaper strengths. Modern, consumer-oriented marketing techniques do that, however, by helping us sharpen the news product to gain wider public support and thus succeed in circulation and advertising.

New business opportunities are opened through the marketing concept. Improved marketing research identifies new consumer needs and desires, among readers and advertisers alike. New editing techniques permit satisfying readers and advertisers, for example, with news and ads tailored in zoned editions or, indeed, by creating entirely new vehicles, such as newsletters, direct mail, magazines and so forth. New production technology permits faster, better printing and distribution. Combining those strengths to attack newspaper problems—and exploit opportunities—is what the marketing concept is all about.

This is clear: A journalistically strong, even superior news product will not succeed automatically in the marketplace. Check those who worked for *The New York Herald-Tribune, Washington Star, Philadelphia Bulletin* and other papers that failed despite being first-class journalistically.

Something else is needed: Belief that a newspaper—a manager—need not be resigned to whatever fate brings but, rather, that your long-range future can be guided in large part through planned effort.

CORE CHARACTERISTICS OF MARKETING

To create a consumer-oriented newspaper you'll need a marketing philosophy with these characteristics.

Total Company Focus

The goal is to spot marketplace demand, analyze how it can be met, plan to meet it, then meet it. In the past, if anyone did that it was the sales arm of a newspaper. Today, that's what every department—including news—must do.

Research Base

Research to identify and measure customer wants and needs must be continual. Whether you buy professional assistance from outside or develop in-house capability, research must guide every department's daily operations and long-range strategy. News wants to add three columnists? Does research say they are needed? Circulation wants to start to push in the northwest suburbs? What does research say about the potential readers there—and whether advertisers would find them attractive?

Profit Orientation

Profit, not volume, is the goal under the marketing concept. Producing and selling more newspapers each day is not necessarily better. Are they being sold to the right readers, those attractive to advertisers? Face it: Your profit-oriented stockholders want to know.

The Marketing Mix

Whatever your management role, you will help fashion a correct marketing mix: creating a product that satisfies consumer needs; pricing it to cover costs, ensure profit and meet competitive prices; distributing it to the right customers, at the time, in the right locations; and promoting it in a manner consistent with the newspaper's overall objectives. For clues on how to arrive at the correct marketing mix, you first must look outward, to the newspaper's external environment.

Monitor the External Environment

Your success (or lack of it) will be influenced heavily by your newspaper's external marketing environment in four important broad areas.

Society's Needs and Expectations

Since Colonial days, the American public's expectation has been clear: Newspapers must do more than make a profit; they must educate, uplift and serve the public interest. Yet, society's attitudes shift constantly, and newspapers often come under attack from that same public as being arrogant, distant, cold, too powerful. Make no significant marketing move without considering society's perceptions of the process.

Government and Legal Issues

Like it or not, as a newspaper manager—or manager of any business—you have a partner: the government. It influences every aspect of newspapering. The law today carries unprecedented importance in newspaper operations.

Competitive Issues

Careful analysis of this influence in the external environment must precede every marketing decision, as you know already.

Economic Issues

The broad national economic picture and the local market and audience are crucial influences in marketing. In all newspaper operations, what to do, when to do it—indeed, whether to do it—depends on your analysis of economic influences.

Launching a costly Sunday magazine to attract national advertising makes no sense if the national economy is in recession; trying to sell subscriptions in a distant area of the state makes no economic sense if advertisers don't care about readers who live there. The only constant in the external marketing environment is change. Be alert for shifting influences.

AUDIT THE INTERNAL ENVIRONMENT

Important internal considerations influence the newspaper's marketing concept.

Resources Available

If research identifies a marketplace need, can you meet it with the money, time, management and staff talent available to you? New methods in management and research *can* stretch resources; the marketing concept *does* give us bigger sales bang for every buck. Research *does* show us where to spend for greatest effect in producing new circulation and advertising revenue. But the parameters of your marketing effort will be limited by the availability of resources.

Financial Goals

Your marketing direction will be established largely by your owner's financial goals. Publicly or privately owned, newspapers must meet the rising tide of shareholder expectations and produce ever-improved dividends. If you could listen to secret strategy sessions at large communications companies, you would hear executives first establishing financial goals, then working back from them to set the marketing and operational objectives required to yield those financial results.

Social Goals and Ethical Standards

What public image do you and the owners want for the newspaper? Your in-house decision will influence greatly the type of and quality of paper you produce. What ethical stance is to be taken? Should the newspaper get involved in community boosterism or limit its role to that of observer?

Technology

Whatever research indicates you should do, whatever marketing goals you establish, your newspaper's ability to perform depends heavily on its technology. Elaborate marketing strategy can be devised to blanket a distant county with your circulation, for example, but all to no avail if your press cannot produce papers on time or your distribution technology cannot get them there. And, obviously, your internal audit must cover whether your newspaper possesses the latest electronic technology which offers you new marketing opportunities or, in the hands of competitors, poses external threats.

STEPS IN THE MARKETING PROCESS

To ensure effective results, you should follow these discrete steps in planning and implementing the marketing concept.

Organizing the Marketing Structure

Drawing a new table of organization to create a "marketing director" will announce the marketing era has arrived. See Figure 5.1 for how that is done. But the new chart won't convince anyone. You must change old ways of thinking and overturn age-old work habits.

Be prepared for conflict. The marketing approach involves new basic tasks for individuals, perhaps new employees. The hierarchy must be realigned, new lines of authority and responsibility established—and that will upset many people. Ad-

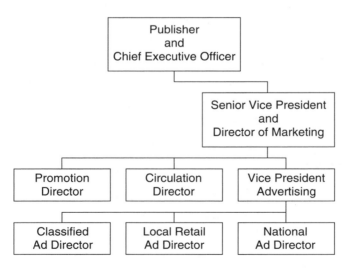

FIGURE 5.1 Typical reporting relationships among publisher, marketing director, and directors of promotion, circulation and advertising.

vertising and circulation executives who reported directly to the publisher now will report to the marketing director. Reporting directly to the top boss is a status symbol. Ending that is seen by many as a demotion.

The marketing director must be a person of outstanding talent who can create and effectively lead a department that serves as the primary business link between the newspaper and its readers and advertisers. Ability to motivate others, externally and internally, is required. Because advertising represents 75 to 80 percent of total revenue for most newspapers, marketing directors often are selected from ad department ranks. In the new job, however, the director must take a broad view of strategic planning, market analysis and leadership of a widely diverse group of employees; normally, he or she is responsible for the performance of both the advertising and circulation departments. Close coordination with production, news and promotion departments is required. The marketing effort also needs top management's total—and visible—commitment. The publisher must sign on with full support.

Analyzing Your Present and Future Position

Get visionary. Think big. Take nothing for granted. If you think newspapers have a heavenly mandate for continued prosperity, remember the railroads. They once were one of America's greatest industries.

What should the marketing department recommend to top management as long-range strategy? Where are today's customers and markets? Where will they be tomorrow? How should the newspaper compete for them, with what product, where and when? Should you stay in the newspaper business alone or branch off into magazines, shoppers, television, cable?

Where is there potential reward—in profit or market share— and what investment is necessary to unlock it? Where do competitors, present and future, fit into the picture? What are their strengths and weaknesses?

Setting Goals

What must be achieved in the short and long term to fulfill strategic objectives or exploit opportunities revealed in market analysis? Precisely what must the newspaper accomplish in profit, market share, social objectives, image? Where in the market must the newspaper be positioned and when—at what cost and for what reward? If your strategic objective in, say, five years is to be the dominant news and advertising medium in a five-county area surrounding the city, what must be done immediately to improve journalistic quality and advertising and circulation operations to achieve that objective?

Planning and Assigning Resources

What financing is required? What is needed in personnel, management talent, time, plant and equipment, newsprint and other supplies? Then, commit them.

Management sets the tone, creating a climate for creative ideas, products, services—solutions to customers' needs and wants. Anything less than total commitment—hedging on resources, for example—can ruin the venture.

Creating the Product

The "product" can be a generally improved newspaper, a Sunday magazine, an overhauled business section—or an entirely new venture into free-circulation shoppers or direct mail. New products create great excitement in a newspaper staff. If everything clicks, the rewards can be enormous. Conversely, failure can be costly in money, market share, competitive position and public image.

Creating a product requires intimate understanding of the intended market, likely competition, probable short-term costs and revenue, and long-term potential. Dry runs and test marketing will help gauge reader and advertiser reaction to the new product and suggest how it can be priced. Your goal is the highest possible price consistent with other objectives. If, for example, circulation is your primary objective, a lower subscription price might be warranted, at least initially. In pricing, know what your own costs will be, what test marketing indicates customers are likely to pay willingly, what competitors charge and what profit levels are required by your corporate policy. In assessing competitors' prices, study their costs as well. How far can they drop their prices to meet your entry into the market?

Monitoring, Controlling, Adjusting

This critical function involves setting standards, evaluating performance and making changes if standards are not met. For a new product, this means determining, for example, whether quality and cost standards are being upheld. Are profits, market share and public reception (image) as planned? If not, move boldly and quickly to improve the performance—or scrap the new product.

Don't carry a loser if your evaluation shows its prospects are poor. Knowing when to kill a new product can be as important as knowing when to launch one. Stay flexible to meet constant change in external and internal environments. New opportunities open, old products wither, fresh competitors appear. Marketing requires continual examination of all variables in the marketing mix.

COMPANIES AND PRODUCTS: THEIR LIFE CYCLES

Companies and their products go through distinct life cycles. From birth to decline, each stage presents its own opportunities and problems. For each, you must organize the appropriate marketing response.

Company Life Cycles

In the development stage, a company is created to win a new market or an existing company undergoes radical overhaul and is repositioned to gain new lease on life.

Many new companies are being created in electronic publishing. Most major daily newspaper corporations are being repositioned as diversified communications conglomerates. Times Mirror Corp., the Washington Post Co., the New York Times Co., Tribune Co.—all grew from a single-newspaper base and now are positioned in related areas such as broadcast, cable and magazines.

The *maintenance* or *balancing stage* involves retaining market position and carefully controlling existing operations rather than launching new major products. Newspapers in this stage are "tuning up" their existing product but not moving boldly into radically new areas.

In the *growth* stage, a newspaper enters a new market or introduces a new product similar to existing markets or products. For example, a daily newspaper launches a weekly shopper. That is close to the newspaper's main business thrust but still offers new growth potential.

In a *new venture,* a company may risk stretching for potentially great reward in an entirely new field. Many large newspaper-based companies are in this stage, diversifying into entertainment, for example, or new communications systems for the "electronic highway."

Product Life Cycles

For most young managers, firsthand experience in life and death cycles will come with individual products. The newspaper's overall strategy will be in place when you hire on and you won't get your hands on that for some years. But you probably will be directly involved in product strategy, for we are in a highly innovative era in American newspapering and new products are being launched continually.

For any product, the *birth* stage is most expensive. Creating the product and introducing it to consumers—promoting it to create consumer demand—is costly. And production and distribution must continue even if initial consumer demand is low. Gannett lost hundreds of millions of dollars—some say $1 billion—in launching its national paper, *USA Today.* Reader demand was substantial but advertiser support was insufficient.

The second stage in product life cycle is *growth*—if introduction is successful. The growth period often yields substantial profits and market share. But success will attract attention, so competitors probably will enter the market. Rapidly growing city and specialized business magazines are examples of competitors flocking to share profit potential that newspapers uncovered in highly affluent areas.

In *maturity,* a product saturates its potential and sales level off. Competitors force costly adjustments or carve out their share of the market and profits drop. This is not necessarily the end. Innovative marketing can find new customers and adjust the product to give it new thrust. Many long-established newspapers are in this stage, vigorously adding new journalistic dimensions (business news sections, for example, or new "lifestyle" pages) and thus attracting new categories of readers and advertisers.

Decline and death of a product can result from fundamental changes in environment or consumer desires. For example, changing American lifestyles put afternoon newspapers under heavy pressure and the flight of affluent residents from cities to suburbs helped kill some.

SEGMENT YOUR MARKET AND FORECAST PROFITS

Take two final—and important—steps before developing your marketing strategy: Target precisely the market you seek and forecast whether your endeavor will be profitable.

Segmenting the Market

No newspaper product will succeed if distributed indiscriminately. *Target marketing* is required. Sort through broad geographic, demographic and psychographic characteristics of your newspaper's market for market segments of smaller, more homogeneous groups or areas that can be targeted. Look for a target audience with similar product interests, people willing and able to buy the product and, for certain, who are attractive to your advertisers. For example, an appealing segment could be a particularly wealthy suburb—a geographic slice within your larger market—that you plan to serve with a weekly suburban news section and, in turn, offer to advertisers as a vehicle for reaching an especially attractive audience (see Figure 5.2).

Or you could target, within your general readership, a bloc of readers particularly interested in money matters—stocks, bonds, investments—and serve them with a once-weekly insert on personal investments. The insert, in turn, could be offered to banks, brokerage houses, realtors and others as an attractive advertising medium.

Stay clear of *undifferentiated marketing* (the creation of a single product and marketing mix for an entire market) and move toward *differentiated marketing* (or creation of several products, each with its own marketing mix) aimed at small, discrete segments of the larger market.

For generations, undifferentiated marketing succeeded by bringing all market segments into the same journalistic tent and thus offering advertisers mass distribution of their messages at a relatively low per-subscriber cost. Two developments today limit the success of that strategy: First, numerous competitors—shoppers, direct mail and others—are segmenting the market and delivering those narrow slices advertisers have come to desire. Shoppers and direct-mail companies can offer a food store, for example, a distribution scheme covering only homes in the immediate vicinity where the store's primary customers live. Second, the costs of the mass-circulation newspaper, especially in labor, newsprint and distribution, are so high that more narrowly based competitors with lower costs can price their advertising below the newspaper's rates.

Concentrated marketing in a narrow market segment with high profit potential is the strategy for some newspapers. *The New York Times,* for example, avoids widespread circulation among readers of low income and educational level; rather, it

Our Towns Micro-zones
Get even more precise targeting with Our Towns Micro-zones.

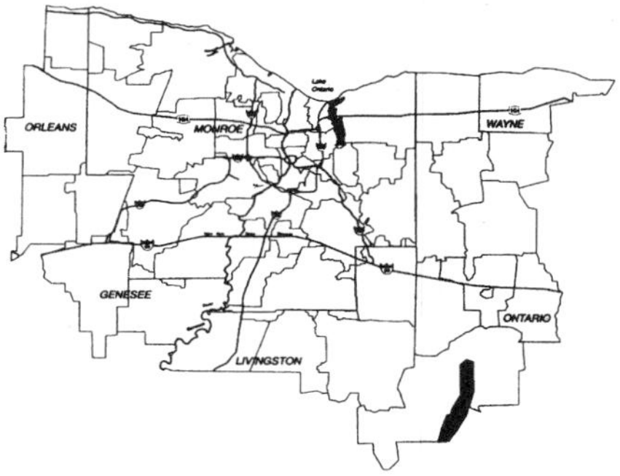

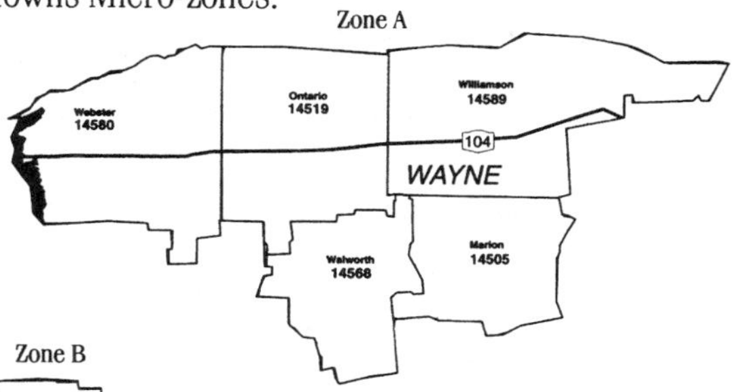

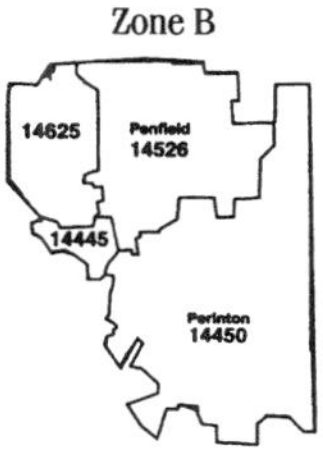

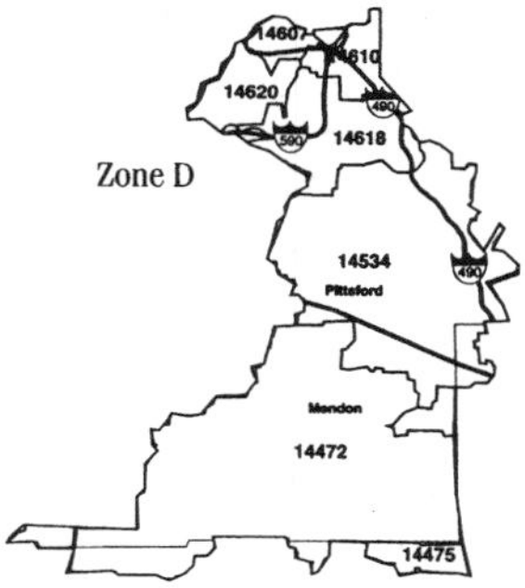

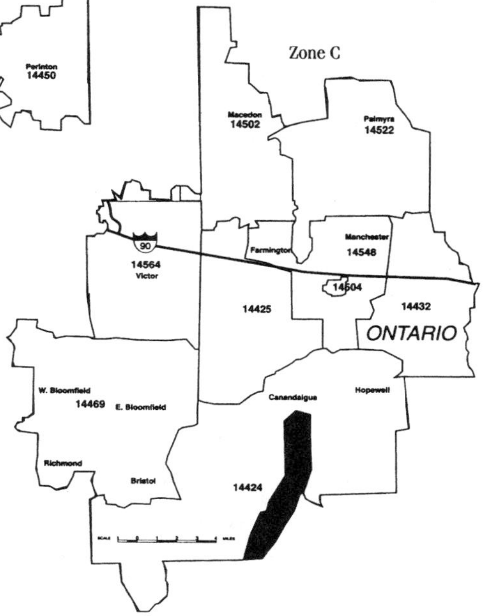

Micro-zone Rates

	Zone A Webster/ Wayne (15,000 HH)	Zone B Penfield/ Perinton (20,000 HH)	Zone C Ontario/ S. Wayne (12,000 HH)	Zone D Brighton/ Pittsford (35,000 HH)
Open	$8.65	$10.04	$9.27	$17.94
Frequency Contracts - consecutive weeks				
6x	7.61	8.62	8.24	14.83
13x	6.06	7.37	7.21	12.76
26x	5.71	6.90	6.18	12.07
52x	4.84	5.99	5.15	10.35
Annual Bulk Volume Contracts				
100"	7.79	8.86	7.73	14.83
250"	7.10	8.50	7.47	14.49
500"	6.06	8.22	6.70	14.11
1000"	5.88	6.93	5.67	12.07
2500"	4.84	6.39	4.64	10.35

Micro-zone Policies

One micro-zone may be purchased at the micro-zone rate, adding the same ad to another micro-zone earns a 10% discount, adding two or more earns a 15% discount. Minimum ad size in a micro-zone is 4 column inches. For full zone pricing please refer to page 8.

FIGURE 5.2   **Gannett's Rochester (N.Y.)** *Democrat and Chronicle* **and** *Times-Union* **segment their total market (upper left) into smaller zones for advertisers interested in focusing on specific areas. Reprinted by permission of the Rochester (N.Y.)** *Democrat and Chronicle* **and** *Times-Union.*

seeks elitist circulation among highly affluent readers valued by advertisers. This will be the strategy for many profit-oriented newspapers in the future. You cannot profitably serve mass audiences that are geographically dispersed and demographically and psychographically diverse. Why? Because costs are too high—and because advertisers don't want dispersed, diverse audiences.

Forecasting Product Profitability

New-product ideas spring from all corners of a newspaper. Some managers set up new-product committees ("skunk works") to develop ideas. Each should be analyzed for how it fits into overall strategy, whether it would be unique or face stiff competition, whether it would achieve desired goals in image or community perception. Then, you calculate profitability.

New-product failure rates can be extremely high, so proceed cautiously. If profit is your primary goal (as contrasted, for example, with image or community service), drop the project unless a sound profit margin is indicated. Analysis of data on similar products launched in the past provides the most reliable basis for forecasts. A new zoned edition, the fourth launched in two years, probably will perform predictably. However, launching entirely new products in new markets can be hazardous due to lack of previous experience. This is exactly where many communications companies are today as they look at the enormous capital investments necessary to be a significant player on the new "electronic highway."

The measurement most used in evaluating profitability is *return on investment* (ROI). This measures new product performance on the basis of invested resources, as follows:

$$ROI = \frac{\text{Net profit}}{\text{sales}} \times \frac{\text{sales}}{\text{investment}}$$

To illustrate, let us say your newspaper must invest \$400,000 in the first year to launch a free-circulation shopper. First-year advertising sales are expected to hit \$1 million; net profit, \$80,000.

$$ROI = \frac{\$80,000}{\$1,000,000} \times \frac{\$1,000,000}{\$400,000} = 0.08 \times 2.5 = 20\%$$

ROI cannot be the only tool in new-product evaluation. The new shopper, for example, may have other and more important goals—achieving market share, protecting the paid-circulation newspaper against competing shoppers and so forth.

In using ROI, you must decide what return is appropriate. Within the context of its other goals, a shopper returning 20 percent might be projected a winner. However, if ROI is the only goal, the 20 percent must be evaluated in light of what ROI is offered from similar investments elsewhere. Perhaps you should invest in a cable television system if you seek higher ROI (although \$400,000 probably would not be enough for a down payment).

CONSUMER BEHAVIOR AND YOUR STRATEGY

Throughout our discussion of marketing, we have headed toward this question: How will readers and advertisers—the consumers—react? Will they buy the new product, support the strategy? As a manager in a consumer-oriented business, you must know a great deal about consumer behavior.

Determining Who Your Consumers Are

The questions are basic but crucial—and often difficult to answer. In auditing readers and nonreaders, we ask: *Who* buys (or doesn't buy) newspapers? *Why* do or don't they? *When* do they buy and "consume"? Precisely *what* do they seek?

Note I refer to "consumers" of newspapers, not simply "buyers." We must get beyond the "buy" decision into how and why newspapers—or parts of them—are consumed or used and by how many people other than the buyer. Your editors need to know so they can tailor the product; advertisers need to know so they can position their ads. In auditing advertisers as consumers, ask the same questions—who, why, where, when and what? The newspaper's lifeblood, its ad revenue, is at stake.

Many behavioral scientists agree that true understanding of consumer behavior lies in a knowledge of basic human needs and perceptions plus the environmental influences that act on them. Needs include *physiological* or primary needs for food, shelter, clothing; *safety* needs, or the need for security; the *social* need to belong; *esteem* needs, or the desire for status; and *self-actualization* needs involving the realization of one's full potential.

As an example of how important is it to understand human needs, let's use them to design newspaper promotional slogans:

- Check your local newspaper for food store ads and where to rent an apartment. (Both are primary physiological needs.)
- Keep up on the news and don't be surprised by what happens in the world around you. (World events often raise safety needs or the wish for security.)
- Join your friends (fulfill your social need to belong) by reading the sports pages daily; read the society pages (and join the social elite).
- Read *The New York Times.* All the intelligent, wealthy people in town do. (You'll gain status.)
- Read *The Wall Street Journal.* All successful business people do. (Realize your potential in the business world.)

Note that the reality of needs is one thing; perceptions of them are quite another. For example, a newspaper in reality is a medium of news, information and advertising. But what it really can do for readers and advertisers is perceived through their eyes, not those of editors and publishers. Thus, to understand consumer behavior you must first understand consumers' perceptions—what they want to believe—about the newspaper. Editors must understand not only how their product covers the news and how it is judged by other journalists but also how that coverage is perceived by readers.

Like all human conduct, consumer behavior can be either rational or emotional. The rational approach involves a reasoned, deliberate evaluation of, for example, the newspaper's usefulness—whether it is reliable and worth its price. Emotional evaluation can lead to hardened attitudes: "The paper is no good and I won't buy it regardless of the improvements those editors try to make." Many influences tug and pull at consumers making such judgments.

Environmental Influences on Behavior

Behavioral scientists identify environmental factors that influence human behavior. Some influence consumer behavior toward your newspaper. It starts with being influenced by family, for example, or other social groups and each individual's status with a group. Each individual has a group role that signals expected behavior.

Behavioral scientists find individuals identifying with a *reference group* and conforming to the group's behavioral standards; they are also influenced by *social class* (family background, residential area, source of income and so forth). *The Boston Globe, Chicago Tribune, Los Angeles Times* and other "establishment" papers have a strong appeal to wealthy, socially powerful readers; readers of the *Bloomington (Ill.) Daily Pantagraph* tell how their fathers and grandfathers read the paper, too. Newspapers large or small can appeal to reference groups or social classes, and simple readership surveys will help identify them.

Equally important but harder to identify are changes in broader *cultural influences* and their effect on newspaper operations. For example, dramatic changes are under way in the American family, its role and structure, social mobility, pace of living, attitudes toward work and leisure time and other values and ideas. The implications are obvious for a newspaper editor trying to put together an appealing news product, a circulation executive trying to create promotion for a subscription campaign or an advertising executive trying to formulate winning sales promotion themes. Let's check how the consumer, influenced by such changing values, makes decisions—and how you, as a newspaper manager, must influence the outcome.

Consumer Decisions: How to Influence Them

Consumers move through identifiable steps in their decision making, and newspaper marketing must be aimed at influencing each step. First, the consumer becomes aware of a need or problem. Perhaps, for example, the consumer recognizes that existing information sources—other newspapers, television, radio—are inadequate or an advertiser realizes the ad medium being used isn't doing the job. Your marketing mission is to understand the other media's weaknesses and position your newspaper, in reality and consumer perception, as a viable alternative. Your newspaper's content and promotional themes, then, would emphasize "all the news—not just bits and pieces offered by television"; you would sell advertisers on the idea that your paper gets into attractive households and, unlike a competing shopper, delivers results.

Second, the consumer takes action, gathering information on what could be done about the need or problem. Here, your promotion must be strong and visible, making every potential reader aware that your news coverage is superior, making certain every nonadvertiser has in hand detailed information on your newspaper's strengths.

Third, the consumer appraises alternative solutions. Does your newspaper cover local news better than television or the other papers available? At this point, your product must prove itself; your local coverage indeed must be superior.

Fourth, the decision is made. The consumer buys. Perhaps an introductory of-fer—six months at a reduced subscription rate—will help swing the decision your way.

Fifth, the consumer makes ongoing appraisal of the choice. Now that your paper has been read for six months, is it still superior to television or that other paper? In other words, once you have the readers, you and your editors must keep them, with coverage that meets their continuing needs.

The consumer may not be aware of a need that is dormant and can be roused only by stimulation. Much of your marketing effort must be aimed at stimulating consumers to recognize that they need your newspaper and must start that five-step process toward becoming your loyal readers.

AUDITING YOUR MARKETING EFFORT

As in all your managerial responsibilities, you must evaluate your performance in marketing by measuring these areas.

Corporate Tone

Has the newspaper, from executive staff to employee ranks, accepted the market-ing concept? Is "consumer first" truly motivating each department? Is the news-room carefully researching reader needs and wants, then constructing a news package accordingly? Or are editors still putting out what they think is important, blind to reader desires? Do the advertising and circulation departments launch forth aggressively each day to satisfy consumer needs, or are they simply out there trying to sell more space or more subscriptions?

People Performance

Without superior performance by each individual involved, the marketing concept will not work. Assign individual responsibility, monitor performance, correct in midcourse, if necessary—then evaluate final results. Do not let individuals hide behind departmental or "collective" responsibility. Later we'll discuss specific tools you can use to measure performance.

Management's Performance

And that includes yours. Have you pitched in to help, made resources (people, financing and time) available? Go back over the basic marketing steps: organizing the market structure, analyzing the market, setting goals, planning and assigning resources, creating the product, monitoring and controlling, adjusting with flexibility. Have you assisted at every step?

Bottom-Line Results

The marketing effort *must* deliver results. There must be measurable progress in sales, profit, market share, community image. Assess what precisely has been accomplished. There also must be long-term advantage. Has there been improvement in formulating strategic objectives, planning and steps taken to achieve them?

The Adjustment Phase

You won't be pleased with answers to all those questions. Completely satisfactory performance would be a miracle. So you now enter the next phase of your management responsibility—adjustment. This will involve primarily five departments: news, advertising, circulation, production and promotion, and tuning each to respond properly to the demands of the newspaper's overall marketing strategy. Now, let's turn to specific techniques you can use to accomplish that.

THE GOALS AND TOOLS OF PLANNING

Planning must establish specific goals at all levels of your newspaper's operations and assign a priority to each task your staff must fulfill to accomplish those goals. Whether you are managing the newspaper's mail room or, as publisher, are responsible for all operations, your planning must spur present and future action. It must be flexible, so you can adjust course as needed in what inevitably will be changing external and internal conditions.

The Three Parts of Planning

Planning is comprised of three parts:

- *Strategic planning* is long range, stating the newspaper's overall mission and major goals. It lays down policy guidelines for reaching those goals, which can be 5, 10 or more years distant. Strategic planning always questions fundamental assumptions ("Will we *always* use newsprint?") and provides alternate

---

BOX 5.1   Planning and the "Daily Miracle"

Publishing newspapers can be so hectic and technically difficult that simply setting one out every day sometimes is called the "daily miracle" (or, "daily agony.") This creates a day-to-day mindset among newspaper people against planning. After all, planning takes time and money, creates bureaucratic paperwork and sometimes takes years to smooth out—so why make the effort? Also (although it's not talked about much) planning represents to some a threat: It forces new methods, and "old ways" are most comfortable; it creates the threat of failure in having to live up to planned goals.

But . . .

Without a plan, a newspaper is a corporate wanderer doomed to drift in disarray. Without a plan, a newspaper cannot anticipate either threats or opportunities. Without a plan, you will live your managerial life reacting to developments—mired in crisis management.

So, sell the planning concept: Point out that for each employee planning provides consistent guidelines plus the advantages of working for a newspaper that, instead of simply reacting to circumstances, anticipates the challenges. If planning strengthens the newspaper over the long haul, everybody wins.

---

avenues for reaching corporate goals. This planning is continuous, changing constantly as external and internal conditions change. Flexibility is key.

- *Intermediate* or *medium-range planning* refines specific activities necessary to reach strategic goals. Managers evaluate the approach most likely to succeed, set the time frame and, importantly, inform employees of goals to be achieved.
- *Short-range planning* for most newspapers covers one year. It is highly detailed and specifies the allocation of resources to be used. Tools include the budget and "management by objectives."

Strategic planning is in top management's hands. Only executives at that level have the information and experience required to take the broad view needed in long-range planning. Intermediate planning must include middle-level executives charged with implementing departmental activities over the next few years so the newspaper moves toward strategic goals. Interdepartmental coordination—true team effort—is crucial in this planning. Managers at the lowest levels participate in short-range planning. They are responsible for operating methods that will move the paper through the next 12-month cycle.

REALITIES OF LONG-RANGE PLANNING

For centuries, it all went Johann Gutenberg's way. For hundreds of years after he popularized movable type in the 1400s, printers made no substantive changes in the way Gutenberg did things. Yet after 1950, it took scarcely a decade for television to leap from birth as a commercially viable medium to enormous economic and social influence in America. The electronic editing of newspapers, a chancy experiment in 1970, went through three completely new generations of editing terminals in its first

18 months, so explosive was the new technology. In just a few years, this new technique transformed the methods and economics of newspaper production.

Today, rapid, traumatic change is a fact of life and newspapers ignore it at their peril. In their long-range planning, newspapers will anticipate change and adapt to it, or perish.

Planning Must Challenge Basic Assumptions

Strategic planning, then, deals with such basic questions as whether in 20 years there will be markets for newspapers as we know them. Planning must look far ahead and ask what business the newspaper should be in, who its customers will be, who will be competitors and how the newspaper can use its resources—both internal and external—to ensure future strength.

As the chief executive officer of Harte-Hanks Newspapers, Robert Marbut searched for any new trends and attitudes that would signal "a red flag to either change our strategy or programs, or even our goals."[1] He monitored these areas:

- The national/international political scene
- The general economy
- Work force trends
- Consumer attitudes and changing values
- New technology's impact
- The role of government and regulatory agencies
- Advertising trends
- Competitive developments

Planning Must Reposition the Newspaper

To meet change, we must reposition the traditional stand-alone community newspaper as a diversified information and advertising center. Only by assuming a new mindset will you and other managers be prepared to use not only newsprint to meet reader and advertiser needs but *any* means, including direct mail and electronic delivery. This concept presumes not merely positioning a newspaper to sell space to advertisers but, rather, accepting the advertiser's business problem, whatever it is, and solving it through a variety of means.

Technological breakthroughs permit managers to make radical adjustments in their competitive stance against other media, and to plan services perhaps unfettered by the severe technical limitations imposed by printing presses, newsprint and 13-year-olds on bicycles delivering the final product. Long-range strategy, then, must develop options for diversification, looking far afield for new areas of service and profit.

Newspapers have broadened their revenue bases with moves into other forms of print, such as free-circulation publications, or widened their geographic base by acquiring newspapers in other markets. But some struck out adventurously into completely new fields. For example, the Tribune Co. of Chicago ranges wide afield by owning the Chicago Cubs baseball team as well as newspapers, newsprint mills, TV stations and a large cable TV operation. Tribune Co. achieves enormous synergistic benefit by televising Cub games on its Chicago station, WGN, which has become a "super station" carried on cable systems nationwide. Other newspaper-based companies are in entertainment, auto auctions, equipment manufacturing—endeavors far removed from their main thrust. But some experts counsel strategic planning must stay closer to the newspaper's traditional business.

After years as senior vice president of the *Chicago Sun-Times,* Paul S. Hirt reasoned: "Through current literature describing the outstanding companies of Europe, Asia and America, many of the same ideas recur: Get back to basics, stick to your knitting, concentrate on value, service and excellence, and the profits will follow; beware of overemphasis on short-term profit to the neglect of future survival; avoid fostering internal bureaucracies; encourage networking [internal communications among peers] and entrepreneurial thinking throughout the organization. Each of these ideas is applicable to newspapers. . . ."[2]

Looking *far* into the future is difficult, obviously. But that doesn't stop many companies from trying. Dow Jones and Co., generally recognized as among the industry's best-managed firms, is one. Sterling E. Soderlind, for years Dow Jones vice president/planning, said:

> We have had systematic long-range planning on a corporate-wide basis since 1975. We have gone through the planning cycle annually, sometimes for three-year periods but most often for five-year spans. The plans contain written statements on corporate objectives and strategies to achieve these goals during the plan period. There are similar sections giving details on objectives and strategies for each of our products, services and subsidiaries. These include The Wall Street Journal, Barron's, *our Information Services Group, the Community Newspapers Group (Ottaway Newspapers). . . .*
>
> To help managers in their planning, the Planning Department provides analysis on demographic, economic and lifestyle trends, in some cases looking ahead 10 years or more *(author's emphasis)."*[3]

Planning Must Project Profits

Future profits must be a centerpiece of long-range planning. A newspaper must generate profits to attract investors with capital necessary for expansion and improvement. The industry, long regarded as "people-intensive," has become capital-intensive. Further, only profitable newspapers attract talented staff and executives; only profitable newspapers can afford the journalistic quality so necessary in today's highly competitive communications world.

Soderlind spoke to the importance Dow Jones and Co. attached to planning for profit: "One corporate long-range objective is to increase net earnings at a rate that equals or exceeds the growth of the economy, including inflation. In the case of some of our divisions, this also is part of their financial objective. But other yardsticks also are used. Thus, some publications and services aim to meet or surpass a certain level in their operating profit margin. A new venture may aim at achieving a specific annual growth rate in revenues during a plan period—and also may set a time period during which the venture is expected to achieve profitability."[4]

Varying routes lead to profitability. One is a strategy of holding down costs by delivering low-quality service to readers and counting on high profits over the short run. Social responsibility and professional ethics aside, this fast route to profit can bleed a newspaper of self-respect and public regard. It can lead to loss of market share, disaffected readers and competitive disadvantage. Nevertheless, the technique is practiced by many newspaper planners.

Another plan involves investing more in the newspaper, guaranteeing high-quality service and projecting over the long haul for greater profit to flow from a satisfied, demographically attractive readership that, in turn, attracts a greater number of advertisers willing to pay higher rates.

Warren Phillips, who as chairman of Dow Jones and Co. helped push that company to international prominence, cast his company's long-range planning for profit against the wider background of service to reader, advertiser and community: "Our number one objective, our primary objective, is to serve the public exceedingly well—i.e., to raise further the standards of editorial content and of service."[5]

In sum, long-range strategy demands immediate action to accomplish change in three, five or more years. But only with a clearly defined strategy can management turn to intermediate and short-range planning and thus move the paper pragmatically toward its overall goals.

INTERMEDIATE PLANNING

In this second broad area of planning, managers focus operational methods necessary to accomplish long-range goals. This involves establishing the time frames and most appropriate methods in these areas:

- Improving journalistic quality to levels that will be demanded by a more sophisticated, discerning audience.
- Upgrading staff quality, including hiring and promoting women and minorities.
- Increasing advertising quantity and quality.
- Deepening circulation penetration of households and raising reader demographics.
- Strengthening the newspaper's competitive posture.
- Constructing production facilities to meet future needs.
- Diversifying in a manner appropriate to the company's main thrust.
- Improving profit levels.

Intermediate planning means informing all employees on the plan. Success depends on everyone's complete grasp of what is expected and the time frame for each task. An upward flow of information—a "feedback loop"—is necessary so comments and suggestions from first-level supervisors and employees get to

CASE STUDY 5.1 Standards to Plan By

OK. You're a publisher. It's time to plan your corporate strategy. And, your entire staff is looking at you for leadership. Where do you start? What goals—what standards for achievement—will you lay down?

Well, for starters, consider four broad strategies developed by a Newspaper Association of America (NAA) study team for a hypothetical 50,000-circulation daily: Your market is being fragmented by competitors. Cable TV is competing for readers' time. Direct mail is offering target marketing to your advertisers.

The local advertising dollar in your city of 100,000 households is divided as shown in the pie chart below.

NAA's four strategies:

1. Continue the newspaper's traditional role of mass market medium. Maintain circulation and ad market share through modest price increases and product refinements.

2. Protect profit margins by targeting upscale readers and advertisers. Aggressively raise circulation prices. Make modest changes in the news product to reflect its narrower target audience.

3. Add demographically targeted print and electronic products to the core, mass market newspaper and thus meet changing reader and advertiser needs.

4. Add direct marketing services to the core, mass market product and thus respond to your newspaper's principal competition.

Cautioning that strategy must vary with your own market and competitive situations, the NAA team said it projected that in the period 1990 to 2000, Strategy 4 would be most successful: It protects the newspaper's advertising base, provides targeting skills and diversifies revenue sources.

The team warned that standing pat on Strategy 1 (maintain the traditional mass medium status) would give the newspaper no new skills, products or revenue sources to stop erosion of the newspaper's basic business.[a]

Now, you'll need specific departmental goals to crank into your corporate planning. Depending on your local market and competition, consider industry averages compiled by Susan H. Miller, then Scripps Howard vice president/editorial:

- Average paper devotes 50 percent of its space to news ("newshole"), 46 percent to paid advertising, 4 percent unpaid ads.

- Household penetration for a newspaper of less than 150,000 circulation, without direct newspaper competition, averages 54 percent in the morning and 42 percent in the evening, in its city zone (CZ) or news

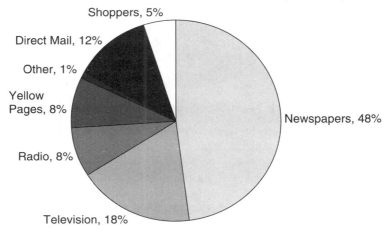

Shoppers, 5%
Direct Mail, 12%
Other, 1%
Yellow Pages, 8%
Radio, 8%
Television, 18%
Newspapers, 48%

Continued

CASE STUDY 5.1   *Continued*

paper designated market (NDM). (Scripps Howard's goal: at least 60 percent daily, 70 percent Sunday.)

- Local retail advertising revenue averages 2 percent of total local retail sales in the market.

- Daily newspapers average 38 percent share of local ad spending (goal: 45 percent).

- Work force is 61 percent male, 39 percent female, 18 percent minority. (Total U.S. work force is 46 percent female. Scripps Howard's goal: percentages of women and minorities comparable to local work force.)

- Newsroom staffing averages 1.1 to 1.2 full-time employees per 1,000 circulation.

- 65.2 percent of men read the previous day's weekday paper; 60.2 percent of women did (goal: raise women's percentage to men's level).

- Readership of previous Sunday paper is 68.8 percent of men in the market, 68.1 percent of women.

- Reading time per issue: 38 minutes daily, 62 minutes on Sunday (goal: 45 minutes daily, at least one hour on Sundays).

- Newspapers average 2.3 adult readers per copy sold.

- In budgeting, total costs are divided as shown in the pie chart below.

- Revenue is 75 to 78 percent from advertising, 21 to 25 percent from circulation, 0 to 1 percent from other.

- Operating profit margins for newspaper divisions of publicly owned companies ranged from 15 to 30 percent of revenue.[b]

There! Now you have standards to plan by.

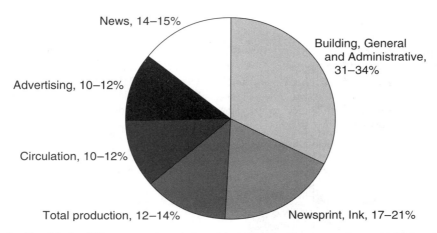

a"Mastering Your Market," Newspaper Association of America, The Newspaper Center, 11600 Sunrise Valley Drive, Reston, Va., 22091, 1993.
bSusan Miller, "Scripps Howard General Managers Newsletter," November 1992.

higher managers. By informing employees, management invites willing, creative participation. And the feeling of being part of an important planning project as well as the sense that management is interested in comments from below can work wonders for employee morale.

SHORT-TERM PLANNING

By contrast with the long view of strategic planning, short-term planning states each manager's goals for only the coming year. Managing under such a plan requires creative and tightly disciplined managerial skill at all levels. But beware: The short-term plan cannot be a rigid list of performance demands laid down unilaterally by top management for subordinate managers. Rather, team goals must be drawn jointly by top management and each manager who must meet the goals.

Properly implemented, short-range planning can elicit enthusiastic participation from every level and move the newspaper ahead on all fronts. However, a plan improperly drawn or arbitrarily presented is worse than no plan; it can harm staff morale and operations. Precision short-term planning affects many employees otherwise only vaguely aware of corporate planning. So, particularly in newsrooms, it often stirs resentment as yet another administrative burden—or even fear that the new program will threaten job security. Careful explanation of planning goals can head off complaints. But planning must proceed despite almost inevitable grousing.

Short-term planning specifies, among other objectives, what the newspaper must achieve in profits, growth and market share. Two primary tools are used:

- Budgets specifying how a manager will employ resources—particularly money and personnel—to meet given objectives. Importantly, budgets also set goals for individuals and measure and evaluate performance. Thus, budgets are motivational *and* control mechanisms. They inform the entire management team of goals and coordinate efforts to achieve them.
- Management by Objectives (MBO), a process popularized by management theorist Peter Drucker. Under MBO, employees and managers collaborate in establishing goals not easily reduced to statistical representations of a budget, such as improving journalistic quality or upgrading staff talent.

Before you can implement short-range planning, you must understand your newspaper's basic financial position. Two instruments, the balance sheet and profit and loss statement, help you do that.

How the Balance Sheet Works

Accounting is for experts. But even nonfinancial managers with "math fright" must learn to keep score in the business of newspapering. Here are a few tips: The *balance sheet* represents financial conditions on a certain date. Conditions change rapidly, so note that the balance sheet reflects your newspaper's assets and liabilities only on that date.

Assets are things of value owned by a business. *Current assets* can be turned into cash within one year; they include cash in the bank, marketable securities, inventory (such as newsprint) and accounts receivable (sums owned by subscribers or advertisers in the next 12 months). *Fixed assets* are such things as land and equipment. *Intangible assets* may not show on the balance sheet but can be extremely

TABLE 5.1   Risk Publishing Inc. Balance Sheet

Assets		Liabilities and Capital	
Cash	$1,000,000	Liabilities	$_____
		Capital	
		Common stock	
		P. Anthony	500,000
		R. Stone	500,000
Total assets	$1,000,000	Total liabilities and capital	$1,000,000

valuable. They include franchises, licenses, trademarks and goodwill. In accounting usage, goodwill is the difference between the actual book value of assets and the higher price a buyer would pay for those assets because the newspaper has a strong reputation in its market and with its customers.

Balance sheet *liabilities* include *current liabilities* (due in the coming 12 months), *accounts payable* (amounts the paper owes creditors), *notes payable* (such as promissory notes held by banks), and *accruals* (such as wages, pension contributions and taxes owed but not yet paid). *Long-term liabilities* are debts such as mortgages due after the current year. The balance sheet also shows *shareholder equity* or the owners' share of the business. It is computed by subtracting liabilities from assets.

In sum, the balance sheet represents things of value the newspaper owns (assets). On the other side are what it owes (liabilities) and the owners' share of the company. The two sides—assets and liabilities—must balance; every entry into or out of one side must be balanced by a corresponding entry on the other side. To illustrate, let's assume you are P. Anthony and, along with a former classmate, B. Stone, you start a newspaper. Relatively inexpensive equipment permits low-cost entry into small-paper publishing, so you each put up $500,000. You divide 50–50 the stock in the new company, Risk Publishing Inc. Your first balance sheet entry is shown in Table 5.1.

The $1 million put into Risk Publishing's bank account is carried on the balance sheet as cash; the value of your stock in the company is carried on the liabilities and capital side.

Now, things look a little tight in start-up. You need newsprint and ink and other supplies. So, you borrow $50,000 from the local bank on a six-month note. Again, entries are made on both sides, as shown in Table 5.2.

Your first purchase is $12,000 in production equipment and $5,000 in newsprint. Delivery is completed, but you have 30 days to pay. Meanwhile, your partner has leased a small building and paid one month's rent, $250, in advance. You record those transactions as in Table 5.3. Note several things about the entries in Table 5.3. All cash is still on the balance sheet except the $250 paid in advance rent. That is listed as prepaid expense. Your $12,000 in production equipment is a fixed asset. The $5,000 in newsprint is listed under inventory.

On the liabilities side, the $12,000 you owe for equipment and $5,000 for newsprint are represented as accounts payable of $17,000. The $50,000 note payable, of course, is your bank loan. Capital is still $1 million in common stock.

TABLE 5.2   Risk Publishing Inc. Balance Sheet

Assets		Liabilities and Capital	
Cash	$1,050,000	Liabilities	
		Note payable	$50,000
		Capital	
		Common stock	
		P. Anthony	500,000
		R. Stone	500,000
Total assets	$1,050,000	Total liabilities and capital	$1,050,000

Each subsequent transaction, as Risk Publishing gets under way, is similarly recorded on both sides, so assets and liabilities always stay in balance. Transactions actually are recorded in journals (chronological records of transactions) and ledgers (records of transactions segregated by area or account—such as cash, accounts payable and so on). At the end of an accounting period—six months, one year or whatever period you choose—entries from journals and ledgers are transferred to a balance sheet.

Table 5.4 on page 126 shows the balance sheet used by an actual small paper of 10,500 circulation.

Understanding the P&L

The *profit and loss statement,* or "P&L"—variously called "earnings report" or "income statement"—summarizes the newspaper's operations for any period but usually for a calendar year or "fiscal" year (which begins and ends on dates other than January 1 and December 31).

In your early years as a manager, you may never work with a balance sheet; indeed, few managers in daily operations are concerned with it. For them, the P&L

TABLE 5.3   Risk Publishing Inc. Balance Sheet

Assets		Liabilities and Capital	
Cash	$1,049,750	Liabilities	
Inventory	5,000	Accounts payable	$17,000
Prepaid expense	250	Note payable	50,000
Fixed assets	12,000		
		Total liabilities	$67,000
		Capital	
		Common stock	
		P. Anthony	500,000
		R. Stone	500,000
Total assets	$1,067,000	Total liabilities and capital	$1,067,000

TABLE 5.4   Balance Sheet
          Small Daily Publishing Co.

Assets	September 30	
	This Year	**Last Year**
Current Assets		
Cash (in bank or readily available elsewhere)	_____	_____
Accounts receivable (amounts owed by customers, less reserve for those unlikely to be paid)	_____	_____
Inventory (newsprint, ink)	_____	_____
Prepaid expenses (rent or insurance paid in advance, for example)	_____	_____
Fixed Assets		
(building, press, etc., less depreciation—that portion of the fixed assets' original cost used up since purchase)	_____	_____
Other Assets		
(includes goodwill)	_____	_____

Liabilities		
Current Liabilities		
Bank note payable (amount due within 12 months on a loan)	_____	_____
Accounts payable (what the newspaper owes its suppliers)	_____	_____
Accruals (salaries, taxes owed but not yet paid)	_____	_____
Long-Term Liabilities		
(mortgage payments and bank debt due after current 12-month period)	_____	_____
Stockholder's Equity	_____	_____
Capital stock (amount investors put in to buy *Small Daily*)	_____	_____
Retained earnings (net profits after taxes, less any dividends paid stockholders)	_____	_____

is most important because it shows the newspaper's revenue from advertising, circulation and other sources; it shows expenses and, on the "bottom line," the result of operations—profit or loss.

Table 5.5 shows the form *Small Daily* uses.

Note in Table 5.5 the P&L has four main sections—sales, expenses, taxes, profit—and that performance is measured against last year in each. The P&L format is the basic form for budgeting. When you become responsible for revenue and expense, you will learn very quickly to spot entries that vary from what you are budgeted to produce. In sum, your job is to increase revenue and decrease, or hold to minimum, expenses. Doing that consistently yields improved profits.

BUDGETING: COMPLEX BUT ESSENTIAL

Budgeting is a complex subject that requires its own book. For our purposes, it can be broken into three types:

TABLE 5.5 **Small Daily Publishing Co.**
Statement of Income
12 Months Ended September 30

	This Year	Last Year	Increase (Decrease)
Sales			
Newspaper (advertising and circulation revenue)	_____	_____	_____
Commercial printing (from doing invitations, business cards, etc.)	_____	_____	_____
Less discounts (given large advertisers)	_____	_____	_____
Cost of Sales			
(Salaries, newsprint, payroll taxes, etc.)	_____	_____	_____
Operating Expenses	_____	_____	_____
(Officers' salaries, property taxes, bank interest)	_____	_____	_____
Operating income (sales minus cost of sales and operating expenses)	_____	_____	_____
Other Income			
(Rental income, interest on cash in bank, sales of waste paper)	_____	_____	_____
Other Deductions			
(Includes payment to former owner acting as consultant)	_____	_____	_____
Net income (loss) before taxes	_____	_____	_____
Income Taxes			
Federal	_____	_____	_____
State	_____	_____	_____
Net income (loss)	_____	_____	_____

The master budget, forecast budget or earnings plan. This is a projection of earnings and maps the newspaper's overall financial goals.

The capital budget, which covers expenditures for land, buildings, equipment and similar assets which will benefit the newspaper over a longer period than the one-year, short-term planning period.

The control budget, which deals with revenue and costs and measures operating performance by individuals or departments. Here, in the generation of revenue and control of costs, aspiring newspaper managers must first win their spurs. We will concentrate on this area of management responsibility.

Looking Backward and Ahead

Cost/revenue budgets are normally broken into 12 one-month segments. They guide managers toward the future but are based largely on the past plus best estimates of what is ahead. So in budgeting, first determine cost/revenue patterns of previous years and months. Although it may be difficult, the budget for the forthcoming year must be constructed against a historical perspective. Some small papers are lax in expense control and it sometimes takes years to develop reliable cost/revenue patterns against which to compare current budget performance.

But before you proceed, decide precisely what type newspaper you want to publish—a function of long-range strategic planning. The key question is whether this budget is correct for this newspaper at this time in this market against this competition. For example, high-quality news is costly; if you want it, the newsroom must budget accordingly.

Avoid Budgeting "Gamesmanship"

Each manager must dovetail his or her 12-month operating goals into the overall plan, then project accurately the resources—the share of total expense—needed to reach those goals. Each manager, in effect, competes with others for resources to do the job in the coming year.

The budgeting process thus easily degenerates into a contest of wills with, say, an operating head hiding a "fat factor" of 10 to 15 percent in the budget proposal and hoping top management will not catch it. Or management plays the game by automatically rejecting as too high each executive's first and second budget proposal, however fat or lean.

Avoid such gamesmanship and avoid arbitrarily constructing a budget without in-depth prior consultation between operating executives. A budget drawn without consultation is likely to be just plain wrong. And it is only human for operating executives to treat cavalierly, in the year ahead, any budget they did not help construct.

Make sure the budget process assigns *accountability*, so that each executive has measurable responsibility for meeting goals. Delineating precisely which executive is responsible for which goals is the fabric of planning in any communications company. Nowhere is it more important than in budgeting.

Some news executives in particular believe that newspaper budgets cannot be drawn with the inflexible finality of budgets in other industries. It is argued that news is not predictable and what looks like a quiet news year ahead could be one of famine, strife and rising creeks—all expensive to cover.

However, even *The New York Times* editors, whose spending on news coverage is envied by editors around the world, today operate under tight budgets. Not long ago, *Times* editors spent as needed to cover the news, then asked the business office for more. Not today. If news coverage emergencies require unusual spending, *Times* editors must shift funds from elsewhere in their budgets.

Start by Forecasting Revenue

A budget can run to scores of pages, with hundreds of individual revenue and cost items, so we cannot reproduce one here. But let's discuss how *Small Daily* goes about getting its financial house in order for the 12 months ahead.

Detailed budgets are drawn for seven departments: editorial, advertising, composing, pressroom, circulation, general and administration, and commercial printing. The beginning point is a revenue forecast for the next year. Advertising must project its sales first, because the amount of ad space sold will determine the number of pages the other departments must create. Circulation must project how many papers will be sold, so accurate estimates can be made for newsprint and ink needed, transportation costs and so forth.

Forecasting sales is tricky, of course. Understanding past sales trends is important, but there will be many variables in the months ahead: Will local business flourish, giving merchants more money to spend on advertising? Or will it slump? Difficulty at a single local factory—a strike, bankruptcy—could create havoc with *Small Daily*'s projections. So could the appearance of a new competitor—a free circulation shopper, for example—or one that suddenly cuts advertising rates. Some variables will lie in the paper's overall plan. For example, if the plan is to put more salespeople on the streets and promote sales more heavily, new costs will occur.

Small Daily's ad manager asks individual salespersons for their thinking on what lies ahead. For major accounts, particularly food and department stores, careful month-by-month estimates are made. For each advertising category (we'll discuss them in a later chapter), the manager projects column inches that will be sold and the rate for each. The two multiplied represent expected revenue. *Small Daily* makes its projections as shown in Table 5.6.

Variables affecting such month-by-month projections include *Small Daily*'s own rate structure; rates in each category will be raised at least once each year. Exactly when to increase rates, and how much, is crucial. Also, there are seasonal

TABLE 5.6   Categories for Revenue Projections

	Local Adv.	Local Color	National Adv.	Contract Classified	Transient Classified	Legal Adv.	Preprint Adv.	Total
Jan.								
Feb.								
Mar.								
April								
May								
(etc.)								
TOTAL								

	Present Rate (per inch)	Proposed Increase (%) and Date	New Rate
Local			
National			
Contract classified			
(etc.)			

fluctuations in advertising. Stores advertise more just before Christmas; other months—January and February, for example—are less active.

Many variables influence projections of circulation revenue. Among the fundamental issues of market economics that a circulation manager must consider are these: If the market's population is expanding, circulation expansion is possible; if tough economic times are ahead, circulation may drop. What sales implications are in the newspaper's overall plan for the year ahead? If, for example, the newsroom plans to begin covering a new suburb, circulation salespeople will have something to sell to prospective subscribers living there. Expected sales must be projected. How much new revenue can be raised through rate increases? *Small Daily* is in a city which isn't expanding in population. Several nearby competitors have vigorous journalistic and marketing strategies that limit *Small Daily*'s circulation growth. For the year ahead, any growth in circulation revenue must come from an increase in per-copy price or subscription rate—or both.

Estimate Expenses Next

With circulation and advertising revenue projections in hand, *Small Daily*'s managers turn to the second major task in budgeting—estimating costs. Each department head must project costs within the context of the paper's overall plan. For example, editorial must calculate the cost of assigning reporters to the new suburb where the paper plans to expand, and circulation must estimate the cost of putting salespeople into the suburb to sell subscriptions. The production manager must project the number of pages to be produced in the 12-month period. The pattern over past years must be reviewed, along with the circulation department's estimate of how many copies will be sold next year and the advertising department's projection of how much advertising will be placed. From that, the production manager must project how many employees will be needed and at what costs. Adequate newsprint and ink must be ordered. Expert production managers know at all times their costs for each page produced, how much newsprint is in storage and what their presses and other production facilities can produce.

Each significant cost must be isolated for examination. Most attention must be paid to "big-ticket" expenses—salaries and benefits, often 46 to 48 percent of a paper's total, and newsprint and ink, 24 to 26 percent.

All departmental managers must decide in advance what salary increases will be granted in the forthcoming year. Each month's salary costs then are calculated before the new year begins—and if the budget is closely followed, an employee scheduled for a raise on September 1 will get it on that date and not a day earlier. Similarly detailed projections are made for other costs. Table 5.7 shows how *Small Daily* does it for the editorial department.

Monitoring Performance

With cost and revenue estimates from department heads, the newspaper's chief financial officer projects an *operating statement*, outlining what the financial picture

TABLE 5.7   Editorial Department, Year 1995/1996

	January		February		March		(etc.)
	1995	1996	1995	1996	1995	1996	
Salaries							
Overtime							
Operating supplies							
Associated Press							
Feature syndicates							
Correspondents (local)							
Travel/entertainment							
Motor vehicles							
Company							
Employee mileage							
Dues/subscriptions							
Misc.							
TOTAL							

should be at year's end. If projections do not satisfy top management (or its board of directors), each department must lower projected costs or increase revenue—or both. Once the budget year begins, management must monitor closely—at least monthly—ongoing budget performance by each operating section.

Year end is too late to discover cost overruns or revenue shortfall. Off-budget performance has a crack-the-whip effect: seemingly minor variances up front snap fiercely at year's end. There must be control, with each variance from budget caught quickly and corrected.

Control, a major duty of each manager, must ensure results match or exceed those planned. Basic to the control function are the following:

Standards for performance established by the budget.

Information to alert a manager immediately when performance deviates from standards.

Action by a manager to correct substandard performance.

Small Daily's managers receive a printout of each month's expense and revenue in their department within days following close of business for each month. The publisher and a few key executives get printouts on all departments. But analyzing the vast amount of information takes time, so the publisher gets two "quick-read" documents that give an immediate picture of how the newspaper is performing. One is a "budget summary" that reports revenue and expense performance in major categories, including a free-circulation shopper published by *Small Daily*. Table 5.8 on page 132 shows how it looks.

The budget summary lists each category with an "actual" figure—the precise total revenue or expense in the month just ended. Alongside is "this year's budget"

TABLE 5.8   Budget Summary

	Actual	This Year's Budget	Dollar Variance	Percentage Variance
Revenue				
Local				
National				
Classified				
Legal				
Preprint				
Weekly/Shopper				
Total Advertising				
Circulation				
Commercial Printing				
Other				
Total Revenue				
Expenses				
Editorial				
Advertising				
Production				
Circulation				
General & Administration				
Depreciation				
Total Expense				
Operating Profit				
Conversion Ratio				

figure. Any variance is expressed both in dollars and percentages. Learn to watch both. A $500 increase in an expense might not look significant, but if that is a 100 percent increase, investigate. Note the budget summary presents the "conversion ratio," the percentage of total revenue converted to operating profit.

The publisher's second "quick-read" document is a weekly summary of significant expenses (see Table 5.9).

This weekly summary also informs top management of performance in advertising, as expressed in column inches, and in circulation. As crucial as it is, the budget, however, is only one step in short-range planning.

MANAGEMENT BY OBJECTIVES

Many newspapers employ management techniques beyond budgeting to establish order, predictability and accountability in operating sectors where those conditions didn't always exist. These programs lay down participatory goals within a 12-month framework but are wider in scope than the budget.

TABLE 5.9 Weekly Summary

Significant Expenses	Actual	Budget	Dollar Increase (decrease)	Percentage Increase (decrease)
Total Salaries	_____	_____	_____	_____
Circ. delivery costs	_____	_____	_____	_____
Circulation postage	_____	_____	_____	_____
Newsprint	_____	_____	_____	_____
Overtime	_____	_____	_____	_____
Total significant expense	_____	_____	_____	_____
Total operating expense	_____	_____	_____	_____
Statistical Summary				

Inches	Actual	Budget	Increase	Decrease
Local	_____	_____	_____	_____
National	_____	_____	_____	_____
Classified	_____	_____	_____	_____
Legal	_____	_____	_____	_____
Shopper	_____	_____	_____	_____
Total				

Circulation	Actual	Budget	Increase	Decrease
Daily	_____	_____	_____	_____
Shopper	_____	_____	_____	_____

The programs—often termed "management by objectives"—have two principal strengths: First, they enable you to measure progress—or lack of it—in areas not easily quantified in a budget, such as quality of reporting and writing or effectiveness of corporate promotion. Second, you can use MBO techniques to make yourself more visible at all operating levels, to reach down into lower ranks with programs that touch individuals and thus create a sense of corporate direction at levels previously untouched by top-level planning.

Frankly, some areas included in MBO programs—quality of writing, for example—are not regarded by some newspaper people as particularly fertile for business methodology. Management's intrusion into them smacks of corporate discipline, a condition studiously avoided by some journalists. And, there are the usual objections that MBO programs, like all planning, take too much time and work and, anyway, the future is unpredictable, so isn't planning useless? But the need for more orderly management is too great and MBO—by that name or another—has joined budgeting as a way of life in progressive communications companies.

Why the MBO Approach?

As chief executive officer of Harte-Hanks, Robert Marbut was an early user of MBO programs. He explained:

Management by Objectives is part of the whole planning process and certainly part of our culture . . . it is done for financial planning, for human resources planning, for organizational planning, for facili-ties and capital investment planning, for product development planning and the like.

It covers a lot of areas that are hard to measure, such as editorial quality and staff quality. However, we do feel that there are ways to get your arms around even those esoteric things.

It is based on the idea that we ought to know on the front end how we are going to measure our results—that way, everyone is happier and tends to be in greater agreement as to where we are.

If the goal is just to have a 'better product,' how do we measure it at the end of a year? But if we say that a better product means more local editorials, more local photographs, a higher rating on the part of readers in the next readership survey, a larger percentage of the total news given to local news, etc., then we can measure what we mean by this.

The same is true with people development. If we set a goal to have people improve certain technical skills, we can identify what they are and then measure at least on some related basis—such as 'better than/about the same as/less effective' than last year. The same is true about a lot of other areas. . . .[6]

Increasingly, editors also are becoming committed to goals programs, though many find it difficult to measure newsroom performance. Burl Osborne, editor (and now also publisher) of *The Dallas Morning News,* said:

We do have a goals program for the news department that we are trying to implement in some form at every management level. It is related to an improved budgeting system that pushes accountability and control down to every subdepartment supervisor.

In general, the goals are combinations of quantifiable matters, budget being chief, and less tangible elements such as writing and editing quality. It is a matter of stated practice that any (staff) replacement must raise the level of the given position, and that, along with other intangibles such as design improvement, better packaging, stronger headlines and the like, are subjective judgments, arrived at by the supervisor and the person with the goal.

It is an imperfect system . . . but we think it can serve the purpose of achieving improvements of which all parties can be proud.[7]

Constructing Your Program

Successful MBO programs feature clear statement of corporate goals and short-term objectives, commitment by top management and enthusiastic follow-through by all managers along the chain of command. Detailed discussion is required of what each individual or unit must accomplish in the year ahead, specific improvement to be made and target dates. Give each individual flexibility in determining precisely how goals will be met. That can elicit imaginative efforts from individuals and is a morale booster.

As in budgeting, there must be interim reporting dates for monitoring and controlling progress. Each manager's goals must be reasonably attainable; goals patently beyond reach simply turn off operating managers and create serious morale problems. Yet goals must be "far enough out" to make each manager stretch to unusual lengths.

Early drafting, say two or three months before the year opens, permits discussion, so a manager can sense how employees regard goals being assigned them. "Feedback" from lower echelons is extremely valuable, and you must listen carefully. Responsive adjustment in goals can launch a finely tuned program with full staff support. You never should stifle questioning or even dissent. Both are essential to progress.

All managers should have uniform reporting dates—say, the first of March, May, July, September and November. This permits control of performance and allows for adjustments during the year which, in turn, makes possible a company-wide survey of problems in a meaningful manner.

Benefits and Dangers

One benefit of an MBO program is the sense of participation—opportunity for creative contribution—it gives junior employees. To make that happen, each manager must delegate significant goals and responsibilities to younger subordinates. However, a warning: More than one MBO program encounters difficulty when managers, misunderstanding the program or feeling threatened by it, refuse to delegate authority as long as they retain responsibility for performance. Explain thoroughly what your MBO is all about and understand any uneasiness among those with responsibility for making it work.

An MBO program can fail if it becomes an end in itself, creating mountains of paperwork and degenerating into meaningless bureaucratic exercises. Keep the program results-oriented, keep paper to a minimum, state goals briefly and precisely. An Associated Press MBO program assigned the executive editor just five goals and required only seven progress reports to higher management during the year. Goals included improving writing and editing, generating monthly sports news projects of substance, invigorating reporting by specialist reporters—and other news projects.

Properly directed, MBO can aid the top-priority tasks of cost control and decision making. We turn to those next.

COST CONTROL: TOP PRIORITY

Yes, I know: You aren't considering a newspaper career so you can spend your days searching for stray nickels and dimes. But if you depart this chapter remembering just one thing, it should be that costs are like a giant tumor, growing almost unseen, and if you ignore them they will sap your newspaper's strength and defeat even your best planning efforts.

CASE STUDY 5.2   Philadelphia: A Planning Triumph

In Philadelphia, it truly seemed, nearly everybody read the *Bulletin*.

But that was before Philadelphia, with many other U.S. cities, felt the full impact of socioeconomic change revolutionizing city life. It also was before many afternoon papers such as the *Bulletin* encountered financial difficulty, due largely to changes in lifestyle. And it was before a determined group of tough professionals from Knight Newspapers (now Knight-Ridder Inc.) landed in town with a long-range strategy for taking over the newspaper scene— a scene dominated by the *Bulletin,* once the country's largest evening newspaper, with more than 700,000 circulation daily.

To general amusement, the *Bulletin* deliberately understated its strength with a promotional slogan that became famous: "In Philadelphia, *nearly* everybody reads the *Bulletin.*" The *Bulletin* was a political, social and economic power and *everybody*—not *nearly* everybody— knew it. In those days, when the *Bulletin* spoke, Philadelphia listened.

In retrospect, it's amazing any newspaper group would pick a toe-to-toe fight with the *Bulletin.* But Knight did, acquiring in late 1969 the morning *Philadelphia Inquirer* and afternoon *Daily News* for $55 million. Some, including *Bulletin* executives, thought Knight wanted only a slice of the pie. Not so. Subsequent developments revealed Knight clearly intended, early on, to dominate and eventually occupy the market exclusively—*and it had a plan for doing so.*

In those days, the *Bulletin* and *Inquirer* represented opposite planning and management styles. (The author, then vice president of the Associated Press, visited both newspapers frequently for conversations with executives.) *Bulletin* managers seemed uncertain of what character the *Bulletin* should assume. With Philadelphia's inner city rapidly changing, they knew its business there was jeopardized. But where to take the paper? How to get there? The paper hesitated, uncertain what to do.

Then it plunged heavily into zoned coverage for scores of communities ringing Philadel-

phia. This significantly weakened its influence as a regional and national newspaper, yet the *Bulletin* never really bested the highly detailed local coverage in the numerous small dailies and weeklies located in those communities.

At the *Inquirer,* there was aggressive confidence that belied Knight's position, then still very much the underdog. The *Inquirer* had been less than distinguished. Indeed, it was a limping old-fashioned city paper that never had been anywhere, and here it was trying a comeback! Yet, at every level of *Inquirer* management there was optimism and a plan— a plan for today, tomorrow and five years ahead.

Years later, Sam S. McKeel, then *Inquirer* president, said: "Despite what seemed to be *Bulletin* strength, we felt as early as 1974 there would be major changes in the Philadelphia newspaper publishing scene. *At that time, we were losing money and the Bulletin was slightly more than breaking even* (author's emphasis)."[a] Knight-Ridder's planning, that is, projected victory even while its *Inquirer* was a losing number two to the profitable *Bulletin.*

Enormous drive, aggressiveness and attention to detail, in strict accord with priorities, characterized the *Inquirer* plan. John Brown, then *Inquirer* senior vice president of circulation: "Our first years in Philadelphia were devoted to learning about the market, and developing a strong editorial product to satisfy our readers' needs.... In a few years we began to see the impact of our changes.... *Philadelphia Magazine,* a long-time critic, in 1973 changed its mind and called the *Inquirer* the best paper in Philadelphia. National and regional prizes began to flow in, culminating in 1975 with the *Inquirer's* first Pulitzer. (Author's note: By 1993, it was 17.) Pulitzer Prize stories don't sell papers in the sense of a next day ad or more voluntary starts, but they are an important symbol of a newspaper's commitment to excellence and to the community.... By 1965, we felt confident enough in our position in the market to begin establishing aggressive, long-range circulation and advertising goals."

CASE STUDY 5.2   *Continued*

Among other things, Philadelphia lifestyles were surveyed. Brown says:

> We wanted to determine how we were viewed ... our perceived strengths and weaknesses, and those of our competitors. We wanted to know more about the lifestyles of our readers, and any ways in which they differed dramatically from those of readers of local papers—ways we could take advantage of in terms of future editorial improvements, and targeted promotional strategies.[b]

The *Inquirer's* journalistic architect was Executive Editor Gene Roberts, a North Carolinian hired from *The New York Times.* Roberts, though affecting a "laid back" down-home style complete with quiet drawl, was a hard-hitting editor with great drive and instinct for a news story. And he was renowned for detailed planning. One observer described him as "a consummate and careful planner ... a devoted student of newspaper detail, right down to the agate lines of the high school sports scores.... The *Inquirer* under Roberts is like the Russian economy: always on some sort of multi-year plan...."[c]

Inquirer executives analyzed their market, their own newspaper's journalistic and advertising strengths and weaknesses, the competitive picture and—having methodically done their homework—laid down long-range strategy that, with their concurrent day-to-day operational plan, guided the *Inquirer's* every move.

Under such heavy pressure, the *Bulletin's* owners gave up in 1980, selling to Charter Co. Charter invested millions of dollars in a game fight. But nothing worked, and in 1982, the 134-year-old *Bulletin,* by then a wizened shadow of the *Bulletin* nearly everybody used to read, closed its doors. It was losing $20 million annually at the end.

Inquirer executives quickly shifted to another plan: "Plan Alpha," laid down several years earlier to ensure that the *Bulletin's* predictable death would be followed immediately by an aggressive *Inquirer* campaign to pick up *Bulletin* readers and advertisers. Plan Alpha included hiring *Bulletin* circulation managers, who, in turn, hired former *Bulletin* carriers to deliver the *Inquirer* or its sister, the *Daily News,* to former *Bulletin* readers.

Plan Alpha even provided for the precise number of new telephone lines (20) needed to handle calls from ex-*Bulletin* readers seeking *Inquirer* subscriptions.

The *Inquirer's* Brown, (modestly): "We were satisfied with Alpha's success. While the *Bulletin* was declaring audited circulation of just over 400,000, by the time of their demise, we estimated their net sale to be close to 360,000—about one-third of which was duplicated with the *Inquirer* or *Daily News.* Of the 250,000 circulation available to us, the *Inquirer* and *News* quickly achieved over 200,000, or 80%."[d]

In sum, Philadelphia offers a classic example of alert professionals fusing short-range operating plans with long-term strategy, all soundly based in research, to seize every advantage in a changing marketplace and achieve a stunning victory.

The payoff?

- In 1992, the *Inquirer* had 502,136 weekday circulation, 976,223 on Sundays. The *Daily News* was at 196,715 on weekdays.

- Combined advertising revenue for the two papers was $295,017,000; circulation revenue, $126,738,000. Those totals were 18 percent of all Knight-Ridder operating revenue that year, far ahead of the company's onetime flagship, the *Miami Herald,* and its 26 other newspapers or, even, its international business news services.[e]

[a]Sam. S. McKeel, speech to Philadelphia Rotary Club, Dec. 15, 1992.
[b]John Brown, speech, April 25, 1983.
[c]Paul Taylor, "Gene Roberts, Down-Home Editor of the *Philadelphia Inquirer,*" *Washington Journalism Review,* April 1983, p. 35.
[d]John Brown, op. cit.
[e]All figures drawn from Knight-Ridder Inc. 1992 annual report.

Cost control—getting firm grip on *every* dollar spent—is a top priority for every manager. During the recession of the early 1990s, when advertising revenue slipped backward, cost control—and cost reduction—saved many newspapers (and managerial careers). Clearly, many managers had let costs get out of control in the booming 1980s and were forced into emergency retrenchment when recession struck. Daily attention to cost control will help you avoid that.

Avoid, Control, Monitor, Reexamine

Best way to handle costs: Avoid them. Question every new expense proposal and insist on a cost/benefit study to, simply, prove what benefit will be derived. It's difficult, obviously, to judge exactly the contribution of a new syndicated column to overall journalistic quality. But ask: Would it demonstrably assist the newspaper in reaching its overall goals? If so, add the new cost to the budget; if it won't improve quality or profitability, reject it.

The second step in controlling costs, if they prove unavoidable, is to make sure they are kept as low as possible. Shop around, compare; *think.* Is there a cheaper way?

Third, monitor all costs against last year's actual costs and this year's expense budget. Correct any overrun immediately.

Fourth, never stop reexamining all costs, repeatedly weighing the cost/benefit balance. Because somebody's grandfather justified a cost in 1940 does not mean it is acceptable today. Arthur Ochs (Punch) Sulzberger is fond of describing how, shortly after he became publisher of *The New York Times,* a study of production costs uncovered highly paid back-shop employees without duties or job descriptions—and neither management nor union knew what they were supposed to be doing.[8] At one point, Sulzberger told shareholders, *The Times* employed 50 percent more production workers than did competing papers—one reason *The Times* for years contributed only 24 percent of the parent corporation's profit, although it contributed 66 percent of total revenue.

Watch costs that could become fixed expenses forever. A one-time cost of $35,000 for new equipment is one thing; a new copy editor at $35,000 annually for an indefinite time is quite another.

A Few Tips

Make sure you have an efficient *purchasing system* to seek competitive bids on supplies and negotiate the best possible prices, particularly for any commodity (like newsprint) that is purchased in bulk. Purchasing should be headed by a tenacious executive skilled in narrowing the gap between asking price and what the vendor will take when pressed.

Contingency plans should be made for cost cutting if business turns suddenly sour. Planning gives each manager the opportunity, without the pressure of a crash effort, to target cost pruning methodically and avoid slicing too deeply into crucial operational areas and journalistic quality.

Cost-reduction goals should be assigned in dollar or percentage terms; managers should strip costs out in a manner they feel will least disturb operations. This preserves accountability—making every manager responsible for his or her operation. It can also motivate each manager to make sure that fat, not muscle, comes out of costs.

Although they represent the largest shares of total expense, labor and newsprint costs should not dominate your cost-control program. Substantial savings can be achieved with disciplined control of variables such as vehicle use, overtime, travel/entertainment, telephone, stringers, postage, electricity and so on.

And beware of seemingly insignificant percentage increases. For example, a 5 percent increase in *The New York Times'* newsroom costs might not sound like much but it would add millions annually to the newspaper's costs.

ANOTHER PRIORITY: MANAGEMENT INFORMATION SYSTEMS

Plan as you will—as you must—but effective management will elude you unless you and other managers receive timely, top-quality information. Management information systems (MIS) must be constructed for the efficient collection, coordination and distribution of internal and external information.

Budgeting and MBO are key in the internal information system. But managers also increasingly use sophisticated computer systems—"decision support systems"—to analyze information from marketing, finance, production and other departments by comparing it with decision models.

Management information systems must provide information in the correct quantity (enough but not too much), of high quality (as accurate as possible), in useable form, at the right time (when needed, not the next day). Much of the needed information is scattered throughout operating departments and is hard to collect.

Management information systems must assist managers in evaluating pertinent information, then in rationally and unemotionally identifying opportunities or problems and alternative solutions. Picking alternatives to follow, then implementing them and monitoring progress complete the process. And that's not simple.

Decision making is a complex matter requiring you to have a high degree of social skills as well as wide experience and the right attitudes and abilities. Conflict and inability to arrive logically at decisions are prime causes of disarray in newspaper managerial suites.

Computers and simulation techniques make it possible to run problems in abstract form and to study alternatives; linear programming allows for mathematical approaches to problems, particularly those involving money, time and people. But it's still fashionable in the newspaper industry for managers to draw on the expertise and opinions of their executive staff, audit the newspaper's external and internal environments, then personally match decisions with existing conditions—the "contingency approach."

SUMMARY

The *marketing concept* is widely accepted in newspapers, and your generation of managers must be adept in its core techniques: publishing newspapers in response to needs and desires of a competitive marketplace, organizing internal systems and motivating people to produce such newspapers. For generations, newspapers were production-oriented, not consumer-oriented. But thinking changed with emergence of new competitors for readers and advertising dollars—as well as growing awareness of newspapers' general inability to achieve household penetration at levels demanded by advertisers.

Marketing theory requires total commitment of the entire company to satisfying consumer needs. The *marketing mix* creates a product, prices it, distributes it and promotes it. The *marketing process* includes organizing the marketing structure, analyzing the market, setting goals, planning and assigning resources, creating the product, monitoring and controlling performance, and adjusting as internal and external variables change. Understanding *consumer behavior* is essential for any newspaper manager. This requires grasp of consumer *needs* that the newspaper can meet and consumer *perceptions* of how well it meets them. Throughout runs one theme: Fundamental changes are under way in the newspaper's environment and one aim of marketing is adjusting to them.

With the marketing concept implanted, managers turn to *planning.* Three stages are crucial:

Long-range strategy positions the newspaper for journalistically effective and profitable operation five or more years hence, whatever the socioeconomic environment may be. Looking externally, planners should question basic assumptions—even whether newspapers will continue to exist in their present form. Internally, managers must plan improved performance by each department. Planning for profit is key, for without profit, newspapers cannot flourish in today's competitive marketplace.

Intermediate-range planning involves setting time frames for projects necessary to implement long-range strategy. Importantly, managers inform each employee of strategic goals and encourage feedback from lower ranks. This can build employee enthusiasm for goals programs.

Short-range planning, for the year immediately ahead, is designed to move the newspaper step by step toward its long-range goals. *Budgeting,* followed with precision and discipline, is crucial. It sets dollar goals that each revenue-generating department must meet. It assigns expense limits for all departments. Thus, accountability is assigned to each manager and department. *MBO programs* are handy in short-range planning for establishing order, predictability and accountability in areas not easily controllable by budgeting. Goals such as improved writing and reporting are assigned.

Cost control is a top priority for every manager. Costs can zoom out of control quickly, negating the most innovative plan for advertising and circulation expansion. Costs should be avoided or controlled, monitored and reexamined in a methodical, disciplined manner.

RECOMMENDED READING

For current newspaper industry thinking on the marketing concept and strategic planning, three groups are your best sources:

Newspaper Association of America, The Newspaper Center, 11600 Sunrise Valley Drive, Reston, Va. 22091-1412, is the leading industry trade organization. Its *presstime* magazine and regular reports to its more than 1,700 member newspapers cover all aspects of newspaper management and planning.

American Society of Newspaper Editors, same address as NAA, is comprised of top editors of the most significant papers in the United States. Its *ASNE Bulletin* and reports to members provide strong coverage in news and editorial issues, freedom of the press and ethical/legal issues.

Associated Press Managing Editors Association, 50 Rockefeller Plaza, New York, N.Y. 10020, is an organization of managing editors of Associated Press member papers but is independent of AP control. This organization's *APME News* and study reports are particularly strong on research into reader attitudes and newsroom planning and management.

Regional and state press associations are valuable to newspaper managers. Notable are the Southern Newspaper Publisher's Association (P. O. Box 28875, Atlanta, Ga. 30328) and Inland Daily Press Association (Suite 802-W, 840 North Lake Shore Drive, Chicago, Ill. 60611).

NOTES

1. Robert Marbut, letter to author.
2. Paul S. Hirt, *Newspaper Marketing: A Time for Reappraisal?* a pamphlet published by International Newspaper Promotion Association, 1983.
3. Sterling E. Soderlind, letter to author.
4. Ibid.
5. Warren Phillips, letter to author.
6. Robert Marbut, letter to author.
7. Burl Osborne, letter to author.
8. Arthur Ochs Sulzberger, conversation with author.

PART III

YOUR OPERATING RESPONSIBILITIES

With your long-range strategy in place, you must turn to managing your newspaper's daily operations. This is a hands-on business, so prepare to plunge in!

First, manage your people. We're a people-intensive industry and you'll need the best people skills to succeed. We'll discuss this in Chapter 6, "The Human Element." In Chapter 7, "News," we'll turn to the soul of your newspaper: the newsroom, its coverage of your market, its creation of the daily news and editorial product. In Chapter 8, "Circulation," we'll discuss how you go after readers—the right readers, those your advertisers desire. This is your first step in the marketplace exploitation of your newsroom's efforts.

Next is exploiting your news and circulation efforts by convincing advertisers your newspaper is the solution to their business problems. This is covered in Chapter 9, "Advertising." Everything you do in the marketplace—in news, circulation and advertising—must be positioned carefully in the minds of your readers and advertisers and in the collective perceptions of your community. We'll address this in Chapter 10, "Image and Promotion."

Finally, we're in manufacturing, as well as news and advertising, of course. Producing about 60 million units of our product every day is no mean feat. We'll discuss your manager's responsibilities in this sector in Chapter 11, "Production and the New Technology."

Now, roll up your sleeves!

6

THE HUMAN ELEMENT

Are you a little uptight about managing people? Concerned that you're not up to supervising the human element?

Relax. You've got some experience already—if you've ever led a Boy Scout troop, coordinated fellow students working on a class project or even motivated, persuaded or cajoled just one other person to accomplish a simple task you've planned.

That is, you may not be as new to managing people as you think.

Of course, there's much difference between leading Scouts or fellow students and managing a newspaper's staff. So, we've got serious topics to discuss in Chapter 6: the theory of motivating men and women; how to monitor and adjust their performance; how to be fair, yet demanding. We'll also look at newspaper unions and their impact on your management role.

Before we start, a bit of advice: People, not machines, produce newspapers; people are your greatest asset—and your largest single cost. So, there is no room, at any managerial level, for anyone indifferent to or unable to deal effectively with the human element. If you cannot motivate and lead people, your career in newspaper management will be a nonstarter.

YOUR BASIC TASK IN PERSONNEL

Your basic task in personnel management is to obtain the best available talent at a cost your newspaper can afford and then establish an environment that will create and motivate a staff of high morale to move the newspaper toward goals of improved quality, productivity and profitability.

Key steps in your basic task: auditing your newspaper's personnel needs and existing resources, planning effective development and use of personnel, hiring and motivating, controlling performance and, yes, disciplining.

Auditing Needs and Resources

As in any planning, auditing is a manager's first step. This means forecasting the human resources your newspaper's operating departments must have to meet their short-, intermediate- and long-range goals. The next step is assessing which resources are available in-house and which must be obtained outside.

Forecasting for the *short term* is relatively easy. The budget and operating plan will authorize certain numbers and types of employees; the audit determines how many already are on staff and how many probably will be lost (through termination, promotion, transfer, etc.). Thus, you determine quickly how many must be hired, trained and put in place. For example, if retirements six months ahead will create two openings on the sports desk, two sports reporters must be hired. Simple enough.

However, over the *intermediate term*, forecasting becomes much more difficult. Looking two or five years ahead, you must decide who is needed, when, where, with what type skills and at what cost. Let us say your intermediate plan calls for general improvement in quality of the entire sports staff and creation of new coverage in prep sports over the next three years. Forecasting personnel resources needed for such a general overhaul of an entire department is difficult, so you and the sports editor must plan precisely where and how to obtain the needed resources. This could involve, for example, a stipulation that each new sportswriter hired must be more experienced and demonstrably abler than the employee being replaced—and that new employees be hired from among the outstanding sports reporters working for highly regarded newspapers.

Human resources forecasting for the *long range*, five years or more, requires your best analytical skills. Your challenge is to assess probable changes in the newspaper's internal and external environment and then fashion appropriate human resources strategy. For example, long-range forecasting should anticipate such trends as societal pressure for hiring and promoting women and minorities. Many newspapers failed to do so in the 1970s and 1980s and even now have not caught up with society's expectations.

Making Plans and Stating Policy

Having audited existing resources and forecast needs, you must establish your human resources policy and clearly communicate it through every supervisory level to each employee. The policy statement should cover the newspaper's intentions in dealing with people. It can be a highly detailed handbook covering your determination to hire and promote strictly on merit, as well as such minutiae as how to join the company softball team. Or you can express the spirit of the policy rather simply, as Al Neuharth did at Gannett, telling his managers to pay close attention to employees because they are "50 percent of our costs and 100 percent of our accomplishments." That was a clear signal to every manager that the company regarded its people as its most valuable resource.

Increasingly, newspapers are swinging away from traditional, tightly centralized authoritarianism based on the "Theory X" concept, that human beings instinc-

---

BOX 6.1   The Handbook Controversy

Sharp controversy exists over whether newspapers should provide employees with handbooks explaining corporate policy and, if so, how they should be written. Some managers say improving internal corporate communications requires that employees be given written explanations of policy, pension plans, health programs and so on. Yet handbooks and written guidelines are interpreted by some courts to be work contracts, and employees have used them in lawsuits against newspapers.

One major difficulty is handbook language referring to the "permanent employee" or in some way even implying guaranteed employment, promotion or wage increases. Newspapers that discharge an individual even for incompetence or to reduce work forces in an economic slump are vulnerable to lawsuit if such a "contract" exists.

Another problem is with handbooks—or even oral statements during hiring—that precisely define work rules or conditions of employment in a manner deemed contractual. A newspaper is vulnerable if it changes rules or conditions by, say, transferring a reporter to night work in contravention of an implied contract.

Some newspapers are withdrawing policy handbooks from circulation. Seek legal advice in writing yours. One remedy is including a handbook disclaimer stating that no contract is implied and asking employees to sign it.

---

tively dislike work and must be forced to perform. Most policy statements take the "Theory Y" approach, that each employee is an individual with special needs who wants to perform well—and will if properly motivated. However expressed, personnel policy should elicit feedback from all managers, including first-line supervisors. There is controversy, however, over whether the policy should be stated in writing (see Box 6.1).

Your personnel policy should enlist employee initiative in the drive to achieve the newspaper's goals. A reporter who is a self-starter in developing story ideas and pursuing them should be rewarded with bonuses, raises or public recognition and compliments. Reward an advertising salesperson for digging up new business. Policy must inspire teamwork, creating an atmosphere in which news and photo departments automatically cooperate in coverage and in which production and circulation cooperate to get papers on the street on time.

Importantly, your personnel policy must assign each manager the task of listening to employees with sensitivity and empathy as well as talking to them. Employees must be able to express their views as well as receive orders; two-way communication is essential.

Recruiting the Best, Wherever They Are

Prepare for your newspaper's future personnel needs in two broad ways: Insert qualified employees into the training pipeline so they will be promotable when needed, and hire experienced talent from outside.

Most papers use a combination approach. For now, let's concentrate on how you can locate, pursue and hire outside talent. Three points to keep in mind:

First, lots of people out there want to work for newspapers but competition for talent is fierce. It won't come to you; you must launch an aggressive search program—and keep it going.

Second, the greatest single attraction for talent in the newspaper business is reputation—yours as a fair and professional manager, the newspaper's as a "hot" paper offering journalistic excellence and sharp competitive instincts. "Hot" papers attract top talent even with wage patterns behind those of other newspapers. For example, *The Washington Post* and *The Philadelphia Inquirer* don't offer the highest salaries for reporters. Yet, both are meccas for thousands of talented journalists across the country, and can pick the best and brightest. Why? Because both papers set standards of excellence in news reporting and writing—and all journalists know it.

Third, a newspaper's personnel needs are diverse, and you must seek talent from many outside sources, not only journalism schools and other media. Get your recruiting lines open to schools and industries where you can find talent in data processing, accounting, the law, science, engineering—the specialized skills needed in the newsrooms and other departments of your newspaper.

When recruiting beginning reporters and editors, concentrate on journalism school students and majors from other disciplines working on university newspapers. Insist that all candidates have some newsroom experience from a college paper or summer job. Ask faculty members to prescreen the best for your interview. Frequently visit schools in your region; establish for your newspaper and yourself a reputation among students by participating in class projects and occasionally lecturing.

Establish "talent banks" of files on prospective employees working on other papers. Follow their careers. Let them learn the basics on somebody else's payroll, then hire when they are ready to work for you. The bylines of star reporters will be on front pages regularly; the work of talented photo editors is there for you to see; energetic advertising salespeople advertise their own presence through the ads they sell and publish; if you need pressroom talent, which newspaper is well printed?

Be as liberal as your budget permits in offering summer internships for college students—and not just in the newsroom, either. Establish programs for students interested in other departments—particularly advertising, circulation and production.

Promoting from within is less expensive than recruiting outside and can create loyalty to your newspaper, but it also can lead to insular thinking and a "comfortable" atmosphere that permits substandard performance. By recruiting outside, you get a double dividend: talent with fresh views that also can shake things up a bit in your shop.

Selecting and Hiring with Care

The hiring process is dominated by three broad considerations: First, greater talent is needed in every department. Marketplace demand for improved journalistic quality is increasing; complex business and technical problems require highly specialized workers. Simply put, each new hire must be a qualitative improvement in staff professionalism. New reporters, for example, must be better educated and more experienced than those they replace.

Second, severe legal and societal constraints cover each step of the hiring and employment process, and expert legal advice is necessary. Because you cannot easily fire a bad selection, the hiring process is critical. Third, most newspapers today employ experts specially trained in sophisticated testing and interview techniques. But you must be intimately involved in hiring.

Throughout the process, you should work from two documents: a *job description* that specifies duties for the position in question and a *job specification* that lists qualifications—education, experience and so on—the job applicant must have (see Box 6.2).

Follow these steps:

1. *Completion of application form.* Get all relevant personal data, a resume and references. For reporters, editors, and photographers, obtain samples of work.
2. *Initial screening and interviewing.* Those patently unqualified should be put aside immediately. For the others, there is no substitute for a detailed interview

---

BOX 6.2   How to Write Job Descriptions and Specifications

The *Louisville (Ky.) Courier-Journal* issued the following "employment opportunity" when an assistant managing editor's slot became vacant. Note the detailed job description and outline of qualifications needed.

Job Description

Will be responsible for overall planning, coordination and critique of news gathering, processing and presentation, within the context of the goals and standards established by the managing editor.

Will work with the city, state, Indiana (a neighboring state where the paper circulates) and business editors, providing direction and problem-solving on a day-to-day basis, and will insure that the activities of all departments are coordinated in the best interests of the total product.

Will serve as liaison with photo, news art, production, circulation, advertising and research and analysis departments, in order to accomplish daily and long-range planning.

Will assume the first-echelon responsibility for preparation of the annual departmental expense and newsprint budget, coordinating the work of each desk and department. Will work with the managing editor's administrative secretary in preparation of budget documents.

Will monitor and evaluate each edition of the newspaper, in order to assist the managing editor in assessing the content of each and the performance of staff members.

Will advise the managing editor on staff needs, recruitment and training, personnel administration, departmental management, research and marketing and news policy.

Will take charge of the newspaper's various operations in the absence of the managing editor, and will assume such other duties in the areas of policy and planning as the managing editor may dictate.

Qualifications (Job Specification)

College degree most desirable. Advanced study desirable.

Extensive, varied experience as a daily newspaper reporter and/or copy editor most desirable. Previous experience in news administration most desirable.

Ability to communicate effectively, in person and in writing, essential.

Ability to work with other news administrators and staff.

by the supervisor involved. Use all the time you can spare. Let applicants talk at will. Ask what they read and about skills obviously needed—language skills for newsroom applicants, an intimate understanding of equipment for pressroom applicants and so forth. But in all applicants look for enthusiasm, commitment and determination. You can train employees in skills; they must light in their own bellies the fire you need.

3. *Testing.* This is a high art and you need tests professionally drawn up and evaluated.

4. *Detailed background check.* Sadly, resumes and letters of reference cannot always be trusted. One study showed that 26 percent of firms surveyed found new employees had falsified their resumes. Check academic credentials and talk with former employers.

5. *Second interview.* On an important new hire, this will require a commitment of considerable time by you. Interview over a relaxed dinner and a drink; then, do it again in the formal, somewhat stressful surroundings of your office. Ask pointed questions—precisely what did the applicant do in his or her last job? Then, ask broad questions that force the applicant to take a wider view, such as "Tell me about your strengths." "What are your weaknesses?" "What job do you want 10 years from now?"

Dos and Don'ts of Interviewing

There are severe legal constraints on questions you may ask in interviews. Attorneys advise the following:

- Do not ask a prospective employee about race, creed, color, national origin, sex, marital status or handicaps *unless* there is justifiable occupational reason.
- Do not ask about height, weight, plans to have children, number of children, arrangements for child care, a spouse's salary, previous arrest records, type of military discharge received.
- Do not outline a specific career path or promise promotions or special benefits.
- Do not speak of benefits, salary or employment in general terms, such as, "You've got a job here as long as you do a good job."

Two additional points of caution: First, does this applicant possess potential for growth? Always fill even an entry-level vacancy with a person talented enough to qualify for promotion. Hire today for tomorrow. Second, have you, in your excessive eagerness to obtain the best talent, oversold the job? Is this an overqualified individual who will not be able to use his or her full abilities? If so, morale problems could arise after employment.

You never can be completely certain you have matched a properly qualified individual with the proper job despite painstaking efforts. So accept the applicant *only* on the condition that a six-month probationary period is completed successfully. Now you must motivate the new hire to help you and the newspaper reach your goals.

Motivation: Theory and Practice

The importance of properly motivating each employee and thus the entire newspaper staff cannot be overestimated. It is central to your career success and to your newspaper's ability to achieve its objectives. Luckily, you have a great deal of scholarly research from which to draw in learning how to motivate people.

The Theoretical Background

Progressive motivational attitudes in newspaper management (as in other industries) are strongly influenced by Abraham Maslow (1908–1970), a psychologist who developed a theory of human needs as an explanation of behavior. Maslow developed the idea of a *hierarchy of needs,* suggesting that as individuals satisfy their needs on a lower level they will move to a higher one and an ever-enlarging range of needs. Your challenge is to understand the employee's shifting view of his or her needs and respond appropriately in the interests of both the employee and the newspaper.

For example, Maslow's theory holds that each individual has basic *physiological needs* such as food, clothing and shelter. In a newspaper, these needs are served by wages, which enable the employee to purchase the minimum necessities of life. But, Maslow theorized, once minimum needs are met, each individual expresses *safety and security needs.* These are met by job security, health insurance and other fringe benefits.

Meanwhile, however, employees develop *social needs,* which Maslow defined as need for group belonging and companionship. If an employee's work environment doesn't satisfy those needs, an unhappy employee could look elsewhere, perhaps joining a union to satisfy them. Gannett executives speak of the "Gannett family" to give employees a feeling of belonging to a group.

Maslow's *esteem needs* represent an individual's desire for self-confidence and wish to be considered important by others. Bolster your employees' self-confidence by giving them authority to act independently and demonstrate how important they are. Corporate status symbols—a title on the door and a rug on the floor—are efforts to meet esteem needs among top executives; a reporter's might be fulfilled with a byline on an important front-page story.

Self-actualization needs, according to Maslow, are those all humans feel to realize their potential, to be creative, to achieve. (Ever wonder why the U.S. Army uses the recruiting slogan, "Be All That You Can Be"?)

Simply put, if you assign a highly creative writer to handling routine obituaries you soon will have an unhappy employee on your hands; an advertising salesperson capable of achieving success with major accounts will become restive if assigned only minor accounts.

Note the Maslow theory is directed at explaining the individual's needs. You must help employees fulfill those personal needs, but within a context of meeting the newspaper's overall corporate objectives. Your goal is to produce not simply a happy employee but one happily and productively contributing to the newspaper's overall effort.

You don't have to satisfy every need—indeed, Maslow's theory holds this to be almost impossible, since human beings, once satisfied on one level, will expand the range of needs yet to be satisfied. But be on the lookout for those *unsatisfied needs* that create frustration, constructive behavior (seeking fulfillment outside the job) or defensive behavior (anger, withdrawal, or bitterness).

Pay Alone Isn't Enough

Building effective personnel policy within Maslow's theoretical framework is complex. Obviously, pay alone will not do it. Newspaper employees (like those in other industries) increasingly point to a complex equation for job satisfaction. Playing a meaningful role in a worthwhile task and being appreciated for it are prime demands these days.

Knowing the newspaper is a meaningful force in the community and that they play key roles in getting it published can be extremely important to employees. From newsroom to circulation loading dock, you should demonstrate to all employees how essential they are to the overall operation.

Helping employees with personal problems is extremely important. Helping a working mother find a day-care center for her children or a new employee obtain a home mortgage can pay huge dividends for you. You can follow many avenues to elicit the desired performance from each employee.

Researcher Frederick Herzberg and others developed the "two-factor" theory, according to which employees obtain satisfaction from "motivation factors" such as the job and its opportunities for promotion, personal growth, responsibility and status but that dissatisfaction results from "maintenance factors" such as pay, company policies, managers, and relationships with others.

For example, a job perceived as important and prestigious will help create a satisfied employee. Pay—even high pay—does not in itself guarantee a satisfied, effective employee. But if pay is too low, dissatisfaction and ineffective performance may result. This led Herzberg to conclude that people are motivated by *job enrichment.*

This concept holds that an employee's sense of recognition and achievement can be more important than pay or working conditions and that managers therefore must design jobs to be challenging and meaningful. The theory does not suggest mere rotation of jobs, each as boring as the other. Rather, it points to task identity—making sure each employee has an entire piece of work to complete and that it is significant. That is, avoid whenever possible job assignments smacking of assembly-line work—putting nuts on bolts all day long.

Give a copy editor, for example, total responsibility for a series of stories on one subject; let an advertising salesperson completely design and implement a campaign for a major retailer. The sense of both starting and finishing something is important. It comes down to you determining, first, what performance is needed, then what rewards are valued by employees and linking rewards to performance. People respond differently to rewards.

Setting Pay Levels

Pay, obviously, is important, but is just one motivational tool at your disposal. The floor for pay levels is set by the federal minimum wage law, but most of a newspaper's work force is paid well above that. Base your salary levels on these factors: Your newspaper's ability to pay. Obviously, financially strong newspapers can pay more. And, what competitors pay. This means not just other newspapers of like size and characteristics but all employers who compete for the talented people needed in newspapering. If pay is too low, talent will move to broadcasting, public relations, advertising and other industries.

Your pay policy must demonstrate clearly a relationship between job and pay for it. That link must be discernible to employees and be perceived as satisfactory. That is, an employee loading newspaper bundles into circulation trucks must understand there is only so much pay available for moving bundles and that higher pay requires promotion to a more responsible job.

In advertising and circulation sales, incentives should be built into the pay structure: more pay, quickly, for more, better work. This is "performance-related pay," which many managers use to ensure their payroll is spent, as best possible, to reward performers. If your employees see pay linked to performance, pay can be an effective motivational tool. Take care in distributing rewards. If pay and other rewards are perceived as being unfairly distributed—and there are few secrets in newspapers on such matters—great dissatisfaction can result.

One researcher into motivation, psychologist B. F. Skinner, fashioned the theory of *operant conditioning* (or *reinforcement theory*), which holds that individuals perform to be rewarded and that their behavior is shaped by reinforcement. Skinner's theory is that positive reinforcement is most effective in shaping desired behavior. That is, you can be much more effective by patting someone on the back, granting public recognition or paying a bonus than by using negative reinforcement such as criticism or punishment.

BOX 6.3   A "Pro" But No "Professional"?

Reporters may consider themselves a newspaper "pro" but a U.S. District Court has ruled a reporter is not a "professional," as defined by law.

The court, in Concord, N.H., ruled in 1993 that reporters are not "professionals" under U.S. Labor Department regulations and that the *Concord (N.H.) Monitor* therefore had to pay 10 reporters and 2 photographers nearly $21,000 in overtime.

The *Monitor* had asked that reporters and photographers be considered professionals and thus exempt from the Fair Labor Standards Act of 1938. The act exempts professionals, executives and administrators from time-and-a-half pay for working more than 40 hours weekly.[a]

[a]George Garneau provided an excellent wrap up of this much-discussed case in "Monitor Loses Overtime Case," *Editor & Publisher,* Nov. 13, 1993, p. 26.

Your next step is to decide where, how, when and in what measure to use motivational tools. For a discussion of that we turn to control, a major responsibility of every manager.

Controlling Employee Performance

To ensure your newspaper reaches desired objectives, you must control employees in the workplace. This requires establishing *performance standards, measuring performance* by each employee and *correcting shortcomings.* The control function is key to your career success at every level of management.

As a first-level manager, directly supervising employees each day, you need strong technical skills. As, say, a copy-desk supervisor, you obviously must know how to edit; if you become a first-level foreman in the pressroom, you must know the nuts and bolts of presses. First-level managers must be skilled in explaining in clear, understandable terms what must be done and how to do it. See Box 6.4 for how the *Louisville Courier-Journal* spells out performance standards. See Box 6.5 on page 157 for a personnel director's view of how first-level supervisors must operate.

Middle-level managers—heads of circulation or advertising, for example—must shift their supervisory emphasis from controlling day-to-day performance by individuals to controlling interdepartmental efforts. Working smoothly and effectively with other middle-level managers is crucial.

Top-level managers—publishers—must be strong on conceptual approaches necessary in controlling the newspaper's overall strategic performance. They must motivate others to view the newspaper as an integrated whole that needs strong teamwork to accomplish its mission.

At all levels, successful control requires continual, systematic and detailed appraisal of each employee's effectiveness. Appraisals must spot weak areas that need correcting and help select employees suitable for promotion.

Performance is appraised in many ways, depending on the employee's job. For example, reporters should be appraised on initiative in pursuing stories, ability to write clearly and well, reliability in handling facts. Reporters—and other employees—should be appraised for ability to use time wisely, solve problems, make speedy decisions and work well with peers.

Appraisals normally rank employees on a wide scale. Knight-Ridder supervisors rank each employee on whether performance is low, below average, average, above average or outstanding. An employee consistently ranked outstanding obviously could be considered for promotion.

At least annually, a supervisor must discuss performance with each employee: pointing out not only shortcomings but also how performance can be improved. If training is required, the supervisor should suggest on-the-job help from a more experienced employee or recommend outside assistance, perhaps at a local college, technical school or one of the many formal seminars and training programs run by Newspaper Association of America, American Press Institute and other industry groups. Most newspapers require supervisors to give each employee a written ap-

BOX 6.4 How to Establish Performance Standards

A prime responsibility of management is to issue clear guidelines for employees on what is expected of them. Can there be any doubt about these standards, which the *Louisville (Ky.) Courier-Journal* established for reporters and copy editors?

Reporters

Writing ability—Grammar and spelling; ability to tell a good story well; use of quotes, anecdotes and descriptive detail; use of active voice and strong verbs; ability to write leads that are inviting and that hit the point of the story; ability to write tightly and to organize information in logical, compelling sequence.

Reporting ability—Pursuit, digging, enterprise, diligence; ability and eagerness to see and pursue promising angles; ability to seek and obtain anecdotes, detail and quotations that provide documentation and add liveliness to copy; ability to see the need for and to get both sides of the story; ability to cultivate good sources.

Speed, productivity and efficiency—Speed on deadline; speed and efficiency in completing non-deadline assignments; ability and willingness to manage more than one assignment at a time; ability and willingness to make frequent, substantive contributions to the content of the paper.

Accuracy—Skill with basic factual information such as names, addresses, dates and figures; ability to identify and make use of the best sources, whether they are documents, references or people.

Work habits—Punctuality, reliability, readiness to go beyond the minimum requirements of the job; interest in assuming and ability to assume more than minimum responsibility; ability and willingness to anticipate and fulfill the demands of an assignment without prompting; ability to deal even-handedly with peers and supervisors, to accept constructive criticism and offer constructive suggestions; interest in all areas of the news operation; knowledge of community, regional, national and international events; regular and thorough reader of the newspaper.

Judgment—Commitment to fairness and balance; ability to recognize and assess possible adverse consequences of actions; knowledge of, respect for and observance of the news department's policies.

Potential—Likelihood that the reporter is a candidate for a more challenging reporting assignment; for a supervisory position; evidence that he or she possesses the characteristics of leadership and supervisory ability expected of supervising editors.

Copy Editors

Editing ability—Grammar and spelling; ability to trim excess verbiage, clarify confusing or contradictory language, improve a story without robbing it of the writer's style; ability to identify and give proper emphasis to important news angles; ability to spot and correct holes in stories; ability to spot and correct errors, libel, unfairness and imbalances; ability to condense stories for use in digests and roundups; knowledge of and adherence to style.

Headlines—Accuracy; ability to convey the essence of the story; ability to write inviting feature heads; knowledge of headline orders and style.

Accuracy—Skill with basic factual information such as names, addresses, dates and figures; ability to identify and make use of the best sources, whether they are documents, references or people.

Work habits—Punctuality, reliability, readiness to go beyond the minimum requirements of the

Continued

BOX 6.4 *Continued*

job; interest in assuming and ability to assume more than minimum responsibility; ability and willingness to anticipate and fulfill the demands of an assignment without prompting; ability to deal even-handedly with peers and supervisors, to accept constructive criticism and offer constructive suggestions; interest in all areas of the news operation; knowledge of community, regional, national and international events; regular and thorough reader of the newspaper.

Potential—Likehood that the copy editor is a candidate for a more challenging editing assignment; for a supervisory position; evidence that he or she possess the characteristics of leadership and supervisory ability expected of supervisory editors.

Versatility—Ability and willingness to learn and perform a variety of jobs on the news desk and copy desks.

Judgment—Commitment to fairness and balance; ability to recognize and assess possible adverse consequences of actions; knowledge of, respect for and observance of the news department's policies.

Design skills (where appropriate)—Mastery of layout and design skill; of typesetting techniques; of the use of photographs; of the development and use of graphic devices such as charts, graphs and maps.

praisal, which the employee is asked to read and sign, attaching comments if desired.

James D. Boswell, vice president for employee relations at the *Los Angeles Times*, said appraisals must be made of all employees, from lowest salary level to highest. He said such measurements meet various needs. For the employee, appraisals answer questions like, How am I doing in my job? What are my strengths? Weaknesses? How can I improve? Where is my career going? For management, appraisals help spot employees who are not doing well and who may need training or, if that won't help, transfer from the job. Consecutively poor appraisals may suggest dismissal. Below-par appraisals serve as documentation for discipline. For both employee and management, appraisals are agreements on each employee's job objectives and when and how to reach them. They also provide recognition for employees. Workers feel proud of consistently being appraised as outstanding performers.

Appraisals help determine whether—and when—wage changes must be made. Being ranked low across the board should be explained as a clear signal that merit increases will be mighty slow in coming; an outstanding employee should get increases. Used properly, then, appraisals are an effective communications medium between supervisor and employee.

The more detail covered in an appraisal, the better. See Figure 6.2 on page 158 for how Knight-Ridder, an industry leader in efficient personnel practices, uses appraisals to draw detailed pictures of each of its more than 20,000 employees (in 1993).

Ideally, appraisals lead employees to adjust their performance to the standards expected of them and become productive workers. But ideal conditions do not al-

---

BOX 6.5   Dos and Don'ts in Supervising People

As corporate personnel director for Morris Communications Corp., a privately held group of newspapers, Bobby Reid said the successful supervisor:

1. Is firm but always fair with every employee.
2. Understands that a supervisor's conduct often determines an employee's motivation.
3. Recognizes that some problems always exist in every group of employees.
4. Uses two-way communications effectively and is available for individual discussions of problems.
5. Brings problems to the attention of the company and pursues solutions.
6. Explains company policy effectively.
7. Sells the company and its policies to employees.
8. Knows employees—their backgrounds and goals—and is interested in them.

9. Uses constructive criticism to help employees prepare for promotion; promotes the qualified.
10. Is impartial and consistent in enforcing rules; plays no favorites.
11. Views employees gripes as an opportunity to solve a problem.
12. Cultivates leadership among employees.
13. Supervises people, not machines.
14. Keeps employees informed of their progress; praises publicly, criticizes privately.
15. Talks with employees, not to them; is a good listener.
16. Terminates poor employees and chronic complainers.
17. Answers questions and seeks answers to those he or she doesn't know.
18. Can clearly explain what is required of an employee and provides the information necessary for doing the job.
19. Backs employees when they are right.

---

ways exist, so managers must be prepared to take firm—sometimes distasteful— steps.

Discipline: The Distasteful Task

Hiring and training talented personnel will be among your most creative and enjoyable tasks. However, one of your most distasteful—disciplining and, sometimes, firing people—can be just as important in constructing and controlling a professionally capable staff.

Unfortunately, mistakes—by an unfit person in applying for a job and by a manager in providing one—sometimes land unsuitable men and women on a newspaper staff. Job counseling or reassignment sometimes sets things right. A writer who doesn't improve may be suited for an editing job; an editor impatient with working on somebody else's writing might make a superb reporter. But there are occasions when consistently poor performance or disruptive behavior will leave you no alternative but harsh discipline or discharge.

Discipline and when and how it is applied must be fair and even-handed. Follow these steps:

Knight Ridder, Inc.
INDIVIDUAL DEVELOPMENTAL PROGRAM

NAME _____   NEWSPAPER/COMPANY _____

POSITION _____   SUPERVISOR _____

A. PERFORMANCE (See Manager's Guide for Definitions)

Rating	Low	Below Average	Average	Above Average	Outstanding	N/A*
1. Utilization of Resources						
• Personnel						
• Capital						
• Budget						
• Facilities						
• Time						
• Professional Knowledge						
2. Reaction to Unforeseen Events						
3. Planning—Objective Setting						
4. Problem Solving						
• Identification						
• Analysis						
• Creativity						
5. Decision Making						
• Basis						
• Speed						
• Quality						
• Follow-through						
6. Attitude Concerning						
• Subordinates						
• Peers						
• Immediate Supervisor						
• Your Newspaper/Company						
7. Dependability						
8. Personal Effectiveness						
9. Overall Evaluation						

B. EVALUATION OF PROMOTABILITY   *N/A — Not applicable

1. Short-Term Promotability

   a. Employee is promotable and ready now ❏

   b. Employee is promotable with additional experience and training. ❏
      Specify additional experience and training needed; then specify positions.

		WHEN	
		Now	# Mos
Recommended Position(s)	Current Department		
Recommended Position(s)	Other Department(s)		

FIGURE 6.2 With 22,000 employees, Knight-Ridder has a mammoth task in evaluating the performance and promotability of its staff. This detailed appraisal form is one step in that process. Reprinted by permission of Knight-Ridder Inc.

If this employee exhibits exceptional potential for development at an accelerated rate, please comment:

Is employee satisfied with present career direction and rate of development?

Is this employee willing to relocate?

2. Not Promotable: Well placed now ❏ In wrong position, needs transfer ❏ Over his/her head ❏
   Should be replaced in job but kept in company ❏ Should be terminated ❏ Too soon to tell ❏

3. Near Retirement (Within 5 Years): Promotable as indicated above ❏ Better utilization could be made ❏
   Performance is slipping ❏ Valuable where placed ❏ Should consider early retirement ❏

C. LONG-TERM CAREER ASPIRATIONS AND POTENTIAL

   1. What are the employee's career aspirations?

   2. How realistic are the individual's goals and are they compatible with your views of his or her capabilities?

D. DEVELOPMENTAL RECOMMENDATIONS

   1. Ideally, what should be done to assist employee in achieving ultimate potential?
      (Skill training and experience; management training and experience; experience outside present area.)

   2. What specific actions will be taken? Specify when action will be taken and who will be responsible.

E. BACK-UP IDENTIFICATIONS

   Considering the employee's present position, identify persons by name and title who might fill the job should the employee move.

Signature of preparer _____   Date prepared _____

FIGURE 6.2 *Continued*

1. Obtain all pertinent facts about the alleged infraction (and it *is* alleged until proven). Get a dispassionate view from the employee's side as well as management's. For example, a supervisor who complains that an ad salesperson is unproductive may be giving that person only dormant, unrewarding clients to visit; your job is to look at the employee's side of the story, as well as the newspaper's.

2. Consider union implications, if any. Under some union contracts, you may be obliged to inform the union that disciplinary action is contemplated. Some contracts require a union representative to be present during discussions with the employee.

3. Talk with the employee whenever possible in a low-key, informal way; ask for his or her views. Often, a chat over coffee is helpful.

4. If facts dictate a warning, consider whether you can keep it oral and still make your point without a written complaint that becomes part of the employee's permanent record.

5. However, if the situation calls for more forceful treatment, issue a written warning that states management's view in detail. Ask for the employee's written response. Both become part of the permanent record. The warning should include specific examples of errors committed or other lapses.

6. If punishment is required, a pay increase or promotion can be denied or, in extreme cases, the employee must be fired. Note: If an employee is genuinely surprised at being fired, management has not done its job properly. The newspaper's statement of personnel policy or supervisors should spell out infractions that can lead to discharge. If the issue is, say, gradual deterioration of performance rather than a single incident, supervisors should be on record as having warned the employee that discharge was inevitable unless performance improved.

Throughout the entire process, from day of hiring onward, there should be a fully documented, written record of the employee's work performance, including copies of any written criticisms by supervisors. Keeping voluminous records, alas, is part of personnel management because numerous lawsuits crop up.

In litigation, a frequent question is whether a contract for employment exists. Courts sometimes rule that even an implied promise of continued employment can constitute a contract which, if broken, opens the newspaper to damages. To discuss an "annual" salary in a hiring interview, for example, might be viewed as promising a one-year contract. Speak only of a "weekly wage."

A pattern of raises, promotions and favorable critiques by supervisors can be held as strengthening the implied contract, particularly if the record shows no criticisms for substandard performance. Neglecting such legalisms can mean years and thousands of dollars spent in litigation over charges of breaking a contract or failing to deal in good faith with an employee. Clearly, there is under way a steady erosion of the tradition that American newspapers—or corporations of any type—can "employ at will" or fire without reason or notice.

Employees gain rights, of course, under any union contract that might exist or under certain laws, such as the Civil Rights Act of 1964, that restrict employers in hiring and firing. But beyond this, courts in many states have defined circumstances which restrict your right to "employ at will." For example, the right to serve in the National Guard or on a jury or to refuse a lie detector test is protected by law. Fire an employee for exercising such a right and you may face a costly lawsuit.

Sometimes you do employees a favor by suggesting they move on. For many people, one of life's great frustrations is to hold a job beyond their capabilities, and a wise personnel manager will find ways of bringing that reality to the attention of employees who are not suited for newspaper work. Many young reporters move on to success in other fields when gently informed that their writing is not good enough for newspaper work.

SPECIAL PROBLEMS: TECHNOLOGY, DOWNSIZING, MINORITIES

Three special problems complicate your human resources management: New technology eliminates thousands of jobs and forces radical changes in the work skills and habits of many employees. Downsizing, or force reduction, requires eliminating jobs to maintain the profitability of many newspapers. Legal and societal pressure forces hiring more minorities and women and promoting those qualified to responsible positions. And, you must construct a level playing field for all employees, one free of sexual harassment and discrimination.

When Technology Displaces Jobs

One of your most difficult problems will be to deal sensitively and fairly with employees displaced by technology, yet protect your newspaper's best interests by pursuing the economies and efficiencies the technology offers. Employees whose jobs vanish through no fault of their own suffer great trauma. This has been apparent for decades as successive waves of new technology swept through newspapers.

Starting in the 1960s, newspapers switched to offset printing and photocomposition from letterpress-stereotype production plants, and many thousands of jobs were eliminated. The 1970s brought more job eliminations as computerized electronic writing and editing swept the industry. Thousands of jobs disappeared in composing and other "back-shop" departments. A third large job displacement is occurring as newspapers switch to pagination—computerized makeup of news and advertising pages. Example: *The Pasadena (Calif.) Star-News* had a composing room staff of 100 before pagination, *nine* afterward.

Some newspapers make expensive "buyouts," providing early retirement or cash incentives for displaced workers. Many newspapers retrain employees for new jobs with the same company. Gannett's Westchester Rockland Newspapers, a group of community dailies north of New York City, transferred 66 displaced composing room workers into almost every other department, including advertising and editorial. Eleven were trained as electronics technicians to service the very machines that displaced them. Retraining employees familiar with general operations proves easier, in many cases, than hiring outsiders and substantially cheaper than a buyout.

Betty A. Duval, for years vice president for staff development of Dow Jones & Co., cautioned managers to be particularly sensitive to staff worries when making technological changes. Because managers initiate change, it is rational and understandable to them, she said; but change can be perceived negatively by employees who think they have no control over developments that threaten them. She cautioned managers to:

1. Explain company goals and what other newspapers are doing.
2. Seek employee input on proposed changes and offer options if possible.
3. Provide training when new equipment is introduced.
4. Realize that cost-cutting measures or new equipment may mean fewer people doing more work, and consider lightening the load.
5. Listen to employee concerns and suggestions; watch for boredom and loneliness due to the introduction of new technology.
6. Implement major changes in stages, involving employees in this and discussing any problems along the way.

Business Is Poor; You're Fired!

Telling this to an employee is one of a manager's toughest jobs. Yet, it's been done on hundreds of newspapers. The newspaper industry's work force was trimmed—"down-sized"—by an estimated 10 percent in the period 1990 to 1993. Some newspapers cut back even more. The *Los Angeles Times* cut its staff of 8,500 by about 2,000—a whopping 23 percent—in that period.[1]

The principal cause, of course, was the national economic recession. Industry advertising revenue dropped from $32.2 billion in 1990 to $30.6 billion in 1992. The *Los Angeles Times* said its 1993 ad revenue was about $150 million under its peak of $1.1 billion in 1990. Circulation was down more than 120,000 from 1.2 million in 1990.[2] In Los Angeles, work force reduction was achieved primarily through buy-outs, incentives for early retirements or, sometimes, outright cash settlements for resignations.

When *The New York Times* reduced staff it attempted to negotiate with unions cash buyouts for employees selected for termination. Failing that, *The Times* laid off news and advertising employees. Wages were frozen at many news organizations.

The very existence of some newspapers depended on their ability to quickly and substantially reduce costs. For others, the goal was to protect profit margins—evidence of the influence the rising tide of shareholder expectations has on yet another sector of your management responsibilities.

Three factors are clear: First, newspapers weren't sufficiently cost-conscious in the prosperous 1980s. Too many people were unthinkably added to payrolls. Want to avoid telling employees they're fired because of poor economic conditions? Carefully control costs so it's not necessary.

Second, newspapers must be more innovative in hiring. Many now hire part-time help, which can avoid huge staff benefits costs (you generally pay about 35¢ in vacation, health and other benefits for every $1 in salary). Some editors hire entry-level reporters on two-year contracts, then retain on full staff basis only those who perform superbly well.

Third, each employee must be more productive. This is your responsibility: hire, train, motivate and control so that you accomplish more with fewer employees.

Meeting Societal Standards

You're under heavy societal pressure to ensure equal opportunity in your newspaper for minorities and women. The societal demands are reflected in a wide range of legislation. The seminal legislation, of course, is the 1964 Civil Rights Act. Under Title VII of that act, the Equal Employment Opportunity Commission (EEOC), a federal body, was formed to investigate charges of discrimination (see Box 6.6 for other applicable laws).

Law aside, it makes business sense for a newspaper, which must mirror its marketplace, to build a staff representative of the people who live there. As chairman of Gannett, Al Neuharth was a leader in building staff diversity. He put it this way: "Promoting and practicing equal opportunity is not only the right thing to do; it's the smart thing to do . . . no newspaper can cover all of the community unless it employs all of the community."[3]

And, what constitutes *all* the community is changing: Fully 87 percent of the nation's population growth in the decade leading up to the year 2000 is expected to come in minority communities.[4] Gregory Favre, *Sacramento (Calif.) Bee* executive editor: "Unless newspapers represent the changing face of their communities, we're not going to have readers. It's quite that simple."[5]

BOX 6.6   You and the Law

Here's a manager's primer on laws and court rulings affecting your human relations policies:

- *Equal Pay Act* (1963) makes it illegal to discriminate in wages on the basis of gender.
- *Civil Rights Act* (1964) outlaws discrimination on basis of race, color, religion, national origin. A 1972 amendment outlaws gender discrimination. The *Pregnancy Discrimination Act* of 1978 makes it illegal to refuse to hire a woman or fire her because she's pregnant or to force her to take a maternity leave.
- *Age Discrimination in Employment Act* (1967) forbids age discrimination in the workplace. The *Older Workers Benefit Protection Act* of 1990 outlaws discrimination against employees 40 or older in benefits programs.
- The U.S. Supreme Court ruled (1986) that sexual harassment is illegal discrimination.
- The *Americans with Disabilities Act* forbids discrimination against people because of their physical or mental disabilities.
- The *Family and Medical Leave Act* (1993) requires companies with 50 or more employees to give employees the right of up to 12 weeks unpaid leave if a close family member is pregnant or ill.

Gannett's early drive for diversity is carried forward by its current chairman, John Curley. The payoff: Minorities held 16.2 percent of professional jobs (as contrasted with clerks' jobs and so forth) in Gannett newspaper newsrooms in 1993, compared with the national average of 10 percent, the company says.[6] As in all things managerial, Gannett's success is due to top-level involvement. Company editors filled 32.4 percent of their newsroom openings with minorities in the period July 1992 to July 1993.[7] That increased minority representation in overall newsroom staffing to 16.2 percent from 14.8 percent the year before.

Some large newspapers do well: Minority journalists at *USA Today* (a Gannett paper) were 20.8 percent of total newsroom staff in 1993, 16.8 percent at *The Wall Street Journal*, 18.5 percent at the *Los Angeles Times*, 21 percent at the *Detroit Free Press* (which has a huge black audience), and 29.9 percent at the *Miami Herald* (with many Hispanic readers).[8]

However, industrywide results are not impressive. A profile of the American journalist was developed by two Indiana University professors and is shown in Figure 6.1.[9]

The Statistical Picture Isn't Good

Slow growth in minority hiring is explained in part by slow growth of overall media jobs: Job growth was 61 percent, 1971 to 1982; just 9 percent, 1982 to 1993.

Nevertheless, the industry obviously doesn't meet societal expectations. Note:

* Daily newspaper staffers were 19 percent minority in 1992, unchanged from 1990.
* Only in 1993 did the number of minorities in daily newsrooms reach 10 percent.
* Minorities in other departments: circulation, 23 percent; accounting and finance, 21 percent; information systems and services, 17 percent; general management and administration, 15 percent; advertising, 13 percent; marketing, promotion and research, 11 percent.[10]

For comparative purposes, the Census Bureau said the 1990 U.S. population was 80.3 percent white, 12.1 percent black, 2.9 percent Asian-Pacific Islanders, 0.8 percent American Indian/Eskimo/Aleut, 9 percent Hispanic, 3.9 percent other.[11]

The newspaper industry's statistics are worse for minority supervisors. Minorities held just 7.1 percent of total supervisory jobs; in newsrooms, the figure was 17 percent.

Women's Numbers Lag, Too

Industry statistics on female employment also show much yet to be done:

* Of total newspaper employees, 39 percent were women in 1992.
* Women, however, unlike minorities, are more successful in gaining promotion. In 1992, women were 30 percent of executives and managers.
* Minority women were 7 percent of the work force and just 3 percent of executives and managers.[12]

FIGURE 6.1   **Managing newspaper people can be a complex task because journalists are complex people, as cartoonist Jack Ohman illustrated for *presstime*® magazine. Reprinted by permission of Jack Ohman and *presstime*.® (Data from "The American Journalist in the 1990s," A Study of 1,400 journalists by David Weaver and Cleveland Wilhoit of Indiana University. Funded by the Freedom Forum, Arlington, Va.)**

Eliminating Harassment: Your Task

To create an effective (and legal) work environment, you must eliminate harassment. It's in *sexual* harassment that the greatest inequities (and legal dangers) lie. For starters, this is how the EEOC defines sexual harassment: "Unwelcome sexual advances, requests for sexual favors, and other verbal or physical conduct of a sexual nature when:

> *Submission to such conduct is made either explicitly or implicitly a term or condition of an individual's employment; OR, submission to or rejection of such conduct by an individual is used as a basis for employment decisions affecting such individual; OR, such conduct has the purpose or effect of unreasonably interfering with an individual's work performance or creating an intimidating, hostile, or defensive working environment.*

Morris Communications Corp. gives its supervisors examples of conduct that can create an offensive (and, perhaps, illegal) work environment:

- Discussing sexual activities or dating.
- Unnecessary touching or brushing against a person's body.
- Commenting on physical attributes.
- Pervasive displays of nude or suggestive pictures.
- Leering or ogling.
- Using demeaning or inappropriate terms ("sweetie" or "hunk").
- Unseemly gestures.
- Graffiti written on walls.

Morris Communications adds this guidance:

A single comment or incident might not be sexual harassment, but a pattern of this type of behavior probably will be. The critical element is whether the behavior is perceived as unwelcome by another person.

The "Reasonable Woman Standard" has emerged as a benchmark for evaluating this perception. Because men and women have different sensitivities, conduct that is unoffensive to men may well be offensive to women. For that reason, some courts apply the "Reasonable Woman Standard": Would the alleged conduct be offensive to a woman of average sensitivities?

In determining if your own behavior might be unwelcome, a rule of thumb is to ask yourself: Would your behavior change if someone from your family was in the room or would you want someone from your family to be treated this way?[13]

Hiring Homosexuals

Some newspapers actively recruit gays and lesbians to expand newsroom diversity. The *Los Angeles Times, Miami Herald, The Washington Post* and *The New York Times* were among newspapers that assigned recruiters to the 1993 convention of the National Lesbian and Gay Journalists Association.[14]

Arthur Ochs Sulzberger Jr., publisher of *The New York Times,* commented: "We can no longer offer our readers a predominately white, straight, male vision of events and say that we, as journalists, are doing our job."[15]

A survey of American Society of Newspaper Editors members showed many editors agreed with Sulzberger: 73 percent of 236 editors responding said their official policies or informal practices were designed to prevent discrimination against gays and lesbians.[16]

MEASURING YOUR SUCCESS

Now, let's see where you are as a manager of human resources. You develop a positive ("Y") attitude toward employees. You study motivational theory and try to open honest, sensitive communications with each of them. *Is it working?*

You better find out. Because if it isn't you are failing to elicit optimum performance from the newspaper's most important and costly asset, its people. And that is what you are paid to do. You may even be unwittingly contributing to worsening morale. So, you must measure your effectiveness in human resources management, whether you are responsible for one person or thousands.

Watch Important Indicators

Excessive Turnover
This is disruptive, harms morale and is costly, because new hires must be found, trained and put in place—with inevitable loss of productivity. When employees stalk out the door, much expensive training and experience goes along. (Scripps Howard estimates it costs $12,500 on average to replace a newsroom professional, about $3,000 to replace an entry-level worker.)[17] And beware: Before they stalk out, there is a great deal of grousing to fellow workers, and their morale suffers, too. Of course, some turnover is good. You can hire new blood—perhaps better-qualified replacements.

How much turnover is excessive? Smaller newspapers, traditionally serving as training grounds for nearby metros, will have high turnover; some, in fact, serve as "farm clubs," hiring new college graduates, knowing they will move to the "big leagues" in a few years. It's not uncommon for small-town editors to promise new hires, "Do the job for me a couple years and I'll introduce you to my friend, the metro editor."

Papers renowned for journalistic quality, good working conditions and high pay naturally will have low turnover. But whatever your paper's size, if turnover exceeds 15 percent annually, you have a serious problem.

Deteriorating Job Performance

This often is a prime indicator of morale problems. Watch carefully, for example, the journalistic quality of the paper; a sudden slump demands investigation. The performance of individual employees should be monitored carefully.

Absenteeism and Tardiness
This can signal widespread difficulties. For individuals, it may mean serious personal problems such as alcoholism or drug usage.

Complaints
Complaints delivered through your own grievance system, if you don't have a union or formally through the union if you do have one, are prime measurements of employee sentiment.

The Grapevine
Speedily transmitting information and misinformation outside the formal chain of command, the grapevine is a barometer of mood. If you are a first-level supervisor

in direct contact with employees, they often will discuss what is on the grapevine; if you have moved up to middle or top management, they won't, so make sure your supervisors are tuned in.

Formal Audits of Employee Morale

Simply keeping an ear cocked to the grapevine is hardly adequate for auditing employee attitudes. You should develop scientific, formal measurements. Written questionnaires and in-depth personal interviews are effective. Both can be employed as your newspaper's pocketbook permits—small papers can conduct homemade surveys at low cost; large papers can call in professional consultants.

Some newspapers use questionnaire surveys every 18 to 24 months, letting employees anonymously answer questions ranging from whether restrooms are kept clean to how well the newspaper is managed.

In-depth interviews can add greatly to measurements of employee attitudes if you keep in mind that it takes planning to elicit desired information. A few hints:

- Go into the interview well prepared with personal background and job performance data on the interviewee and the subject to be discussed. Have a plan and stick to it, gently pulling the conversation back on track if it strays.
- Establish a relaxed atmosphere by interviewing in private and without interruptions. Set a friendly tone by operating informally, chatting easily and reassuring the interviewee (who may be alarmed by the whole process).
- Always be courteous. And if you can handle it, use humor, too! Nothing shuts employees up like brusque, humorless treatment. If you want information, you should relax.

Warning: Employees often are reluctant to respond frankly in attitude surveys. Some fear that doing so will jeopardize their position or anger a supervisor. In interviews, some employees are incapable of expressing themselves on complex problems. You must create an atmosphere of trust that will embolden employees to speak frankly, without fear of retribution.

Follow Through

One key to effective audits of employee attitudes is careful record keeping. Whether you are auditing one employee or a thousand, you must gather information through surveys and interviews and verify it by cross-checking through additional contracts with the staff, asking the same question another way or running more surveys. Then, correlate it and pull it all together for interpretation.

Detailed record keeping permits you to chart staff behavior, establish norms and then spot future variances from the norm that might signal changes in employee attitudes. For example, suppose absenteeism, charted over a period of years, comes to an average of six days per year per employee. If that figure should suddenly jump to 10 days, you must determine why.

It is essential for you to act whenever possible on the information gathered. If you ask an employee what is wrong, you have raised the expectation that what is wrong can be fixed. If it isn't, the letdown can cause even greater morale problems. If you ask a circulation truck driver how his job is going and he says the brakes on the truck are no good—and you don't get the brakes fixed—you have destroyed your credibility with that employee.

Sometimes, a departing employee can provide valuable information for you to follow through on. *The Athens (Ga.) Banner-Herald* and *The Daily News* ask outgoing employees these questions in interviews conducted by appropriate department heads:

- What did you like most about your job?
- What did you like least?
- What did you like most about the company?
- What did you like least about the company?
- Was your job training adequate?
- What problems did you encounter on your job?
- Further comments or observations?

Such "exit interviews" can provide meaningful views of the newspaper's workplace efficiency and morale. Of course, their validity is limited if an employee is leaving under pressure or won't be frank for fear of jeopardizing references for future jobs.

In your follow-through, don't hesitate to adjust your own performance on what you learn. Look at it this way: As a supervisor, you establish standards for your employees, you monitor their performance—and you require them to make adjustments if performance falls short. So isn't it only fair (and logical) that you should adjust your performance if employee (and ex-employee) attitude surveys so dictate? If you don't act openly and responsively, you may find yourself no longer dealing one-on-one with individual employees but rather with groups of employees that have coalesced against you.

GROUPS: LEARN AND WORK WITH THEM

As you will learn quickly in your first supervisory job, your influence on an employee is just one of many. One of the most important is group pressure. It's human nature. People form groups. There are many kinds, not just the formal groups—the work sections, the departments—represented by your newspaper's table of organization.

You must learn to recognize and work with the informal groups that evolve naturally in any work situation. They may be groups of employees who see economic benefit in sticking together (this, of course, can lead to unionization) or who seek sociopsychological benefits, such as a feeling of security. Such groups may se-

CASE STUDY 6.1   Why Is Your Newsroom Unhappy?

You're personnel director for a 100,000-circulation daily. You and the executive editor know dissatisfaction permeates your newsroom. But precisely why are staffers unhappy? Is dissatisfaction unusually high? What can you do to build staff morale?

Start with a survey of 627 journalists from 29 newspapers, conducted in 1993 by one of the industry's leading researchers, Kristen McGrath of MORI Research, Inc., and commissioned by The Associated Press Managing Editors Association.[a]

First, the survey found dissatisfaction widespread: Of respondents, 19 percent planned to leave newspapering within five years; 44 percent wanted to work for a different newspaper; only 35 percent planned to work for the same newspaper (and 2 percent didn't have plans or declined to answer). Second, staffers who planned to leave were those editors want to keep—ambitious, serious professionals. Third, principal reasons for unhappiness generally are things you can fix.

McGrath's survey showed you should investigate employees' attitudes in five areas that "drive" job satisfaction.

Management Issues

In predicting job satisfaction, most important is how journalists answer questions on newsroom management: Are you appreciated? Do you get the direction you need? Are you fairly evaluated? Does your supervisor respect you?

Opportunity for Growth

Second most important are two questions: How do you rate your newspaper on chances for advancement? Do you have opportunity to grow within the company?

Newspaper Quality

Journalists clearly were concerned with how their paper ranked in quality, whether it performed public service by helping people—and, importantly, whether journalists were required to perform at a high standard of excellence.

Autonomy

In your newsroom, investigate whether employees feel free to manage themselves and use their own good judgment. The McGrath study showed great dissatisfaction over *micromanagement*—heavy-handed supervision of the smallest details.

Job Demands vs. Resources

McGrath found more than 1 in 5 journalists responded negatively to these questions: Do you have access to the resources needed to do your job well? Are expectations placed on you consistently excessive? Obviously, staff cuts to protect profits left many employees feeling overworked and unable to produce quality work.

Now, check your staff's attitudes in five areas McGrath found are *not* strong predictors of satisfaction:

- *Co-worker considerations.* Staffers don't like turf battles or co-workers who don't pull their own weight. But by 3 to 1, journalists said their co-workers were qualified.
- *Compensation.* McGrath found journalists "not ecstatic" about pay and benefits but concluded "these issues were not related statistically to people's levels of job satisfaction."
- *"Team" qualities.* Journalists reported little "empowerment"—sharing of responsibility for decision-making in newsrooms. But McGrath found this not strongly related to job satisfaction.
- *Job security and "fit".* This wasn't a factor in job satisfaction, McGrath found, and journalists felt their jobs were secure and they were accepted by co-workers.

CASE STUDY 6.1 *Continued*

• *Marketing considerations.* Journalists were "strongly negative" to newspaper marketing and agreed: Newsrooms increasingly are forced to "sell out" to the business side and if journalists concern themselves too much with what readers think, the quality of their work will suffer. But these feelings were not related to overall job satisfaction.

Now, if your newsroom staff responds along those lines, what can you do? McGrath suggests: First, appoint only the best newsroom managers and train them well—the most important thing in improving job satisfaction. Second, too few promotion opportunities are available, so improve "professional and intellectual development." Third, address journalists' concern about quality, increasing their understanding that newspapers must change content and presentation because audiences are changing. Fourth, grant more autonomy to journalists. Fifth, watch for "job burnout" and ensure sufficient resources are available.

[a]"Journalist Satisfaction Study," a national study commissioned by the Associated Press Managing Editors Association and conducted by MORI Research Inc., Minneapolis, Minn., Sept. 1993.

lect one member to come forward and tell you that the air conditioning is inadequate. Or a group may form out of the purely social desire to form friendships.

Group formation can have positive or negative effects on your efforts to achieve goals. On the negative side, for example, groups can pressure individual members to reduce production, to write fewer stories per day, and thus create a slower, more comfortable pace for all reporters. As a manager, you make a mistake if you ignore the reality of such disruptive group behavior.

On the positive side, the thoughtful manager will recognize the desire for group membership is very human and that you can turn the dynamics of group behavior to good effect. Behavioral scientists find group members derive satisfaction from certain activities. For example: Membership in an elite, highly regarded group helps meet the individual's need for self-esteem and self-actualization. Creating a special team of investigate reporters can fulfill this need for members of the team; so can membership on a select task force assigned to reducing newsprint waste in the pressroom. Group membership gives the individual the perception of being part of the decision-making process, of participating in judgments that affect his or her own life. This leads to a feeling of being valued. Assigning employees to help design a new electronic news service or lay out new circulation routes they will service are example of how you can turn group activity to your advantage.

Working through groups has other advantages. It brings into play the expertise of the group and uses the natural strengths of group activity to generate ideas and collect and disseminate information.

But working through groups has its dangers. Group members tend to rally together when pressured by management, and one wrong move by you can turn an informal, loosely structured group into a disciplined, antimanagement force. Also, if improperly directed, groups can indulge in "groupthink," the tendency to avoid any controversy that might destroy group unity. That can lead individual members to subordinate their own judgments—or reservations—to the group.

And group membership can mean, for some individuals, opportunity to slip comfortably into a group to avoid full effort on the job or to avoid any decision making at all.

The Quality Circle Concept

With regularity of geese honking their way south in the fall and north in the spring, management fads sweep through American industry.

In recent years, we've had:

Total quality management, which lets employee teams devise ways of improving their own productivity.

Benchmarking, or sending employees to other companies to find new ways of solving business problems.

Process re-engineering, or dramatically revising a table of organization to create new ways of doing old things.

Broadbanding, or eliminating multiple pay scales and tying compensation more closely to each individual's performance.

Gainsharing, a team-based incentive program that groups employees in a given activity, then rewards them with part of the new business or savings they achieve.[18]

Each fad has one purpose: Find more efficient, less costly ways of doing a better job. Well, it's no longer a fad, but I like the *quality circle concept.* This concept originated in Japan and was imported to the United States in 1971 by Lockheed Aircraft. Some newspaper managers view it as an excellent tool for improving job performance by harnessing the positive strengths of group interaction and avoiding the negatives that groups sometimes create.

Quality circles are groups of 10 or so employees doing similar work who meet on a voluntary basis for an hour or so each week to solve problems in their workplace. This usually is done on company time and a member of management usually is present. The group's leaders are selected by the members and any subject except the personal affairs of other employees is open to discussion.

Quality circles at some newspapers have discussed, for example, how to arrange electronic editing terminals in the newsroom for most efficient use by staff. Others have dealt with the lighting in the workplace, how group members will share the workload, even when best to take a coffee break. Anything goes.

The aim is to improve relations between managers and employees, let employees participate in decisions affecting them and the newspaper, and elicit from individuals the valuable suggestions many would make if only they were asked.

Quality circles also give you opportunity to recognize and reward achievement, spot rising talent and consider for promotion the most capable.

Knight-Ridder uses quality circles, and tells employees frankly why. Circle members, it says, will get:

- Training in problem-solving techniques.
- An opportunity to identify/solve problems "no one seems to care about."
- A chance to "make your department and newspaper a better place to work."
- Recognition "as an expert in your work area."
- An opportunity to present recommended solutions directly to management.

However, not all group relations are smooth. Some result in conflict.

Group Conflict: Causes and Remedies

Because your manager's job includes coordinating the activities of groups as well as individuals, you must understand the sources of conflict within and between groups.

Within a group, conflict is likely to arise if there is lack of clarity on what task must be performed and when. This underlines the importance of, say, a first-level supervisor in retail advertising being crystal clear in laying out each salesperson's client list or territory. Conflict also erupts when group members have difficulty communicating with each other; hence the same supervisor should hold regular staff conferences to give salespeople an opportunity to discuss their problems—to let off steam with each other.

Conflict within a group is certain to arise if the members have widely differing interests and attitudes. A group of printers will erupt in conflict if half are serious about high-quality printing and half couldn't care less. In both instances, you must weed out the unenthusiastic.

Conflict frequently arises over competition for limited resources. You make a grievous mistake if, for example, you distribute pay increases that are dramatically uneven for members of the same group. Giving some member better tools—and, thus, a better chance to succeed—can create serious conflict, too.

Conflict between groups can arise, also. Competitive patterns often develop when two groups strive for third-party recognition or favor. For example, if two investigative reporting teams in the same newsroom strive for the editor's favor (or most of the travel budget), a competitive condition exists.

Some newspaper managers strive to create this condition. Ben Bradlee, when executive editor of *The Washington Post,* sometimes was perceived as pitting groups against each other, expecting that to improve efficiency and quality. Thus, two newsroom teams were urged to outperform each other in producing important front-page stories. It's called building "dynamic tension," a sense of controlled competition.

However, conflict—outright hostility—can develop between groups if competition gets so hot that one tries not only to outperform the other but destroy it. In many newsrooms, for example, the quarrel between different desks to get news into the paper's limited newshole can become downright vicious. The wire desk competes with the local news desk and both compete with sports.

Also, if "dynamic tension" creates too much pressure on employees, mistakes can occur. Because of such pressure at *The Washington Post,* reporter Janet Cooke was able to get past editing-desk safeguards and into print with a gripping—and entirely false—story about a child heroin addict. The story won a Pulitzer Prize, which Bradlee returned, along with public (and embarrassing) acknowledgment that his staff had made terrible errors under intense pressure to produce high-impact stories.

Is Group Conflict Inevitable?

Some management theorists say conflict between groups is inevitable. A manager's task, they say, is to control the conflict as well as possible and channel it in creative directions. Thus, you should permit group conflict in your newsroom as long as it truly creates superior reporting and writing. But if conflict begins eroding the newsroom's overall performance, you should halt it. Other theorists say conflict between groups can and must be avoided entirely if the newspaper is to move efficiently toward its goals. There are three broad paths for solving conflict:

Domination. This solution leaves one group satisfied but the other dissatisfied—an outcome not normally acceptable at any newspaper. A group of reporters who feel shunted aside in favor of another group can lose effectiveness or, worse, openly rebel.

Compromise. This is a supervisor's effort to arrive at a resolution that, although it doesn't completely satisfy everybody, doesn't leave anybody terribly dissatisfied, either. Compromise isn't the ideal solution if it leaves two groups of people smoldering with dissatisfaction.

Integration is the attempt to make everybody happy, admittedly a difficult thing. This calls out the best in any supervisor, requiring creative resolution of competing demands. Perhaps, for example, the local news desk can be given its day in the sun—major front-page display—for an important series in a compelling local story, while the wire desk is given equally prominent display later for a series on a national or international story.

One very real danger of uncontrolled group conflict is that it can create such ill will that employees turn to an outside party—a union.

UNIONS: THE MANAGER'S ROLE

If you accept management responsibility, you implicitly agree to support management attitudes and efforts. That includes helping management avoid unions or, if they are unavoidable, helping fashion a relationship with them that will ensure management attitudes prevail. The fundamental management attitude is that unions insert a third party—a union lawyer or organizer—between manager and

CASE STUDY 6.2　Standards to Plan By

You're publisher of a 50,000-circulation daily and you must lay down strategic goals for your personnel director. Where to start?

You first could order your staff structure brought in line with industry averages revealed in a 1992 Scripps Howard survey:

- You should have about 5.3 employees per 1,000 circulation.
- Payroll should be 31 to 39 percent of your total revenue.
- Benefits (insurance, vacations, etc.) should be 30 to 35 percent of total payroll.[a]

Your second strategic directive could be to reduce employee costs as a percentage of revenue. Order use of new technology to eliminate people wherever possible; also, reduce nonessential layers of managers.

Industrywide, departmental costs averaged as a percentage of revenue as shown in the pie chart below.[b]

Third, order aggressive training programs. They'll help employees be more productive and meet an almost unanimous staff demand.

A survey by the Freedom Forum found 93 percent of journalists strongly desire midcareer training, but 40 percent said their newspapers offer no in-house workshops and 31 percent said no outside seminars are offered.

Journalists want training in these subjects (in this order): ethics, writing, law of privacy, management, libel, reporting, computer-assisted reporting, editing, government/politics, freedom of information, environment.[c]

Fourth, set goals for instituting modern part-time and job-sharing policies. *The Wall Street Journal,* for example, permits employees to work part-time for up to five years after maternity/paternity/adoption leave. In 1993, *The Washington Post* had three married couples sharing foreign bureau duties.[d]

Fifth, consider seriously whether executive compensation (including yours) is out of line with what you're paying your staff. One study shows media CEOs in 1992 earned an average of $2,407,000 or *48 times* the average top pay for reporters ($50,000).

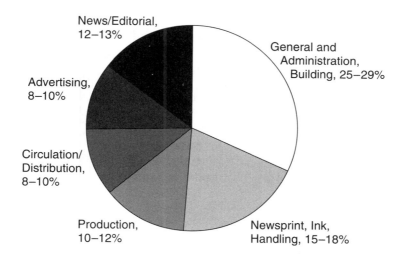

News/Editorial, 12–13%

General and Administration, Building, 25–29%

Advertising, 8–10%

Circulation/ Distribution, 8–10%

Production, 10–12%

Newsprint, Ink, Handling, 15–18%

Continued

CASE STUDY 6.2   *Continued*

At *The Wall Street Journal*, the union employees proposed shareholders vote on resolutions linking reporters' pay to that of CEO Peter Kann. That year, the union said, Kann's compensation hit $885,000, up 21 percent from 1991. Employees got a 5 percent contractual raise and the average wage was $45,000, the union said. It insisted CEO compensation be no more than 20 times the average salary for employees.

The union got nowhere—but it made a point: You'll destroy morale if you limit or cut employee salaries while enjoying huge increases for yourself.[e]

[a]"Scripps Howard General Managers Newsletter," Nov. 1992, p. 6.
[b]Ibid.
[c]"No Train, No Gain," a Freedom Forum advertisement, in *presstime*, July 1993, p. 37; note the Freedom Forum's insert in the same *presstime*.
[d]See Barbara W. Selvin, "Do Newsrooms Value Families?" *Columbia Journalism Review*, Oct. 1993, p. 42.
[e]See Graef Crystal, "The C.E.O. Factor," a compensation survey, *Columbia Journalism Review*, Nov./Dec. 1993, p. 49. Also see "Workers Propose Link to CEO Pay," *USA Today*, Sept. 9, 1993; and George Garneau, "Dow Jones Union Targets Executive Pay," *Editor & Publisher*, Sept. 25, 1993, p. 13.

employee. That reduces the manager's ability to make decisions unilaterally—to run things.

Unions are costly because they force higher wages and benefits and even can threaten a newspaper's financial stability with economic demands or strikes. In many newspapers, even first-level supervisors are expected to reject union membership for themselves and to support management. If you cannot accept that, a manager's career is not for you, because few areas of management require such deep commitment.

Despite occasional instances of cooperation, union-management attitudes come essentially from a history of tension and struggle. Management's stance primarily has been one of strong-willed owners who dominated the American newspaper scene until, in the 1960s, they began selling to communications groups. Those often highly individualistic owners built a tradition of fighting to keep wages low, to protect profits and management prerogatives.

With similar—but perhaps more subtle and realistic—determination, managers of publicly owned companies strive today to prevent union interference in those same profits and prerogatives.

Early union attitudes were set in picket-line confrontations and there won't soon be any change in the basic union attitude that the way to deal with management is to build membership in an adversarial context and bargain hard—to strike, if necessary.

Union Power Is Weakening

Union membership is dropping dramatically and, unlike in days past, most newspapers now can withstand heavy union pressure and, if necessary, continue publishing despite strikes.

Union power is waning primarily for these reasons:

- Newspaper shutdowns in large cities, where unions had their major strength. This deprived unions of thousands of members and, thus, financial support from dues.
- Technology, such as electronic editing and pagination, eliminates many union-covered jobs and, importantly, permits newspapers to publish during strikes.
- Tough, skilled managers are providing better pay and benefits and succeeding in getting unions "decertified"—rejected by unionized employees (who object, among other things, to high dues) and thrown out.

Nevertheless, unions represent an estimated 19 to 20 percent of newspaper employees, compared with 16 percent nationwide in other industries.[19] The newspaper industry was one of the first organized by unions in their heydays, in the late 1890s and early 1900s, and a union tradition continues in many newspapers, particularly metros. Some have 10 or more unions.

Unions to Watch

The *Newspaper Guild* was organized in 1933 by reporters and copy editors but also now represents clerical and advertising employees. Guild membership is dropping precipitously. In 1993, it had 26,202 dues-paying members, down from 34,828 in 1987. In 1992, the *Guild* fired four of its 14-person headquarters staff to reduce expenses.[20]

Communications Workers of America has over half a million members, mostly in other industries. It absorbed the *International Typographical Union* in 1987, as part of an effort to expand in newspapers. The ITU represented primarily composing room workers and mailers, and had been hard hit by automation. The ITU was one of the earliest—and toughest—unions in America.

Other unions include the *Graphics Communications International Union*, representing production employees, such as press operators, photoengravers, paper handlers. The *International Brotherhood of Teamsters* has fewer than 10,000 members in newspapers but can shut some down by interrupting deliveries. The Teamsters struck the *Pittsburgh Press* in 1992, and the paper was closed permanently.

Present but less active in newspapers are the *International Association of Machinists* and *International Brotherhood of Electrical Workers*. In 1992, a new union appeared in newspapers: The *United Auto Workers* won the right to represent employees of the *Sault Ste. Marie (Mich.) Evening News!* It wasn't a big win; the staff voted 25–14 in favor of the union.

Unions: Cause, Prevention, Treatment

Withdrawal of labor—the strike—is the primary weapon of any organized work force, of course. And the strike traditionally was effective against newspapers. Advertising lost during a strike is lost forever, and a newspaper's "inventory" of news and advertising cannot be built up in anticipation of a strike, as can inventory, such as autos, in many industries.

For employees, a union's basic appeal is that they are virtually powerless to influence management individually but, by combining forces, can protect and improve their lot. And, unless you address employee's fears and meet their nonmonetary but very real needs, unions can grow strong even if you provide high wages and ample benefits. Although high wages won't always prevent union activity, low wages and inadequate benefits can create morale problems that lead employees to invite unions. This is true particularly if wages are perceived as being unfairly distributed or if employees see inequity in their manager's treatment of employees.

Historically, American newspaper unions grew out of unfair, even harsh treatment in the workplace; there, they struggled almost exclusively to improve wages and working conditions. For the most part, employees didn't organize for ideological purposes. However, some unions broadened their demands. In the early 1970s, for example, the Wire Service Guild began demanding, albeit perfunctorily, a seat on the Associated Press board of directors. The Newspaper Guild demanded legislation to limit the number of newspapers a single company can own.

When union activity erupts, three factors frequently are behind discontent:

- Poor communications between managers and employees, preventing the work force from gaining any idea of where the newspaper is going, what its plans are and what goals are to be achieved. Employees cannot express their views to management or gain any voice in the way things are run.
- Management neglects—or is perceived as neglecting—adequate and fair pay, or there is a feeling that unhealthy or unpleasant working conditions exist. Management is perceived as neglecting the dignity of the individual, job security and quality of life—highly important to men and women working on newspapers today.
- There is poor, uninformed supervision, often by young, inexperienced first-level managers.

Because of the large economic stakes involved and tricky legal environment, specialized management skills are needed if the newspaper is unionized or threatened by unionization. Some newspapers with unions establish a separate labor relations department whose executives are experienced in union relations.

Unless you are alert, seemingly insignificant problems can fester, with tension among employees then overriding even good pay, benefits and working conditions. This is proven repeatedly in newspapers that paternalistically pay some of the highest salaries in the nation yet have unending labor unrest because there is no responsive communication directly between management and staff. (Quality circles can create communication by giving units of co-workers frequent contact with responsive management.)

A common error is for managers to think that because they take an enlightened attitude toward employee needs and desires, the newspaper's personnel policy automatically is being communicated correctly to the staff. But for most employees, "management" is the immediate supervisor—and if that supervisor, often young and inexperienced, cannot skillfully represent corporate policy in daily contact with your staff, your most carefully drawn personnel program will fail. Train supervisors to ensure that top management's policies are implemented and that management, in turn, receives an upward flow of employee feedback. Let the first-level supervisor, not a union official, be the "lightning rod" to hear about—and correct—employees' problems.

If your strategy for dealing with unions is formulated only when union organizers arrive in your office, it may be too late. Each manager must create a work environment that makes it unnecessary for employees to join unions. The entire human resources program—from hiring to firing—must be constructed with avoiding unions as a prime objective.

Some newspapers encourage independent—or "company"—unions because they are often less militant than international unions. *The Wall Street Journal,* for example, has negotiated for years with an "Independent Association of Publishers' Employees." Smaller newspapers often avoid organization because the relevant bargaining unit, say, a newsroom of five or six persons, is too small for an international union. But metros sometimes operate without unions, too. Both the *Los Angeles Times* and *Miami Herald* have fought off unions by offering attractive personnel policies.

In sum, union avoidance—using preventive labor relations— is an acceptable management technique. You must *not* try to defeat a union's organizing attempts illegally or discriminate against pro-union employees. Both have legal rights.

When Union Organizers Arrive

Union organizers often are invited in by disgruntled employees. They then establish local organizing committees to win support in the targeted "bargaining unit" or department before management even learns they are at work. Legal and often very effective steps can be taken to beat back organizing efforts. But your first step has to be consulting an expert labor lawyer because union-management relations must be conducted within a highly technical legal framework.

The *National Labor Relations Act of 1935*—also known as the *Wagner Act*—provides employees the legal right to join unions and bargain collectively. The *Taft-Hartley Act of 1947* protects management's rights to campaign against unions and urge employees not to join as long as certain guidelines are followed.

The *National Labor Relations Board* (NLRB), a federal agency, watches over the relationship—or, if it comes to that, the battleground. The rules are precisely defined and the NLRB has major powers. The NLRB zealously protects labor's basic right to organize and bargain collectively and will monitor attempts to organize a

newspaper, ensuring fair elections and making certain management does not inter-
fere illegally.

You cannot infringe on labor's rights without risking NLRB action. Those
rights include being able to contact and talk with individual employees in private,
free of management interference. Unions are permitted to post bulletin boards on
the newspaper's premises. Names of employees must be given to union organizers. Infringing on those rights can be costly in both money and lost management prerogatives. For example, the NLRB can force you to rehire an employee
illegally discharged, fine your newspaper for unfair labor practices and influence
every area of personnel policy.

By law, a union can petition the NLRB to schedule an employee election on
union representation if 30 percent of the targeted units's employees sign *authorization cards* designating the union as their collective bargaining representative. Organizers normally seek signatures from substantially more than 50 percent support
in any election that follows.

Managers may react vigorously (and legally), before the NLRB is petitioned,
by raising wages or changing working conditions— provided they act for proper
business reasons and without discrimination for or against any employee on
grounds of his or her union sentiments. Once a union petitions the NLRB with sufficient authorization cards, there are severe legal restrictions on what management
can say or do.

Management Must Counterattack

When an election is scheduled, management must launch a vigorous campaign to
win. Even if union organizers have been long at work, even if you and other managers have been laggard in communicating effectively with employees in the past,
you now must solve problems that inspired the organizing effort.

Campaigning by both sides often gets heated. Expect union charges that management neglected employees—underpaid and overworked them. You must respond effectively to even the wildest charge and each complaint raised. A single vote
has swung many a union election. Let no employee's complaint go unanswered.

One crucial element of the battle is precisely which employees belong in the
relevant bargaining unit. The union will attempt to include as many employees as
possible, even some you might regard as managers: desk editors with supervisory
duties, for example, or circulation employees directing other employees and handling money. Your goal must be to hold to a minimum the number of employees permitted to vote—and concentrate on persuading them to reject the union at the
NLRB ballot box.

Managers should emphasize, in daily conversations and bulletin board announcements, your desire to deal fairly and directly with individual employees,
not through an outside third party. Managers should inform workers about the
union, its financial strength, salaries of paid officers and, importantly, dues and
fees it charges each member. Such information can be obtained from forms designated IM-2 or IM-3 that each union must file in Washington with the Department

of Labor. Facts about a union often reveal quite a different picture than the one organizers paint for employees.

Managers *cannot* discharge union supporters or threaten them in any way. Raises or preferential treatment *cannot* be promised for anti-union vote. But managers can and must react vigorously in early stages of any organizing effort.

What to Do If the Union Wins

If a union wins the right to represent your employees, you have lost only the first skirmish, not the battle. The law forces management to negotiate in good faith, but *not* to accept union demands blindly. Unquestionably, however you face a dangerous new element: threat of an organized strike now is very real. Each manager, therefore, must immediately prepare to continue publication if a strike occurs. That means training supervisors or outsiders to replace employees who might strike. Assume all union employees will walk out in event of a strike. The more detailed your strike preparations are and the more obvious it is that publication can be continued, the less danger of a strike.

Your next step, with advice of legal counsel, is for your management team to construct a bargaining strategy. Supervisors should be consulted on staff feelings toward the union and the union's likely objectives. A bargaining team, normally three or four experienced, strong-willed executives, then prepares to go to the table with the union. Bargaining often is heated, lengthy and tiring. So your strategy must be developed in detail and followed carefully and coolly. Intemperate, careless moves in negotiations must be avoided.

The Prebargaining Audit

Before talks open, audit external and internal factors likely to affect bargaining. Internally, audit your strengths and weaknesses. What is the newspaper's true bargaining power? Is it financially capable of taking a strike, or if it must reach accommodation with the union, how rich a contract can it afford? Each manager, particularly first-level supervisors, should review attitude surveys, past grievances and other indicators of how strongly employees will back union negotiators. Are employees prepared to walk out or are they likely to press for a reasonable settlement?

Externally, audit public attitudes, which cannot be ignored by any newspaper. Preparing for money talks, you must forecast business conditions, inflation and unemployment to get a fix on the economic context in which any contract will be enforced. Carefully study the union's general attitudes and strategy. What agenda did it push in negotiations with other newspapers? What is the union's bargaining power? Is the international union present and supportive with negotiating expertise and money? Is a strike fund established? Valuable background on comparable contracts and settlements is available from Newspaper Association of America.

A Few Negotiating Hints

Your bargaining strategy should be firmly fixed before negotiations open. Set parameters for all economic discussions likely to occur: How much is management willing to offer in pay increases, fringe benefits and other dollars-and cents areas?

Beware of what union negotiators call noneconomic issues. They ostensibly deal with such things as workplace rules and not with money, but they can end up costing the newspaper a great deal. For example, a "noneconomic" request for two coffee breaks, not one, in the composing room means management must pay somebody extra to work during the second break. Calculate the dollar cost of that.

Pin down timing. Negotiating is fatiguing and stressful, so plan to start and end talks at reasonable hours. When should management put forward each proposal? What does management want to achieve and, frankly, what is it likely to attain? A spokesperson must be selected (and only he or she should speak for management). Some newspapers prefer the spokesperson be in insider; others call in labor lawyers or professional negotiators.

You (the CEO) may direct negotiations from behind the scenes, but stay fresh and clear-headed by keeping out of the talks and avoiding the long hours of often highly emotional confrontation with union negotiators. And by staying out, you reserve flexibility to move in at the last minute with an offer for settlement. Your negotiating team can vary in composition but must include a person thoroughly acquainted with labor law and a financial expert who can calculate the costs of various union and management proposals. Other team members can include managers familiar with operational matters being discussed.

There are countless approaches to negotiating, ranging from "take it or leave it" to the more widely used "bid and ask." The former is just that: an offer dropped on the table without negotiation. This can create political problems for union negotiators with their own members, who expect tough bargaining for advantage; it often leads to impasse and strike.

"Bid and ask" involves making an offer (which everybody recognizes as being preliminary and, thus, low), then negotiating offers and counteroffers until a mutually acceptable agreement is reached.

The management team must tailor its approach to its own objectives, strengths and weaknesses. A few things to keep in mind throughout the bid and ask process:

- Always protect management's right to manage, protect profitability, hire and fire for cause, change and improve operations, control size and composition of the staff. Unions cannot be permitted to chip away at these management prerogatives and responsibilities.
- Beware of union demands for a voice in work rules. They limit your ability to decide who works where and can lead to underutilization of employees.
- Never assume existing wages and benefits are a base and that the whole exercise is how far upward they will be negotiated. When a union takes management to the table, an entire new package of wages and benefits must be negotiated.
- Avoid automatic "escalators" in wages or benefits tied to cost-of-living increases or other external indexes. They can take your costs up at a time when your profits are going down.

- Resist attempts to win union seats on your board of directors or jointly administered pension and health plans. Both would admit the union to management's inner council and reveal its innermost secrets, destroying your flexibility in policymaking.
- Never make a concession without getting something in return. A management proposal that is greeted with a simple "no" from the union should stay on the table until the union responds in good faith with a counterproposal.
- *Never* open with your best offer. If a wage increase of $18 per week over a three-year contract is your goal, don't open with $18. Try $10.
- Keep proposals in writing and take detailed minutes of the meeting, thus preparing a record for any subsequent lawsuit or arbitration.
- Prepare package offers with wages and benefits tied to other negotiating goals. Offer, for example, the $18 weekly *if* the union gives ground by dropping demands for another vacation day. Union rejection of any single element invalidates the entire proposal and you are free to withdraw it.
- Be alert for the cumulative or "rollup" effect of fringe benefits, pay differentials for working different shifts and so on. In total, they can add substantially—easily 30 to 50 percent—to the cost of the contract, even though each in itself may appear insignificant.
- Signal the union's chief negotiator where management will go in negotiations and where it won't go. Step out in the corridor for off-the-record talks, particularly if the negotiator is a professional from the international union. Often he or she will want to get on to other things and will help you find a reasonable settlement.
- If settlement is reached, insist that union negotiators recommend acceptance to their membership. Too often, union leadership throws management's offer before its members without a recommendation for approval, hoping members will reject it and give union negotiators greater clout in a second round of bargaining.

If There Is an Impasse

If settlement is not reached, management's negotiators must tune in to the words and actions, even the body language, of their counterparts. Signals of readiness to settle may be coming across the table. A casual comment such as, "We sure hate to walk away from this table . . ." can be a signal to try once more for settlement. Absent such signals, you can try to break the logjam by stating you will make a "final offer"—maybe another dollar in wages or an extra holiday. You must truly mean you will offer no more inducements and the union must understand that.

Sometimes, management's total offer, economic and noneconomic, can be restructured to make it more attractive to the union yet no more expensive to your newspaper. For example, if management has made an offer of, say, a 10 percent pay increase over two years, perhaps each year's increase can be juggled or their effective date changed. One technique is to switch some of your total money offer to fringe benefits from pay, thus giving union negotiators something they can take back with pride to their members—a non-taxable gain, in this case.

If all else fails, the dispute can be given to a mediator from the Federal Mediation and Conciliation Service, a similar state body or a private expert in labor affairs. These professionals frequently engage directly in negotiations, shuttling back and forth between union and management hotel rooms, suggesting compromises and pointing out ways to break deadlocks. Often, their mere presence as dispassionate outsiders is enough to cool negotiators and speed solutions. *Mediation* is not biding by law, however, and you and the union still must agree on a solution. If a true impasse exists and mediation doesn't work, both parties can argue to *arbitration* which is binding.

Sometimes, if negotiators break down, management's choices are to take a strike or give in. The prebargaining audit should have answered the question, but if not, this is the time for you to decide whether your newspaper can afford a strike.

Living with the Union

Once signed, a union contract must be followed, of course. Departures from it can leave your newspaper vulnerable to lawsuit or NLRB action—and both are expensive to defend against. Even seemingly insignificant departures can be dangerous. If, for example, a supervisor agrees independently with a handful of employees to change even slightly the work rules spelled out in the contract, a "past practice" can be created. This is a practice permitted to exist over a period of time that thereby can become an accepted contract change. Any departure from contract should be made only after consultation with counsel and deep thought about its long-range implications. Management then should have a letter exchange with the union, spelling out the change and whether it is permanent.

Once under contract, management must set the tone for living with the union. Will it be a cat-and-dog fight all the way? If so, your newspaper will be a tense place to work. Some unionized newspapers strive for a harmonious relationship in which the interests of both sides are recognized. Sometimes, though infrequently, there is true cooperation, with both sides working together to achieve the same goals.

Unions Can Be Thrown Out

Living with a union need not be forever. In addition to monitoring employee organizing efforts, the NLRB oversees *decertification* of unions when at least 30 percent of the bargaining unit's employees no longer desire union affiliation. By law, it is not management but employees who must file with the NLRB for decertification. Management must stay out of the matter until decertification is under way and, even then, must avoid any offered or threats in campaigning for it.

Decertification proceedings frequently start when employees decide the union is not making gains for them. Union dues are expensive and employees may decide they can do better for themselves by negotiating with management individually. Decertification is a prime reason for unions' current loss of membership. Decertification also is caused, in part, by economic recession; union organizing efforts are less successful when employees fear for their jobs.

But in great part, newspaper management teams are creating their own successes against unions through professional personnel policies that make it more difficult for unions to find enough employee dissatisfaction to support their efforts. And newspaper managers simply are negotiating more aggressively, denying unions clear-cut victories at the negotiating table that justify, in their members' eyes, the unions' continued existence.

SUMMARY

A top priority for every young manager is learning how to manage the human element effectively. It is a core function at every level of management and at every newspaper, large or small. Expert personnel management can achieve fast improvement by quickly infusing a newspaper with new, winning talent. And because tomorrow's newspaper will be a mirror image of today's new hires, it is in personnel that a manager can put a stamp on the newspaper's long-range character.

The challenge in managing human resources, by far the newspaper's most important and costly asset is auditing the newspaper's personnel needs, planning their effective development and use, establishing policy, recruiting and hiring and then motivating. Then there is the control of performance and, at times, the distasteful but necessary job of disciplining or firing.

Motivating employees to perform according to plan, thus helping move the newspaper toward its overall goals, is a function of every manager. Its key is understanding employees' often shifting view of their needs, then helping each individual satisfy them in a manner that will benefit both the individual and the newspaper.

Challenges ahead include increasing minority hiring and promotion (an area in which many newspapers fail), and preparing for the inevitable displacement of many jobs due to automation and work force reduction.

A priority for management is union strategy—how to avoid unions or how to work with them if you must. Despite recent signs of accommodation by unions, relationships with management are based on a history of tension and struggle. The National Labor Relations Board tightly supervises union-management relations and newspaper managers are wise to seek legal advice on how to work within the guidelines.

RECOMMENDED READING

For current developments in newspaper human relations, watch *presstime* and *Editor & Publisher,* and trade journals that do an excellent job of staying abreast of newspaper operations.

The Newspaper Personnel Relations Association is an excellent source of research in human relations. It is at The Newspaper Center, 11600 Sunrise Valley Drive, Reston, Va., 22091-1412.

Outstanding research is available from the American Society of Newspaper Editors' *ASNE Bulletin* and periodic reports by The Associated Press Managing Editors, 50 Rockefeller Plaza, New York, N.Y., 10020.

Also see Paul Hersey and Kenneth Blanchard, *Management of Organization Behavior* (Englewood Cliffs, N.J.: Prentice-Hall, 1982); and Raymond Hilgert, Sterling Schoen and Joseph Towle, *Cases and Policies in Personnel/ Human Relations Management* (Boston: Houghton Mifflin, 1982).

NOTES

1. This was widely covered as symptomatic of metro newspaper troubles. A detailed wrap up is found in William Glaberson, "The Los Angeles Times Steps Back from a 'Sky's the Limit' Approach," *The New York Times*, Dec. 13, 1993, p. C-6.

2. Ibid.

3. Gannett Co. management report to annual meeting of shareholders, also reported in special supplement to *USA Today*, May 25, 1983.

4. William Glaberson, "Minority Hiring as a Financial Necessity," *The New York Times*, Nov. 30, 1992, national edition, p. C-8.

5. Ibid.

6. Celeste James, "One Voice," *Gannetteer*, Sept. 1993, p. 11.

7. Laura Dalton, "Briefly...," *Gannetteer*, Oct. 1993, p. 1.

8. Alicia C. Shepard, "High Anxiety," *American Journalism Review*, Nov. 1993, p. 19.

9. The research, by David Weaver and G. Cleveland Wilhoit of Indiana University School of Journalism, is described in "Job Discontent Rises in Newsrooms," *The Forum*, Jan. 1993, p. 7.

10. "Diversity," *Facts About Newspapers '93*, Newspaper Association of America handbook, p. 25.

11. Carolyn Terry, "The Color(s) of Power," *presstime*, Nov. 1993, p. 36.

12. "Diversity," *Facts About Newspapers '93*, op. cit.

13. "Sexual Harassment Policy Introduced," *The Morris Communicator*, Winter 1992, p. 14.

14. William Glaberson, "Gay Journalists Leading a Revolution," *The New York Times*, national edition, Sept. 10, 1993.

15. Ibid.

16. Reid Maccluggage, "Newspeople," *ASNE Bulletin*, Oct. 1992, p. 14.

17. "Scripps Howard General Managers Newsletter," Jan. 1991, p. 4.

18. These fads—and the fact that few experts find they increase productivity—are discussed in Fred R. Bleakley, "The Best Laid Plans," *The Wall Street Journal*, July 6, 1993, p. A-1.

19. Newspaper Personnel Relations Association. Also see, "Unions Feel the Heat," *U.S. News & World Report*, Jan. 24, 1994, p. 57.

20. George Garneau, "Union Clout Waning," *Editor & Publisher*, May 1, 1993, p. 16; and Mark Fitzgerald, "Facing the Future," *Editor & Publisher*, July 18, 1992, p. 7.

7

NEWS

It's time you started turning management theory into efficient daily management techniques that you can use in the newsroom. You'll need those techniques in all operational areas—including circulation, advertising, production and promotion—but we will start with news because in a very real sense news is the soul of a newspaper, its historic rationale. The newspaper's unique status among our societal institutions flows from its role in collecting and disseminating the news and information needed to keep our democracy viable. From the business perspective, of course, a newspaper's financial foundations rest on news—the quantity and quality of news sold to readers who, in turn, are sold to advertisers.

Regardless of where in newspaper operations your career starts and whatever your future responsibilities may be, understanding the news process is crucial to your success. You need not be a great reporter or editor to be a newspaper manager; you do need to understand news and how men and women who dedicate their careers to it make the news process work.

In Chapter 7 we'll discuss designing the news organization, researching and planning news content and managing newsroom resources. We'll conclude with two case studies on subjects important to your career: the competition between metro and suburban papers, and the role you would play as future editor of a "news and information center."

THE IMPORTANCE OF NEWS SUPERIORITY

Readers regard substantive news and information—in volume and detail, quality, topicality and pertinence—as the core of a newspaper's strength and appeal. Marketing research into reader habits shows newspapers *should* be entertaining and colorful, *should* be aesthetically pleasing, but *must* be newsy and informative. Nothing underlines this better than newspaper experience in the 1980s and 1990s.

In its death throes, the *Cleveland Press* was fundamentally weak in news content and tried to camouflage that with racy layout and handsomely packaged sections. The *Press* blossomed, splashing color on its front pages and, critics say, becoming a colorful "daily comic book." But bright hues did not disguise lack of basic news-gathering resources. The *Press* died.

In Minneapolis, Cowles Media Co. experimented, sometimes wildly, for five years to save its afternoon *Star,* dropping standard hard news coverage of the city council's activities, speeches and news conferences and, instead, substituting magazine-style feature "takeouts" that sometimes ran to many thousands of words. Readers seeking news gradually turned away from the *Star;* even loyal readers had not much to give up when it folded.

Newspapers die for complicated reasons and "stunting" with layouts and features did not kill the *Press* or *Star.* Rather, they were symptoms of frantic last-minute efforts to find a new lease on life. But both papers failed the basic job of a newspaper: *to inform.*

It is not enough, however, to produce a newsy, informative newspaper. *The Washington Star* was full of strong reporting and editing right up to its death; so was the *Philadelphia Bulletin* in its decades of gradual decline. The weekly *Georgia Gazette* in Savannah died the year it won a Pulitzer Prize.[1] Even a newspaper that's strong journalistically must be marketed properly if it is to succeed.

Journalistic excellence must be fashioned within an overall marketing scheme to fulfill reader needs. Marketing must exploit superior news coverage by obtaining appropriate reward—advertising and circulation revenue—for the newspaper's investment. Content must do more than discharge the newspaper's historic responsibility to cover the news and inform the public; it must do more than meet professional standards of editors and publishers. It also must meet standards set by the marketplace to ensure the newspaper's commercial viability.

BOX 7.1   What Is "Journalistic Excellence"?

Newspaper people argue a lot over how to define journalistic excellence. Is the *Seattle Times* a "better" newspaper than the *St. Petersburg Times?* Is the *Boston Globe* "superior" to the *Chicago Tribune?*

Argued that way, the basic question has a faulty premise: that there is a universally accepted definition of excellence. No such agreement exists, among editors, readers or advertisers. After all, in New York City thousands of readers buy the flashy, sometimes zany *New York Post* at the same newsstands offering *The New York Times,* with its deliberate coverage of world politics, and *The Wall Street Journal,* with

its sober reflections on money. In most cities, you can get the flamboyant *National Enquirer* and *The Star* in supermarkets, along with your local community newspaper.

Clearly, tastes differ widely among readers, advertisers and editors alike. What is good for Seattle may not be—and probably isn't—good for St. Petersburg.

The argument over "excellence" is entertaining. But don't let it divert you from the central question you must ask about your newspaper: Is this newspaper and its content right for this market at this time?

Some argue marketing news reduces the newspaper business to something akin to marketing soap—searching for a market opening, then designing a product with a special aroma to fit it—when, say these critics, newspapers should react to news, not passing whims of readers, and should let editors design news packages that meet their own professional standards.

This argument need never occur. First, editors sometimes lose touch with readers and need modern marketing methods and surveys to regain contact. Second, newspaper editors need not let marketing experts take over the newsroom. Marketing technique is one tool, old-fashioned journalistic instinct and method another.

Dallas: A Case in Point

It was *Time* magazine that dubbed it "Shootout in the Big D," triggering a spasm of Western analogy on copy desks across the country. "Shootout at the Lone Star Corral," headlined the *Washington Journalism Review*. "Texas-style Shootout at the Dallas Corral," said *Editor & Publisher* magazine.

The "shootout" was a rip-roaring fight in Dallas, one of few head-on newspaper confrontations of such intensity anywhere in the United States and, without doubt, the liveliest. The fight is instructive for aspiring managers because it involved two wealthy, marketing-oriented communications companies that assign high priority to news quality in the battle for market supremacy.

On one side of the corral was *The Dallas Morning News*, flagship of A. H. Belo Corp., a communications conglomerate then owned mainly by Texas families (and now publicly owned). On the other was the *Dallas Times Herald*, owned by Times Mirror Corp., with headquarters in Los Angeles. The shooting was over the rich Dallas market, one of the nation's fastest-growing in the 1970s and 1980s.

Times Mirror acquired the *Times Herald* in 1970 for $91 million and threw into the fight much executive talent and money, lots of money. In just five years, 1975 to 80, the paper's newsroom budget was increased 157 percent. In one six-year period, all but about 50 of 203 news staffers were replaced.[2]

Belo Corp. did not react until 1980 and then brought in, at age 29, Robert Decherd, son of a former Belo chairman, as executive vice president. One of his first moves was raiding the Associated Press and hiring Burl Osborne, its managing editor, then 43, as executive editor.

Superior News: A Marketing Weapon

The battle was fought as classic newspaper battles should be fought—over circulation and advertising turf, with superior news coverage the primary marketing weapon. Both newspapers spent heavily to hire more and better staff talent, open bureaus, assign correspondents to far-off places, launch new sections. Both scrambled for features.

Why all the fuss? Both papers, after all, were profitable; Why not relax, minimize costs and maximize profits? Well, newspaper marketing experts suspected that even rich Dallas, like most U.S. cities, one day would support only one vigorous metro daily. Osborne said at the time:

I believe the economy of the Dallas market can support two metropolitan dailies for a long time. Eventually, though, the economy will mature and no longer will have the rapid growth rates that have characterized the past two decades.

When that might happen is hard to say. . . . I do wonder, though, whether the basic character of the business is any different here than in Philadelphia or Washington or Cleveland [where metro papers failed]. An interesting question to explore is whether, in fact, metropolitan newspapers are natural monopolies and that, left in a free market, will eliminate all but one by natural selection. Further, I wonder if those conditions exist in Dallas as elsewhere, and are merely masked by the rapid growth of the economy.

I also question whether it is possible for two newspapers to compete vigorously and remain in equilibrium at more or less parity. I think one will emerge as dominant and the other as clearly in a second position. I don't think that means No. 2 must go out of business but rather that it will have to pick its market segment and concentrate on it, forgetting about trying to achieve overall superiority. . . .[3]

To the Dallas combatants, then, long-term stakes were survival, no less, and success that could be achieved only through the production of a superior news product that would increase circulation and advertising.

Simply put, *News* executives did a better job of that than did their *Times Herald* counterparts and, importantly, they marketed their product more shrewdly in consonance with Dallas and its times. By 1986, the *News* had 390,275 daily circulation, 521,727 on Sunday—and leads of 145,646 and 173,643, respectively, over the *Times Herald*. The *Times Herald's* ad share dropped to 42.7 percent and *Times Mirror* sold out (for $10 million) and left town, licked. The new owners couldn't turn the tide and they folded the *Times Herald* in December 1991.

A Look Back at Victory

In 1993, Burl Osborne, by then publisher as well as editor, analyzed the *Morning News'* triumph:

We felt the first requirement was to be active and not reactive in the competition. We concluded that we must focus on what we needed to do, and that we could not be distracted by whatever our competitor was doing. Mostly I think we were successful in that.

Next, we concluded that our market would support a newspaper of distinction, that offered high absolute and relative levels of content quality and service. This was consistent with, and helped to implement, our view that we had to be the circulation leader, especially Sunday. Around 1980, we had a small daily lead and Sunday was pretty much even. Within Dallas County and within what then was the SMSA (Standard Metropolitan Statistical Area), we trailed by substantial margins both daily and Sunday.

We believed that we must leverage our strengths and opportunities. We had the fortuitous advantage of having "morning" in our name. The AMS (morning) field opened up opportunities in both sports and business as well as in general news. Our research suggested that all of these franchise areas were up for grabs. So we invested and invested some more, in people, content, new products and promotion. But we tried never to just throw money at a problem; we always wanted to know what we would get for what we might spend. Then we priced advertising aggressively as the notion of our quality penetrated the market. We were less aggressive in circulation pricing because we wanted the growth.

We institutionalized the notion of continuous improvement. There is no finish line in the race for quality. We concluded that high production values, especially for color reproduction, would be essential for newspapers that succeed in the future. We also believed that we must maintain the deadlines that by then had given us the lead in sports as well as the press off-times that permitted circulation to achieve high satisfaction levels with delivery times. Those were central reasons for construction of a new printing plant that opened in 1985 and now is built out with eight press lines. Even with 500,000-plus daily and 800,000-plus on Sunday, our home and box edition printing window remains under three hours.

Finally, we held the course. We were not jerked around by quarter-to-quarter changes in direction. We made decisions locally, and quickly, while our competitor did not. We operated under a fairly brief set of goals that have been in place from the beginning:

1. *High quality of people, content, marketing, production, distribution and service. The notion of fair and balanced and accurate journalism is central.*
2. *Margins that are high enough to keep shareholders happy, but not so high as to preclude reinvestment in people and other resources.*
3. *Leadership in our market, industry and against all competitors.*
4. *Planning with one eye on the horizon so that short-term decisions don't imperil long-term goals.*[4]

Postscript

The *Morning News'* rewards for victory were quick: The paper's circulation increased a phenomenal 26.4 percent daily and 31 percent on all-important Sundays the year following the *Times Herald's* demise. And, the parent company's stock hit an all-time high ($46.87 a share) on Sept. 1, 1992, and profit for the year reached $37.2 million, nearly triple the prior year's results.[5]

Robert Decherd, now Belo chairman and CEO: "More than any other year in the Company's experience, 1992 validated the concept that journalistic quality and a patient business strategy will ultimately produce greater profitability then a limited, near-term focus."[6] Clearly, the *Morning News'* victory didn't just happen. It took planning and organization.

Designing the News Organization

In designing your newsroom's organizational structure and philosophy, you create an apparatus that must fashion your newspaper's relevancy to present and future readers—and that, in the process, will account for 12 to 13 percent of the newspaper's total costs.

Great care must be taken in your design, obviously. Three factors to keep in mind: First, insure the news organization's structure, personnel and attitudes effectively mirror your marketplace. Newsroom employees, their duties and titles, type of news covered, style of writing—all must meet your readers' needs. A Southern small-town daily with mainly farm readers should not staff its newsroom entirely with reporters raised in Northern big cities whose primary news interest is opera and modern dance. Some must be interested in agricultural news and high school football.

Second, integrate the newsroom into the overall marketing operation. Seat the chief news executive at top-management planning sessions and protect every editor's managerial prerogatives. A publisher who "end runs" the sports editor by telephoning compliments directly to a football writer for a story well done or who accosts a city hall reporter in the elevator for a story poorly done is a publisher who has destroyed an editor's credibility. Design a clear-cut hierarchy and make sure it is followed.

Third, design for efficient management of resources—people, time and money. Businesslike methods must be accepted routine in the newsroom as in advertising, circulation or other departments. Let's look at how two completely different newspapers design quite different news organizations.

Metro Newsroom Design

Newsday, Times Mirror's East Coast flagship, is a truly world-class journalistic product. That's the judgment of journalists but, more importantly, also of *Newsday*'s market. More than 700,000 copies of the paper are sold daily.

Newsday's primary market—affluent Nassau and Suffolk counties on Long Island—is composed of scores of upscale communities. Thousands of residents commute daily to work in New York City. That audience is demographically superior, particularly in education and household income. It demands sophisticated coverage of art, music, entertainment, books and other "culture" news, in addition to expert coverage of sports and hard news.

An unusual twist: In most big city markets, metros attack outward, chasing into affluent suburbs after affluent residents who fled the core city's socioeconomic deterioration; *Newsday*, a suburban paper that grew into a regional giant, attacks into New York City with *New York Newsday*. This competes against *The New York Times*, the market leader, but, more particularly, seeks to carve out an upscale city niche by grabbing the most affluent readers of the New York *Daily News* and *Post*.

Newsday obviously faces an enormous challenge in meeting the diverse news needs and desires of an audience so geographically dispersed and demographically sophisticated. A multifaceted newsroom design is the result. At the top, the newsroom management hierarchy is heavier than at many newspapers and, importantly, *Newsday* editors have strong voices in corporate affairs. The editor, for example, is one of three corporate senior vice presidents, and among general management executives is listed below only the publisher/CEO and associate publisher. That's a clear signal that in addition to running the newsroom, *Newsday*'s editor has concurrent responsibilities on an integrated management team that designs and executes overall strategy. The two other senior vice presidents represent finance and marketing.

Newsroom Lines of Authority

In the newsroom, authority descends from the editor/senior vice president to first-level supervisors along both subject and geographic lines. For example, the next six executives on the ladder are a vice president/editorial administration (budgeting, personnel matters, etc.), the editorial page editor, the *New York Newsday* editor and three managing editors—for operations, news and *New York Newsday.*

There are eight assistant managing editors—for investigations (*Newsday*'s investigative reporting is superb), business news, Long Island, *New York Newsday*, national/foreign news, features. Two assistant managing editors carry no specific subject title. Thirty-six other editors handle special-subject coverage—environment, entertainment, education, books, food, travel and so forth. Geographic areas are assigned to individual editors—New York state's capital bureau, Albany; New York state news and Suffolk County.

Newsroom Design for Smaller Papers

For smaller papers, newsroom design can be much less complicated. Figure 7.1 on page 194 shows the structure at the *Columbus (Ga.) Ledger-Enquirer,* which has 56,000 daily and 70,000 Sunday circulation.

The *Ledger-Enquirer*'s top newsroom manager has a corporate title and responsibilities, as does *Newsday*'s. The *Ledger-Enquirer* is a Knight-Ridder paper, and that company is a strong proponent of including editors in an integrated, newspaper-wide total marketing effort. In Columbus, the executive editor concurrently is a newspaper vice president and member of a five-person management team that designs overall strategy.

Note in Figure 7.1 that just two newsroom executives report directly to the executive editor—the editorial page editor and managing editor. The managing editor, responsible for day-to-day creation of the news product, has enormous responsibilities that, as at *Newsday,* span both subject and geographic areas. Subject areas, however, are straightforward and, compared to *Newsday*'s design, few: sports, photos, hard news (under the "news editor"), arts/entertainment, food, features, business.

For a paper its size, the *Ledger-Enquirer* has complicated geographic areas to cover. Its circulation spills over into neighboring Alabama, so the paper maintains a bureau in Auburn-Opelika, Ala. It shares an Atlanta, Ga., bureau with sister Knight-Ridder papers in the state, in Macon and Milledgeville, and a Washington bureau. Other areas' responsibilities are uncomplicated. Individual editors are in charge of news from the Columbus metro area, city, state and nearby LaGrange, Ga.

Key responsibilities under the executive editor and managing editor are signaled by titles that carry "clout": executive sports editor, assistant managing editor

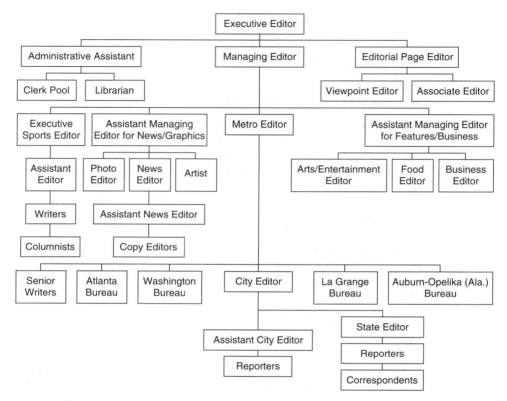

FIGURE 7.1 *Columbus (Ga.) Ledger-Enquirer* **newsroom organization, as adapted from information provided by Publisher Billy Watson.**

for features/business and assistant managing editor for news/graphics (note the latter integrates control of news stories and accompanying graphics under one editor's control).

A key feature of the *Ledger-Enquirer*'s newsroom design: It isn't top heavy with executives. The design is lean, efficient and consistent throughout with the paper's small circulation and its market, which is uncomplicated, compared to *Newsday*'s.

Design News into Marketing

Large or small, newspapers must truly integrate the newsroom into the overall marketing thrust. Important: Design to facilitate two-way communication between news and other departments. Unlikely as it seems today, this is a fairly new concept. As recently as a decade or so ago, for example, many editors had no idea what their newspapers' revenue, costs or profits were.[7]

As we've seen, *Newsday* and the *Ledger-Enquirer* solved that problem by giving the top editor concurrent corporate responsibilities. But many newsrooms still are isolated from the commercial realities of newspaper life—and how can their editors, lacking any overall understanding, feel they are equal partners in a team effort? Frequent meetings between publisher and editor help break down such barriers, as does automatic inclusion of the editor in cross-departmental strategy sessions. The alternative to such integration is an isolated newsroom "doing its own thing" and not efficiently supporting the marketing concept.

While directing news coverage and getting the next edition on the streets, the editor—as a member of management's strategy team—simultaneously must look 10 years ahead to the future shape of the newspaper. Add the need for wise expenditure of, sometimes, tens of millions of dollars annually in a newsroom budget, and the chief news executive's responsibility assumes awesome proportions. It's a stressful job (see Box 7.2).

Just as news executives must be involved in operational areas outside news, so must other managers—particularly in circulation and advertising—be kept current on what news is doing.

BOX 7.2   Stress Goes with the Turf

Editors say they enjoy their work, finding it challenging and well paid; but they warn that stress-related health problems go with the job. Of 902 editors responding to an Associated Press Managing Editors Association survey, 39 percent report health problems they believe linked to job-related stress: 33 percent specify ulcers, asthma, hypertension, cancer, heart disease, arthritis, stroke, alcoholism, or drug abuse. Most editors report being stimulated by the need to meet deadlines, manage newsroom competition between highly talented newspaper people and produce quality newspapers.

Their biggest frustrations come from bosses who ignore their advice and weaken their power or who decline to allocate sufficient resources to do the required journalistic job. Major stress follows any conflict with a boss who compromises newsroom integrity with decisions aimed only at producing higher profit.

Stress also comes from a fundamental change in their job function. Robert H. Giles, as editor of Gannett's *Detroit News,* supervised the survey. He explained at the time:

Fifteen years ago, editors were editors. Today, they are editor-managers. They direct the editing of the newspaper with one hand and, with the other, they are deeply involved in business management.

The editor is expected to carry on in the best traditions of journalistic excellence, but also is expected to share responsibility for the newspaper as a "profit center." Many editors discovered that this dual obligation created unfamiliar stresses, stresses born of a conflict between the need to be good and the need to be lean.

You'll note the irony: Gannett later gave Giles the dual title of "publisher and editor"—with full responsibility for *both* business and news operations.

Most editors report working more than 40 hours weekly: 22 percent say they put in 40 to 45 hours; 34 percent, 46 to 50 hours; 25 percent, 51 to 55 hours; 18 percent, more than 55 hours; and 53 percent say they work more than five days weekly, often at home.

Stress or no, jobs as editors of America's leading newspapers are highly coveted, and for each there are hundreds of eager aspirants.

Caution: Involvement in news by managers from outside the newsroom is a sensitive subject for many editors. Such editors say news must be covered almost instinctively in accord with standards developed through experience by professional reporters and editors and that intrusion by the "business side"—with its marketing, advertising and circulation considerations—is disruptive at best, prejudicial at worst.

This is a historic and very strong feeling, deeply rooted in some newsrooms, that stems in part from examples—every newspaper person knows several—of coverage being distorted for business reasons. As an aspiring manager, you must understand that this feeling pervades the very psyche of many experienced editors. It must be dealt with sensitively and carefully. But it cannot prevent dovetailing the newsroom, its executives and its goals into the newspaper's overall mission.

Design Research into News Values

The marketing concept requires, of course, tight focus on meeting reader needs, hence newsroom managers at all levels must research precisely what those needs are and then plan carefully to fulfill them.

As discussed in Chapter 2, you must know the geography of your market and who lives there. You must now go beyond that, into a detailed audit of reader and nonreader thinking, interests and attitudes—plus systematic research into how the newspaper as a product relates to them (Table 7.1).

It is important, for example, to research how readers are likely to receive change—a new section, a new feature, redesign of content. In Dallas, Burl Osborne recalls once trying to save space in the *Morning News* by not running in all editions high-school sports results from throughout the sports-crazy city. For one day, results were "zoned"—included only in editions sent to areas near the school mentioned. "The readers damn near stormed the gates," Osborne says, "and we repented the very next day."[8]

Aside from subjecting the newspaper's gates to such wearing trial-and-error methods, you have other means of sampling readers and nonreaders.

BUY RESEARCH OR DO IT YOURSELF

Research aids range from complex and expensive to simple and cheap: *Professional readership studies*, for those papers able to afford them, provide valuable guidance through personal, in-depth interviews with scientifically selected probability samples of the public. Such studies can be expensive and take months to conduct and analyze. Papers such as the *Los Angeles Times* spend millions researching reader and advertiser attitudes. This type of research is so important that many companies, Dow Jones among them, acquired their own research firms.

Subscriber questionnaires can be published in smaller newspapers or mailed to readers (and nonreaders), if your corporate purse requires do-it-yourself surveys.

TABLE 7.1   **Well-managed newspapers conduct detailed research into their audience, for use by advertisers and editors. Note the detailed demographic information that Gannett's** *Rochester (N.Y.) Sunday Democrat and Chronicle* **publishes on its readers. Reprinted by permission of the** *Sunday Democrat and Chronicle.*

	Readers	% Composition
Total	500,000	100%
Sex:		
Male	239,900	48%
Female	260,100	52%
Women Employed	144,600	56%
Age:		
18–24	59,500	12%
25–34	107,700	21%
35–44	108,800	22%
45–54	79,600	16%
55–64	53,400	11%
65+	91,100	18%
Median Age	*42.6 years*	
Household Income:[a]		
Less than $25,000	118,300	27%
$25,000–$34,999	68,200	16%
$35,000–$49,999	95,400	22%
$50,000–$74,999	93,000	22%
$75,000 +	56,100	13%
Median HHI	*$39,550*	
Education:		
High School Graduate and less	180,100	36%
Some College/Technical	133,500	27%
College Graduate +	182,100	36%
Race:		
White	454,000	91%
Black	31,900	6%
Household Characteristics:		
Married	311,600	62%
Two-Income	123,000	25%
Own Home	373,300	75%
Have Children (under 18 years)	196,000	39%
Live in Monroe County	422,400	85%

[a]Composition based on those responding. Note: Some columns may not add to 100% due to rounding or some other response not displayed. Source: 1993, SRBI./Base: 648,700 NDM adults

Affordable research expertise can be as close as the nearest business or journalism school.

Circulation department feedback is invaluable. This department contacts readers and nonreaders daily, yet many newspapers have no systematic feedback to the newsroom. Every subscriber who halts delivery should be asked why; every non-subscriber who declined the paper should be asked why; and the news department should hear why.

Reader complaints or praise should be analyzed carefully. Letters plus memos on telephone calls should be circulated to editors as indicators (not, of course, totally reliable proof) of public mood.

Encounter groups provide excellent feedback if true cross-sections of readers are selected. Some papers hold coffee-and-doughnut meetings so editors and readers can discuss the newspaper in depth. Knight-Ridder's *Detroit Free Press* had its group study a competing paper, *USA Today*. (The 78-person study group liked *USA Today*'s color reproduction, shorter stories and TV listings but not its lack of local news and local advertising.)

Personal contacts number in the hundreds each week for managers of even a small paper—and each manager should listen to what is said about the newspaper.

Newsroom managers should be involved in such research from start. The goal is information needed to operate effectively, and news managers should help decide what that is. But also, editors tend to deprecate as inaccurate—or reject as interference—readership research in which they have no part.

Research IS Needed

Editors and publishers clearly need scientific research. Surveys repeatedly show that instinctive interpretation by both of reader views on news often can be very wrong.

A Lou Harris poll, for example, shows that publishers often hold news values quite different from those of their readers: 19 percent of publishers said readers are very interested in international news, while 49 percent of readers said they were; 98 percent of the publishers said readers are very interested in local news, but only 72 percent of readers said they were.[9]

Editors don't score much better in a survey by United Media Enterprises, a Scripps Howard company: 92 percent of 101 senior editors polled said it is very important for a newspaper to provide community information, but of 1,000 members of the general public polled, only 76 percent agreed; 81 percent of the editors rated national/international developments a close second, but only 69 percent of the public agreed; 73 percent of editors said analyzing complex issues is a very important newspaper function, while only 42 percent of the public agreed.[10] Unless they are careful, then, publishers and editors can produce newspapers that appeal to them or other publishers and editors yet miss the public's desires by a wide margin.

Working journalists, editors and reporters on the beat often err, too. For example, seminal work on the public's view of newspapers was done by 16 newspaper organizations in the Newspaper Readership Project. Journalists were found to be so fundamentally misjudging the public's reading and lifestyle habits as to raise questions whether they could produce newspapers precisely tuned to their audiences: News staffers estimated 51 percent of adults read a newspaper on an average day, at a time when research placed the national average at 67 percent; news staffers estimated front-page readership at 89 percent, while research placed readership of an average hard news item at less than 50 percent.

Journalists generally overestimated by far reader interest in sports, nongovernmental local news, fashion, food, society, homemaker topics, celebrities, and personalities and they substantially underestimated interest in national government, environment and energy news. In practice, many news executives combine careful research with a news instinct born of years in the business.

Recommendations for using both, and a warning against sole reliance on surveys, come from Harold W. Andersen, then president of the *Omaha (Neb.) World-Herald:*

> *Surveys often give conflicting signals—quite different answers when the same basic question is phrased differently and sometimes very vague or generalized answers from those being surveyed.*
>
> *Personally, I rely less on surveys (although we do surveys) than on keeping my eyes and ears—and mind—open to all signs of what interests the people of Omaha and our region. . . . This "feel" for the needs and interests of our readers can be developed in a variety of ways, including surveys and occasional luncheon meetings with various groups of readers. Another useful source: A careful reading of the newspaper itself, observing what writers are telling us in letters to the editor, what people are asking from their school board and city council and the state legislature, what various neighborhood groups are discussing at their meetings and what goods and services are being offered by advertisers in response to, or in development of, various consumer needs and tastes.[11]*

Whatever your methodology, you need detailed, accurate research in hand before embarking on your principal function as a manager: planning.

PLANNING IN THE NEWSROOM

Newsroom planning is a multidimensional responsibility for the manager. Two broad areas are most important:

- Planning effective use of human resources. *No* newsroom can rise above the quality of its staff, and every newsroom manager's first responsibility is planning recruitment, hiring, training, motivation and effective use of top-caliber people.
- Planning overall journalistic tone and the drive for quality.

A Planning Checklist for Quality

Let's look at a manager's checklist for planning journalistic superiority. We'll relate it to what Burl Osborne does at the *Morning News* in Dallas.

Make Financial Commitment

There is no cheap route to journalistic superiority. In the first two years of Osborne's editorship, Belo Corp. doubled the *Morning News'* newsroom budget. The company then spent continuously—but wisely—until it won in Dallas. To correct journalistic weakness, then build a winning product, newsroom executives must have sufficient financial resources.

Strengthen Newsroom Management

Stealing Osborne from AP is only one example of Belo's aggressive search for management talent. The *Baltimore Sun* was raided for Carl Leubsdorf, a skilled political writer who became the *Morning News'* Washington bureau chief. Dave Smith, superbly talented editor of *The Boston Globe*'s prizewinning sports section, was recruited as sports editor. Other talented managers were found in newsrooms across the country.

Strengthen Newsroom Staff

This often, but not always, requires additional personnel. It *always* requires upgrading the staff's experience and ability—its general talent. In three years, the *Morning News* expanded its news staff to nearly 300 from 185. Says Osborne: "It is a matter of stated practice that any replacement must raise the level of the given position...."[12]

Cover the Ground

The best way to cover news is to have people there when it breaks. When Osborne joined the *Morning News* it had bureaus in Fort Worth, Austin, Houston, Mexico City and Washington. In three years, it opened new bureaus in San Antonio, El Paso (to cover West Texas), Tyler (East Texas), Mid-Cities (between Dallas and Fort Worth), Plano (a demographically attractive growth area north of Dallas), North Dallas, Toronto, New York City, Tel Aviv, and Oklahoma City. The Washington bureau's new chief expanded his staff to seven from three, and the state capital bureau in Austin was strengthened.

Few newspapers are able—fewer are willing—to spend the enormous sums necessary for such sudden bureau expansion or provide newshole for additional coverage. But you must identify your newspaper's area of *opportunity*, where investment in staff will bring appropriate return, and its area of news *responsibility*, which must be covered if the newspaper is to claim journalistic validity. Then you must plan for sufficient reporters on the ground.

Reexamine Coverage Strategy

Frequent and fundamental reexaminations of which areas are covered and why are mandatory, because, as you have seen, a market's demographic character can shift rapidly. For reader and advertiser alike, management must move quickly into areas of new opportunity.

The *Morning News* made a major staff expansion into rapidly growing high-income suburbs south, north and west of Dallas.

Reexamine Newspaper Structure/Content

Just as demographics shift rapidly, so do readers' needs. Managers must frequently sample readers plus nonreaders and produce newspapers for them, not for other editors and not just because that's the way newspapers always were produced.

The *Morning News* overhauled its content and structure in what Osborne calls *internal zoning*. It blossomed with new sections, new features, new approaches to coverage—from local high school sports to international oil news.

Improve Packaging/Layout

Internationally renowned for journalistic quality and businesslike precision, *The Wall Street Journal* sells extremely well to its special audience (nearly 1.8 million copies daily in 1995) despite layout and design that are yet to emerge from the 18th century. Few newspapers, in this era of television and color, could do so. The *Morning News* redesigned to use color and catch readers with a wider, more open appearance. Attractive packaging, well-edited photos and graphics are musts.

Plan for Hard News

Research into reader desires sent shifting signals to newspaper editors over the past two decades. One leading researcher, Ruth Clark, found readers in the late 1970s most wanted "local" news—useful news to help them cope with a complicated world. Clark's research was clear: Readers wanted newspapers better organized, easier to read, more relevant to their lives, more personal—and less time-demanding.

This research kicked off a new approach to newspaper design, including integration of written copy with photos, charts, and graphics of all kinds to give readers better, quicker comprehension. *USA Today*'s colorful, snappy design, revolutionary for its time, was one result. Many of *USA Today*'s design innovations are incorporated in newspapers across the country today.

Clark's continued research found reader desires in the 1980s shifting to "hard" news—daily, fact-filled coverage of such things as health, science, technology, diet and nutrition, and child-rearing—as contrasted with soft, featurish coverage of less essential subjects. Clark also found a desire for a broadened mix of local, national, state and regional news. Clark attributes the reader shift to the many traumatic events that occurred between surveys: U.S. inflation and recession, unemployment, international crises.

The studies, both sponsored by the American Society of Newspaper Editors, underline how quickly reader views can change and how editors, and the entire marketing effort, must move quickly with them. One controversy is whether readers, distrustful since Vietnam of distant conflicts and large institutions, are turning inward, restricting their news interests to local life; indeed, some say the reader wants only local news—Main Street, not Afghanistan; school boards, not the United Nations. All this inspires a paroxysm of seminars and studies dedicated to the proposition that if it is not "local," it is not relevant news.

Define "Local" Broadly

Too often, "local" is given a parochial geographic definition: If it does not happen within the city limits, its news value is suspect at best. Calmer heads should prevail. "Local" should include any news development anywhere that affects "local" life.

Your challenge is building a staff capable of sifting through the world of news and extracting those items—regardless of dateline or subject—with bearing on the lives of your newspaper's readers, then reporting and writing those stories to properly highlight their relevance and meaning. A guerrilla war in Afghanistan *is* of "local" importance if it might someday involve U.S. tax dollars and young Americans; a school bond fracas in California has meaning in Newark if it parallels school controversies in New Jersey.

Hard news is what newspapers should be all about in the 1990s. The earlier preoccupation with soft, featurish approaches was, in part, an overreaction to the perceived threat of television. Electronic journalism, some thought, would take the edge off hard news, leaving newspapers to featurish, in-depth, "explanatory" journalism. That proved wrong. Television has not become a satisfactory news medium—although, of course, a great many viewers perceive it as satisfactory.

Many leading newspapers that virtually became magazinelike are swinging back to hard news. It is a return to what a football coach might call the fundamentals, the journalistic version of blocking and tackling—precision identification of important issues plus in-depth reporting and clear writing that explains the news in terms meaningful to readers who are overwhelmed by daily developments. Surveys repeatedly show readers seeking information to help them cope, to handle complex social and economic problems.

Plan "Showcase" Improvement

Plan for news superiority in these showcases.

Front Page

The explosive growth of "inside" sections—lifestyle, business and so forth—rivals the front page for reader attention. But the front page still is where the day's best stories and photos are displayed and is extremely important in establishing public perception of the newspaper. The tone for the entire paper is set on the front page. It is a reader lure that the newspaper's best layout designers should construct carefully.

One commendable change at many newspapers is to open the front page to all types of news, not just stories from Washington, London or state capitals. Smart editors "front" outstanding stories—business, sports, real estate—that in the past were consigned to deep inside play regardless of news merits.

Business Section

Probably the greatest single improvement in recent years is in business, financial and economic news. This responds to how everyday life is influenced for millions of Americans by the money supply, interest rates, the Federal Reserve Board and other esoteric business once thought meaningful only to stockbrokers and bond traders.

But smart editors also know that outstanding business coverage can deliver readers who are demographically attractive to advertisers. Business coverage is not only necessary if a newspaper is to discharge its obligations to readers—it also is good business. Make sure your business reporters are skilled "interpreters," capable of reducing highly complex stories to understandable terms meaningful to readers.

Editorial Page

As the front page showcases your newspaper's best reporting, the editorial page displays its conscience. Unfortunately, some newspapers attempt to serve all factions with dispassionate editorials exploring all sides of an issue, never venturing to express an opinion. The result is deadly dull editorial pages and a withering of the leadership spirit many newspapers once displayed to the good of their communities. To assert leadership, a newspaper should explore thoughtfully all dimensions of a subject but then take a hard-hitting stand that makes a choice. Op-ed pages are expanding as reader soapboxes featuring guest writers, letters to the editors and columnists.

Sports Sections

Sports fans are insatiable. They want to know who batted first in the fourth inning of a local Little League game, as well as the sports editor's opinion on the Super Bowl. And, these sports fans, though difficult to satisfy, are a hard core of readers cherished by newspaper editors the country over. To meet the fans' needs, expanded sports sections carry yards of statistical material plus in-depth, analytical behind-the-scenes coverage. With television showing the game in living color, newspapers must not rush out with who won—but how they won.

"News of Record"

The newspaper is the best easily accessible source of life's statistical detail in any community. It alone records births, school graduations, marriages, deaths. Regardless of your newspaper's journalistic character or overall mission, you must devote significant resources to providing news of record.

Plan Special Sections

It is a formidable task to sift the entire range of newsmaking events, collating and packaging the most important in orderly fashion for readers with many news interests, needs and desires. Planning the hard news elements is comparatively simple. The day's top story often is obvious and gets page one's top spot; the number two story gets subordinated and so forth.

But how to handle thousands of other important stories that pour in daily? In many newsrooms the answer is an explosive but carefully planned proliferation of special sections. Special sections give you strength in two areas:

- They permit in-depth reporting of subjects of compelling interest to some—but not all—readers. Many newspapers, for example, run weekly sections variously titled "Wheels" or "Autos" or "Style," "Fashion," "Entertainment" and so forth. There are readers out there eager to learn the horsepower and other precise details of the newest sports cars. Many readers would be bored stiff by such coverage, so meet the car buffs' needs in special selections or "pullouts."
- Special sections, of course, also are perfect vehicles for advertisers. Car dealers courting car buffs know they are getting a targeted audience in "Wheels"; department and clothing stores flock to "Style" and "Fashion."

Most newspapers carry seasonal special sections or run special editions tied to shopping patterns. Seasonal sections are designed principally as advertising vehicles, and at many newspapers are edited by the advertising department or other non-newsroom personnel.

Testimony to the value of seasonal special sections: *Newsday* runs at least 76, including such favorites as "Back to School" and "Holiday Gift Guide" but also showing innovative planning, with such as "Kitchen & Bath," "Nurse Recruitment" and "College Directory." The smaller *Columbus Ledger-Enquirer* schedules about nine seasonal special sections—"Bridal" in February, "Football" in August and so forth.

Importance of Sunday Planning

Sunday newspapers—attractive, bulky and profitable—are the single most important edition for many managers and are sure to become even more important. Sunday papers grew explosively in numbers after World War II, while their Monday through Saturday brethren were shrinking (see Table 7.2).

Sunday growth results in large measure from advertiser awareness that readers have more time to leaf through their papers on Sundays and thus can be exposed to more ads for longer times. And the Sunday paper can be designed to "pull" all occupants of a household—children, in for comics today but serious readers tomorrow; teenagers, prime targets for advertisers because they are big

TABLE 7.2   Sunday Papers Growing Rapidly

	1946	1993	Change
Daily papers	1,763	1,570	−193 (−10.9%)
Sunday papers	497	893	+396 (+79.6%)
Daily circulation	50,927,505	60,083,265	+9,155,760 (+17.9%)
Sunday circulation	43,665,364	62,542,031	+18,876,667 (+43.2%)

Source: Newspaper Association of America

spenders; homemakers, who—with their food and other expenditures—virtually control the budget in most households; and heads of household who make "big-ticket" purchases—cars, boats, houses.

The Sunday paper is so popular with advertisers that its ad content outruns ads in Monday–Saturday papers. Total ad content in 1992 was 66.3 percent on Sunday, 55.3 percent in daily morning papers, and 54.8 percent in evening papers (it was 58.8 percent for all papers—morning, evening and Sunday).[13] Sunday ad lineage is 22 to 35 percent or more of some metros' total for some weeks. Circulation often runs substantially ahead. For the *Dallas Morning News* it is 54.4 percent higher; for the *Philadelphia Inquirer,* it is nearly *double* weekday circulation.

The Sunday paper's contribution to total revenue is a tightly held secret in most management suites, but for some it's 30 to 40 percent. Costs for a bulky Sunday paper can run 30 percent or more higher than for a weekday edition, but the Sunday paper still often delivers a higher percentage of profit.

The title "Sunday Editor" is escalating in pecking-order importance in hundreds of newsrooms. The Sunday editor's challenge is quite different from that of daily newspaper colleagues. The Sunday editor must plan to cover spot news breaking Saturday for Sunday and also sum up, with in-depth analysis, the past week's top news for thousands of readers not taking the daily paper. The Sunday editor must project ahead into what the coming week's news might be and delve into areas that are outside the news mainstream but are of compelling interest to demographically upscale readers: the arts, food, wine, books, "inside" business and sports, travel—all the informative esoterica that draws leisurely Sunday readers.

This requires an acute sense of timing. To spread out printing demands and not strain press facilities, the Sunday editor plans to put many relatively timeless sections "to bed" early in the week or, sometimes, weeks ahead.

The hard news content of many Sunday papers shrinks as their sheer bulk forces earlier press times for even the front page ("Sunday" editions become available early Saturday evening in many cities). But to be valid as a *news*paper, the Sunday edition must have substantial hard news content, and that demands vigilant last-minute monitoring of news agency wires and local spot news beats before the presses roll on Saturday.

Because of this timing problem and the Sunday reader's leisurely reading habits, the Sunday paper is evolving strongly toward background and entertainment copy. That gives rise to special Sunday feature writers, columnists, book and arts reviewers, and home maintenance specialists—and the Sunday magazine.

Not long ago, many newspapers produced their own local Sunday magazines. Today, few do, because weekly magazines tend to simply bleed ad revenue from other sections, rather than produce new revenue. Weekly magazines also tend to degenerate into second-rate journalistic efforts. Many Sunday editors, therefore, contract to carry nationally distributed *Parade* or *USA Weekend* (formerly *Family Weekly*).

In sum, the weekly magazine generally proved too costly for results delivered. As in all things journalistic, magazines that are poorly executed detract from editorial quality throughout the paper and are expensive. It will be safer for you, an aspiring manager, to learn it here, in this book, rather than in the real world of newspapering: Your newsroom planning must safeguard against wasteful spending. Failure to learn that early can cost you heavily when you launch your career. Wanton spending isn't permitted.

HOW TO MANAGE NEWSROOM RESOURCES

A newsroom manager commands four basic resources. You must employ each with telling precision:

- First, *human resources*. Any newsroom manager responsible for more than two staffers is a manager of people—and their time—as much as an editor or journalist. If you don't like managing people, solving their problems and motivating them to produce, you don't belong in management. Most of your time will be spent making sure their time is used efficiently and effectively.
- Second, *money* for salaries, bonuses, travel—money to get the right people in the right place at the right time.
- Third, *external resources,* such as news services and syndicates, all major contributions to any newspaper's content (and costs).
- Fourth, the *newshole,* precious space accorded the newsroom for each day's coverage, from Afghanistan to Main Street, from politics to "Dear Abby."

From an editor's view, there never is enough of the four; the business office often feels there *is* enough. That difference of opinion can preoccupy both news and business managers.

Managing Internal Resources

In the newsroom as elsewhere in the newspaper, your basic task is to recruit the staffers required (or permitted by the budget), train and motivate them to perform in accord with plan, then control and adjust their performance. Chapter 6 covers principles of the basic human resources task. We will zero in here on specific newsroom issues.

It's often said you need one staffer per 1,000 circulation. But that's a rule of thumb not applicable everywhere: Newspapers employ anywhere from 0.7 staffers per 1,000 circulation to 1.4 or more. The difference ties back to two issues: First, the overall strategic goals of the newspaper, its competitive strength and the financial strength it enjoys and is willing to commit. In a competitive fight, with a goal of winning through superior news coverage, more staff obviously must be employed. In its drive for market supremacy, the *Dallas Morning News* added staffers so quickly that the ratio dropped from nearly one staffer per 1,000 circulation to about one per 950 in just months. Second, the state of the newspaper's technology. When first introduced, new technology tended to reduce the newsroom staff through automation. However, subsequent automation in production and other departments shifted to the newsroom new functions in manufacturing the newspaper as well as producing journalistic content. That tends to force increases in newsroom staff.

Training for Quality Results

The newsroom manager aggressively recruits the most talented staff available, of course. But then what?

Proper training can have great impact on quality performance. In-house training by senior reporters or editors is fine, but in reality deadline pressure often limits the number of experienced trainers available. Key staffers should be given outside training.

Some of the best programs available are at the following:

- Newspaper Association of America, The Newspaper Center, 11600 Sunrise Valley Drive, Reston, Va. 22091.
- American Press Institute, 11690 Sunrise Valley Drive, Reston, Va. 22091. (Strong on training for small-paper community journalism.)
- National Newspaper Association, 1627 K St., NW, Suite 400, Washington, D.C. 20006. (Its members are weekly and small daily newspapers and it often conducts programs with state press associations.)
- Inland Press Association, Suite 802 West, 840 N. Lake Shore Drive, Chicago, Ill. 60611.
- Southern Newspaper Publishers' Association, 6065 Barfield Road, Suite 222, Atlanta, Ga. 30328.
- Suburban Newspapers of America, 111 E. Wacker Drive, Chicago, Ill. 60601.

Trained news specialists can yield great dividends in readership. The general-assignment reporter, the journalistic switch-hitter who (some say with varying degrees of accuracy) quickly can get atop just about any type story, is still welcome in the newsroom. But in covering and "translating" enormously complex stories in law, medicine, science and other highly technical areas, a reporter must have solid academic background or proven expertise, developed on the beat, in reading or patient, time-consuming digging.

Indeed, with newspapers dispensing advice on everything from health of the heart to health of the mind, stories are too crucial to life itself to be left to amateurs.

Planning Staff Time Carefully

With salaries rising steadily and the work week getting shorter, the newsroom manager must budget staff time for effective use of every minute. A reporter hanging around the coffee machine waiting for the next assignment is a valuable resource not being used effectively. A copy desk without time management will be overstaffed at some times and understaffed at others.

Union contracts or company policy establish work regulations—how many hours, how many days, whether the night-side staff works fewer hours than the day side, how much vacation time to grant and so on. But within the confines of such policy, each newsroom manager must establish detailed time management. A few essentials:

Time is money, and you never have enough of either. Look upon time, yours and the staff's, as one of your most valuable resources. Don't waste it.

Lay down a written plan for how your staff will be employed. Schedule workdays and hours in advance, two weeks or more, if possible, so employees can organize their personal lives and lay down their time management plans.

Write a daily budget assigning each on-duty staffer. Be specific: story (or other task), time, location, approximate time to be spent, results expected.

Be demanding. It's your managerial responsibility to obtain optimum payback from every resource utilized. Demand effective payback for time spent.

Caution:

Newspapers don't manufacture widgets and newsroom staffers aren't unthinking robots paid for piecework. Creativity is the newsroom's business, and it doesn't come in planned, predictable bursts Monday through Friday, 8 A.M. to 5 P.M. Be flexible in time management, and when you smell a good story let them run after it without punching a time clock. And be prepared for them to come back dry occasionally, without the story; that's the news business.

Reporters, writers and editors are highly individualistic in talent and abilities. Consider each staffer's very own strengths and weaknesses and budget time accordingly. Staffer A will whip through a complicated financial story in no time flat; Staffer B will sweat for hours over it. In news, unlike a factory production line, a body is not just a body.

Plan Your Money Management Carefully

Even on small papers editors today spend a great deal of money; unless you can handle it effectively, you don't qualify for newsroom management. A basic accounting course gets you over "math fright" and enables you to construct a budget as an evaluation and control tool. But to employ newsroom funds effectively, you must learn through experience where to use your money resources and when.

How much money is enough? That depends on the newspaper's overall financial condition and its goal in journalistic quality and profit. Editors of the largest papers spend many millions annually; editors of smaller dailies and weeklies obviously make do with considerably less. As you learned in earlier chapters, newsroom costs industrywide are about 12 to 13 percent of a newspaper's total *costs,* 14 to 15 percent of total *revenue.* To put that in perspective, the *Los Angeles Times* has about $1 billion in revenue annually and, of course, 14 to 15 percent of that is $140 million to $150 million.

The weakness in using industry averages is apparent: They don't reflect such extremely important variables as competitive posture, market share, sense of journalistic mission, and desire for quality. Newsroom money management, in effect, is people management (see Box 7.3).

BOX 7.3   Standards to Plan By

In designing your newsroom, take guidance from these industry averages developed by Scripps Howard Newspapers for papers with 50,000 to 100,000 circulation:

- Staffing averages 1.1 to 1.2 FTEs (full-time equivalent employees) per 1,000 circulation.
- Staff allocations (excluding clerks, copy aides, etc.): 24 percent supervisors, 16 percent copy editors, 50 percent reporters, 10 percent photographers (Scripps Howard's goal is fewer supervisors and more copy editors).
- Distribution of beat reporters: 19 percent sports, 16 percent miscellaneous, 13 percent general assignment, 13 percent govern-

ment/politics, 8 percent family/lifestyle, 7 percent business, 6 percent arts/entertainment, 4 percent education, 4 percent social issues, 4 percent police/crime, 4 percent courts (2 percent other).

- Newsroom budget: 76 to 80 percent employee costs, 10 to 15 percent features and wire/supplemental services, 2 to 5 percent free-lancers.
- Total newsroom/editorial costs per subscriber (total "subscribers" equals average daily paid circulation): $42 to $50 per year.[a]

Following are pay rates developed in a survey by the American Society of Newspaper Editors:

Median Base Pay[a]

Position	Circulation			
	5,001–10,000	20,001–30,000	100,000–150,000	500,001—Over
Publisher	$56,238	$92,750	$173,800	$340,000
Editor	31,900	54,600	109,179	200,000
Managing Editor	28,000	39,249	73,918	154,720
Sunday Editor	NSD	30,734	49,140	78,520
Editorial Page Editor	21,850	35,776	58,532	118,000
City/Metro Editor	22,565	33,059	50,781	82,500
Business/Finance Editor	NSD	27,560	47,268	84,650
Lifestyle Editor	17,576	28,201	48,958	76,175
Sports Editor	19,188	31,430	48,906	87,750
Assistant City Editor	NSD	29,664	40,192	56,446
Editorial Writer	NSD	31,225	43,170	61,714
Copy Desk Chief	20,062	29,900	46,750	76,162
Copy Editor (0–4 yrs.)	20,280	22,034	26,988	41,410
Art/Graphics Director	22,980	28,916	49,095	84,240
Director of Photography	19,376	29,224	46,657	78,000
Senior Reporter (5-plus yrs.)	19,500	25,996	36,038	59,644
Experienced Reporter (1–4 yrs.)	16,583	22,807	27,508	49,650
Entry Reporter	15,080	18,900	21,320	30,246
Photographer	16,950	22,464	34,239	55,808

[a]"Scripps Howard General Managers Newsletter," Nov. 1992, p. 8. Figures for 1993
NSD—Not Sufficient Data
Source: Wanda Lloyd, "Top Editors Lead Newsroom in Pay Raises," *ASNE Bulletin*, Nov. 1993, p. 14.

So, to achieve dollar effectiveness, look to people costs. Three expense problems relate to how people are managed:

1. The number of employees inevitably expands without plan. Part-time employees show up on a full-time basis; temporary hires for a single project suddenly become indispensable. No addition in either category should be made without careful study of need and formal approval by the newsroom manager.

2. Overtime. Paying one and a half to two times regular salaries for overtime can raise costs quickly. Often, managers try to avoid adding a regular staffer, who can be paid at regular rates, by filling schedule gaps with overtime assignments—at a cost much above an additional salary. Calculate which costs less.

3. Variable costs—telephone, travel, expense accounts—can get out of hand quickly.

The newsroom manager—whether the title is executive editor, editor or managing editor—carries final responsibility for constructing the department's budget and ensuring it is followed. However, many newspapers delegate day-to-day monitoring of budget performance to an administrative assistant—a person with news background plus a bent for financial detail. This person helps draw up the budget, approves all expenses, tracks down and corrects any unfavorable variances from the budget and has authority to cut back in one expense area to compensate for unfavorable variances in another.

Managing External Resources

You have seen that a table of organization sketches control of internal news-gathering resources. For the *Columbus Ledger-Enquirer*, it leads from publisher to executive editor and, eventually, to a stringer paid by the published story for community news.

A newspaper also marshals major external news-gathering resources for their readers. These resources can be formidable in size and quality, costly and pivotal in news operations. Each manager must understand clearly how they operate.

They are *news agencies*, primarily the Associated Press; *supplemental news services*, such as the New York Times News Service and the Los Angeles Times–Washington Post News Service; and *syndicates*, such as United Features Syndicate, King Features and scores of others.

MANAGING NEWS SERVICE RELATIONSHIPS

The Associated Press—the name dates to the 1840s—was reorganized in 1894 as a nonprofit cooperative and is the world's dominant general news agency. It serves, as of 1994, 1,556 U.S. dailies—98 percent of those large enough to use a news service. AP's worldwide revenue in 1993 was $365 million. Its competitive strength stems from its cooperative nature, which gives even the smallest newspaper member representation on a 24-person board of directors and a direct vote at the annual meeting in AP affairs.

Member newspapers are obligated contractually to contribute their news to the cooperative. That means AP's news-gathering resources include the 1,556 U.S. newspapers and 5,925 radio and TV stations. News exchange agreements with thousands of overseas newspapers and broadcast stations, directly or through national news agencies, give AP unrivaled news-gathering resources. The newspaper desiring AP news or photo service must be voted into membership by the cooperative and must agree to pay weekly assessments levied as the newspaper's proportionate share of AP's costs.

Broadcast members and overseas subscribers contribute much of AP's revenue. Newspaper members in the United States contribute about 43 percent. AP service costs substantially more than that of other agencies. Some newspapers, *The New York Times* and *Los Angeles Times* among them, pay more than $1 million annually for AP services, although assessments of $150 to $200 weekly or so are common for small dailies.

Two factors are particularly operative for you as a manager:

1. AP member newspapers large or small are entitled to call on AP for special coverage—a story on a local man injured skiing in Switzerland, for example, or national and state divorce rates as background on a local story about divorce. Make sure all editors are aware of this.

2. AP's membership contract requires two years' notice of intent to cancel, and the contract is an open-ended commitment to pay whatever assessments the board levies. That means there is no negotiating AP's basic membership fee.

AP provides many services, including high-speed computerized general news wires, full-time sports and photo services, and state news circuits—all at a cost that's low compared to what coverage would cost if generated through a newspaper's internal resources. For example, studies in the 1980s showed newspapers on average were filling 37 percent of their newshole with AP copy for 17 percent of their newsroom budget. The *Baltimore Sun* at that time was filling 24 percent of its newshole for 4 percent of its newsroom (not total newspaper) budget. Smaller papers can get a combined service of international, national and state news for the cost of a full-time reporter or two. Danger: Your editors can fill yards of newshole with AP copy at very little cost, leading to serious weakening of all-important local coverage. Other agencies include United Press International, once but no longer a strong rival of AP, and Reuters, historically owned primarily by British and Commonwealth newspapers but publicly owned since 1984.

Dealing with Supplementals and Syndicates

A number of U.S. newspapers operate strong supplemental news services, competing against AP and offering high-quality news and photo coverage to even small papers. The supplementals started as salvage services, selling news and feature copy prepared for their mother papers. They gradually moved into true agency operation and today originate copy exclusively for their wires.

Important supplementals are operated by *The New York Times*, jointly by *The Washington Post* and *Los Angeles Times,* and by Dow Jones and Knight-Ridder.

The supplementals' attractiveness is threefold:

- They carry excellent copy from some of the world's most prestigious papers.
- Clients can get exclusivity in a market (AP by law must serve all qualified applicants).
- Unlike AP, most supplementals will negotiate rates and contract terms.

Syndicates operate in a highly competitive environment and negotiate their prices wildly for thousands of offerings—comic strips, crossword puzzles, horoscope features, you name it. Small papers pay as little as a few dollars weekly for even nationally syndicated columns; large papers pay hundreds or even thousands. Popular comic strips ("must" Sunday reading for more than two-thirds of child readers, polls show, and more than half the adults) draw substantial prices. Large papers pay thousands of dollars weekly for popular strips such as "Peanuts" or "Calvin and Hobbes."

THE EDITING FUNCTION

From many internal and external resources, then, news flows into the newsroom in great volume. AP alone can deliver millions of words daily without strain. So as a newsroom manager you must carefully use your precious resource, space. The newshole can range from 25 percent of a large metropolitan daily on heavy advertising days to 60 percent or more of the small daily.

Newshole size varies widely, but *not* in direct response to news availability; it is determined by the advertising department. On the basis of advertising sold, the ad department calculates number of pages needed. Ad layouts are made on page forms and given to the newsroom, which only then learns how many columns it has to fill and which pages are "open" for news and photo copy. For many papers, the size of the day's paper is set by food and department store advertising, two of the largest sources of ad revenue. Food stores traditionally advertise on Wednesdays or Thursdays—"food day"—and that creates "big" papers; Monday and Saturday papers often are "thin." News coverage planning revolves around such advertising considerations.

The key to efficient use of news resources and newshole lies in selecting which stories and photos to print and basing their length and display on news merits. It is a delicate process. Initial winnowing and sifting of copy is extremely important. The immediate task is to quickly discard the irrelevant and unimportant and begin "working" copy that might qualify for publication. Direct your sharp attention to this point in the copy-handling chain, examining both the efficiency of the systems for selecting copy and the professionalism of the men and women doing it.

BOX 7.4   Setting USA Today's "Tone"

USA Today, Gannett's national daily, boasts a colorful "with-it" tone that created the fastest circulation success of any American newspaper: In seven months after launch, in 1982, it grew to more than 1.3 million circulation (it claimed 1.8 million in 1995).

The paper's start-up editor, John Curley (now chairman/CEO of Gannett), says the experience gives him a few clues to editing a national newspaper:

- Keep stories short. Upscale readers have many demands on their time and desire brevity.
- Edit for clarity, particularly in sports.
- Hire more editors even at the expense of reporters.
- Stories should inform and be interesting, not boring.

- Emphasize graphics that help tell a story. Crop photos effectively and make sure cut lines make sense.
- Do more stories on personal finance, new technology and gimmicks that people can use in daily life.
- Don't always run negative stories.
- Weather news is important.
- Readers want portions of newspapers at different times for different things—in the morning for sports and hard news, later for leisure reading of feature copy.

Curley tells editors faced with the daily challenge of producing a paper amid chaos and disorganization: "Regain control of the asylum from the inmates."

Call them "copy tasters," "gatekeepers" or "editors," the desk people who handle those thousands of words minute by minute greatly influence a newspaper's content and its journalistic stance (see Box 7.4 for the views of Chairman/CEO John Curley of Gannett.)

Controlling Copy Flow

Many "copy flow" charts and systems exist for ensuring smooth operation in the newsroom.

You should develop a system for your newspaper's needs and, importantly, for the editing talent available to you. The traditional approach is based on separate "desks" (or control points)—city, state, national (or "wire desk") and so on. Reorganization in many newsrooms, however, is aimed at breaking down the traditional desk system, on grounds it creates artificial barriers between departments and simply doesn't lend itself to creating a modern news product properly attuned to reader needs.

Some newspapers are breaking down the "beat system" under which reporters are assigned to covering the structure of government—city hall, sheriff's department, board of education and so forth. Instead, reporters are assigned to "government," "law enforcement," "learning" or even broader subject areas—"leisure," "quality of life" and so forth. Whatever your system, you must ensure efficient control of the torrent of news flowing over the various desks (or through subject areas), reporting on international, national, state, regional and local affairs—in general news, sports, business and so forth.

As deadline approaches, so does another point in the copy-handling system where you must ensure firm control. This is the story conference. It is a daily brawl at some newspapers; a quiet, scholarly discussion at others. Whatever the level of emotion, it is the time when editors from various departments begin competing seriously to get their copy into that day's paper. The newsroom manager must intervene decisively to avoid deadlock if, say, the foreign editor demands front-page lead position for the latest guerrilla attack in Afghanistan while the city editor argues that last night's city council meeting is the lead.

Managing the Newspaper's Tone

The newspaper's journalistic tone is set in the process of selecting which stories to publish, how they will be written, which headlines to run and how pages will be laid out. Choices are infinite—anything between rape, pillage and burn in bold colors beneath shouting headlines on the one hand and, on the other, routine stories written by uninspired writers under sleepy headlines for a gray front page.

There is no universal standard of what is correct and what is not. The *New York Post,* its red-daubed front page screaming about the day's icepick stabbing in Central Park, would wither corn and dry up cows if sold on street corners in Bloomington, Ill., where the *Daily Pantagraph* adopts a quiet, conservative stance attuned to its small-town and rural audience. Conversely, the *Daily Pantagraph* could only murmur ineffectually at thousands of harried New Yorkers streaming past subway newsstands.

Don't copy another paper's approach. Design your paper's tone to meet its market's needs. Matching tone to market helps determine your paper's success in circulation, advertising, and profitability. If the newspaper is designed as a more attractive news and information tool that readers can use effectively, logical packaging of both news and ads will pull readers more deeply into the newspaper and hold them there longer. And the more time readers spend going through pages, the happier your advertisers will be.

Increasingly, newspapers use design specialists called art directors, creative directors or design editors. Their tools are photos, graphics of all kinds, color and creative thinking about layout and design. The pressure to achieve better design stems primarily from three sources: (a) improved production techniques, permitting more and better color throughout a newspaper; (b) *USA Today*'s example of successful graphics; and (c) market research showing that readers want newspapers that are better looking and easier to use.

Newspaper design and layout truly are art forms, deserving their own book (or books). Here, however, are a few things to keep in mind:

- Design and lay out pages to emphasize content, not overshadow it with artistic stunting. Warren Watson, managing editor/operations of *The Portland Press*

Herald and *Maine Sunday Telegram* and a design expert, says, "Smart design is based on content."

- Strive for simplicity, a newspaper that's easy to read, and for what Watson calls "dignity." ("Our typography, layout and color use will have purpose and substance. Color will not be decorative.")
- Be consistent. Help readers cope with the information explosion by "anchoring" fixtures (news briefs, roundups and so forth) in the same place daily.

As assistant managing editor/graphics, Nanette Bisher helped to design the enormously successful *Orange County Register* of Santa Ana, Calif. Her advice:

1. Design pages for simple reading; lead readers to stories and steer them through.
2. Strive for horizontal design; don't revert to the traditional up-and-down design.
3. Fit design to reader habits. Modular makeup, constructed block by block, helps readers concentrate on one element at a time.
4. Avoid continuing stories to another page; if "jumping" stories is unavoidable, jump as many as possible to the same page.
5. Build each page around a dominant story, signaling readers which story editors regard as most important.
6. Use dominant art—one story strong or a story/photo/graphic package.
7. Balance the page and design the entire page, not just the top half ("above the fold") or the dominant element.
8. Organize material with boxes, but don't overuse this device; two per page is probably the limit.
9. Typeface helps determine a newspaper's personality, so don't confuse readers by varying it too much. Use type creatively and consistently; it's effective in breaking up gray areas.
10. Have fun.

Evaluating Your News Product

So, you design what you hope is an effective organization, you motivate people and you plan efficient use of money, time, newshole. Are you succeeding? Perhaps nowhere else in the newspaper is answering that so difficult.

Your principal evaluation, of course, must be whether household penetration meets your (and your advertisers') expectations. Bottom line, your news product must meet the demands of a competitive marketplace, or you fail. And reader acceptance of your product is the objective measurement of that.

But your evaluation process is more complex. You must make subjective judgments in evaluating newsroom performance and controlling the effort to reach planned goals. Oh, you can evaluate your work schedules and employee motivation by whether people show up for work on time. And comparing costs to budget will objectively determine whether the staff is spending beyond your means for telephone calls or travel. But what you must really evaluate at the end of each day, week and month is whether your newspaper's overall impact in news—its professionalism, its tone—meets your audience's needs and meshes with the overall marketing effort. To judge, run down the following checklist.

The Busy Manager's News Checklist
Ask these questions:

- Is the paper accurate in minor as well as important detail and does it enjoy reader trust? Does it have credibility?
- Is it balanced and fair, reporting all sides of an issue in an objective, dispassionate manner?
- Does it cover the local scene? Can your readers learn what is happening in their hometown?
- Is it geographically complete, covering area, state, national and world news? It is well rounded, with full subject diversity, covering all types of news?
- Does the newspaper demonstrate enterprise, going beyond the routine to seek out and explain meaningful developments?
- Does it capture life's drama or is it dull, unexciting? And does it have that occasional humorous story to make readers smile?
- Acknowledging that news values vary, does the paper display judgment in emphasizing meaningful news and ignoring trivia?
- Is its writing professional and grammatically correct? Is copy clear, concise, readable?
- People are news. Are people of all ages in the newspaper?
- Do photographs, cut lines and graphics help tell the story? Does the paper have professional, understandable graphics?
- Does layout make efficient use of newshole? Are headlines clear and well written?
- Is the paper competitive? To win in this business, a newspaper must beat somebody. Did you beat somebody today?

CAREER HINTS: TWO MAJOR PATHS OPEN

Let's conclude this chapter by examining two areas of modern newspapering that offer you major career opportunities. First, we'll examine metro vs. suburban newspaper competition, the hottest sector of "action" in print management today. Second, we'll look at how you can start adapting now to two developments certain to open major career opportunities: newsrooms will become "information centers" and newspapers will evolve into "profit centers," distributing news/information on newsprint, as always, but also using electronic and other means. To get your career started in the right direction, think deeply about opportunities offered you in the following two case studies.

The Surburban Action: A Case in Point

So many metro dailies have folded that surviving big city newspapers enjoy comfortable monopolies. Right? Wrong.

Throughout the country, in virtually every city, the principal competitive between print media has shifted to *metro vs. suburban*—a battle between a single downtown daily and packs of small dailies and weeklies in surrounding towns and rural areas.

A case in point is in northeast Georgia. As you learned from earlier case studies, the *Atlanta Journal* and *Constitution,* like regional dailies elsewhere, withdrew from distant (and unprofitable) circulation frontiers in the 1980s and focused on a target market with a radius of 50 miles or so from downtown. Then, in the "Second Battle of Atlanta," the *Constitution* and *Journal* in the 1990s beat off a major challenge from the New York Times Co. in suburban Gwinnett County.

Time for *Journal* and *Constitution* editors to relax? Don't believe it. Knocking on Atlanta's suburban gates are other dangerous opponents. They are personified by Otis Brumby, publisher of the *Daily Journal,* a seven-day morning paper of 30,000 circulation produced in Marietta, 15 miles northwest of Atlanta.

You don't think a 30,000-circulation daily threatens two metros with over 500,000 circulation? Well, Brumby has linked *18* small free-circulation weeklies to his paid-circulation daily and rings Atlanta with hometown news offerings for readers—and tightly zoned audiences for advertisers. First, note below the list of Brumby's "Neighbor Newspapers" in Table 7.3 on page 218. Then match the list to the map in Figure 7.2 on page 219 to understand how he has a noose around Atlanta's most affluent suburbs.

Brumby's publishing formula is classic for small suburban papers: For readers, concentrate on local news and create a sense of community—even neighborhood—identity. Leave to others the "big-picture" role—and expense—of covering world, nation, state. For advertisers, do what they want. Dedicate up to 75 percent of total content to ads (the post office maximum for preferential mailing rates) and expand distribution via mail to any areas advertisers want to reach. Ad rates are based on a total of 506,000 circulation (the *Marietta Daily Journal* plus all *Neighbor* papers) *or* on a zoned total as small as 11,000 (*The Paulding Neighbor*).

Because so many affluent residents have fled Atlanta for the suburbs, Brumby is positioned smack in the middle of a market the *Journal* and *Constitution* want—and need. (This means, of course, that the *Journal* and *Constitution* inevitably will throw their massive journalistic and marketing strengths into a fight for Brumby's turf, just as they attacked—successfully—an earlier penetration of their suburban market by New York Times Co.'s *Gwinnett Daily News.*)

Across the country, the pattern repeats: Tight rings of suburban publications sprout in rich markets literally created anew in the 1970s and 1980s, as upscale population shifted. For example, in those two decades, the *Miami Herald* and now-defunct *Miami News* increased their combined circulation just 14,000. In the same period, paid and free circulation of suburban papers increased from 157,000 to 999,000. In St. Louis, suburban newspapers played major roles in forcing Newhouse Newspapers to sell its profitless *St. Louis Globe-Democrat* (whose new

TABLE 7.3   Brumby Neighbor Newspapers

Market	Newspapers	Circulation
1. Cobb County	*Marietta Daily Journal*	29,628
2. North Cobb	*The Kennesaw Neighbor*	45,596
	The Acworth Neighbor	
	Cherokee Tribune and Plus	
North Cobb	*The Kennesaw Neighbor*	16,364
	The Acworth Neighbor	
Cherokee	*Cherokee Tribune and Plus*	29,232
3. East Cobb	*The East Cobb Neighbor*	45,184
4. Smyrna	*The Smyrna Neighbor*	10,584
5. South Cobb	*The Mableton Neighbor*	20,857
	The Austell Neighbor	
	The Powder Springs Neighbor	
6. Douglas	*The Douglas Neighbor*	22,566
7. Paulding	*The Paulding Neighbor*	11,995
8. North DeKalb	*The Dunwoody-DeKalb Neighbor*	24,064
	The Chamblee-Dekalb Neighbor	
	The Doraville-DeKalb Neighbor	
9. Mid DeKalb	*The Decatur-DeKalb Neighbor*	54,306
	The Tucker-DeKalb Neighbor	
	The Stone Mountain-DeKalb Neighbor	
10. South DeKalb	*The South DeKalb Neighbor*	38,558
11. Rockdale	*The Rockdale Neighbor*	14,340
12. North Fulton	*The Roswell Neighbor*	35,397
	The Alpharetta Neighbor	
13. Northside/Atlanta Sandy Springs	*The Northside Neighbor*	25,210
	The Sandy Springs Neighbor	
	The Vinings Neighbor	
14. South Fulton	*The South Fulton Neighbor*	26,788
15. Clayton	*The Clayton Neighbors*	43,313
	The North Clayton Neighbor	
	The South Clayton Neighbor	
16. Fayette	*The Fayette Neighbor*	18,205
17. Henry	*The Henry Neighbor*	19,239
18. Bartow	*The Bartow Neighbor*	20,637
19. Suburban	All Newspapers	506,467

owners later folded it). It's the population shifts that create major news coverage problems for metros, of course—and growth opportunities for suburban papers.

Metros must cover not only their inner cities but also those numerous small communities proliferating sometimes on a 360-degree perimeter around the city. Small suburban papers use relatively inexpensive new technology to lower the "cost of entry" into the competition and, by restricting coverage, keep their costs low. Important new career opportunities are opening on both sides of this metro vs. suburban battle. Let's look at some suggestions on how you can succeed.

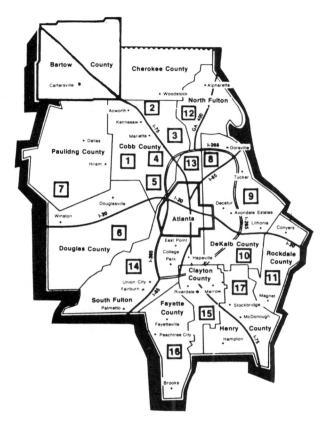

FIGURE 7.2 Neighbor Newspapers encircles Atlanta
with free-circulation weekly newspapers.
Reprinted by permission of Neighbor
Newspapers Inc.

How to Win in the Suburbs

If you enter suburban journalism, these are among steps you can take to win:

1. Because each suburban audience tends to be socially and economically homogenous, you must ensure fine tuning of your editorial product and marketing strategy. It is counterproductive for a suburban paper to fashion, as many metros do, broad-based news products designed for audiences widely varying in educational background and interests. Suburbs tend to attract people of similar lifestyles; you must be certain to meet their precise news needs.

2. Make sure your advertising rate structures are competitive, particularly with those offered by metros for their zoned editions or part-run advertising. Lower op-

erating costs permit many suburban papers to set rates substantially below the metros' and still enjoy profit ratios higher than the metros'. Lower costs are possible because relatively inexpensive, labor-saving technology is available for small papers, and lack of unions permits its widespread introduction without a costly "buyout" of displaced staff.

3. As a suburban manager you must structure your operations to take full advantage of relatively simple distribution. Suburban papers already are located in the rich areas that metros must reach via traffic-clogged highways. Home delivery is easier and cheaper for suburban papers. Use this competitive edge decisively to achieve the home delivery so highly attractive to advertisers.

4. Your operation must be structured to exploit the enormous advantages that time/distance factors give suburban papers. Many suburban afternoon papers, for example, can hold for a press run of, say, 1 P.M. and deliver fresh, same-day news to front porches by 4 P.M. Distant afternoon metros are forced into early press runs, sometimes 8 A.M. to 9 A.M., to enable trucks to get papers to the suburbs for 4 P.M. delivery. That means suburban readers of an afternoon metro often see, at 4 P.M., a warmed-over rehash of last night's news. The advantage this gives suburban papers must be highlighted in both your news operations and sales promotion. Suburban morning papers have similar time/distance advantages over metros. They can hold press runs to well past midnight, then deliver night sports scores and other late-breaking news to breakfast tables. Distant morning metros must go to press early, often at midevening, and they, like afternoon metros, often arrive with outdated news content.

5. As a suburban manager you must, above all, focus sharply on local news, for neither the neighboring metro nor evening television can match you in quantity and quality. Many successful suburban papers treat lightly most news from world, nation and state, concentrating instead on local schools, the village council, Little League baseball. For householders concerned with their immediate surroundings, your suburban paper must be a necessity, not simply nice to have.

However, metros have strengths, too, and if you enter management of a large city daily, there are steps you can take to fight suburban papers.

How Metros Can Counterattack

Metros, if managed wisely, can meet suburban competition with confidence. As a metro manager, you should:

- Deploy your paper's relatively massive resources in all sectors—news, advertising, promotion, circulation—to put suburban papers under heavy pressure. Through zoned editions, focus on narrow geographic market slices and offer detailed local news plus somewhat lower ad rates.
- Offer broad news coverage with world, national, regional and state dimensions, appealing to well-educated, cosmopolitan suburban readers for whom the local paper's offerings of Little League baseball and church socials are not enough.

BOX 7.5   Don't Lose Sight of Basics

"If one afternoon a reader hears an ambulance or firetruck siren roaring down a nearby street, he should find out why in his community newspaper the next day. Even if it is a false alarm."

John Morton, newspaper analyst, in "The New Meaning of News Competition," *Washington Journalism Review,* Jan./Feb. 1993, p. 52.

- Feature high-quality reporting and writing that can make suburban papers look amateurish by comparison. Special-interest sections—science, art, business—are particularly strong showcases for a metro to display reporting depth.
- Strike into suburban markets with Sunday papers, those bulky, colorful and often highly profitable papers that give many metros strong competitive advantages. Suburban papers, with their small staffs and limited budgets, cannot publish matching Sunday papers, with panoramic news coverage, entertainment sections and advertising.
- Fully use the increasingly effective mechanical and distribution flexibility now available to metros for zoning news and ad content. Satellite production plants in suburbs and morning publication (permitting predawn distribution over empty streets) give metros opportunities to compete in suburbs. The *Oklahoma City Oklahoman and Times* leap-frogs outside its core city to a $50 million production facility eight miles from the downtown news, advertising and circulation offices. This puts small papers throughout the state under heavy pressure as the morning *Oklahoman* prints a much later—and thus more journalistically valid—edition for distant regions of Oklahoma. Following affluent readers to small towns around Dallas is *The Dallas Morning News'* strategy with its $57 million satellite plant in Plano, a rapidly growing suburb. Among other metros establishing satellite production facilities: The *Atlanta Journal* and *Constitution!*

Many metros possess managerial expertise in news, advertising and circulation that small papers cannot match. It was managerial genius that devised *The New York Times'* strategy: Skim off the most attractive readers, demographically, in the prime city market but then leap-frog over a constricting ring of small suburban papers (19 dailies are published within 40 miles of New York City) and achieve national newspaper status with satellite printing plants coast to coast.

Although it publishes some suburban coverage, *The New York Times* chooses not to compete head-on against vigorous dailies and weeklies in Long Island, Connecticut and New Jersey. Rather, *The Times* maintains one of the finest newsgathering staffs in American journalism, turns it loose on substantive matters important to an intellectual (and economic) elite, and uses new technology to reach across the nation.

Brilliant newsroom management led *The Philadelphia Inquirer* attack against the then-dominant *Philadelphia Bulletin* and a near army of local dailies and weeklies in greater Philadelphia (by some counts, 200 print competitors were out there). Eugene L. Roberts, then *Inquirer* executive editor, first strengthened his paper as a metro daily, then as the region's best package of international, national and state news. Finally, he added suburban news.

"The *Inquirer* can't do everything the local papers do but distinguishes itself by running stories on trends relating to all the suburbs," he said. That included stories on taxation, education, street crime—news of pertinence in all Philadelphia suburbs. Roberts said the *Inquirer* approached readers on many levels, claiming it had the best general news, best TV and movie listings, "and on top of that you don't neglect their high school basketball team."[14]

The *Atlanta Journal* and *Constitution* fight suburban competitors with detailed local news plus total market coverage. *Journal* and *Constitution* vehicles:

The "extras," tabloid weekly papers heavy with local news and zoned many ways for ads. Extras are inserted in the *Journal* and *Constitution* for the inner city and for county areas where suburban papers are most vigorous.

ZAP (zone-area preprints), permitting advertisers to target any or all of many zones for inserts on Sundays or in Wednesday's *Journal* and Thursday's *Constitution*.

REACH which delivers preprinted newspaper supplements to nonsubscribers via shared mail in ZIP code areas with as few as 5,000 or as many as 400,000 households.

Second-Layer Growth in the Suburbs

Some suburban markets mature so richly that they open competitive possibilities for new entrepreneurs. For example, *Newsday* not long ago was the epitome of a suburban daily. Now that it's a 700,000-circulation monster of national stature, legions of small dailies, weeklies and shoppers are springing up in Long Island towns and neighborhoods.

On the other side of Manhattan, in New Jersey's rich, suburban Bergen County (average annual household income over $67,000 in 1993), the Hackensack *Record,* also once a small suburban daily, has 165,000 daily circulation and 231,000 on Sundays. Like *Newsday,* it is complete in all dimensions: international, national and state news as well as local.

In journalistic quality and sheer bulk, these "suburbans" match most metros and surpass many. But as suburban dailies mature to *Record* or *Newsday* levels, they come under attack by yet another layer of suburban publications tucked tightly beneath their shadow. As the *Records* and *Newsdays* broaden their news horizons to include Kabul and Katmandu, small local weeklies—of free or paid circulation— spring up to serve the narrow local news demands of small communities.

Old versus New Thinking: A Case in Point
Envisage this scenario: You're editor of a 90,000-circulation daily, with 51 percent household penetration in its city zone and 29 percent in its retail trading zone. In your weekend reading (editors *always* read during off-hours), you stumble across this: A national survey shows that when asked about life's worst "little stresses," 42 percent of women mentioned fear of car breakdowns.[14] Interesting, right? Now, what will you do with that revelation?

Well, if you're old-fashioned, you think you're editor of a "mass-circulation" medium. So come Monday morning, you order your "Women's Page" editor to do a story on how housewives should carry a notebook of telephone numbers for auto garages and road-side repair services. The story will be "full-run," for all 90,000 circulation.

Now: "With-It" Thinking

However, if you're a with-it editor—the kind in demand on quality newspaper everywhere—you must move in entirely different ways. First, you dismiss "mass-circulation" pretensions. Your paper reaches over just half your city zone (CZ) households; nearly three-quarters in your retail trading zone (RTZ) don't take your paper. You obviously don't edit a "mass"-circulation medium. Second, you dismiss that housewives/women's page bit. Women more than likely work outside the home; Housewives' page gave way years ago to something more in tune with the New Woman—a "Working Woman" page, perhaps, or "Life" or "Coping." Third, you put your in-house research department on the idea. Your paper is deeply into database marketing, and you have full demographic and psychographic detail on readers and non-readers in both the CZ and RTZ.

Now, if you're *really* a with-it editor—one who wants to run a big news operation—you follow *this* course: First, you inform the newspaper's marketing committee that working/commuting women might constitute an entirely new niche audience. (The newspaper's *integrated management team* is constantly searching for new niche audiences attractive to advertisers because the old concept of mass-audience loyalty is dead.)

Second, you present refined research showing that because your newspaper's market is in the Northeast, subject to heavy snow and other weather dangers, working/commuting women in your area are even more fearful of auto break-downs than the national survey shows. Your researchers' instant telephone poll shows 62 percent of working women in your market mention auto breakdowns as a real fear.

Third, you order your "Transportation" or "Public Safety" editor (not the long-gone "Women's Page" editor) to do a story on dangers of commuting. Research shows the story won't be of interest to inner-city readers; they commute primarily by bus or train. So, you say, direct the story at the suburban woman niche—and ensure it is personalized: What *you*, the working women, can do when *you* have a car breakdown on a lonely road at night.

At this point, your staff has computer-assisted reporting under way. (Your research department's database and several national databases are on-line with the newsroom.) But your emphasis on personalized writing ensures that reporters using the new technology will, as always, strive for the human touch in their copy.

How to Use the News Product

Now, how will you use the resulting five-part series on commuting dangers facing women? Here we go:

- You use the story in the newspaper, as your old-fashioned colleague would, but only in two zoned editions with 47,000 total circulation in affluent commuter suburbs.
- You order the story incorporated in your electronic newspaper. You use flat-panel (or "tablet") technology, a hand-held device about the size of *Time* or *Newsweek.* Subscribers plug it in at home, day or night, for updated electronic "feeds." They view the news on the panel's screen, touching the screen to summon up what they want, much as you use a "mouse" on a Macintosh computer.
- You also add telephone numbers and addresses of 24-hour auto garages to the audiotext daily-up services your newsroom offers (at 50¢ per telephone call).
- Detailed do-it-yourself instructions on car repairs are inserted in the information database your newsroom provides. Subscribers interrogate this videotext service via interactive circuits and personal computers or their "household information center," installed by your business partner, the local telephone company (its technology delivers your news/information for a flat fee of $45 monthly for unlimited use or 75¢ per call.)
- Your fax newspaper department adds pertinent road and safety information to the facsimile services transmitted daily to special subscribers.

By now, you've used the same basic news and information five different ways—and suddenly the economies of scale are dramatically improving your newspaper's profitability.

Create More Spinoffs
But, you're still not finished. You now consider whether your burgeoning database on commuting dangers can be used to create yet more *spinoffs.* A few ideas:

- Check the newsletter department on whether it could issue a regular mailing (at a substantial per-subscriber fee) to car owners. (Be certain to check whether the Spanish-language desk should create a special newsletter for Hispanics.)
- Ask the city magazine division if it wants to use your database for the magazine's own look-ahead cover story on what must be done to improve road safety.
- Your newspaper's book division probably won't be interested in a follow-up, but check. Lots of newspapers have profitable book operations.
- Your newspaper's independently run regional business journal certainly will be interested in this story. It likely will do a story on the business implications of commuting, traffic, autos, safety and highway construction.

Why, You've Created an Information and Profit Center!
Now, step back and consider how you've transformed your newsroom: First, it has become an *information center,* collecting information through old-fashioned, hard-nose reporting, combined with new computer-assisted techniques. The big difference: You distribute news in many ways, not just on newsprint. Second, your newspaper has become a *profit center,* using in a variety of profitable ways its understanding of readers, its unrivaled strengths in collection, collation, analysis and

distribution of information. Third, with new services based on subscriber usage fees, you have shifted much of your operation's economic burden to the reader/user and, importantly, off the shoulders of advertisers, bitter over your newspaper's never-ending rate increases.

However, aren't there even more ways to make a buck off this commuter/travel database? Think: Your original research identified 47,000 households where 62 percent of working women fear auto breakdowns while commuting. What else can you do with that? A suggestion: Perhaps your advertising department could sell access to those homes to auto repair garages, towing services and other similar local businesses.

Working with the circulation department, ad salespeople could deliver advertiser messages to those homes in these ways:

Traditional ads in the zoned editions reaching those 47,000 homes, or via your newspaper's direct mail service, or, via the newspaper's alternative distribution service, which (for a substantial fee, of course) will hang on doorknobs of each of those 47,000 homes a plastic bag filled with reprints of the newspaper ads plus other flyer material advertisers want delivered. (Alternative delivery is a secondary—and profitable—usage of the newspaper's unique seven-day household delivery system; *no other industry,* including the U.S. Postal Service, delivers *every* day.)

Finally, lists of targeted households are valuable assets. Should you sell your lists (and your database backup) to other businesses? Think carefully about whether that invades the privacy of your subscribers. But this might be a source of additional revenue.

Well, there is a vision of the editor's future. It's certain to be part of your future if you want a career in big-league newspapering.

SUMMARY

A newspaper's survival ultimately depends on whether its news content meets its readers' needs, and your news effort must be dovetailed into the overall marketing concept. Whether your competition is another paper of like size and characteristics or an entirely different medium, news is at the tip of the marketing spear. The design of your news organization must adapt to your marketplace and the coverage it requires. For a metro or small daily the table of organization must bring the newsroom and editors into the mainstream of planning.

Planning for quality must include a willingness to spend for newsroom resources; the hiring of strong news managers, reporters and editors; identification and coverage of the newspaper's areas of opportunity; researching reader needs and desires; and then designing the paper for its own particular market.

From all this, plus the responsibility of spending sometimes millions of dollars annually, comes an expanded definition of the newsroom manager's job. Top editors today are deeply involved in "business" affairs and the efficient use of newsroom resources—people, money, time and newshole. Editors often misjudge reader needs and desires. Detailed readership research is a must, whether you obtain it through expensive or do-it-yourself techniques such as encounter groups.

Plan to personalize your paper, organize its content, make it more readable, particularly the showcases: front page, business section, editorial page, sports edition and those pages of statistics on birth, death and life in your town. Plan for efficient use of internal news resources, such as staff and stringers, plus external resources such as news agencies and syndicates. Then, decide whether your newspaper's news content and design/layout—"tone"—match needs of its market and its time.

Career hints: Competitive "action" in newspapering is largely between metro dailies and surrounding suburban dailies and weeklies. Significant career opportunities exist on either side of such fights. And, successful editors of the future will redesign their newsrooms as "information centers" that distribute news/information on newsprint, as usual, but also via electronic and other means. Newspapers thus will become "profit centers" operating many niche products.

RECOMMENDED READING

Best sources of continuing (and excellent) coverage of newsroom management: Newspaper Association of America's *presstime*, American Society of Newspaper Editors' *ASNE Bulletin,* Associated Press Managing Editors Association's *Continuing Studies* and *APME Red Book.*

Also see *American Journalism Review, Quill, Columbia Journalism Review,* and for related subjects, *Advertising Age.*

To keep watch on the competition: *Folio* has excellent coverage on magazines; *Broadcasting and Cable Magazine* covers television, radio and cable. *Journalism Quarterly* presents scholarly analysis of newsroom issues. For an excellent summary of modern trends in layout and design, see Mario Garcia, *Contemporary Newspaper Design,* 3rd ed. (Englewood Cliffs, N.J.: Prentice-Hall, 1991).

NOTES

1. The *Georgia Gazette* folded in 1984, the *Star* and *Press* in 1982.
2. "Shootout in the Big D," *Time,* Sept. 7, 1981, p. 58.
3. Burl Osborne, letter to author.
4. Ibid.
5. *Belo 1992 Annual Report,* "Chairman's Letter to Shareholders," p. 2.
6. Ibid.
7. See "Newsroom Management Committee Report, 1979, Continuing Studies," Associated Press Managing Editors Association.
8. Osborne letter, op. cit.
9. "Readers Give Newspapers Higher Marks Than They Did Eight Years Ago," *Southern Newspaper Publishers Association Bulletin,* May 12, 1983, p. 2.
10. "Reading the Newspaper Ranks Second Among Favorite Leisure Activities," *Southern Newspaper Publishers Association Bulletin,* June 16, 1983, p. 3.
11. Harold W. Andersen, letter to author.
12. Osborne letter, op. cit.
13. Newspaper Association of America, 1994.
14. C. David Rambo, "Suburban vs. Metros: Newspaper Civil War," *presstime,* August 1982, p. 38.
15. *Scripps Howard General Managers Newsletter,* March 1992, p. 7.

8

CIRCULATION

You'll recall from Chapter 7 that creating the right news product for your marketplace is a costly and time-consuming effort. Well, it's payback time! It's time for you as a manager to begin extracting reward from the marketplace for the effort you and your staff put into the product.

That brings you to circulation: selling the newspaper and gaining the readers your product deserves and your advertisers demand—and, of course, pulling in substantial revenue at the same time. In circulation, you must get that "right" product of yours to the right consumers at the right time, and if you think this involves only a simple sales and distribution project, think again. Newspaper circulation is highly complex, and so important that it's a career path into marketing and, for many, onward to the publisher's chair.

In large measure, the complexity in circulation ties to a change in advertiser thinking. No longer is the sophisticated advertiser interested merely in how many papers you sell. Today, that advertiser wants, first, assurance you are selling a newspaper which will satisfy reader needs and thus be closely read and, second, that you are delivering it in timely, reliable fashion to the right people—those ready, willing and able to purchase the advertiser's goods or services.

Your challenge is to thoroughly integrate your circulation effort into the newspaper's overall marketing strategy and then, at acceptable cost, get the paper to sufficient numbers of consumers that your strategy identifies as primary targets. It is worth emphasizing that the marketing concept requires tightly coordinated, interdependent effort by all principal departments: news, advertising, production, promotion and circulation. So, we turn to circulation, an immensely complicated, important part of the newspaper's integrated marketing thrust.

WHAT YOU FACE

Fashioning circulation strategy requires fresh thinking. Traditional methods are outmoded by these developments:

1. Advertisers have redefined what is attractive circulation and what isn't. They want to pay for delivering their message primarily to prospective customers living close to retail outlets and ready and willing to buy. For many newspapers, distant circulation built over decades at enormous cost is suddenly "inefficient" and must be terminated.

2. Readers pay billions of dollars annually for daily and Sunday newspapers but they provide only about 23 percent of most paper's total revenue and often do not cover newsprint costs, let alone the costs of news collection, printing and distribution. Reader contributions to revenue must be increased.

3. Soaring distribution costs, particularly for labor and transportation, raise to 30 percent or more the circulation department's share of most newspaper's total costs, thus sharply threatening profits.

4. Changing American lifestyles, particularly the expansion of single-parent households, could invalidate newspaper content and distribution techniques tailored for traditional households of stay-at-home mother, father and children.

5. Broadcast media, shoppers and direct mail challenge newspapers by offering both total market coverage (TMC) to reach all households in a market and selective market coverage (SMC) to reach narrow market segments or just the affluent readers so desired by advertisers.

If you aspire to any manager's role you must understand the impact of these changes. Let's look at what happened to newspapers in the Twin Cities of Minneapolis and St. Paul, Minn., as such changes swept those markets.

The Upper Midwest: A Case in Point

In the 1930s, John Cowles Sr. thought big in planning a circulation market for his *Minneapolis Star and Tribune*. The entire Upper Midwest would be his turf; his newspapers would span Minnesota's forests and the Dakota prairies, perhaps reaching even beyond. Cowles succeeded, establishing by the 1960s a complex system of more than 14,000 carriers covering thousands of square miles and offering doorstep delivery in far-flung outposts, including Igloo, S.D., 700 miles from Minneapolis. By 1973, combined circulation for Cowles' morning and afternoon papers topped 485,000; their editorial voices were powerful throughout the region. But beneath the rosy surface, all was not well.

Newsprint, $179 a ton in 1970, skyrocketed to over $500 in the early 1980s (and hit $700 by 1994). Gasoline and other distribution costs rose rapidly. Wages, crucial in labor-intensive circulation work, jumped ahead. Subscription prices, however, lagged. And, local retail advertisers, the single most important source of newspaper revenue, lost interest in paying for circulation in Igloo or anywhere else far away. Suddenly, yesteryear's circulation triumph was today's expensive liability.

The company had not adjusted gradually to change—had not shifted circulation priorities to meet new marketplace realities—and now it was forced into Draconian measures. John Cowles Jr., who succeeded his father as president, began a full retreat toward home base, vacating the vast marketplace the elder Cowles had built so painstakingly. Like many regional papers, the *Star Tribune* found the circulation empire's outer reaches no longer tenable. In 1982, Cowles merged them into a single paper, the *Star Tribune,* with 360,000 initial circulation, down a whopping 25 percent from 1973. By 1993, circulation was 410,000—still far below 1973 levels. Even in its shrunken form, however, the *Star Tribune* tried to handle a huge circulation territory—a seven-county metro area around Minneapolis and St. Paul. It still was too big.

In neighboring St. Paul, meanwhile, Knight-Ridder's *Pioneer Press Dispatch* was anticipating change and adjusting, not reacting, to it. Key to *Pioneer Press Dispatch* strategy was intensive cultivation of a tight three-county area around St. Paul. In light of cost/revenue realities, that was wise. Donald Dwight, then presiding as Cowles' publisher in Minneapolis over an extremely high-cost operation, was envious: "St. Paul's distribution costs are just so appreciably lower than ours because they distribute in a much smaller area—wisely, because the profitability has got to be much better."

Outcome: Today, at about 190,000 circulation, the *Pioneer Press Dispatch* (now combined into a single morning paper) achieves over 36 percent household penetration in its Newspaper Designated Market (NDM), the area the paper regards as most important to its advertisers. The higher (and more costly) circulation of the *Star Tribune* achieves just *under* 36 penetration in its NDM. In sum, circulation success traditionally meant selling more and more newspapers, regardless of who bought them or where they lived. No more.

Circulation today must be established among customers in areas carefully selected for advertiser needs. For, without advertising support, circulation is a cost factor, not a profit generator. Cowles didn't recognize that early enough; Knight-Ridder did. Lesson: In attitudes and structure, the circulation organization must be designed to look anew at how newspapers are sold and distributed.

DESIGNING YOUR CIRCULATION ORGANIZATION

The circulation department's primary objective is planning, then achieving circulation expansion in accord with the newspaper's overall strategy. It is a formidable challenge requiring that the department be organized properly. First, organizational design must ensure that circulation pulls effectively with news, advertising, production and promotion departments. Second, circulation must receive sufficient resources, including truly outstanding managerial talent. The department is key to marketing success and cannot be starved for resources.

The Table of Organization

Changes under way externally in the newspaper's marketplace, plus internal adoption of the marketing concept, require transforming the circulation department from a semiautonomous unit reporting directly to the publisher into one that reports to the chief marketing executive. Top management must grant circulation managers major voice at the policy-making level. For many newspapers, this means circulators for the first time will help plan strategy. Top managers themselves must get involved in circulation—its planning, strategy and execution. Many managers never have done this. Barriers between departments must come down—something other departments, particularly news, often resist. Marketing managers must keep circulation aware of what advertisers want; news managers should receive feedback from circulation salespeople on how the public regards the product.

Within the circulation department, thinking must expand beyond selling and distributing newspapers into entirely new dimensions of marketing strategy. For example, sales pushes cannot be made into new neighborhoods merely because, like mountains, they are there to be conquered; rather, sales efforts must be made in areas that are attractive to advertisers and covered by the newsroom. (That may sound painfully obvious but it hasn't been part of circulation efforts at many newspapers.)

Departmental design must establish a hierarchy along unequivocally clear lines. The organization itself need not be complex, though the task is. See Figure 8.1

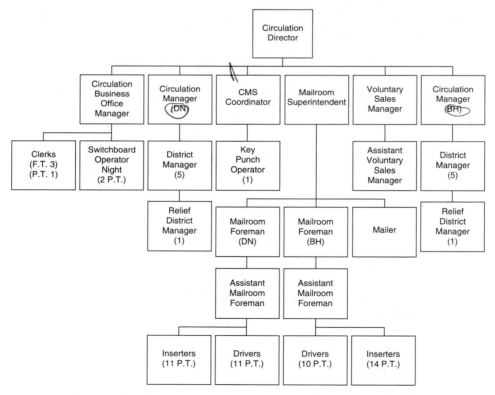

FIGURE 8.1 **The circulation department at the *Athens (Ga.) Daily News* and *Banner-Herald*.**

for a simple but effective table of organization for the *Athens (Ga.) Daily News*, a morning paper of 12,300 circulation, and *Banner-Herald*, which has 13,700 afternoon circulation. Note six subordinates report directly to the circulation director who, in turn, reports directly to the publisher. At these papers, the publisher serves as chief marketing executive.

Management Job Description

The most important single resource of any circulation department is a highly professional circulation director backed by trained, capable middle-level managers and first-level supervisors.

The director must be a master of marketing strategy at the highest levels and be able to plan and manage circulation operations on a daily basis. This requires the ability to use modern research, fight competitors head on, motivate people and deliver profitable results. The job is a pressure cooker of responsibilities. In keeping with the newspaper industry's early production (rather than marketing) orientation, circulation managers traditionally were expected to be primarily distribution experts. No more.

Today, general management skills are needed at all levels in circulation. Many newspapers recruit college graduates for first-level and middle-level management positions. That's a change. Older circulators, reared in another era, are mostly a different breed. For example, the International Circulation Managers Association in the mid-1980s found only 34 percent of circulation directors had college degrees. Behind them, however, 69 percent of younger middle managers had degrees. Many newspapers retire the old title "circulation manager" for "circulation director" or "vice president/circulation" to recognize the increased interdepartmental responsibilities that go with the job today.

Other job descriptions:

1. A *business office manager* supervises clerks and telephone operators taking "start" orders for new subscriptions and "stop" orders for cancellations. Part-time operators are available at night to customers with delivery complaints.
2. *Circulation managers* (one each for the *Daily News* and *Banner-Herald*) supervise district managers (DMs), who in turn recruit, train and supervise carriers. (If you're interested in a circulation/marketing career, DM could be your entry-level job.)
3. A *circulation management systems* (CMS) *coordinator* is responsible primarily for computerized lists of subscribers and nonsubscribers essential in database marketing.
4. A *mailroom superintendent* handles mail circulation, of course—but much more, including all functions between the press and delivery to carriers and single-copy sales points.
5. A *voluntary sales manager* ("single-copy sales manager" at some newspapers) is responsible for sales at newsstands, drugstores and vendor boxes.

Other important functions are also part of circulation work at larger papers. The 120,000-circulation *Lexington (Ky.) Herald-Leader* has these:

State managers, who supervise circulation outside the city, a challenging job of efficiently planning motor routes and other distribution schemes to reach far-flung subscribers.

City managers, who supervise home delivery, a formidable task of recruiting, training and motivating carrier youths. (Long Island's *Newsday* at one time had 10,000; the *Detroit News,* 12,000!)

Marketing managers in circulation, who coordinate promotion through house ads, sales literature for carriers and other media.

Transportation managers, who supervise truck and car fleets. Big job? Remember, about 60 million copies of U.S. newspapers must be transported each weekday. The *Des Moines (Iowa) Register & Tribune's* circulation vehicles used in delivery, sales and supervision in the 1980s drove 1.2 million miles annually.

Phone-room supervisors, who manage a sales force that works exclusively by telephone. It's the most important source of "starts" plus cross-checks on delivery service and "stops."

Design for Newsroom Coordination

For the circulation director, a tough challenge is opening effective relations with the newsroom, where editorial prerogatives are zealously protected and outside influences sometimes rejected out of hand as unwholesome efforts to distort the news process. But the sales force's view of the product must be considered in news planning; those who sell newspapers develop, from contacts with the public, keen insights often valuable to the newsroom's decision-making process.

Circulation managers should be aware they tread here on sensitive ground. Nevertheless, the news process must consider circulation's needs. If the marketing concept calls for a sales push in a suburb north of town, reporters obviously must cover that suburb. But the daily judgment calls on what is news and what isn't must be made in the newsroom by seasoned editors, not in circulation or any other department.

Some newspapers design formal procedures to get circulation's feedback into news planning. Under Bingham family ownership, the *Louisville (Ky.) Courier-Journal* (now Gannett-owned) was widely applauded for journalistic excellence and independence, yet its managers made sure circulation was consulted on where deployment of new reporters likely would yield greatest benefit.

As circulation manager of the *Santa Barbara (Calif.) News Press,* Russell Barcroft maintained circulators could be helpful particularly to the newsroom in judging whether the "personality of the newspaper meets the personality of the community...." Barcroft also urged close coordination with the research, advertising and promotion departments in mapping sales drives. Research should spot areas likely to be receptive to new sales efforts and sales themes; advertising must ensure advertisers' needs are factored into sales strategy; promotion must use television, radio, direct mail and other media to prepare the way for high-intensity sales drives in narrowly focused geographic areas.

Said Barcroft: "The circulation and promotion departments that use the shotgun approach are apt to be doomed for failure . . . with a rifleman's technique, the chance for success is great."[1]

The circulation department is heavily dependent on the production department: Late press runs mean missed schedules all along the distribution chain and angry subscribers at the end of it. Circulation veterans say no publisher would permit late press runs if he or she ever were held personally responsible for delivering bundles to trains, buses, airplanes or teenagers on bicycles—none of which wait for newspapers that arrive late.

Pulling all your departments into an integrated marketing thrust to accomplish marketing objectives may create personality clashes or turf battles between strong-willed and previously autonomous departments. If so, you must step in forcefully. Waiting for consensus to develop—waiting for them to sort things out— can waste valuable time. Strong managers set things right immediately when they spot trouble.

As Always: Get Involved!

Many publishers and other top managers pay detailed attention to newsroom and advertising operations but, amazingly, ignore the effort to get the papers to paying customers. Many feel ill at ease in circulation work because they lack hands-on experience.

One publisher with that experience was Virgil Fassio of the *Seattle Post-Intelligencer.* Said Fassio: "Circulation is probably the area of least practical working experience (for) most publishers. As a result, circulation executives get less input on how to run their operations, but more second guessing from publishers. . . ."[2] Not many managers have Fassio's background, which included being circulation director for several major newspapers. But departmental design—in both structure and attitudes—must be such that managers supportively put their hands on key links in the circulation chain. Here are five of these links.

Sales Strategy

Too many circulation departments, under strong deadline pressure, are driven by a frenetic spirit of grabbing bundles of papers from the pressroom and trucking them wildly to distant sales points. Make sure there is a strategy designed to reach the right readers at the right time. Any circulation manager who cannot present, on paper, a strategy for the next three to five years—in addition to specific sales goals for the next 12 months—is failing.

Sales Techniques

Things can go badly wrong in sales. One survey showed 64 percent of nonsubscribers in metro areas *never* were asked to subscribe to a newspaper.[3] There must be precise techniques for canvassing target areas on a block-by-block basis, methodically and regularly. A circulation manager must plan in detail how available sales resources—people, time, money—will be used for optimum results.

Salesperson Training and Motivation

Ill-equipped salespeople not personally motivated to sell effectively will do worse than not sell the paper; they will create a negative image that can be extremely difficult to overcome. Sales trainers should be selected internally, from the ranks of experienced circulators, or imported from outside. There is a science to selling, and good trainers can teach it.

Check carefully your existing incentive plans. They can vary in detail but must link reward to sales performance and be attractive enough to inspire hard selling. Be aware: It is costly to sell effectively.

Pricing and Payment Collection

This is such a key link in the circulation chain that we'll discuss it later in detail; for now, suffice to say that if a newspaper is priced unprofitably low or if collections are inefficient, the entire circulation exercise is wasted.

Effective Distribution

This, too, warrants detailed discussion later, but of course any newspaper—even if beautifully crafted by the newsroom, jammed with attractive advertising and then printed with loving care—is worthless if not delivered to the right people at the right time. Ensuring that the trucks, rural route drivers and 13-year-olds on bicycles do their duty is the responsibility of every manager. All that is a full plate for any manager, but there's more.

Design for Diversification

Circulation departments today must be more than simply a service arm of the newspaper. They must be a "profit center" as well. No longer can circulation be permitted to operate at a financial loss—accounting for, say, 30 percent of the newspaper's total costs but only 23 percent or so of revenue—even if it sells and distributes the newspaper properly.

Rather, circulation must be required to also generate a departmental profit and view itself as an operating entity with responsibilities beyond just keeping 13-year-olds happily mounted on bicycles and delivering newspapers. That requires circulators to initiate and operate TMC or direct mail services or find other profitable uses for departmental resources normally only partially used in delivering the paid-circulation newspaper.

Alternate delivery (or "distribution") is an attempt by circulation departments to turn a profit by using existing delivery systems to place products other than newspapers before householders. Consider: Delivery to the American front door is talked about by many—magazine publishers, advertisers, producers of goods and services of all kinds. But now that the iceman, grocer and milkman have dropped out, only the U.S. Postal Service and the daily newspaper deliver door-to-door on a regular nationwide basis.

And only the newspaper does it on a seven-day basis. But the newspaper's elaborate, expensive and unrivaled delivery capability is used just once daily in limited fashion. Carriers and drivers fan out across a market with newspapers for 30 or 40 percent of households. They walk, ride or drive past nonsubscriber homes—homes thousands of firms want to reach. Because not enough newspapers exploit the opportunity in that, vigorous direct mail and independent alternate-delivery competitors spring up. For competitive purposes and profit, circulation strategists must investigate carefully the possibilities of offering alternate delivery themselves.

Early experimenters delivered magazines inserted in their papers. *Time, Newsweek* and others find, however, that such delivery is only minimally cheaper—or sometimes more expensive—than mail and also inaccurate. Magazine delivery appears to offer low profit potential. There often *is* profit and protection against competitors, however, in delivery of preprints and other advertising. Some newspapers deliver material from a number of advertisers in a single plastic bag or wrapped in grocery store preprints.

The competitive threat from independent alternate-delivery companies is illustrated in Columbus, Ohio, where a firm started operations during a newspaper strike. The company quickly grew to $3 million annual revenue and held important food advertisers even after the strike ended. The *Columbus Dispatch* eventually bought the company for about $5 million.

In the 1990s, alternate delivery experiments took a new direction: Some community papers began delivering national publications, including *The New York Times* and *The Wall Street Journal*. The *Journal's* deputy circulation director, Michael Sheehan, welcomed the move: "The (community) newspaper has the opportunity to leverage its delivery network and earn extra revenue, and the *Journal* is able to make its newspaper available to its subscribers early in the morning."[4]

The *Journal* developed its own alternate delivery subsidiary, National Delivery Service. Dow Jones, the *Journal's* parent, reported in its 1992 annual report that 932,000 *Journal* subscribers were getting early morning delivery to homes and offices through NDS—and, the company also was delivering nearly 6 million publications annually for other firms.

RESEARCH: THE CRUCIAL FUNCTION

An ongoing social revolution in America forces circulation managers to research their strategy carefully. Metropolitan daily newspaper circulators must use research to predict the newspaper's socioeconomic environment a decade ahead. Will inner-city deterioration spark further flight of affluent residents to suburbs? If so, should the newspaper follow? Who will remain behind as prospective readers? How can the newspaper—its marketing strategy, its sale techniques—meet inner-city lifestyle needs *and* appeal to suburbanites?

Small dailies and weeklies must research equally important unknowns: What will suburban and small-town life be like a decade ahead? What will the traditional family household unit look like? How will it spend its time and money? How can the newspaper penetrate the household and meet its need? These are enormously important questions because, like army generals preparing to fight the last war, many newspapers are suited for a socioeconomic environment that was, to someone extent still is, but in the future might not be.

Focus Research on Household Strategy

Basic circulation strategy must be to penetrate the household with home delivery. The household is where buying power is and that's where advertisers want sales messages delivered. It is when they form traditional households that most readers take up the newspaper habit, particularly when they must know about schools, taxes, street crime and the cost of groceries.

The problem: Fewer Americans today form traditional households. Those who do wait much longer to start. And when they do, they don't act the way they used to. Particularly significant is the rapid growth of alternative living units, such as single-parent households. During the 1970s, married-couple families headed by householders age 35 or younger *grew* by about 147,000 annually. In the 1980s, the number *declined* by about 220,000 each year. There were 13,867,000 such households in 1983, down 343,000 from 1982. One-parent families by 1984 constituted 25 percent of all families. Mothers headed 89 percent of one-parent families. In 1985, the Census Bureau reported nearly half the households added in the United States since 1980 consisted of people living alone or with nonrelatives.

Now, how can such research be applied to circulation strategy? Well, consider the American newspaper: Except for a few big-city papers that depend primarily on single-copy or street sales, most newspapers aim at traditional households of father plus mother and children. For delivery, this package of news and advertising directed at householders is printed attractively and dropped on front porches before 6 A.M. or, for afternoon papers, around 4 P.M.

Circulation success is measured largely in number of households thus "penetrated." Advertisers are assured that once in the living room, the paper is easily disassembled and parceled out—sports to father, comics to children and a favorite section for mother, too. It's all perfect for leisurely reading. But will that content meet the needs of an unmarried 30-year-old mother who hurries to put her children in a day-care center while she works? How about the 30-year-old single male who has no head-of-household responsibilities and whose leisure time is spent in fishing, golf or tennis? What content will attract him?

And is throwing the paper on the front porch the way to reach either of them? They might, in fact, not have a front porch. Nearly one-third of U.S. housing units are multifamily structures, high-rise buildings or condominiums. Penetrating them with newspaper delivery is like attacking a fort, because many are built like forts to protect residents from crime, inconvenience and interruption. They offer no opportunity for a smiling 13-year-old carrier to walk onto the front porch and clinch a sale. Collections suffer too. Carleton Rosenburgh, when circulation director of Knight-

Ridder's *The Philadelphia Inquirer* and *Daily News,* said his company's bad-debt write-offs ran about 8 percent in multifamily dwellings as against 3 percent elsewhere.

Research should be sensitive to such lifestyle changes. Papers such as the *Inquirer* and *Daily News,* whose research spotted Philadelphia's trend to multifamily buildings, can adjust news strategy and circulation techniques accordingly. For example, high-rise "forts" can be penetrated by enlisting building personnel to sell subscriptions for hefty commissions. A building superintendent can be paid for making door-to-door deliveries or distributing newspapers through boxes in the lobby. Particularly in retirement communities, some circulators develop social get-togethers to introduce residents to the paper and entice them into pressuring building managers to permit effective delivery.

Continuing research is needed on the following:

The impact of education and income on reading habits. They are, in that order, the most accurate predictors of newspaper readership, more so than race or other factors. The higher the education and income, the greater the readership.

Age as a factor in readership. You'll recall from Chapter 1 that 62.6 percent of adults surveyed are weekday readers (it's about 68.2 percent on Sundays) but that young adults 18 to 24 years old are far less loyal to newspaper reading than older adults (72 percent of those 55 to 64 years old read papers on both weekdays and Sundays). Young readers clearly are among readers at risk—and our research must map ways to correct that.

Readers in demographically attractive suburbs who are highly desirable circulation targets for both small suburban and larger metro papers. Suburbanites enjoy incomes and educational levels higher than those of most Americans. If suburbanites commute into a nearby city, the metro daily often can attract them with city coverage. But fewer use trains or buses and more drive, so they are difficult to reach. If a suburb becomes a self-sufficient community, offering jobs as well as bedrooms, suburbanites tend to shift preference to a local daily. That happened for *Newsday* when its market, Long Island, developed into a self-contained commercial and industrial center. It also happened for the *Bergen Record* in northern New Jersey suburbs of New York City. When their markets thus "mature," many suburban readers favor a local paper, particularly if it broadens its content beyond strictly local news to include national and international coverage, plus TV news. Both suburban and metro papers need more research on the precise balance of content that will attract suburban readers.

Growing leisure time and money to enjoy it change reading habits. The householder who once settled into an easy chair with the paper after work now can ski, hunt, fish—intrusions into reading time are countless. (Saturday afternoon papers are casualties.) Newspapers, once primary sources of entertainment as well as news and information, now compete against many affordable entertainment options such as home movies and cable TV. What content mix, promotional themes and sales approaches are needed? Conduct research to find out.

Disappearance of the two-newspaper habit from most households narrows the circulation potential. It's not just lifestyle that's causing this; newspapers are bulkier and more comprehensive in content, eliminating need to buy more than one for ample news and advertising.

In sum, it may seem an entire lifestyle is the circulator's principal competitor. That's not totally true, of course; there are other, vigorous competitors. But lifestyle changes *do* pose enormous problems for circulation directors because of rapid shifts in where and how Americans live. Alert researchers must track each shift carefully, for news content and circulation strategy must shift equally fast.

The Research Scenario Ahead

Consider this scenario: Your circulation and advertising managers jointly visit the city's leading department store to solicit advertising; they learn the store is launching special efforts to bring in residents with 75,000 or more annual income—people who drive Cadillacs, ski in Switzerland and buy fur coats and expensive perfume. Direct mail firms can locate and reach people of that demographic profile, store executives say; so can specialty magazines. Can the newspaper?

Your circulation manager must be able to say yes, along these lines:

> *There are 48,932 such households in our retail trading zone, almost all in three ZIP code areas on the northwest side.*
>
> *Our computer has matched your demographic targets with our subscriber list, and your ad in our paid newspaper will reach 78 percent of them. The addresses of the others are also in our computer and we will reach them for you in our own direct mail program.*

Now, that is far from handing the paper to a 13-year-old carrier headed in the general direction of the wealthy northwest suburbs. But circulation departments must develop such precision-target marketing to remain competitive. Some already can.

As Harte-Hanks corporate director of market research, Beverly Barnum reported considerable success with computer analysis of census materials to identify household characteristics that correlate tightly with newspaper circulation. Thus, Harte-Hanks could identify target areas where circulation sales drives were likely to succeed or, conversely, where results would not justify the time and expense involved. Many newspapers retain outside research firms every two years for probing studies of population trends in their markets.

Computers are used widely in circulation work. Many newspapers computerize subscriber and nonsubscriber lists, circulation accounting and billing. Managers of even small papers must computerize circulation record keeping. Knowing precisely who lives where in the market, how much they earn and how they spend their money and what they like and dislike about the newspaper is a fund of information the circulation department needs.

The circulation department, then, needs research tools to operate as a problem solver for advertisers. It must meet the advertiser's needs, perhaps with its own shopper or direct mail effort, and not simply offer a single vehicle, the paid daily paper, on a take-it-or-leave-it basis.

PLANNING CIRCULATION STRATEGY

You must plan circulation strategy for effective performance in three broad areas:

1. Plan to protect—enlarge—your newspaper's franchise as principal source of printed news, combating other newspapers, specialty publications, magazines.
2. Protect your newspaper's dominance as an advertising vehicle by fighting off radio, television, shoppers and direct mail.
3. Guard your newspaper's role as an effective door-to-door delivery vehicle against competition from the U.S. Postal Service and independent alternate delivery systems.

All this must be accomplished while selling subscriptions, delivering the paper efficiently and on time to keep subscribers happy, and collecting and pushing single-copy sales. It takes a great deal of planning.

Key Elements of Strategy

With adjustments for local conditions, strategy for any newspaper, large or small, must include key elements.

Improve Household Penetration
This requires continuing research to determine the news needs in households, traditional or nontraditional, then constructing a news product to meet them. Sales resources—people, time, money—should be concentrated on selling home-delivery subscriptions. Convert casual, several-times-weekly buyers to the seven-day habit with, again, research determining their news needs and helping the newsroom to construct a product to fulfill them.

Increase Prices
You must elicit from readers greater revenue and thus relieve the burden on advertisers, who contribute 75 to 80 percent of a newspaper's total revenue. The basic necessity, of course, is a news product that readers perceive as essential, so that higher prices will become a secondary consideration or at least will seem palatable. It can be done: Magazine editors often succeed in delivering content deemed crucial and, consequently, the magazine industry as a whole obtains 51 percent of its revenue from readers, 49 percent from advertisers.

Improve Selling Techniques
For generations, the primary sales force for this multibillion-dollar industry was the teenage carrier (whose sales pitch was something like, "You wouldn't want to

buy the newspaper, would you?"). Devise new ways for reaching prospective subscribers effectively, using the latest promotion and marketing techniques that must be used by any multibillion-dollar industry. Simultaneously, the carrier sales force must be converted to adults whenever possible and trained and motivated to sell better.

Improve Customer Service
A major reason for subscription cancellations is poor customer service—late or missed delivery, papers thrown in trees and mud puddles, billing foul-ups. Where would General Motors be if it built a beautiful, high-quality car, promoted and advertised it expertly, but couldn't deliver it on time to the buyer?

And remember: Newspapers are perishable products. Today's paper delivered tomorrow is worthless.

Improve Management
The increased responsibilities—and importance—of the circulation department mean it must be ignored no longer by top management. Publishers *must* get involved. The department itself must be infused with men and women highly skilled in marketing and professional human resources supervision and training. Down to the front lines—to district manager level—effective training must be continual.

Develop Profit-Center Concept
Two musts: First, find new profit-making activities that can create a profit center out of what for most newspapers is a costly service department. And second, control costs for the basic function of circulation. The department's costs will increase as the cost of transportation and labor increases and will absorb more than the current 30 percent or so of the newspaper's total costs—unless effective cost-control measures are in place.

Penetration: Number One Goal

The statistics are dismally clear: Paid newspaper penetration of U.S. households is falling far behind household growth and, certainly, behind advertiser demands. This "silent crisis" of U.S. newspapering is a circulation weakness—an inability of the industry to fulfill its basic mission for advertisers. The problem will not be disguised by increasing newspaper profits, innovative news coverage or improved production technology. The plain facts are that an industry which sold 124 papers per 100 households in 1950 sold just 64 per 100 in 1993.

Katherine Graham, as Washington Post Co. chairman in the 1980s, sounded the warning: decline in household penetration leaves newspapers vulnerable to competitors "ranging from shoppers and (direct) mailers to any variety of target marketing and total market coverage schemes." Newspapers must rebuild penetration or face "encroachments by the electronic media as well."[5]

Many metros have shallow penetration—25 to 30 percent in the city zone is not unusual for even journalistically strong dailies. Even some small-town dailies, which traditionally penetrated deeply into their markets, today claim only 50 percent or so. Yet, many retail stores demand penetration of 80 percent or more. One traditionally huge advertiser in newspapers—J. C. Penney—added its warning to Katherine Graham's: Improve your penetration or else.

James F. Boynton, overseer of $270 million or more in annual Penney advertising in the 1980s, said he would consider using "direct mail or some other media option when paid circulation drops below 50 percent penetration, and where we are getting less than 55 to 60 percent from the newspaper, we will add broadcast."[6]

Faced with such advertiser demands, your circulation strategy must include invigorated efforts over the long term to expand paid circulation plus immediate total market coverage (TMC) programs. Your problems will be many.

To deliver deep penetration, the circulation of free papers must be double or triple your paid circulation—and that creates huge operational difficulties. Costs leap upward, and achieving accurate, on-time delivery to all households becomes complicated. But no problem is larger than staff attitudes. Generations of newspaper people grew up thinking of shoppers as rather shabby devices. Some newsrooms disdain any publication devoid of news and thrown free on doorsteps; ad departments long preached that advertising adjacent to quality news in a paid-circulation paper is the way to sell products. Even upper management, whose view of the penetration crisis should be the clearest, often is reluctant to publish shoppers.

If your newspaper has such attitudes, it lags behind its public in comprehending that shoppers have arrived. Most U.S. adults live in communities with free papers and get them delivered regularly to their homes—and read them. A startling reality: For many consumers it matters little whether you deliver a "traditional" newspaper or a free-circulation shopper. What counts to them is whether their needs are fulfilled by a publication's cost, content and usefulness. Increasingly, the readers' verdict gives the shopper a place in the American home despite its lack of news content.

Many paid-circulation papers were late in recognizing the necessity of TMC as a competitive tool, but now converts to TMC include some of the best and brightest names in American publishing: Times Mirror, Tribune Co., Knight-Ridder and the New York Times Co. When they finally enter the field, paid papers often find they have many strengths in TMC operations: They know their markets, have advertiser contacts and their sales forces are ready to sell the new medium. They have printing presses, newsprint sources, trucks—the necessary production and circulation structure exists. TMC operations often prove highly profitable. Converting 35 to 40 percent of revenue to operating profit (double the performance of many paid dailies) is not unusual. TMC vehicles also can protect your newspaper's franchise against outside attack and serve as promotional vehicles for selling paid newspaper subscriptions.

Hints on Launching Shoppers

If you launch a TMC operation, carefully select the format and marketing plan to suit your own marketplace and competitive needs. In style and quality, free-circulation papers and shoppers vary widely. Some are full-size or "broadsheet" papers, others are tabloids or $8\frac{1}{2}$ by 11 inches, the *Pennysaver* format.

There is no "typical" shopper operation but research by Belden Associates and other researchers identifies commonalities:[7]

- Most newspapers publish TMC products once weekly, usually on Wednesday or Thursday ("food day").
- Most broadsheet TMC products are distributed by carriers; direct mail is used for many TMC products.
- Most newspaper TMC operations face entrenched competition from direct mailers or "marriage mailers" (which include advertising materials from several customers in the same mailed envelope or hand-delivered plastic bag).
- Newspaper TMC efforts are directed primarily at regaining the business of discount houses already among the heaviest users of TMC: Sears, K-Mart, Wal-Mart and others.

Warning: If your newspaper is the dominant advertising medium in your market, *never* launch a TMC operation against competitors without expert legal advice. We'll discuss this later in Chapter 12 with press law, but there are important antitrust implications in how you launch TMC vehicles.

Despite all the problems, many leading newspapers launched vigorous TMC efforts in the late 1980s. The *Rocky Mountain News* in Denver offered TMC by delivering preprints to any or all 45 metropolitan ZIP codes, and inserting them on Wednesdays in the paid paper. Nonsubscribers got theirs in plastic bags hung on doorknobs by Wednesday evening. Advertisers could have preprints delivered to all homes, just single-family units or apartments, multifamily units, or combinations. The *Orange County Register* in Santa Ana, Calif., delivered preprints to any or all of 69 ZIP code areas through a combination of the paid paper and four-color tabloid mailed second class to more than 400,000 nonsubscribers. The *Los Angeles Daily News* offered delivery to 461,000 homes in 60 ZIP code areas. The *Baltimore Sun* offered "Sun Plus," claiming nearly 93 percent household penetration in five counties—371,000 subscribers of the morning and afternoon *Suns* and 320,000 nonsubscribers reached via mail.[8]

Using Direct Mail for TMC

Operating a direct mail effort must be part of your circulation department strategy. It builds household penetration, constructs yet another defense of your paid newspaper's franchise, provides valued advertisers with one more service and, if operated properly, can be profitable.

Direct mail, long a selling technique, blossomed in the 1970s when lower third-class postage rates made it a viable alternative to newspapers for distributing preprints. Direct mail is a *huge* business (1993 revenue: $27.4 billion), so the potential for newspapers is huge.

Computers permit circulation departments to provide cost-effective service with high accuracy and reliability. Address lists covering most U.S. households are available commercially. Computers can cull them for the demographic and geographic markets demanded by advertisers.

For example, Lifestyle Selector of Denver was an early innovator in selling address lists. Its computers hold millions of names and can cross-check them for many characteristics such as age, sex and occupation plus lifestyle interests such as outdoor sports, foreign travel, gourmet foods, wine and so on. Retailers like direct mail, of course, because it reaches primarily only those audiences of real value to them.

James Hollis, then with Newspaper Advertising Bureau (subsequently incorporated into Newspaper Association of America), was among the first to recognize the danger direct mail poses to newspapers. In the early 1980s he said the average discount store had about $7 million in annual sales volume and "25,000 circulation is all that is needed to generate sales far above this average . . . generally, a store will not draw from an area larger than the area its employees come from. . . ."[9] And, of course, targeting such well-defined markets is direct mail's strength. William McConnell, executive vice president/sales for Advo-Systems Inc., the nation's largest direct mail firm said, "If I'm K-Mart and want to buy all households within a mile and a half, I should get marriage mail . . . most newspapers would force me to buy a larger area."[10] Direct mail is particularly threatening, then, for newspapers with high advertising rates and low household penetration. Retailers often view direct mail as offering immediate sales assistance at reasonable cost.

Your major operational problem in starting a direct mail effort probably will be establishing address lists. Many papers begin by purchasing lists from commercial mail firms. Newspaper carriers or special teams make house-by-house checks. Once you have 90 percent accuracy in street names and addresses collated by ZIP codes, the post office (under Section 945 of the *Domestic Mail Manual*) is obligated to make corrections, additions and deletions for a minor fee.

The *Los Angeles Times* entered direct mail early, establishing a sophisticated system of 109 grids covering 2.7 million households in Southern California. Advertisers were offered zoned groups as small as 6,126 households, but zones averaged 40,000 addresses. On average, about 10,000 of those 40,000 subscribed to the *Times;* that is, 30,000 were direct mail candidates.

By offering small zones, and thus lowering costs, direct mail attracts many advertisers previously unable to afford newspaper advertising. A *Times* count in 1983 revealed 650 advertisers used the program to distribute 400 million pieces. Small newspapers that publish a free-distribution shopper can broaden ad client support with mail delivery in rural areas.

Direct mail services should be promoted heavily. A competitor's direct mail may be "junk mail," but *yours* is exciting, effective advertising. Note the picture emerging from promotional efforts by the *Atlanta Journal* and *Constitution* to counter doubts about their direct mail:

Doubt: Direct mail is junk mail, with no image, no firm readership. *Answer: Our* direct mail isn't just any mail advertising. It is produced by the *Journal* and *Constitution* and carries their reputation.

Doubt: Direct mail is too costly. *Answer: Our* program affords efficient, selective market targeting by using mail in tandem with the newspapers. Cost compares to regular direct mail postage rates.

Doubt: Direct mail via third class cannot be guaranteed for timely delivery. *Answer: Our* program was developed in consultation with the U.S. Postal Service and at least 75 percent of each mailing will be delivered on the target date, the balance the following day.[11]

*Un*answered, however, in Atlanta and elsewhere, are several fundamental questions: Is direct mail's attraction due to basic strength as an advertising medium or to perceived weakness in newspaper penetration? Is direct mail simply attractive as stopgap TMC, and will it lose appeal if newspapers gear up both their combined paid-circulation efforts and free-distribution papers to offer much demanded TMC?

In sum, whether you choose direct mail, shoppers or other means, your circulation strategy must combat the "silent crisis" of shallow household penetration. TMC must ensure five basic strengths: ability to reach large numbers of households, concurrent zoning capability to focus on small segments of the market, highly accurate delivery, a competitive rate structure and credibility among discerning advertisers as a cost-effective vehicle.

The best long-term strategy is improving journalistic content and marketing practices to open sufficient doors for the paid newspaper, for paid newspapers *are* better read than free-circulation papers or direct mail circulars and *do* offer the best possible advertising environment. But increasingly paid circulation is a long-haul proposition requiring major investment in content, promotion, sales—and time. So short-term TMC remedies must be planned.

Basic Strategy Question: Elitism?

Your basic strategy must determine how narrowly your paid newspaper will focus its circulation. More readers are wanted, all right, and advertisers do demand TMC. But there is simultaneous pressure, often from those same advertisers, for *selective market coverage* (SMC), delivering readers particularly attractive in income and buying habits or who live in precisely delineated areas targeted by retail advertisers.

Many advertisers put it simply: It's better to reach families with $50,000 annual income living close to my store than those with $15,000 living far away. Other media—direct mail, specialty magazines—can deliver to attractive households and eliminate the cost of reaching those less attractive. Can newspapers? A concurrent question for circulation strategists, of course, is whether, with newsprint and other distribution costs rising, newspapers can afford to serve readers who are unattractive to advertisers.

These questions are enormously important for newspapers in philosophical as well as strategic terms. A traditionally mass-medium industry is going elitist. Should it label some readers unwanted? What would that do to the newspaper's historic role in raising the public's educational and social consciousness? Some newspapers frankly create "elitist" strategies to skim demographically attractive readers off the market.

Metropolitan dailies such as *The New York Times* and *Los Angeles Times* offer advertisers a class of readers with very high incomes and education and make no pretense of deeply penetrating the "mass" market. At a time when the *Los Angeles Times* penetrated only 24.5 percent of Los Angeles County households, the *Times* claimed its Sunday issue in the county reached 73 percent of those with annual incomes of $50,000 or more and 80 percent of college graduates.

An Elitist Success Story

The Wall Street Journal's circulation strategists are unrivaled in gathering readers of high demographic appeal. They engineered a circulation of 1.8 million—largest among dailies—yet built such demographic "purity" that the *Journal* is a premier advertising vehicle for some of the world's largest companies.

An architect of that circulation strategy was Warren Phillips, chairman in the 1980s. Said Phillips:

> *We have been careful as our circulation has grown to monitor very carefully whether the quality of our demographics is being diluted—whether . . . we will retain [our] hardrock businessman subscriber. We have found that our demographics have actually been growing stronger in recent years, rather than the reverse, and we can provide the research to document this. As we enlarge the content of the* Journal, *we take care not to turn it into a general newspaper but rather to try to strengthen its appeal to our basic business audience by improving the paper's coverage of business matters . . . and at the same time supplementing this core coverage with news of foreign politics, leisuretime activities, health, education and other matters that have strong impact on the lives of our business subscribers. We believe the* Journal *is a long way from reaching any saturation level in its circulation.*[12]

The *Journal*'s success unquestionably flows from *integrated management effort.* The news product isn't slapped together haphazardly by editors isolated from reader desires or thinking. Rather, the *Journal* newsroom painstakingly constructs it five days weekly for a hand-picked audience whose news needs are identified through precision research. The *Journal* is promoted shrewdly as *the* quality newspaper of its class, and the circulation department seeks out, one by one, those demographically attractive buyers. To ensure prompt, efficient delivery, 17 satellite printing plants are located strategically around the country, and the paper typically is available at breakfast almost everywhere on the business circuit, coast to coast.

Having accomplished that stunningly difficult journalistic, production, sales and distribution task, *Journal* strategists focus on big-league advertisers willing to pay high ad rates that make the newspaper as successful financially as it is journalistically. *That* is success in elitist circulation strategy.

The Market Segmentation Strategy

Few newspapers can focus strategy as narrowly as does the *Journal.* Not many want to. Their markets are often homogeneous and can be served with a single advertising strategy. Nevertheless, circulators who look into the future see that obtaining *widespread general circulation* probably will be (a) extremely expensive and (b) not all that attractive to advertisers anyway. Many see a strategy of market segmentation—*geographic zoning* and, perhaps eventually *interest zoning*—as a solution.

Geographic zoning, of course, attracts many advertisers, small and large, by reaching market segments with editions tailored in news and ads for those areas. For large papers, this can be enormously complicated. Richard Capen, publisher of the *Miami Herald* in the 1980s, explained:

> The Miami Herald publishes 11 editions circulated throughout the state of Florida, plus an International Edition air-shipped each day to some 40 cities in the Caribbean and Latin America. We have developed a weekly Business/Monday tabloid section. To serve the needs of our local communities, the Herald publishes, twice a week, 11 Neighbor editions circulated in 20,000–40,000 subscriber increments.
>
> As we look at the future, our success will be based on our willingness to adjust to change while giving high priority to the expanding needs of our readers and advertisers.[13]

The *Chicago Tribune* offers many advertising zones daily for both display and classified plus four-way zoning of local news for Chicago and suburbs. Geographic zoning is a strategy primarily for papers in large markets, such as Chicago, with great cultural or economic diversity and sprawling geographic areas to cover. A sense of neighborhood uniqueness in, say, the wealthy suburbs north of Chicago makes that area a prime target for a zoned edition.

Zoning is less attractive in smaller, more homogeneous markets. Residents in a small town, for example, have common news interests and merchants feel no need to zero in on a special market segment; they draw shoppers from throughout the town. Also, many small papers lack the production and distribution flexibility necessary to split a press run of 15,000 copies into three runs of 5,000 each—and to deliver different, tailored news packages to narrow slices of their market.

For newspapers large or small, getting the right papers to the right zone at the right time is a difficult logistical task in geographic zoning. Papers must by bundled by zones and trucks must take the right bundles to the right drop-off points. An edition zoned for the northwest suburbs is of no value delivered on the southeast side.

Interest zoning is an increasingly attractive idea—if not yet an operational reality—as new production and distribution techniques promise at least the technical capability for publishing daily editions zoned for special reader interests. It is possible, for example, to split press runs into segments aimed at business-oriented readers, sports fans or arts-and-leisure audiences. Computerized subscriber lists segmented by reader interest are feasible; on the drawing boards are inkjet, plate-less presses that could switch easily and cheaply from running papers heavy with business news to some designed for sports fans or science buffs.

Does it all point toward computer-sorted bundles being dispatched so carriers can throw the sports-heavy paper to the first house on the block, the business-oriented paper to the second and so forth? Technically, it will be feasible. But in addition to fearing that this could create a distribution nightmare, many circulation strategists argue the newspaper is a mass-distribution product of wide-ranging news and advertising content for general, not specialized, audiences, and that tinkering with that could undermine its strongest quality.

In sum, geographic zoning will be an essential strategy for dailies whose advertisers demand the servicing of narrowly focused market segments. However, interest zoning probably will be restricted to direct mail or perhaps newspaper use of the envisaged "electronic superhighway." For certain, your circulation strategy must involve eliminating circulation unwanted by advertisers.

A Must: Cut "Inefficient" Circulation

Your circulation strategy must eliminate "inefficient" circulation—circulation that is too costly or unwanted by advertisers.

The Washington Post, for example, avoids reaching out too far despite the temptations of going national, like *The New York Times.* The *Post*'s cost/benefit studies in the 1980s were negative, showing, among other things, that an average daily issue then priced at 25 cents contained 26 to 27 cents worth of newsprint alone. Potential *subscribers* to a national edition wouldn't begin to cover costs, and *The New York Times* and *The Wall Street Journal* were established solidly with *advertisers* as major national newspapers. So the *Post* stays profitably home (although it does distribute nationwide a weekly publication covering mainly national politics).

Some newspapers historically burdened with inefficient circulation now charge more for copies distributed 50 miles or more from home base; most, however, simply eliminate such circulation. The *Miami Herald* is among major regional papers trimming distant circulation. "We're concerned about the readers that matter to advertisers," said James Batten, now chairman of the *Herald*'s parent, Knight-Ridder.

The *St. Louis (Mo.) Post-Dispatch* once trucked 400 papers daily across Illinois to distant Indianapolis, Ind., at a huge annual loss. Not anymore. Nicholas Penniman IV, now publisher, said out-of-state circulation was built by publishers with big egos but became unaffordable. He said it was too showy and costly—"Buffalo Bill circulation."

The Boston Globe, which once considered most of New England its turf, changed strategy under Editor Thomas Winship, who said: "We do strive to continue our presence in the distant areas of New England but on rather a limited basis. We have found that from a realistic advertising point of view, that we should concentrate within a radius of 50 miles of Boston...."[14]

Some managers let inefficient distribution wither, not replacing losses, or they gradually redeploy news and circulation resources in more attractive areas. The *Tulsa (Okla.) World*'s Executive Editor Bob Haring: "The *World* is not pulling out of any circulation areas, but we are concentrating in the newsroom on expanding our efforts where they make most economic sense . . . for example, changing the focus of our mail edition to appeal more heavily to those prospects who live near Tulsa but who, for reasons of distance, etc., cannot be efficiently served by carrier and thus must get the paper by mail. We will spend more money to cover Bartlesville, where we sell 7,500 papers a day, than we will Muskogee, where we sell 1,500."[15]

For a few newspapers, some widespread circulation is attractive for strategic reasons. The *Dallas Morning News* in the 1980s sought enhanced regional stature but only with distant readers who were special. Publisher Burl Osborne: "We sell some papers in Texas and other areas of the Southwest outside of Dallas but . . . to very high-demographic groups. We sell very well in Midland, Texas, an oil center [290 miles southwest of Dallas]. The readers are people who get on their private jets and come to Dallas to shop at Neiman-Marcus and Saks. The advertisers don't complain."[16]

Today, however, most *Morning News* circulation is distributed tightly around Dallas, within the Newspaper Designated Market. Ironically, circulation's changing economics can mean a dramatic negative impact on newspaper profits due to sudden growth.

The year the *Washington Star* folded, the surviving *Washington Post* quickly increased circulation by 25 percent. There was a day when that would have been a bonanza. For the *Post*, it had short-term contrary meaning: Serving the larger number of subscribers—buying extra newsprint, driving delivery trucks extra miles—raised the *Post*'s operating costs so much that its third-quarter pretax operating earnings dropped about $2.5 million. Newly gained circulation revenue did not cover the cost of the new circulation and the *Post* could not raise ad rates quickly enough to make up the difference.

The *Philadelphia Inquirer* suffered similar temporary dilution of earnings when circulation soared following the death of the competing *Philadelphia Bulletin*. Of course, both the *Post* and the *Inquirer* now profit from increased circulation and have emerged as the only major dailies in their markets.

Target "At-Risk" Readers

Circulation strategists must work closely with editors to expand readership among "at-risk" readers. They include:

- Young adults, who aren't picking up the reading habit, as did their elders.
- Minorities. Black and Hispanic readership is substantially below white readership.
- Women, whose readership is below male readership, and dropping.

Newspapers have important societal responsibilities to fashion news and advertising to these "at-risk" readers. And their numbers and future demographic attractiveness make reaching these groups a business imperative, as well. Leo Bogart, one of the industry's premier researchers, found in 1979 that 72 percent of whites read a daily paper "yesterday"; 70 percent read the previous Sunday's. For blacks, the figures were 50 and 61 percent, respectively. In 1985, the Newspaper Research Council put average daily white readership at 74 percent and black readership at 67 percent. The council attributed the difference to disparity in education and income, suggesting black readership will lag until blacks catch up with whites in both areas. Bogart suggested some blacks perceive newspapers as part of the "system" that makes them feel indifferent or even alienated. However, newspapers themselves may contribute to the lag. How?

First, with affluent suburbs offering greater and more immediate potential reward, news and circulation strategies often are oriented away from city inner cores, where many blacks live. Content fashioned for middle-class suburbanites will lack relevance to blue-collar inner-city residents. Also, street crime and traffic congestion in core cities complicate the delivery and sale of newspapers.

Second, newsrooms and management ranks are predominantly white, making it difficult to execute news, promotion and circulation strategies that will capture black readers. Until more reporters, editors and managers are drawn from black communities, the weakness will continue.

To capture readers in burgeoning Hispanic communities, many newspapers publish Spanish-language inserts, editions or stand-alone daily newspapers. The imperative: The size and growing affluence of the Hispanic market attracts advertisers who, in turn, require newspapers to reach the market.

Attracting young adults to reader ranks may seem less complex because there is evidence the newspaper habit comes with maturity and the assumption of adult or head-of-household responsibilities. Circulation managers have traditionally banked on it: A 19-year-old doesn't read newspapers because the newspaper isn't needed at that age. But, the argument continues, once married and concerned about taxes, children's education and shopping bargains, the former teenager will need it.

That traditional argument may be unrealistic in this era of changing lifestyles. Head-of-household responsibility is not accepted by some young people today; others delay it into their late twenties or early thirties. And the longer the delay, the greater the chance that alternate sources of information will be developed, with the newspaper never becoming integral to the individual's daily life.

Your newspaper must provide content immediately attractive to young people, starting with comics and school news pages for children and then for all age groups leading to adulthood. For example: Music is an obsession with millions of American teenagers; billions of dollars are spent annually for records, tapes and music festivals. Yet few newspapers boast even adequate coverage of that music world in appropriate language and style for a teenage audience. (This led Jon Katz to comment in *Rolling Stone:* "What earthly reason would kids have to consume a medium that thinks the most interesting things in their lives are dumb and dangerous...?")[17]

Given appropriate content, circulation departments must get the paper before young people with promotion underlining its usefulness in terms that young people understand. One excellent avenue is the Newspaper in Education (NIE) program, under which papers are provided free or at low costs to schools as teaching aids. Teacher usage of newspapers is strong. The *Atlanta Journal* and *Constitution* surveyed teachers using their papers and found 99 percent regarded them as viable teaching tools; 63 percent used papers in teaching English or language arts; 61 percent, reading and writing; 53 percent, current events; 47 percent, social studies; and 26 percent, math.

Most papers in the NIE program also use other means of attracting student readers, including publication of school news written by students or examples of student art. Details are available from Manager/Educational Services, The Newspaper Center, 11600 Sunrise Valley Drive, Reston, Va. 22091-1412.

MANAGING THE CIRCULATION EFFORT

Circulation management is a never-ending process of planning, making decisions, setting goals, organizing resources, motivating people, and monitoring and controlling performance.

Let's discuss applying that process in three areas particularly crucial to any newspaper, large or small, and to your success as a manager in circulation:

- Selling the newspaper.
- Pricing the newspaper to achieve market dominance and profit.
- Distributing and collecting.

Unless you are aggressively successful in those three areas, you will fail in the short term, and so will your newspaper in long-term strategy. A fourth area, circulation promotion, is so important that we will cover it later, within the context of the newspaper's overall promotion effort.

The core of the circulation effort is obtaining readers, both through delivery and single-copy sales; retaining them with proper service that holds their loyalty; pricing the paper at attractive yet competitive levels that are profitable for your newspaper; collecting from subscribers; and replacing subscribers who move away or drop the paper for other reasons.

Selling the Newspaper

In planning circulation strategy, you define the geographic areas and demographic characteristics advertisers want brought into the fold. Selling starts with devising a marketing mix of type and quality of product needed by the market targets as well as price, promotion, type of sales effort, distribution network—all the devices for achieving either household-delivery subscriptions or single-copy sales.

Two factors should dominate your thinking in establishing selling "tone" and managing the sales structure: First, sell not merely the newspaper but rather solutions to readers' needs. Newspapers will not sell over the long haul if they are merely nice to have; newspapers must become crucial to readers in daily life. Second, in most complex, heterogeneous markets, successful selling cannot be based on a single "product." For advertisers, offer a variety of products, perhaps a shopper or direct mail service in addition to the paid paper. For readers, the sales force must differentiate the newspaper's wide variety of offerings as a solution to a variety of their needs—business section for the business executive, for example, sports for one group, arts and leisure section for another.

Selling must entice householders to subscribe but, equally, persuade them to continue subscribing. Too many sales programs are aimed solely at gaining new subscriptions, and the turnover rate ("churn") of existing subscribers is extremely high. It's a closely guarded secret at many newspapers, but churn exceeds 50 percent annually at some metropolitan dailies. Churn presents a significant problem: Advertisers seek continuity of readership and distrust newspapers with high churn.

It has been fashionable among circulators to say circulation departments can only sell new subscribers and that the newsroom must hold them. That cop-out is no longer acceptable. The circulation department must keep subscribers happy with on-time delivery and correct billing procedures, using continuing promotion to "resell" subscribers on the merits of continuing to take the paper.

Focus on Narrow Markets

Focus sales campaigns on narrow market segments. Maximum impact is gained with alert promotion and hard selling in, for example, a single ZIP code area or similarly narrow target selected in consultation with news and advertising. Trying to sell in an area ignored by the newsroom is futile; people want to buy a paper with news from their area. And selling in an area of no interest to advertisers is counterproductive. They won't pay for your achievements there. ZIP code areas commonly are targeted for sales efforts because they increasingly are used by advertisers in their sales campaigns.

Many newspapers concentrate sales efforts in affluent areas, not only because residents there are favored by advertisers but also because high-income families, once sold, tend to continue subscribing. Often, higher incentives are paid to salespersons for subscriptions signed in those areas.

For some papers, carriers are the basic sales force. At the *Milwaukee Journal*, for example, three-fourths of "starts" are sold by carriers. Young carriers require basic instruction on how to make a sales pitch. Your circulation department must provide promotion material that even a tongue-tied 13-year-old can use effectively. Sales crews of youths other than carriers can effectively flood an area under adult supervision and knock on doors. Intensive training by newspaper employees is vital.

Adult salespersons also are used, particularly in high-rise or other multiple dwelling units where negotiations with building managers are necessary. Adults

Our Towns

Target your ad message with any combination of the four Our Towns zones.

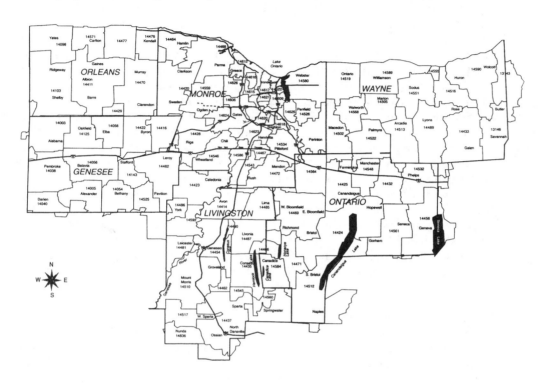

NORTHEAST

Monroe County
14617 Irondequoit
14622 Irondequoit
14580 Webster
14580 Webster Village
          Northeast Rochester

Wayne County
14505 Marion
14519 Ontario
14568 Walworth
14589 Williamson

NORTHWEST

Monroe County
14464 Hamlin
14430 Clarkson
14420 Brockport
14420 Sweden
14559 Ogden
14559 Spencerport
14616 Greece
14612 Greece
14468 Hilton
14468 Parma
14606 Gates
          Northwest Rochester

SOUTHEAST

Monroe County
14618 Brighton
14450 Fairport
14526 Penfield
14534 Pittsford
14450 Perinton
14445 East Rochester
14472 Honeoye Falls
          Southeast Rochester

Ontario County
(entire)

Wayne County
14502 Macedon
14522 Palmyra

SOUTHWEST

Monroe County
14428 Churchville
14428 Riga
14606 Gates
14624 Chili
14618 Brighton
14623 Henrietta
14467 Henrietta
14543 Rush
14546 Scottsville
14546 Wheatland
14511 Mumford
          Southwest Rochester

Livingston County
(entire)

FIGURE 8.2 Many retailers target consumers by ZIP code areas—so newspapers do, too. This is how the Rochester (N.Y.) *Democrat and Chronicle* and *Times-Union* offer target marketing to their advertisers. Reprinted by permission of the Rochester (N.Y.) *Democrat and Chronicle* and *Times-Union*.

must be better compensated and thus are expensive, particularly in rural or low-density areas where they must spend a great deal of time to obtain a few subscriptions.

Telephone crews—"phone rooms" in industry parlance—are kept in continual operation by many newspapers. Adult solicitors are used. Smaller papers often achieve good results with occasional telephone efforts, either using employees or outside solicitors paid on a percentage basis.

Direct mail is useful with scattered prospects or those difficult to reach otherwise, in apartment buildings, for example. Magazines successfully sell subscriptions and renewals by mail. But it is a technique considered coldly informal by some newspaper circulators and likely to get lost in the river of direct mail flooding most households.

Whatever techniques are used—and most papers use several simultaneously—there must be intensive, concurrent promotion in the target area. Radio, television and outdoor advertising can create a sales environment helpful to the carrier who knocks on a door, order blank in hand. "Sampling," delivering free copies to non-subscribers for a week or so, often is successful.

A smaller paper, the *Corinth (Miss.) Daily Corinthian,* increased circulation by 25 percent—to 9,100—in a 22-month sales campaign featuring a variety of methods. "We have done everything you can do to seek new business," said Publisher John Fitzwater. "Four nights a week we telephone area residents. We ask first if they have home delivery of the *Daily Corinthian.* If 'yes' we ask about service. If 'no,' we go into a sales pitch."

In an effort to convert casual readers into regular subscribers, the circulation department inserted mail-back subscription cards in each copy sold in racks. Cards were inserted in the paper's shopper, mailed to 13,000 households in five counties. Door-to-door sales were made by carriers. The newspaper also provided free delivery tubes to subscribers.

Develop Single-Copy Sales

Your newspaper's basic circulation strength must come from home subscriptions, of course, but single-copy sales are important for these reasons:

- Single-copy sales can add circulation numbers in key areas.
- Single-copy sales increase revenue.
- Single-copy sales racks, coin boxes and displays make your paper visible throughout the market.
- Single-copy sales give you sales access to the casual reader, important because you must make a vigorous effort to convert single-copy buyers to the seven-day habit (preferably with home delivery).
- And, sales costs are lower in single-copy sales. Each home-delivery subscription is costly in promotion, sales commission and other expenses.

The biggest challenge in single-copy sales is that those who purchase the paper today must be convinced to buy again tomorrow. Bringing single-copy buyers back day after day challenges the entire staff: Editors and reporters must fill the front page with substantive, attractive news; advertising salespeople must provide

BOX 8.1   The Selling of USA Today

Though the paper struggled a long time toward profitability, adroit promotion helped *USA Today* achieve the most rapid circulation success of any American newspaper. After spending more than $2 million in market research, Gannett Co. launched the national newspaper on Sept. 15, 1982. It jumped to over a million circulation in one year. Expensive, tightly coordinated promotion and sales boosted *USA Today.* Highlights:

Advertising through newspapers, radio, TV and billboards introduced *USA Today* two or three weeks before it was "rolled out" in each market. Promotion stressed its delivery via satellite to nearby production plants; the paper's use of color; its lively, exciting, fresh approach to the news.

Special displays in shopping malls before launch showed TV commercials and promotion tapes on TV monitors and videocassettes. Gannett reports signing substantial numbers of subscriptions in malls. Free samples were distributed at strategic locations throughout the market. Newspaper ads described where they were available and touted the mall displays. Launch events—dinners, breakfasts, cocktail parties—were held (at great expense) to create excitement and get people talking about the new paper.

Gannett's other papers (then numbering 85) were enlisted in focusing total resources on market-by-market launch. Some papers held subscription contests, giving employees prizes for signing customers. Promotion brochures that included order blanks were delivered to homes. Gannett Tel-Sell, a subsidiary, sold subscriptions nationwide by telephone.

Extensive door-to-door sampling and selling followed. Customers received thank-you notes and money-back guarantees. Colorful, modernistic coin boxes were set out by the thousands, appearing quickly throughout the selected markets and providing opportunities for purchase. The per-copy price was kept low, at 25 cents, in the first two years, after which it was raised 40 percent to 35 cents and then to 50 cents in 1985.

high-interest ad copy; production managers must get the paper off the presses on schedule; and circulation managers must get it to sales points on time.

Missed objectives in any department—a dull front page or late delivery—can mean thousands of sales missed. A big-city paper aimed at single-copy sales among commuters has a disastrous day if papers reach train and bus stations after the commuter rush.

Yet expertly run single-copy sales campaigns often yield faster results than subscriptions sales efforts. Attractive newspapers that are made easily accessible sell quickly on heavily traveled street corners, in train and bus stations, hotels, shopping malls. About 28 percent of all daily papers are sold one copy at a time. About 80 percent of the *Boston Herald*'s circulation is single-copy sales; the *New York Post* and *Daily News* are sold mostly one copy at a time. Some large cities have a strong tradition for street sales because many potential buyers, mostly commuters, can be reached quickly. However, even small newspapers have great opportunity for expanding single-copy sales after decades of emphasizing home subscriptions at behest of advertisers. In some markets, particular lifestyles improve single-copy sales. Florida cities with seasonal influxes of vacationers, for example, are prime areas for single-copy sales.

Important buyer psychology is involved in single-copy sales. Some readers prefer paying 25 to 30 cents for a single copy rather than a dollar or so for a weekly subscription—even though the latter is significantly cheaper.

Interestingly, research shows 7 out of 10 single-copy buyers read a paper every day. They are "habitual" single-copy buyers. However, single-copy sales often catch occasional readers who say they don't have time to read a paper every day or those who buy only on certain days for special reasons—on Wednesday or Thursday for food ads, for example.

A problem is that street newsstands are disappearing and, as large supermarkets and chain stores prosper the number of small retail stores drops, reducing over-the-counter sales outlets. This forces wider use of vending machines—"news racks"—to get newspapers before the public. Vending machines are expensive. Gannett paid over $200 for each of more than 10,000 futuristic boxes used to launch *USA Today* (and reports more than 1,000 were destroyed or damaged by vandals in nine months in the Philadelphia–New York City region).

Loose change in boxes tempts vandals and dishonest employees. "Returns"—papers placed out for sale but returned unsold—are another expense. Accurately predicting the number needed for each box is an inexact science at best.

Successful single-copy sales require the following:

Attractive front-page layout that makes the passerby dig down for coins. Many circulators insist the news department strive to make the front page particularly inviting above the fold—the portion that shows through the vending machine's window.

Heavy promotion of that day's front-page news plus banners or other visuals that draw the buyer's eye to the vending machine or stack of papers.

On-time delivery. Be there when readers are—or else. The late Dolly Schiff told me, before she sold the *New York Post* to Rupert Murdoch, that she nearly created her own navy to get the paper out on time. *Post* trucks could not penetrate Manhattan traffic to catch the afternoon commuter rush, and she investigated using speedboats on the East and Hudson rivers. That didn't work; neither did her later study of using helicopters to fly papers over the traffic.

Another crucial factor in both home delivery and single-copy sales is price. It merits careful study.

Top Priority: Aggressive Pricing

Your pricing strategy should either maximize profit or achieve maximum sales volume and share of market. Of relatively minor concern in newspapering is pricing to achieve a certain quality image (the Cadillac auto high-price strategy) or to serve ethical or social considerations—sometimes factors in other industries.

In newspapering, *profit-oriented pricing* aims at halting just short of that point where price increases cause disproportionate decreases in sales. Your pricing strategy fails, obviously, if an increase designed to raise $20,000 in new circulation rev-

TABLE 8.1 Why They Say "No!"

Here's what *former readers* say when they drop the newspaper:

Prefer another news source	37%
Poor service	20
Papers pile up ("Not enough time"?)	17
Too expensive	15
Not enough interest	10

This is what *nonreaders* say in refusing to subscribe:

No time to read	39%
Prefer TV news	21
Papers are boring/dull	19
Already read a weekly	12
News just comes to me	9

Source: Helen Cochran of Urban and Associates, and Scripps Howard Newspapers, "Building a Competitive Advantage," *Scripps Howard General Manager's Newsletter,* May 1993, p. 5.

enue annually so angers readers that they cancel subscriptions worth $25,000. Your strategy succeeds if it permits your newspaper to both raise prices and increase circulation.

There is no industry formula for achieving that happy result. You must judge where price increases will meet reader resistance. The old Newspaper Advertising Bureau had this simple advice: "If we sell our paper for less than our readers think it is worth, we may be losing revenue. If we sell it for more than our readers think it is worth, we may be losing circulation. If we hit the bull's-eye, we may be maximizing both revenue and circulation." (In my view, the newspaper industry generally is stricken with pricing timidity and unnecessarily shies away from aggressive, profit-oriented pricing.)

Volume-oriented pricing aims for maximum sales or market share as more desirable long-range objectives than immediate profit. This approach often is used in competitive situations. Due largely to its competitive past—but also (I contend) because newspapers fear they aren't perceived by the public as worth more—the newspaper industry emphasizes volume-oriented pricing.

External influences on pricing, then, include competition and custom. Unfortunately, the newspaper industry permits the ingrained custom of buying a newspaper for a stray coin or two. Newspapers sell their costly wrap-up of news from around the world—plus pages of interesting advertising—for pocket change! Competition influences pricing not because newspapers generally battle head-to-head against other papers of like size and characteristics but because there are many other competitors for reader time and attention—and pocket change.

In terms of pricing theory, many newspapers may appear to enjoy monopoly status because they are the only paid daily or weekly in their market. But most are engaged in *pure competition*—fighting large numbers of competitors, some of whom can enter the market easily and clamor for reader attention and all of whom can restrict your newspaper's pricing flexibility.

Nevertheless, many newspapers are trapped by decades of unimaginative efforts to meet all marketplace challenges simply by keeping prices low. Ask yourself: Has low pricing been an expedient answer to, say, quality lapses in news content or breakdowns in distribution?

Whatever the cause, prices are deplorably low. In 1992, if you were lucky enough to find a restaurant cup of coffee still priced at 50 cents you didn't have to worry about finding inexpensive reading material while you drank it: Exactly 1,200 U.S. daily newspapers were priced that year at 45 cents or under—less than a cup of coffee!

The picture worsens when rate discounts are used to induce householders to subscribe, further reducing realized revenue. Discounting rates for 50 percent of total circulation is not unusual for some metro dailies. For example, in 1985 Knight-Ridder sold its journalistically outstanding *Free Press* for the low rate of 20 cents daily or 75 cents on Sundays at newsstands; $1.90 for seven-day home delivery. Yet it acknowledged discounting prices on 132,942 daily copies (20.5 percent of the total) and 173,081 copies (21.5 percent) on Sundays. The *Free Press* was in head-to-head competition with the *Detroit News,* also a journalistically outstanding paper. The *News* was priced at 15 cents daily (20 cents outside the city), $1.40 for home delivery per week, and 75 cents on Sunday. Knight-Ridder claimed the *News* was discounting prices on 394,873 (or 60.6 percent) of its daily circulation, 431,823 (or 50.2 percent) of Sunday sales.[18]

Obviously, the Detroit papers are special cases. Their fight was for survival. Each lost money and feared that if it fell too far behind it would be assigned permanent number two position in a Detroit market that eventually might support just one paper. In 1989, the warring papers received U.S. Justice Department exemption from certain antitrust laws so they could combine production and business operations under a single roof in a *joint operating agreement* (which will be discussed in Chapter 12).

Deep discounting of subscription rates is particularly damaging because it greatly dilutes the primary source of circulation revenue—home delivery. The typical U.S. daily delivers 72 percent of its circulation to homes. In setting prices, remember that you deliver comprehensive news, information and entertainment plus colorful, detailed advertising to the door each day for pennies! The subscriber must be made to understand what a bargain that is.

The daily newspaper's price must be edged up to and past the cost of that cup of coffee. After all, magazines commonly are priced at $2 to $4 or more and get 51 percent of their total revenue from the reader (compared to 23 percent for newspapers). Cable TV fees are rising; book prices are up. This inevitably cheapens the newspaper's image in the public's eye, for it reveals our deep concern that our product has only a tenuous hold on its market position. Unless the entire industry moves quickly, ridiculously low prices will be so ingrained in the newspaper's relationship with readers that significantly higher prices will be impossible.

Why You Need Rate Increases

Three basic concerns militate for higher prices to readers: First, escalating advertising rates throw an increasingly inequitable share of newspaper costs onto advertisers, and that is unacceptable in this competitive world. Second, even minor circulation price increases can yield significant new revenue. A 5 percent increase in Knight-Ridder circulation revenue in 1992, for example, would have yielded more than $24.2 million additional. Third, circulation costs are rising rapidly, particularly in labor (often 60 percent of the department's total) and energy (sometimes 20 percent of total). Unless circulation departments convert to "profit centers" and bring in more direct revenue, they will fall even more deeply into deficit operations.

Some evidence suggests that the public generally feels rate increases would be justified. In her major readership survey (*Relating to Readers in the 80's*), Ruth Clark found 85 percent of the public regarded newspapers as "one of the biggest bargains there are these days." Clark quoted one housewife: "Our paper costs only a nickel or dime more than it did 10 years ago. Show me any product in the supermarket that can make the same claim."

Belden Associates found in a study of metro markets that 60 percent of adult respondents considered newspapers "inexpensive"; only 29 percent termed them "expensive." The *Orlando (Fla.) Sentinel* determined that 72 percent of its readers found the paper "a good value for the money" (vs. "poor value"). So, is the public already psychologically prepared for increases? Some managers think so.

When the *Los Angeles (Calif.) Daily News'* market research revealed that readers regarded the paper worth more than its price, the paper raised prices 11 times in seven years.

The Wall Street Journal was emboldened way back in 1984 to test an important psychological barrier: It raised its annual subscription over $100—to $101. The percopy price was raised 25 percent, to 50 cents. The *Journal* said $100 *was* a psychological barrier and that circulation dipped 2 percent in the second quarter of 1984, but growth resumed quickly. (In 1993, a one-year subscription to the *Journal* cost $149; single-copy price was 75 cents.)

USA Today, from its first day a hit with readers, dropped 9.5 percent in circulation when it increased its single-copy price from a quarter to 35 cents in 1984. Circulation recovered quickly, however, and Gannett executives are confident they crossed a psychological barrier with buyers: The public *would* dig down for two coins (a quarter and a dime) as easily as for one (a quarter alone). That proven, Gannett increased *USA Today*'s price to 50 cents—and circulation today is second-highest among all U.S. newspapers. (Gannett now is quietly experimenting with sales boxes that will accept $1 bills or credit cards.) The pricing lesson in *USA Today*'s experience: Offer attractive content deemed crucial by buyers and you can push prices upward.

The New York Times is deemed so important by readers that it commands $1 per weekday copy in the city, $2 on Sundays—the highest price ever for a U.S. newspaper. And, across the country, *The Times* Sunday readers are something akin to cult followers. They pay $3 to $5 in some cities.

Prepare Readers for Increases

The New York Times and *The Wall Street Journal* are aggressive pricing leaders in the industry. Implicit in that leadership is confidence in their competitive strength, confidence their news and advertising are worth more and that readers perceive both newspapers as so crucial to their daily lives that they will pay, within reason, the prices demanded.

Reader reaction to price hikes depends in large measure on how well newspapers serve their readers—and the availability of media alternatives. Certainly, no circulator can increase prices boldly without preparing the public carefully. You must coordinate a fully integrated effort by all departments to improve the product so as to warrant increased prices; promote it effectively to ensure the public will agree; and deliver it smoothly and on time. Then, prices can be hiked.

As circulation director of the *Anderson (S.C.) Independent-Mail,* John Truitt had this advice:

- Never call it an "increase," always a "price change."
- Schedule change for early fall, when demand for the paper is highest (because of back-to-school news interest, shopping activity, etc.).
- Alert carriers two weeks in advance; give subscribers three days notice, on the front page. The less advance notice to subscribers, the better.
- Don't stop the paper even when subscribers order it halted because of the price change; keep the paper arriving and give subscribers a cooling-off period to adjust to the new price.
- Any subscriber who insists on a halt in delivery should get a "preferred-customer kit" that includes a letter from the carrier, requesting reconsideration.

Some Circulators Disagree

Some circulators say the reading public simply will not accept aggressive pricing and that newspapers cannot stand any drop in household penetration resulting

---

BOX 8.2   Pricing: A New Approach

Jeff Hively, Scripps Howard corporate director of circulation and marketing, is a proponent of *aggressive pricing.* He says 1993 research shows:

1. Consumer demand for newspapers is *inelastic.* Despite traditional fear of losing circulation when prices are increased, only slight decreases occur if prices are raised annually and at a rate slightly higher than inflation.

2. Newspapers that raised their prices annually achieved operating profit margins of 26 percent, compared with 11 percent for newspapers that held prices in check.

Hively's goal is $115 in *annual* circulation revenue per subscriber. That requires a seven-day subscription price of $15 monthly, or single-copy prices of 50 cents daily and $1.75 on Sundays.

Source: "Circulation Pricing: New Strategies," *Scripps Howard General Managers Newsletter,* May 1993, p. 4

from higher prices. Jack Butcher, circulation director for the *Tampa (Fla.) Tribune*, said, "Direct mail is now a major competitive price comparison [for advertisers]. Penetration declines can be reversed in the absence of circulation price increases. On the other hand, it would appear that every price increase causes a permanent penetration percentage decline."

Some circulators say the pricing leaders, *The Wall Street Journal* and *The New York Times*, are special cases and that the marketplace has room for few newspapers of their types. These circulators say that if most newspapers were priced appreciably higher, they would be denied the mass-market acceptance that has traditionally been their basic appeal to advertisers.

Low-price advocates note television and radio are "free" to viewer or listener and that their cost is borne by the advertiser. They cite proliferating free-circulation publications and direct mail, also free to recipients, as competitive reasons for keeping newspaper rates low.

Distributing the Newspaper

Manufacturing more than 60 million copies of a product that is acceptable in quality and on time each day would challenge many industries. Most would be stunned at the idea of giving their expensive product to teenagers to distribute. But despite growing conversion to adult carriers, daily newspapers nationwide as recently as 1990 still used 360,000 carriers under age 18.[19] So, you must become expert in the "little merchant" teenage carrier system and other ways of distributing newspapers to the right people at the right time and collecting for them.

Handle Little Merchants Carefully

Most teenage carriers are *independent contractors*, not employees, who buy newspapers at wholesale prices, deliver and collect—thus they are known as "little merchants."

Your newspaper's contractual and working relationship with carriers must be crafted carefully with legal advice. Little merchants are exempt from minimum wage laws. Their independent status exempts the newspaper from pension and benefits responsibilities and other legal burdens. Inappropriate contract language or job supervision can create an employer-employee relationship requiring the newspaper to shoulder enormous financial responsibility and exposing it to penalties under the law.

First make sure contract language for carriers explicitly states they are independent contractors, not employees, and that the contract meets other current needs under state and federal law. The law changes, so stay alert. Essentially, you must protect the little merchants' independent status by compensating them for services rendered, but you may control only the result of their labor, not how it is accomplished. The newspaper cannot set prices, for example, or delineate sales territories or otherwise tightly supervise daily sales and distribution activities. It's a tricky area, hence legal counsel is required. Although the law doesn't require it, you should make sure carriers receive compensation close to the legal minimum wage. Compensation below that contributes to turnover in carrier ranks and draws trouble. (Other important legal questions affecting circulation strategy are discussed in Chapter 12.)

Effective programs for recruiting, training and motivating carriers are necessary to make sure delivery keeps those valuable subscribers happy. Circulators perforce become expert in dealing with juvenile carriers and the problems of youth. Carriers are difficult to recruit, sometimes hard to motivate and often fickle about staying on the job. Turnover is high, with 90 percent annually nationwide, 200 percent or more at many newspapers.

A nationwide trend toward smaller families means fewer children for carrier jobs, an important factor for newspapers needing hundreds or thousands. Growing affluence means larger child allowances, so dollars earned as a carrier are less enticing. Schools, churches, YMCAs, scoutmasters—all are sources of serious, reliable youngsters. Motivational training, financial incentives and adult supervision are crucial. Most newspapers conduct contests and award prizes—cash, stereos, baseball tickets, vacation trips—to carriers who sign the most new subscribers.

District Managers Are Key

The key first-level supervisor in all this is the district manager (DM), who recruits, trains, motivates and supervises carriers. DMs themselves should be recruited and trained very carefully. They can make or break circulation efforts.

The *Detroit News* in 1994 had 1,500 youth carriers (down from *12,000* in the mid-1980s!). Still, it's a formidable task to supervise each of the 1,500, and DMs are needed particularly in three essential tasks: sales, delivery and collection. Recruitment and training are executed carefully, and each year the DMs lead special sales efforts, with major promotion campaigns, motivational meetings, contests and prizes. *Milwaukee Journal* DMs use slide shows featuring rock music and teenage humor. The idea is to put fun into selling.

Delivery problems often are complicated by rapid turnover among DMs themselves. As circulation director for Scripps Howard, Tony Delmonico reported one of his group's papers, the *Rocky Mountain News* of Denver, had 89 percent turnover among its 91 DMs in one year. He said it cost the company about $7,500 to recruit and train each replacement. Screening and better training of new DMs dropped turnover to 61 percent and saved $427,000.

The *News'* circulation director, R. J. Myatt, said he knows the problem: A district manager must be a sales manager, teacher, psychiatrist, truck driver, public relations person, bill collector and accountant—"we're looking for a Superman or Superwoman, and too often we hire a nerd."[20] The basic difficulty, of course, is the type work DMs must do. Often, that includes delivering a "down" route—one dropped without notice by a teenage carrier. As a manager, you can do little to change the nature of the DMs' work. But you *can* bring to bear leadership and motivational skills to keep them posted on the newspaper's strategy and circulation goals. Pay your DMs appropriately and make them feel members of the management team.

The hassle of collecting is the reason carriers give most frequently for quitting. The collection process also irritates subscribers and leaves loose change rattling around, a temptation for the dishonest. Many papers switch to *payment-in-advance* (PIA) and bill by mail. This eliminates the administrative burdens teenagers feel in weekly door-to-door collecting and is attractive from your viewpoint because it actually gains interest-free loans from subscribers. A severe drawback is that PIA reduces personal contact between carrier and subscriber, in effect withdrawing the newspaper's front-line sales staff from frequent contact with customers. Some newspapers report this has a negative effect on subscription renewals.

Managing Other Distribution Systems

Newspapers sometimes contract with *independent agents* who handle all distribution, from press to subscriber household or point of single-copy sale. Often, independent agents handle many newspaper and magazines in the same area. Over the short run, working through independent agents might appear the most profitable and certainly easiest option for circulation departments. It avoids the need for large staffs, since recruiting and maintaining carriers are someone else's headaches.

Beware: The independent agency system can cause a newspaper to lose ultimate control of its product, pricing, distribution and—importantly—customer relations.

Courts have ruled under antitrust legislation that once an independent agency buys newspapers for resale it may set its own prices and sell wherever and to whomever it pleases. Thus, a newspaper may find its product is being handled by several agencies which are selling at various prices in competition with one another in the same general area. Also, newspapers can have no precise idea of who their subscribers are or where they live if distribution is handled by independent agencies (or loosely supervised nonemployee little merchants).

There are strong reasons, then, for every manager to study closely a third option: *employee distribution.* Newspapers increasingly use only employees for moving papers from press to street sale points, stores and vendors. Some also convert little merchants to employee status and pay them hourly wages. Under little merchant or independent agency systems, carriers typically keep about 30 percent of subscriber revenue. Calculate whether employee delivery would increase your newspaper's percentage.

Another major consideration is that computers permit you to maintain accurate subscriber lists. With employee delivery, this gives your newspaper close adult contact with subscribers, and that is attractive. Robert Whalen of Whalen Computers, specialists in circulation systems, spotted a trend: "A lot of newspapers have come to the conclusion that it is too dangerous to have their only contact with customers come through a 12-year-old boy."[21]

Some circulators argue the day of youthful carriers is passing—that legal, operational and cost factors dictate a shift to adults. Others, however, feel little merchants are the newspaper industry's greatest circulation strength and that, in selling newspapers, nothing beats the smiling teenager who lives down the street.

Mail delivery is used for 6 to 10 percent of all daily newspaper circulation. This is attractive, particularly for morning papers with substantial rural or apartment house circulation. Papers taken in presorted batches to post offices before dawn can be delivered the same day. Afternoon papers, of course, have little chance for same-day delivery by mail.

Many weeklies distribute exclusively by mail because it is inefficient to maintain expensive carrier systems for once-weekly use. Economical delivery by mail generally is possible only under second-class rates, based on distance the newspaper is mailed and its weight. To ensure qualification for a second-class permit, management must attest that the paper, among other things, is published on a regular schedule at least four times annually, has legitimate subscribers and devotes not more than 75 percent of its space to advertising in more than half its issues over a 12-month period. Mail delivery is extremely important in TMC operations. But relatively high costs and postal delays threaten timely delivery at acceptable cost. Understanding and conforming to postal regulations is extremely important, and you should establish personal ties with the local postmaster and stay informed on changes in regulations through the *Postal Bulletin* and *Domestic Mail Manual,* both on file at your local post office.

CASE STUDY 8.1   You're in Charge! (Now What?)

Once again, fate thrusts you into a leadership position. (Or, I prefer to think, you win it with thorough career preparation and hard work on the job.) However you got there, you're in charge of circulation for a large daily and, as always, the staff is looking to you for both strategic planning and daily operational guidance.

Now what? Well, start with planning goals, always the manager's first responsibility. Look first at what other newspapers accomplish in circulation, then plan your goals program to stretch your staff a bit to accomplish even more. We'll run through a scenario based on the industry averages for newspapers in the 50,000 to 100,000 range. Research was done by Scripps Howard, which in goals programs for its newspapers tries to outdo average performance.

Standards to Plan By
Penetration

It's your major circulation problem (and the industry's, too). Scripps Howard found dailies under 150,000 circulation, *without* head-to-head newspaper competition, average 54 percent morning penetration in their city zone or newspaper designated market. Evening papers av-

erage 42 percent. AMs paper over 150,000 circulation average 58 percent; PMs, 36 percent. Scripps Howard's goal: 60 percent penetration daily, 70 percent on Sundays.

In multiple-dwelling units, Scripps Howard wants 20 percent household delivery and an additional 15 percent of households buying single copies from on-site vending machines. (The industry averages 17 to 18 percent home delivery in multiple-dwelling units. Total industry circulation is 72 percent home delivered, 28 percent single-copy sale. Increased home delivery is your advertisers' desire and, thus, should be yours, too. "Natural" churn annually averages 30 percent of home subscribers industrywide. This is turnover due to lifestyle changes—household moves and so forth. Total churn, including for delivery or service problems, can run 50 to 75 percent.

Profit

Scripps Howard wants to retain 46 percent of *gross circulation revenue* with 30 percent going to carriers. Of the remaining *net revenue,* 35 percent should go to noncarrier expenses. Companywide, Scripps Howard sets this pricing

Continued

CASE STUDY 8.1   *Continued*

goal: Charge 50 cents daily, $1.50 on Sundays (improving over industry averages of 35 cents and $1).

Sales

Industrywide, it costs $6 in sales commission and other expenses to sign a daily newspaper subscriber. Sunday subscribers cost $4 each. Lesson: Don't lose subscribers you now have. They're too costly to replace. And, find ways to reduce your per-sale costs.

Here's where the industry gets *new subscription orders;* 36 percent from telephone solititation, 22 percent are voluntary, 20 percent from carriers, 14 percent from sales crews, 4 percent from direct mail, 4 percent other (district managers, promotional inserts and so forth). Obviously, one of your priority goals must be an effective "phone room."

Industrywide, *discounts* for new subscriptions are 2 percent of total revenue—an enormous sum of money. Scripps Howard tells its managers: Get discounts down to no more than 1 percent.

Paid-in-advance (PIA) subscriptions are sought by all newspapers, with varying success. For nonmetros, 25 to 75 percent of total subscribers pay from 3 to 12 months in advance; for metros, 15 to 65 percent. Scripps Howard wants 75 percent PIA for its nonmetro dailies, 65 percent for its metros.

Single-copy sales industrywide are 50 percent through dealers, 46 percent from vending machines, 4 percent others (hawkers and so on). Scripps Howard aims for 60 percent of single-copy sales through dealers, 35 percent from machines, 10 percent through other sources. One reason: sales per vending machine average only five copies per day and return of unsold copies, an expensive proposition, averages 30 percent. Supplying vending machines is not only an inexact science—it's expensive, too.

Single-copy returns overall, including from dealers, are 15 percent daily, 12 percent on Sundays.

Customer Satisfaction

Percentage of penetration in your city zone and retail trading zone is your best measure of whether your newspaper meets its marketplace's demands. But there are other measurements:

- Industrywide, 70 percent of customers respond "very satisfied" to the question, "How satisfied are you with weekday delivery service?" Scripps Howard wants 85 to 90 percent of its customers responding that way.
- We know customer satisfaction ties directly to on-time delivery. Industrywide, newspapers achieve morning delivery at 6 A.M.; for afternoon papers, 5 P.M.; and 6:30 A.M. on Sundays. Scripp Howard's goal: 5:30 A.M. for morning papers, 4:30 P.M. for afternoon papers, 6 A.M. on Sundays.
- The more adult carriers you have, the better your on-time accuracy—and customer satisfaction. Industrywide, 65 percent of papers now are delivered by adults, 35 percent by youth carriers. Scripps Howard wants "gradually" increased percentages of adults—"gradually," presumably, because adults are more expensive.
- Service errors (failure to deliver and so forth) industrywide now run under 1 per 1,000 subscribers daily, fewer than 1.5 per 1,000 on Sundays. That's very good, of course. But what a shame to lose any customers through service errors!

So, even if you've unexpectedly been thrust into (or even clawed your way into) circulation department responsibility you now have standards to plan by!

Source: "Newspaper Industry Performance Averages and Goals," *Scripps Howard General Managers Newsletter,* Nov. 1992, p. 6.

SUMMARY

Under the marketing concept, the circulation department must be truly integrated with news, advertising, production and promotion in a focused thrust toward the newspaper's overall goals. Advertiser redefinition of what is attractive circulation plus rising distribution costs forces many newspapers to eliminate circulation distant from their home markets. Advertisers want to pay only for circulation that reaches prospective customers living near retail outlets. Circulation without advertising support is a cost factor, not a profit generator, and thus is "inefficient" circulation.

Lifestyle changes force changes in circulation thinking. The newspaper is packaged and marketed under the basic strategy of penetrating the traditional mother-plus-father-plus-children household. Growth of other types of family units—single-parent families, for example, challenges long-held assumptions about the content and sale of the American newspaper. With new competition springing up, circulation strategy must protect the newspaper's franchise as principal source of printed news, dominant advertising source and door-to-door delivery vehicle.

Circulation accounts for about 30 percent of a newspaper's total expense but about 23 percent or less of total revenue. Increasingly, circulation managers are expected to launch TMC or direct mail operations and generate departmental profit as well as perform more traditional distribution tasks.

An industrywide problem is fear that higher prices will lead to circulation loss. Improve content and launch aggressive promotion to make sure the public perceives the paper as being worth more. That's key to raising prices.

"Selling" the newspaper involves obtaining readers, servicing them to retain their loyalty, collecting from them and replacing those who cancel. The manager must intervene in the process at key points and times to ensure the staff quality and operational smoothness needed to accomplish those tasks.

RECOMMENDED READING

Newspaper Association of America was formed in 1992, in the merger of seven industry associations. It absorbed the International Circulation Managers Association and thus became the leading source of industry research in circulation. ICMA resources now at NAA headquarters include a wide variety of research reports, circulation case histories, training films and so forth. Contact NAA at the Newspaper Center, 11600 Sunrise Valley Drive, Reston, Va. 22901-1412, telephone (703) 648-1000.

Another valuable source is the Audit Bureau of Circulations, 900 N. Meacham Road, Schaumburg, Ill. 60195. ABC issues periodic research reports and case histories.

Some of the most timely (and important) research and analysis is published in *Scripps Howard General Managers Newsletter,* Scripps Howard, P.O. Box 5380, Cincinnati, Ohio 45201. Also watch *presstime, Editor & Publisher.*

GLOSSARY

Many newspaper managers rise through news or advertising departments without hands-on circulation experience. Any manager who seeks to be a circulator—or who seeks credibility among them—should learn their language, some which is defined here.

Alternate Delivery. Use of a newspaper's delivery force to distribute products of other companies, including magazines, advertising flyers and so forth.

Audit Bureau of Circulations (ABC). A nonprofit cooperative that audits and publishes member newspaper circulation figures for advertisers and others. Each member circulation department must keep daily and monthly records in accordance with ABC rules.

Blitz. Free delivery (also known as "sampling") to nonsubscriber homes for a week or so, followed by intensive sales effort.

Bootjacking. A term of yesteryear for selling single copies on the streets.

Bulk Sales. Distribution of bundles trucked in large quantities for sale to, for example, hotels or airlines; there is disagreement over whether bulk sales should be counted as paid circulation under ABC rules.

City manager. Supervises street sales manager, district manager and others responsible for city circulation.

Contract haulers. Independent truck owners, not employees, who deliver bundles.

County manager. Supervises district managers, motor route drivers and others distributing outside the city.

District (or "branch") manager. Responsible for a specific territory; hires, trains and supervises the carriers in it.

Door knockers. Sales crew, usually young people other than carriers, who sell subscriptions door-to-door on a commission basis.

Draw sheet. Count of copies ordered each day by each carrier, dealer or others who distribute papers. Incorporates each new "start" or "stop" of subscriptions for that day.

Honor racks. Contrasted with coin-operated racks, these put buyers on their honor to leave money for the papers; a high theft rate is normal.

Little merchants. Boys and girls, not employees, who buy papers at discount, then deliver and collect. Check local/state laws for minimum ages, work hours and other regulations.

Motor route drivers. Adults who drive distribution routes, throwing papers or placing them in roadside "tubes"; normally they are independent, not employees.

Ownership statement. Federal law requires the publisher of each general-circulation paper with a second-class postal permit to submit by Oct. 1 of each year a sworn statement of paid circulation, ownership details, executives' names and addresses and point of publication. Statement must be published in first or second issue of the paper following submission.

Payment in advance (PIA) or pay by mail (PMB). Payment through office, not carrier; is designed to sign subscribers to longer periods, usually three, six or twelve months and relieve little merchants of collection hassles; the number one cause of carrier turnover.

Phone room sellers. Employees or outside salespersons who canvas for subscriptions by telephone.

Promotion manager. Designs, supervises sales campaigns by carriers, phone rooms, outside sales crews, direct mail, other media.

Returns. Newspapers returned unsold to the circulation department; an important indicator of a newspaper's circulation success in single-copy street sales. A high return rate can be enormously expensive.

Route list. A carrier's list of subscribers, usually requested annually by ABC.

Sampling. Free delivery to nonsubscribers for a week or so, followed by sales contact. This is expensive and must be tightly controlled.

SMC. Selected market coverage, circulation designed to reach a narrowly focused area of prime interest to advertisers.

Start. An order for delivery to a new subscriber.

Stop. An order to halt delivery.

Stuffing. Inserting preprinted material, often manually on smaller papers, prior to delivery.

Throwaway. A free-circulation paper or "shopper" with little news content; often thrown on front porches.

Total market coverage (TMC). Distribution system designed to reach all or nearly all households in a market; it often combines the newspaper's paid circulation with a free-circulation companion publication or direct mail.

NOTES

1. Russell A. Barcroft, "The Circulation Perspective," speech to International Newspaper Promotion Association, Chicago, May 15, 1983.

2. Celeste Huenergard, "Publisher Tells Circulators, 'Don't Be So Defensive,'" Editor & Publisher, June 25, 1983, p. 8-B.

3. "Newspapers Must Hustle for More Readers: Bogart," report on Newspaper Advertising Bureau survey, *Editor & Publisher,* June 25, 1983, p. 8-A. (The bureau was incorporated into Newspaper Association of America in 1992.)

4. "Nationals Use Alternates Too," *presstime,* June 1993, p. 25.

5. "Household Sales Plagues Daily Papers," *Editor & Publisher,* May 1, 1982, p. 12.

6. "How J. C. Penney Uses Newspaper Audit Reports," *Audit Bureau of Circulations Case Book,* 1983, p. 5.

7. Belden was early to recognize the importance of research in this area. Note "Belden Reports Results of TMC Product Survey," *Editor & Publisher,* July 24, 1992, p. 15.

8. Celeste Huenergard, "Upscale Shopper Eyes National Distribution," *Editor & Publisher,* Nov. 20, 1982, p. 20.

9. "Newspapers Urged to Embrace Shared Mail TMC Programs," *Editor & Publisher,* July 31, 1982, p. 8.

10. "Marriage Mail: A Letter-Perfect Match," *Advertising Age,* May 30, 1983, p. m-15.

11. These themes run through *Journal* and *Constitution* promotion. See particularly their 1983 promotional brochure, *Product Profile.*

12. Warren Phillips, letter to author.

13. Richard Capen, letter to author.

14. Thomas Winship, letter to author.

15. Bob Haring, letter to author.

16. Burl Osborne, letter to author.

17. Jon Katz, "The Media's War on Kids," *Rolling Stone,* Nov. 25, 1993, p. 47.

18. *1984 Annual Report,* Miami, Fla., Knight-Ridder Inc.

19. Though impressive, this figure is down dramatically in recent years. The International Circulation Managers Association reported 362,470 carriers under 18 on the job in 1990, down from 823,746 in 1980. See Peter T. Kilborn, "Paperboys and Papergirls Turn a Last Corner," *The New York Times,* Aug. 16, 1992, p. 22.

20. "Newspapers Told to Hire Better DMs," *Editor & Publisher,* June 25, 1983, p. 8A.

21. Elise Burroughs, "Computerized Circulation Comes of Age," *presstime,* Dec. 1982, p. 28.

9

ADVERTISING

I'll be candid: You can be a successful newspaper manager even if you can't write a Pulitzer Prize-winning news story—even if you don't understand the inner workings of a press or how computers are programmed. But if you don't understand—completely, thoroughly—newspaper advertising, your manager's career will be short and unspectacular.

Advertising is the financial heart of the newspaper. Every manager at every level in every department must understand that and help create a newspaper that is a successful advertising medium, because readers alone don't come close to fully supporting the newspaper. It is advertisers, contributing 75 to 80 percent of total revenue, who determine whether a newspaper will succeed financially.

In this chapter, we will discuss managerial principles you can use in designing and leading the advertising department. Those principles include designing organizational structure, planning ad strategy and then managing and controlling performance.

WHY ADVERTISING MATTERS

If simply selling more papers was the only newspaper game, the newspaper death list in the 1980s would have been considerably shorter. The *Washington Star*, after all, had a very substantial 340,000 circulation when it failed. The *Cleveland Press* claimed 316,000, 19th largest in the nation, just before it died. The *Philadelphia Bulletin* went down with close to 400,000, fourth largest for any afternoon paper in the country.

Reader loyalty in those cities translated into millions of dollars in circulation revenue each year. In other cities, in different competitive and cost environments, circulation of that magnitude would mean immensely profitable operations. What went wrong? How could those newspapers fail financially when thousands and thousands of subscribers plunked down cash to buy them each day?

The equation of failure in newspaper publishing is extremely complex, and disaster wore many faces when it struck in Washington, Philadelphia and Cleveland. Yet a common theme ran through those sad stories: Each failed newspaper lost advertiser loyalty and share of advertising market. For each, there came a time when revenue would not cover out-of-control costs, management error, journalistic weakness, onrushing competitors—all the ills that can afflict a newspaper—and those papers starved to death financially.

Loss of advertising market share is a manifestation of ills, *not* the cause; often, when share deterioration becomes glaringly visible, the newspaper's situation already is precarious. Large or small, published in village or metropolis, the newspaper then is vulnerable to internal disruption or error, such as a strike or management fumble, and to external forces, such as an economic downturn or competition from other papers or media. An example was the *Cleveland Press* in its final months.

The Cleveland Press: A Case in Point

The *Press* demonstrated under ownership of E. W. Scripps Co. how resilient a stricken newspaper can be. It somehow survived years of internal and external affliction until rising costs and faltering revenue brought it to the breaking point.

With its 45.1 percent share of Cleveland's metro daily circulation but at best only 35.5 percent of its daily advertising, the *Press* was caught in the classic Catch-22 of a number two newspaper: It sustained high costs to maintain large circulation but had only low advertising revenue to support those costs.

Then came economic recession. Cleveland businesses shut down; unemployment skyrocketed. Retailers, still suffering from the city's 23.6 percent population loss between 1970 and 1980, were in agony. The *Press* was ravaged. Real estate advertising, for example, dropped one-third. Costs did not fall, however, and *Press* executives announced a 12 percent raise in local retail ad rates. A 12 percent increase for hard-pressed retailers in a stricken city buffeted by recession? It couldn't fly—and didn't.

The *Press*, now owned by local entrepreneur Joseph E. Cole, announced rebates aimed at making rate increases more palatable. At the same time, it tried to improve news content and the paper's overall competitive posture. But time ran out and the newspaper shut down.

Says owner Cole: "With better economic conditions, I believe we could have made it. But the economic environment, combined with . . . depressed real estate, automobile, housing and retail sales, contributed to our inability to secure sufficient advertising revenues. The times were simply against us."[1]

Strangely, Cole's eulogy did not mention competition, for in its extremity the *Press* battled formidable competitors for a share of Cleveland's shrinking ad revenue:

- The *Cleveland Plain Dealer,* then 380,000 daily and 450,000 Sunday circulation (and now 446,000 daily and 570,000 Sunday), owned by well-financed, nationwide Newhouse Newspapers.
- Eleven suburban weeklies and shoppers, with 273,000 free and paid circulation, owned by Com Corp. Sun Newspapers Inc., plus three independent weeklies with 45,000 combined circulation.

- *Cleveland Magazine* plus four TV stations and 20 radio stations (more in nearby suburbs and towns).
- Other competitors included 16 foreign-language newspapers aimed at the city's ethnic groups, 46 business and trade periodicals published in Cleveland, 7 local college publications, vigorous direct mail and outdoor advertising companies, plus a tight ring of dailies and weeklies in smaller cities around Cleveland.

The *Press* had to fight desperately for market share, because every ad dollar spent with a radio station, Hungarian neighborhood weekly or suburban shopper was an ad dollar the newspaper did not get.

In sum, to understand advertising's role in newspaper operations you must consider several key points:

- Unless reader loyalty can be translated into advertiser support a newspaper is doomed.
- A circulation/advertising imbalance—high circulation costs, low ad revenue—creates a cost structure so high that the newspaper is vulnerable to disruptions in internal operations or external environment.
- Regardless of size, whether weekly or daily, a newspaper must have an advertising organization that, with help from all other departments, can compete against competitors of all types on all sides.

Now, how can you design an advertising organization capable of dealing effectively with those complex challenges?

DESIGNING THE ADVERTISING ORGANIZATION

The advertising department is "betwixt and between" at any newspaper. It is the crucial link between the newspaper's need for revenue and the prime source of it, the competitive marketplace.

But, it is totally dependent on other departments—news, circulation, production—for what it sells: solutions to advertisers' problems.

Take great care, therefore, in designing your advertising organization to operate efficiently in both its internal and external environments. Try to create new attitudes to motivate managers, in advertising or out, to nurture the advertising organization, giving it appropriate human and financial resources and supporting its efforts. And, importantly, design to accommodate internal changes in the way newspapers do things.

Design for Change Within

Newspapers in early days gained all their revenue through circulation alone. By 1887, when the American Newspaper Publishers' Association (now Newspaper

Association of America) was formed and began keeping records, about half of newspaper revenue came from circulation. By 1909, it was down to one-third; by the early 1990s, it was 20 to 25 percent or less. The change reflects slow circulation growth and a reluctance to risk offending readers by charging them more. Many newspaper managers fear readers will not accept higher costs, and the main burden, therefore, falls to advertisers.

Advertising's contribution to total revenue has risen, consequently, to 75 to 80 percent or more at most newspapers, although it is one of the least expensive departments to operate—only 10 to 12 percent of total expense. To survive without advertising newspapers would have to increase their circulation rates fivefold or more *and* maintain present circulation levels. Of course, newspapers priced that high and lacking full advertising—a reader draw, just like news—would lose circulation speedily.

The first reality in designing your advertising organization, then, is its relative position within the newspaper's structure: It is crucial in generating revenue and comparatively inexpensive to operate.

A second reality is that you must integrate advertising with other departments and ensure they work together smoothly. The ad department must be involved in every step of the marketing effort, including creation of the news product, production and distribution. That's still a revolutionary idea at some newspapers, particularly in newsrooms where *any* suggestion that advertising considerations enter the news process can create immediate tension. Start by clearly explaining to editors the financial importance of advertising, but stop well short of suggesting the newsroom sell its journalistic soul to advertising. That won't work and it's wrong.

In the corporate hierarchy, the advertising department must report directly to the chief marketing executive: the marketing director in larger papers, general manager or publisher in smaller papers. Looking downward, the advertising director must plan and continually evaluate, control and adjust as necessary the performance of important sub-units. Depending on newspaper size, sub-units vary in number and character.

Figure 9.1 shows the organizational structure of the ad department at the jointly owned *Athens (Ga.) Daily News* and *Banner-Herald*, which have 12,000 morning circulation and 13,800 in the evening. These sub-units report directly to the papers' ad director:

The *national ad coordinator* seeks all available national or "general" revenue. Relative to other sources of revenue, it won't be significant on a newspaper this size. The coordinator works through a "national rep," a firm that sells space, on a commission basis, to national advertisers for many newspapers.

The *retail manager* runs the single most important sub-unit. Retail or "local retail" ads from local merchants provide most revenue for all newspapers except those national in scope.

The *chief artist* directs layout and design services for advertisers. Vital to the sales effort is the speculation or "spec" ad created by artists to entice advertisers into signing a contract. Advertising graphics that are aesthetically pleasing—in addi-

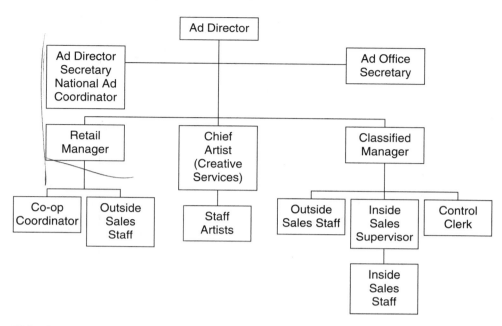

FIGURE 9.1 Organization of advertising for the *Athens (Ga.) Banner-Herald* **and** *The Daily News.*

tion to being persuasive—contribute greatly to a newspaper's readability and appeal. Increasingly, ads are being laid out, graphics and all, on computer screens. This process is being dovetailed into pagination—the computerized layout of pages.

The *classified manager* directs a booming sector of newspaper advertising. Classified is 35 percent of all newspaper ad revenue, and 50 percent or more of the total for some papers.[2]

Design for External Change

Design your advertising department to meet rapid changes outside the newspaper. Three are key: First, although newspapers still are the nation's leading advertising medium, you will recall from Chapter 1 that newspapers' share of the ad revenue pie is getting smaller. Design to gain a larger share in your local market.

Second, the number of competitors for ad dollars is increasing *and* competitors are offering target marketing precision and comprehensive total market coverage (TMC)—two challenges newspapers meet only with difficulty. Design for zoned (or "part-run") advertising and launch special advertising vehicles that offer your own target marketing; design free-circulation products or direct mail services to offer your own TMC.

BOX 9.1   Just What Do Advertisers Want?

Distill speeches and comments by executives of leading retail firms and you'll find them demanding top-flight performance from newspapers. These demands keep cropping up:

1. Retailers want to advertise their products in publications that have a quality appearance and a competitive edge over other media.
2. Newspapers must break down circulation by ZIP codes and guard against duplication—charging advertisers twice to reach the same reader through different media.
3. Advertisers demand accurate, timely demographic and psychographic research from newspapers in standardized form to ease dealing with two or more papers.
4. Advertisers want new, innovative ways of reaching new customers and old, using the newspaper itself but also alternate means.
5. Advertisers also buck at time delays inherent in the newspaper production process. They want ability to telephone in or fax ad copy the day before publication (delays of 3 to 4 days now are standard).
6. And, of course, advertisers want all this done at minimum cost with value-added programs that create extra incentive to use newspaper advertising. (Some newspapers, for example, offer "extra cards," which resemble credit cards and entitle subscribers to discounts on products and services sold by local retailers.)

Third, retailers are changing their advertising and marketing tactics—seeking more than simple exposure of their message to large numbers of diverse ("undifferentiated") readers. They now demand meaningful impact on potential customers through newspapers that join in solving business problems, not simply selling space.

And, yes, advertisers have demands for your newsroom, too. They want your news and feature copy to create believability and reliability, thus lending credibility to ads and motivating response.

Note the promotional themes of high-quality newspapers (or magazines). They boast their pages offer an environment of high-quality journalism that delivers upscale readers who believe the publication they hold in their hands. *The New York Times* uses this theme of "high-quality environment" to capture the great bulk of print ad dollars in New York City, despite vigorous competition from *New York Newsday, The New York Daily News* and The *Post.*

Another external factor you must watch: Advertisers are analyzing media costs carefully, watching "cost-per-thousand" rates ("CPMs" in the trade), which newspapers and their competitors charge to deliver an advertising message to 1,000 readers. Whatever the quality of your newspaper's journalism or its other attributes, CPM comparison is an important advertiser yardstick in judging the relative cost effectiveness of competing media. You must design an organizational structure capable of meeting competitors on that battleground.

As newspaper CPMs escalate due to higher costs—plus shareholder profit demands—and as alternative media become more attractive, some advertisers withdraw from newspapers or seek a "mix" of, say, one newspaper supplemented by television, radio, direct mail or other. For example, Jewel Food Stores, a major advertiser, announced in the 1980s an advertising mix of about 52 percent newspapers, 23 percent television, 13 percent radio, and 12 percent direct mail and other vehicles. In 1992, supermarkets nationwide were using only 44.5 percent newspapers. Direct mail's share rose to 31.5 percent. Television was hit worse than newspapers: Its share of supermarket dollars dropped to 4.8 percent.[3]

In two-newspaper towns, some advertisers withdraw from number two paper on grounds they can reach desired audiences more economically through one newspaper, the market leader, plus a mix of other media. For the advertiser, this eliminates the cost of "duplication"—advertising in two newspapers whose circulations overlap and to some extent deliver the same readers. It also helps kill number two newspapers. It certainly did in Washington, Cleveland and Philadelphia.

Increasingly, all this no longer is sorted out one to one between newspaper salesperson and corner grocer. More than half of all newspaper advertising is planned or bought outside the local market, at distant headquarters of store chains, where research-oriented specialists demand precise information on newspaper markets, audiences and competitors. Traditionally, many newspapers sent backslapping sales people into the fray equipped with little more than pleasant personalities; these same papers now scramble to deliver computer-generated market studies to this new breed of advertising executive.

Designing Advertising Research

You'll recall from earlier chapters the first steps in strategic planning: first, research your own newspaper's strengths and weaknesses, second, investigate your market and, third, research your competition. Now, add a fourth step: you must research your advertisers' businesses to determine their needs and how your newspaper can meet them.

Research must be continuous, using "intelligence" generated internally and externally by government or research bodies. Larger papers must have research units with computer capability to digest vast amounts of raw information. Smaller papers can and must make sure they also have research capability, no matter how primitive technologically.

BOX 9.2   Practice "Smart Bombing"

"The current mass media practice of undertaking B-52 overflights and conducting 'carpet bombing' of consumers will give way to targeted, 'smart bombing' whereby a specific message is delivered to a specific household on a one-to-one basis.

"The B-52s are old technology. Newspapers must learn the new technology and be able to deliver it seven days a week if they hope to survive."

Alf Nucifora, chairman of Nucifora Consulting Group, specialists in strategic planning and marketing, in "Newspapers' Future Depends on Their Sensitivity to Customers," *presstime,* July 1992, p. 44.

Always focus research on marketing the newspaper better and more profitably, suggesting practical steps toward basic objectives: identifying marketing opportunities or problems, designing tentative solutions and then helping the decision-making process move ahead. Research for external use should be designed to solve advertiser needs and assist you in what advertising sales is all about: getting signed contracts. Base your sales efforts on solidly researched information and facts, not the personality of salespeople.

The *Rocky Mountain News* of Denver gave clients a 54-page market analysis by Belden Associates, a Dallas research firm used by many newspapers. As an example of the report's detail, Belden found there were 71,000 widows in the Denver-Boulder market or 11 percent of all women, and that 54 percent of these read the *Rocky Mountain News.*

Market surveys by outside firms can be expensive. *The Atlanta Constitution* and *Journal* paid more than $200,000 to Scarborough Research Corp. of New York for one market study. Was it worth it? Ferguson Rood, then vice president for marketing and advertising, said:

> *Research such as Scarborough is essential to the sale of advertising. It is necessary that we measure our markets in terms of readers rather than simply count circulation. Knowing who our readers are in terms of their demographics and lifestyles helps us and our advertisers target advertising messages for everyone's benefit.*
>
> *We have found through years of experience that when we relate our readership to shoppers at specific stores, we help advertisers buy more space more efficiently, thus making their advertising an investment rather than an expense.*

If you cannot afford outside research, do-it-yourself kits are available. Suburban Newspapers of America distributes readership survey materials complete with sampling methodology and questionnaires.[4] However it is obtained, your research must help advertisers find the geographic or demographic targets they want to reach, then assist in precision delivery of the client's message via target marketing.

Donald R. Hartley, as ad director for the *Montgomery (Ala.) Advertiser,* said, "I can see the day when we'll be able to hit all the left-handed cigar-smokers on the left side of the street whose names start with 'M.' Nobody else is better suited to do it."[5] That sort of competitive confidence presumes, of course, that newspapers will develop target marketing services, such as direct mail. Research must determine how the newspaper is performing in its market. Without this, strategy can go astray. Sometimes, for example, huge chunks of newspaper circulation become unattractive to advertisers. Such a development must be picked up in research so managers can adjust accordingly.

Cleveland: More Lessons

At the *Cleveland Press,* that sort of development wasn't picked up in research, managers didn't react in time—and that compounded the *Press*'s problems. To explain: *Press* circulation penetrated 47.9 percent of households in its ABC City Zone. That ranked an impressive sixth among the 25 largest-circulation U.S. newspapers in the early 1980s. However, Cleveland's core went through a decade of wrenching socioeconomic change, and many demographically attractive customers fled to suburbs in the Retail Trading Zone (RTZ). Out there, the *Press* ran into Com. Corp.'s 11 suburban weeklies and shoppers, each entrenched in its narrow local market, plus zoned editions launched earlier by its alert cross-town rival, the *Plain Dealer.*

The *Press* was late in detecting the shift to the suburbs; when it finally reacted, the competitive situation had deteriorated beyond repair. The *Press* never penetrated more than 14.6 percent of those desirable RTZ households and was able to offer its advertisers only circulation that was mainly in relatively unattractive inner Cleveland. Advertisers insist on lower ad rates for unattractive circulation—if they pay for it at all—so the *Press* was forced to lower rates and then provide rebates, which reduced revenue even more. Lessons for all managers: Research must pick up trends such as those that trapped the *Press* early enough so adjustments can be made.

Press ad salespeople were ill equipped to meet advertisers' objections that they were not interested merely in large circulation, that they wanted the *Press* to deliver the right kind of readers—the affluent, ready-to-spend readers who lived near suburban retail outlets. The *Press*'s research should have found those readers so the newsroom could develop a product for them and circulation, in turn, could deliver them for the advertising department to sell to clients.

A different but equally instructive research problem plagued Gannett's *USA Today* in its early years. The paper enjoyed astounding circulation success, but many advertisers complained that 70 percent of sales were single copies from newsstands and racks and that, therefore, there was no reliable research on precisely who the readers were. Advertisers want continuity among readers, and they asked for research on whether the same people were buying the paper each day. Some wanted to know whether readership was heavily sports-oriented—drawn by the paper's outstanding sports section—and whether as a daily *USA Today* had a "shelf life" of several days, as did *Time, Newsweek* and other magazines.

Breaking through the image problem and selling advertisers on the value of *USA Today*'s very substantial circulation was frustratingly difficult for Gannett executives. Their inability to plan an advertising strategy that answered those questions satisfactorily contributed to *USA Today*'s losses, which over a decade approached $1 billion.[6]

Planning Ad Sales Strategy

Now, one of your most important responsibilities: planning a dynamic sales strategy to achieve your advertising department's assigned goals. This must be done for major advertising categories—local retail, national and classified—and, as well, for preprint/insert advertising. All are important revenue sources.

As you study each category in detail, in pages ahead, you may easily lose sight of the overall strategic picture. So keep in mind that advertising sales strategy must be planned in complete consonance with strategies of other departments, particularly news and circulation.

Here is an example of what can happen when that underlying principle of the marketing concept is ignored.

New York Post: A Case in Point

When Australian publisher Rupert Murdoch first bought the *New York Post*, he laid down a news strategy featuring highly sensational coverage—rape, murder, pillage and arson were standard fare. His circulation strategy aimed at New York City readers left behind by the *Daily News* in its climb to somewhat higher journalistic ground and, certainly, by the high-toned *New York Times*.

Murdoch's advertising strategy? Well, a story (perhaps apocryphal) illustrating his dilemma made the rounds. It had Murdoch trying to convince an executive of an upscale New York City department store to switch advertising to his *Post* from *The Times*. Murdoch's flamboyant afternoon tabloid was, after all, then delivering more readers than *The Times*. "Mr. Murdoch," the executive is said to have replied, "*The Times*'s readers are our shoppers. The *Post*'s readers are our shoplifters."[7]

True or not, the story damaged the *Post*. As the paper tried to carve out a share of an advertising market crowded by the *Daily News*, then the largest general-circulation daily in the country, and *The Times*, perhaps the most prestigious, the tale was circulated by, among others, *Advertising Age*, a trade publication widely read by advertising executives and retailers nationwide. The magazine quoted "one New York media buyer" as follows: "I look at their numbers [the *Post*'s readership research] and I see that they reach more college-educated readers than the *Daily News* and that they have a younger audience than the *Times*, but just when I think that—maybe—I should recommend the *Post* to a client, I look at those screaming red headlines, and I think, God, no I just can't go in there."[8]

The failure of the *Post*'s advertising strategy seriously detracted from one of the industry's great circulation success stories up to that time—from 400,000 to 960,000 in just six years. Circulation plummeted to 732,000 in 1987, and by 1994, the *Post* was barely alive. It was self-defeating for one *Post* department, news, to create a sensational newspaper and for another, advertising, to try to sell to advertisers on fashionable Fifth Avenue the type of readers that content attracted.

Now, let's look at where advertising dollars come from, how the competitive battle for market share is heating up and where newspaper strengths and weaknesses lie.

Local Retail Display Advertising

Local retail merchants, who sell directly to consumers, are mainstays of newspaper advertising. Television is the newspaper industry's closest single competitor in local retail, but a distant one. Radio's share is smaller.

For all but national newspapers, local retail dominates revenue. Often, 50 percent of the total—70 to 80 percent or more on smaller papers—comes from local retail. So the local retail fight is one in which newspapers battle rising numbers of vigorous competitors lusting for their very lifeblood.

Direct mail companies, using computerized address lists to seek out tightly stratified, demographically attractive advertising targets, certainly are in the forefront of competitors. So are free-circulation papers. They offer, of course, highly sophisticated selective market coverage (SMC) plus ability to blanket geographic areas with nearly 100 percent TMC penetration.

BOX 9.3 The Real Competitive Foe?

"Despite all the concern about the competitive threats from the electronic superhighway and other manifestations of the digital age, the reality of the here-and-now for the newspaper business is that the U.S. Postal Service is the most formidable newspaper competitor for local advertising. This is likely to be true for years to come."

Newspaper analyst John Morton, commenting on Safeway Stores' decision to pull its grocery ads from the *Washington Post* and use direct mail instead, in "The Mail Animal," *Newspaper Letter,* Sept. 30, 1993, p. 1.

Because newspapers traditionally dominated local advertising, some managers even today project their local revenue as a guaranteed fixed percentage of advertisers' store sales. This is changing as local merchants increasingly seek media alternatives. Also changing is the attitude, among some managers of small- and medium-size papers, that they can raise rates nearly at will. Advertisers started rebelling in the late 1970s and early 1980s over automatic increases designed to cover rising newspaper costs. Some papers were passing along double-digit, twice-annual increases that totaled substantially more than inflationary cost increases.

Your sales strategy, then, must recognize that newspapers face an unprecedented challenge in local retail due to strengthening competitors, advertisers' increasing sophistication in media affairs, and the inability of some editors and circulation managers, as at the *Cleveland Press,* to shift journalistic and marketing strategies to meet socioeconomic changes in their markets. Don't overlook, either, pressure created by advertisers who got quite an education when newspaper companies that went public were required to publish financial results. Advertisers learned the ad rates they were paying supported newspaper profit ratios higher than those enjoyed by many industries and, indeed, often by advertisers themselves.

Your Strengths in Local
Your newspaper has strengths in the fight for local retail advertising. Here's how you can bring them to bear:

1. As the primary, often unrivaled source of substantive local news, community newspapers generally can demonstrate reader acceptance promising widespread and credible exposure of advertisers' messages to their primary consumer target—local residents. Indeed, many readers buy newspapers for advertising as well as news. Sell your newspaper as a family tool actively used in the search for shopping guidance by serious, habitual readers.

2. Point out to advertisers that the very nature of a newspaper, as contrasted with television or radio, permits graphic display of detailed local retail shopping information—full page ads of grocery prices, for example, or dozens of hardware items.

3. Newspaper readers generally are upscale in education, income and buying habits. Research of your own market should reveal this; then, demonstrate how your integrated marketing effort creates and distributes products that reach attractive consumers.

4. Merchants selling consumables (foods or drugs, for example, not autos or refrigerators) tend to advertise at predictable levels in good times; yet they also advertise even in bad times just to maintain their institutional image and market share. Newspapers have "shelf life" or availability and usefulness in the home— all day for a daily, five or six days for a weekly—that is well suited for that type of advertising. Make it a selling point.

5. Alert newspapers can meet, better than any competitor, the pressing need of core-city advertisers by "chasing" affluent customers who move to the suburbs and beyond. *The New York Times* does this for Fifth Avenue merchants by delivering demographically attractive readers via its circulation in rich suburbs of New Jersey, Connecticut and elsewhere. Smaller dailies can offer target marketing, particularly if they provide TMC with a combination of their paid-circulation plus a free-circulation paper to nonsubscribers. Television, a mass-appeal medium, cannot focus its efforts that way. It casts a net for scattered millions. Radio can "zone" with programming—rock music to draw young listeners, "golden oldies" for older listeners—but it still cannot match newspaper zoning.

6. Newspapers require less "lead time" than television for ad copy, so advertisers can quickly exploit an event (a swimsuit sale, for example, soon after unexpectedly good spring weather). Television requires lengthy lead times for commercials and commercials are far more expensive to produce than are newspaper ads.

Beware Your Weaknesses
However, newspapers battle for local retail ads with a number of weaknesses:

1. Paid circulation generally penetrates too few households. Your strategy must be to improve news content to eventually attract more paid readers while also providing TMC with a separate vehicle.

2. Because it is essentially a news medium, the newspaper cannot attract the huge audiences lured by television's entertainment. Your strategy must be to show advertisers (through research) that you, however, deliver demographically attractive albeit smaller audiences.

3. Newspapers, unlike television or radio, use a very expensive commodity— newsprint—and, also unlike broadcast, are labor intensive. This drives up costs, which, in turn, forces newspaper ad rates higher until competitors sometimes can undersell. Free-circulation papers have costs substantially lower than those of a paid-circulation newspaper: Shoppers have no expensive news staffs. To counter both low-cost competitors, you must sell advertisers on the fact that paid circulation papers (a) attract more affluent readers and (b) are read with greater care and thus are a better advertising medium.

4. Newspapers suffer competitively due to their cumbersome, expensive distribution process—kids on bicycles, adults on motor routes. Contrast flicking a dial to tune in an anchorperson to retrieving a newspaper thrown in the bushes by an

errant teenager (and newspaper ink smudges readers' hands—a serious reason, incidentally, why some people avoid reading newspapers). Your best response is to create a capable circulation organization to ensure timely delivery and efficient subscriber service.

5. And, to be blunt, some newspapers lose local retail simply because they are archaic in marketing strategy, sales techniques and research. Often, television just outsells them.

Now, Counterattack!

In counterattacking, particularly against television, many newspapers find great opportunity in part-run local retail advertising—ads that run in just some editions.

In Dallas, the *Morning News* offers part-run advertising techniques that are models for all managers. Witness:

1. Dallas is a sprawling "metroplex," and huge portions of the *Dallas Morning News* circulation are of no interest to many small advertisers. A store owner in southwest Dallas, whose customers come from the immediate neighborhood, does not need to advertise in distant northwest Dallas.

2. Rising costs, particularly of newsprint, push ad rates based on total circulation beyond the reach of small advertisers.

3. Competing media, particularly shoppers or neighborhood weeklies and small dailies, deliver narrowly focused circulation zones suited to small advertisers and at lower rates.

What to do? The *Morning News* offers lower-cost space in just a portion of total circulation, rather than only "run of paper" (ROP) advertising in all editions. Many papers are turning to part-run advertising because it reverses a dangerous situation: As full-run rates get higher, newspapers appeal only to larger advertisers and thus must depend on a shrinking handful of clients. Part-run broadens the revenue base to include smaller advertisers and makes newspapers less vulnerable to economic dislocation or the whims of a few large ones.

Part-run advertising, in sum, is just good business. Wall Street analyst C. Patrick O'Donnell Jr., examining for his investor clients the finances of a 75,000-circulation "model" newspaper, pointed out that incremental cost increases for part-run "are not burdensome . . . and such advertising revenue adds to the overall operating margins of any newspapers." O'Donnell's model paper would charge $2,000 for one-time insertion of a full-page ad that goes to all 75,000 subscribers, $800 to deliver the same ad via part-run to 15,000 subscribers.[9]

National (General) Advertising

Your strategy in this category must be to expand by attacking the dominance of television. Stakes nationwide are huge. National advertising in newspapers, mostly by firms offering mass-produced goods and services for multi-outlet sale, approached $4 billion in 1993. However, network television got more than $10 billion. National ads placed directly with local TV stations ("spot" national) passed

$16 billion. In just those two sectors of national, then, television's take was over $26 billion. Getting more for newspapers will be a tough fight.

Television has great strength in advertising products such as, say, razor blades or beer—products mass-produced and sold coast to coast to demographically diverse audiences. After all, more than 98 percent of all U.S. households have TV sets and at least three out of five have one or more turned on during prime viewing hours.

However, you *can* sell against TV competition: Newspaper Association of America says research shows television is "background noise" for many adult Americans: 2.2 percent are out of the room when a set is on during prime time, 27.6 percent pay "some" attention and 70.2 percent pay full attention. NAA says television doesn't deliver for commercials the audiences it attracts for entertainment programming: One-third of adult viewers don't see commercials during prime time; they're out of the room, talking, reading or flipping channels.

Switching channels to avoid commercials reaches such dimensions that advertisers have a name for it: "zapping." It's particularly easy with a remote control device operated from a favorite armchair. General Foods counterattacked—at heavy cost—with "roadblocking." That involves running the same commercial on other networks and cable TV—so channel jumpers would have a good chance of seeing it whenever they switched. (However, that doesn't catch viewers using VCRs to record programming and eliminate commercials by "zipping" past them.) In sum, says NAA, advertisers pay a higher CPM to reach viewers than TV salespersons quote.

TV viewers cannot easily recall commercials. NAA says only 4 percent can immediately recall either the product or brand name they have just seen advertised on television.

The TV audience, says NAA, "is hard for advertisers to reach." Cable TV penetrates (1994) 61 percent of TV homes and the average TV home receives 35 channels. Where in that fractionalized jungle of channels must an advertiser spend money to reach viewers?[10]

Point out also that 20 percent of the population does 43 percent of total television viewing. Any advertiser who relies solely on television reaches only one-fifth of the population.

Television has difficulty "selling" socioeconomically upscale segments of the population. With improved zoning and sophisticated marketing, newspapers can offer national advertisers a precision vehicle for reaching demographically attractive consumers—particularly since television's CPMs are soaring. (NBC charged $850,000 for a 30-second commercial during its broadcast of Super Bowl XXVII in 1994. For the finale of the show "Cheers," the cost was $650,000.)

Two other factors give newspapers strength: Consumers are better educated than ever, more demanding and require more information before buying many products, such as cars. Newspaper advertising is best suited to deliver factual detail. Also, newspapers are best suited for advocacy and institutional advertising, the type that discusses public issues in thoughtful detail.

Be Aware of Your Weaknesses
However, your national ad sales strategy must recognize that newspapers have weaknesses: First, the big dollars available draw many competitors, and the news-

paper industry's share is slipping. With a generation of television-oriented advertising executives, it will not be easy to reverse that trend. Second, newspapers spend heavily to modernize plant and equipment, but many still cannot provide the reproduction quality—particularly in color—demanded by national advertisers in this era of crystal-clear TV transmission. And third, there lingers an old newspaper habit of charging more—as much as 65 percent more—for national advertising than for local. Avarice aside, newspapers argue their costs are higher and that they must compensate national sales reps. Also, newspapers say, national advertisers benefit from all circulation—even out-of-state circulation that is of no value to local advertisers. All that justifies for newspaper executives a higher rate schedule for national advertisers. But it goes over poorly with advertisers. The prestigious *Advertising Age* warns that "pricing arrogance" is the greatest barrier to increased national advertising for newspapers.

The Industry Campaign for National Advertising

The newspaper industry campaigns strongly for increased national advertising, and you can dovetail your sales strategy into a nationwide effort by the Newspaper Association of America. The goal: Make it easier and cheaper for national advertisers to use newspapers.

A key element in the campaign is the *standard advertising unit* (SAU) system. Participating dailies—virtually all in the United States—accept uniform formats to make it easier for advertisers to use the same ad copy in many (or all) newspapers.

To fully conform, full-size ("broadsheet") newspapers accept a format of six columns, each $2\frac{1}{16}$ inches wide with $\frac{1}{8}$ inch between columns. Columns are 21 to $22\frac{1}{2}$ inches deep. Printed pages are 13 inches wide. Ad rates are based on the column inch (not agate line, used generally by newspapers since the early 1800s). Tabloid pages are $10\frac{13}{16}$ inches wide and 14 inches deep, with five columns, each $2\frac{1}{16}$ inches wide and $\frac{1}{8}$ inch apart. Some tabloids have minor variations (see Figure 9.2 for an illustration of SAU "specs").

The SAU system involves 57 standard ad sizes, 56 of which fit full-size newspapers; 16 fit tabloids. This permits advertisers to create a single ad for all SAU newspapers throughout the country. Newspapers are free to accept other sizes, too.

Even smaller newspapers which normally attracting little national advertising should adopt SAU standards, because major regional and even local advertisers seek standardization among newspapers. Regional advertising headquarters for food or discount stores, for example, exert pressure for conformity. Classified advertising is exempt from SAU standards.

A second industrywide bid for national ads is "Newsplan," under which more than a thousand newspapers offer 3 to 30 percent rate discounts to national advertisers who contract to buy 6 to 104 pages annually.

Other features of the campaign to increase national advertising are *standard invoicing forms* containing basic information elements to reduce paperwork headaches for national advertisers and a *standardized rate card*. See Figure 9.3 on page 285 and Box 9.4 on page 286 for the standardized invoice and Box 9.5 on page 288 for the rate card.

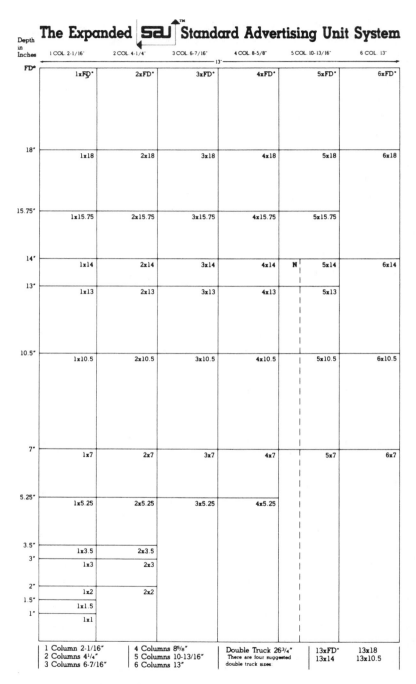

FIGURE 9.2 Using the SAU system, advertisers can create a single
advertisement that meets the mechanical
specifications of newspapers nationwide.

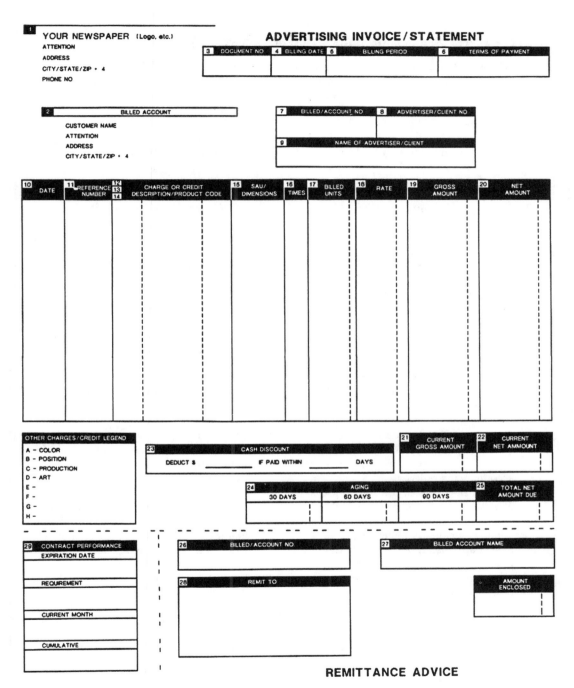

FIGURE 9.3 The standardized Advertising Invoice/Statement, used by papers nationwide, is part of the newspaper industry's effort to make it easier for advertisers to use newspapers.

BOX 9.4   The 29 Elements of the Standard Advertising Invoice (SAI)*

1. **Name of Particular Newspaper, Address and Phone No.:** The name of your newspaper and contact person with mailing address, including provision for nine digit ZIP codes and phone number, including area code.

2. **Billed Account Name and Address:** Name of the advertiser or advertising agency that placed the advertising, and the complete billing address.

3. **Invoice/Document Number:** A numerical control procedure that will provide a unique number for each individual invoice, invoice/statement or document.

4. **Billing Date:** Last day of current billing period or cycle.

5. **Billing Period:** Period of time covered by the invoice (week[s], month, etc.)

6. **Terms of Payment:** A statement of when the invoice becomes due and payable.

7. **Billed Account Number:** The unique number or letter/number sequence assigned to each advertiser or advertising agency by the newspaper. This number would generally be part of the newspaper's accounts receivable control system.

8. **Advertiser/Client Number:** If different from account being billed.

9. **Advertiser/Client Name:** If different from account being billed.

10. **Date of Insertion or Transaction:** Date(s) of publication of the advertisement (month and day[s]), or a transaction date for other items (payments, adjustments, etc.).

11. **Newspaper's Reference Number:** A newspaper's internal reference number for document retrieval, cash application, or for other purposes.

12. **Other Charges or Credits:** Identification of transaction such as color charges, position charges, production charges, art charges, zone area, penalty carrying charges, etc. (A legend identifying any codes used should be shown on the invoice.) If code legend is not used, explanation of transaction should be provided as part of description.

13. **Description of Ad:** Identification of the ad for the advertiser. Description may include the advertiser's insertion order number, advertiser's name, key words in the ad, products advertised, a number furnished by the advertiser or advertising agency used to identify the advertising order, etc.

14. **Product/Service Code:** A number identifying both manufacturer and product, or service.

15. **SAU/Dimensions:** For display ads, the self-descriptive nomenclature of the columns by inches (e.g., 3 x 14 inches would be the SAU number for a three-column-by-14 inch display ad). For other ads, appropriate dimensions (eg., 1 x 6 lines for a classified ad).

16. **Number of Times Published:** The total number of appearances of an ad.

17. **Billed Units:** The size of the ad in column inches, lines, number of preprints or other billed units.

18. **Applicable Rate:** The rate per inch, line, number of preprints, or other billable unit charged based on the rate card and contract in effect.

19. **Gross Amount:** The extension of total billed units at the applicable rate before agency commission and cash discounts.

20. **Net Amount:** Gross charge less agency commission.

21. **Current Gross Amount:** Total of the gross charges for advertising, color, production charges, art charges, position charges, etc., appearing on the invoice for the current billing period.

22. **Current Net Amount Due:** The total of net charges for advertising, color, production charges, art charges, position charges, etc., appearing on the invoice for the current billing period.

23. **Cash Discounts:** A discount allowed for the early payment of amounts due. This may be included in the terms of payment or shown separately, if applicable.

24. **Aging of Past Due Amounts:** An aging of overdue charges according to billing terms,

BOX 9.4   *Continued*

based on the number of days outstanding from the billing dates, usually stated in 30-day increments (e.g. 30-60-90). This is a statement item and is optional for those newspapers that prefer to send separate statements of account.

25. **Total Net Amount Due:** The total of all current net charges plus those charges still outstanding from previous billing periods. This is a statement item and is optional for those newspapers that prefer to send separate statements of account.

26. **Billed Account Number:** Optional repetition of item 7 if remittance stub is used.

27. **Billed Account Name:** Optional repetition of name part of item 2 if remittance stub is used.

28. **Name and Address for Remittance:** The name and address to which payment is to be sent. A return payment document may be included with the invoice.

29. **Contract Performance:** Information regarding contract period and requirement as well as current billing period and cumulative performance. This information can also be supplied in the description portion of the invoices or on a separate statement.

*These invoice elements represent minimum data requirements. Individual newspapers may, at their option, include or incorporate additional data relevant to their publications and customers.

Using National "Reps"

Many large newspapers and groups maintain their own national sales staffs. Knight-Ridder, for example, has offices in many cities; Tribune Co. sells space for its *Chicago Tribune* and other group newspapers from offices across the country. Most papers, however, rely on agencies representing scores of newspapers. One of the largest "reps," Landon Associates Inc., bases sales forces in New York City and 21 other cities to sell for newspaper clients in 50 states.

Standard commissions paid to agencies range from 10 to 15 percent under contracts continuing automatically from year to year unless they are canceled by either party. Groups with many papers negotiate more favorable terms.

Managers of small papers, individually representing a tiny fraction of any agency's total revenue, must be certain they don't get overlooked by sales reps obsessed with the "big view" from New York City or Los Angeles. Although national revenue often is only 5 or 6 percent of total revenue for small papers, it can, given due attention, be expanded considerably.

Small-paper managers must open personal contact with their reps to ensure the reps receive a steady flow of information about the paper. A significant increase in circulation, a competitive improvement, news content restructuring—all should be passed to the rep. Send along a *fact book*; it need not be expensive. The best such books state, simply and clearly, the market's strengths and the paper's ability to exploit it for the national advertiser. "Any rep is as good as your push," the ad director of one small paper told me.

Whenever possible, small papers should join statewide or regional groupings of papers that offer national advertisers a single buy covering many markets. National advertisers don't often reach down to make a single buy in, say, a daily of 25,000 circulation. But that daily is attractive if, with 10 others, it offers 250,000 or

BOX 9.5   The Rate Card

A rate card must state advertising policies and rates with clarity and precision in a format that promotes the newspaper's value to advertisers. In an industrywide effort to make it easier for advertisers to use newspapers the Newspaper Association of America recommends a standardized $8\frac{1}{2}$ X 11 inch rate card. It presents data in sequence used by the Standard Rate and Data Service, which publishes monthly rate information from newspapers nationwide. The recommended order:

1. Personnel
    Publisher, marketing director, ad manager, and so on.
2. Representative
    Name, address of "rep" firm selling space to national advertisers.
3. Commission and Payment Terms
    Whether cash discount is offered; agency commission.
4. General Policy
    Policy on forbidden ad copy, days of publication, contract dates, rebates.
5. ROP/Reprint Rates
    Black-and-white rates for Standard Advertising Units, insert rates, discount policy, delivery specifications.
6. Group Combination Rates
    Rates for ad in two or more jointly owned newspaper; also co-op rates.
7. Color Rates
    Available days, rates for color.

8. Special ROP Units
    SAUs; see number 5.
9. Split-Run Ads
    Rates for ads in less than full circulation.
10. Special Services
    Creative services, market research newspaper provides advertisers.
11. Special Days/Pages/Features
    Guide for advertisers who want copy to run on days when certain news copy is featured.
12. ROP Depth Requirements
    Minimum size for ads.
13. Contract and Copy Regulations
    See number 4.
14. Closing Times
    Deadlines for receipt of copy.
15. Mechanical Requirements
    Column depth in lines; number of columns to page, other mechanical information.
16. Special Classification Rates
    Rates for guaranteed position; rates for special advertiser groups.
17. Classified Rates
    Sometimes presented in separate rate card.
18. Comics
    Rates, policy covering ads for comic pages.
19. Magazines
    Rates, policy for ads in television or other magazine published by newspaper.
20. Miscellaneous
    Circulation, market information, audience demographics, etc.

more circulation. Many state press associations offer such "ad networking" of weekly or small daily papers.

Classified Advertising

Your ad strategy should assign some of your newspaper's brightest talent to classified advertising. Here is why:

- Newspaper classified revenue in 1993 surpassed $11 billion. That's almost triple revenue just 13 years earlier, in 1980.

- Industrywide, classified is about 35 percent of total newspaper ad revenue; it's over 50 percent for some metros.
- Classified yields the highest per-page profit for most newspapers; more than 50 percent of new incremental revenue can go directly to profit.[11]
- Although newspapers today have a near monopoly on this extremely valuable ad revenue sector, you must plan now for intense competition from electronic services that will deliver computerized classified directly to homes.
- Classified provides more than ad revenue; it ranks strongly with readers as favorite *news* coverage. Research indicates readers view classified as a sort of guide to what is happening in town—who is having a garage sale, what used cars are worth and so forth.[12] One study shows 53 percent of all adult readers see some classified on a weekday. It's 54 percent for Sunday or weekend papers.[13]

Other attractions of classified: Its low cost to the advertiser and its proven ability to sell products and services.

Profit Tips

Classified provides a high profit ratio because no expensive news coverage is necessary for its pages (although some papers position news in classified—an auto maintenance column in the used car section, home building hints in real estate, etc.). You can use two other tactics to boost the profit ratio in classified: First, economical

---

BOX 9.6   Want More National Revenue?

Here is what Walter M. Haimann, president of Jos. E. Seagram & Sons, a major advertiser, had to say on ways newspapers can increase national advertising:

- Improve reproduction, change formats to reduce page "clutter" and "fill-ins, small-space" advertising that surrounds ads and "cheapens the image of my product"; reduce the "incredible" 60/40 ad-to-news ratio.
- Provide an "editorial environment that stimulates interest in a product" and do not place an ad next to "blatantly unacceptable" editorial matter (i.e., a Seagram liquor ad next to a story on drunk driving).
- Create a newspaper that "stimulates an immediate sales reaction," one consumers will "shop" for information on product availability and price; newspapers "shine" in this area.

- Produce a newspaper giving a national advertiser "impact against his target . . . and color is impact; newspapers with good color will be read all over, even the ads."
- Guarantee "competitive product protection"—separation between his ad and a competitor's; Seagram insists on at least six pages separation in magazine advertising, which newspapers try not to promise because it creates page layout and production problems.
- "Research is the name of the game," and newspapers must provide better target audience data for comparison against other media, so advertisers can determine optimum ad sizes, how many times to run an ad, and so on.
- Stop charging national advertisers "rates that are sometimes 50% over the local rates." National advertisers insist on advantageous or at least competitive pricing.

layout can cram maximum ads into minimum space. Many papers with standard six or eight column formats for other pages go to nine or 10 narrow columns per page for classified. This greatly increases revenue per page when classified is sold on a per-column-inch or per-line basis. Second, sophisticated computerized systems permit efficient, low-cost order taking via telephone. Typesetting and billing can be automatic. The reduction of staff adds to classified's profit.

Three categories of advertisers provide most classified: auto (43 percent), employment (18 percent) and real estate (also 18 percent). But new categories, arranged by classification (thus, "classified"), develop all the time. "Garage Sale" arrived relatively recently, for example, but is significant business for many newspapers.

Some advertisers prefer to use photographs or illustrations with word copy. This creates "classified display," particularly in auto and real estate. It is welcome revenue if it is new business; unfortunately, much is merely shifted from local retail and does not represent any net increase in business.

A major problem is classified's vulnerability to economic downturn. If the local economy sneezes, classified gets pneumonia. Classified is so reflective of the nation's economy that the "help wanted" category is used as a leading indicator of economic activity nationwide. If you depend on classified for major share-of-profit performance you must be ready with contingency plans so that, if an economic downturn should dislocate classified volume, immediate cost reductions can be put into effect to protect margins.

Preprint (Insert) Advertising

Delivering preprints tucked into newspapers is *big* business—a multibillion-dollar, highly profitable business. Some newspapers get $50 or more for delivering 1,000 of the colorful, different-size inserts that readers shake out of their daily and Sunday newspapers. And, almost no incremental new costs are involved. Carriers deliver bulkier papers stuffed with preprints for the same fee.

Preprints arrived on the newspaper scene after World War II, when discount houses began demanding well-printed, colorful advertising—almost minicatalogs—delivered to households in their markets. Many newspapers cannot offer precision color printing but are efficient distribution vehicles. So retailers ship preprints in bulk to newspapers for insertion and delivery. Newspapers get about 45 percent of total preprint revenue; 55 percent goes to commercial printers.

The primary competitor is direct mail, which Kmart, Sears, and other large advertisers use to obtain total market coverage. Newspaper executives argue that U.S. postal rates are lowered to accommodate direct mail firms and that first-class postage subsidizes the mailers, including Advo, the nation's largest direct mail company. (Advo, with annual revenue exceeding $900 million, claims it reaches 53 million homes each week with packages containing an average of seven fliers or circulars.)[14] Advo executives—and postal officials—deny direct mailers are subsidized.

Despite high profits in carrying inserts, newspaper executives worry about the long-term effect. Haven't newspapers for generations told advertisers that tight adjacency of ad and news copy best assures high readership? Isn't the basic appeal to advertisers that news copy pulls readers into reading ads? And don't preprints destroy adjacency? Don't they turn newspapers into simple delivery vehicles?

Editors worry, too: Switching advertising from advertising in the newspapers itself (ROP) shrinks newshole. After all, newshole—the space available for news—is established by the amount of ROP scattered throughout the pages. Some editors seek a guaranteed number of columns for news to maintain their newspapers' journalistic integrity, even if there isn't ROP advertising to support them. But that is expensive—a direct drain on profits, and few such guarantees are forthcoming from publishers.

The threat to newspapers is clear: In the 1970s, 73 percent of Sears' local print advertising was ROP; in the 1980s, it dropped to 19 percent. Sears complains that newspaper rates for ROP are too high and, as far as insert are concerned, that newspapers cannot penetrate sufficient households or improve color reproduction.

Today, there is massive use by large retailers of direct mail, shoppers or door-to-door delivery through alternate delivery systems. Increasingly, the newspaper is eliminated as a delivery system for preprints.

To improve your preprint business, take these steps: Maintain sufficient household penetration by your paid-circulation paper, of course, but also by combining its circulation with marketplace coverage obtained through your own direct mail or free-circulation vehicles. Simultaneously provide target marketing to deliver preprints to attractive households in tightly segmented blocs, such as ZIP code areas. Use zoned editions of the paid-circulation paper in combination with other vehicles. Constantly promote the value of news-ad adjacency and sell the theme that including ads in a news-and-feature package lends credibility that direct mail and shoppers lack. Direct advertisers' attention to the relatively poor readership of preprints and shoppers that arrive on the tide of hundreds, if not thousands, of pieces of direct mail delivered to a household annually. Many direct mail preprints go unread from mailbox to garage pail.

Co-Op Advertising

An important revenue sector is co-op, under which national manufacturers reimburse local retailers for much—sometimes all—of the cost of advertising their products. Using co-op, retailers double or triple their ad budgets but increase their own direct costs only 10 to 20 percent. Much co-op revenue comes from makers of cameras, jewelry, home maintenance products, and furnishings and apparel who want to advertise their specific products and simultaneously identify local retail stores where they are available.

Many newspapers overlook this revenue source, and local retailers often do not understand it either. By some estimates, only two-thirds of available co-op support is spent each year. Competitors are not slow in lunging for co-op dollars. Much of the loss goes to direct mail.

You should establish a special co-op department; the results can be spectacular. Newspapers often print special forms that retail clients can use for claiming co-op reimbursement from suppliers. Anything that helps merchants in your town extract co-op support from manufacturers is money in your newspaper's bank.

Coupon Advertising

Every shopper, it seems, heads for the supermarket clutching coupons snipped from the local paper. *Billions*—85 percent of all coupons—are distributed annually in newspapers. Coupon values range from a cent off a bar of soap to $2,500 to $10,000 off prices of foreign cars imported by a car dealer in Richmond, Virginia (21 of his coupons were redeemed, one for a $10,000 reduction in the $48,174 price of a Porsche 928).[15] The total value of coupons in any daily's paper can range into hundreds of dollars in major metro markets. The *Athens Daily News* and *Banner-Herald* often carry $100 worth or more each week. Four of five coupons are placed by the grocery industry. For all newspapers, large or small, they are significant readership attractions. Direct mail poses severe competition.

Selling advertisers on your newspaper as a coupon vehicle is part of the overall challenge of positioning the newspaper effectively in its marketplace. Start by offering advertisers free trial with a coupon—buyers coming through the front door clutching the coupon will convince many retailers.

Legal (Public Notice) Advertising

This advertising is important, particularly for small dailies and weeklies. For papers with a daily circulation of 10,000 to 15,000, legals often are 1 to 2 percent of total revenue. The $10,000 or so sometimes available annually in small towns can make the difference between profit or loss for weeklies. Legals cover many subjects—bidding for city contracts, executors of wills seeking survivors, new laws, divorce notices.

This advertising sometimes is awarded by government jurisdictions on a bid basis, sometimes on a rotating basis between two or more qualified newspapers. Qualifications vary between states, but normally legals are awarded only to newspapers of general news content with paid circulation and second-class postal permits that publish on a continuous basis, at least in part in the city where the newspaper office is located. In some states, including California, publications must be adjudicated as bona fide newspapers for legal advertising purposes. Rates for this type advertising are set by the awarding governmental body.

HOW TO MANAGE AD SALES

Picture your favorite football team with the ball on the opponent's one-yard line in the year's most important game. Your team worked hard to get there, organizing, planning and scouting the opponent's strengths and weaknesses. If your team gains that last yard and scores, it succeeds. If it doesn't, all the hard work fails.

And so it is in managing newspaper advertising. You can organize, research and plan, but if your department doesn't sell, you fail. And you don't get applause for merely playing the game well, either. It's what's profitably on the scoreboard—the advertiser's signature on a sales contract—that counts.

There are many routes to the one-yard line—many approaches to organizational design, research, planning. But one thing is clear: To score, there must be professional, hard-hitting sales work. Without hard selling, a paper can make all the right moves in circulation, news and other areas and still not reap full benefit in advertising.

But, let Tom Vail, who was publisher and editor of the *Cleveland Plain Dealer*, describe what happened when he launched his paper on a campaign to overtake the *Press:* "At the time we were 80,000 a day behind the *Cleveland Press* [in circulation], although we were the only Sunday paper in Cleveland, and we trailed on a daily basis our competitor in both retail and national advertising....When we passed the *Press* in daily circulation, I thought the advertising leadership would shift to us automatically. How wrong I was! Not only did it take us eight more years to get the advertising leadership, but of course we had to show circulation leadership not only in the total area but also in our home county, city, zone, the Standard Metropolitan Statistical Area, and other categories of circulation leadership interesting to advertisers."[16]

American advertisers, economic underpinnings of the world's largest, most active free press, have become a demanding, discerning force. They know what they want and must be served, or they will go elsewhere. Those advertisers have to be sold. Your sales campaign must be multidimensional, ranging from institutional promotion of print as an effective medium to tailoring an ad schedule to a local retailer's needs and budget.

You must be not a seller of space but a solver of problems. Successful selling requires having an imaginative variety of products and services rather than, say, simply trying to push a full page ad in Wednesday's food section. That requires thorough research of the market, the newspaper's position in it, and competitors. It requires understanding the advertiser's needs and business so solutions to those needs can be put forward.

Harte-Hanks employs this concept as a fine art, operating a consumer distribution marketing (CDM) division, in addition to its newspapers. Harte-Hanks bills CDM as a "complete publishing/distribution support system that helps advertisers target their messages to their prime prospects in the most cost effective way."[17] CDM offers commercial printing and distribution of printed advertising via private carriers and mail, which it claims can reach 90 percent of all American homes via computerized address lists. CDM also offers research services and, importantly, publishes shoppers zoned for 300 separate editions reaching 3.2 million households weekly.

Former president and CEO Bob Marbut put it this way: "We have the ability for newspapers and CDM salespeople to jointly call on major advertisers such as Sears and Kmart, and the like."[18] Thus, a Harte-Hanks sales team can offer full-run advertising ROP in one of the group's paid-circulation papers, space in its shoppers, plus inserts which Harte-Hanks will print and distribute in its own publications, via direct mail handled by the company or, if the client wishes, in a plastic bag hung on doorknobs by one of the company's direct-distribution units. Harte-Hanke's own research companies can survey the client's market and suggest efficient ways to advertise.

CASE STUDY 9.1   Database Marketing and You

Time: Ten years following your graduation. You're already marketing director of a major daily.

Scene: A crucial conference with your largest auto advertiser, who threatens to switch to direct mail.

"Here," says the advertiser, "is my problem: I have two product lines, one (Fords) for households in the $25,000 to $30,000 annual income range, and another (Cadillacs) for those earning $50,000+. But I don't know where those households are or how to reach them."

"Simple," you respond.

Simple, that is, *if* you're an expert in *database marketing* and thus able to pull from your briefcase a computer printout listing every household in your market.

In database marketing, that printout must list not only household addresses but also complete demographic and psychographic characteristics of all who live in them. You must know who buys what—and why. You must know their habits, attitudes, likes and dislikes. For two reasons: First, as marketing director you are a business partner of your advertisers. You must know their product lines and how to match them with their customers and noncustomers. You must locate those $50,000+ households for your advertiser's Cadillac sales effort and know where the advertiser's family Ford sedans can find a home in those $25,000 households.

Second, your newspaper colleagues—in news, circulation and advertising—must use your database internally to design a variety of news and advertising products to reach your advertiser's customers and noncustomers with great precision.

So, spread your printout before your advertiser and say something like this:

- There are 26,000 $50,000+ households in this market. We will reach 23,245 with full-page ads in zoned editions of the newspaper, to which they subscribe. We will reach the remaining 2,755 with a high-quality direct mail program which we will design and distribute.
- Of the $50,000+ households, we have identified 76 percent, or 19,760, as buying cars primarily for status. Our newspaper ads and direct mail pieces for them will emphasize that Cadillacs are status symbols. Sales material directed at the remainder will emphasize the Cadillac's long-lasting quality and high resale value—thus emphasizing economy for those who won't buy for status alone.
- Incidentally, Mr. Advertiser, our analysis of credit card transactions in our market shows 82 percent of Cadillac owners purchase repairs and service at non-Cadillac garages. Why not let us design a campaign to help you recapture that business? We can use our city magazine to reach high-income households. Oh, also, we'll use our free-circulation shopper to sell your repair service to low-income, Ford-owning households.

That's database marketing.

Is it really necessary? Well, here is what an executive of the ad agency BBDO told a panel on newspaper advertising: "There's got to be a way to more finely target advertising in mass media. A shampoo ad doesn't do much for a bald man...."[a]

[a] Ron Harrison, media director of BBDO San Francisco, "How's the View from the Catbird Seat?" SRDS Report, vol. 6, no. 8.

Not many sales managers, particularly in early years, run operations that complex. But the principles of sales management are the same if you are supervising a $500 million corporation or a two-person sales staff on a weekly. You can follow the same checklist.

The Sales Manager's Checklist

Let's look at organizing—and energizing—an effective sales force to accomplish your top-priority responsibility in sales management: getting through the prospect's front door and coming out with a signed advertising contract. Key steps:

- Analyze market, types of advertisers, competitive situation, your own newspaper's strengths and weaknesses, formulate attack plan.
- Recruit and train sales force.
- Organize individual salesperson tasks and assign client lists.
- Lead, motivate, compensate.
- Evaluate, control and adjust individual sales efforts.

Plan Your Sales Attack

A painstaking audit of significant advertising prospects in the market comes first. Who is out there? Where do they now advertise? What potential revenue do they represent? Now, lay that intelligence against your sales goals developed in corporate and departmental strategy sessions. Where can you get business needed to improve revenue, increase number of advertising clients and boost your market share?

List your competitors' accounts and those they share with your newspaper. Target theirs for special attention by your sales force. Analyze sales themes and techniques competitors use against your paper, and equip each of your salespersons with telling counterarguments (listed in my earlier discussion of different advertising categories). Compare rates, CPMs and rate increase histories. Are yours dangerously high—or low enough that an increase will be palatable to advertisers? Establish programs penetrating new areas of business, not simply reworking old ones. For example, newspapers opened new major revenue sources with banks and other financial institutions.

Your attack plan must cover the relevant geographic market and focus on prospects with true potential for significant revenue. Select prospects who need to advertise (whether they recognize it or not) and who have the business volume to support the cost of advertising.

Recruiting and Training Salespersons

Libraries full of books have been written on the selling process. But what makes one person effective at it and another ineffective is still a bit of a mystery. Some successful salespeople rely on personality—the ability to approach an advertising prospect with poise, tact and good cheer. Others rely primarily on the ability to manipulate and persuade, to identify the prospect's needs and demonstrate persuasively how the newspaper can fulfill them. Still others can adapt to any situation, zeroing in on the prospect's wants and demonstrating understanding of them.

Whatever the technique, successful selling requires the salesperson to listen carefully to the prospect—to understand and sense the prospect's thinking and react accordingly. Importantly, the salesperson must need to succeed in selling—must be ego-driven and goal oriented. Look for those characteristics in recruiting a sales force.

Talent is all around: at smaller newspapers nearby (don't overlook competing papers), in other sales business, in junior ranks of your own newspapers, among recent college graduates. Beware of job-hoppers, whose records show personal instability or have unexplained gaps. Don't be diverted by the old argument over whether it's the product's quality that sells or the salesperson's ability. You need both.

Training is a continual process, regardless of the experience or success of your sales force. Start by ensuring a smooth flow of information to the staff on overall corporate goals and departmental objectives; any improvements in the newspaper—new sections, new columnists—and circulation and penetration successes; and what your competitors are doing.

Training aids include lectures, training films, one-on-one assistance, role-playing, guest speakers. Experienced salespersons may balk at training on the grounds they know it all. They don't. Bring them into refresher courses.

Organizing the Salesperson

This is a particularly crucial function for every sales manager. First, you must organize each salesperson's efforts in a fail-safe system that ensures regular sales calls and all prospects. If you don't, some prospects and clients will be neglected. Salespeople must become "account executives" assigned to "accounts" or customers.

Second, salespeople need direction and standards against which to judge their own performance. As sales manager, you can nudge—prod, if necessary—each individual to reach personal sales goals.

Third, good salespeople are thoroughbreds and ego-driven self-starters. But they need lots of attention. Don't forget to stroke their psyches a bit.

Fourth, in organizing sales territories and prospect lists, you will, to a great extent, be determining the salesperson's earnings potential and whether he or she qualifies for advancement. You will ruin a salesperson's morale if you consistently provide only low-quality prospect lists.

You must make sure that each salesperson organizes time, planning each day's effort efficiently. It wastes time to make a few calls that are widely scattered throughout a large territory; it's better to bunch them. Even telephone calls should be organized methodically. Each salesperson must be organized each day to represent the newspaper properly. An ill-prepared sales call wastes the prospect's time and can damage the newspaper's image.

Make sure each salesperson has a clear understanding of precisely what performance is required. That includes not only signing new prospects but also increasing revenue from existing clients. It includes the administrative duties involved in selling—writing regular summaries of activity and submitting expense accounts on time. Don't overdo it, however. Don't keep those thoroughbreds off the sales track just to shuffle irrelevant paper.

Lead, Motivate, Compensate

The Marine Corps motivates people with flag, country, patriotism. Coaches lead football teams by invoking the alma mater's name. With a sales force, leadership based on such appeals inspires team spirit and drive. Momentum is built by the challenge of competition. Appeals to pride motivate individuals to improve their personal sales records.

Those techniques—and others discussed in Chapter 6—will help you assemble aggressive, professional salespeople and train and lead them well. As sales manager, you must determine each individual's needs and help fulfill them. Be supportive in both a personal and an organizational sense. But whatever factors enter your motivational strategy, the central ingredient must be worthwhile compensation. Best is a commission plan tied directly to performance plus careful assignment of client lists from which commissions are earned.

The advantages of commission-based compensation are many: It is a strong incentive for salespersons because it relates pay directly to results. Each salesperson easily understands a compensation system based on performance. Your newspaper's costs in base salary are reduced and sales costs rise only proportionately to revenue gained.

Some disadvantages are these: Heavy reliance on commission payment feeds the sales force's already strong money orientation and doesn't build company loyalty. Salespeople tend to "work" only active accounts likely to yield quick sales, and neglect the service of existing customers or the spadework to open new accounts. They tend to neglect administrative duties. And a few highly talented salespeople—or those with the best account lists—will earn more than their colleagues, creating tension in the department.

Strive for balance to maintain the motivational value of commissions, yet build loyalty to the newspaper with salary. *The Dayton (Ohio) Daily News* pays outside salespeople 75 percent salary, 25 percent commissions; inside telephone salespersons, 60 percent salary, 40 percent commission.

Evaluating and Controlling

Evaluation and control of performance must occur on two levels—with individual salespersons and for the entire department. First, evaluate the individual primarily on whether sales goals are met—that is, on dollar volume of sales brought in.

There are few valid excuses for a salesperson who consistently fails to meet goals. Conversely, high sales volume can make other shortcoming irrelevant.

Dollar results aside, evaluate individuals for:

- Time spent in office. Sales are made in clients' offices, not at the newspaper.
- Personal neatness, including hair and clothes.
- Number of calls on existing accounts. No efficient salesperson permits accounts to languish.
- Number of new accounts opened. Each salesperson must constantly open new sales prospects.
- Promptness and accuracy; completeness of sales orders, call reports, and other administrative procedures.
- Cost of sales, including entertainment, travel.
- Salesperson's knowledge of newspaper industry, your newspaper and its circulation, readership and demographic strengths. Important: Does the salesperson know the competition and sell effectively against it?
- Efficiency in planning the work day, including routing and frequency of calls.
- Persistence in pursuing the sale, asking for the order and then the reorder.[19]

TABLE 9.1   Sales Costs as Percentage of Revenue

	High	Low	Mean
Retail	11.3%	2.9%	6.2%
National	21.2	0.3	7.9
Classified	26.2	1.2	10.3
Miscellaneous	1.0	0.1	0.63
Total	12.7	6.9	9.8

Source: "Company Average Sales Costs to Revenue for Advertising," *Newspaper Controller,* Washington, D.C., Institute of Newspaper Controllers and Finance Officers, Dec. 1982, p. 3.

Continuing evaluations spot individuals who need help and perhaps retraining and those who consistently fail to perform. Terminate the chronically unproductive, reward your producers. Shift inactive accounts to new salespeople. Evaluation of departmental performance rests on whether goals are met. But that doesn't mean relying solely on revenue measurements. Quite the contrary.

To be an effective sales manager, you must hold cost of advertising sales to efficient levels. What is "efficient" varies with market, competition and operational factors. However, the Technical Advisory Board of the International Newspaper Financial Executives surveyed its newspaper members in the 1980s and drew up some guidelines based on the composite of sales cost as a percentage of advertising revenue (see Table 9.1).

Let's take that approach to a "typical" 75,000-circulation daily with annual advertising revenues of $14,750,000 and advertising department costs of $1,150,000.

$$\text{Cost/sales ratio} = \frac{\$1,150,000}{\$14,750,000} = 7.7\%$$

That 7.7 percent compares favorably with the mean of 9.8 percent in Table 9.1. But what ratio is satisfactory to your newspaper depends on the competition you face and other local conditions. For one measure, compare your ratio against those of previous years, then factor in such subjective considerations as whether new competition entered the market or whether other external factors have raised costs, for example, or lowered revenue.

Note the cost/sales ratio will signal difficulties or successes in the department. But it doesn't reveal causes. For that, you must compare each salesperson's performance against standards for sales and expenses.

Check These Off, Too

Your sales manager's checklist is incomplete if you don't check off a few points:

- Do you walk through the ad department frequently ("management by moving about") and insist on an alert, well-dressed, cheerful staff that spends most of its time outside the office? Unkempt, downbeat salespersons gathered around the coffee machine are not representing your newspaper properly.

- Do you personally make sure your national ad rep is being fed new and frequent descriptive material on the newspaper's market and competitive position? Is the rep getting selling hints on properly representing your newspaper?
- Do you monitor the Newspaper Association of America and other trade groups for selling hints?
- Importantly, are you doing your share by calling on major advertisers and nonadvertisers, offering them information about your newspaper and obtaining guidance for your own staff? Are you involved in your department's main role?
- Have you organized—and energized—an effective sales force to get through a client's front door and come out with a signed order? That, after all, is your top priority responsibility.

Listen to Walter M. Haimann, president of Jos. E. Seagram & Sons, a major national advertiser, on newspapers in the 1980s: "Quite frankly, a lot of us are beginning to wonder if newspapers don't *want* national business. You certainly don't give any indication of it by your actions. And I can't tell you how long it's been since my people or I have even had a newspaper rep knocking on our doors. I see magazine people in our offices constantly."[20]

Setting Advertising Rates

In establishing ad rates, you must perform with high professionalism, mustering judgment plus keen insight into your marketplace, the competition and the newspaper's marketing objectives. Pricing can have several objectives: profit, market share or high sales volume for competitive purposes, and it can be influenced by social or ethical considerations. Rates also can be influenced by legal factors (which will be discussed later).

Rates pegged too high kill the most imaginative, energetic sales efforts if they provide openings for competitors or are rejected by advertisers. Pegging rates too low makes a mockery of your entire sales effort. If costs are not covered, if no profit is forthcoming, why go through the exercise?

You must shoot for a spot somewhere between those extremes. Precisely where the point is and how to find it is much discussed among advertising managers. Some maximize profit by edging rates upward until there is a disproportionate drop in volume of ad dollars. Others sacrifice immediate profits to maximize sales and achieve long-range improvement in market share.

Another approach is cost-plus: adding relevant costs plus a percentage for profit. But calculating relevant costs, particularly a percentage of fixed overhead costs such as rent or utilities, is difficult. And cost-plus doesn't consider competitive rates or other realities of the marketplace. So managers speak of establishing "feel" rather than "formula" for setting ad rates. In gaining your "feel," consider this checklist.

A Rate-Setting Checklist

Costs. Key here is understanding precisely what and where costs are in your newspaper's operations. Managers who don't know what costs must be covered are crippled. You also must judge where costs are likely to move in the period ahead for which rates are being established.

Profit level required by the ownership—whether a single individual, family or thousands of shareholders represented by a board of directors. The *operating statement* (see Chapter 5) approved by the ownership should state the newspaper's specific profit goals for the forthcoming year. Your *departmental goals* will state revenue and cost objectives. Absent such precise direction, performance appreciably "better than last year's" is a good rule of thumb if you like your job. Set rates accordingly.

Quality of service. Rates should reflect whether the paper is performing as advertisers demand. Set high rates with confidence if your paper penetrates sufficient homes in the relevant market, reaches the right, demographically attractive readers, and stimulates sales. Managers who cannot claim such performance must be more tentative in setting rates. Note there sometimes is image advantage in high rates; the higher the rates, the higher the perceived value of the advertising service.

Competitive rates. You cannot raise rates far above a serious competitor's—be the competitor another paper, a radio or TV station, direct mail or whatever. Only with clear competitive superiority can your newspaper greatly outstrip competitors' rates. Advertisers are mobile, capable of shifting quickly to any medium promising better results at lower costs. Try to determine your competitors' costs and rate histories; if things get tough, how far can they lower rates?

Inflation indices. Many advertisers compare your rate increases with inflation, the Consumer Price Index or other cost indices. Rate increases that consistently outstrip the inflation rate will draw advertiser ire.

Rate-increase history. Regardless of other factors, too many increases too frequently will draw trouble. Pacing and a sense of timing are crucial. If possible, peg increase to improved service, better journalistic content, expanded circulation.

Sell your rates. Expert selling plays a huge role in demonstrating the value of newspaper advertising, its strengths over competitors, its ability to get results. It is not enough for rates to be competitive, fully justified and logical from your newspaper's cost point of view. Each advertiser must be sold on the idea that all this is true.

Whatever the market will bear. It all comes down to what the advertiser will pay. Stay in close touch with advertisers and react quickly to any shift in sentiment. Know what they think about your rates.

"Flexible" Pricing Is In

Facing competition plus advertiser resistance to rates, newspapers increasingly use "flexible" pricing tactics. This amounts to solving the advertiser's problems with imaginative sales assistance—through rates and other devices—rather than a take-it-or-leave-it sales posture and rigid price structure.

A manager's aim in this is to attract more advertising but also to address specific problems that crop up for newspapers. For example, some businesses concentrate advertising on certain days—Wednesdays for food stores, Sundays for department stores and so forth. This leaves some issues, particularly on Mondays and Tuesdays, short of advertising. Perhaps your newspaper should offer discounts for advertising on weak days.

Substantial discounting is aimed at attracting advertisers to ROP use of the newspaper's pages themselves rather than preprinted inserts. This creates a larger newshole and, for many papers, solves a difficult problem of physically inserting preprints. Inserting equipment is expensive and often cranky mechanically.

Newspapers traditionally have offered volume discounts: The more you advertise, the lower the rate. Under flexible pricing, that practice is extended. For example, newspapers with zoned editions or TMC programs offer discounts for placing ads in those special products as well as ROP. Special positioning of ads in the newspaper is offered in "flexible" pricing. A special section on real estate is the place for a realtor's ad, restaurant ads belong in "Arts and Leisure," auto ads in sports or business.

Design Effective Rate Cards

Pay special attention to how your newspaper, rates and policies are presented to the marketplace. Of particular concern is "drop material" provided for salespeople to use and leave behind during sales efforts. Without detailed, hard-hitting and colorful promotion material, few salespeople can be fully effective.

Key pieces are rate cards. They range in size and complexity from a single four-page, 3- by 8-inch black-and-white pamphlet to slick, highly detailed color brochures of 12 to 16 pages. Rate cards must cover local retail, classified and national advertising plus specialty business such as preprints and job printing. The essential element in any rate card is clear, understandable statement of rates, production schedules and advertising policies. Make sure your advertiser does not need a lawyer and pocket calculator to understand the rate card.

Rate cards should include any conditions—such as prohibited advertising (some papers refuse ads from fortune tellers, tobacco and liquor companies or others)—and a clear statement that rates may be changed with notice (usually 30 days) for advertisers with volume contracts and without notice for noncontract advertisers.

Circulation figures and other facts about the paper must be completely accurate. You'll lose marketplace credibility and invite lawsuits with inaccurate rate cards. The *Sacramento (Calif.) Union* agreed to reimburse advertisers up to $2 million after it was charged that a former circulation manager had inflated the circulation figures on which ad rates were based.[21]

HOW YOU CAN SELL

You undoubtedly will be introduced to advertising by selling it, not managing the department. So you need personal selling skills for use in the marketplace. Anyway, you cannot manage other people who spend each day pounding the bricks unless you understand what it is like. If you have management aspirations in ad-

BOX 9.7   Standards to Plan By

The scenario: You're thrust into a leadership position in advertising. Your challenge: Lay down standards—a plan—for your department.

Suggested first move: Plan in accordance with standards established by other successful newspapers. Some hints follow.

Salesperson Compensation

A study by Newspaper Association of America reveals this total compensation for a "typical" ad salesperson in the table below.

TMC and Niche Capabilities

- Plan a *non*subscriber distribution program (direct mail, shopper, etc.). An NAA survey shows 81 percent of U.S. daily newspapers have such programs.
- Target narrow market niches. Of newspapers with *non*subscriber products, 68 percent zone by ZIP codes or even more narrowly.
- Build databases on your market's households. Subscriber databases are maintained by 94 percent of dailies; *non*subscriber databases are kept by 76 percent. This information is computerized by 95 percent of dailies.[b]

Interactive Capabilities

Plan now for electronic delivery of advertising to households. *The Washington Post, The New York Times* and many other papers have *interactive* systems through which customers, using personal computers or household terminals, make restaurant reservations, buy entertainment or sports tickets, etc.

Your newspaper somehow must cooperate with major retailers and cable systems offering *home shopping*, a burgeoning sales area. Saks Fifth Avenue sold $570,000 worth of clothing in *one hour* on QVC Network in 1993. Macy's plans all-day selling via cable home shopping, and estimates annual revenue will be $50 million.[c]

Enlist Help

Every newspaper faces competition from multi-billion-dollar telephone companies and cable TV conglomerates. BellSouth's revenue in 1992 was $15.2 billion. Its Yellow Pages revenue alone was $1.4 billion. Even the largest newspaper's resources are puny by comparison.

So, smart newspaper managers are joining forces with each other *and* telephone companies. You should plan to do the same. For example, Cox Enterprises (*Atlanta Journal* and *Constitution* and many others) formed a consortium with major Southern newspapers to work with BellSouth in developing new electronic information services based on newspaper classified and telephone company Yellow Page advertising.

Annual base earnings rate (Includes pay for vacations, holidays)	$30,000
Bonuses	9,000
Newspaper's matching contribution to employee's 401K retirement plan (50-50 up to 6% of base earnings)	900
Company's annual cost for employee benefits (included Social Security tax)	11,400
Total value of working for the newspaper	$51,300[a]

BOX 9.7 *Continued*

Remember the Basics

Throughout your planning, remember your basic goals:

- Keep your *existing* customers.
- Add *new* customers.
- Keep *all* customers happy.
- Do this *profitably.*

[a]Walt Potter, "Salary, Benefits, Incentives," *presstime,* Sept. 1992, p. 12.
[b]*Facts About Newspapers '93,* Newspaper Association of America, p. 13.
[c]Stephanie Strom, "Telemarketing's Impact on the Bottom Line," *The New York Times,* June 20, 1993, p. 4-E.

---

vertising, seek on-the-job selling experience. What follows can be the basis of a training program for salespeople you manage or for selling a client yourself.

Let's set forth on a typical selling mission:

Psyche yourself up. Ready for a hard day's work? Do you want to succeed, to win? Check your time-management plan. Telephone ahead for appointments and arrange your visits with the most efficient routing.

Organize your presentation. Who precisely is your target? What is their business? How can your newspaper solve their sales problems? What sales resistance will you encounter? Where do they now advertise? How can you counter that? What can your newspaper do that competing media cannot? Make certain your presentation will be delivered to the prospect's decision maker.

Check your briefcase. Rate cards and contracts? "Drop" material on your newspaper's strengths, circulation, advertising volume? Tear sheets illustrating how your target's competitors advertise? "Spec" layouts of ads you think your target should buy? A copy of the newspaper?

Now, you are ready for the prospect. Let's follow a five-step procedure recommended by the Newspaper Advertising Bureau (the NAB was folded into the Newspaper Association of America in 1992, and the selling procedure is henceforth referred to as the "NAA Plan"). The procedure is used by many newspapers.[22]

Selling Retail Clients—I

As either a salesperson or ad manager, you must understand retailing and your target's business. The NAA averages in Table 9.2 on page 304 show you and your target how much other store owners spend on advertising.

Selling Retail Clients—II

Gauging household spending flow is crucial in any advertiser's decision on when—and how much—newspaper advertising should be bought. Table 9.3 on page 305 shows monthly patterns of spending by the average U.S. household in representative stores. You can show them to your target. These figures can be multiplied by the number of households in your market to yield the market's sales potential.

The NAA plan recommends convincing your retailer target to spend for advertising when customers are in a buying mood ("shoot when the ducks are flying").

TABLE 9.2   What Retailers Spend on Advertising

Type of Business	Average Percentage of Sales Spent on Advertising
Air conditioning, heating, refrigeration	1.8
Amusement/recreation	4.4
Apparel	1.9
Beverages	8.5
Cable/pay TV	1.7
Cigarettes	3.5
Department stores	2.8
Drug stores	1.4
Electric housewares/fans	4.9
Family clothing stores	2.3
Furniture stores	8.6
Grocery stores	1.3
Hotels/motels	3.2
Jewelry stores	3.2
Movie theaters	3.2
Radio/TV stores	4.7
Shoe stores	4.0
Women's clothing stores	3.7

Source: Developed from NAB (now NAA) *Newspaper Advertising Planbook*, 1991.

Establish monthly buying patterns using the national figures in Table 9.3 and each store's own pattern, then suggest your target spend for advertising in the relationship depicted in Figure 9.4 on page 306.

The relationship of sales to advertising should *not* look as it does in Figure 9.5.

NAA suggests alerting the target advertiser that a store department that is efficiently delivering maximum buyer traffic at the lowest possible advertising cost will have a sales-to-ad ratio similar to that depicted in Figure 9.4. Sales and advertising activity should proceed hand-in-hand.

Selling Retail Clients—III

You must help your target understand the store's sales-to-ad ratios. Use the monthly planning schedule shown in Figure 9.6 on page 307.

The procedure is this: Write in column 1 the retailer's monthly sales last year. Divide last year's total sales into each month's sales, entering the resulting percentage in column 2. In column 3, enter each month's advertising last year (in dollars or column inches). Divide last year's total into each month's figure, entering the percentage in column 4.

TABLE 9.3　When Households Spend Money

	JAN	FEB	MAR	APR	MAY	JUNE	JULY	AUG	SEPT	OCT	NOV	DEC	TOTAL
Department Stores	$99	99	133	134	141	139	129	146	137	145	183	280	$1,765
Women's Apparel Stores	$23	21	28	27	29	26	26	29	29	29	33	48	$349
Furniture Stores	$24	22	24	24	25	25	24	25	24	24	26	27	$293
Appliances, Radio/TV	$26	24	27	26	28	30	28	29	28	28	31	45	$352
Grocery Stores	$273	261	294	284	303	304	309	307	300	292	297	326	$3,548
Variety Stores	$5	5	6	6	6	6	6	6	6	6	8	13	$77
Hardware Stores	$9	8	10	11	12	12	12	11	11	11	11	12	$130
Auto/Home Supply	$22	21	26	27	29	30	29	31	30	30	29	28	$333

Average dollar purchases by households. Multiplying figures by number of households yields your market's *approximate* sales potential.
Developed from NAB (now NAA) *Newspaper Advertising Planbook*, 1991.

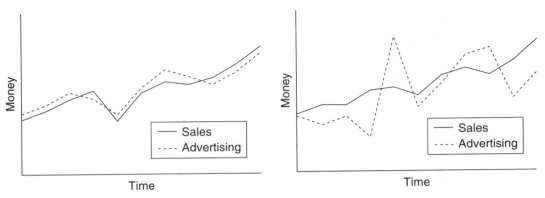

FIGURE 9.4 A good relationship of sales to advertising.

FIGURE 9.5 A poor relationship of sales to advertising.

Plot monthly sales and advertising percentages on the graph (column 5). If sales and advertising lines don't run close to each other, advertising is too late or too early—and sales are being missed.

Selling Retail Clients—IV

Help your target judge proper allocation of ad dollars to different departments or merchandise lines using Figure 9.7 on page 308. Write in column 1 a randomly selected month, in column 2 the store department or line. In column 3, write each department's (or line's) sales last year, then total. Divide the month's total sales into each department's (or line's) sales, writing the percentage in column 4.

In column 5, enter each department's (line's) advertising expenditures during the month. Divide month's total advertising (figured in step three) into each department's (line's) advertising, and enter in column 6 the percentage of advertising run.

Examine two departments, and (in column 7) shade in bar graphs representing sales percentages, along with advertising percentages. Has proper advertising emphasis been given each department (or line)? Are some departments under-advertised?

Selling Retail Clients—V

Counseling your retailer to use methodically planned advertising campaigns of lengthy duration should be your strategy. The NAA recommends that, having helped the retailer understand the store's past performance, you try to become the retailer's partner in planning the store's sales strategy and advertising spending. A four-step plan:

Step 1: Set Goals. Starting with last year's sales for one month, consider market changes in population, income and employment since last year. Figure in special sales or merchandise events planned for the forthcoming month (special holiday

	Sales Last Year $	% of Year's Sales	Advertising Last Year $	% of Year's Advertising
Jan.	_____	_____	_____	_____
Feb.	_____	_____	_____	_____
Mar.	_____	_____	_____	_____
Apr.	_____	_____	_____	_____
May	_____	_____	_____	_____
June	_____	_____	_____	_____
July	_____	_____	_____	_____
Aug.	_____	_____	_____	_____
Sept.	_____	_____	_____	_____
Oct.	_____	_____	_____	_____
Nov.	_____	_____	_____	_____
Dec.	_____	_____	_____	_____
TOTAL	$ _____	100%	$ _____	100%

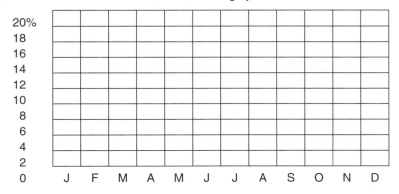

Distribution of the Year's Total Sales
and Advertising by Month

FIGURE 9.6 The monthly planning schedule.

sales and so on). Judge as best you can what competing stores are doing and estimate their relative success. Consider any expanded or new departments in the retailer's own store and instill determination to advertise and sell more aggressively. Enter in Figure 9.8 on page 309, for the relevant month, last year's sales in dollars (or column inches) plus percentage and market plus competitive conditions, then rough in sales goals for the same forthcoming month.

Step 2: Set Advertising Budget. Determine next month's advertising expenditures, first checking co-op dollars available from suppliers. New or expanding stores should

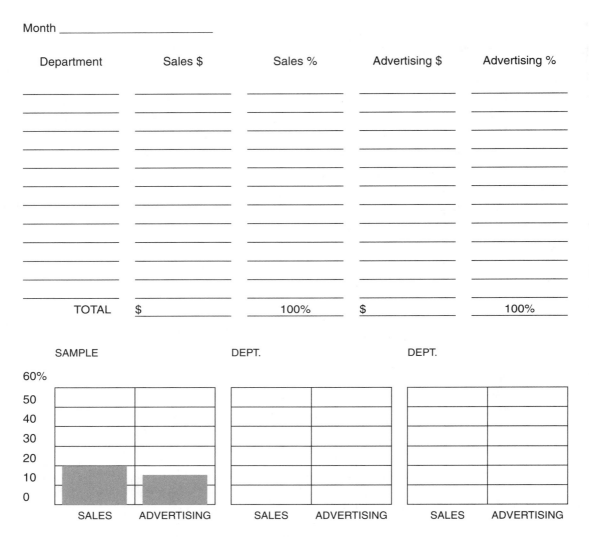

FIGURE 9.7 Department by department planning.

advertise more, as should any in less favorable locations. Larger budgets are required for stores with strong competition or whose primary appeal is low prices. Special dates or events offer additional sales opportunities and should be budgeted for.

Using Figure 9.9, enter (1) percent of sales invested in advertising for same month last year. Write in (2) dollars, including co-op, invested last year. Enter (3) inches (or lineage) bought last year.

Enter (4) month's sales goal, and (5) multiply it by percent planned for advertising. That yields (6) the month's ad budget. Dividing the budget by the newspaper's space rate will give (7) the inches (or lineage) available to promote the store for the month.

Next Month Is _____

Department of Merchandise Group	Month's Sales Last Year $	% of Total Store's Sales	Month's sales goal this year $	% of Total Store Sales Goal
TOTAL	$ _____	_____ 100%	$ _____	_____ 100%

FIGURE 9.8 Next month's goals.

Step 3: Decide What to Promote. In helping the retailer determine which departments or products to advertise, consider the sales goal for each. "For instance," says NAA, "if the sales goal of Department A is 9 percent of the total store sales

---

Next Month Is _____

1. Write down the percent of sales you invested in advertising for LAST YEAR:

_____ %

2. For the month you are now planning, write in LAST YEAR'S dollar investment in advertising:

$ _____

3. Write in the number of inches this bought:

_____ inches

4. Now, write in this year's sales goal for the month you are planning:

$ _____ ×

5. Multiply it by the percent you plan to invest in advertising for this month this year:

_____ % =

6. This gives you your ad budget*:

$ _____

7. Dividing your budget (from 6)…

$ _____ ÷

8. by your earned rate…

_____ =

9. will give you the amount of inches you have to promote your store next month:

_____ inches

FIGURE 9.9 Monthly ad budget.

Month _____

Department, Merchandise Group or Profit Center	% of Month's Sales	% of Month's Advertising	Inches
_____	_____	_____	_____
_____	_____	_____	_____
_____	_____	_____	_____
_____	_____	_____	_____
_____	_____	_____	_____
_____	_____	_____	_____
_____	_____	_____	_____
_____	_____	_____	_____
_____	_____	_____	_____
_____	_____	_____	_____
_____	_____	_____	_____
TOTALS	_____ 100%	_____ 100%	_____

FIGURE 9.10   Monthly sales and advertising.

objective this month, then earmark for it something like 9 percent of the month's planned advertising space."

Using Figure 9.10, draw up a flexible outline factoring in items likely to attract shoppers in the month ahead (no snow tires in July). Consider "sleepers" or products that are currently hot but which didn't show up in last year's figures. Again, determine which goods have co-op support. Plan to promote new or expanding departments plus products that are seasonal and likely to face decreased sales next month.

Step 4: Complete a Day-to-Day Schedule. Using a large calendar, calculate ad expenditures for each day in coming month. Consider such things as when large local firms pay employees and thus make money available for shopping; days when traffic is heaviest; nights when the store is open; merchandising events, local or national, when shopping traditionally is done; departments to be opened or expanded; current prices and stock on hand. Enter items, prices and ad sizes for each day. You should urge a trial period of at least four months for this four-step program of increasing a retailer's advertising. Anything less is unlikely to prove the value of consistent advertising.

Ask for the Order!

A sales presentation should focus on the prospect's needs (never, "*I* sure need a good order today") and how your newspaper can fulfill them. Concentrate on a central theme, avoiding too many sales points. Don't confuse the issue. Keep your presentation simple. Always be honest with every claim. State your case briefly; if you waste the prospect's time, you will not be welcomed again.

Stay flexible, ready to depart from your planned presentation if it isn't going well (watch your prospect for signs of impatience) or if your prospect presents you with an unexpected opening. For example, if you go in with a presentation on advertising shoe sales and the prospect starts talking about boots, you switch signals too.

Opinions vary on how hard to sell against competition. Some sales managers say competition never should be mentioned; others say a presentation that doesn't bounce off competition is inadequate. On balance, talk positively about your newspaper and its strengths and not too much about competitors' weaknesses.

Be sure you state the cost of the advertising program you propose and quickly translate that into likely effectiveness. That includes CPMs and how they compare to other media. Always describe advertising as a necessary *investment* by the retailer in improved business, *never as a discretionary expense.* Ask for the order, *always.* You know that's why you're there. So does the prospect. Get a signature on that contract!

FOLLOW THROUGH WITH EFFECTIVE ADS

Only if advertising is effective will the client return to the newspaper. So your job includes making certain that ads are well done. NAA guidelines for effective ads:

1. *Create an identity* with distinctive artwork, layout and copy. This attracts more readers. Don't look like the competition.
2. *Use simple layout.* Be clever but not cryptic. Move the reader's eyes logically from headline to illustration to explanatory copy to price to store name and logo.
3. *Have a definite focus.* Newspapers are a visual medium and readers' eyes are drawn to well-chosen photographs or interesting artwork that, in turn, leads then to read about what you are selling.
4. *Feature consumer benefits.* Answer the customer's question "What's in it for me?" If it's lower price, feature that.
5. *Avoid congestion.* Use white space to separate your ad from the print surrounding it.
6. *Tell the whole story.* Cite color, size and price in appealing, enthusiastic, complete sentences and with illustrations.
7. *Name the price.* List the item's outstanding features to justify higher price. With lower prices, mention "closeout" or "clearance sale" to dispel any notion of low quality. Explain credit and layaway options.
8. *Specify branded merchandise.* Capitalize on the manufacturer's previous advertising to establish a brand name. Enhance the store's reputation by featuring known brands.
9. *Include related items.* Strive for two sales instead of one by, for example, showing a clothes dryer in an ad featuring a washer.

10. *Urge readers to buy now.* Stimulate prompt action with "limited supply" or "this week only."

Warning:

- Don't forget store name, address, telephone number and hours. One out of 10 American families moves annually and may not know the store. Even if the store is long established, mention its name several times in the ad.
- Don't be too clever. Some consumers distrust cleverness in advertising, as they distrust glib salespeople. Straightforward copy is most effective.
- Don't use unusual or difficult words. Many consumers won't understand "couturier" or "gourmet" or technical terms. Use simple language; everybody understands it.
- Don't generalize. Shoppers want facts; facts sell.
- Don't make excessive claims. The surest way to lose customers is to make claims the store cannot back up.

SUMMARY

Advertising market share, more than circulation share, tells the tale in newspapering today. Dailies in Washington, Cleveland and Philadelphia died even though they had substantial reader loyalty. For smaller dailies and weeklies as well as metros, financial success depends on achieving sufficient ad share against many competitors—television, radio, shoppers, direct mail—and not simply fighting off competing newspapers of like size and characteristics. Advertising departments must compete for ad dollars and reader time against all media.

Newspapers continue strongest in *local retail* and *classified* advertising. Opportunities are opening for expansion of *national* advertising as cable TV and other electronic systems fractionalize the network TV market. But television's entertainment value delivers huge audiences that are attractive to many national advertisers, so the battle will be tough.

Research is fundamental to effective advertising strategy. Advertisers want newspapers to deliver selected affluent, ready-to-buy prospects living near retail outlets. Research must find those prospects. Newspaper advertising strategy must include target marketing. More so than broadcast, newspapers are superbly equipped for zoning editorial and advertising content to deliver pinpoint marketing.

Newspapers' biggest single problem is the relatively shallow household penetration that many deliver in their primary markets. Managers must offer total market coverage (TMC) to quickly deliver all or nearly all households for demanding advertisers while simultaneously improving news content to improve paid circulation. Each manager must develop modern marketing leadership, integrating sales-related functions and launching highly motivated, well-trained sales forces into the marketplace.

GLOSSARY

Adjacency. Ad copy placed next to news copy (or, in TV, commercial time slot immediately preceding or following programming).

Advertorial. An ad advocating a commercial, political or philosophical concept—often controversial because it may be interpreted by readers as regular news content.

Agate line. A space measurement, one column wide and 1/14 inch deep.

Agency commission. Usually 15 percent, paid to recognized ad sales agencies for selling space to national advertisers.

Better Business Bureau. A local watchdog group supported by businesses to guard against business fraud and deceptive advertising.

Broadsheet. A "standard" newspaper page, normally 13 inches wide and 21 inches deep (measurements vary).

Center (or double-page) spread. Ad space on two facing pages.

Checking copy. Ad copy sent advertiser to prove publication.

Circular. An ad printed on a stand-alone single sheet or folder.

Classified. Ads arranged by "classification" such as help wanted, autos for sale, etc.

Column inch. A space measurement one column wide and an inch deep.

Combination (or combo) rate. A reduced rate offered advertisers for also using another publication, usually one owned by same publisher.

Cooperative (or co-op) advertising. Ads for which a national advertiser, usually a manufacturer, pays some or all of the local costs to promote a product jointly with a local retail outlet.

CPM (cost per thousand). Advertiser's cost for ad reaching a thousand readers (or, in television and radio, viewers or listeners).

Cumes (cumulative audience). The total of unduplicated persons or homes reached in given time by an advertising schedule; used mostly in television.

Demographics. Vital statistics of a population, such as age, income, occupations.

Direct mail. Mail-delivered direct-response advertising.

Display advertising. Ads other than classified often set in type larger than body type and "displayed" in larger spaces to attract attention.

Double billing. A billing method whereby an advertising medium gives a retailer two invoices for the same ad. The retailer pays the lower one and sub-units the other to the manufacturer for co-op funds (which are actually unjustified). Highly unethical.

Double truck. A single unbroken ad on two facing pages.

Drive time. Time during which commuters drive to and from work and for which radio charges the highest rates; normally 6 A.M. to 10 A.M. and 3 P.M. to 7 P.M.

Due bill. The exchange of ad space for goods or services from restaurants, theaters, etc.

Duplication. Number of persons exposed to more than one medium.

Ears. The upper corners of front pages, often boxed and sold for ads.

Federal Trade Commission (FTC). Monitors interstate commerce to, among other things, prevent unfair competition and fraudulent or deceptive advertising.

Flat rate. Space charge without quantity or frequency discounts.

Following (or full) position. Ad space next to specified editorial matter, for which the newspaper charges a premium rate.

Food and Drug Administration (FDA). The federal agency with, among other things, authority over the labeling of products.

Forced combination. The selling of ad space only if space in another publication is purchased. May be illegal.

Frequency. The number of times readers or household is exposed to an ad within a specified period.

Full (or following) position. Ad space in preferred space, next to certain reading matter or at the top of a page.

General (or national) rate. Rates for nonlocal advertisers.

Gross rating points (GRP). A measure of overall effectiveness of an advertising medium—percentage of audience reached and how frequently. Each point equals 1 percent of households or persons being measured; usually used in radio, TV or outdoor advertising.

Gutter. Blank inside margins of printed page.

Inserts. Preprinted ad matter delivered in newspapers, normally for a fee per thousand.

Island position. Ad space completely surrounded by editorial matter.

Layout. Finished design or rough sketch showing how an ad will look.

Legal (or public notice) advertising. Ads fulfilling legal requirements that certain governmental reports and statements, such as new laws or election notices, be published; also, ads by individuals or institutions on divorce, financial statements, bankruptcy proceedings, etc.

Lineage. Total ad lines printed or lines in an individual ad (14 lines to a column inch.)

Local advertising. Ads from local merchants, as distinct from national (or general) advertisers.

Makegood. Free ad to correct error or other problem in previous paid ad.

Marriage (piggyback) mail. Mail in which two or more advertisers use the same cover and share costs in a direct mail campaign.

Milline rate. Cost for one line in ad appearing before 1 million readers; used to express ad rates in relation to circulation.

National advertising. For products or services sold through many outlets, as contrasted with single-outlet local advertising.

National "reps." Agencies that sell national advertising for newspapers on a commission basis.

Newsplan. Industrywide effort under which individual newspapers offer quantity/frequency discounts to national advertisers.

Open rate. Highest ad rate, paid by users who don't qualify for discounts; also called basic, transient or one-time rate.

Preferred position. Special position for which advertiser pays premium rate.

Prime time. Peak TV viewing hours, usually 7 P.M. to 11 P.M., for which higher rates are charged.

Psychographics. Market description in terms of lifestyles, attitudes, opinions, etc.

Publisher's statement. Usually sworn statement by publisher of circulation, on which ad rates are based.

Rate card. Listings of rates, mechanical specifications, advertising policies and other matters affecting advertisers.

Rate holder. Used normally in local advertising to indicate ad published to maintain time or quantity discount guaranteed under contract.

Reach. A newspaper's total audience.

Reading notices (advertorials). Ads set to look like editorial matter. Many newspapers refuse them or require clear labeling as advertising.

Rebate. A payment to an advertiser whose increased activity qualified for a larger discount, or payment by a newspaper when circulation falls below guaranteed levels.

Retail advertising. Ads placed by local merchants who sell directly to users.

Robinson-Patman Act. An FTC-enforced federal law to protect smaller merchants by ensuring that they receive same ad discounts given to larger advertisers in same market.

Run of paper or run of press (ROP). An ad position anywhere in the paper at the discretion of the publisher.

Scotch double truck. One ad taking up two facing pages, bordered on each side and at the top with editorial matter.

Short rate. A rate applying to the payment of an advertiser who enjoyed space discounts but failed over the contract period to buy the minimum space required under contract.

Space buyer. Ad agency employee who selects print media for advertising clients.

Space discount. A discount given for a contractual agreement to buy certain amount of space.

Standard Advertising Unit (SAU) system. An effort to standardize newspaper advertising sizes and dimensions and increase national advertising by making it easier to plan, order, create and pay for a newspaper ad space.

Supplements. Preprinted inserts distributed in newspapers.

Till forbid (or, run TF). Normally used in local advertising to order continuous publication until the advertiser withdraws the order.

Transient rate. See "open rate."

NOTES

1. I talked with Cole and other *Press* and *Cleveland Plain Dealer* executives many times during this period. This quote, however, is from "We Gave It Our Best—Joseph Cole," *Cleveland Press,* June 17, 1982, p. 1.

2. Christy Fisher, "Newspaper Call to Arms in Fight over Classified," *Advertising Age,* April 26, 1993, p. S-1.

3. John Morton, "The Mail Animal," *Newspaper Letter,* Sept. 30, 1993, p. 1.

4. *Market Research,* a kit from Suburban Newspapers of America, 111 E. Wacker Drive, Chicago, Ill. 60601.

5. Elise Burroughs, "More Dailies Offer Advertisers Chance to Reach Target Markets," *presstime,* Aug. 1983, p. 19.

6. Gannett announced *USA Today* turned profitable in 1993. Published estimates on losses range from $600 million upward. Many start-up costs were hidden, however, so it's impossible for outsiders to get true accounting. For example, Gannett assigned journalists from its other papers to the *USA Today* staff but left salary responsibility with home papers—thus avoiding, it appears, assignment of those costs to the new paper.

7. "*Post* Has the Numbers, But Lineage Trails," *Advertising Age,* Nov. 29, 1982, p. 26.

8. Ibid.

9. "The Business of Newspapers: An Essay For Investors," industry review by Patrick O'Donnell Jr., senior publishing analyst, E F. Hutton, Feb. 12, 1982.

10. "TV Advertising: Is It Money Down the Tubes?" a "Marketing Smart" series, Newspaper Association of America, 1992.

11. "The Business of Newspapers," op. cit.

12. *Changing Needs of Changing Readers,* a study commissioned by the American Society of Newspaper Editors and conducted by Ruth Clark, then vice president of Yankelovich, Shelly and White Inc., May 1979.

13. "Classified Receives High Performance Rating," *International Newspaper Advertising and Marketing Executives News,* Dec. 1982, p. 11.

14. CEO Robert Kamerschen of ADVO, quoted in, "Don't Look Now—Advo Has Your Ads," *American Journalism Review,* Dec. 1993, p. 11.

15. "Competitors Eye Newspaper Bonanza as Advertisers Expand Use of Coupons," *presstime,* April 1983, p. 35.

16. Tom Vail, letter to author.

17. Harte-Hanks Communications, San Antonio, Texas, 1981 Annual Report.

18. Robert Marbut, letter to author.

19. For additional helpful details see *Measuring Salesforce Performance,* Management Aid No. 4,003, Fort Worth, Texas, U.S. Small Business Administration, 1981.

20. Walter M. Haimann, speech to International Newspaper Advertising and Marketing Executives, Las Vegas, Nev., Jan. 23, 1983.

21. The *Union* folded in 1994. The $2 million agreement was reported in, "Sacramento *Union*'s Advertisers will Get $2 Million Settlement," *Wall Street Journal,* Aug. 16, 1983, p. 16.

22. NAB activities and resources now are available through Newspaper Association of America.

10

IMAGE AND PROMOTION

Why, you might ask, are we interrupting our study of operating newspapers to discuss "image and promotion"? Here's why:

- Newspapers are fighting for their existence in the *commercial marketplace*. They must get more advertiser dollars and more reader time or face slow but inexorable decline.
- *Public regard* for newspapers is low. Newspaper motives and methods are distrusted. Of Americans polled by the Roper Organization, 43 percent said reporters put self-interest first, a dramatic worsening from a decade earlier when 61 percent said reporters put public interest first.[1]

You may think this evidence of trouble in the marketplace and in public opinion leads newspapers to give image and promotion a high priority. Not true. On average, newspapers spend just 3.1 percent of their total revenue for self-advertising and promotion. That contrasts with 17 percent spent by television, 11 percent by radio, 5 percent by outdoor advertising.[2] For a very long time, promotion was taken lightly among publishers and editors. A fashionable wisecrack: "For people in advertising, we sure do a lousy job of advertising our business."

Well, times changed. Promotion today is an extremely important managerial responsibility and must be integrated into every newspaper's marketing effort. Image in the marketplace must be built carefully and protected devotedly. So, if you're headed for a career in general management, circulation, advertising or news management, don't separate promotion or image in your mind from your most fundamental priorities.

We will look first at the wider newspaper industry image and then at how you can organize and manage a promotion effort to improve your newspaper's general image, increase circulation and augment advertising sales.

YOUR FIRST PRIORITY: PROTECT YOUR NEWSROOM'S CREDIBILITY

Skillful promotion can strengthen your newspaper's standing with advertisers simply by explaining in accurate detail how ads in your pages will sell goods and services. Slick brochures and sincere, well-planned public service programs will help pull public opinion and readers your way. But the core strength of your newspaper—and the principal thrust of any promotional effort—must be the credibility of your newsroom. And, it's so easy for that credibility to be damaged.

The Wall Street Journal: A Case in Point

On February 27, 1984, *The Wall Street Journal* published an item favorable to Chicago Milwaukee Corp. Next day, the company's stock value jumped more than $7 per share. It was another example of investors' extraordinary faith in the *Journal*'s accuracy. It was commonplace, this investor willingness to bet large sums of money on the *Journal*'s insightful reporting. Generations of dedicated reporters and skilled editors, schooled in the *Journal*'s ethics of handling sensitive news, labored to build that trust.

So Chicago Milwaukee's $7 jump raised no suspicions at the *Journal*. But it did at the Securities and Exchange Commission. Unknown to the paper's management, the SEC was tracking the market impact of stories written for the paper's "Heard on the Street" column by 35-year-old R. Foster Winans, author of the Chicago Milwaukee story. The SEC had been informed by the American Stock Exchange that suspicious trading patterns surrounded mentions of companies in "Heard."

In sum, the SEC later reported, Winans on many occasions leaked to associates advance word of what "Heard" would say. They traded before the paper was published and well before the general investing public could react. Large profits were made and Winans shared them, the SEC said.

The story was big news, the talk of Wall Street. Radio, television and other papers ran detailed accounts. The *Journal*, writhing in anger and embarrassment over what it called this "betrayal," published thousands of words on the affair, even describing Winan's sex life, obviously determined that whatever surfaced would see first light in the *Journal*, not a rival paper.

It was a dagger in the heart of the *Journal*'s only strength in the advertising and circulation marketplace—its credibility—and a blotch on its image as *the* source of accurate and reliable financial, business and economic news. (Winans later was sentenced to 18 months in prison.) The *Journal* is not the only paper hurt in this way.

The Washington Post was hoaxed by a staffer who tugged at readers' heart-strings with the piteous story of a child heroin addict who, it eventually was revealed, did not exist. *The New York Times* ran a beautifully written, first-person account of a guerrilla war in Cambodia by a reporter who got no closer to the jungles of Southeast Asia than a comfortable seaside resort in Spain. Many other papers must acknowledge that momentary breakdowns in editing safeguards let raging errors—or outright hoaxes—slip through.

So in a very real sense, the first line of defense in newspaper promotion must be placing the entire staff on guard against journalistic lapses that will cause the newspaper great embarrassment.

Every member of the staff must make sure that:

- Reporting is perceived by the public as presenting all sides of an issue and giving all principals in a story, particularly those accused of wrongdoing, opportunity to respond.
- Writing is as objective and dispassionate as possible and clean of bias. Make certain Republicans don't "smile" in your columns while Democrats "smirk" or vice versa.
- "Informed sources" and "observers" aren't quoted too often. Even casual readers understand those terms often cover only the writer's own opinions.

Simply put, the entire staff must ask, "Is that story just too good to be true? Are those quotes just a little too slick?" Had those questions been asked at *The Washington Post, The New York Times, The Wall Street Journal* and other newspapers, some major blemishes on newspaper credibility would have been avoided. However, even the most alert newsroom has difficulty preventing betrayal by an individual.

In the cases cited, the *Journal, Times* and *Post* had formal codes of ethics or standards of professional conduct that were betrayed by individuals. What counts when that happens is how the newspaper in the short term handles the explanation to readers and advertisers and how, over the long term, it rebuilds its image. There can be no haphazard approach to image and promotion. It must be a professional, ongoing effort. And as with any of your managerial responsibilities, you first must turn to planning and organizing the effort.

PLANNING AND ORGANIZING PROMOTION

As a key player on the integrated marketing team, the promotion department pursues planned goals. Two are most important: First, the department conducts *institutional promotion* of the overall character of the newspaper—its business and editorial philosophies. This establishes the paper's "tone" in its market. Second, the department conducts *marketing promotion* to increase sales by informing readers and advertisers of the newspaper's availability, stimulating their needs and convincing them the newspaper's advertising and news fulfills those needs. Promotion also is a competitive weapon to compare the newspaper with competing media, drawing distinctions and differentiating the media.

Guidance for promotion activity comes from two sources and can cover both short-range and long-range activity: First, overall strategic guidance comes from the newspaper's long-range planning process. This should include, for example, general guidelines on how to "position" the newspaper in "image" or public and consumer perception five or 10 years in the future. Second, the newspaper's short-term plan must assign specific immediate activities that are tightly coordinated with the circulation and advertising departments to increase sales or achieve other objectives within the year ahead.

Promotion takes various forms: *advertising* in the newspaper itself (house ads) or other media; *publicity,* such as news releases for other media; *sales activities,* such as trade shows booths and displays. There also must be for salespeople effective "drop" or *promotion material* focused on the selling function.

In organizational structure, promotion should report to the marketing director and have easy access to the directors of advertising and circulation. Close coordination with other departments, particularly news, is important. Top management must assign appropriate human and financial resources to promotion. Avoid the common error of running a low-budget promotion department headed by a powerless third-rank executive who gets the job only because he or she doesn't quite fit in elsewhere.

Such a promotion director never is admitted to decision-making circles, of course, and promotional considerations never enter overall executive strategy. This type of promotional executive never is asked to help fashion the news and advertising strategies that create a newspaper's image but is asked, occasionally, to clean up a public relations mess—explain away major error or hoax. And the publisher will wonder why the paper has low credibility in its market.

Deciding how much to spend on promotion is difficult. Should the figure be a percentage of sales, a little bit more (or less) than last year or pegged to what competing media spend? In practice, many newspapers give promotion a bit of what is left over after other departments share next year's budget pie. But if you are a promotion-smart manager, you will assign precise goals to the promotion department, then provide the financial resources needed to meet them. If you manage a small paper, you cannot afford a large promotion organization. But you must think promotion and maintain effective efforts even if you can assign promotion only as a part-time responsibility for a manager.

Increasingly, as you know, research into reader and advertiser attitudes is used to identify what is liked or disliked about the newspaper. That means the promotion director *can* define departmental objectives and plan means of accomplishing them. Two thoughts: First, all the promotion in the world cannot explain away basic flaws in a newspaper's journalistic content, advertising practices, or production and delivery systems. The best way to create a quality image is to produce a top-flight journalistic product and business operation. And second, absolute honesty in promotion is essential. Promotion *never* should step beyond facts into unfounded claims. The newspaper industry has a serious credibility problem and promotion must be part of the solution, not part of the problem.

Understand the Industry's Image

To effectively manage a newspaper's image, you must understand the industry's image. For although polls show readers hold their own paper in higher esteem than the "media," no individual newspaper is free from the rise or fall of public esteem for newspapers as a whole.

Your basic challenge in this image business is that your newspaper sells readers and advertisers something difficult even to define, let alone achieve and maintain: credibility. But it's all that you have to attract readers and advertisers. It takes generations to build credibility and unceasing vigilance to protect it. But in a flash, despite constant watchfulness, grievous damage can be done to it.

A single hoax or error might not destroy credibility, but it can draw down the reservoir of public confidence to dangerous levels. Probably more serious over the long haul is gradual erosion of public confidence due to errors in fact or to perceived bias in handling news, lack of good taste, or insensitive and unfair invasions of privacy. All find their way into daily and weekly papers large and small, and though each may seem insignificant, their cumulative impact can be devastating and long lasting.

Polls reveal many negatives in public perception of the press. And, contrary to long-held industry belief, polls show the criticism is not simply of the press as a messenger of bad tidings but rather as an impersonal, arrogant and manipulative element that intrudes into political, social and economic life. The press often is seen as a self-appointed participant in—not merely an observer of—the decision-making process. And some critics ask: Who elected the press to run my life?

Design Your Promotion Strategy Carefully

Research is nearly unanimous in finding the public generally distrusts the press and has severe doubts about its motives. And it's against that gloomy background that you must design your promotion strategy. By the early 1980s, journalists became acutely aware of the "credibility gap" developing between them and the public. With slight fluctuations of theme, subsequent research revealed deep problems.

For example, a major study by Ruth Clark for the American Society of Newspaper Editors (ASNE), *Relating to Readers in the '80s*, revealed that:

- Three-fourths of adults surveyed had problems with news media credibility; one-fifth deeply distrusted the media.
- Three-fourths said reporters only want a good story and don't worry about hurting people.
- One-sixth said the media are biased—that they sensationalize, invade people's privacy and emphasize bad news too much.
- Half said they would turn to television if forced to choose a single source of local news; only one-third chose newspapers.

Belden Associates, a leading newspaper research company, found these criticisms of newspapers:

- They are biased in handling news, carrying "slanted" news and too much "bad" news.

- They are guilty of inaccurate reporting (both typographical and factual errors).
- Content is "irrelevant."
- Not enough news is local.
- Then, mechanical problems: stories are too long, there are too many jumps (continuation of a story to another page), there is poor organization within the paper.[3]

Public opinion can be fickle, changing at least superficially on short notice. For example, researcher Clark found improvement in one sector since an earlier study (*Changing Needs of Changing Readers,* in 1978): Readers liked newspapers and their editors, and a majority found newspapers indispensable (though younger readers were less sure). A Times Mirror Corp. survey released in 1986 found wider than expected public support for newspapers and that vociferous critics were in a minority.

Nevertheless, design your promotion against this finding by Clark: "We (readers) still question, however, whether you are fair and unbiased when it comes to covering and allocating space to all your constituents. And we sometimes think you are trying to manipulate us."

Clark found the industry generally was judged more harshly than each reader's own newspaper:

- Fifty-seven percent expressing opinions did *not* feel newspaper stories were usually fair; only 39 percent believed their own paper was biased.
- Fifty-three percent did *not* believe newspapers were usually accurate; 84 percent described their own paper as accurate.

"While the perception of bias among newspapers in general has immense implications," Clark said, "it is apparent that the problem is one for the industry as a whole rather than for individual newspapers. One reason, of course, is that people's ties to their own papers are far stronger and warmer; 88 percent believe that the paper they read most often really cares about the community." However, 42 percent expressing opinions said even their own newspaper attempts to manipulate them.

Other researchers were finding problems, too. Gallup found that newspapers as an institution ranked in public confidence far down the list, behind organized religion, the military, banks, the U.S. Supreme Court and public schools. (Television came dead last, behind Congress, big business and organized labor.)[4] Gallup also found only 11 percent of the public had "a great deal" of confidence in newspapers. Among those polled, 41 percent had "some" and 18 percent "very little."[5] Harris polls showed similar slippage in public confidence in the press.

The public's view is even more mixed on confidence in the men and women collectively called the "press." Harris asked, "As far as people in charge of running [the press] are concerned, would say you have a great deal of confidence, or hardly no confidence at all in them?" As an institution, newspapers gained a higher confidence rating than television. But in confidence in the men and women behind the scenes, newspapers were rated substantially below TV news.

Studies show the public does not know much about the men and women who publish newspapers. Contrast that with viewer identification with a TV anchor who comes across as a real person, even a friend, invited into the home each evening to read the news. Consider the total anonymity of most publishers and editors or, indeed, save a few bylines, most reporters.

Contrast that with how CBS anchor Dan Rather drew solemn comment in the trade press and even in general-circulation papers when he first chose to read the news occasionally wearing a sweater under his jacket. Only the naive believe Rather wore a sweater because he got cold under those bright (and very hot) studio lights. TV strategists select such sartorial touches to build personal linkage between anchor and viewers.

Conversely, it's a newspaper tradition to scorn such trivialities, to glorify the copy desk's anonymity, to root out of a writer's reporting little touches of warmth and personality that could fashion personal links with readers. (Homer Bigart, whose reporting won two Pulitzer Prizes, once told the author in Vietnam that he had survived unscathed when bullets hit every other man he was riding with in a helicopter. Bigart could tell only another correspondent, not his *New York Times* readers. *The Times* copy desk, he said, edited from his account all personal references to his narrow escape. Picture how TV news would handle it: Correspondent in tailored bush suit breathlessly describing the firefight while camera pans across bullet-riddled chopper. And guess which account would come alive for the public back home.)

By neglecting such personal touches, the newspaper industry demonstrates that it doesn't understand readers. Ruth Clark found that 56 percent of her sample group wanted to know more about editors and reporters who publish the local paper; only 40 percent wanted to know more about production technology—a favorite promotional theme for scores of papers for decades.

Make Believability a Major Goal

Without believability, the newspaper industry cannot function as the credible primary source of in-depth information so essential in a democratic society. An individual newspaper lacking believability cannot succeed in circulation or advertising. Achieving believability is a complex challenge.

A Gallup poll on news believability asked, "If you got conflicting or different reports of the same news story from radio, television, the magazines, and the newspapers, which of the four versions would you be most inclined to believe?" Television received 51 percent favorable response, newspapers, 22 percent.[6]

However, polls consistently rank newspaper advertising more believable than TV ads. One poll—published by the industry's chief advertising promoter at the time, the Newspaper Advertising Bureau (now part of the Newspaper Association of America)—found 42 percent of those surveyed regarded newspapers the most believable advertising medium; 26 percent said television was most believable (it was 11 percent each for magazines and radio; 5 percent for direct mail.)[7]

What accounts for the different believability scores of news and advertising? In part, the difference stems from basic difference between newspapers and television: Some TV viewers think they "see" news develop on TV. Could a camera lie? Would the anchor, "Mr. Sincere Himself," shade the truth? In contrast, 33 percent of those surveyed by *Newsweek* magazine said newspaper reporters—unfamiliar, anonymous, impersonal—"often make things up." In advertising, TV commercials are intrusive and often avoided by viewers; recall of specifics is difficult after even a short time. Newspapers, conversely, are purchased by many *for* advertising. They carry detailed ads that can be clipped for future reference. They are not burdened by the strident hucksterism that plagues so much TV advertising.

Focus on Other Problem Areas

Polls reveal problems in three other areas: First, the public, better educated and more sophisticated, makes an important distinction between what the press does and *how* it does it. For example, there is strong support for investigative reporting in concept but firm disapproval of undercover techniques in practice. Gallup asked, "As you probably know, the news media—TV, newspapers and magazines—often do what is called investigative reporting: uncovering and reporting on corruption and fraud in business, government agencies, and other organizations. In general, do you approve or disapprove of investigative reporting by the news media?" The results:

- Seventy-nine percent of U.S. adults surveyed *approved* of investigative reporting in *concept*.[8]
- Sixty-five percent *disapproved* of reporters disguising their identity as reporters; 58 percent *disapproved* of using hidden cameras and microphones; 56 *disapproved* of paying informers; 52 percent *disapproved* of quoting unnamed sources.[9]

Second, there is important evidence that the newspaper industry should not speak of *its* First Amendment rights, but, rather, of the *public's*. That, Clark says, could translate directly into greater public support for what the press attempts to do. For example, Clark found a high percentage of adults feel the press must be present when U.S. military forces are sent to another country. Yet, there was widespread public support of the Reagan administration's decision to bar correspondents from landing with troops during the Grenada invasion in 1983.

Why? Clark: "Newspapers might have obtained stronger public support against their exclusion from the Grenada invasion if the issue had been expressed differently: as the right of the public to know, rather than the right of the press to be there."

Despite fears of many journalists that they alone defend the First Amendment, Clark found 86 percent of her sample agreeing with the statement, "If the government tried to close down a newspaper and stop it from publishing, I'd be upset enough to do something." Only 25 percent agreed that the president has a right to stop a newspaper from printing a story he feels is biased or inaccurate.

Third, much public criticism of the "media" really is directed at television, not newspapers, and many in the newspaper industry feel promotion efforts should make this distinction. Creed Black, then chairman and publisher of Knight-Ridder's *Lexington (Ky.) Herald-Leader,* in his final speech as president of the American Society of Newspaper Editors, said: "I come to what I have become increasingly convinced is one of the major reasons our public standing seems to have declined while our performance as an institution has improved. It is that the public lumps the printed press and television together in something called 'the media' and makes little if any distinction between the two. The result is that we are blamed for the sins and shortcomings of what television—which remains basically an entertainment medium—calls news."[10]

Black criticized what he termed television's "show-biz" approach to news, saying much of its offering is not news at all. He urged newspapers not to include themselves in "the media"; newspapers are "the press."

Ben Bradlee, then executive editor of *The Washington Post:* "Television has changed the public's vision of the reporter into someone who is petty and disagreeable, who has taken cynicism as an unnecessary extra step."[11] TV cameras, lights and recording devices are much more intrusive than a reporter with notebook and pencil. And, the process of getting a television news story can become part of the story itself in a dramatic, prying way.

In sum, your newspaper's promotional strategy must take into account public perceptions that newspapers are biased. Some readers fear newspapers attempt to manipulate them. Consequently, newspapers as an institution do not have the complete confidence of their readers. However, readers generally rank their own hometown papers much higher.

HOW TO BUILD YOUR NEWSPAPER'S CREDIBILITY

Against a backdrop of public suspicion of "the media," you must plan a detailed campaign to build your own newspaper's credibility in its marketplace. Then, allocate the necessary resources and execute the campaign over a prolonged period. You can make the effort pay off. The *Orlando (Fla.) Sentinel* did.

Concerned that a "credibility gap" existed between their newspaper and its readers, *Sentinel* managers launched a major image-building campaign that yielded enormous dividends in just two years.

First, daily circulation rose 6.1 percent (Sunday's was up 8.6 percent) in the two years, significant growth even for a newspaper in the prosperous Sun Belt, where circulation increases generally outstrip those in many other sections of the country. Second, and more significantly, research proved *Sentinel* readers noted and approved the Sentinel's self-improvement campaign. Importantly, research showed the promotion campaign helped readers note the newspaper's improved news coverage, appearance, design and organization.

TABLE 10.1   How the *Sentinel's* Image Improved

The *Sentinel* is	Positive	Neutral	Negative
Believable	74%	21%	5%
Has integrity	70	23	7
Fair/objective in reporting	60	27	13
Accurate in reporting	65	26	9
	Agree	**Disagree**	**Don't Know**
The *Sentinel* insists on the public's right to know	84%	10%	6%
The *Sentinel* is a positive force in community	85	9	6
The *Sentinel* has made some good changes in the paper in the past year or two	88	8	4[a]

[a]H.R. Lifvendahl, letter to author, and the newspaper's study, "Attitudes Toward the *Orlando Sentinel* in the Central Florida Market."

After the campaign, a study of the market by Belden Associates revealed the public's view of the paper's credibility and the public's attitudes toward how the paper operated (see Table 10.1).

Belden reported in 1984, at conclusion of the campaign, that 44.4 percent of survey respondents said the *Sentinel* was "better than it used to be," a 45 percent increase over those who said that two years earlier. David Burgin, then the paper's editor, said, "I can't say we've closed the (credibility) gap, but certainly the results show we've narrowed it dramatically."

Importantly, the *Sentinel* continues to attack that "gap." It launched strong image campaigns in the 1990s to maintain promotional momentum developed in the 1980s. One successful device: a bimonthly page giving readers behind-the-scenes looks at how the newspaper gathers news, produces and delivers each day's paper. Reporters, editors and columnists are profiled; the newspaper's literacy programs, recycling and charitable giving are explained.

"We're informing readers about ourselves, showing them the many ways we get involved in the community—through events and educational programs, for example," said John Blexrud, vice president and director of marketing. "Telling readers about ourselves isn't part of our normal newspaper beat, but (the bimonthly page) is a chance to tell our story."[12]

An Image Improvement Checklist

You can draw important lessons from the *Sentinel's* campaign in structuring your promotion department and planning improved image:

Ensure top management's full commitment. Sentinel President and Publisher H. R. (Tip) Lifvendahl was deeply involved in the campaign, along with the editor, circulation director and others.

Listen to readers. Research into readers' views must be the foundation for promotion strategy. The *Sentinel* listens through Belden's continuing market study. Less costly polls can be run by smaller papers, along with focus groups (see Box 10.1 for how they operate) or personal interviews that can reveal how readers and nonreaders perceive a newspaper.

Improve image through substantive improvement in news and advertising. Effective image building is more than a new 15-second radio jingle boosting the paper, sponsoring a soapbox derby or handing out T-shirts to joggers. It is enlarging the newshole, increasing story count, reorganizing and redesigning the paper to aid readers, improving reporting and writing. The *Sentinel* did all those things during its campaign.

Spend money. How much obviously depends on your available resources. The *Sentinel*, a wealthy Tribune Co. paper, added 30 experienced writers and editors during its campaign, increasing its total news staff to 270 people.

Exploit every positive development. The *Sentinel*'s campaign exploited a $40 million conversion to offset printing by promoting improved color and reproduction capability. The paper's name was changed from *Sentinel Star* to *Orlando Sentinel* to build stronger market identification. Opening a new bureau, adding a new feature or column or a major series of articles—all are positive developments you can exploit through promotion.

Warm up the paper. The *Sentinel*'s index now says, "Good morning" every day. The paper doesn't order readers to turn the page if a story jumps; it says, "Please

---

BOX 10.1   Why Use Focus Groups?

Readership surveys sometimes return conflicting signals on public perceptions of newspapers. For example, respondents to one survey divided in three almost equal groups: One considered the press unbiased in business coverage; a second, biased for business; a third, biased against business. So, many editors augment surveys with in-depth meetings with readers. Thus, the focus group.

If moderated expertly in a relaxed atmosphere, focus groups can provide valuable feedback. Focus groups are simple to conduct and provide inexpensive contact with readers. However, participants often are selected unscientifically and sessions yield unrepresentative information. So beware drawing sweeping conclusions from them.

It's best to seek reader input on a specific subject, say women's pages or the sports section. Invite appropriate groups of 15 or so readers to the newspaper office or to a neutral meeting room for a chat, perhaps over coffee and doughnuts. Participants tend to be reticent if newspaper personnel are present, so many sessions are conducted by an outside professional. Or, invite newspaper personnel in for a roundtable discussion during the second half of the meeting. Two hours is considered the effective maximum for such meetings.

The main benefit of such informal sessions is that, if skillfully run, they give small groups of readers a chance to speak their minds about the paper. But directing informal conversation into useful channels can be a challenge for even an experienced discussion leader. So, again, results must be weighed cautiously.

see...." And, Burgin directed the staff to "squeeze in as much wit and charm as we can...." He assigned critics to cover movies, restaurants, classical music, art and architecture, all to make the paper a useful and readable friend to each reader.

Talk about yourself. Many newspapers are reluctant to brag a bit in public. Such reticence is a bad habit. The *Sentinel* states in its masthead, "The Best Newspaper in Florida." It issues slick promotional packets on its credibility campaign. Publisher Lifvendahl signs cover letters sending packets to advertisers, journalism schools and other newspapers across the country. Explaining to both reader and advertiser what you are doing to improve your newspaper is essential in any image-building effort.

Avoid Extremes in Promotion

Two dangerous extremes in newspaper promotion must be avoided. First, when major errors appear or hoaxes slip into print, many papers publish guarded "explanations" that cannot possibly be confused with an apology or even a correction. Other editors and publishers will understand, but readers are left confused about just what did happen.

For many editors, it is most important that there be ritualistic (and, of course, symbolic) disembowelment by a responsible editor who courageously steps forward to accept blame at the annual convention of ASNE or another professional forum, appropriately out of view of readers and advertisers. Resolutions should be passed, codes of ethics reexamined and each editor, upon return home, must send to the editing desk a memo to "tighten up" and guard against hoax and error. For many editors, that fixes the matter. But, of course, for readers it doesn't.

The guarded "explanation" at best treats only symptoms of an image problem, not the cause, and at worst adds to public doubt and suspicion. Too often, the entire exercise is internal, almost fraternal, conducted by editors for other editors.

Clear, detailed explanations to readers of what went wrong are the only course. No reader could fail to understand what went wrong at *The Wall Street Journal* in the Winans case *or* doubt the *Journal*'s determination to avoid another such lapse.

A second extreme to avoid is managing the newspaper with the "image factor" primarily in mind, sacrificing the journalistic fundamentals of printing the facts and exercising community leadership in an effort to be "liked." Never should a newspaper grovel for favor. Credibility comes not from being "liked" but rather from being respected for courageous, high-quality professionalism. Promotional considerations must enter strategic planning but they cannot override the professional judgment of editors, advertising directors or circulation managers.

Themes to Stress

Research into reader views clearly suggests promotional themes you can use to improve your newspaper's credibility. Examples:

1.   The newspaper is the best possible source of complete, accurate, meaningful news and information. Stress "complete" to contrast with television's shallow treatment of news, "meaningful" to contrast with its "show-biz" tendencies and frothy stories used simply because they look fine in pictures. Stress "accurate" because factual errors in newspapers are a prime cause of loss of reader confidence. Donald Jones, experienced editor for the *Kansas City Star and Times,* said factual errors "do more to undermine the trust and confidence of readers than any other sin we commit...the smallest error of fact (will) cast doubt on the whole story...."[13]

2.   The paper must fairly and openly judge itself. Some newspapers appoint an "ombudsman" to handle reader complaints and judge, on the public's behalf, the newspaper's fairness and professionalism. Ombudsmen, drawn often from senior editor ranks but sometimes from outside the paper, achieve success directly proportionate to how seriously management views its credibility problem. If you are serious, your ombudsman will have credence and be helpful. If you don't care, neither will the public. A measure of your seriousness: Does your ombudsman have full rein to print sharp criticism of your paper? Ben Bradlee, executive editor of *The Washington Post* at the time, gave his ombudsman space for thousands of prominently displayed words to berate the *Post* for mishandling the child heroin addict who did not exist. Only another editor can understand how each word, in his own paper, took a bite out of Bradlee. Not many newspapers take such self-inflicted punishment. Many played with the ombudsman concept in the 1970s and 1980s, then quietly retired it. By the 1990s, only about 30 newspapers—about 1.8 percent of the total—had an ombudsman. A major reason: A survey by the Organization of News Ombudsman showed 58 percent of editors at the largest 100 dailies said they—*editors*—should handle the ombudsman function.[14]

3.   Make the newspaper accessible to its public and thereby attack a widely held view that editors and reporters hold themselves apart and are "arrogant." Promote letters to editors and invite guest columnists. Emphasize that no other medium can give readers such opportunities to have their say. If your paper has no ombudsman, switchboard and desk personnel should be schooled in handling telephone complaints or comments responsively. Use focus groups, kaffeeklatsches and building tours to give readers access to newspaper personnel. Above all, correct errors promptly and fully. Reveal all. There can be no coverup, no holding back. Take your lumps and then get on with rebuilding reader confidence. If a questioned story is correct, say so—and say why it is. Don't simply publish that lame old, "The *Daily Bugle* stands by its story."

4.   Promote "good" news content to counter persistent complaints that newspapers print only "bad" news. Research consistently shows readers feel newspapers pay too much attention to "bad" news, not enough to "good things." One reader told Ruth Clark: "If there is a drug bust in the high school, it is on the front page. If we raise money for the band to take a trip, it is not in the paper." If that is true for your paper, you have an internal problem with story selection that must be corrected. But most newspapers print plenty of "good" news—awards, scholarships, humor columns. Promote it.

5. Explain the newspaper's responsibilities to cover the news, push for facts and, on occasion, seemingly pry into private lives. This is to counter complaints that reporters are insensitive and invade privacy just to "sell newspapers." Don't simply retreat behind what the First Amendment and the law permit reporters to do: Explain *why* the newspaper must serve as community watchdog and professional adversary of government. Promote the paper's role as defender of the public's right to know.

6. Emphasize the fairness and balance of coverage. Present all sides of controversy. Cover all elements of the community, particularly minorities and the young. Be fair—and promote the fact that you are. Clark: "If there is a gap between newspapers and the public, it is on the fairness issue."

7. Promote the newspaper's usefulness as a tool in everyday life. Want to know where to go for entertainment, how to get there, and how much it will cost? Health columns, recipes, TV listings, how to cope? It's all in the paper, so promote it.

8. Underline the newspaper's independence from pressure groups, including advertisers. Ruth Clark said 57 percent of her respondents say advertisers and other business interests influence news coverage.

9. Identify with the community. This does *not* mean unthinking "boosterism." It means promoting the paper as a constructive—and sometimes critical—force for community involvement. It means editorials on local issues, not always Afghanistan. It means translating world and national issues into local terms—and promoting the paper as complete, well-rounded and watching the world of news for local readers. Group-owned papers must avoid acting like local franchise outlets for some distant, impersonal publicly owned corporate giant. Gannett for years promoted the theme, "Gannett, A World of Different Voices Where Freedom Speaks." (See Box 10.2 for another promotion activity important to publicly owned companies.)

By the mid-1990s, efforts to identify with the community gave rise to "civic journalism" (sometimes called "public journalism"), a move to not only report on societal problems but to help find solutions. Proponents urge editors to meet with civic groups and, even, public officials they are covering to discuss ongoing reporting on poverty, crime, the economy and other local hot topics. Opponents argue this carries newspapers into covering stories they help create—in effect, transforming reporters from observers and commentators into political activists and participants in a process better left to voters and their elected representatives.

Promotional Vehicles to Use

Promotion managers tend to agree basic promotion strategies are applicable among all papers, large and small. Donald B. Towles, then vice president and director of public affairs of the *Louisville (Ky.) Courier-Journal* and *Times*, said, "Newspaper promotion is basic. What will work for a 250,000 circulation daily will work just as well for a 25,000 circulation daily or 2,500 circulation weekly."[15]

BOX 10.2   Investor Relations: A Career?

Growth of publicly owned media corporations creates a top priority task for management: keeping Wall Street informed on company operations. That, in turn, creates a new career specialty for men and women who understand the media and have a flair for explaining their complex operational and financial methods. This is important "image" work and carries substantial career reward.

Gannett gives vice presidential status (and salary) to its director of investor relations, Susan Watson. She explains her job:

> Investor relations is essentially a marketing function. My department communicates the company's plans and priorities to the institutional investment community, which recommends or evaluates stocks for their clients.
>
> We keep our investors informed about business developments so that their expectations about revenue and earnings are realistic. We make every effort to prevent surprises. The stock market hates surprises.
>
> In most cases, our individual shareholders, including employee shareholders, deal with the Law Department or the company's transfer agent, First Chicago Trust Company of New York, which coordinate shareholder services, such as replacing lost certificates, or enrolling shareholders in our dividend reinvestment plan.[a]

Knight-Ridder also has a vice president in charge of relations with Wall Street analysts and investment portfolio managers who forecast the company's performance. Those forecasts influence the price of Knight-Ridder stock on the New York Stock Exchange and the exchanges in Tokyo and Frankfurt.

Frank Hawkins Jr., who held the job for years, explained:

As part of the process we, like other publicly traded companies, spend a good deal of time and effort keeping the analysts informed about Knight-Ridder, its activities and prospects. Our investor relations effort is based on the premise that we have a fundamentally good story and it is in our interest and the interest of our shareholders to tell it thoroughly and well.

We rely to a large degree on written communications such as our annual report to shareholders, quarterly reports, press releases, a fact book we hand out at analyst presentations and, occasionally, letters or other printed material.

But, ultimately, it's personal contact that sets the tone for how analysts judge Knight-Ridder. This personal contact comes from not just from me, but also from Chairman and CEO Jim Batten, President Tony Ridder (and other company executives)."

Unquestionably, this is corporate promotion that requires hard work—and fast thinking. Hawkins:

I spend a good deal of time on the phone or meeting with the analysts to supplement this information, answering their questions as they track our earnings prospects through elaborate spreadsheets that permit them to make sophisticated guesses about how much money we are likely to earn in the future.

Their estimates are the primary element in helping Wall Street set the price of our stock. The price generally reflects some multiple of anticipated earnings. This is also known as the price earnings or P/E ratio. Obviously,

Continued

BOX 10.2   *Continued*

the higher the earnings estimate, the higher the price of the stock is likely to be.

The trick is not to let any favorable expectations get out beyond reality. The worst mistake any company can make with the Street is to surprise analysts in an earnings release with a disappointing result. That means it's in our interest that the analysts not expect the company to earn more than it actually will.

So how's our stock going to do in the future? Ultimately, it depends heavily on how well we do on the bottom line.[b]

[a]"Q and A: Ask Susan Watson," *Gannetter*, July/Aug. 1991, p. 25.
[b]Frank N. Hawkins Jr., "How High Will Knight-Ridder Stock Go?" *Knight-Ridder News*, Spring 1993, p. 10.

That is, whether you are spending a million dollars or more annually to promote a metro daily or promoting a weekly on a low, low budget, you can use essentially the same approach. Some vehicles for spreading the message follow.

Your Own Pages

Large or small, a paper can use "house ads" to reach readers and advertisers. However, *non*readers and *non*advertisers, important targets, are not reached. So house ads cannot be the sole vehicle for successful promotion. But they are relatively cheap to fashion and can be run as space becomes available. House ads constitute 2.5 to 3.5 percent of total content in some newspapers. Use your shopper or TMC product to reach nonreaders.

Radio and Television

Some managers say using competing media might be endorsing them as advertising tools. However, radio and television are widely used, and should be. William J. White, *Philadelphia Inquirer* promotion director, said, "Using other media is the only way to reach out beyond our own readers."

Radio is favored because of its relatively low cost and target marketing capability. E. Russell Donnelly, promotion manager of the *Worcester (Mass.) Telegram and Evening Gazette* in the 1980s, compared radio and television as promotional vehicles: A 30-second TV commercial for a New England station costs $20,000 to produce, up to $3,000 to run once—and was viewed by thousands in four states too far away to subscribe to his papers. A 60-second radio commercial cost under $1,000 and could be aired for $15 to $18 each time. And local radio, with programming targeted at different age and income categories, reached the people his papers wanted to reach.[16] Radio offers quick promotion of, say, a news exclusive in today's paper. Some papers telephone commercials to radio stations on just minutes notice.

Outdoor Advertising

It often is used for photos of individual columnists or reporters to "humanize" an otherwise anonymous news-gathering staff. But relatively few people see any single billboard and copy must be limited to those few words motorists can catch while zipping by.

Direct Mail

Direct mail is a promotional medium that can target *non*subscribers. But large papers find it prohibitively expensive to use direct mail for reaching vast audiences of demographically diverse groups of nonreaders. Magazines use direct mail heavily. But most use nonsubscriber address lists carefully screened for demographic and psychographic characteristics that make recipients likely targets for buying subscriptions. Newspapers with strong database marketing techniques can locate households with characteristics that make them likely to subscribe. Once that capability is more widespread, the industry could find direct mail cost-effective in the future.

Other Vehicles

These include magazines, cable TV, rack cards (printed promotion placed on coin boxes) or posters on circulation trucks. Many papers use other newspapers, particularly in New York City, to reach East Coast ad agencies and major advertisers. *The Wall Street Journal* is used by papers trying to reach advertisers likely to read the *Journal.*

In sum, building a newspaper's institutional credibility is extremely important. But the true goal of effective promotion is increasing readership and ad revenue. And that requires hard-hitting promotion aimed at specific circulation and advertising audiences.

PROMOTING CIRCULATION GROWTH

It was a promotion manager's dream—a photograph of smiling Al Neuharth, then chairman of Gannett Co. Inc., holding up a copy of his new baby, *USA Today.* At his side, also smiling, were no less, President Ronald Reagan, Senate Majority Leader Howard Baker and House Speaker Tip O'Neil.

Neuharth, thus having boldly obtained virtual endorsement by the nation's then top three political leaders, was launching *USA Today* in the first "market rollout" in Washington on Sept. 15, 1982. Published prominently in leading newspapers and trade journals, the photograph set the tone for the costliest, most aggressive—and most successful—circulation promotion campaign ever conducted by a U.S. newspaper.

Just eight months after Neuharth and friends were photographed, a survey for *Advertising Age* magazine found 51 percent of the U.S. population had heard of *USA Today* and 46 percent had read it at least once. The paper at the time was available in just 15 major markets.[17] By 1993, *USA Today* had over 1.5 million paid circulation and was the nation's second-largest daily. Gannett doesn't say how much it spends promoting *USA Today,* but Joe Welty, then vice president for advertising, said the company spent $1 million *per market* to introduce *USA Today.*

A Circulation Promotion Checklist

Whatever your circulation promotion budget, take lessons from *USA Today*'s campaign:

Achieve a high degree of visibility. *USA Today*'s name, its distinctively colored nameplate, and its futuristic coin boxes are everywhere. The nameplate is on coffee cups, cereal boxes, matchbooks, T-shirts, TV, radio and other newspapers and magazines. It is difficult for literate, aware people in any primary market not to know of *USA Today.*

Reach great promotional intensity quickly and then maintain it. The shock value of *USA Today*'s campaign was unmistakable. The message quickly inundated target audiences; it wasn't dribbled out.

Make the newspaper readily available for purchase. Intensive promotion of a newspaper that readers cannot find to buy is a waste of money. *USA Today* blossomed overnight at thousands of sales points. Aside from coin boxes, Gannett pushes single-copy sale at newsstands, hotels, airports and other high-visibility places. The company sells many thousands of copies at reduced rates to hotels, airlines and others for free distribution to customers. This "bulk sales" circulation is highly controversial among newspaper executives who complain that *USA Today* unfairly inflates its circulation figures by "giving away" the paper. Gannett reports that its technique gets *USA Today* into the hands of demographically desirable people who frequent hotels and airlines, a goal of all newspapers. Whatever the merits of "bulk sales" as valid and verifiable paid circulation, the free distribution certainly promotes *USA Today* by getting it to people who might not otherwise read it.

Relate circulation promotion directly to the paper's overall strategy. Gannett proposes *USA Today* as a unique national newspaper for traveling upper-income executives and other demographically appealing audiences. Promotion speaks directly of the paper's usefulness to that type person.

Tie promotion to the paper's distinctive appearance, characteristics or features. Gannett's promotion touts *USA Today* as a different kind of paper, bright, fast-paced, with-it. Gannett does *not* promote *USA Today* as a me-too version of *The Wall Street Journal, The New York Times* or any other publication.

Promotion must stick to facts. *USA Today*'s circulation growth, the industry's fastest ever, is documented carefully each step along the way. An Audit Bureau of Circulations imprimatur certifies Gannett's claims. *The Washington (D.C.) Times,* by contrast, launched itself with the claim that it was "a newspaper second to none," when in fact any knowledgeable observer could see it was a distant tenth to its competitor, *The Washington Post.* The *Times* claimed "unquestionable excellence," which was patently open to question. Ads boasting a "talented, award-winning staff of experienced journalists" carried photos of staffers who appeared to be in their teens. In 1991, when the Gulf War erupted, the *Los Angeles Times* published full-page ads with the headline, "Persian Gulf War: When Experience Counts, Southern Californians Count on the *Times.*" *That* ad contained photos of six correspondents of obvious maturity. Cutlines explained their award-winning experience.[18]

Avoid the trite, routine approach. Try for the unusual, catchy theme or idea.

Promote Fulfillment of Reader Needs

Successful circulation promotion stresses that readers can fulfill important needs by reading the paper. The best copy does so in direct, explicit terms.
Examples:

- *The Wall Street Journal* sells itself as a tool for business success, a newspaper that will "save you from missing something that could help your career a lot."
- *The Milwaukee Journal* prides itself in its comprehensive international, national, state and local news: The *Milwaukee Sentinel* makes a virtue of its smaller size by promoting itself as "tightly edited" and more manageable for the busy reader. In 1995, the papers merged to become the *Journal-Sentinel.*
- *Newsday* promotes, among other things, its ability to reproduce photos and ads in four colors: "There's a More Colorful New York in *New York Newsday.*"
- *The New York Times* even promotes the difficulty of its crossword puzzle: "If you thought today's crossword puzzle was challenging, see what the *Times* has in store for you tomorrow!"

Attack Problem Areas Directly

National polls or even your own low-budget research can uncover reader doubts, suspicions and complaints. Your promotion should attack them directly.

The *Dayton (Ohio) Daily News* attacked feelings that they were distant from readers, perhaps arrogant or out of touch:

- Dayton residents were invited in for "Coffee with the Editor." Staff members spoke to groups and answered questions.
- Telephone calls to a special number were taped and published in "Speak Up Dayton," a regular feature letting citizens speak their minds.
- To personalize the staff, full-page ads featured photos of staffers and listed city area or suburb where they lived—all under the headline, "Your Neighbors Cover the News." Said promotion Director Ken Walters: "The ad showed that the 'downtown paper' was really staffed with people who live throughout the Miami Valley—they are neighbors."[19]

As chairman and publisher of the *Miami Herald,* Richard G. Capen said newspapers "have problems with alienation from their readers and the public at large," so his paper took steps to stay close to readers. The *Herald:*

- Held monthly "Meet the Press" meetings of readers to help them "understand some of the things we do and create a substantially improved awareness on the part of our editors and reporters as to the sensitivities of our coverage and the problems we cause when errors are made."

- Held regular breakfasts and lunches with community leaders and opinion makers, asking "top business people, cultural and civic leaders, top black, Hispanics, women and related segments of our community to discuss current problems and ways in which our newspaper can meet the needs of our readers."
- Carried an expanded "Reader's Forum" to publish reader letters.
- Offered space for guest editorials and feature articles on many issues.
- Ran a "Speakout" series in which readers challenged *Herald* editorials and op-ed articles.

Many papers publish detailed stories about their newspaper operations, picturing staffers at work and identifying them by name, title, and function. *Milwaukee Journal* articles said, "This is another in a series of Sunday pages intended to help you become better acquainted with the *Milwaukee Journal.*"

When he was editor of the *Detroit Free Press*, David Lawrence, now *Miami Herald* publisher, frequently wrote his own letters-to-the-editor column in response to reader complaints. "People are scared of us," Lawrence said, "and think we have all the power and have to have the last word. Readers want to know we're human, imperfect and not very different from them."[20]

At times, circulation promotion must anticipate reader complaints. For example, like all newspapers, *The New York Times* expects complaints, even lost circulation, following a price increase. Anticipating this, *The Times* publishes an explanatory news story prior to any increase in single-copy or subscriber prices.

Crucial elements in such an explanation include why the price is being increased (newsprint prices are up, transportation expenses are rising and so forth); how long it's been since the previous increase; and value-added improvements that give readers more, despite the increase. In 1993, to explain an increase to $2 from $1.50 in the single-copy price of the *Sunday Times,* Publisher Arthur Sulzberger Jr. pointed to recent improvements in metro and sports coverage, and the introduction of two new sections ("Styles of the Times" and "The City"). He explained the company built a color printing facility and planned more improvements.[21] The more such detail you include, the better your chances of preventing grumbling over a price increase from turning into cancellations.

Any major change in operation should be fully—and publicly—explained. Many papers in recent years closed afternoon editions, creating much unhappiness among readers wedded to evening reading. When it did that in 1993, the *Augusta (Ga.) Chronicle and Herald* wrote to subscribers with a detailed explanation making these points:

- Subscribers are "precious" so "we felt we should contact you directly with this letter. . . ."
- The staff "exhausted all methods of maintaining the circulation and readership" of the afternoon *Herald.*

- "This is not unique to Augusta. In the past decade more than 400 afternoon papers have closed, switched to morning publications or merged with their morning sister papers. . . ."
- "We have accepted the fact that we can better serve the Augusta area by putting all our resources into one (morning) newspaper."
- "The death of any institution is a somber event but we view this more as a celebration of better things to come for our readers."

The letter was signed by Publisher William S. Morris III and General Manager Julian Miller.[22]

Go After Nonreaders

One specific target of your promotion campaign should be residents who don't read your newspaper. You've got plenty of research to draw from.

Deanne Termini, senior vice president of the research firm Belden Associates, identified reasons frequently given in polls for not reading newspapers. I've adapted her list to themes you can use in countering complaints:

No time to read. This is a critical complaint among time-starved, ever-busier Americans. Take it seriously. Your promotion could emphasize section-by-section news compartmentalization and indexing to aid the harried reader. Even *The New York Times,* hardly a "quick read," addresses this complaint. One of its slogans for the 1990s: "You're in a hurry? Need the news in a flash? Check page 2 every day for the 'News Summary' in the New York Times." Present your newspaper as a menu from which readers quickly can select desired items. Above all, promote your paper as containing information crucial to readers and, thus, well worth the time spent reading it.

Too expensive. Compare relatively low price—35-cent paper with 50-cent restaurant cup of coffee. Stress the paper's shopper coupons, sometimes worth hundreds of dollars in a single issue. The *Athens (Ga.) Banner-Herald* publishes house ads totaling coupon values in the previous week's issues, adding "it's like having money delivered to your door."

Poor delivery service. Aside from bearing down on the circulation department, establish a customer service unit and promote use of trucks to get copies to complaining subscribers who missed theirs; always follow up with a telephone call the next day.

Prefer TV/radio news content. First, ensure that local news is covered, then promote its exclusivity and depth. No other medium records births, marriages, deaths and other local news as does the newspaper.

Dislike of content. Too much bad news, bias. Ensure bias does not exist, then promote "good news" content, highlighting it in the paper itself and in promotional themes. Have a local humor columnist? Put his or her photo on billboards advertising the column's cheery message. There is content for everyone in the paper; promote it.

Dislike of editorial policy. Promote the difference between news columns and the editorial page; I *never* would carry an editorial on news pages, particularly the first page, and only rarely a "news analysis" anywhere but on the editorial or op-ed page. Many readers do not distinguish between straight news and editorial pages. Promotion should highlight that an editorial point of view does not mean news stories are slanted.

In sum, promotional preemptive strikes should be launched against known reader doubts even if they have not yet manifested themselves in written complaints—or declining circulation. Find out what problems exist, fix them, then explain with frank, detailed promotion.

The Importance of Carrier Promotion

Much of your promotion must be directed toward recruiting and motivating carriers and acquainting the public with their importance. House ads detailing potential earnings can help attract carriers. Gannett's *Wilmington (Del.) News* published photos of carriers along with job application forms. Many papers direct carrier recruitment promotion at parents, pointing out the value of instilling the work ethic in their teenagers. The *Lynchburg (Va.) News and Daily Advance* struck a community service theme and promoted carriers' efforts to raise money for United Way. "We do more than just deliver newspapers," the ads said.

Promotional material for use by carriers in door-to-door selling is extremely important. Not many 13-year-olds are accomplished salespeople. The *Bakersfield Californian* provided its carriers with selling hints written and illustrated like comic books. One showed how to explain a price increase to subscribers.

The Contest Controversy

One controversy in circulation promotion is over the value of sweepstakes, cash giveaways and other contests variously called Bingo, Zingo or other racy names. Rupert Murdoch's *New York Post* heavily promotes cash contests and attributes much circulation growth to giveaways. The New York *Daily News* and *Chicago Tribune* also have used cash contests to ignite reader interest. In New York City in 1983, the *Post* and *Daily News* took their bitter contest for circulation into the contest arena, offering a total of $225,000 in weekly prizes. Games involved lucky numbers printed daily by each newspaper. (The *Post* promptly tricked *News* Publisher James Hoge into being photographed holding a *Post* Wingo promotional card; the photos were duly published in the *Post*.)

Atlanta Journal and *Constitution* executives found to their surprise that 24 percent of Atlanta's adults participated in their Zingo contest. The players' demographics matched those of *Journal* and *Constitution* readers, although players were slightly older.[23]

Cash contests attract primarily nonreaders with only temporary interest in the paper and bring little permanent increase in circulation. Warns management guru

Peter Drucker: "Of the top marketing lessons for the highly competitive '90s, the most crucial one may well be that buying customers doesn't work."[24] However, contests do entice nonreaders into trying the paper, and hard-hitting promotional follow-up and, most importantly strong news content, can help hold some cash-oriented players.

Ask for the Order

The entire point of circulation promotion is to hold current readers and sell the paper to nonreaders. Surprisingly, many promotion efforts don't directly appeal to either group. Promotional ads should carry telephone numbers or addresses where subscriptions can be ordered. Include coupons that can be clipped and sent in. Don't avoid the point of it all: Ask for a subscription order.

PROMOTING ADVERTISING GROWTH

Turning to advertising promotion, you must shift gears. A completely different audience must be wooed with different themes. The targeted audiences are advertisers or their surrogates, the ad agencies. Both are sophisticated in advertising strategy and market research. Without question, they are discerning in where, when and how to spend their advertising budgets. Make sure your promotional messages aimed at these audiences are tightly researched, factual and of high quality.

Advertising promotion revolves around the number of your readers, where and how they live—their demographic appeal—and your newspaper's ability to elicit from them shopper/buyer response to the advertisers' message. Thus, the fundamental theme of advertising promotion is that the newspaper is a tool for advertisers in improving their own business fortunes. Sometimes, however, promotion must start with a much more basic theme—that a market indeed exists.

First Delineate the Market

Drive through Chicago's suburbs all you want. Ask at every gas station. You'll not find "Herald City." But it's there. The *Daily Herald* of Arlington Heights, Ill., says so. The *Daily Herald* mapped out a market of 16 communities in Chicago's northwest suburbs, called it Herald City, and tells advertisers that only the *Daily Herald* can "deliver" affluent suburbanites who live there.

It's possible to argue that Herald City is in fact 16 distinctly separate communities, that they lack commonality to constitute a single market, and that the *Daily Herald* isn't exclusive in delivering them. Other newspapers, including the Chicago metros, so argue. But despite vigorous attack from competitors, the *Daily Herald* has had enormous success in creating, through promotion, the concept that this market exists, that it is demographically attractive and that the *Daily Herald* and its free-circulation sister, *This Week,* deliver it.

How successful? Between 1969 and 1986, the *Daily Herald* expanded from a twice-weekly with a limited marketing view to a seven-day morning paper with paid circulation over 62,000 daily and once-weekly TMC of 280,000 nonsubscribers households. Daily circulation in the 1990s surpassed 85,000.

Daily Herald Editor Dan Baumann said of the $200,000 Herald City promotion campaign: "The theme was to build the idea that this is a market that can be defined and separate from the amorphous [city plus suburban] mass."[25]

Times Mirror Corp. had similar promotion under way in Connecticut towns north of New York City, attempting to instill in advertisers' minds the idea of a suburban regional market served by the company's *Stanford (Conn.) Advocate* and *Greenwich (Conn.) Time*. This has been Times Mirror's strategy since acquiring both papers in 1978. Neither the *Advocate*, with morning circulation of 30,000 (1993), nor *Time*, with 13,000, fits the profile of a typical Times Mirror paper (such as the *Los Angeles Times* or *Newsday*, both huge metros).

But Times Mirror saw rich opportunity for expansion in those rich Connecticut suburbs, and the *Advocate*'s news desk turned out stories of regional interest that tended to knit together communities throughout the area. The promotion department delineated the area as a single market the *Advocate* alone could serve well. Sometimes, smooth promotion cannot create a rewarding market.

For example, Gannett saw a rich demographic market available in affluent, much-traveled business executives, and heavily promoted the concept that *USA Today* could reach them anywhere in the United States. But advertisers were slow to accept the claim after the paper was launched in 1982, and not until 1993 did the paper have a profitable year.

Promote Your Market's Attractiveness

With the market delineated geographically or demographically, your promotion must convince advertisers of its attractiveness. Because most newspaper ad revenue is local/retail, your first task is to promote effectively on Main Street.

Promote population size and attractiveness in the market, households, personal and household income, retail sales and other indicators of wealth and willingness to spend it. For smaller papers, promotion materials can be simple collation of vital statistics in a low-cost pamphlet. Larger papers should produce expensive promotion in a full range of media. Whatever your paper's size, a "market fact book" or "marketing kit" is essential (see Box 10.3).

Prove You Deliver the Market

The third step, after delineating the market and demonstrating its attractiveness, is to prove your newspaper reaches the advertisers' potential buyers in the market. Key elements are your newspaper's household penetration in a geographic market, such as city zone or retail trading zone, or its readership in demographic markets.

At this point, your promotion must position the newspaper competitively in its market. Some small-town publishers position their paper as "The only newspa-

BOX 10.3 The Marketing Kit

Call it a "marketing kit" or "fact sheet," your newspaper should have a core packet of promotion highlighting for advertisers the market's strengths and how the paper exploits them. Some papers publish slick, expensive market books for ad agencies, ad reps and advertisers. Smaller papers can make do with inexpensive fact sheets. Whatever your budget, include key information:

- Market description, including retail sales, households, population and an explanation of the geography. Maps showing ZIP code areas covered by TMC or zoned editions are helpful. Ages of the population, educational levels, incomes, buying habits—all are essential.
- Competitive situationer, including how your paper and principal competitors reach the market. This should be expressed in total and ZIP code area penetration plus circulation by demographic groups, such as women 18 to 35 or $50,000-plus income categories.
- Readership profiles giving a clear picture of who reads the paper—expressed in age, education, occupation, whether they own their own home or rent and so on.
- Newspaper growth records are helpful when they show expanding circulation and increasing ad content.
- Shopping mall and store studies showing who shops and where—all related, of course, to newspaper circulation and reading habits.

- Statement of source and methodology for any research or survey material. Undocumented claims are unacceptable to sophisticated advertisers.
- Background on newspaper and key personnel can personalize both the institution and its staff.
- And, of course, rate cards and contracts.

Promotion you design to highlight your market's value must tie closely to your newspaper's overall strategy. For example, *The New York Times* doesn't pretend to be a mass-consumption newspaper—indeed, it studiously avoids being so considered. So, *The Times*'s promotion stresses the high incomes and educational levels of its carriage-trade audience. The *Times* promotes its national market as a relatively narrow but highly attractive demographic slice just 1 or 2 percent of the U.S. population that is most affluent.

More frequently, however, your newspaper promotion will stress the attractiveness of your geographic market and the quality of its readership. Ensure that your promotion presents truly important information in a form easily understood by busy, preoccupied advertisers and their agencies. Promotion material then must be placed in the proper hands—preferably by a salesperson directly or via direct mail, or, often, ads in periodicals likely to be read by advertisers. Precision tailoring and delivery is a key link in the promotion chain.

per in the world that gives a damn about our town." That's not a bad statement of confidence, saying that any advertiser wanting to reach "our town" must do it through our pages.

One way or another, often at enormous cost, many papers position themselves through promotion as the number one medium in delivering the market. Promotion executives differ on whether promotional positioning should mention competitors by name. Some argue naming competitors graces them with advertiser awareness they otherwise would not achieve. *USA Today* doesn't mince around. It positions itself against *Time, Newsweek, Sports Illustrated* and *U.S. News and World Report*—and names them in promotions designed to prove that *USA Today's* audience is more attractive demographically than theirs.

Prove That You Create Response

Demonstrating that your newspaper reaches an audience doesn't convince many advertisers today. This brings you to the fourth step in advertising promotion: proving your newspaper can pull response, proving an ad will draw customers into a store and move merchandise.

Nothing succeeds like a trial run of ads (always strive for more than one) to demonstrate response. But if the advertiser is unwilling to experiment, there always are testimonials and the judgment of peers. A list of your advertisers, showing how long they have been customers and how much space they buy, can convince holdouts their peers see the newspaper as effective and that they must jump aboard.

USA Today floods advertiser prospects with lists of companies, arranged alphabetically and by type of business, that use the newspaper. Testimonials from advertisers should describe the response from customers who see their ads in the paper. *USA Today* creates testimonials on number of customers as well as telephone calls or orders resulting from ads in the paper. ("*USA Today* is an action medium," promotion reads, "bold, inviting and uncluttered. If you send in the coupon, we'll send you actual case studies that'll knock your socks off!")

To prove reader interest, promote time spent by the average reader with each issue and the number of consecutive issues read. A newspaper skimmed for just a few minutes once every week or so by the occasional reader is not attractive to advertisers. *USA Today* uses one poll showing 41 minutes average reading time by respondents and that they have read, on average, 3.7 of the past five issues.

Don't Overlook National Advertisers

You must create effective promotional material to boost national ad sales, providing it either directly to major advertisers and ad agencies or through your newspaper's own national ad rep. But be aware that promoting national is particularly difficult.

National advertisers and agencies generally have headquarters in distant cities. Their decision-making executives often are preoccupied with the quick, single buy of TV or magazine advertising. Most lack personal contact with your newspaper or awareness of what it is doing to capture your market.

To counter this, Lou Hagopian, when chairman of N. W. Ayer ad agency in New York City, said promotion aimed at national advertisers should:

- Stress circulation totals, particularly any saturation coverage available though TMC vehicles, but *avoid* total preoccupation with circulation numbers.

- Show the demographic quality of your circulation, not just totals. Advertisers seek special-interest blocs of readers, so promotion must describe the diverse groups comprising your total circulation and how your newspaper reaches each. For example, demonstrate that your business section reaches highly affluent readers seeking personal investments information (of interest to bank or broker advertisers). Show you attract sports readers (of interest to liquor and car advertisers).
- Simplify the national agency's job in buying newspaper ad space. Include standardized rate cards and promote use of Standard Advertising Units and Newsplan, devices to remove mechanical barriers to newspaper advertising.
- Speak to your own strengths and don't attack competing newspapers. Some newspapers, Hagopian said, are "forever cutting down their competitors and, thus, themselves." A newspaper's strengths, he said, are couponing ("unbeatable"); TV support advertising; new-product introductions; local retail; and ads for tobacco, liquor, financial and food products.
- Get copies of your newspaper into the hands of national advertisers and agencies, along with personal information on the men and women who produce it. Personalize the image.

Promote Classified Advertising

Here are some successful themes for advertisers:

- It's simple to use classified. Just telephone us and we'll handle everything; we'll bill you, or you can drop off a check.
- It's cheap to use classified. A few dollars will sell your used car or get rid of those surplus kittens.
- Classified ads draw a fast, meaningful response.

Testimonial promotion stressing number of responses to a single ad or quick sale of an item can be very effective.

Target two basic audiences for classified promotion:

- High-volume or "contract" advertisers, such as real estate firms, employers and car dealers (largest three users of classified).
- Occasional or "transient" or "voluntary" user of classified.

Obviously, different approaches must be used to reach prospects who range from real estate firms that spend thousands of dollars annually in classified to the householder who wants to advertise, for $4.50, the once-in-a-lifetime garage sale. Streetwise, aggressive salespeople are the primary force for selling classified to high-volume advertisers, and they must have leave-behind or "drop" material, including rate cards and contract forms that are easy to understand and use. Promote classified's attractive rates for those prospects who find retail display rates prohibitively high but who, if convinced to use classified, can be attractive revenue contributors.

House ads in your own pages are the most widely used form of classified promotion. Your paper's existing readership, shown by research to frequently browse classified pages, is the largest, most attractive and most easily reached audience available. Promotion campaigns built around house ads should have continuity and frequency—a front-page teaser, for example, alerting readers to an amusing or particularly interesting ad. Radio, outdoor advertising, direct mail—all are used, but generally less than for promoting local/retail or national advertising.

Persistent, imaginative promotion, in sum, can build classified success. "I got my job through the *New York Times*" is a promotional theme that made *The Times*'s classified employment section famous—and added millions of dollars to *The Times*'s coffers.

CASE STUDY 10.1   Promotion: Ideas for Planning

Once again, you're thrown unexpectedly into managerial responsibility—promotion, this time—and you have no experience to lean on. Where to start?

Your First Move

Turn first to Newspaper Association of America, the industry's principal trade group. NAA was formed in 1992 through merger of the American Newspaper Publishers Association, Newspaper Advertising Bureau and five other marketing associations: the Association of Newspaper Classified Advertising Managers, International Circulation Managers Association, International Newspaper Advertising and Marketing Executives, Newspaper Advertising Co-Op Network, and Newspaper Research Council. NAA provides operating and promotion expertise from its headquarters at The Newspaper Center, 11600 Sunrise Valley Drive, Reston, Va., 22091–1412, telephone (703) 648–1000.

If your newspaper is one of 1,700 newspaper members of NAA, you can call on the association for help in any promotion campaign you want to run. On a national level, NAA focuses on four areas:

• Government, legal and public policy (such as lobbying against telephone company

desires to enter into the news/information business).
• Marketing, including a high-powered effort on behalf of newspaper advertising.
• Technology and telecommunications (including research and development).
• Diversity (primarily minority hiring).

Don't be bashful asking for NAA help. Your paper, like all members, pays hefty dues—up to $100,000 annually.

Your Second Move

Build a promotional strategy around basic NAA themes for dealing with competition:[a]

Counter television in advertising as an expensive, fractionalized medium. NAA research shows even highly popular TV programming (and thus adjacent commercials) suffers badly in the electronic scramble for viewers. Thus, even highly popular cable channels have only limited penetration of TV homes—2.5 percent for WTBS, 2.4 for ESPN, and 2.2 for USA, according to NAA research.

Promote to counter radio on grounds it, too, is fractionalized, with many stations clamoring for listeners—and, NAA says, point out that many listeners are unattentive to radio pro-

CASE STUDY 10.1   *Continued*

gramming and actually "shut out" commercials.

Promote against direct mail on grounds newspapers already offer total and selective market coverage, and that direct mail is wasteful— only 14 percent of most households read direct mail ads, NAA says, whereas people pay to read newspapers.

Your Third Move

Start public service programs. Two are particularly important: Newspaper in Education, a nationwide plan for getting newspapers used as teaching tools in schools, and adult literacy.

Many newspapers build promotion strategies around those two programs. Both have high visibility and fulfill a newspaper's role of being a good citizen in its community, as well as looking out for its own long-term business interests. Sponsoring arts festivals, soap box derbies and other events is image-building, too.

Your Fourth Move

Design uniqueness into your promotion; make it different, to ensure you catch the attention of readers, nonreaders, advertisers and nonadvertisers.

The *New York Daily News*, competing against newspapers with overwhelmingly superior resources, got widespread attention with a promotion campaign directed against

Newsday: It featured photos of a cow grazing in a Long Island field that, as *Editor & Publisher* commented, was "presumably a mere cowchip's toss away from the office of *New York Newsday*'s publisher."[b] You decide whether that wisecracking approach is effective, but it certainly made the *Daily News'* point: We're streetsmart and zippy while *Newsday* is, well, bucolic and bovine.

The *Chicago Sun-Times,* number two in its market, went straight for the jugular in promotion commenting on a price increase to 50 cents from 35 cents by the *Chicago Tribune:* "Budget cuts. Plant closings. Mass layoffs," a *Sun-Times* radio commercial said. "With news like this, how can a paper raise its price over 42 percent? Maybe it's time to choose one that's sensitive to the issues. The *Chicago Sun-Times.* Still only 35 cents. Smart choice."[c]

The *New York Post* struck hard, fast and much to the amusement of thousands when *The New York Times*, in a most un-*Times*like move, launched a promotion contest. The *Times* hid a photo of Kevin, star of the movie "Home Alone," in its pages and gave prizes to readers who could find him. The *Post* launched a promotion counterattack, printing each day, next to its table of contents, where Kevin could be found in the *Times*.

Promotion is important? Yes. Promotion can be fun? Yes!

[a] See "Sales Presentation Maker," NAA publication, based on various research in 1991–1992.
[b] Dorothy Gibbons, "Ads Aimed at Starting a Tabloid War," *Editor & Publisher*, Dec. 25, 1993, p. 24.
[c] Mark Fitzgerald, "Price War," *Editor & Publisher*, Oct. 3, 1992, p. 11.

SUMMARY

Polls show the newspaper industry is perceived by the public as guilty of bias in handling news or, by some readers, of intentional fabrication. When expressing confidence in American institutions, the public ranks the newspaper industry substantially below organized religion, the military, banks, the U.S. Supreme Court, and public schools (but ahead of Congress, big business, organized labor and television). The public has less confidence in the men and women who collectively make up "the press" than in the individual newspapers they read daily or weekly.

The industry obviously has an image problem as it strives for the credibility newspapers must have to discharge First Amendment responsibilities and achieve commercial success in advertising and circulation. Each individual newspaper must bolster its own image through professional, imaginative promotional campaigns. Research—listening to readers and nonreaders—must be the foundation of all promotion. Promotion cannot gloss over journalistic or product weakness; there must be substantive improvement in product quality, which promotion then highlights and exploits.

However large or small your promotion budget, one goal must be making the newspaper warmer, friendlier—personalizing it and its staff. These themes are important: The newspaper provides complete and reliable news and information; the paper is accessible to its public, responsive to its needs; "good news" is available along with the bad; the paper has a duty to probe and push for news and doesn't needlessly invade personal privacy; it is fair and balanced in coverage.

In promoting circulation growth, the paper should quickly achieve a high degree of visibility; it must be talked about. Promotion should stress benefits to readers that come with subscribing. It should avoid exaggeration. And without fail, promotion should ask for the order; it should urge purchase of the paper.

Advertising promotion is directed at a different audience, the advertiser or ad agency. Most are sophisticated in advertising, and promotion must be first-rate in pertinence and quality. Promotion should delineate the market, describe its attractiveness, prove that the paper delivers it and prove it pulls response from advertisers' prospective customers.

NOTES

1. "Whose Interests Do They Serve?" *presstime,* March 1993, p. 19.

2. "Industry Standards," *Scripps Howard General Managers Newsletter,* Nov. 1991, p. 7.

3. Deanne Termini, senior vice president, and Sheila Miller, research associate, Belden Associates, Dallas, in a paper delivered to Southern Newspaper Publishers Association editorial clinic, Dallas, April 3, 1984.

4. Gallup Report, Aug. 1983.

5. Ibid.

6. Ibid.

7. *Key Facts About Newspapers and Advertising, 1984,* Newspaper Advertising Bureau, p. 23.

8. Gallup Report, Aug. 1983.

9. Ibid.

10. Creed C. Black, "Our Image Problem: A Paradox," speech to ASNE, Washington, D.C., May 9, 1984.

11. "Journalism Under Fire," *Time,* Dec. 12, 1983, p. 77.

12. "Orlando Community Looks Behind the Scenes," *Newspaper Marketing,* May/June 1992, p. 14.

13. *Excerpts,* pamphlet from Organization of Newspaper Ombudsmen, distributed by now defunct National News Council, March 8, 1983.

14. Frank Wetzel, "Listening to Readers Through an Ombudsman," *presstime,* June 1990, p. 30.

15. Donald B. Towles, "Mailing Promotion Work," speech to National Newspaper Association, Louisville, Sept. 22, 1983.

16. Elise Burroughs, "Airwaves, Billboards and TV Tout Newspapers," *presstime*, Oct. 1983, p. 46.

17. *"USA Today* Scores Well in AA Survey," *Advertising Age,* July 1983, p. 46.

18. "Persian Gulf War," advertisement in *Los Angeles Times*, Jan. 18, 1991, p. A-25.

19. "Editorial Staffers Introduced as Neighbors," *INPA Idea Newsletter,* International Newspaper Promotion Association, Reston, Va., April 1984.

20. Knight-Ridder Inc., *First Quarter Report,* 1984, p. 11.

21. New York Times Co. news releases, Sept. 13, 1993, p. 1.

22. Letter to *Augusta Chronicle and Herald* subscribers, April 17, 1993.

23. Minor Ward, president of Atlanta Newspapers, conversation with author.

24. Peter F. Drucker, "Marketing 101 for a Fast-Changing Decade," *The Wall Street Journal,* Nov. 20, 1990, p. A-20.

25. Joanne Cleaver, "Making Herald City Come Alive," *Advertising Age,* Jan. 30, 1984, p. M-21.

11

PRODUCTION AND THE NEW TECHNOLOGY

We turn now—with *very* good reason—to "Production and the New Technology." First, the newspaper industry creates about 60 million units of its product every day, which makes it a manufacturing industry, as well as a news and advertising industry. That reality will influence your career, whether you focus on news, advertising or another department.

Second, ours is a capital-intensive industry. Newspapers spend enormous sums of money on plant and production equipment. We face even greater costs ahead for research and development in new electronic technology. Financing that at your newspaper will be a pivotal consideration for you as a manager, whatever your department or level of responsibility.

Third, fulfilling careers are available within production, and some managers who start there reach significant general executive positions with top companies. Who knows? This might be where you start your march to the top.

Caution: Detailed treatment of production is far beyond the scope of *Strategic Newspaper Management*. Entire books could be written on the subject. So, I concentrate in pages ahead on only the most important technology and the basic understanding you need of the production process.

THE SPACE AGE AND BEYOND

Space-age technology has transformed newspapering. And, it's not just the production department that benefits. New technology gives every department better, more cost-efficient ways of meeting reader and advertiser needs. Some examples follow.

Growth of National Newspapers

Without satellite communications, national newspapers could not have gained strength in the United States. Other countries, notably Britain and Japan, developed national newspapers long ago. But those relatively small countries have efficient railroads to transport newspapers overnight from central production sites to virtually every section of the land.

The huge U.S. land mass prevented that here until satellite technology arrived. Today, *The Wall Street Journal, USA Today* and *The New York Times* are edited at central locations—and the finished prepress product is delivered by computer-driven systems to printing sites throughout the country. Signals are transmitted from central editing desks via satellites 22,300 miles above earth.

Result: High-quality national newspapers are available at breakfast almost everywhere in the United States. Readers get unique treatment of world news; advertisers get access to demographically attractive readers; local and regional dailies come under substantial competitive pressure—and American journalism is forever changed!

The Satellite Concept Down Here

If national newspapers can leapfrog thousands of miles through space to reach important audiences, why can't metro dailies leapfrog out of their core cities to reach affluent suburban audiences? They can—and they do.

Knight-Ridder's *Philadelphia Inquirer* and *Daily News* in 1992 opened a $229 million production facility 14 miles from the papers' downtown editorial and advertising headquarters. The *Phoenix Gazette* and *Arizona Republic* that same year opened a production facility 18 miles west of Phoenix and the *Richmond (Va.) Times-Dispatch* began printing papers at a $175 million plant eight miles from downtown.

At all three new facilities, complete press-ready pages are received via facsimile (or "digital fax") on fiber-optic cable from downtown editorial departments. (Fiber optics is a communications technology using circuits of thin glass, which can carry huge amounts of information at much faster speeds than can conventional copper circuits. See the glossary at end of this chapter.)

The result:

- It's easier to get thousands of tons of raw newsprint to suburban printing facilities via truck or railroad than to navigate crowded downtown streets.
- Finished newspapers are more easily distributed throughout affluent suburbs if presses are located outside downtown.
- It's cheaper to build new facilities in suburbs. Many localities grant tax breaks and other benefits in their eagerness to attract capital investment and new jobs. Real estate is cheaper, too.

Zoning Is Made Easier

The new technology enables newspapers to meet advertiser and reader demand for zoned news and ad content. For example, *The Philadelphia Inquirer* and *Daily News* plant produces a news section for readers in New Jersey, across the Delaware

River from Pennsylvania. Four other zoned editions, all containing late-breaking news, are produced for Philadelphia suburbs.

The *Inquirer*'s zoned sections are full-size and are published daily, a huge improvement over its former zoning effort—tabloid "Neighbors" sections inserted two or three times weekly. For readers, zoned editions provide a *daily* reason to buy the *Inquirer*. For advertisers, the zoned editions offer targeted audiences and, because they are buying smaller segments of circulation, lower ad rates.

A key decision in establishing satellite plants is location, of course. The *Atlanta Journal* and *Constitution* studied population and demographic shifts throughout metropolitan Atlanta before locating their new satellite plant in the northeast suburbs—smack in the center of projected growth in that area.

Multiproduct Strategies Are Possible

New production facilities are being built with enormous printing and handling capabilities, which gives newspaper strategists exciting new options for serving readers and advertisers. For example, *Phoenix Gazette* and *Arizona Republic* presses spew out nearly 70,000 newspapers hourly. *The Philadelphia Inquirer*'s facility produces about 700,000 newspapers daily, nearly 1 million for Sundays. It processes almost 1 billion inserts annually.

Strategists thus gain in two critical areas: speed of production and flexibility in handling varied products. Result: Vastly improved tailoring of niche products and services and, importantly, better capability for offering total market coverage. In sum, we are gaining production capability to meet the newspaper's marketing needs.

Color Reproduction Is Enhanced

Research is unmistakable: Readers want better color in their newspapers; advertisers demand it. Tons of catalogs move through direct mail each day, carrying high-quality color on glossy paper that highlights advertisers' messages. Television's color, as well as its "see-it-now" action, draws ad revenue that once went to newspapers.

And, the newspaper industry itself, which once despaired at ever meeting the competitive threat in all that, now sees proof that outstanding color *can* be produced on newsprint: *USA Today* does it, day in, week out. So, your newspaper—like all newspapers—now is judged against the competitive standard of color reproduction marketed by media inside and outside the newspaper industry.

To measure up against that judgment, by readers and advertisers alike, newspapers are spending millions of dollars for the expensive and technically complicated equipment necessary to move into a new era of color reproduction. Even the "Grey Old Lady," *The New York Times*, is moving into color. So is *The Wall Street Journal*. Both newspapers previously marketed themselves successfully for their content, not how they look.

Reporting and Editing Are Improved

New technology gives reporters and editors flexibility and speed unheard of just a decade or so ago. Reporters write on portable "laptop" computers and "file" via telephone circuit into master computers in their home offices. Writers once tied to office desk and typewriter now write virtually anywhere—in airplanes, aboard ships, in bed, even, and almost instantaneously "dump" their copy into the editors' computers. Editors, in turn, "work" the copy (without touching pencil or paper) and submit it directly to the production department.

The speed is awe-inspiring: Sports reporters write game stories and file virtually before spectators leave the stadium. Associated Press reporters need only *seconds* to reach wires that, in turn, transmit thousands of words per minute to newspapers and TV and radio stations throughout the world. And the system is relatively inexpensive: Portable laptops cost just hundreds of dollars and telephone circuits are a low-cost transmission system. And, there's no rushing back to the office to write, just a quick "dump" from the nearest telephone in press box or motel.

For Weeklies: A New World

Electronic editing and modern pressroom equipment used by dailies are available also to weeklies—in slimmed-down versions and, importantly, at acceptable cost.

And what a change! Robert Tribble, publisher of small-town weeklies in Georgia and elsewhere, recalls the Linotypes, hot-metal composition and sheet-fed flatbed presses of the 1960s, when he entered weekly newspapering:

> *The publisher, editor, ad salesman and many times bookkeeper had to spend long hours in the back shop around the hot metal. What you really had in those days was not a newspaper editor but a printer. His time had to be spent in production rather than newswriting and sales. I know of several old-time editors and publishers who never wrote a story or called an advertiser. The stories and advertisements that ran in each edition of the weekly press "walked" in the front door. Editors and publishers were too busy in hot metal composition and job printing to bother with too many news stories or ads.*[1]

WHAT IT ALL MEANS FOR YOU

Space-age technology has arrived, then, in an industry still celebrating itinerant printers who, legend says, could arrive in town with a "shirttail of type" and go into the newspaper business. As young men and women, many of today's senior managers entered an industry chained to slow, clanking Linotypes; in just the span of their careers, it has become an electronically complex, capital-intensive industry with the hum of computers hanging over the newspaper landscape.

Implications for you, an aspiring manager, are many:

- New technology raises the newspaper's fundamental cost base yet it also promises better cost control.
- It shifts production work to departments, particularly news, that never before were involved in manufacturing, yet it also permits dramatic improvements in journalistic quality.
- For advertising and circulation, it opens entirely new marketing opportunities.
- And, clearly, new technology yet undreamed is a certainty within your career span.

At Hearst, they're planning for all this with a committee called "Hearst New Media and Technology Group." D. Claeys Bahrenburg, president of Hearst Magazines, says the committee's mission is "to actively explore ways in which our various products—newspapers, broadcasting and cable TV programming, our books and magazine editorial franchises—can be adapted to and merged with these new technologies."[2]

Career hint: Wherever you work, whatever your job, get on your newspaper's version of the "New Media and Technology Group." That will be on the cutting edge.

DESIGNING YOUR PRODUCTION ORGANIZATION

Managing the present and preparing to wrestle with the future—whatever its shape—takes careful planning. Not too many years ago, if you were designing a production organization you would walk quickly through the news and advertising departments to the "back shop," where it all happened.

Today, you start by studying the entire newspaper for efficient, profitable ways to use new technology in a production chain running from the front door through all departments to loading docks out back where trucks pick up bundles and speed off. The target is a *unified system* tying together the computer and data processing needs of all departments and thus achieving maximum efficiency and compatibility of equipment plus lower initial cost and economical operation. Computerized writing and editing have transformed newsroom operations. VDTs and PCs "capture" reporter and editor keystrokes to drive high-speed electronic typesetters—eliminating the slow, costly Linotype operators once so crucial in production.

Many production functions such as typesetting now fall to the newsroom. The wire desk, which once received news agency copy via land lines, at 66 words per minute, or by mail, now catches it with a satellite receiver on the newspaper's roof. Copy pours into newsroom computers at thousands of words per minute. Newsroom "morgues," those dusty libraries filled with ragged envelopes of decaying clips, are computerized for instantaneous recall on VDTs. In classified advertising, customers telephone copy to clerks who write ads on VDTs, proofread, check credit references, submit copy to typesetting and issue bills—all in minutes.

Circulation uses mobile radios and telephones to maintain contact between home office and district managers; computers handle subscriber and nonsubscriber address lists. Business office inventory, accounts receivable, financial data of all kinds—the details on which enlightened managers move—are "massaged" by sophisticated electronic equipment and made available to decision makers when they need them.

In sum, efficient design of your production organization must integrate the missions, needs and resources of many departments, not just the back shop. Maximize your exploitation of three major technological breakthroughs: computerized capturing of keystrokes, offset printing and cold-type process, and pagination.

Design to Capture Keystrokes

Newspapers save millions of dollars because technology permits computer capture of keystrokes made by reporters, editors and ad copywriters. This must be central to any organizational concept for your production department.

In precomputer days, a reporter typed stories on a sheet of paper that the copy desk pencil-edited and passed to Linotype operators, who produced the type used in page makeup. Similarly, all ad copy was "rekeystroked" in laborious and costly typing and retyping. A cost-reduction breakthrough came in the 1960s with optical character readers—"scanners"—which can read copy prepared on special typewriters and convert it into electronic impulses that drive automatic typesetters. Scanners were short-lived as primary typesetting devices. VDT writing and editing became feasible in 1970 and spread rapidly thereafter.

VDTs virtually eliminate expensive rekeystroking. Reporters' keystrokes go into computer storage. The copy desk uses its own VDTs to edit reporters' stories and resubmits them to computer storage. Stories then go into phototypesetters. Using light flashed through negatives, or images formed on cathode-ray tubes, phototypesetters spew out columns of type—"cold type"—to be pasted up in page layouts from which offset plates are readied for presses. Phototypesetters create the equivalent of a full-size newspaper page of type in seconds. "Capturing" the original keystrokes of reporters and editors is a basic, extremely important cost-reduction offering of the new technology.

Design for Offset's Advantages

A second major technological advance central to your organizational concept is offset printing. Offset is based on cold-type processes that employ high-intensity light or laser beams to reproduce page layouts on light-sensitive plates. Once mounted on presses, the plates are treated with water and oil-based ink. Ink adheres to images on the plates, which transfers ink to "blankets" or cylinders which, in turn, transfer—"offset"—ink to newsprint running through the presses. Most U.S. daily papers are printed by offset.

The offset and cold-type process is a major advance from hot-metal printing. In hot metal, Linotypes create type for page layouts that are locked into a "chase" or metal frame. Papier-mâché mats are made from the chase and, in turn, 40-pound hot metal stereo plates are locked on presses, inked and run against newsprint—

the raised typeface creating inked images. Offset printing is cheaper, faster and cleaner than hot metal. A fast Linotype operator can set five or six column lines of hot type per minute; computer-driven typesetting machines in cold type spew out over a thousand per minute.

Facing fewer union roadblocks to new technology and able to reequip at lower total cost, smaller papers switched to offset relatively easily. Metro dailies, however, faced union restrictions and enormous replacement costs. *The New York Times* spent millions in a "buyout" of union-covered composing-room employees displaced by new equipment. The *Chicago Tribune* spent $80 million in 1982 for 90 new Goss Metroliner presses. Most of the 133 displaced old Gross units were sold for scrap.

Relatively inexpensive equipment modifications permit some papers to use older presses for modern printing processes. Modified presses use special plates developed by DiLitho, Letterflex, NAPP and other companies.

Some newspapers convert from letterpress to "flexographic" printing, around for years but used primarily by book printers. Flexography prints water-borne inks directly on newsprint, without offset's intermediate "blanket." Proponents claim that "flexo" promises high-quality printing plus cheaper color. Flexographic units are less complicated mechanically than other press units and somewhat cheaper. They waste much less newsprint, are quieter and cause less "show-through" of ink (thus reducing ink smudges on readers' hands). However, "flexo" users report continuing problems with quality control.[3]

Design for Pagination

It was the dream of newspaper managers for years: If only they could eliminate those time-consuming, expensive steps in the production chain between newsroom and press—if only editors and ad layout artists could handle the total appearance and production of the newspaper—it would revolutionize production economics, reducing manpower and lowering costs. Great technical expertise and huge sums of money were thrown into pursuing the dream. First came cold type and offset, then VDT editing.

Next came *pagination*—electronic makeup of pages. It eliminates composing and platemaking departments and is a third major technological innovation around which your production organization must be designed.

Pagination works like this: News and ad copy created on VDTs by reporters and advertising personnel go directly into computer storage without additional rekeystroking. This copy then goes to a computer terminal operated by an editor or, if ads are being laid out, an advertising artist. Entire pages are laid out—stories, headlines, photos and artwork, ads, and all—on the VDT. Then, pages go directly to the platemaking process (see Figure 11.1 on page 356.)

Some composing rooms, which account for half of all production costs, are eliminated. The *Long Beach (Calif.) Press-Telegram* installed pagination in 1985 for about $3 million, including equipment, building remodeling and separation incentives paid to displaced workers. Composing room staff was reduced to 21 from 56

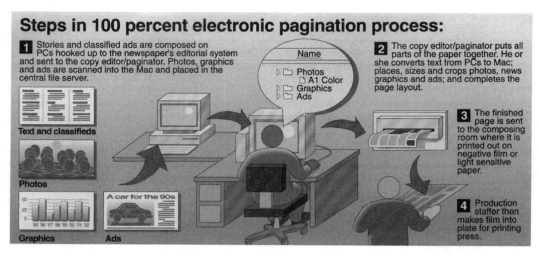

Steps in 100 percent electronic pagination process:

1 Stories and classified ads are composed on PCs hooked up to the newspaper's editorial system and sent to the copy editor/paginator. Photos, graphics and ads are scanned into the Mac and placed in the central file server.

Text and classifieds

Photos

Graphics   Ads

Name
▷ ☐ Photos
  ☐ A1 Color
▷ ☐ Graphics
▷ ☐ Ads

A car for the 90s

2 The copy editor/paginator puts all parts of the paper together. He or she converts text from PCs to Mac; places, sizes and crops photos, news graphics and ads; and completes the page layout.

3 The finished page is sent to the composing room where it is printed out on negative film or light sensitive paper.

4 Production staffer then makes film into plate for printing press.

FIGURE 11.1   Pagination eliminates expensive and time-consuming links in the production chain by permitting news and advertising computers to automatically create plates for the pressroom. Reprinted by permission of Gannett Co. Inc.

full-time employees; engraving department personnel fell from 8 to 6. Four positions were added in the newsroom, which took on tasks formerly handled in other departments. Editor Larry Allison said the newsroom got total control of content, design and layout as well as better color and faster production.

A disadvantage for the newsroom is that it must assume additional and very complex equipment and tasks. While this permits the design of smaller production departments, it requires adding staff in newsrooms, which must now take over many tasks that were formerly assigned to production.

Lester Wiltse, production manager of the *Pasadena (Calif.) Star-News,* a 52,000-circulation paper which went to 100 percent pagination of news and classified ads, said: "In 1973, when we abandoned hot metal, we had 100 composing room employees. In late 1981, when we were still pasting pages, we had 22. Today, after (using pagination) we have only 9, and the number will drop more ... with hot metal, we required 7 composing man-hours per page. With [pagination], the figure is down to 0.6."

The *Niagara Falls (N. Y.) Gazette,* a 31,000-circulation Gannett paper, reduced its 18 composing room employees to six in 11 months after installing pagination and cut to $1\frac{1}{2}$ from nearly 3 the number of per-page man-hours needed in composition. The system saved 18,000 work hours per year.

Joseph M. Ungaro, then president of Gannett's Westchester Rockland, N. Y., Newspapers and an early experimenter in pagination, said the process could save the newspaper industry more than $2 billion annually. Most medium-size newspapers could save $100,000 to $150,000 annually in materials, eliminate 15 to 17 jobs and, he said, achieve sufficient cost reduction to pay off pagination in three years.

Production department design can take many forms and its managers can take different approaches to achieving their objectives. Whatever your style, make sure your department is structured to exploit the cost-reduction and product-improvement potentials of capturing keystrokes, offset and cold-type printing, plus pagination.

Start with a Table of Organization

The *Atlanta Journal* and *Constitution* designed a production table of organization useful as an illustration (see Figure 11.2) of the complexity, today, of what was once a simple, straight-line hierarchical arrangement. Note how it assigns functions:

General manager. Newspaper's chief business (as distinct from news) executive; reports directly to the publisher.

Director of operations. Normally found only on larger papers, where broad-based technical *and* managerial skills are required.

Production manager. Supervises traditional production sub-units (composing, platemaking, pressroom, mailroom) and is responsible for newsprint, shipping/receiving and returns (newspapers brought back unsold) plus the newspapers' marriage-mail program, "Reach."

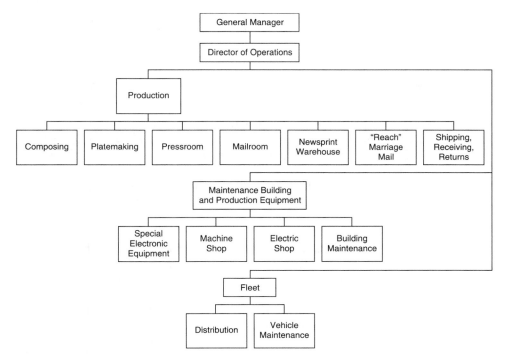

FIGURE 11.2   The *Atlanta Journal* and *Constitution* operations department.

Maintenance manager. Has the very important function of supervising electronic equipment—computers and VDTs—plus machine shop, electric shop, building.

Fleet manager. In addition to vehicle maintenance, supervises distribution of papers from loading dock to branch offices or other distribution points.

Small dailies feature much less complicated organizational designs. The *Athens (Ga.) Daily News* and *Banner-Herald* produce 27,000 copies daily in a comparatively simple production organization led by a "production director" who reports directly to the publisher and supervises four sub-units. Design your production organization for your needs; don't duplicate somebody else's chart.

The production department requires massive resources—in money and managerial talent, particularly. At a typical daily with 50,000 to 100,000 circulation, production *operating* costs are 12 to 14 percent of *total* costs, and newsprint, ink and handling are 19 to 21 percent.

In *capital* investment, production plant and equipment are the walkaway leaders. Recall the $229 million facility Knight-Ridder built for its *Philadelphia Inquirer* and *Daily News.*

WHO MAKES A GOOD PRODUCTION MANAGER?

Special skills are required to manage the expensive equipment involved in such important, complex functions. Who makes a good production manager? It varies. Consider two award-winning production managers described below.

Norman P. Dusseault

Dusseault was operations manager of the *St. Petersburg (Fla.) Times* when it built a national reputation for technical (and news) excellence. Dusseault had an unlikely background for production work: He graduated in social science from Holy Cross College, served in the U.S. Marines as a personnel and legal officer, and then joined the newspaper in 1957. He worked successively as personnel assistant, employment manager, assistant manager/classified advertising and in 1974 became operations manager, responsible for all production activities.

Dusseault:

> *I am decidedly nontechnical, although I surround myself with top technicians and together we get the job done. I suppose a better technical orientation on my part would be a help, but the job is far too complex technically to be mastered by any one person anyway.*
>
> *I suppose some ability to draw together the diverse management and technical people toward common ends is important. So management training that emphasizes team building, the ability and the willingness to delegate, etc., would be important preparation. I frequently find my own background in personnel management, promotion, written and verbal communications helpful.[4]*

Ken Kniceley

Kniceley followed a different route in becoming production director of Charleston (W. Va.) Newspapers and winner of awards for printing the *Gazette* and *Daily Mail.* Kniceley worked for the *Daily Mail* in high school and became a composing-room apprentice after graduation in 1950. Along the way, he crammed in two years in print management at West Virginia Institute of Technology and, after serving as manager of the advertising and composing-room departments, was made production director in 1977.

Kniceley's techniques:

> *Produce the very best paper possible on time, and at the most reasonable cost; place the right manager in the right job in each work area; properly train all managers; cross-train all employees, even between departments; stress neatness and cleanliness in all areas, which shows up in the final product; make sure all employees are made aware of all goals and give directions to achieve these goals.*
>
> *Each individual should have leeway to achieve these goals so that they can use their own abilities.[5]*

Note Kniceley's emphasis on *goals.* Planning them and supervising their achievement is a major function for any production manager.

PLANNING THE PRODUCTION MISSION

Planning years ahead is difficult in all newspaper management but probably most difficult in production. First, production's basic mission shifts rapidly over the short term as the departments it supports—news, advertising, circulation—adjust operations to meet changes in the marketplace, competition and reader and advertiser demands. Second, never before has there been such a rapid flow of technological change affecting newspaper operations, and there is more radical change ahead.

Third, it is imperative to long-range strategy that production planners pin down the expected cost of new technology, but this has proven almost impossible. Costs simply change too quickly. A fourth difficulty: Planning is particularly difficult because great lead time is required. In equipment development, laboratory breakthroughs normally take years to reach production trials, many more years to reach widespread commercial application. But plan we must.

Plan for Long-Range Needs

A new production chain will have to be constructed for coming decades. It could start with reporters "talking" stories into computers equipped with voice recognition logic, then proceed to editors sitting before VDTs and fulfilling all production functions short of the pressroom. A dream: impactless printing by computer-controlled inkjet systems using laser imaging. Technically, this could permit editors to produce as many different newspapers as there are subscribers. From dream to reality: Production *will* have to automate mailrooms and customize newspapers by inserting special-interest sections for different subscribers.

Efficient pagination systems and presses will be needed in satellite locations, perhaps even by some medium-size papers. The mission will be to produce a multiplicity of zoned editions, total market coverage publications and other tailored journalistic and advertising products at several sites other than the main plant.

Production will have to satisfy unrelenting demands from news and advertising for ever-improved color reproduction. *USA Today* proved high-quality color is feasible and that it sells. There will be no turning back. Many weeklies now share production facilities—central printing plants—which will become faster and more economical with the spread of electronic editing, pagination and high-speed movement of copy by circuit from newsroom to remote printing plant.

On all papers, pressure will increase for the production department, through automation and other efficiencies, to save time and money. Competition and more sophisticated readers will require more timely, better researched news content. Production will have to help provide it. Even the smallest daily's production department will need a satellite receiver to pull in news copy from news agencies and obtain ad copy from national advertisers and agencies. National ads will be prepared just hours in advance and sent to newspapers by satellite.

Newspapers already sell information to customers other than subscribers. Some production departments maintain databases—"information centers"—capable of turning out newsletters, direct mail and electronic transmissions to homes and offices.

There will be major changes in ink and, perhaps, newsprint. Researchers are seeking less expensive substitutes for wood pulp now used in newsprint production. Ink that greatly reduces rub-off is being developed, although it currently is very expensive.

Keep Basic Goals in Mind

As you look ahead to production management and all those dazzling possibilities, it will be easy to forget basic goals and to buy new technology for the same reason some people climb a mountain—simply because it is there.

Stick to these basic goals:

1. Seek higher profits through automation and resultant work force reduction. This is essential in production and maintenance, which account for 45 to 48 percent of total employees for many papers. New technology offers unprecedented cost reduction. Plan for it.

2. Improve the news product with technology offering clearer printing, sharper photographs, vastly improved color. Construct systems, for example, to ensure that skilled journalists, not unskilled typists, are the last to touch news copy. That will improve accuracy and reduce typographical errors.

3. Strengthen management's hand with unions by reducing back-shop work forces and installing equipment that is automated or can be operated by nonunion supervisors. Design production systems that unions cannot shut down.

4. Improve research capability and give editors better information on reader likes and dislikes, marketplace demographics, competitors' strengths and weaknesses; give advertising managers retailing trends, lifestyle developments.

5. Plan product diversification as new technology frees the news, advertising and production departments to create zoned editions, free-circulation publications and direct mail services. Smaller papers particularly should plan to attract lucrative outside job printing. As never before, newspapers can establish themselves as "profit centers" offering new, profitable services to reader and advertiser. Some newspapers will sell access to their market research, for example, or permit users to dial into computerized morgues via telephone.

6. Improve distribution flexibility with new technology permitting news, advertising and circulation departments to target small segments of their markets, then deliver with great accuracy. Plan, for example, for presorting newspapers so motor route drivers can insert a plastic identity card at the loading dock and automatically receive newspapers sequenced and bundled for fast delivery.

7. Strive for overall improvement in management efficiency, probably the greatest payoff for decision makers from the computerization of record keeping. Financial officers must be able to offer, quickly, the meaningful, understandable data essential for any management team trying to calculate where a newspaper is financially and project where it likely will go. Computerized inventory records, for example, can give some managers their first-ever accurate picture of raw materials in storage and any impending shortages or expensive oversupply.

To exploit this great potential, a technology committee should be established to formulate long-range strategy. This committee should meet frequently with managers of all departments and seek for every dollar spent at least one dollar in cost reduction or product improvement. Proceed carefully, for although new technology opens opportunities undreamed of just a few years ago, it also opens traps.

Beware the Technology Trap

With just a misstep or two, you can take a wrong and very expensive fork in the technological road. The stakes are so huge that the manager who errs in this way very likely will suffer a career setback. Some dangers:

1. The capital investment required for new technology can throw a paper deeply into long-term debt and add heavy interest payments that strap current operations. It's basic stuff but easily forgotten: Interest of 9 percent on a $50 million loan for new equipment will total $4.5 million the first year. If you're managing a weekly grossing $350,000 annually, can you afford $2,250 annual interest to borrow $25,000 at 9 percent for new equipment?

BOX 11.1   Standards to Plan By

Production is one newspaper department that can express performance standards in precise figures—the exact number of employee work-hours most efficient for certain functions. For example, a Scripps Howard survey of newspapers in the 50,000 to 100,000 circulation range shows the following averages.

Total employee work hours in the composing room for each broadsheet ("standard") page produced are two. In the plateroom, hours per page are .15 for newspapers printing with offset presses, .60 for letterpress. In the pressroom, employee work hours per page are three. If your production department requires more work hours than those averages, you've got an inefficient, costly department.

Another performance standard watched carefully is the number of times presses start or finish late—a problem if it causes the circulation department to get papers to subscribers late. The industry average for late starts and/or finishes: no more than three per month.

Important: On average, production departments costs are 12 to 14 percent of newspapers' total spending budget. Newsprint, ink and handling are 19 to 21 percent. As percentage of total revenue, the averages are 10 to 11 percent and 15 to 17 percent, respectively.[a]

Here is another—and crucial—factor your generation of production managers must crank in to your planning: Like all businesses, newspapers are subject to societal demands—none more so than the demand that our environment be kept clean and safe.

For newspaper production managers, the principal culprit is ONP—industry parlance for old newspapers. ONP is what's left after millions of tons of newsprint are used annually to carry news, information and advertising into U.S. homes. (Annual consumption surpassed 11.6 million metric tons in 1993!)[b]

In days bygone, ONP was dumped in landfills or left skittering through wind-swept streets. No more. Extraordinary pressure is building on the industry to recycle ONP.

And, it's not just mother-earth environmentalists who are concerned. One recent poll showed 41 percent of respondents were "very likely" or "somewhat likely" to cancel subscriptions if they knew their newspaper didn't use any recycled paper.[c] Early pressure for recycling was rejected by many newspapers and, particularly, newsprint manufacturing companies, which faced enormous costs for building plants (about $100 million for retooling an existing plant to handle recycled newsprint; $500 million or so to build a new one.)[d]

By 1986, ONP occupied about 8 percent of total space in U.S. landfills, the Environmental Protection Agency estimated. ONP doesn't biodegrade quickly, either. If packed tightly newspapers can be dug up and easily read decades later.

Some newspapers argued that any governmental pressure for collecting and recycling ONP was an attack on freedom of the press. As late as 1991, the Southern Newspaper Publishers Association published an article—quoting Thomas Jefferson—that stated that requiring newspapers to use recycled newsprint was an "illegimate intrusion into the activities of the press."

By 1993, however, 58 percent of ONP was recycled (32.7 went into production of new newsprint, 20.8 percent was used in manufacturing paperboard, and the rest was used in making home insulation and other products.)[e]

Society establishes other standards for production managers to plan by:

- Reduce the amount of volatile organic compounds your newspaper releases into the environment by using petroleum-based ink. Use soy-based inks.
- Insure you could survive a surprise visit by agents of the federal or state Occupa-

---

BOX 11.1 *Continued*

tional Safety and Health Administration. They'll be looking for such things as unsafe pressrooms and jobs that put employees at risk, due to heavy lifting or repeti-

tive-motion tasks that create carpal tunnel syndrome, a painful condition that can affect hands and arms.

[a]*Scripps Howard General Managers Newsletter,* Nov. 1991, p. 7.
[b]*Facts About Newspapers '94,* published by Newspaper Association of America, p. 16.
[c]"The Green Revolution," *Advertising Age,* Jan. 29, 1991, p. 10.
[d]Michael L. Coulter, "Newspaper Recycling Laws Threaten Press Freedoms," *SNPA Bulletin,* Feb. 20, 1991, p. 21.

---

2. Unleashed, American technical genius develops complex systems, some offering—at justifiable cost—far more capability than needed. There is an inherent temptation to overbuy systems with bells, whistles and flashing lights when just a buzzer or two would do. Beware of consensus systems planned by interdepartmental committees, each clamoring for costly, tailored equipment that is no more functional than cheaper, off-the-shelf systems already successful at other papers. For most papers, standardized electronic editing systems—proven through years of experimentation elsewhere—are quite sufficient. Don't pay to reinvent the wheel. And beware the danger of planning a system for what it will do, not for what the newspaper needs done. Why pay limousine prices if an economy car will do?

3. There is, conversely, danger in planning technology only for today's needs, without consulting all departments on what tomorrow's expanded needs likely will be. Whether you're buying a building, a press or a computer, allow for incremental additions that won't force you to rip out walls, replace entire lines of presses or switch to new computer systems in future years. However modern, your new building or electronic system will not stay long at the tip of the technological spear; improvements are coming and your needs will change.

4. Guard against newsroom and production department appetites for more and more new technology that can pressure you to invest without reward in systems that are ahead of their time. In the 1970s, some papers wasted millions on pagination, though they learned quickly that its time had not yet arrived.

5. Never plan hurriedly. Analyze functions suggested for new equipment and obtain interdepartmental agreement on what they are. Invite at least three vendors to study those functions, design a solution and submit cost estimates. Do not reverse the equation by buying a system, then attempting to adapt functions to it. Always haggle over prices. Tippen Davidson, general manager of the *Daytona (Fla.) News-Journal,* put out specifications for VDTs and computers to handle news and ad copy. Bids ranged from $350,000 to nearly $1 million. After settling on a $600,000 system, he advises: "Assume the initial proposal from any vendor is for his 'Cadil-

lac' model and question him closely about less expensive alternatives... don't be bashful about dickering over prices." Carefully select a single integrated "total system" to serve all departments. Incorrectly choosing even one piece of equipment can lead an entire newspaper toward a costly, soon-to-be-obsolete system.

In sum, the technological "Great Leap Forward" can do wonders for profitability, efficiency and product quality *if* it is carefully researched and planned for proven application to your operating problems. But, the Great Leap also can take you over a cliff if you don't accurately calculate application, cost and payback.

How long your newspaper can wait for payback—recovery of cost of new equipment—depends on many variables, including the newspaper's financial condition and tax situation. Seek expert counsel from your chief financial officer on this, but here is a rule of thumb: Calculate the average annual *net* savings the equipment will produce through staff reductions, increased efficiency and so forth. Divide that into the new equipment's cost to obtain the years to payback. You then must make a business judgment on whether the payback period is acceptable. In the early days of electronic editing and photocomposition, payback was sometimes extraordinarily fast—two years or less for entire new systems—because deep staff cuts were possible. Some composing room staffs were cut 50 percent or more; often, 75 percent of full-time proofreading staffs were cut.

Today, such opportunities come less frequently. Ken Kniceley, at the *Charleston Gazette and Daily Mail*, sought payback in five to seven years for most electronic equipment, 20 years for presses.[6] Norm Dusseault at the *St. Petersburg Times* sought payback in about two years for most equipment, but he said, "this is not the only factor involved in deciding to buy new equipment. For example, we went into offset printing years ago, and are currently expanding again, not solely based on a proven cost justification formula, but rather because of our interest in producing quality. Ultimately, of course, this cost justifies in the general health of the newspaper."[7]

Gannett ranks its managers' capital investment requests from "must have" to "nice to have," then calculates the impact each will have on cash flow. If the investment promises an immediate return of 15 percent or so, approval is given. Dow Jones takes a longer view, seeking quick payback, of course, but also considering the long-range strategic value of the capital investment.

Obtain expert financial advice on tax implications: Make *no* capital expenditure without exploring depreciation schedules under which the IRS permits tax deductions over a period of years for newly purchased equipment. Tax consequences frequently are pivotal in deciding whether a capital investment should be made. Any purchase contract should be checked by the paper's attorney before it is signed.

Of course, in production planning, you must balance cost of equipment and payback against the support role your department plays for other departments. You don't manage production just for the sake of managing it; you manage production to assist news, circulation, advertising and other departments.

HOW TO MANAGE PRODUCTION

You may approach production and new technology with weak technical background and strong trepidation. You're not alone. Many aspiring managers fear its technical complexities and high costs. So, let's discuss how you can get along in performing the technical duties of a production manager and handling the human element.

Hints for Nontechnical Managers

How can the nonengineer manager get atop all this? In the words of Michael G. Gartner, an experienced news executive and publisher,

> *That's a problem. "It used to be," a publisher told me not long ago, "that the circulation department was the place the publishers avoided because they couldn't understand it. Now, it's the production department." The good publisher has to do two things: First, educate himself about the new technology; second, hire a bright young engineer to run the production department. Between the two of them, then, they'll be able to stay abreast of developments and override the old-fashioned thinking that pervades the department. When the new technology came to the newsrooms, an editor I know went to night school to learn about computers. He learned. "A wonderful thing just happened," he told me one day. "One of these young computer whizzes tried to get by with something, and I looked him in the eye and said, 'B. S.' I knew enough so I couldn't be walked over by those guys." The good publisher and the good editor and the good ad managers must now keep abreast of technology, too, so that the computer people don't take charge of the other departments. Business and editorial and advertising decisions should not be made on the basis of what machines can do.[8]*

Advice, then, for the nontechnical manager in this technological age:

Get involved. Don't avoid technology; it will not go away. As publisher of the *Miami Herald*, Richard G. Capen Jr. said, "There must be willingness to learn about new technology, to not be afraid of it and to accept it willingly and enthusiastically."[9] Read trade publications, particularly the technology sections of *presstime* and *Editor & Publisher* and *Newspapers & Technology*. Attend the Newspaper Association of America's Annual Research Institute Production Conference, *the* showplace for new equipment. Attend training programs offered by numerous trade associations, visit other papers, stay in touch with equipment vendors.

Hire carefully. Select employees who know the new technology and understand that production fulfills service functions for other departments (avoid those so enamored with new technology that they want the technical tail to wag the newspaper dog). Assign staffers with strong technical orientation to those departments, such as news, that might need assistance.

Do not be awed by the new gadgets. Check what other papers are doing, listen to your vendors. But don't follow them blindly. As in all crucial management decisions, step back, take a deep breath, and ask: Is this system, at this cost and this payback, best for this newspaper at this time?

In daily operations, look for key indicators of high quality: on-time performance in all functions, particularly press runs; minimum downtime of equipment, a sign of good maintenance that reduces breakdowns; good printing, with sharp color reproduction, clean inking (no smudges), and minimum showthrough of ink from the other side of page.

Dusseault of St. Petersburg listed his priorities this way:

1. *Quality—This is the religion around here and so I hear a lot about poor-quality products. Also it hurts my pride to turn out poor work. Quality is elusive, however. There are so many variables, and so many people involved. I would say that this is my major challenge, to keep quality standards high.*
2. *Maintaining good morale—This involves a host of activities, ranging from communications to good pay programs, to safety, etc. Mostly it is trying to get across that we care about our people working here, that they are important as individuals. We don't always succeed, but we try.*
3. *Planning equipment and processes and staffing to keep abreast of surging [market] growth in our area. We can get behind in a single season, and we have to look ahead intelligently or be drowned.*
4. *Cost control, staying within budget, holding down waste, and at the same time being flexible enough to change the budget when it makes sense.*
5. *Daily operations, meeting deadlines, spotting and correcting problems, etc.*[10]

Managing the Human Element

Managing people in any department is a challenge. It is even more so in production, because new technology brings with it traumatic change that deeply affects employees' lives. A fundamental redistribution of work is under way. Employees are being assigned new, sometimes bewildering tasks. Some jobs are disappearing; many employees are worried, some are hurt. Many newspapers reduce production staffs through attrition, waiting for retirements and resignations over a period of time. But papers that must move quickly or are restricted by union agreements use the "buyout"—paying workers to leave.

Job displacement will continue, particularly with pagination. To be humane *and* achieve maximum benefit of new technology, you must treat gently those whose lives feel the impact. This is necessary particularly with systems that transform job functions. Providing adequate information and training makes a huge difference. Newspaper employees, regardless of their age or experience, can take smoothly to new technology. This was proven with VDT writing. Careful training equipped thousands of reporters and editors who used typewriters all their professional lives to take quickly to VDTs.

To avoid fear of or resistance to new technology, you should:

Explain overall strategy. Describe the newspaper's goal and how new equipment or systems fit into the larger operational picture.

Immediately and frankly describe impact, if any, on jobs. If jobs will be eliminated, say so—and simultaneously announce how you will care for the displaced. Be candid about redistribution of workload. If, for example, the newsroom must accept tasks formerly performed in production, explain how they will be shared.

Stress positive attributes of new technology. Many reporters and editors quickly took to VDTs over typewriters because they make jobs easier. Highlight such benefits.

Whenever possible, let employees help design new systems. They often make sound technical contributions, learn what is happening and, importantly, help quiet the fears of others.

Always be careful to minimize shock or newness. In early conversion to electronic editing, for example, many newspapers would change only an editor's tool—a new VDT for an old typewriter. Job function wasn't changed. That meant the editor had to wrestle only with training on a new tool, not a new job as well.

Address authoritatively and in detail any fears that technology will affect health. Early on, rumors swept newsrooms that VDTs injure health, and newspapers eventually produced expert medical testimony that they don't. Include such evidence in your initial announcement that new technology is coming.

Create liaison teams for effective coordination in newly realigned departments. Quickly iron out any operational problems.

Listen to your staff. If there are even seemingly minor complaints—that the positioning of VDTs creates glare, for example, or cricks in the neck—move rapidly with a remedy (in this case, mount VDTs on swivels so employees can adjust them comfortably). Don't let cricks in the neck sour your staff on a multimillion-dollar system that will jump your technology ahead a generation.

Manage Newsprint Resources Carefully

Newsprint management is high among any production manager's priorities. Every effort must be made to lower newsprint costs and reduce waste. Why? See Table 11.1.

Of all costs, only personal expense is larger. And none is as subject as newsprint to marketplace pricing pressure. Newsprint prices have increased steadily and in 1995 hovered around $700 per metric ton. No price plateau is in sight.

Ensure effective cost control, particularly in three areas:

At purchase. Newspapers or groups that are large consumers must negotiate quality discounts. Even if yours is a medium- or small-size newspaper, negotiate.

In handling and storage. A careless forklift operator who pokes a roll can destroy many dollars of newsprint; rolls that become wet or too dry represent money

TABLE 11.1   Newsprint: The Costly Raw Material

Daily Circulation	Newsprint Percentage of Total Costs
1,000,000+	19.3
250,000	25.6
50,000	18.8
9,000	23.3

Source: *Newspaper and Newsprint Facts at a Glance, 1992–93,* published by Newsprint Information Committee, 420 Lexington Ave., New York, N.Y. 10017, p. 9.

wasted (NAA recommends storage at 60 to 70 degrees Fahrenheit and 45 percent relative humidity).

In usage. Money is saved if presses are operated by trained (and cost-conscious) press crews. A "web-break"—a newsprint tear while presses are running—will cost you severely and delay your press run.

Depending on printing process and other variables, waste ranges from about 2.2 percent of total newsprint used to 5.3 percent or more. For papers in the 50,000 to 100,000 circulation range, Scripps Howard found waste running 2.9 percent for newspapers using letterpress, 3 percent for those with flexo systems, 4.1 percent for offset presses. Many newspapers pay bonuses to pressroom employees who reduce waste below those industry norms.

One newsprint-conservation step is reducing "web width"—the width of each page. *The New York Times* reduced its width from 58 to 56 inches in 1981, then to 55 inches in 1983. The annual newsprint saving (at 1984 prices) exceeded $8 million.

Some newspapers use lighter, less expensive newsprint. The standard basis weight is now 30 pounds. Newsprint is weighed in pounds per ream, or five hundred 24-by-36-inch sheets. In metric terms, weight is expressed in "grammage" (weight in grams of one sheet of newsprint measuring one square meter). A 30-pound basis weight is equivalent to a grammage of 48.8. Shifting to even lighter newsprint, with technology at hand, causes ink "bleed through" and severely impairs readability. But stay alert for new techniques that might make it possible.

Newsprint waste reports from hundreds of newspapers are analyzed by NAA's Research Institute. The institute also monitors newsprint from Canadian and U.S. mills for variations in physical properties that influence printing quality. Published results identify each mill only through a confidential code. You can obtain details from NAA, The Newspaper Center, Box 17406, Dulles International Airport, Washington, D.C. 10041.

To ensure newsprint availability and influence prices, some newspapers invest in mills. Canadian mills outproduce U.S. mills by far. In 1992, for example, Canadian capacity was 10.2 million metric tons; U.S. capacity, 6.6 million. U.S. newspapers and other users consume nearly double the U.S. production. About 50 percent of the newsprint used in the United States comes from Canada, 49 percent from U.S. mills and 1 percent from other countries.

Your newsprint prices are sure to rise, for the newsprint industry's economics are stunning. It costs hundreds of millions of dollars to build production plants. Costs are high for raw materials, labor (strongly unionized) and energy. As many as 22,800 gallons of water are used to produce one ton of newsprint, along with huge amounts of fuel oil.

And because mills must be located close to wood supplies, the cost of transporting newsprint to U.S. papers is high. Abitibi-Price Inc., North America's single largest producer, says its costs are as follows: wood, 25 percent; labor, 23 percent; energy, 15 percent; other mill costs, 21 percent; delivery, 16 percent.

All this inspires search for new raw materials. Some experts say the answer may be kenaf, a nonwood fibrous plant that matures in four or five months—compared with 25 years for trees used in wood pulp—and provides a per-acre yield nine times that of forest land. It grows well in the South, Southern California, and Arizona. Importantly, it produces high-quality newsprint. Some futurists predict that new technology using kenaf will permit construction of small mills, close to U.S. newspapers, producing 25 to 50 tons daily.

Managing Building and Site

Newspapers traditionally have been located in the city's center, close to business activity, government and other news sources that must be covered. However, many city centers are deteriorating, readers and retailers are moving to the suburbs, news sources are dispersing—and many newspaper buildings are inadequate for new equipment or for storing tons of newsprint.

It all raises questions: Is there a *social responsibility* to remain in the city's center, to support the core of the paper's market? Or is there a *business imperative* to move to cheaper land (and lower taxes) outside town?

Or should the operation be split, keeping editorial and business departments downtown and establishing production in a satellite location outside town? The *Atlanta Journal* and *Constitution* made what is becoming a standard move for many metro dailies: It constructed a $50 million satellite printing facility northeast of Atlanta but left other operations downtown. This locates some production capability in a growing population area and leapfrogs inner-city traffic.

If your paper contemplates moving all operations outside the city, consider whether the newspaper risks losing identity in its market core. Also consider the cost. Experts suggest 1 to 1.5 square feet of building are needed for each copy of the newspaper sold. Downtown real estate often is more expensive than suburban land.

In picking a new site, make sure good transportation is available. Delivery trucks must have quick access to major highways leading throughout the market; easy commutes will mollify employees disgruntled over moving to a new plant. Considerations of taxes, topography (presses weigh tons and must have solid foundations) and availability of utilities all go into site selection and planning. If possible, arrange multiple service by utilities. Don't let a single power failure shut down a new multimillion-dollar plant.

In designing a plant, make sure all department heads are consulted on projected long-term needs. Design today for tomorrow's needs. Use an architect experienced in the construction of newspaper plants. Obtain building and fire code requirements in advance. They vary and you don't want a new building declared unsafe the day after it opens.

PRODUCTION'S ELECTRONIC FUTURE

So, to produce newspapers we're bouncing signals off satellites in space. Down here, we're using hugely expensive, high-speed technology. And, what's at the end of that production chain? Teenagers on bicycles or adult drivers, all poised to grab bundles of newspapers and head off—with varying speed, accuracy and efficiency—toward house-to-house delivery. Isn't there a better way... can't there be a better ending to the costly, high-tech production process?

The thought that there *must* be a better way drives production and circulation executives to explore the possibilities of electronic home delivery. That same thought motivates telephone and cable companies to bet many millions of dollars that there indeed *is* a better way and that they, not newspapers, can provide it.

How all this will shake down is unclear. But three factors are obvious: First, the new technology is capable of delivering enormous quantities of information to households, at extremely high speeds and with great accuracy. Discerning information users will be able to interact with distant databases and gain access to far more information, in more timely fashion, than any newspaper can deliver.

Second, as the cost of newsprint, production and newspaper delivery soars, the cost of computer memory and electronic communication is falling. Particularly if information services are "bundled" in electronic systems with other services (banking at home, cable TV and so forth), the per-unit cost of delivering news electronically may drop dramatically below the cost of putting it on newsprint, then delivering it to doorsteps.

Third, it's obvious that newspaper production departments are central to how newspapers use the new technology. That requires production executives to expand their technical skills beyond putting ink on paper. Some factors to watch follow.

Digitization of Information

Most transmission circuits have been made of copper, carrying electrical or *analog signals* that are severely limited in speed and capacity. Digitizing information reduces it to numbers or "bits." The process permits compressing signals so more data can be transmitted with a high degree of accuracy. What takes hours to transmit via analog signals takes just seconds via digital systems. Plan your production strategy on the assumption that if your newspaper "goes electronic" you'll have virtually unlimited capability of dumping huge amounts of information in subscriber homes.

FIGURE 11.3
New technology raises an old question: Is
putting ink on paper the best way to
distribute news and advertising?
Newspapers, which handle tons of paper
daily, are investigating electronic home
delivery as an alternative. Courtesy *Dallas*
Morning News **(photo by Don Tremain).**

Smart Information Centers for Homes

Today's newspaper reader plows, on average, through 200,000 or so words of information preselected and packaged by editors responding to their own news values and judgments of what's important. Tomorrow's reader will have greater personal control over news selection by using a combination of media—perhaps the newspaper itself backed by a "smart" TV set or television-plus-laptop computer. Perhaps the newspaper, judged "complete" by today's standards, will be used by many readers tomorrow as only the starting point for an information search that will lead via interactive circuits from the "smart" household information center into distant databases and libraries.

In other words, plan your production strategy around the concept of (a) producing your newspaper in combination with auxiliary information services, or (b) competing against information *(and advertising)* suppliers that digitize information and feed it via interactive circuits into household information centers.

Fiber-Optic Systems

Some futurists bet on direct broadcast satellite (DBS), sending information via satellites to special rooftop antennas atop individual homes. Others wondered whether the future was in low-power television (LPTV)—establishing low-power TV stations for over-the-air broadcasting to homes. However, most large communications companies—particularly telephone and cable companies—are betting on fiber optics. This involves, of course, underground circuits of glass strands, each of which can carry 150,000 to 200,000 times as much information as a copper circuit. Lesson: Your strategy should be to seek partnership with companies financially strong enough to build the hugely expensive fiber-optic transmission systems. (Wouldn't your information and advertising and their technology make a fine package?)

At minimum, your strategy must be to seek access to such transmission systems. No newspaper company even approaches the big players—the regional Bell operating companies—in financial strength, and building independent, newspaper-owned transmission systems reaching into the households of America will be impossible.

NOW, BE CAREFUL!

If past experience is a guide (and it *should* be), some companies will lose a lot of money up front as newspapers try to step onto the "electronic superhighway." Knight-Ridder spent at least $50 million trying to develop videotext, the delivery of computer-generated information over two-way interactive circuits. Times Mirror invested millions in a similar effort. And both companies shut down these efforts in 1986. They were technically strong but unable to arouse sufficient consumer interest.

What the two companies attempted—and why they failed—are important to newspaper managers facing today the challenge of creating viable electronic home-delivery information systems.

Knight-Ridder's system, Viewtron, linked user homes with computers to provide not only news, information and advertising but also banking and shopping service, educational programs, games, community bulletin boards and many other services. Hand-held keyboards summoned Viewtron services over telephone circuits and displayed them on home TV screens (a major disadvantage that put both telephone and TV temporarily out of action) or personal computers.

The strategy was to build a nationwide network of allied papers and jointly make Viewtron available on a widespread basis. Each local participant was to own 75 percent of its joint venture and contribute local news and marketing expertise.

Linking the powerful news-gathering resources of 20 or 30 major newspapers through high-speed computerized networks was a mind-boggling idea, but consumers would not pay for it and the advertiser would not support it.

The system aimed at high-income, demographically attractive users and, in raw numbers at least, the potential market was large. Researcher Ruth Clark found 68 percent of all regular newspaper readers already were participating in the "communications revolution" through cable TV or video games, personal computers or video cassette recorders.

However, users proved extremely cost-sensitive. Customers would not pay substantial fees for general news also available, albeit somewhat later, in a 35- or 50-cent newspaper; few wanted to use a costly personal computer and telephone hookup for baseball or football scores they get free on radio or television, or in tomorrow's paper.

There was—and today is—some doubt that the householder will adapt easily to a computer-based keyboard for such tasks as banking and shopping. Will shopping electronically from the kitchen be considered essential? Or will it take some of the fun out of life? Will the buyer want to leave home to *feel* the fabric of a new dress, *sniff* the freshness of meat? And after all, how many need to use an electronic system for banking from home at midnight? Note the target markets in past experiments were "typical" (if upscale) households and the services offered general news and information.

Beyond doubt, a substantial *business* audience is eager for electronic delivery of news. Dow Jones, Reuters, Bloomberg and other news services profitably serve tens of thousands of brokers, traders and bankers. The distinction: Those services transmit news on which business—and profits—turn.

Nevertheless, even general news and information *are* a valuable commodity. And, newspapers are unrivaled in their ability to collect and analyze it. Plan your strategy around the reality that your newspaper must—somehow—take advantage of that in the electronic future.

SUMMARY

Technology is transforming American newspapers into a capital-intensive, computerized industry, promising national dailies and country weeklies alike exciting new ways to improve content and reduce costs. Three basic techniques are the core of a modern production chain: computerized writing and editing that captures newsroom keystrokes, offset printing and cold-type processes, and pagination or computerized layout of pages. Each offers staff reductions, higher profits and improved journalistic quality.

There are dangers: The high cost of new technology can create heavy debt; it is easy to buy too much technology or, conversely, too little.

Even managers lacking technical background must get involved in the new technology. But buy carefully and never without haggling over prices or obtaining expert financial advice. Newspapers must plan to sell news and information to customers other than subscribers. But most publishers say that electronic systems will supplement—not supplant—newspapers.

The general public doesn't easily adapt to high-cost delivery of news via home terminals. However, delivery of news in a "bundle" of other services such as telephone, burglar/fire alarms and so on might be a possibility. Certainly, the delivery of tightly focused "news to profit by" to the business community can be highly successful. In serving business, newspapers may find new uses for existing staff, facilities and the huge databases they build each day.

RECOMMENDED READING

Technical bulletins issued by the Newspaper Association of America are the best available source of up-to-date information on newspaper production. Contact NAA, 11600 Sunrise Valley Drive, Reston, Va. 22091. *Presstime* reports regularly on studies by NAA standing committees on newsprint, telecommunications and technical research. *Editor & Publisher* and *Newspapers & Technology* are good sources on technical developments. The Southern Newspaper Publishers Association issues weekly technical bulletins.

GLOSSARY

Access time. Delay between receipt of material and the instant the computer was ordered to deliver it.

Audiotext. Automated telephone services providing sports scores, stock prices and other information.

Bandwidth. Width of a communications circuit; expresses volume of information that can be carried.

Cable television (or community-antenna television, CATV). Delivery of TV signals via wired circuits.

Cathode-ray tube (CRT). Vacuum tube that displays information on a screen, as in VDTs, or transmits images to photocomposition equipment.

Cellular radio. Telephone system that passes mobile user from one transmitter to another in a city; transmitters cover "cells."

Central processing unit (CPU). Computer element that fulfills instructions from programming.

Coding. Successive instructions assigned computer for processing.

Database. Information in computer storage.

Digital. Transmitting/interpreting information as discrete "bits" of binary information.

Direct broadcast satellite (DBS). TV signals to satellite for relay to earth stations; permits long-range broadcast.

Direct lithography. Process of converting letterpress to offset with special plates, avoiding the cost of replacing the press.

Electronic data processing (EDP). Processing data electronically, especially with computers.

Electronic mail. Computer exchange of messages.

Federal Communications Commission (FCC). Licenses radio and TV stations, assigns wavelengths and monitors public interest in broadcasting.

Fiber optics. A technology of circuits derived from glass with much larger transmission capabilities than copper wires; such circuits convert a signal into a light wave, which is reconverted to signal at receiving end.

Flexographic printing. Applies water-borne ink directly to paper without offset's intermediate "blanket"; presses are cheaper, less complicated, waste less newsprint.

Front-end system. VDTs and computers that handle news and advertising copy.

Gravure printing. Printing using images etched below the nonprinting surface to cup ink in hollows; noted for high-quality reproduction.

Halftone. Photo or other continuous-tone art specially screened with crisscrossing lines so reproduction appears as small dots.

Hardware. Computer components, including mechanical and electronic.

Interactive. System that both sends and receives.

Kenaf. Nonwood fibrous plant that some experts feel could replace wood as the primary raw material in newsprint.

Letterpress. Now nearly extinct newspaper printing process; uses hot-metal typesetting and prints from raised surface of type.

Linotype. Keyboard machine for mechanical typesetting from hot metal; displaced from newspapers by photocomposition.

Low-power television (LPTV). Limited to 10 watts for Very High Frequency stations and 1,000 watts for Ultra High Frequency stations; designed to diversify TV ownership and permit reaching audiences in a 10- to 20-mile radius.

Management information system (MIS). Internal system for making pertinent data available to decision makers.

Microwave. High-frequency electromagnetic wave transmission in straight line of sight.

Multipoint distribution service (MDS). Service whereby microwave transmitters send pay-TV programming to subscribers equipped with special antennas.

Offset. Prints image transferred from plate cylinder to "blanket" or second cylinder which, in turn, transfers to paper; widely used in newspapers for clean reproduction at lower cost than letterpress.

On-line services. Provide subscribers with information/entertainment via personal computers and modems.

Optical character reader (OCR or "scanner"). "Reads" typewritten copy and translates it into electronic impulses that drive typesetters; has largely given way at newspapers to VDT editing.

Pagination. Computerized page layout on screen; promises eventual elimination of composing and platemaking departments.

"Payback" period. Time in which reduced costs and other efficiencies cover expense of new equipment; crucial in decision whether to buy.

Personal computers (PCs). Important in newspaper production because they cost less than most VDTs and are both lightweight and transportable; many are interactive with other systems.

Photocomposition. A method of typesetting involving a light-sensitive photo process.

Plateless printing. Goal of many newspapers that hope to eventually switch to lower-cost inkjet printing; obviates the need for heavy presses and permits rapid changes in the material being printed.

Satellite earth station. Receiver for signals transmitted from communications satellites.

Satellite plant. Production facility distant from the news and advertising offices; typically, a suburban plant linked by microwave or fiber-optic circuits from downtown headquarters.

Software. Programmed instructions (tapes or disks) used in conjunction with a computer.

Subscription television (STV). Television programmed for subscriber sets equipped with special decoders enabling them to receive special pay programming delivered by standard signal.

Teletext. One-way transmission of characters and graphics, usually via TV frequencies.

Video display terminal (VDT). A terminal enabling user to type material on screen for transfer into a computer; newspapers use thousands in news, advertising, administration.

Videotext. Two-way teletext; user can interrogate distant computer.

Web printing. Printing whereby continuous rolls of paper are fed to a cylinder press, as in newspaper production.

"Wired city". Term indicating high degree of household penetration by cable TV or other forms of electronically delivered programming.

NOTES

1. Robert Tribble, letter to author.
2. D. Claeys Bahrenburg, "Face the Digital Future Without Fear," *FOLIO*, Feb. 1, 1994, p. 21.
3. Jim Rosenberg, "Users Assess Flexo in '92," *Editor & Publisher*, Jan. 30, 1993, p. 28.
4. Norman P. Dusseault, letter to author.
5. Ken Kniceley, letter to author.
6. Kniceley, op. cit.
7. Dusseault, op. cit.
8. Michael G. Gartner, letter to author.
9. Richard G. Capen Jr., letter to author.
10. Dusseault, op. cit.

PART **IV**

EXTRA DIMENSIONS

So, you now have a firm grasp of the operating responsibilities you'll have in newspapering and you're ready to launch your career. Right? Not so fast. You still must consider two extremely important extra dimensions of management: the legal and ethical environments in which managers and newspapers operate today.

We'll turn first, in Chapter 12, to the law and you. It's no exaggeration to say that you must consider the legal implications of every significant decision you make in management. Then, in Chapter 13, we'll consider the newspaper's social responsibilities and each manager's need to develop a personal sense of ethics.

The law, in a sense, is a fairly precise road map you'll need to follow. Ethics, on the other hand, is a subject filled with nuances, subtleties and, often, self-doubt. Now is the time for you to start sorting out how you'll operate in both extra dimensions, the law and ethics.

12

THE LAW AND YOU

We turn now to a constant companion you'll have in newspaper management: the law. Don't think that delaying discussion of this subject until now means you can assign it secondary importance. Quite to the contrary. It's a legal jungle out there for you aspiring managers, and we've held our study of this subject until now only because it requires the coherence and emphasis that a separate chapter can give it.

Newspapers operate today in a litigious, legally belligerent environment. They are under legal attack in virtually every operating sector. Emboldened by a public mood often critical of the press, plaintiffs seek and sometimes receive huge judgments. Suing a newspaper, if not entirely fashionable, is at least an increasingly acceptable enterprise.

Losing a suit—or paying the often enormous costs of defending against one—can destabilize your paper financially and chill its reportorial ardor. It can blemish careers. Losing to a union or government regulatory agency can create third-party intervention in your newspaper's conduct of its own business.

Currently active areas of newspaper law include libel and invasion of privacy, open records and freedom of information, antitrust, advertising and circulation, and personnel and labor. Each merits a book by a lawyer (which I am not). So for aspiring newspaper managers, some advice: As a first step, you must retain competent legal counsel (a) to construct preventive programs designed to avoid legal difficulties and (b) to defend you when litigation threatens. Not every manager can or should be a lawyer. But every manager must learn when to call one.

IN THE NEWSROOM: WATCH FOR LIBEL

For you as a manager, the stakes are very high in libel law. You must ensure that your entire staff—particularly in news, down to newest cub—understands that. Here's why: If a libel case goes to trial, you stand a good chance of losing. In the early 1990s, the media won only about 27 percent of libel cases. And, you can lose big. Awards against the media averaged $1.1 million in 1992–1993, $8.3 million in

1990–1991. In recent years, awards of $58 million, $34 million and $29 million were made against three media companies.

Reflecting public disdain for the media, juries frequently award punitive damages, which are designed not to compensate plaintiffs for actual losses but, rather, to punish newspapers, magazines and broadcast stations. In the early 1990s, juries handed out punitive damages in 76.2 percent of cases in which damages were awarded. The punitive awards averaged $8 million.

About the only good news on the libel front is that 90 percent or so of libel actions are dropped, settled or dismissed before going to trial. But even that good news has its dark side: It can cost hundreds of thousands of dollars—millions, even—to defend against a libel action. One result can be a newspaper management team preoccupied not with running your newspaper but, rather, fighting off financial disaster. Another result can be a newsroom whose reportorial ardor is "chilled" by fear of stumbling into another expensive libel suit.[1]

Alton Telegraph: A Case in Point

At the time, the *Alton (Ill.) Telegraph* was a prosperous 38,000-circulation evening paper known for vigorous, award-winning investigative reporting. Its crusading editors brought home awards and commendations. The paper's market value was $3 million or so. Then, the shock: A local businessman filed a $10.5 million libel suit based on a memo, never published, that two *Telegraph* reporters sent to a federal agency while they were researching a story. After a legal battle for nearly seven years, the *Telegraph* lost in 1982. A jury awarded the businessman $9.2 million—$6.7 million for actual damages and $2.5 million in punitive damages. The *Telegraph* sought protection under bankruptcy laws. Then, with legal costs mounting ($100,000 simply to prepare a never-delivered appeal), the *Telegraph* settled out of court by paying the businessman $1.4 million, much of it borrowed.

The paper's owners nearly lost everything, not just jobs but almost the paper itself. A chill descended over the *Telegraph*. Salaries were frozen. Newsroom vacancies went unfilled. Cautious editors banned the use of anonymous sources; reporters often destroyed notes after use lest they be subpoenaed in any future lawsuit.[2]

All of which is good reason for you to take a close look at libel law—and another potential legal trap, invasion of privacy.

AVOIDING TROUBLE: A CHECKLIST

First, you—and your entire newspaper team—must understand the law of libel and privacy.

Libel

Libel is injury to reputation, a false statement communicated to a third person without consent or privilege that injures or tends to injure an individual's reputation by lowering community estimation and causing him or her to be shunned or avoided or exposed to hatred, contempt, or ridicule. Damages against newspapers often result when stories cause monetary loss to an individual or business.

Provable truth is the only complete defense, but some state laws require truth with good motives or justifiable ends. Check with local counsel for a precise interpretation. In some circumstances, newspapers have privilege. They are immune if they fairly and accurately cover certain sources—judicial, legislative, public and official proceedings and most public records, even if those proceedings or records contain libelous statements. This is a tricky area; what constitutes "judicial proceedings," for example, can vary. Again, consult a local attorney. The *right of fair comment* permits factually true, fair comment without malice on matters of public interest.

Invasion of Privacy

An increasingly active sector of law concerns invasion of privacy. Newspapers have been found liable for unreasonable intrusion into the seclusion or privacy of an individual because they publicly revealed embarrassing or objectionable private facts or held the individual in a false light. Stories held to shock or outrage the "reasonable person" are dangerous.

Intrusion can include use of hidden cameras or microphones or theft of documents. Such tactics can be legally (and ethically) indefensible. In general, courts hold that individuals lose the right to privacy when they are involved in a news event or story of legitimate public interest, even against their will. But this is a gray area. Newspapers have been found liable for digging up distasteful, sordid details from the past of a person who currently lives a private life that is not newsworthy. That is, truth is sometimes *no* defense if there is no current newsworthiness or if the truth is sufficiently private and embarrassing.

Another dangerous area is appropriation without consent of a person's name or photograph for commercial gain. This could include using a person's name or photograph in an advertisement endorsing a product, for example. It's all so complex that safeguards must be developed.

How to Build Safeguards

These are steps a nonlawyer manager can take:

- Hire a lawyer expert in libel (not contract law, not real estate) who can explain current law in lay language. Let the lawyer construct your defensive program against libel. Whenever possible, retain the lawyer to read dangerous copy prior to publication or take telephone inquiries from your news desk—even at midnight.
- Hold regular staff seminars on libel, with both counsel and top executives participating to underline the subject's importance. Give staffers the background of recent court rulings (see Box 12.1).
- Make sure that a libel manual is available in the newsroom and that each staff member *signifies in writing* that it has been read. A fine manual for the working journalist is in *The AP Stylebook* (The Associated Press, 50 Rockefeller Plaza,

BOX 12.1   Landmark Cases

Libel is a changing, evolving sector of the law. You need expert legal counsel to keep you current—and out of trouble. But here is background on U.S. Supreme Court landmark cases that helped establish current libel law.

New York Times v. Sullivan (1964)

The U.S. Supreme Court ruled that public officials must prove actual malice to collect damages for a story on their official conduct. Malice was defined as publishing despite knowledge that the story was false or in reckless disregard of whether it was.

Associated Press v. Walker (1967)

This case extended *Times v. Sullivan* to include not just public "officials" but also public "figures" in whose "public conduct society and the press had a legitimate and substantial interest." In *AP v. Walker* and a consolidated case, *Curtis Publishing Co. v. Butts,* the court made a distinction between "hot news" stories and investigative reporting. Careful substantiation of all facts is doubly required in the latter.

Rosenbloom v. Metromedia (1971)

The court ruled that a private individual (as well as a public official or public figure) must show malice to recover libel damages when coverage is on matters of public interest.

Gertz v. Welch (1974)

Here, the court signaled that it felt it went too far in *Rosenbloom v. Metromedia.* In cases not involving punitive damages, it said, private individuals did not have to prove malice, only fault by the newspaper. It left open to state courts the definition of what constitutes fault or negligence. The court also left it up to lower courts to decide who is a "public figure." In this case, it ruled that a well-known Chicago attorney was a private individual.

Time Inc. v. Firestone (1976)

The court ruled that a prominent socialite who held press conferences and used a clipping service to collect stories about herself was a private individual in libel law. This decision seemed to limit the protection the press won in *Times v. Sullivan,* confining it to cases involving public officials and public figures who willingly step into the limelight.

Other Decisions

Starting in 1979, a series of decisions created concern among newspaper executives that the Court was taking a conservative view of the press. Among other things, the Court began to allow libel plaintiffs to probe the "state of mind" of reporters and their conversations with editors prior to publication of an alleged libel.

However, two decisions in 1986 were interpreted as granting newspapers additional protection: In *Philadelphia Newspapers Inc. v. Hepps,* the Court ruled that a person suing a news organization for libel must prove damaging statements to be false, at least on "matters of public concern." Until that ruling, the burden was on news organizations to prove that contested statements were true.

In *Anderson v. Liberty Lobby,* the Court ruled that libel suits filed in federal courts by public officials and public figures must be dismissed before trial unless evidence suggests that libel can be proved with "convincing clarity." That was hailed as encouraging judges to dismiss weak cases and avoid expensive trials.

In an important case in 1987, a federal appeals court in Washington threw out a jury award of $2 million that had been won by William Tavoulareas, a former president of Mobil Corporation, in a libel suit against *The Washington Post.* The *Post* had reported Tavoulares "set up his son" in a shipping firm doing business with Mobil.

The appeals court ruled Tavoulares was a "public figure" and thus must prove the *Post* defamed him with "actual malice." The court ruled the *Post* story was "substantially true" and said it agreed with the newspaper that "the First Amendment forbids penalizing the press for encouraging its reporters to expose wrongdoing by public corporations and public figures."

New York, N.Y. 10020), but it should be amended by counsel for local applicability.

- Wage unrelenting war on careless, sloppy reporting and writing. This is the cause of most libel cases. Demand accurate handling of *every* story. Even the most routine, seemingly innocuous story can be libel dynamite. Insist that reporters assigned to highly technical stories—crime, law, medicine, business—have the expertise to write balanced, accurate stories.

- Weed out activist reporters who carry their causes into what should be dispassionate news columns. Beware of tendentious, argumentative, imprecise language. Some words—"Nazi," "communist," "liar," "drunkard," "fraud"—are libel per se in some circumstances.

- Discourage overuse of "informed source" or unnamed "official source" who gives your reporter a damaging story about someone. What are the motives behind the anonymous attack? Is the story of meaningful, substantive interest to readers or simply malicious? Is it provably worth the risk? Sometimes, you might insist that if anonymous sources must be used, they sign statements authenticating their information so there can be no reneging in court. Always make sure that a responsible editor knows the identity of the reporter's anonymous source.

- Carefully monitor investigative stories alleging criminality or malfeasance. Again, you may have to prove truth. Warn against unseemly haste. It can cause errors and errors may spell libel.

- Extend your libel watch to all pages—letters to the editor (your newspaper is legally responsible for *all* content), photographs, births, hospital notes, marriages and that column called "Our Town 30 Years Ago Today" (you can be in big trouble if you resurrect the drunk driving arrest, 30 years ago, of a person who subsequently lived a blameless life).

- Strive for sensitive handling of stories that are journalistically unfair—that hurt, embarrass or cause monetary loss. Those stories are libel bait. Get balancing comment; be fair.

- And check the libel insurance. It's expensive, but you cannot be without it. Companies specializing in libel are Safeco of Seattle; Mutual Insurance Co., Ltd., of Hamilton, Bermuda; and Employers Reinsurance Corp. of Overland Park, Kan. The Libel Defense Resource Center of New York City, a media-supported group, can provide additional background.

What to Do When Trouble Erupts

Assume every threat of a lawsuit—even implied—is serious. Columnist William Safire of *The New York Times* terms libel lawsuits the "rich man's relief." Those who threaten to sue may be able to afford following through.

A second recommendation: Be professional and courteous to any complainer. Persons who feel offended by what's printed about them often are looking only for a chance to let off steam, to complain. Listen carefully, take notes and promise to look into the matter. However, if an attorney telephones about a story, you, the layman, *never* do the talking. Instead, your attorney talks law with the complaining attorney.

What is said or written following alleged libel can be crucial to a lawsuit's outcome. When danger flags go up, especially if the words "libel" or "lawsuit" are mentioned, give the matter to your attorney. Anxious young reporters trying to "straighten things out" themselves with an attorney or offended individuals can dig your newspaper deeper into trouble. You must create a newsroom climate that encourages reporters to discuss libel threats with their superiors rather than acting independently.

In any discussion, admit nothing. Libel law is complex and what appears libelous to the complainant or even to you might not be libel at all. Listen courteously, then call your attorney. In delicate situations, consult your attorney in negotiating and writing corrections; never publish a retraction without counsel's advice.

Retractions can be held later to be admissions of falsity or wrongdoing. Also, a retraction can repeat the defamation and thus increase the newspaper's liability. The best way to defend against a libel suit is not to let it get into court.

There is danger that you may so frighten the newsroom staff—or yourself—about libel that self-censorship settles over the newspaper. The rising number of suits filed by corporations may be aiming to do just that. Examples are lawsuits over stories critiquing new products or even reviewing books or restaurant food. Mobil Corp. in 1982 insured 100 top executives for up to $10 million in legal fees should any of them sue for libel.

Achieving correct balance in alerting employees to libel but not alarming them is a delicate matter for any manager. You must come down on the side of aggressive but fair, courageous but careful journalism. Threats of multimillion-dollar libel judgments must be a business consideration but cannot be allowed to dampen your newspaper's reportorial efforts or the independence of its editorial pages.

Is Offense the Best Defense?

Weary of what they regard as unfounded libel suits, newspapers increasingly are going on the offensive. Two tactics are employed: First, newspapers spread word they won't settle any lawsuit out of court. That's designed to ward off suits by plaintiffs who don't really want to go to court but who hope a newspaper will pay maybe $10,000 or so just to get rid of the nuisance. The *Des Moines Register & Tribune* spread word through the Iowa Bar Association that it wouldn't settle any suit even if that would save money.

Second, some newspapers countersue plaintiffs' lawyers who file libel suits without merit. The late W. E. (Ned) Chilton III, when publisher of the *Charleston (W. Va.) Gazette,* set the policy for his newspaper, saying, "I decided this newspaper would not sit back and allow baseless suits to remain unanswered. I wasn't going to file against the plaintiff because he didn't know the law. I went against the lawyer."[3] Chilton advised: "If enough lawyers are forced to pay for their unmeritorious lawsuits against newspapers, caution will grow among lawyers and fewer unnecessary libel suits will be filed."[4]

Dow Jones & Co. and Cowles Media also counterattack. Both won back some legal costs from plaintiffs who sued them and lost.

LET THE SUNSHINE IN

Who cared when the Knoxville, Tenn., school board elected officers secretly? The *Knoxville News-Sentinel* did. It sued under the state's "Sunshine Law" to force the board to conduct public affairs in full public light.

Not one network TV crew rushed to the story in Knoxville; no national newspapers or magazines covered it. It was left to the *News-Sentinel* to make a fuss—one of uncounted legal actions taken at considerable expense by newspapers throughout the country to protect the public's right to know what its government is up to and to guard the press's right to cover it.

The effort must extend up the government ladder to highest federal levels. If the press doesn't force light into those bureaucratic dark corridors, who will? As a manager, you must participate aggressively in this effort if your reporters are to have free access to news and if your newspaper is to be a responsible community leader. Many government officials want to shield themselves and their official activities from public view. But federal and state laws give you strong weapons to fight this.

Here are some sources of help:

Reporters' Committee for Freedom of the Press. It has an FOI Service Center (800 18th Street, N. W., Washington, D.C. 10006) that instructs reporters on how to use the federal FOI Act. A telephone hotline (202-466-6312) gives free aid in press law matters. The center provides sample letters for requesting government information (see Box 12.2) and will even tell you how much federal agencies charge for assistance (how much per hour, for example, for clerical help at the Central Intelligence Agency).

State press associations usually retain legal counsel and provide Sunshine Law assistance. The Georgia Press Association, for example, publishes a tiny ($2\frac{1}{2}$ inches by $3\frac{1}{2}$ inches) booklet on state public records and open meeting laws. It fits easily into reporters' wallets (Georgia Press Association, 1075 Spring Street, N. W., Atlanta, Ga. 30309).

The Society of Professional Journalists operates a legal defense fund for First Amendment cases (840 N. Lake Shore Dr., Suite 803, Chicago, Ill. 60611). Other active press groups include ASNE, NAA and Inland Press Association.

Gannett Co. and the New York Times Co. are among communications companies often arguing for open access in FOI battles. Gannett expects its reporters to object if a courtroom is closed to them. They carry small cards they can read to the judge (see Box 12.3). The Gannett statement objects to courtroom closure on behalf of "my employer *and* the public. . . ." It is a *public* right the press defends.

The issues, of course, are free press and fair trial, a clash inevitable at times between the First Amendment and the Sixth Amendment guarantee to criminal defendants of speedy and public trial by an impartial jury or the Fourteenth Amendment guarantee of due process under the law. Judges sometimes rule that news coverage prejudices juries, making fair trial possible; they therefore close courtrooms or issue "gag orders" restricting coverage.

BOX 12.2   FOI Sample Request

This letter is recommended by the Reporters' Committee for Freedom of the Press for requesting information under the Federal Freedom of Information Act. The committee's FOI Service Center in Washington, D.C., provides guidance also for journalists in appealing FOI decisions or taking legal action.

> Telephone No. (business hours)
> Return Address
> Date

Name of Public Body
Address

To the FOI Officer

This request is made under the federal Freedom of Information Act, 5 U.S.C. 552.

Please send me copies of (Here, clearly describe what you want. Include identifying material, such as names, places, and the period of time about which you are inquiring. If you wish, attach news clips, reports and other documents describing the subject of your research).

As you know, the FOI Act provides that if portions of a document are exempt from release, the remainder must be segregated and disclosed. Therefore, I will expect you to send me all non-exempt portions of the records which I have requested, and ask that you justify any deletions by reference to specific exemptions of the FOI Act. I reserve the right to appeal your decision to withhold any materials.

I promise to pay reasonable search and duplication fees in connection with this request. However, if you estimate that the total fees will exceed $_____, please notify me so that I may authorize expenditure of a greater amount.

(Optional) I am prepared to pay reasonable search and duplication fees in connection with this request. However, the FOI Act provides for waiver or reduction of fees if disclosure could be considered as "primarily benefiting the general public." I am a journalist (researcher, scholar) employed by (name of news organization, book publisher, etc.), and intend to use the information I am requesting as the basis for a planned article (broadcast, book). (Add arguments here in support of fee waiver.) Therefore, I ask that you waive all search and duplication fees. If you deny this request, however, and the fees will exceed $_____, please notify me of the charges before you fill my request so that I may decide whether to pay fees or appeal your denial of my request for a waiver.

As I am making this request in the capacity of a journalist (author, scholar) and this information is of timely value, I will appreciate your communicating with me by telephone, rather than by mail, if you have any question regarding this request. Thank you for your assistance, and I will look forward to receiving your reply within 10 business days, as required by law.

> Very truly yours,
>
> (Signature)

BOX 12.3 "Your Honor"

Gannett Co. equips reporters with wallet-size cards carrying guidelines on how to object if a judge closes a courtroom and expels the press. The message is short, respectful of the court, and to the point:

Your honor, I am _____, a reporter for _____, and I would like to object on behalf of my employer and the public to this proposed closing. Our attorney is prepared to make a number of arguments against closings such as this one, and we respectfully ask the Court for a hearing on these issues. I believe our attorney can be here relatively quickly for the Court's convenience and he (she) will be able to demonstrate that closure in this case will violate the First Amendment, and possible state statutory and constitutional provisions as well. I cannot make the arguments myself, but our attorney can point out several issues for your consideration. If it please the Court, we request the opportunity to be heard through Counsel.

Most such restraints are eventually struck down by the U.S. Supreme Court. But unclear is whether *pre*trial hearings are subject to closing. In this era of plea bargaining, pretrial hearings often are the only forum for criminal proceedings. If your newspaper is to operate with a sense of social responsibility, reporters should use the Gannett approach and lodge a protest at any judicial closing.

SHIELD LAWS, SEARCHES, THE SEC

Shield laws, adopted by about half the states, give reporters some protection against being forced to divulge confidential information or testify in court or before legislative and administrative groups. However, laws vary widely and are open to judicial interpretation. Sometimes, they are not much help.

New Jersey has a shield law, but *New York Times* reporter Myron Farber spent 40 days in a New Jersey jail for refusing to turn over notes subpoenaed in a murder trial. It cost *The Times* $286,000 in fines. *The Times* recovered $101,000 when it was pardoned, with Farber, by the governor in 1982—but the courageous stand on principle by Farber and his paper was expensive.

Newsroom searches by police were held by the U.S. Supreme Court in 1978 (*Zurcher v. Stanford Daily*) to be constitutional if performed under a valid search warrant issued to obtain evidence that was reasonably thought to be at the newspaper office. This rose from a search in 1971 of the Stanford University *Daily*.

The Privacy Protection Act of 1980 says that newsrooms can be searched only in rare circumstances, as when officials have reason to believe a search is necessary to save a life or prevent destruction of materials or when a subpoena would be ineffective. Remember: A search warrant authorizes police to use force if necessary. You may refuse to cooperate, stall, ask questions, call your attorney—but don't resist physically.

Securities and Exchange Commission regulations and how they affect the press are controversial and evolving. The subject became heated with SEC charges in 1984 that *Wall Street Journal* reporter R. Foster Winans and four others had profited illegally from his advance knowledge of stories the *Journal* would publish. It was charged that they traded stocks, later benefiting when the stories caused prices to rise or fall.

There was some sentiment in Congress and elsewhere for classifying reporters as "insiders"—people the SEC judges to have advance information that could move market prices. An insider is supposed to reveal inside information publicly or refrain from trading.

The Wall Street Journal, like many newspapers, prohibits employees from buying or selling securities or sharing inside information until two days after an article about a stock is published. *Journal* reporters are not supposed to trade at all in the securities of companies they cover.

IN THE MARKETPLACE: BEWARE ANTITRUST

Antitrust law enters your study of newspaper management principally for two reasons: First, as a manager, you must make no significant move in your marketplace, with new products or campaigns against competitors, unless you have expert counsel on any antitrust implications. It's that dangerous out there. Second, a number of failing newspapers have sought financial relief in exemptions from antitrust law, and the competitive and societal implications of that are becoming heated. Let's look first at what antitrust law can mean for your newspaper.

Antitrust and Your Operations

It's easy, in newspaper management, to make operational mistakes that leave you vulnerable in antitrust lawsuits. Attorney's fees in the hundreds of thousands of dollars are not unusual. And, losers in civil antitrust cases can face treble damages. You also can be forced to change your newspaper's competitive posture and operate under severe restrictions in the future.

Here are examples of what that can involve: The 5,600-circulation *Manteca (Calif.) Bulletin* was awarded $6.3 million damages from a competitor, the *Manteca News,* in an antitrust suit charging that advertising was sold illegally below cost and that secret discriminatory discounts were offered to some advertisers.

Gannett opted for an expensive out-of-court settlement when its *Salem (Ore.) Statesman and Capital Journal* was charged in a multimillion-dollar suit with using illegal, predatory means to drive a shopper out of business; some Salem advertisers sued them on grounds the newspaper (now consolidated into the *Statesman-Journal*) thus deprived them of an alternative outlet for print advertising.

The Chicago Tribune Co. agreed to sell two shoppers and three weekly paid papers in Osceola County, Florida, when the Justice Department charged that their purchase by the Tribune Co.'s neighboring *Orlando Sentinel* would have the "probable effect" of substantially lessening advertising competition in the county. The

Tribune Co. bought the publications in 1980 for $4.1 million, and the Justice Department started an investigation within three months, saying the *Sentinel* had 40 percent of the county's print advertising and the five smaller publications had 20 percent.

Antitrust cases often arise from shifting competitive patterns that throw established dailies and weeklies into direct competition with shoppers, direct mail and other newcomers. Along with radio, television and other media, all are fighting for essentially the same advertiser dollar. And some losers extend the war into the courtroom with antitrust charges.

The Legal Background

Federal and state antitrust laws are many and complex, covering wide areas of newspaper operations. Federal laws spring from these acts:

The Sherman Antitrust Act (1890) is designed to protect free competition in business. It prohibits unreasonable restraint of trade involving a conspiracy of two or more persons. This includes competitors as well as buyers and sellers who conspire in such matters as price fixing, dividing markets, or boycotting or illegally damaging a third party. It prohibits monopolizing a market or conspiring or attempting to do so for illegal purposes. Generally, a newspaper with 70 percent of the "relevant" advertising market is presumed to possess monopoly power, although even 50 percent can trigger suits. These days, an ill-defined "substantial" share of the market—if unfairly gained—can run risk of suit.

The Clayton Act (1914) broadens Sherman by prohibiting activities that could illegally stifle competition. Clayton prohibits discriminatory pricing that injures other media. It prohibits "tying arrangements" that force a buyer to purchase a product just to get another—ads in a shopper to get space in a newspaper, for example.

The Federal Trade Commission Act (1914) created the FTC to enforce federal antitrust laws. Its scope includes business practices violating consumer interests regardless of competitive factors involved. The FTC watches for deceptive advertising.

The Robinson-Patman Act (1936) prohibits price discrimination in interstate commerce (in which newspapers are generally found to be engaged).

A key word throughout all of this is "conspiracy." You or other employees must avoid any contact with competitors that could be construed as aiming at an agreement to fix prices, divide markets or otherwise contravene antitrust laws. This includes meetings at trade association conventions or other seemingly innocuous affairs.

Take Care with Shoppers

Much antitrust litigation revolves around shopper publications, often when an established daily or weekly launches one or otherwise responds to the arrival in the market of an independent shopper. No established paper should field a shopper without expert legal advice. Factors to consider:

The law does not frown on any newspaper launching a "fighting ship," a new publication designed to improve or regain competitive position. The law, indeed, is structured to promote vigorous, fair competition. However, from day one in the planning process you must demonstrate you desire only to improve your newspaper's own economic interests—that your motivation in launching a shopper is to respond to advertiser demands for a new publication. Detailed memos must be kept showing clearly that the shopper, its marketing strategy and its ad rates are not structured to harm any present or future competitor. Launching a shopper with the intent of driving a competitor from the marketplace is reckless, dangerous and—in most cases—illegal.

Understand that however pure your intent, you can still be sued. In some particularly competitive markets, established papers *assume* they will be sued if they launch a shopper. Juries sometimes vote their emotions in antitrust cases, which can be so complex that even skilled lawyers have difficulties understanding the law. And sometimes, juries identify established papers as the "big guy," the wealthy, powerful villain; the shopper publisher sometimes comes off as the favored "little guy," the underdog.

So, even though you may intend to compete fairly and legally, you need legal counsel from the start in establishing the structure and operating patterns of any total market coverage product. The thrust of many antitrust suits is that a newspaper uses illegal, predatory tactics to achieve or maintain a market monopoly. Ensuring fair intent plus legal operation of a shopper might not keep you out of court, but it could improve your chances of eventually winning if you do get sued.

Monopoly position is not illegal as such. Recent newspaper history demonstrates that papers die for many reasons, leaving a single paper the natural victor (still facing other types of media competitors, to be sure). But illegal use of monopoly power thus gained has a high probability of drawing fire.

So, first, you must be doubly cautious if you manage the only paid-circulation daily or weekly in your market. Newspaper strategists point out that this does not constitute monopoly, that the newspaper still faces competitors such as radio, television and direct mail. But chances are that an antitrust-minded plaintiff will move against a dominant newspaper and its shopper, not against, say, a radio or TV station or city magazine.

Second, you must plan to operate your shopper at a profit as quickly as possible. Do not plan to run it at a loss indefinitely, subsidizing it from the established paper. That can be construed as intending a low-cost operation to ensure low ad rates that unfairly undercut a competitor's rates. And that is *predatory pricing,* an illegal tactic. Unfortunately, courts have not clarified how long a newspaper could reasonably subsidize start-up costs of a new shopper before being guilty of predatory pricing.

Third, be certain advertisers are entirely free to buy space in either the dominant paper or its companion shopper and are not forced or coerced unfairly to buy in one publication to obtain space in the other. Such forced combination buys are illegal "tie-ins." It is legal to offer an advertiser a discount to buy in both—but the discount must reflect the newspaper's cost saving when, for example, it uses the same ad mechanical in both publications. Obviously, antitrust cases often revolve around the definition of "reasonable" cost savings.

Fourth, be extremely careful in setting shopper ad rates. When there is even a whiff of potential antitrust action in the air, let legal counsel assist.

Crucial: Costs and Rates

Antitrust actions involving shoppers often focus on ad strategies and rates. A villain in the piece can be predatory pricing—selling advertising below cost with the intent of driving competitors from the market and eventually monopolizing a market to obtain abnormally high profits in the future. In many antitrust cases revolving around this principle, a key is determining a newspaper's true costs in operating its shopper.

Accountants use different approaches in determining this. Whatever the approach, your shopper must be allocated a fair, equitable portion of *fixed costs* plus *variable costs*. That is, the shopper should be charged a fair portion of, say, fixed building expense and administrative overhead as well as variable costs, such as newsprint, labor and other supplies for operating the shopper.

Courts have not established precise cost allocation guidelines. But you must make sure that you allocate costs fairly and equitably to the shopper and intend that it produce a profit. Obviously, these are areas where it is unsettling to be at the mercy of lay jurors—after all, what is fair and equitable cost allocation in a highly complex newspaper operation? And what is a reasonable time for a newspaper to expect its shopper to turn a profit?

At this point in any trial, the plaintiff might ask the jury to consider your newspaper's overall profit picture, and its reputation in the community—an appeal to emotion, not law. You must be sure that your newspaper is not discriminatory in pricing, secretive or arbitrary in ad rate implementation, or coercive. The risk of attracting an antitrust lawsuit—and losing—increases significantly with such tactics.

A few hints:

- Combination rates granting advertisers discounts for using both newspaper and shopper cannot be so heavily biased for such "combo" buying that they constitute coercion or an illegal tying arrangement.
- Off-card selling—departing from a published rate card—can be highly dangerous if it grants more favorable treatment to one advertiser than to others. That's price discrimination. Insist that your salespeople avoid secret or arbitrary deals. Publish a rate card and stick to it with all advertisers.
- Discount for frequency or volume of advertising, long a fixture of newspaper policy, has come under scrutiny by the Federal Trade Commission. Get an antitrust expert to look over your discount policies.

Launching and operating shoppers, then, is legally tricky if your newspaper is dominant in your market. Dominant papers simply must accept that they have to operate under restrictions—self-imposed or otherwise—that other competitors do not face. It is a price of success and all employees must be aware of it. It can be help-ful in any later lawsuit to demonstrate that your awareness included establishing an antitrust compliance program. This should be a formal, documented effort proving that top management committed itself to fair and legal competition in the marketplace and that reasonable moves were made to inform the full staff. Despite the danger of antitrust action arising out of the marketplace, some newspapers benefit—hugely—from antitrust law. Let's look at that.

Joint Operating Agreements

As Hearst Corp. pictures it, the group's *Seattle Post-Intelligencer* was not long for this world: It lost $14 million in 1970–1981, and $8 million in 1982 alone. By mid-1983, Publisher Virgil Fassio says, the 191,000-circulation morning paper was hem-orrhaging $175,000 in *weekly* losses.

Hearst's solution was a joint operating agreement (JOA) with the competing *Seattle Times*, combining all operations except editorial of both papers. The *Times* prints the *Post-Intelligencer*, sells it ads, distributes it and performs business func-tions. In return, the *Times* takes the first 6 percent of profits as a management fee, then the two share the remainder—66 percent to the *Times*, 34 percent to Hearst.

Congress agreed as early as the 1930s and, most recently, in the Newspaper Preservation Act of 1970, to permit two newspapers in one city to combine all but their newsrooms, yet remain free of antitrust considerations *if* one is probably fail-ing financially and faced with closing down. Congress's intent is to maintain sep-arate editorial voices in such cities.

Predictably, JOAs are highly controversial. The U.S. attorney general must ap-prove each and, as in Seattle, there are sometimes stiff court challenges. Opponents argue that JOAs give participants monopoly shares of a market and unfair advan-tage over competitors, particularly suburban papers but also radio and television. A developing controversy is over whether JOAs should be permitted to jointly pro-duce a shopper or other nonnewspaper product. Shoppers, opponents say, carry little or no news and should not be covered by legislation aimed at preserving in-dependent editorial voices. Opponents also argue that JOAs keep ad rates artifi-cially high and don't serve readers well, either. Supporters argue that many papers survive to serve reader and advertiser only because a JOA gives them a new lease on life.

Precise corporate outlines of a JOA—the division of duties, costs and profits—are negotiated separately in each case, subject to Justice Department review.

In most cases, dramatically improved financial results follow. In Seattle, Hearst said it reduced losses the first year under the JOA, then made a profit in the second, 1984. Publisher W.J. Pennington of the *Times* said his already profitable paper en-joyed even higher profits. As in most JOAs, the key to this financial turnaround was staff reduction. Net staff reduction approached 200.

In 1989, Knight-Ridder, owner of the *Detroit Free Press,* and Gannett, which had acquired the *Detroit News,* received approval of a 100-year JOA for the two papers. They said the *Free Press* had lost $35 million in five years, the *News,* $20 million.

TABLE 12.1   Existing Joint Operating Agreements

City	Year Began	Partners
Albuquerque, N.M.	1933	Scripps, independent
El Paso, Texas	1936	Scripps, Gannett
Nashville, Ind.	1937	Gannett, independent
Evansville, Ind.	1938	Scripps, independent*
Tucson, Ariz.	1940	Pulitzer, Gannett
Chattanooga, Tenn. (Dissolved in 1966, renewed in 1980)	1942	Two independents
Madison, Wis.	1948	Lee, independent
Fort Wayne, Ind.	1950	Knight-Ridder, independent
Birmingham, Ala.	1950	Scripps, Newhouse
Salt Lake City, Utah	1952	Two independents
Charleston, W.Va.	1958	Thomson, independent
San Francisco, Calif.	1965	Hearst, independent
Cincinnati, Ohio	1979	Scripps, Gannett
Seattle, Wash.	1983	Hearst, independent
Detroit, Mich.	1989	Gannett, Knight-Ridder
Las Vegas, Nev.	1990	Stephens, independent
York, Pa.	1990	Buckner, Garden State Newspapers

* Scripps announced it would not renew this agreement at expiration in 1998.

They agreed under a five-year sliding formula that Gannett would receive 55 percent of the profits, decreasing to 50 percent after the fifth year. They agreed to split profits 50–50 for the next 95 years. Gannett published—and thus tacitly endorsed—an estimate by securities analyst John Morton that operating profits under the JOA would be $13.5 million the first year, $40 million the second, $57 million the third. However, the Detroit papers did not enjoy immediate profitability—indeed, there is considerable doubt the city, experiencing serious socioeconomic deterioration, will support two dailies over the long term, despite the enormous cost advantages of JOA status.

Combining in JOAs hasn't prevented major dailies from failing in other cities—St. Louis, Miami, Pittsburgh, Tulsa, Shreveport and Cincinnati, among them. See Table 12.1 for cities where JOAs remain.

IN ADVERTISING: LEGAL TRAPS AWAIT

Legal traps await the unwary in many sectors of newspaper advertising. Make sure all your advertising employees are sensitive to possible problems in libel, Federal Trade Commission regulations covering misleading ads, lottery advertisement, liquor ads, and, particularly, ads that discriminate on basis of race, color, religion, sex or national origin.

Laws on discrimination in advertising exist at the federal, state and local levels, and they bear close study. Two examples why: Gannett's *Jackson (Miss.) Clarion-Ledger* and *Daily News* were hit with a U.S. Justice Department complaint, and signed a consent decree that permanently enjoins them from using words such as "white male," "female only" or "gentleman" in advertising.

The New York Times was sued by a fair-housing advocacy group that charged there was racial bias in the newspaper's real estate advertisements. The group charges the pictorial ads depicted mostly whites as potential residents and blacks as doormen, maids and building maintenance employees. *The Times* settled in 1993, agreeing that future ads would "reasonably represent" the ethnic breakdown of metropolitan New York. Since then, many newspapers have taken steps to eliminate language, photos and illustrations that might be regarded as discriminatory.

There also can be problems in publishing ads that make false or fraudulent claims, that promote illegal activity or that encourage activities harmful to health and safety. It is impractical to retain legal counsel to clear each of the thousands of ads a newspaper publishes. But each employee should be trained to recognize those occasional ads that must be viewed by supervisors and possibly the paper's attorney before publication.

Beware: Three Danger Areas

First, all employees should understand that the newspaper can be as legally responsible for ad copy published as for news or editorials. Second, a newspaper has the right to refuse an ad, but the circumstances under which that is done and how it is done can be extremely important. Third, in some cases, merely accepting an ad handed over the counter or telephoned in can constitute a contractual agreement to publish, even though the ad taker may have private reservations and intends to submit the copy for higher view.

Libel and invasion of privacy considerations, discussed earlier as they relate to news, apply fully to ad copy. It was an *advertisement* that triggered the lengthy, costly *Times v. Sullivan* case. Advertising employees must be included in your libel training program.

Be certain rate cards, contracts and classified ad pages carry *disclaimers of financial responsibility* for ad copy or for photographs that libel or invade privacy. Contracts should make advertisers and ad agencies responsible for indemnifying the paper and holding it harmless for an ad's contents. Your attorney should draft the language, of course, but see Box 12.4 for an example.

A newspaper's right to refuse an ad is founded in the First Amendment and the right of a company to decline to enter a contract. However, that right is not unconditional. Antitrust law, for example, prohibits a newspaper from conspiring with a third party to refuse ads from another. It is illegal to agree with your largest food store advertiser that you will reject ads to drive an upstart fruit store operator out of business. Also, antitrust law can limit a newspaper's right to reject advertising that might compete with its own advertising business if the newspaper has a clearly dominant position in its market. Issues are far from clarified, but papers strongly dominating their advertising marketplaces must be careful.

BOX 12.4   Indemnification Clause: A Must

All rate cards and advertising contracts must carry language under which advertisers and ad agencies agree to indemnify the paper for legal problems arising from published ad copy. *The Macon (Ga.) Telegraph and News* uses this:

"Advertiser and advertising agency will indemnify and hold harmless *Telegraph and News*, its officers, agents, employees and con-tractors, for all contents supplied to publisher, including text, representations and illustrations of advertisements printed, and for any claims arising from contents including, but not limited to, defamation, invasion of privacy, copyright infringement, plagiarism, and in the case of a pre-printed insert, deficient postage."

Once you alert employees to types of copy that, for legal reasons, will not be published, you must make sure that no dangerous copy is accepted under terms that constitute a contract. To accept copy but then not publish it can invite lawsuit for breach of contract.

This is troublesome particularly in classified, because many ads are tele-phoned in or casually accepted for cash over the counter. If not handled properly, both techniques can constitute a contract to publish. There are two steps to take. First, publish daily in the classified section an appropriate disclaimer. The *Schenec-tady (N.Y.) Gazette* uses this:

"The *Schenectady Gazette* reserves the right not to accept an advertiser's order. Only publication of an advertisement shall constitute final acceptance of the adver-tiser's order." This gives supervisors time to read and, if necessary, reject any dan-gerous ad even though the ad was taken by telephone.

Second, drill employees in proper techniques of taking ads. NAA recommends these steps if an ad taker senses copy is unacceptable:

- Tell the customer the ad must be reviewed by a supervisor before it can be ac-cepted.
- Do not give the customer a reason or respond to questions. What is said at this point may be pivotal in any later lawsuit.
- Do give the customer a copy of the rate card (which contains standards of ac-ceptability).

Beware of Other Problem Areas

The U.S. Supreme Court, in a 1993 ruling, reaffirmed that advertising is a form of speech with strong First Amendment protection. The Court held that the City of Cincinnati violated the rights of two companies when it withdrew their permits to maintain, on city streets, vending machines for free advertising publications. The city had continued to permit newspapers to place vending machines on the streets, thus drawing a distinction between news and advertising media—a distinction the Court ruled was incorrect.[5]

So, your newspaper advertising carries strong constitutional protection. But there are other problem areas. For example, liquor advertising is a controversial subject. Press groups argue any bans abridge commercial free speech rights. So be prepared: Rising public opinion against drunk drivers could bring pressure for restrictions on liquor advertising, similar to pressure now apparent on cigarette advertising.

New technology is introducing new legal headaches, and their cures won't be sorted out easily. For example, some newspapers have been sued by free-lance writers whose work was distributed on electronic information systems *after* first appearing in the newspapers' pages. Free-lance writers normally retain a copyright on their work; the work of staff writers usually is owned by the newspaper.

New photo-editing technology, permitting easy construction of photo montages, creates the danger of unauthorized reuse of photos. Some newspapers have been sued on grounds they digitally scanned photos and made unauthorized secondary use by extracting elements from them to create computer illustrations. Another problem area is an old one: lottery advertising. State lotteries have been exempted but postal regulations forbid mail delivery of newspapers advertising other lotteries.

Generally, the advertiser, not the newspaper, is responsible under federal law for claims and promises made in advertising. However, you must guard against ads that blatantly promote illegal activity or are false, fraudulent or misleading.

Local counsel must be consulted on local and state laws concerning ads that discriminate because of race, color, religion, sex or national origin. Laws vary widely and are complex. Under federal laws, the Equal Employment Opportunity Commission could move against your newspaper if ads discriminate in employment or housing matters.

IN CIRCULATION: ANTITRUST BREEDING GROUND

In circulation operations, you must avoid antitrust difficulties in three areas particularly: relationships with distributors, price setting, and assignment of circulation routes or territories.

Sounds as if it covers all of circulation? Correct.

Circulation is a breeding ground for antitrust problems. Antitrust suits often follow marketplace changes that draw new competitors, particularly shoppers, into a field occupied by an established daily or weekly. Others arise from newspapers' efforts to gain control of the ultimate pricing, sale and delivery of their own products. And many papers have simply become large, financially successful businesses that constitute attractive targets for antitrust action.

Take Care with Distributors

Most newspapers use adult or teenage independent contract distributors who buy newspapers and put together their own distribution schemes. Out of that arise major operational problems.

Some papers face subscriber discontent over faulty delivery handled by independent distributors. Some distributors aggressively sell new subscriptions, some don't. They set their own retail prices, which sometimes vary within the same general area. Some set prices higher than the paper's "suggested retail price," seeking higher profit by delivering fewer papers at higher prices, and that can contradict the newspaper's strategy of seeking greater circulation.

Distributors establish their own routes and territories; sometimes the results fit the paper's overall circulation and advertising strategies and sometimes they don't. In extreme cases, management virtually loses control over its own product. Once lost, control of pricing and sale of the paper can be difficult to regain.

Any attempt to force independent contract distributors to do things the newspaper's way can significantly increase exposure to antitrust charges. Courts have long held that in certain circumstances a newspaper's efforts to control retail prices that independent distributors charge subscribers can be an antitrust violation per se. A price agreement between a newspaper and a distributor can be construed as a "vertical agreement" to fix prices, which is prohibited by Section I of the Sherman Act. ("Horizontal" agreement—say, conspiracy between two distributors in adjacent territories to fix prices—also is prohibited.)

If you use independent contract distributors, you must restrict yourself to issuing "suggested" retail prices, and be careful how you do that. You will be tempted to subtly, indirectly force distributors to toe a price line or try to set mandatory upper and lower price ranges. Resist the temptation. It is dangerous.

You must seek expert legal counsel if you want to establish territorial boundaries for your independent contract distributors. Dividing a market between them can be illegal under Section I of the Sherman Act if it tends to lessen competition. Under some circumstances, particularly if competition is increased, a vertical agreement between newspaper and distributor on territorial boundaries may be acceptable. But don't make a move without counsel's approval. Note that prohibited division of a market can include not only cutting it up along territorial boundaries but also by types of products to be sold within the market or types of subscribers or purchasers to be approached.

If you use independent contract carriers, new approaches to circulation strategy dictate that you should at least study switching to another system. But changing can create problems.

First, there are operational problems of terminating arrangements that may be decades old. Choices for a new system are an employee carrier force, under which you are free to set retail prices and fix territories, or an agent system, under which you hire independent individuals or companies to merely deliver papers. Note the distinction: An agent does not purchase papers for resale, thus you can control pricing as well as territorial and other operational factors.

Second, independent contract carriers sometimes sue a newspaper that terminates their contracts, demanding compensation for routes or territories. Courts generally have not found routes to be tangible property for which compensation is due. But suits have demanded tens of thousands of dollars and are costly to defend against. Seek counsel before risking suit by terminating agreements.

Third, your newspaper could be vulnerable to FTC action if competition is lessened in any way by terminating agreements with independent contractors and taking over their territories.

Other Problem Areas

Other potentially troublesome areas in circulation to watch:

1. Antitrust laws on tie-in agreements can prohibit forcing a distributor to purchase one product to get another—for example, a morning paper to obtain the afternoon paper if the papers are separate products and competition would be lessened. Courts generally hold that separate editions of the same newspaper are not separate products. The issue arose when one paper was charged with illegally tying its Saturday edition to the Monday–Friday editions; the issue was decided in the paper's favor. A suit brought in Maine by three subscribers charged a paper with illegally tying its Sunday edition to the weekday editions. Many daily papers "force" their Sunday editions, meaning, in newspaper parlance, that they automatically include it in a subscription for the daily paper. This could be legally delicate in the future.

2. Refusal to deal with, say, an uncooperative independent contract distributor can be prohibited if the newspaper has consulted third parties—subscribers or other distributors, for example—and if courts find the newspaper has illegal objectives. This can arise if a newspaper refuses to deal with a distributor who will not follow "suggested" pricing, for example, or who refuses to handle both morning and afternoon newspapers. Generally, however, a newspaper is free, unilaterally, to refuse to deal with a buyer of any kind.

3. News racks and vending machines can create problems because some municipalities try to limit their numbers and locations for aesthetic reasons or, more importantly, tax them to raise new revenue. Absent larger legal issues, local counsel should handle such incidents on a case-by-case basis.

4. Sampling or free distribution of a newspaper as an inducement to subscribe occasionally ends up in court. Some courts hold that, under certain circumstances, intense sampling in the sale area for, say, five to ten weeks is excessive; two weeks has been held to be usual. The issue in longer sampling is whether a newspaper is unfairly undercutting competition by giving away papers.

IN POSTAL LAW: WORDY COMPLEXITY

Thousands of words are used in regulations governing first-, second-, third- and fourth-class mail. Second class is the primary vehicle used to mail most paid-circulation newspapers. Regulations frequently change.

So your first mission is to stay current by maintaining effective relations with the local postmaster. Second, you must watch NAA and other trade groups for early signals of shifts in regulations that affect newspapers.

Papers relying heavily on mail delivery should obtain the *Domestic Mail Manual* and subscribe to the *Postal Bulletin,* which announces manual changes. A "Book and Pamphlet Order Form" is contained in Publication 113, which may be obtained from your local post office. Order both the manual and bulletin from the Superintendent of Documents, U.S. Government Printing Office, Washington, D.C. 10402. Improper use of the mail can increase your newspaper's costs tremendously or even jeopardize its mailing permit.

The Rate Controversy

The hottest controversy over postal regulations stems from newspaper competition with direct mail. Because this involves both the costs of your newspaper and those of your competitors, you must be alert to its implications.

Watch these factors: Relatively low second-class rates and expeditious delivery are available to newspapers (and other publications) that are issued at least four times annually at stated intervals (daily, weekly, monthly, etc.), are formed of printed sheets (not stenciled or mimeographed), and are sold for more than a nominal price.

To qualify, newspapers must have a list of subscribers more than half of whom pay ("51 percent rule") and must disseminate information of a public character. The newspapers must not contain more than 75 percent advertising in more than half of their issues in any single year and must meet certain other Postal Service requirements.

Second-class rates for newspapers meeting those specifications are calculated from factors including weight, distance and number of pieces mailed. Since Colonial days, when Congress decided for the public good to encourage the dissemination of information through mail, second-class rates have been lower than those for other classes.

With expansion of direct mail competition has come explosive growth in third-class mail, the category used by most direct mail companies. Some newspaper strategists say the Postal Service tries to increase its own revenues by creating specially favorable conditions for third-class users. A Postal Task Force, operated by NAA to counterattack, argues the Postal Service carries a great deal of third-class mail for too little revenue. One study showed third-class was 34 percent of mail delivered but yielded only 15 percent of Postal Service revenue.

The Postal Service keeps third-class rates low so its competitors, including newspapers, won't take over delivery of advertising circulars, the task force says. Those circulars, of course, constitute much of direct mail's business. Postal Service executives respond that third-class mail pays for itself, isn't subsidized by first-class rates (as the task force charges) and that newspapers simply are complaining about an aggressive competitor, direct mail.[6]

Check Controlled-Circulation Rates

If you are publishing free-circulation papers—or competing against them—investigate controlled-circulation mail rates, a special rate category established for newspapers without sufficient paid circulation to qualify for second-class rates. Controlled-circulation rates give a free-circulation paper the enormous cost advantage of second-class rates, which are substantially lower in general than third-class rates, plus what postal regulations describe as "newspaper treatment"—that is, faster delivery.

To qualify for controlled-circulation rates, a publication must be issued at least four times annually at regular intervals. Each issue must contain at least 25 percent nonadvertising content and have at least 24 pages. It cannot be published primarily to promote the main business of an individual or company. It must be able to prove to postal officials that more than 50 percent of its recipient households want to receive it (many establish this through return mail cards enclosed in the newspaper or recorded telephone surveys).

Other Postal Issues to Watch

"Red-tag" handling in post offices gives newspapers and weekly magazines special fast delivery because of their timely content. Make sure your newspaper is, in fact, receiving it. Since 1984, all publications mailed second-class, not just dailies and weeklies, get red-tag treatment and you must be certain that delivery of your paper isn't delayed by the increased volume. Have a copy of your paper mailed to your home as a cross-check on delivery delays.

If you are launching a newspaper and newly requesting a second-class postal permit, you must mail via third class until the Postal Service approves the request. In the interim, be sure the local postmaster records your third-class costs on Form 3503. When the second-class permit is in hand (the process can take months), you are due a refund on the difference between your actual third-class costs and what second-class postage would have been. If no Form 3503 is kept, the refund may be impossible to collect.

When the second-class permit is issued, be sure your newspaper conforms to postal regulations by publishing each day, somewhere in its first five pages, this information: date of issue, frequency of publication, consecutive issue number, subscription price, name, address of office and the statement: "Second-class postage paid (city, state, zip code)." If mailed from other offices, the statement should add, "and additional mailing offices."

The name and publication number must be carried on the front page of each issue, along with the number of sections in the issue. Each section, in turn, must carry on its front page the publication's name. Annually, on or before Oct. 1, a newspaper using second-class mail must file a statement of ownership and circulation. Obtain forms from the local postmaster. Throughout, your primary concern must be to protect the newspaper's second-class permit and rates.

Special problems can arise from the insertion and delivery in the newspaper of advertising supplements—material that might otherwise be mailed third class. Postal regulations specify in great detail the types of material that may be carried as supplements, how they are to be labeled and the rates that can be charged.

Carrying unacceptable material as a supplement can result in higher third-class rates being charged for the entire paper. Sit down with the local postmaster and get guarantees that your newspaper's approach is correct. If things cannot be worked out, there are appeal avenues on all subjects, including classification of mail, rates and cancellation of privilege.

IN PERSONAL MANAGEMENT: A MYRIAD OF LAWS

Yet another legally complex responsibility awaits you in labor matters. You have three broad areas of concern:

- Discrimination in hiring and employment
- Terms and conditions of employment
- Regulations of workplace environment, health and safety

Many federal, state and, often, local laws are important to you as a manager in labor matters. There is aggressive government intervention to be concerned about. Also, individual employees are willing, if not eager, to sue for real or imagined wrongs on the job. Work with counsel on programs that ensure your newspaper conforms to the law and, if trouble occurs, that it defends itself properly.

Root out Discrimination

There is enormous legal (and societal) pressure on newspapers, like all businesses, to eliminate discrimination based on color, race, sex, religion, national origin or age. The Equal Employment Opportunity Commission (EEOC) additionally requires you to take affirmative action in hiring and promoting women, blacks and other minorities. The EEOC's basic task is enforcement of Title VII of the Civil Rights Act of 1964, the seminal legislation for federal involvement.

Take affirmative action that not only ensures conformity with law but also strengthens your paper operationally by including in the work force and promoting to upper management qualified individuals of merit and skills from all sectors of the newspaper's environment. Top management must be directly and enthusiastically involved. A written statement of policy should be issued to all employees and made a permanent part of the newspaper's public stance.

To ensure accountability, a senior manager should be assigned responsibility for making the program work. Specific goals should be set for recruiting and training minorities. Periodic monitoring of progress should be part of the program.

Cleanse Hiring Practices

Charges of discrimination often arise from interviews of prospective employees and from hiring practices. If 20 persons apply for a single vacancy, 19 are disappointed, perhaps hurt or angrily thinking they were discriminated against. This, then, is one of those particularly sensitive links in the management chain where careful handling is needed.

EEOC guidelines require that your selection process not only be nondiscriminatory but avoid the "adverse impact" of screening out individuals by establishing standards not tightly tied to job performance. That is, requiring a college degree for a forklift operator's job could draw trouble. With counsel's assistance, you should review your entire hiring process. Some pointers:

1. Put the hiring process in the hands of experts sensitive to the human factors involved as well as disciplined in the law's requirements. Those who interview, particularly, must be personally committed to your affirmative action program.

2. Be sure that advertisements or announcements of job openings conform to EEOC guidelines on nondiscrimination. Avoid language seeking, for example, "young" applicants. Age discriminant suits are increasing in number.

3. Examine all form letters, applications, tests, job specifications or other documents used in the hiring process and eliminate language that might be discriminatory or have "adverse impact."

4. Be sure application forms state they will be void after a specified period. Inform all applicants new forms must be submitted by anyone desiring consideration after the specified period that ends in, say, 30 or 60 days.

5. Be sure your system and employees who direct it treat people professionally and whenever possible, gently. The lawsuit is a club for an angry employee. Let counsel establish procedures for informing unsuccessful applicants they won't be hired; you make sure that however the response is cloaked in legalisms, the unsuccessful are let down gently.

Check Pay, Terms and Conditions

You also must examine terms and conditions of employment to ensure that nondiscriminatory and affirmative action procedures continue in the workplace. Here are some areas to watch:

Pay scales and job assignments must be nondiscriminatory. That means *no disparities* based on race, sex, color, religion, national origin or age in any sector—overtime, fringe benefits, vacation and so on. Much litigation stems from alleged discrimination between male and female, black and white employees. Be certain that differences in work conditions or treatment are not founded in race or sex.

There is controversy over the "comparable worth" theory, which holds that comparable wages must be paid for different jobs if the skills used, responsibility required and effort put forth are similar. The issue sometimes arises when women working as secretaries feel underpaid in relation to, for example, truck drivers. The theory hasn't been raised often in the newspaper industry, but be aware of the controversy.

There must, of course, be no sexual harassment in the workplace. Yesteryear's crude, offensive "macho" remark to a woman employee today can be all of that—and decidedly illegal as well.

Training opportunities must be made available to employees on a nondiscriminatory basis. On-job performance must be monitored and appraised with equality.

Promotion possibilities should be opened without regard to race, sex, color, religion, national origin or sex. Discipline or discharge must be handled similarly.

Here are some general guidelines:

Taking affirmative action is not only the right thing to do but also makes business sense. Better that you implement progressive personnel policies conforming to society's expectations and the law than wait for visits from unfriendly EEOC investigators or lawyers representing disgruntled employees. Look on affirmative action with enthusiasm as a modern management tool you can turn to good advantage.

An affirmative action program is only as effective as your front-line supervisors. If they are not enthusiastically implementing the program, it can collapse or, worse, create conditions that cause lengthy, expensive and damaging lawsuits. Monitor their implementation of your policies.

Don't get so enthusiastic that you become trapped in reverse discrimination. Don't open so many rich opportunities for one group of employees that you unwittingly discriminate against another. The same balance and standards for all are an absolute must.

Remember: Nothing is off the record anymore—not a casual remark in the cafeteria, not a hurriedly typed memo slipped into a forgotten file. In a lawsuit, anything on paper—and a lot more—can be dredged up.

Watch Other Labor-Legal Areas

EEOC is not your only legal concern in labor policy. The federal Fair Labor Standards Act, enforced by the U.S. Labor Department, sets stringent regulations for minimum wage and overtime payment. Work above 40 hours in one week must be compensated at the rate of $1\frac{1}{2}$ times base pay. The Labor Department's Wage and Hour Division will act against papers that don't properly compensate employees for overtime worked. Beware the editor who works reporters overtime but, to keep the newsroom budget in shape, quietly discourages them from claiming overtime pay. The Wage and Hour Division can sue for reimbursement plus hefty damages and penalties.

The overtime issue has long been troublesome with journalists who work irregular hours. Under "Belo" contracts, newspapers are permitted to reach individual agreements with employees and to gain certain exemptions from wage and labor laws. These contracts, initiated by Belo Corp., owner of *The Dallas Morning News,* involve newspapers and employees who work varying hours agreeing on certain compensation arrangements which include overtime pay.

The overtime issued surfaced when the *Concord (N.H.) Monitor,* charged with not paying appropriate overtime, went into court to argue reporters, photographers and nonsupervisory editors should be considered "professionals" exempt from overtime laws. The *Monitor* lost.

Also beware of child labor laws. You may be in trouble if a well-meaning 15-year-old carrier jumps on a forklift to move bundles in the mailroom. The Fair Labor Standards Act prohibits that and closely regulates employment of persons under age 16. Carriers are exempt from the act's regulations on pay and its child labor provisions provided they deliver the paper exclusively to the final consumer. Any other kind of work can be a serious violation of state and federal laws.

The Employee Retirement Income Security Act of 1974 (ERISA) regulates benefit plans and some pension plans. It does not require the establishment of programs but lays down voluminous guidelines for those papers that do.

The Occupational Safety and Health Act of 1970 (OSHA) opened newspaper plants to an aggressive new government agency determined to improve the job-related safety and health of workers. Armed with warrants, if necessary, OSHA inspectors can check a plant for unhealthy, unsafe conditions. Fines are meted out for violations. States also set safety standards.

New technology—particularly the switch from hot metal to cold type—removed many dangerous jobs from newspaper production. But OSHA demonstrates concern over noise levels, particularly in pressrooms, and dangers from fast presses. OSHA regulations require employers to record injuries and illnesses among the work force. Details are available in the Compliance Operations Manual, OSHA No. 2006, obtainable from the Superintendent of Documents, Government Printing Office, Washington, D.C. 20402.

IN COPYRIGHT: BEWARE

Copyright protection is available automatically with publication of the paper. Two additional steps should be taken: First, publish on the front page each day the statement, "Copyright © (year) The Daily Herald." Sending two copies of the newspaper via second-class mail within three months to the Library of Congress, Washington, D.C. 10559 fulfills the requirement. Second, the copyright should be registered. Only with registration will a paper be able to sue for copyright infringement. Registration, for a nominal fee, is accomplished through the U.S. Copyright Office, Registrar of Copyrights, Library of Congress, Washington, D.C. 20559.

The Copyright Act gives an author exclusive right to control publication and distribution of a work. Under federal law, the "fair use" doctrine grants an important exception: Copyrighted material may be used under certain conditions for "criticism, comment, news reporting, teaching, scholarship or research. . . ."

Until 1985, newspapers widely reprinted brief excerpts of copyrighted material (up to 300 words was a rule of thumb) and claimed "fair use" protection. In 1985, however, the U.S. Supreme Court held that *The Nation* magazine had infringed on former President Gerald R. Ford's copyright on his memoirs with unauthorized publication of quotations from his book before it was published. The ruling strengthens the copyright holder's right to first publication. Newspapers and others may be in legal jeopardy if they "scoop" the copyright holder—if they publish material and then claim a First Amendment right on the grounds that it was newsworthy.

SUMMARY

Every manager should be keenly aware of the litigious environment in which newspapers operate today. Lawsuits against newspapers are proliferating. Huge judgments are sought; simply paying defense costs can be financially destabilizing. The most dangerous legal threats come in libel, antitrust and Equal Employment Opportunity violations. Newspapers also face legal difficulties in advertising and circulation operations.

Legal counsel must ensure the paper's policies conform to the law. Detailed libel instruction must be given to both newsroom and ad staffs. Most libel stems from sloppy reporting; root it out. Libel manuals must be on all news desks; seminars in libel should be given by the paper's lawyer.

Antitrust violations are potentially dangerous. Suits often follow the introduction of new competitors, such as shoppers, into a market occupied by an established daily or weekly. Be sure legal counsel helps plan any significant move you make in your marketplace under such conditions. Advertising and circulation departments must be certain their operations do not include activities prohibited under antitrust law.

In *all* matters even remotely smacking of legal difficulties, call in the lawyers. Law as it affects newspapers is extraordinarily complicated, and it is getting more so every day.

RECOMMENDED READING

The Newspaper Association of America regularly flags important legal developments with articles in *presstime* and announcements by its vice president/general counsel. *The New York Times*, *The Wall Street Journal* and *Baltimore Sun* carry superb legal coverage, particularly of the U.S. Supreme Court. Also note *American Journalism Review, Editor & Publisher,* and *Columbia Journalism Review,* all of which cover legal affairs.

A very effective textbook is Kent R. Middleton and Bill F. Chamberlin, *The Law of Public Communication,* 3rd ed. (White Plains, N.Y.: Longman, 1994). For quick updates on libel and privacy contact the Libel Defense Resource Center, 708 Third Ave., New York, N.Y. 10017.

NOTES

1. Libel actions and awards are tracked by Libel Defense Resource Center, a group located in New York City and supported by the newspaper industry. Its findings are used in this section of Chapter 12. For details, see Alex S. Jones, "Libel Study Finds Juries Penalizing News Media," *The New York Times,* national edition, Sept. 26, 1991, p. A-13; "Average Libel Award Skyrockets Upward," *presstime,* Oct. 1992, p. 35; "Update," *New York Law Journal,* Feb. 7, 1994, p. 1; Junda Woo, "Juries' Libel

Awards Are Soaring With Several Topping $10 Million," *The Wall Street Journal,* Aug. 26, 1992, p. B-3.

2. John Curley, "How Libel Suit Sapped the Crusading Spirit of a Small Newspaper," *Wall Street Journal,* Sept. 29, 1983, p. 1.

3. Steve Weinberg, "Libel: The Press Fights Back," *Columbia Journalism Review,* Nov. 1983, p. 65.

4. *"Charleston Gazette* Continues Fight Against Unwarranted Suits," Southern Newspaper Publishers Association *Bulletin,* June 1, 1984, p. 2.

5. See P. Cameron DeVore, "Commercial Speech's Second Chance," *presstime,* June 1993, p. 62; and

Steven W. Colford, "Big Win for Commercial Speech," *Advertising Age,* March 29, 1993, p. 1. The case was *Cincinnati v. Discovery Network, Inc.,* decided March 24, 1993.

6. The issue surfaced strongly in 1984. See Otto Silha, "The Impact of 'Junk Mail' on Postal Rates and the Newspaper Business," a speech to the International Newspaper Advertising and Marketing Executives annual conference, New Orleans, Jan. 29, 1984. For the Postal Service view see William F. Bolger, "The Post Office Point of View," speech to American Newspaper Publishers Association, Montreal, May 1, 1984.

13

PUBLIC TRUST AND MANAGER ETHICS

Your study of management in this book necessarily focuses on the *business* of newspapering. But no manager can forget that ours is a business with unique historic and societal responsibilities to operate newspapers for much more than making a profit and keeping shareholders happy.

Since the days of the Founding Fathers, newspapers have assumed—and been given by society—responsibilities to inform and enlighten, to foster public discussion, to create a marketplace of ideas and facilitate the democratic consensus that guides the nation. As a newspaper manager, then, you must not only guard the bottom line—you must be in the front line of fighting for the public's First Amendment rights, serving the public's need to know and acting as surrogate of the governed in their relationship with those who govern.

At times, meeting those obligations can be burdensome for a manager and, even, harmful to the bottom line. So, why add concern for public trust and ethics to all the other managerial matters you must worry about? Three reasons: First, a newspaper has enormous power in both the marketplace of ideas and the commercial marketplace. Using that power in an ethical, socially responsible manner is the *right thing to do.*

Second, free-circulation advertising shoppers don't assign watchdog reporters to the county courthouse. Direct mail companies don't investigate bureaucratic inefficiencies in Washington. Radio and television, with notable exceptions, race to entertain but lag in defending the people's right to know. Cable TV doesn't walk patrol. You and your newspaper must. Third, keep in mind that ethical, journalistically sound newspapers have the best chance of flourishing over the long term. Simply put, *responsible business practices are good business.*

So, rejoice in the heavy social responsibility that falls to newspapers. By accepting the public trust with sincere, professional dedication, you can help your newspaper meet its historic imperative and secure for itself a meaningful and prosperous future.

ETHICS: THE COSTS AND BENEFITS

You'll soon get frustrated if you take to ethics the same cost/benefit approach you apply to other sectors of newspaper management. Simply put, it's impossible to prove that short-term, bottom-line benefits pay back the often steep costs of ethically and responsibly serving readers, advertisers and community.

The *costs* of responsible management are stiff, immediate and can be calculated with precision. For example, adding another seasoned county courthouse reporter will cost a newspaper, say, a minimum of $30,000 to $35,000 in annual salary, plus perhaps $10,500 to $12,500 in benefits and other related costs—somewhere around $40,500 to $47,500 to hire one reporter to shine light in dark corners over there. Assigning a single foreign correspondent to Hong Kong can cost easily $300,000 to $350,000 annually.

The *benefits* of socially responsible journalism are less tangible. After all, how many extra subscriptions will be sold because of better courthouse coverage? Are readers really interested in staff coverage of Hong Kong and can that $300,000 to $350,000 cost be translated into new, commensurate advertising revenue?

And, as you consider your ethical responsibilities, you inevitably will ask yourself this question: Don't some newspapers skimp on news coverage, rejecting any larger societal responsibility, and *still* do well financially? Conversely, haven't some fine newspapers, strong in news coverage and courageous in editorial stands, failed in recent decades?

The answer to those questions, of course, is yes. There is strong evidence that a newspaper's faithful, long-term pursuit of excellence and unswerving service to public trust will help assure financial success over the long term. But there is no *proof.*[1]

So, you may ask, is ethics and societal responsibility an area where the dollars-and-cents cost/benefits approach extolled in this book comes up lacking? Is this an area where you, as a manager, should instinctively accept the proposition that a newspaper has a greater responsibility than simply seeking ever-improved profits? I suggest the answer is yes, that practicing high-quality, principled journalism is a newspaper's *duty* and that to reject that duty is to commit treason against higher ideals.

Ethical ideals, however, must be related to the everyday reality that your newspaper must show a profit. One depends on the other. An ill-managed newspaper that cuts newsroom staff becomes a mockery; a newspaper that fails financially fails totally.

Early in their careers, young aspiring managers must sort all that out and construct an ethical approach relating higher ideals to daily reality. As a first-line supervisor, your task will be to demonstrate for every employee your personal commitment to ethical, socially responsible journalism and business methods. As a member of top management—an owner, perhaps—you will set the tone for the newspaper's ethical stance. If top management is not committed, the staff will not be either.

FIGURE 13.1   New technology creates new ethical problems: computerized editing makes it possible to rearrange, add or delete elements in a photo. Note that in the doctored version (bottom) a reflection is removed from the background window in the original photo (top.) Can you spot three other changes? Editors generally agree that such manipulation of photos is highly unethical. Experimental manipulation by Dick Van Halesma, *Charlotte (NC) Observer,* courtesy Knight-Ridder.

In days past, managers often created a shareholder-oriented newspaper dedicated to profit with little regard for societal responsibilities much beyond sponsoring the local Soap Box Derby each year. True, many newsrooms took a wider view that journalistically a newspaper had deeper responsibilities. But as businesses, many newspapers were run in a much narrower way.

Today, enlightened self-interest is a necessity in your managerial duties. Boards of directors must be reconstituted to reflect more accurately the social and ethnic composition of newspaper marketplaces. Companies must structure a modern outlook on questions of social responsibility and ethics. These questions arise in all sectors of management.

ETHICS FOR THE MANAGER

When *The Washington Post* led journalism's investigation of the Nixon administration during Watergate, then publisher Katharine Graham had widespread backing among press peers plus significant (but far from unanimous) public support. So did Arthur Ochs Sulzberger when he and his *New York Times* editors defied the same powerful Nixon administration and published the previously secret Pentagon Papers, with their revealing insights into U.S. conduct of the Vietnam War. With dramatic boldness and the public spotlight full on them, both publishers made decisions that gained their newspapers secure places in U.S. journalism history.

For you as a manager, the tests of ethical resolve, the crises of professional conscience, probably won't come with such historic clarity. And in meeting the test, you may stand alone; the world may not take note, may not care.

Your test, for example, may be the town's leading citizen pleading (demanding?) that his name, heretofore unblemished, be withheld from tomorrow's "Court Notes" column, where *all* arrests for drunk driving are normally recorded. He *is* a nice fellow; what's the harm? It may be the chamber of commerce suggesting that your newspaper back off its investigation of local toxic waste dumps. It's bad for business and, after all, what is bad for business *is* bad for the newspaper. Or the test may be the leading advertiser in town subtly hinting at an off-card rebate, just a quiet little deal recognizing his importance to the paper. He *is* important, and who is to know? Your test may be an urge you feel to invest privately in a controversial real estate development your newspaper supports editorially.

Thus, in various forms and guises, often innocent in appearance and cloaked in good intentions, ethical challenges sneak up on today's newspaper manager. As a manager, you must do more than take steps to ensure that the paper avoids unethical conflicts of interest. You must ensure that it avoids even the *appearance* of an ethical lapse.

How about an Ethics Code?

Many newspapers have written codes of ethics. Most are for newsrooms; fewer for the management suite. There is legitimate concern that reducing ethical principles to a comprehensive, written code is dangerous in this litigious era. Some lawyers say a paper could be vulnerable in a libel suit, for example, if its coverage of a story provably strayed from its own written guidelines. Would not that in itself be damaging evidence of error or malice? Or, some editors say, widespread voluntary adoption of a written code could lead to demands by government and others that the code be used for regulation—or licensing—of the press.

But press critics ask: Absent written, enforceable codes, who watches the watchdog? The answer, of course, is that with each edition, a newspaper subjects itself to scrutiny anew. Day after day, reporters and editors put their best and worst on full public display and risk economic retaliation in the marketplace. The critics number 60 million—those who buy daily papers every day; more than 55 million judge weeklies each week. Their ability to stop buying tomorrow is a powerful incentive for you to serve them well.

So, the watchdog is watched in a very real sense by millions of other watchdogs. Yet, there is no formal, disciplined or truly effective critique of the press from any widely respected groups outside the industry itself. In large measure, this stems from the reluctance—outright refusal, mostly—of newspaper editors and managers to cooperate in establishing formal watchdog groups or to listen seriously to those that spring up independently. Submitting to reader and advertiser judgments daily is sufficient for many editors and managers; others are unimpressed with the professional quality of outside criticism or sense that much of it comes, tainted, from highly partisan groups. Probably most important is the fear that submitting voluntarily to even informal judgment by outsiders inevitably will lead to formal licensing or other infringements on First Amendment rights.

The National News Council, funded in 1973 by the Twentieth Century Fund, tried for a decade to establish effective monitoring procedures with press cooperation. It failed from lack of media support. Accuracy in Media, with conservative principles and backing, spends millions to critique the press but is regarded by many editors as highly partisan. Journalism schools generally lack effective links with newspapers in this regard. Much academic research and commentary never finds its way into newspaper strategy.

Journalism reviews—*Columbia Journalism Review* and *American Journalism Review* among them—win some credence among editors and publishers. But few journals focus on ethics outside the newsroom.

Effective critiques of *newsroom* management come from the Associated Press Managing Editors Association and the American Society of Newspaper Editors, but those insider groups are not perceived by the public as truly dispassionate critics. Newspaper Association of America, the leading trade organization for publishers and managers, concentrates mostly on effective operating methods, not principally on ethics and societal responsibility.

In critiquing themselves, only about 30 newspapers (out of 1,570 dailies) create internal watchdogs—ombudsmen—and let them represent the public by reporting on ethical questions arising out of daily newsroom operations. Even fewer newspapers assign significant staff resources to cover journalism or the business of journalism as a news story. (Among those that do are *The New York Times, The Washington Post, Los Angeles Times,* and *The Wall Street Journal.*)

In sum, it is only in the marketplace, in the daily decision on whether or not to buy, that there is any external and effective watch on the watchdog. However, whether ethical principles are enunciated orally or in writing, newspapers increasingly are shaping internal standards of conduct in advertising, the publisher's office and news. Let's look at each sector where you might want to direct your manager's scrutiny.

Ethics in the Newsroom

Newspapers never have been without critics. But, like many institutions in modern society, newspapers are coming under attacks more numerous and serious than ever. It is the newsroom, of course, that each day places its efforts before the public and thus receives the brunt of criticism. And it is in the newsroom that you will find managers indulging in very heavy self-criticism and analysis on ethical issues.

There is no rulebook of ethics. Newspapers have come up with a few general guidelines, but even they are far from unanimously accepted. For you as an aspiring manager, the importance of what follows is not that I provide *answers* but that, perhaps, I *sketch some questions* that you should start asking yourself as you firm up your own approach to ethical issues.

INVASION OF PRIVACY

This is a troublesome area for many newsroom managers who attempt to balance respect for the individual's right to privacy against the newspaper's duty to inform the public about matters of significance.

A general subscription to both seemingly conflicting principles is as far as any ethical code can go. There must be case-by-case decisions on where to draw the line between desire to shield the innocent from the glare of unwanted publicity and the professional commitment to shine the public's spotlight in truly important dark corners.

Few ethical problems create so many gray areas. For example, Bill Clinton's character and qualifications to be president of the United States *were* matters of public interest. But was it necessary for reporters to pursue lurid details of the private life he lived years before he became a candidate? A woman held hostage by her estranged husband in Florida *was* involved—unwillingly—in news of public significance. But was it in the public interest to publish a photograph of her—nearly naked—fleeing her home? In both instances, newsroom managers decided to publish—and, as in similar incidents, drew intense public criticism that sent many editors into agonizing reappraisal of the privacy issue.

Most editors, however, stop short of any definitive policy statement, aiming instead at sensitizing their staffs to weigh the individual's right to privacy against the public's right to know—and, in a close call, to come down on the side of serving that larger constituency, the public, with full disclosure.

Free Press and Fair Trial

You've seen the photographs, of course, and read the stories: *accused* rapists, in handcuffs and eyes downcast, being led from police cruiser to jail; *accused* child abusers—from Catholic cardinal to day-care center employee—protesting innocence before the unbelieving cameras.

Many press critics, lawyers and also editors see such coverage as a conflict between the First Amendment guarantee of a free press and the Sixth Amendment guarantee of a fair trial. The issue is not the public's *right* to know; rather, it's a question of *need* to know, if publication precludes fair trial. Editors frequently argue that the Sixth Amendment guarantees trial by *unbiased* jurors—not jurors totally ignorant of the case—and that there need to be no conflict with the First Amendment.

Nevertheless, extensive coverage that tends to convict a defendant in the public eye before trial bothers many jurists and news executives alike. On this issue, there surely will be increased tension between the press and the courts.

Covering or Making the News

Just as geese fly north each spring, so do predictable news stories break into print on an almost seasonal basis. A typical one might come in springtime from a bass-fishing lake in the Deep South, reporting that a renowned left-hander, possessor of the world's best-ever fastball, won't report to baseball training camp until his salary is increased. Back come reports from team headquarters that the salary demand is outrageous, that the holdout can continue fishing until the lake freezes over. Thus starts the bargaining—and the press injects itself into the process as a vehicle for the public exchange of demands and counterdemands.

Is that reporting or *making* the news? Do political reporters report or make news by carrying charges and countercharges from candidate to opponent and back again? When a business news writer initiates an interview and develops news that moves stock prices, is that reporter making or reporting news?

Business reporting creates ethical problems with increasing frequency. The problems stem not so much from those occasions when reporters betray the trust of their newspapers (and public) by trading and profiting on inside information before sharing it with their readers. As spectacularly unethical (and perhaps illegal) as such practices are, these betrayals are clear violations of trust and punishable by discharge. The code—written or unwritten—is clear on that. Rather, problems arise in gray areas, such as the following.

Business-world rumor can be self-serving and can cause profound marketplace changes. A rumor of a corporate takeover attempt, for example, can boost or depress stock prices in minutes. Yet business news sections regularly publish rumors (often upgraded to "industry reports"). Should they? If the answer is no, how does that square with the press's responsibility to dig out the news, wherever it is, and publish it?

Should business writers, like political candidates, disclose their personal finances? Should they avoid any suspicion of insider trading by refusing to handle a story about a company in which they have invested? Some publications require reporters to inform management of their holdings and to step aside from stories that would involve potential conflicts of interest. None requires reporters to inform the reading public.

Some business stories can be self-fulfilling. Reporting a withdrawal run on a bank, for example, can create panic. Yet newspapers have a responsibility to inform readers of developments affecting their lives, and many editors agree that this might have to include shouting "financial fire" outside the bank. But it is a heavy responsibility that causes grave editors concern for many business news editors and their publishers.

Personal Involvement in the News

There is, obviously, life outside the newsroom and editors and reporters must live it. Can you as a manager dictate *how* they should live it? To greater or lesser degree, many managers say yes. Examples:

- A reporter wins election to a school board. Even if that reporter doesn't cover education news, has the reporter changed hats and become an activist? Importantly, has this created doubt about the newspaper's objectivity? The *Knoxville (Tenn.) News-Sentinel* answered yes to both questions and fired a reporter newly elected to the school board of Alcoa, Tenn.
- Should a newspaper move to avoid appearance of conflict of interest involving even *spouses* of staff members? The *Seattle Times* did. It told its managing editor he would lose his job if his wife became the mayor's press secretary. She declined the job.

Some newspaper people become the news—for example, reporters and columnists who use fame achieved through newspaper publication to command huge fees for lectures. Washington columnists sometimes earn $10,000 or more for a single speech, and some become national "personalities."

Columnist George Will was the center of one celebrated flap over outside activity. It was revealed that he helped Ronald Reagan's staff prepare for debates with President Carter. The *New York Daily News* promptly dropped Will's column, saying he had violated journalistic ethics (the *News* later reinstated the column). Other papers said Will was a declared conservative paid to express his views, and that they saw no ethical problem. Many managers prohibit employees from taking outside employment that might create conflict of interest.

You should prohibit conduct that casts doubt on your newspaper's objectivity. Accepting gifts from news sources or participants in the news must be prohibited, and so must free press tours. "Junkets" are out.

Cooperation with Authorities

Press cooperation with police or other authorities can cause grave editorial dilemmas—as when, for example, lives are at stake and the press, like any citizen, is asked to help save them. A *New York Daily News* reporter served as intermediary between police and a prisoner holding hostages in a Brooklyn hospital. An AP reporter was the link between Washington, D.C., police and a man threatening to blow up the Washington Memorial.

At risk to themselves, other reporters have played similar roles. Should they? Should reporters step out of observer ranks and become participants? Can a press that participates in the news-making process hope to be impartial or to be perceived by its reading public as impartial?

There is a long history of press cooperation with police in certain crime situations. Newspapers often cooperate by withholding precise details of tactics used by antiterrorist police to enter skyjacked airlines to free hostages. They do so to prevent future terrorists from benefiting.

But such *cooperation* is quite different from *participation* as a prime mover. And while the former is generally deemed acceptable—indeed, necessary—by many newspapers, the latter often is not.

The question of press cooperation arises frequently in matters of national security. There has long been an adversarial relationship between many reporters and government. Tension flared when reporters were excluded from the U.S. invasion of Grenada in 1983. Uneasy accommodation followed during the Gulf War, in 1991, with the Pentagon agreeing to carry pool reporters to represent the entire press corps on operations, consistent that is, with mission security and troop safety.

The controversy over reporting on Grenada and, earlier, Vietnam is multifaceted and includes charges that reporters were unpatriotic. Reporters have known and held military secrets in every U.S. war in this century, and there is no documented case of the press causing failure of a mission or death of U.S. troops. However, reporting has sometimes been embarrassing politically to the government, and that is a major factor in the adversarial relationship.

Sometimes, ethical problems arising from cooperation with authorities are resolved easily: It is possible for a newspaper to discharge its obligation to readers by alerting them, for example, that a murderer is on the loose and simultaneously accede to police requests not to publish exact details of his gory methods that might inspire "copycat" criminals.

Generally, however, questions of cooperation with authorities defy such easy answers. Each case requires careful consideration in light of what role the press plays: Is it simply an objective, dispassionate observer whose mission is to serve that broadest of constituencies, the public, or is it an observer that on occasion must become a participant?

As a manager, remember: On the firing line, when events are moving rapidly, the judgment is often difficult to make.

Sources: Revealing and Protecting Them

Major ethical problems often surround news sources. A newspaper is obligated to tell readers the source of news stories and, importantly, the motives the source has in revealing news. It is unfair to ask readers repeatedly to take on blind faith news attributed to "officials" or "sources who declined to be identified." However, sources not granted anonymity sometimes won't reveal important stories—and *that* isn't in the public interest.

So, sparingly, grudgingly, quote anonymous sources selectively when there is real need. A source should be granted anonymity only after much deep thought and agreement between reporter, editor and publisher that the secrecy pledge will be kept. For it might mean jail for somebody on the staff and heavy fines for your newspaper if a judge demands the source be revealed.

Many editors prohibit secret tape-recording of sources, hidden cameras or other "undercover" reportorial techniques except in highly unusual cases. Secret taping, illegal in many states, smacks of dishonesty and fraud. Your newspaper's strength will be built on being a forthright, open and honorable journal of news, information and opinion.

How to Say You're Sorry

Despite rigid editing safeguards and eternal copy-desk vigilance, the hoax, the lie and the distortion have penetrated the pages of many newspapers. What to do when that happens? Come clean. Level with readers. Disclose all. Explain what happened and, yes, you might even say you're sorry.

Some newspapers avoid candid explanations. A "damage control" syndrome calls for quiet internal investigation, private remedial efforts and, at most, guarded discussion with peers at professional meetings of editors. Too often, readers are left in the dark—not that something went wrong; that's obvious. Rather, too often readers don't know why it went wrong or what the newspaper is doing to prevent recurrence. And that carries the stench of cover-up. Probably nothing is more damaging to a newspaper's credibility.

Not much is done for credibility, either, with a coy dismissal of error—"Oops, our slip is showing." And how should readers take the incomplete, unhelpful "The *Bugle* stands by its story"? Refreshingly, some newspapers practice candid full disclosure: *The New York Times* published a story plus editorial explaining how it was hoaxed by a freelance writer on a story about Cambodia. Said *The Times,* in part: "When a newspaper uses precious front-page space, as the *Times* did yesterday, to expose a lie in its own columns, it is trying to do much more than confess a procedural lapse. The point is to reaffirm a compact with the reader: that any credible challenge will be rigorously examined, and that serious error will get prompt and conspicuous notice."[2]

When an airline objected to inaccuracies in a *Wall Street Journal* story, the *Journal* published a lengthy letter from an airline official clarifying the facts, and attached an editor's note acknowledging error. "The Journal stands corrected . . . ," it said.[3]

Many newspapers address possible reader perceptions of unfairness and imbalance even when major error is not involved. For example, when it became clear from reader reaction that a *Milwaukee Journal* story on home buying, carried in an inside section, was misleading, the *Journal* published on its *front* page an article explaining how the story was reported, where its facts came from and why, under later examination, it appeared that, yes, the story was partly misleading. Key to the *Journal*'s treatment was precise dollars-and-cents detail on exactly what was misleading.[4]

Clear the record. Be accountable. That is what we of the press force every day from the institutions and individuals we cover. And that is what we must do with our readers. It's the ethical thing to do.

In sum, a considered, principled approach to newsroom ethics is essential for any newspaper manager today. Whether that approach should be codified in writing is arguable. But written or oral, ethical guidelines must be laid down and the entire staff must be sensitized to your newspaper's responsibility to operate within them. As an aspiring manager, you'll do well to construct your personal code of newsroom ethics around two goals of any newspaper—to search out the truth and serve readers.

ETHICS IN ADVERTISING

As in the news, ethical, principled methods in advertising are foundations of your newspaper's credibility.

Not only for reasons of right or wrong must you fashion credibility in advertising; it is imperative for business reasons.

A *New York Times* veteran, Robert P. Smith, put it this way: "The character of a newspaper is determined not only by its news and editorial content, but also by the advertising it publishes. Those that accept inaccurate, misleading, deceptive or offensive advertising can run the risk of demeaning their most valuable asset—their credibility. That's just plain bad business."[5]

At that writing, Smith had directed *The Times*'s Advertising Acceptability Department for 11 years. Reporting only to the publisher (not the advertising director), Smith was responsible for ensuring that advertising was not illegal or in violation of *Times* policy.

The Times had a detailed code of acceptance for advertising. Smith said it was "nothing more than an accumulation of value judgments—decisions, made on a case-by-case basis, where certain types of advertisements were found to be contrary to the best interests of the *Times* and its readers.... Our decisions in this area are sometimes arbitrary and subjective. We don't deny that. But these decisions, arbitrary or not, must be made if we are to protect the character of our own product. There is no alternative. Either we accept everything that is submitted to us or we're selective. We don't hesitate to be selective."[6]

Among unacceptable ads were those for X-rated movies, mail-order weapons, bust developers, devices to cure illnesses, escort services, speed radar detection devices and fur products made from endangered species.

The Dallas Morning News, like many papers, publishes its code in general terms in its rate card, disclaiming responsibility for ad copy that is legally actionable:

> The Dallas Morning News *reserves the right to reject or revise any copy which it considers not in the public interest, either because said copy is not in keeping with usual newspaper advertising acceptability standards or for any other reason deemed material by the publisher. . . . advertising set to resemble news matter must carry the word "Advertisement" at the top of the advertisement. Newspaper news department type cannot be used in reader ads.*

Managers Must Take the Lead

A selective approach to advertising won't work unless management is strongly committed to it, for rejecting advertising means rejecting money. The *St. Joseph (Mo.) News-Press Gazette* estimated that rejected ads total less than 1 percent of annual ad revenues.[7] That doesn't seem like much, but rejecting 1 percent of the, say, $80 million or $90 million ad revenue that a large daily enjoys could mean, of course, turning away $800,000 to $900,000. All ad takers should be taught to spot questionable ads and send them to the individual charged with reading for acceptability.

Delicate Areas to Watch

Most newspapers refuse to vouch for goods or services offered in advertising. How could any paper check the credentials of all advertisers? And yet, if a newspaper takes pains to present accurate, believable news to readers, does it not have the same moral responsibility toward readers of advertising?

Some newspapers say they do. In Florida, for example, some check whether advertisers of home-improvement services are licensed for competency. The *St. Petersburg Times* started this when two of its reporters discovered that 25 percent of advertisers of roofing, plumbing and electrical services in a *Times* special supplement were not properly licensed. The *Miami Herald* requires such advertisers to show a county occupational license, which is granted only if an applicant is certified in his or her field.[8]

Advocacy advertising can be dangerous and should get full scrutiny in an acceptability program. A full-page ad attributing anti-Israel sentiment to six relief organizations appeared in *The New York Times, Chicago Tribune, The Washington Post* and *Atlanta Journal* and *Constitution.* It was a bogus ad and neither the newspapers nor the ad agency that placed it with them had checked out its originators.

Opinions differ on whether advertising from extremist political groups should be accepted. Some newspapers reject it; not Smith of *The New York Times:* "We've published opinion advertisements representing a wide range of public discourse— from the John Birch Society to the Communist Party. In our view, the First Amendment does not only guarantee a newspaper's right to disseminate news or publish editorials and commercial messages, but it also guarantees the public's right to enter into open discussion in the realm of ideas."[9]

Liquor and cigarette advertising, a major source of revenue for newspapers, is highly controversial. Cigarette advertising must, by law, carry statements of the health hazards of smoking. Newspaper Association of America, among others, argues that First Amendment issues will be raised if stronger warnings are required. NAA says that would result in "substantial expansion of governmental control over the commercial speech of advertisers and, indirectly, over the newspapers printing that speech. . . . Congress should proceed with extreme sensitivity when it considers regulating speech as a method of regulating the use and sale of an entirely legal product." NAA also objects to any move to ban liquor advertising, saying that would abridge commercial free speech and have serious First Amendment implications.

Legal questions aside, it's likely societal pressures, particularly against cigarette advertising, will increase. You make the call: Do newspapers have a moral obligation to refuse advertising for cigarettes, a product which, science says, will kill if used as directed? Front pages carry the latest news on links between smoking and cancer; editorial pages underline the warning. Should advertising pages follow suit? If you think tobacco advertising should be rejected, how about advertising for other products that can kill—guns, for example, or fast cars or speedy motorboats?

The *Seattle Times* banned tobacco ads in 1993, becoming the largest U.S. newspaper to do so. The cost was $100,000 to $150,000 in annual revenue, said President H. Mason Sizemore. The paper's ad base was about $200 million annually. Sizemore recounted the link between smoking and cancer and heart disease, saying, "We just couldn't in conscience be a part of it any more."[10]

Another controversial subject is advertorials, which are ads designed to resemble news stories. Their purpose, of course, is to mislead readers into believing they are reading advertising. Advertorials are regarded as highly successful by some ad agency executives. Pieter Verbeck, executive creative director of Ogilvy & Mather Partners, said people are *five times* more likely to read editorial than ad matter, "so the idea of advertorials is probably a pretty good one." Robert O'Donnell, president of O'Donnell Organization, said, "They're attractive because they look like news . . . no law says advertising has to look like advertising."[11]

For the newspaper, advertorials blur the line between news and advertising and in the long run can harm credibility of both news and ad content. Consequently, many papers have devised signals to readers that they hold an ad, not news, in their hands.

The New York Times publishes a notice that preparation of an ad supplement "did not involve the *Times* reporting or editing staff." *The Wall Street Journal* runs advertorials with body and headline type that is noticeably different in style from that used for *Journal* news copy. Many papers insist on a clear "advertisement" slug atop each advertorial. If readers can peruse an advertorial and not be aware that it is advertising, the newspaper has not met its ethical responsibility.

Sooner or later, pressure from advertisers hits all newspaper managers. Two researchers reported in 1993 that 89.8 percent of 150 editors surveyed said they had been subjected to advertiser pressure—advertisers who pulled ads over news coverage or tried to influence stories.[12]

Resisting such pressure will be a major test of two things: (a) your sense of ethics and responsible, independent management and (b) your ability to diplomatically say no to advertisers who try to buy your news columns (and you *must* say no).

In sum, the best thing you as a manager can do for advertisers is to establish your newspaper's credibility as a principled source of believable news and information that attracts and holds readers. Any advertising practice interfering with that is not in the long-term interests of either newspaper or advertiser.

A MANAGER'S BASIC DILEMMA

It was none other than Katherine Graham, heroine of free press resistance to Nixon pressure during Watergate, who was lobbying hard at the White House and in the halls of Congress. It was the 1980s and Graham was lobbying on behalf of the newspaper industry. The mission: keep telephone companies out of electronic publishing.

The newspaper industry's leading trade group (then American Newspaper Publishers Association, now renamed Newspaper Association of America) hastened to say the lobbying was not what it appeared to be—an attempt to use political persuasion to knock out potential competition; rather, it really was an effort to defend the First Amendment, to prevent telephone companies from using their enormous resources to publish their own news and advertising and transmit it over their own wires and perhaps thus gain monopoly control over the free flow of information.

The lobbying by Graham, then publisher of *The Washington Post*, and her publisher colleagues highlighted a basic dilemma for newspaper managers: The newspapers they manage are sideline observers and critics of society, but also an integral part of it; they are recorders of news but also makers of news—and, crucially, they are an institution claiming special legal and societal status as watchdog surrogates of the people but also businesses out to make a profit.

The newspaper industry's argument sounded disingenuous to Sen. Robert Packwood (R-Ore.) when he was visited by a group of publishers led by Mrs. Graham. Packwood opined that what really worried publishers was that telephone companies might offer electronic "Yellow Pages" and thus destroy newspaper advertising. Responded Mrs. Graham: "You're damn right it is." So much for defense of the First Amendment.

Scott Low, publisher of the *Quincy (Mass.) Patriot-Ledger*, present at the meeting, later said, "It was a disaster, a complete disaster." To some members of Congress, he said, "We come on as fat-cat heavies trying to protect our turf."

All this was reported in elaborate detail by *The Wall Street Journal* in a front-page article headlined, "Newspaper Publishers Lobby To Keep AT&T From Role

They Covet." The article also reported that Warren Phillips, *Journal* publisher, helped draft an industry statement on the issue.[13]

Some publishers disassociated themselves from newspaper-industry lobbying that was so nakedly motivated by self-interest. Said Barry Bingham, then publisher of the *Louisville Courier-Journal:* "I break ranks with the publishers' group when they say in the name of the First Amendment they're going to abbreviate Bell's right to publish."[14]

The newspaper association's efforts spread far beyond Washington, providing background material for editorials in many newspapers. *The Wall Street Journal* reported that only about half the editorials told readers outright of newspapers' commercial stake in the issue.[15]

It was a very public and, to some, embarrassing example of how ethical considerations are not limited to the newsroom or advertising department. Publishers must establish standards of conduct for their own office and in that be no less demanding, no less conscientious. For it is performance in the publisher's office that will set the ethical "tone" for the entire newspaper.

The publisher's code also must look outward, to the newspaper's external relationships and its public image, as well as inward, to internal operating procedures.

Examples of how complex this can get:

- Should publishers lobby government for special privilege, such as sales tax exemptions, while knowing full well that newspapers—their news columns, their editorial pages—are feared for their political clout? Many publishers do.[16]
- Should a publisher practice "civic journalism" or join, say, the chamber of commerce or otherwise engage in "boosterism" of public activities the newspaper must cover?
- Should publishers claim special status and First Amendment rights for companies that, though once newspaper-oriented, are now widely diversified business conglomerates?

The Trap: Conflict of Interest

Here are areas where you'll encounter conflict of interest as a publisher or be perceived by the public as sacrificing higher ideals for naked self-interest.

Joint Operating Agreements (JOAs)

Special-interest legislation maneuvered through Congress years ago exempts some newspapers from antitrust laws and, as explained in Chapter 12, permits them to form joint operating agreements. Only the newspaper industry enjoys exemption in that form.

If one newspaper can prove, to the satisfaction of the U.S. attorney general, that it might otherwise fail financially, JOAs can be negotiated. If they promise to maintain independent news and editorial operations, two competing newspapers then are permitted to share production facilities, advertising and circulation staffs, a building and so on. Even a hint of such cooperation in, say, the auto industry would draw immediate attention from the antitrust division of the U.S. Justice Department.

In passing JOA legislation, Congress was motivated, of course, by a desire to maintain separate editorial and news voices in cities. Many financially weak papers have been propped up in JOAs.

Questions: Did Congress really intend to build a safety net into which enormously profitable groups could dump their losers? Gannett, Knight-Ridder, Newhouse and Hearst, hugely profitable all, are among groups with papers in JOAs. Did Congress really intend to preserve newspapers as journals of facts and ideas, or today's communications conglomerates that are so widely diversified in non-news operations? Many groups with JOAs own free-circulation shoppers, cable TV systems and other non-news enterprises.

Clearly, some cities—Detroit, for example—have two newspapers only because of JOAs. But JOA opponents argue, of course, that when Congress passed the original exemption there were no victims, only beneficiaries. Now, the opponents say, JOAs give participating papers unfair advantage over television, radio, suburban newspapers, shoppers and other media that didn't exist in appreciable numbers way back then. In effect, JOA opponents are saying that competitive and marketplace conditions have changed and that society should rewrite the *social contract* giving newspapers this unique exemption.

Child Labor Laws

Newspapers receive exemptions from certain child labor laws so teenage carriers can deliver papers, and exemption from certain minimum wage regulations and Social Security payments covering adult carriers. The industry uses its considerable clout to lobby strongly for continuation of this. Its argument? "Good citizens" are trained by youthful labor as newspaper carriers (as contrasted, presumably, with youthful labor as gas station attendants or hamburg flippers).

Those Coin Boxes Again

Newspapers often win special status for news racks and coin boxes on streets and in public places, despite frequent attempts by municipal authorities to get them withdrawn or to tax or license them. The newspaper industry's defense? *The First Amendment.*

The First Amendment Umbrella

Increased diversification of newspaper-based companies into wider fields in search of profit adds complex dimensions to the discussion of corporate ethics.

Tribune Co., publisher of the *Chicago Tribune, Orlando Sentinel* and other papers, obviously should shelter beneath the First Amendment umbrella and enjoy the special societal and legal advantages that provides. But how to distinguish *that* Tribune Co. from the one that owns the Chicago Cubs baseball team and newsprint manufacturing assets in Canada?

Dow Jones, Cox and other companies that resisted telephone companies entering the information business have since made partnership deals to assist those telephone companies. So, what's going on here? Are telephone companies threats to the First Amendment, or not?

Should *The New York Times* and *The Washington Post,* which, like many companies, own TV stations, assign reporters to cover the TV industry and the Federal Communications Commission which regulates it? Thus does conflict of interest—or public perception of it—enter the newspaper manager's life.

The Challenge You Face

None of this is to suggest there is flagrant misuse of the press's political clout or its First Amendment status. Neither is it meant to imply that a newspaper should not enter the marketplace in vigorous defense of its own business interests. It *is* meant to suggest that the next generation of newspaper managers will face new, complex questions in constructing an ethical relationship between their newspapers and the society within which they operate.

Some ethical questions have been around for a very long time. That doesn't make them any easier to solve. Consider, for example, boosterism—a newspaper backing local community and industry with chamber-of-commerce fervor, or a publisher joining local business or professional groups and serving charitable organizations. If the publisher isn't careful, that can mean the newspaper drops its role as a dispassionate observer and becomes an advocate *or* that the public perceives the newspaper as having joined forces with certain groups.

Pressures from boosterism are enormous, particularly in small daily and weekly journalism where the publisher is known to all in town ("I go to church with all those folks," one weekly editor says). The question, of course, is whether boosterism leaves the newspaper free to report what is wrong in town and editorialize on how it should be fixed. If the publisher is on the United Way advisory board, is the editorial writer really free to comment on how money is raised and spent?

It is hoped, of course, that publisher and newspaper will find ways to be constructively involved in their community and still maintain journalistic and editorial independence—and if straddling both those responsibilities is not possible, to opt for the historic role of reporting as facts dictate and commenting editorially as conscience orders. Those that so opt can expect problems occasionally.

Witness the *Fort Worth Star-Telegram,* which published articles on safety problems with Huey and Cobra helicopters manufactured by Bell Helicopter. Bell, which has a plant in Fort Worth, publicly attacked the series and banned *Star-Telegram* employees from servicing newspaper coin boxes in the plant. The company's union organized a campaign against the paper and 1,200 subscriptions were canceled. The army grounded 600 Hueys and ordered new parts for 4,500 other helicopters. The *Star-Telegram* won a Pulitzer Prize—and many headaches—for the series.[17]

The question of whether newspapers should endorse political candidates (a very old controversy) assumes new ethical overtones as many editorial pages strive for a centrist, objective position. Centrists argue that a newspaper must present all sides of controversies and comment editorially on issues—but avoid endorsements and thus leave the decision to voters. Papers that are alone in a market often feel greater responsibility to represent all shades of opinion.

USA Today declared it would not endorse candidates because as "the only general-interest national daily... our mission is to inform, to enlighten, to provide debate, but not to dictate. We seek neither to be king-makers nor king-breakers."[18] To some, that is an ethical lapse, a failure to provide leadership, waffling rather than taking a stand.

Endorsements, of course, may not change voters' minds. Franklin Delano Roosevelt won the presidency four times despite thousands of unfavorable editorials. But whether endorsements change minds is irrelevant; the issue is newspaper leadership in the community.

USA Today asked Senator Robert Dole (R-Kan.) whether papers should endorse candidates. Dole said: "Yes. Newspapers choose up sides in everything else. If they can speak out on every public issue from fruit flies to traffic stoplights they can spare a little space for the most important issue of all—the presidential race."[19]

There is deep meaning in that; editorial pages that take stands on fruit flies, which will create no enemies for a newspaper, but that bob and weave on a presidential election, a subject that will, have trivialized their historic role and failed their ethical responsibility.

BOX 13.1   Standards to Plan By

As a manager, your words, actions and policies will set the ethical tone for your newspaper. Even a casual comment or hurried, unthinking act may be taken by staffers as your guidance. So, you must decide whether to risk keeping your guidance informal, for dissemination by word of mouth—or put your guidelines down on paper.

In advertising, precise standards are written by many newspapers covering libel, good taste and ethical issues that arise in the words, photos and illustrations in thousands of ads published annually. But it's impossible to anticipate every ethical dilemma that can arise in a newspaper's *general business* attitudes. So, what to do?

John McClelland Jr. faced that dilemma as owner/publisher of the *Longview (Wash.) Daily News*. He decided to issue to his staff a written statement expressing generally his newspaper's attitude toward its ethical and social responsibilities:

Our newspapers' only license to publish is the freedom of the press clause in the Constitution. As such, their first obligation is to publish the news, to broadcast the truth, to keep the people informed. Their primary obligation is to serve the readers.

Secondly, they are business and manufacturing enterprises depending on the sale of their products for the financial success which enables them to continue publishing the news. That success is necessary to provide compensation for employees, to furnish reserves for improvements in productive capacity, to provide for the payment of taxes necessary to maintain the government, and to allow the shareholders whose capital has made the business possible a reasonable return on their investment.

BOX 13.1 *Continued*

To assure this success, it is essential to produce newspapers that are as good as we are capable of producing, to increase continually our family of readers and to provide, through well planned advertising, a means of serving effectively the sales objectives of our customers.

Talented, truthful, energetic journalism; well prepared advertising and the finest printing our employees and machines are capable of producing—these shall be our objectives.[a]

At *The Washington Post,* Executive Editor Ben Bradlee wrote an ethics code that included a statement by Eugene Meyer, who bought the paper in 1933 and whose descendants manage it today.

The First mission of a newspaper is to tell the truth as nearly as the truth may be ascertained.

The newspaper shall tell all the truth so far as it can learn it, concerning the important affairs of America and the world.

As a disseminator of the news, the paper shall observe the decencies that are obligatory upon a private gentleman.

What it prints shall be fit reading for the young as well as for the old.

The newspaper's duty is to its readers and to the public at large, and *not to the private interest of the owner* (emphasis added).

In the pursuit of truth, *the newspaper shall be prepared to make sacrifices of its material fortunes, if necessary for the public good* (emphasis added). The newspaper shall not be the ally on any special interest, but shall be fair and free and wholesome in its outlook on public affairs and public men.

In addition to thus setting the general tone, both McClelland and Bradlee issued detailed written guidelines for their newsrooms. Here, from Bradlee's "Standards and Ethics," are standards you could plan by:

Condition of Employment

Conforming to ethical as well as journalistic standards is a condition of employment at the *Post* (as at many other papers).

The Basic Goal

Bradlee put it squarely:

The *Washington Post* is pledged to an aggressive, responsible and fair pursuit of the truth without fear of any special interest, and with favor to none.

We fully recognize that the power we have inherited as the dominant morning newspaper in the capital of the free world carries with it social responsibilities:

- to listen to the voiceless.
- to avoid any and all acts of arrogance.
- to face the public politely and candidly.

Conflict of Interest

The *Post* code warns employees to avoid even the *appearance* of conflict of interest. Staffers must avoid freebies, of course, but also shun even off-duty involvement in community or political affairs. Employees are required to discuss with superiors any involvement by *family members* that might "compromise our integrity."

The Reporter's Role

It's simple: cover the news, don't make it—and "make every effort to remain in the audience, to be the stagehand rather than the star. . . ."

Continued

BOX 13.1   *Continued*

Errors

Bradlee warned the staff to minimize the number of errors made and pledged the paper "to correct those that occur."

Attribution of Sources

The *Post* is pledged to "disclose the source of all information when at all possible. But, "When we agree to protect a source's identity, that identity will not be made known to anyone outside the *Post*."

Plagiarism and Credit

Attribution of material "must be total." The code adds, "Plagiarism is one of journalism's unforgivable sins."

Fairness

"Reporters and editors of the *Post* are committed to fairness."

Opinion

"Separation of news columns from the editorial and opposite-editorial page is solemn and complete."

But, the code is not intended to eliminate from news columns "honest, in-depth reporting, or analysis or commentary when plainly labeled."

National and Community Interest

"The *Post* is 'vitally concerned' with both, and, we believe these interests are best served by the widest possible dissemination of information. The claim of national interest by a federal official does not automatically equate with the national interest. The claim of community interest by a local official does not automatically equate with the community interest."

Taste

The *Post* "respects taste and decency, understanding that society's concepts of taste and decency are constantly changing."[b]

Now, before you rush to write *your* code, a word of caution: Many lawyers oppose detailed written codes. David R. Morgan, counsel for the Pennsylvania Newspaper Publishers' Association, put it this way:

"As a lawyer, I'm not a fan of industry codes. No matter how many disclaimers like 'proposed' or 'suggested' you put into them, they still come back to haunt you. Such professional codes inevitably become 'industry standards'—benchmarks for plaintiffs' lawyers everywhere to hold unsuspecting defendants' conduct up to in court."[c]

[a] *General Policies*, a handbook, Longview Publishing Co., P.O. Box 189, Longview, Wash. 98632.
[b] I discuss this code in more detail in Conrad C. Fink, *Introduction to Professional Newswriting* (White Plains NY: Longman, 1992.)

SUMMARY

Newspapers have historic responsibilities beyond making shareholders happy. They must inform, enlighten, lead opinion and serve as the people's surrogates. That is a heavy burden but no other medium is as well equipped to do it.

In newsrooms, compelling ethical issues include balancing the individual's right to privacy and the public's right to be informed, free press vs. fair trial and the press's tendency to make news, not simply report it. Many newspapers insist that staff members' outside work or activities not jeopardize the paper's objectivity or public perception of its objectivity.

In advertising, many newspapers establish standards of acceptability and reject ads that fail certain ethical tests. This involves subjective judgments on whether ads are likely to cause financial loss to readers, to injure their health or otherwise to be contrary to the best interests of the newspaper and its readers. Advertorials—ads made up to look like news copy—are met increasingly with disfavor because they blur distinctions between news and advertising. That damages the newspaper's credibility, which harms advertiser interest as well.

In the publisher's suite, ethical concerns range from lobbying at the White House in the newspaper industry's own naked self-interest to whether an individual paper should endorse political candidates. For ethical questions, there are no rulebook answers. The burden for you as aspiring manager is to begin, now, working out where you stand on compelling issues of the day.

RECOMMENDED READING

An ongoing industry dialogue over ethics is covered thoroughly in reports from the Associated Press Managing Editors Association (note its annual *Journalism Ethics Report*) and in the American Society of Newspaper Editors' *ASNE Bulletin.*

Editor & Publisher, presstime and other trade journals provide strong coverage, too.

Watch *Advertising Age* for developments in advertising ethics. *Journalism Quarterly* and the *Newspaper Research Journal* frequently publish scholarly research in ethics.

I cover ethics in the newsroom, in the manager's suite and in the media as an institution in *Media Ethics* (New York: Macmillan, 1995).

NOTES

1. Journalists generally agree, for example, that Knight-Ridder newspapers publish some of the best journalism in the country. The company's papers are big winners of Pulitzer Prizes and other peer awards. Yet, Knight-Ridder's profit margins are far from the industry's best. I discuss this in Conrad Fink, *Media Ethics* (New York: Macmillan, 1995).

2. "A Lie in the *Times*," editorial, *New York Times*, national edition, Feb. 23, 1982, p. A-22.

3. "Eastern Airlines on *Journal* Article," letter to editor, *Wall Street Journal*, July 20, 1982, p. 24; "A Fair Press?" *Detroit Free Press*, Aug. 27, 1984, p. 4-A.

4. Russell Austin, "Advice to Delay Buying Home Was Not Meant For All," *Milwaukee Journal*, Feb. 22, 1982, p. 1.

5. Robert P. Smith, "Advertising Acceptability Policies Protect Newspaper's Credibility," *INAME News*, June 1984, p. 11.

6. Ibid.

7. "Missouri Paper Organizes Convenient Manual for Ad Codes," *INAME News*, June 1984, p. 13.

8. "St. Petersburg Papers Start Checking Advertisers for Necessary Licenses," *SNPA Advertising Bulletin*, Jan. 10, 1983, p. 1.

9. Robert P. Smith, *INAME News*, op. cit.

10. Dan Bischoff, "Smokeless in Seattle," *American Journalism Review,* Oct. 1993, p. 35.

11. Stuart J. Elliott, "Advertorials: Straddling a Fine Line in Print," *Advertising Age,* April 30, 1984, p. 3.

12. Ann Marie Kerwin, "Advertising Pressure on Newspaper is Common: Survey," *Editor & Publisher,* Jan. 16, 1993, p. 28, reporting on a study by Professors Lawrence C. Solely and Robert L. Craig.

13. Margaret Garrard Warner, "Newspaper Publishers Lobby to Keep AT&T From Role They Covet," *Wall Street Journal,* July 9, 1982, p. 1.

14. Ibid.

15. Ibid.

16. A good roundup on this subject is Patrick M. Reilly and Pauline Yoshihashi, "More State Lawmakers Decide All the News Is Fit to Tax," *Wall Street Journal,* July 23, 1991, p. B-1.

17. Jonathan Friendly, "Paper Assailed For Exposing Faulty Army Copters," *New York Times,* Aug. 5, 1984, p. 30.

18. "We Say You Should Pick Your President," *USA Today,* Sept. 21, 1984, p. 10.

19. Robert Dole, "Papers Have Opinions, So Why Not Endorse?" *USA Today,* Sept. 21, 1984, p. 10a.

PART V

YOU AND THE WEEKLY NEWSPAPER

Is your study of newspaper management beginning to give you ideas—*big* ideas, such as running a newspaper early in your career or even owning one?

If so, check out the weekly newspaper. It can be important to you for two reasons: First, if you want quick experience in all dimensions of management, weekly newspapering gives you the best opportunities. In weekly publishing, a manager "does it all." Second, if it's ownership you want, weeklies offer best chances for entrepreneurship early in your career and at relatively low cost (*relatively,* mind you; there is no inexpensive entry into newspaper ownership).

Even if daily newspapers are your goal, you'll need to know much about weeklies. Many daily publishers offer weekly publications—shoppers, entertainment magazines and so forth—in addition to their daily papers. And as a daily manager you'll almost certainly compete against weeklies; indeed, many dailies are encircled by aggressive weeklies clamoring for a share of reader time and advertiser dollar.

It's with good reason, then, that we conclude *Strategic Newspaper Management* here in Chapter 14 with an examination of weekly newspaper publishing.

14

THE "NEW" WEEKLY NEWSPAPER

Weekly newspaper publishing, where it all began back in Colonial days, has a "new look." Witness:

Weekly circulation and readership are growing strongly. More than 7,400 paid and free weeklies churn out over 55.4 million copies each week (see Table 14.1). With "shelf life" of five or six days in most households, weeklies generally draw four readers or more per copy (compared with 2.2 to 2.5 for most dailies).

Weekly ad revenue is difficult to calculate but it approached $5 billion in the early 1990s and is growing rapidly. In many small towns and suburbs, weeklies dominate local advertising; in many larger competitive markets they are serious challengers for

TABLE 14.1   U.S. Weekly Newspapers 1960–1993*

Year	Total Weekly Newspapers	Average Circulation	Total Weekly Circulation (millions)
1960	8,174	2,566	20.9
1965	8,061	3,106	25.0
1970	7,612	3,660	27.8
1975	7,612	4,715	35.8
1980	7,954	5,324	42.3
1985	7,704	6,359	48.9
1990	7,550	7,309	55.1
1993	7,406	7,487	55.4

Source: National Newspaper Association
* Includes free and paid-circulation newspapers.

major slices of the advertising pie. Free-circulation weeklies, particularly those offering total market coverage, are becoming increasingly popular with many advertisers.

Compared with, say, 30 years ago, weeklies are generating much larger circulations, on average (see, again, Table 14.1). Average circulation of 7,487 in 1993, compared with 2,566 in 1960, means weeklies in general are much more strongly positioned in their individual markets.

Some weeklies are highly profitable, with margins at times exceeding those of daily newspapers. Consequently (and also because few dailies are available for purchase) attractive weeklies command prices of 1.5 to 2.5 times annual revenue. That compares with one times revenue, or less, in the late 1980s. (Dailies, when available, generally command prices of 2.5 to 3.5 times revenue.)

Weeklies flourish best today in two environments: (a) In affluent suburbs of major cities, offering readers highly detailed local coverage that metro dailies cannot match and providing advertisers deep household penetration; and (b) in a group owned by a publisher who achieves economies of scale by publishing two or more from a single administrative facility and under one roof for all production, sales and news functions.

Modern technology and managerial techniques are characteristics of successful weeklies today. Rapidly disappearing: "Ye Olde Country Editor" of lore, an independent owner struggling with a single ill-equipped, underfinanced weekly based on a narrow (and perhaps shrinking) rural or small town market.

STANDARDS TO PLAN BY

There is no truly "average" weekly newspaper in the United States. Like dailies, many weeklies uniquely reflect their own market and competitive conditions and the news and management strategies of their individual owners.

However, whether you want to buy your own weekly newspaper or manage somebody else's you'll need standards to plan by. So, compare your newspaper's characteristics to those that emerge from a 1991 Inland Press Association survey of 42 weeklies.

Circulation and Size

In one study group of weeklies averaging 3,580 circulation, Inland found 99 percent of circulation was paid. These papers annually averaged 74 issues, each with 15.5 broadsheet pages. Of total content, 52 percent was editorial.

For weeklies averaging 9,601 circulation, less circulation— 79 percent—was paid. These weeklies annually published 82 issues, averaging 25.6 pages per issue. Just 38 percent of content was editorial.

TABLE 14.2   Revenue, Expense and Profit

Revenue	1,850–5,035 Circulation	5,756–13,816 Circulation
Advertising	$302,403	$707,364
Circulation	62,593	143,192
Total Newspaper Revenue	364,996	850,556
Commercial printing	382,432	294,133
Shopper	222,161	406,307
Other (interest, rent, etc.)	11,144	53,302
Total operating revenue	589,169	1,143,617
Total operating expense	521,303	1,044,492
Total operating profit	$67,866	$99,126

Profits and Productivity

You can measure your financial success in terms of profit per employee. "FTE" or "full-time equivalent" signifies one average workweek (even if two or more part-time employees do the work). The Inland study found this:

	1,850–5,035 Circulation	5,756–13,816 Circulation
Total FTEs	11.4	22.4
Total payroll	$209,789	$470,291
Average payroll per FTE	18,256	22,031
Operating revenue per FTE	51,269	52,124
Operating profit per FTE	5,906	3,956

Newsroom Standards

For both circulation groups, Inland found these characteristics:[1]

	1,850–5,053 Circulation	5,756–13,816 Circulation
Number of FTEs	3.1	4.3
Total payroll	54,265	111,087
Payroll per FTE	17,234	24,929
Outside services and free-lancers	4,361	10,952
Other expense	3,211	4,815
Total editorial expense	63,870	128,341

Continued

Continued

	1,850–5,053 Circulation	5,756–13,816 Circulation
Editorial expense as percentage of newspaper revenue	19.4%	16%
Annual expense per copy printed	17.74	14.02
Editorial pages per FTE	173	198

Advertising Department Standards

The bulk of your newspaper revenue comes from advertising, of course, so you must pay close attention to how this department is operated. Standards to plan by:

	1,850–5,035 Circulation	5,756–13,816 Circulation
FTE	2.1	3.5
Payroll	$47,714	$86,893
Total department expense	54,352	104,154
Ad expense as percentage of ad revenue	20.1%	14.6%
Ad sales per FTE	147,160	199,000
Annual ad revenue per newspaper page	286.15	368.33
Ad expense per newspaper page	52.15	55.88
Ad revenue as percentage of total revenue	79.4%	82.54%
Local ad revenue	219,967	463,130
National ad revenue	12,169	15,258
Legal revenue	16,006	31,477
Classified revenue	42,107	132,065
Revenue per column inch		
local	3.94	5.41
national	4.22	9.90
legal	4.20	3.80
classified	3.29	6.94
average	3.77	5.30

Circulation Department Standards

Circulation revenue is extremely important for weeklies. Note in the standards below that circulation accounts for 20 percent or more of some weeklies' revenue, and about 10 percent of expense.

	1,850–5,035 Circulation	5,756–13,816 Circulation
FTEs	1	1.6
Payroll	$10,415	$27,339
Total department expense	33,850	87,256
Circulation sales per FTE	80,644	95,688
Revenue as percentage of newspaper revenue	20.6%	17.4%
Expense as percentage of newspaper revenue	10.7%	10.7%
Revenue per copy sold	18.17	16.00
Expense per copy sold	9.56	9.54

Pre-Press Costs

When your newsroom and advertising department have created copy it goes to the pre-press department for composition and preparation for printing, then to the press department. That's a costly process:

	1,850–5,035 Circulation	5,756–13,816 Circulation
FTEs	2.7	2.7
Payroll	$51,929	$49,795
Total expense	54,243	63,021
Cost per composed page	46.89	31.45
Prepress expense as percentage of total newspaper revenue	11.5%	8.1%
Press Department Costs		
FTEs	2.5	4.0
Payroll	$30,877	$42,189
Newsprint/ink	23,764	82,992

Continued

Continued

	1,850–5,035 Circulation	5,756–13,816 Circulation
Total expense	50,578	120,086
Cost per published page	48.51	61.55
Press expense as percentage of total newspaper revenue	14.1%	14.9%

General and Administrative Department Costs

Costs are high because they include the publisher's salary and expenditures for rent, utilities and other services provided for all departments. Among the costs:

	1,850–5,035 Circulation	5,756–13,816 Circulation
FTEs	1.8	2.8
Payroll	$47,075	$89,319
Rent	14,761	18,462
Utilities	7,105	8,704
Total expense	$151,019	$327,131
G&A expense as percentage of total newspaper revenue	44.7%	42.2%[a]

[a]Survey results used with permission from Inland Press Association, Inc., 777 Busse Highway, Park Ridge, IL 60068.

Pay Levels

These are median compensation figures, as of Jan. 1, 1993, from 72 newspapers surveyed by Inland:

	Base Pay	Total Direct Pay	Employees Supervised
Publisher	$60,000	$80,000	23
General Manager	41,980	57,490	22
Ad Manager	29,600	36,350	5
Classified Mgr.	19,552	35,000	3
Ad Salesperson	18,000	26,915	N/A
Circulation Mgr.	18,756	22,150	5
Business Mgr.	26,250	28,414	4
Production Mgr.	30,000	34,000	6

	Base Pay	Total Direct Pay	Employees Supervised
Press Manager	28,600	28,900	5
Managing Editor	28,510	26,603	4
Reporter (entry level)	15,600	18,000	N/A
Reporter (experienced)	21,000	22,000	N/A[a]

[a]Survey results used with permission from Inland Press Association, Inc., 777 Busse Highway, Park Ridge, IL 60068.

SO, YOU WANT TO BUY A WEEKLY?

Thinking about a career in "Main Street" journalism? Does owning and publishing your own weekly sound like a good idea? Before you answer, consider three factors:

First, do you want a career of reporting on the county commission and Little League baseball, rather than the White House or the major leagues? Weekly journalism gets right down to the nitty-gritty of community life—school lunch menus, honor rolls, garbage pickup (*always* controversial), whether the village should buy a new fire engine. This type of journalism will take you closer to readers than any other kind. But many young journalists find it too parochial, too confining.

Second, are you prepared to incur substantial financial risk and to concentrate primarily on the *business* of newspaper publishing, rather than *journalism*? Weekly publishers spend far more time on advertising, circulation and production than in the newsroom. And, despite hard work, many fail financially.

Third, the best place to prepare for publishing your own weekly is on somebody else's payroll. Work for a publisher whose journalistic and business success you admire and you can pick up the skills necessary to build your own success story. Hands-on experience also will demonstrate to you whether a career in weekly publishing is for you.

Now, if you still are interested in owning a weekly, read on.

HOW TO BUY: AN ACQUISITION CHECKLIST

Proceed carefully toward your goal of owning a newspaper. Buying one may be the biggest investment of your life, and you'll need help from an attorney and, importantly, an accountant to help you judge the financial soundness of any deal you make. Negotiate their fees in advance. Then, take the following steps.

Research Market and Product

Before opening serious talks with an owner, carefully research the newspaper, its market and competition. Know as much about the newspaper as any outsider can.

Study the market's economic strength—its geographic, demographic and psychographic characteristics. Talk with bankers, chamber of commerce officials and others.

You're buying access to a market, as much as a newspaper itself, so remember: No newspaper regardless of how well you manage it, can perform above the basic economic strength of its market. Study the newspaper's circulation and advertising history, its competitive status. Once you define and evaluate the market, determine which media competitors will be fighting you for that market.

Even publishers of remote country weeklies know the value of newspaper properties. You probably will pay a handsome price, so your research should concentrate on the growth potential of the paper and its market. Will you be able to pay the cost of acquisition? Research will yield educated guesses about growth potential. However, this is not the time for guessing. You must obtain financial statements from the owner. A few pointers:

- Don't trust financial statements that are not audited by a reputable outside accounting firm which vouches for their accuracy (and be careful even then). Look for written assurance in the statements by certified public accountants that they examined the financials "in accordance with generally accepted auditing standards" and that the statements "present fairly" the company's financial position "in conformity with generally accepted accounting principles applied on a consistent basis during the period...." Unaudited statements often are unreliable.
- At minimum, obtain a balance sheet and profit and loss statement for the immediately preceding three years plus interim results for current year to date. You can't project trends accurately with less.
- Make analyzing the statements a team effort. Your chief financial adviser must search out accounting esoterica that can disguise a company's true condition. You must search for ways to increase revenue and decrease expenses. If you're a beginner without a staff, go outside and hire, if only on a consultant basis, the expertise you need.

How to Analyze a Balance Sheet

Let's examine a balance sheet as if you are thinking of acquiring a large weekly (or arriving to take over its management for the owner). Note Table 14.4, a hypothetical balance sheet adapted from actual operations of a paper.

Pay particular attention to these factors:

Current assets (cash or assets that can be turned into cash within one year) come with the newspaper unless specifically exempted in a sales contract and are key in determining what price you can afford. Nearly $500,000 worth would be in a deal for Dream Publishing predicated on its Dec. 31, 1995, balance sheet.

Total accounts receivable (what the paper is owed) minus reserve for *bad debts* can help you determine that paper's track record in collecting debt. Frankly, reserve for

TABLE 14.4   Dream Publishing Co. Balance Sheets 1993, 1994, 1995

Assets	1993	1994	1995
Current assets			
Cash	43,780	37,534	45,132
Accounts receivable, net of allowance for doubtful accounts of $17,780, $18,380, $6,506 in 1993, 1994, 1995 respectively	377,838	439,312	391,574
Other receivables	————	4,860	19,440
Inventories	53,422	35,904	47,410
Prepaid expenses	12,608	16,468	7,102
	487,648	534,078	510,658
Fixed assets, at cost	1,592,678	1,547,248	1,540,922
Less: accumulated depreciation	1,195,976	1,152,612	1,102,032
	396,702	394,636	438,890
Other assets			
Goodwill	388,750	401,670	422,634
	1,273,100	1,330,384	1,372,182

Liabilities	1993	1994	1995
Current liabilities			
Bank note payable	11,000	30,000	
Accounts payable	144,752	201,802	109,886
Deferred subscriptions	13,180	13,180	13,180
Accrued wages	25,210	26,664	22,576
Payroll taxes payable	6,170	7,062	4,190
Sales tax payable	792	488	354
Estimated corporation income tax liability	12,862	————	220
Current portion of long-term debt	164,884	144,210	111,600
	378,850	423,406	262,006
Long-term debt, net of current portion	750,002	881,172	1,014,531
Stockholders' equity Capital stock	73,954	73,954	73,954
Retained earnings (deficit)	24,530	18,358	(14,195)
Net income (loss) for years ended December 31	45,764	(66,506)	35,886
	70,294	(48,148)	21,691
	144,248	25,806	95,645
	1,273,100	1,330,384	1,372,182

Dream Publishing's doubtful accounts looks low, and some of those receivables should probably be written off as uncollectible. Guideline: If accounts receivable are more than $1\frac{1}{2}$ months of annual business, you, as new owner, might have trouble collecting. In your forthcoming price negotiations with the power, don't "buy" accounts receivable you cannot collect.

Inventories, particularly in newsprint, should be valued on the balance sheet by the more conservative approach of cost or current market value, whichever is lower. Watch that you're not buying old, useless newsprint. Determine number of days of operation for which newsprint and ink exist. Sufficient?

Fixed assets, such as plant and equipment, should be valued at cost minus depreciation (their decline in useful value due to usage or obsolescence). Most widely accepted is "straight-line" calculation of depreciation. That is, equipment that costs $20,000 and is expected to last five years should be valued after one year at $20,000 minus $4,000 or $16,000; after two years, at $12,000, and so forth. So look for *net fixed assets*—cost of assets less depreciation. Ask the owner for a *depreciation schedule.* It will list each piece of equipment. Unless you are an equipment expert, hire one to examine major items, such as presses. Failure of a $200,000 press six months after acquisition can create havoc with your expense projections.

Prepayments for such things as insurance or equipment leases often constitute assets of considerable value. Note them carefully.

Intangibles such as goodwill are important in newspaper acquisition. Goodwill is the difference between the net value of the newspaper's tangible assets and its total worth due to reputation in the marketplace, customer loyalty and so on. It will play a major role in the price eventually set for the paper.

In studying liabilities on the balance sheet, note the following:

Total current liabilities of $378,850 will fall due within the coming year.

Accounts payable, or amounts the paper owes creditors, total $144,752.

Notes payable, including promissory notes, are of particular concern. Interest paid on notes is often high for short-term money. Unless you specify otherwise, you will be paying off those notes.

Accrued expenses payable, such as wages owed employees, pension contributions and so on, can be a significant liability for you to undertake.

Long-term liabilities, or debts due after one year, such as mortgages, must be studied. Unless specifically exempted, you will be assuming those debts. What is the interest rate on them?

Retained earnings are profits not distributed to shareholders as dividends. They are normally invested in various assets of the company and not held as cash.

Here are some particularly important balance-sheet indicators:

Working capital (total current liabilities less current assets) shows what will be left if current debts are paid and thus signals how flexible the company will be in expanding and operating to its marketplace potential. This can indicate whether you, as the new owner, will have to transfuse cash.

The current ratio (current assets to current liabilities) determines whether a company has sufficient working capital. Many managers feel comfortable only with about $2.50 current assets for $1 current liabilities.

Quick assets are available for meeting current liabilities immediately. They include cash and easily convertible securities (but not, for example, newsprint, which must be sold). Some financial officers say $1.30 or so in quick assets for $1 in current liabilities is about right.

Shareholder equity is the company's net worth after liabilities are subtracted from assets. It is what owners would receive were the company liquidated. It will be a factor when you get around to negotiating price.

In sum, the balance sheet presents the newspaper's financial picture on a specific date. But it doesn't reveal much about its operating profitability. For that you must turn to the profit and loss statement.

How to Analyze the P&L Statement

Whether you should buy and, if so, at what price can be decided only after determining how much the newspaper makes (or loses). The paper obviously must be profitable enough—or you must be able to *make* it profitable—to cover acquisition costs.

Table 14.5 on page 442 is a profit and loss statement adapted from the paper whose balance sheet we studied. For space reasons we'll limit our analysis to results over a two-year period. When you actually start buying newspapers or managing them, however, always look at the most recent *three* years plus interim results for the current year.

On the sales or revenue side of the P&L, look for:

Advertising revenue, which must be broken down into local, preprint, classified and legal. If it isn't (and for space reasons it isn't here), ask for a detailed "schedule of newspaper and commercial printing sales" that provides year-by-year results in each category. Steady revenue growth throughout the period is a good sign. Match past performance with your analysis of the newspaper, its competition and its market, then estimate how revenues can be increased with your superior management and marketing effort.

Circulation revenue also must be viewed over a three-year period. If revenue increased, was it from higher circulation or price hikes? You might be able to increase revenue substantially through carefully staged price increases if the former owner did not institute regular increases.

Printing and miscellaneous revenue should be analyzed carefully. Experience indicates that job printing revenue is uncertain, often built by the former owner through personal contracts. As much as 50 percent or more likely will disappear when he leaves.

TABLE 14.5   Dream Publishing Co. Profit & Loss Statement for Years Ended Dec. 31, 1994/95

	1995	1994	Increase (Decrease)
Sales			
Newspaper advertising			
Display	1,205,822	994,188	211,634
Classified	171,160	157,888	13,272
Circulation			
Subscriptions	206,638	223,740	(17,102)
Single-copy sales	151,370	147,954	3,416
Commercial printing and composition	1,098,828	1,034,410	64,148
	2,833,818	2,558,180	275,638
Less discounts allowed	(24,550)	(28,042)	3,492
	2,809,268	2,530,138	279,130
Cost of sales	2,200,632	1,996,956	203,676
Gross profit	608,636	533,182	75,454
Operating expenses	622,734	564,876	57,858
Operating income (loss)	(14,098)	(31,694)	17,596
Other income			
Rental income	45,096	46,228	(1,132)
Sale of used plates	5,342	4,562	780
Bad debts recovered	19,714	20,030	316
Interest income	3,182	4,990	(1,808)
Miscellaneous income	644	1,406	(762)
Insurance dividend	12,958	5,326	7,632
	86,936	82,542	4,394
Other deductions			
Write-off goodwill resulting from discontinuance of *Northside Shopper*		58,712	(58,712)
Noncomplete covenant to former owner	32,616	32,616	
	32,616	91,328	(58,712)
Net income (loss) before income taxes	40,222	(40,480)	80,702
Provision for state franchise tax	4,336	2,166	2,170
Net income (loss)	35,886	42,646	78,532

Turning to expenses, you won't find sufficient detail on the P&L. You'll need further conversations with the seller. In those talks and on the P&L, look for the following:

Costs should grow consistent with inflation and newspaper operating conditions. Lengthy periods of no growth may mean that the owner has not raised wages and that you will face demands for huge increases. Conversely, large year-to-year jumps may signal inefficient administration and opportunities for you to trim costs. Circulation and editorial expense must be matched with your understanding of the owner's operating style, the paper's journalistic quality and your strategy for improving it. As owner, you may be forced to increase spending in these sectors to improve market acceptance of the paper.

Administrative expenses must be dissected dollar by dollar. They may yield your greatest savings after taking over. Plan on replacing the often inordinately high salary the owner pays himself or herself with an appropriate salary for yourself. Deduct private cars, country club memberships and other perks owners often let the company pay for. They're all in "administrative expense," often one of the largest cost categories on a small- or medium-size privately owned newspapers.

Operating income (net revenue or sales minus all operating costs) is a prime indicator of how efficiently a paper is being run and, importantly, what you will be able to do with it.

Conversion ratio of net revenue or sales to operating income is a common measurement of operating efficiency. High conversion ratios may mean the paper is starved for resources and isn't properly serving the reader, advertiser or community. Buying such a paper may confront you with formidable rebuilding in news quality and advertiser service. Of course, a low conversion ratio sometimes means gross inefficiencies that you can eliminate—and still improve the paper. That, the happiest of all conditions, permits you to raise journalistic quality and still increase profits.

Total income (operating profit plus dividends or interest from company investments, etc.) is important. Many independently owned papers have substantial income from "other" sources.

Net income is all income minus all expenses, federal income tax and any interest paid to bondholders.

Cash flow (net profit plus depreciation) should be followed through to how funds were used—for dividends to owners, investment in plant and equipment or whatever. Total cash flow minus total funds used yields "working capital," and charting this over three years will show whether the paper's financial health is improving.

Footnotes are integral to any financial statement. Search them carefully for extraordinary factors. For example, a one-time sale of real estate or equipment, reported in footnotes, could pump up profit in any given year and make the paper look stronger than it really is.

In sum, the balance sheet and P&L indicate even to the uninitiated that Dream Publishing Co. is not highly profitable. For its size and track record, Dream Publishing's accounts receivable are too high; long-term debt too heavy.

On the P&L, there was growth in display advertising 1994–1995, but there is no legal. Is the paper on the outs with the local government jurisdictions that award contracts for legal advertising? Note also the extremely large contribution to total sales by commercial printing and composition. This is a highly competitive sector of newspaper operations, and a new owner of Dream Publishing should not count on carrying forward that revenue.

On an operating basis, the paper is losing money ($14,098 in 1995). It shows net profit of $35,886 in 1995 only because it had $86,936 in "other" and "miscellaneous" income. Note also that Dream Publishing discontinued *Northside Shopper* in 1994. Clearly, not all is well.

However, though crucial to any acquisition analysis, financial statements tell only part of the story. It may be, for example, that Dream Publishing's owner is discouraged by an inability to improve the paper's profitability and thus is open to a low price offer. If you can see ways of improving profitability, buying what may appear to be a faltering paper could prove to be a good deal. So let us assume that you find positive factors in the market and the newspaper itself and are encouraged to continue negotiations.

Other Areas to Probe

Determine precise ownership details. Is the company a *sole proprietorship*, with all business assets owned by a single individual? If so, your strategy must be to construct an offer attractive in that owner's individual tax situation.

If the company is a *partnership*, be sure the person you are negotiating with actually can deliver the company in a sale. (Is there a recalcitrant partner waiting in the background to kill your deal or jack up the price?) Also, note that owners in a partnership generally report net income or losses from the newspaper on their individual tax returns. So, to construct a tax-attractive offer, you must know each partner's overall tax situation.

If it is organized as a *corporation*, the newspaper is taxed separately as a business entity. Some newspapers are *Subchapter S corporations*, *not* taxed as separate entities; shareholders report on their individual returns any pro rata income, losses or credits from the corporation.

In negotiating for any company, be certain the principal can deliver 80 percent of the company's stock. You need at least 80 percent to consolidate the new operation with any existing business you have for tax purposes. Consolidation can be crucial, for if the newspaper has been operating at a loss or is projected to for a couple years, you can write off those losses against profitable operations you might have elsewhere.

Get details on *retirement programs, employment contracts* and any similar commitments you will assume with ownership. If a couple of employees have lifetime job contracts at fat salaries, your operating flexibility will be constricted, to say the least.

Union contracts, news service contracts and all other *contractual obligations* should be investigated carefully. You may have to operate under those contracts.

Watch for *pending lawsuits* or threats of lawsuits. Under certain purchase terms you will accept responsibility for them. To be safe, insist on seller warranting in the sales contract that no lawsuits or threats exist and, additionally, that seller will be responsible for any that develop out of conditions arising before your ownership.

Don't accept the present owner's revenue and cost budgeting or market projections. Even honest sellers put forward optimistic views. *Let the buyer beware.*

Buy Stock or Assets

Now you are close to a decision. Your financial adviser is integral to the next steps. And, again, if you don't have one, hire one—if only for this task. It's essential.

Begin this way: Decide whether to buy the stock of the newspaper company or its assets. If you buy stock, you get the entire company, including liabilities (some of which may be hidden or unknown at time of sale). *If you are uneasy about liabilities, buy assets, not stock.*

Your negotiating strategy must be based, of course, on your own best interests. But be prepared to bend. If you are willing to structure an offer to meet the seller's tax needs, you have the best chance of succeeding. Remember, to the seller it is after-tax dollars received that counts.

Now that you have studied market, product, competition and (in the financial statements) the owner's track record and reputation, you must project how the paper will perform under your ownership. You must estimate how much you can increase revenue and reduce costs in years ahead. Watch those "big-ticket" items— retail, classified and circulation revenue and, in expense, personnel and newsprint. Error in any can invalidate your analysis.

This is tricky business, for you must estimate how the overall economy will develop in years ahead—a difficult task indeed. Also, project your future capital expenditures. Your expert's inspection of presses and other equipment will provide guidelines on what equipment you might have to buy, when and at what cost. If all signals still are "go" you must decide how much you will offer for the paper—and how you will raise the money to pay for it (see Box 14.1 on page 446).

You then must decide how to structure your offer. Structure can influence dramatically your true cost in the purchase price.

Structuring Your Offer

There are many ways to structure your offer. Here are two that are popular among acquiring companies—100 percent cash, or some cash down with the balance paid over a number of years. (Publicly owned companies, of course, can offer a third option, swap of their own stock for the newspaper's. This often is attractive to owners who can defer tax on sale proceeds until they dispose of the newly acquired stock.)

For most buyers and sellers, cash down plus notes over 10 years for unpaid balance is attractive. For sellers, payment stretchout can keep taxes lower. For buyers, inflation can mean paying down the road in cheaper dollars earned by the newspaper itself.

The interest rate you agree to pay on notes is crucial. There are two concerns: First, a shrewd seller will trap you early in negotiations with discussions that get inordinately high interest rates on the table. Early loose talk will haunt you later on.

Second, beware of paying banks' adjustable or "floating" interest rates if you borrow to make the acquisition. They can rise sharply over a 10 year stretchout and increase significantly your cost of acquisition. A 1 percent increase on 1 million dollars over 10 years means real money.

BOX 14.1   Writing a Business Plan

Contrary to what you might think, bankers *want* to lend money to new entrepreneurs. The catch: You must convince them you're a good bet, that they will get their money back plus interest.

Two factors are of compelling concern to any banker or investor you ask to finance your entry into newspaper ownership: First, are you a proven quantity, an experienced, reliable and reputable individual who can make a business prosper? Did you learn publishing on somebody else's payroll? Are you experienced in all dimensions of the business of publishing? Have you cautiously and methodically prepared for ownership?

Second is the newspaper you propose to buy a good bet? Does it hold a "franchise" in its market—does it have strong grasp on readers and advertisers and can it resist competition? *Or,* can you convince the banker that you have the skills to reposition the newspaper to dominate its market?

As a first-time borrower, you must present a detailed written business plan that requires the financing you need and explains why you feel qualified for a loan. Let your attorney and accountant help write it. Warning: Although your business plan should "sell" you and your idea, be careful that you divulge fully all operative details. Don't disguise any negatives. You have a legal responsibility to disclose any known risks your banker or investors might incur. Your banker wants to know who assisted you, so write a cover letter naming your attorney, accountant and others involved in your project.

An *executive summary*—two pages, at most—should cover your more detailed proposal, recapping highlights in a form easily understood by a busy banker (who probably receives many similar proposals). Do your best selling job in the summary.

Organize your proposal logically and clearly. Provide a table of contents.

Other things your banker wants to know:

- Details on your target newspaper, its market and competition. Demonstrate keen grasp of market geography and demography and, particularly, the potential for economic growth.
- Financial analysis, covering at least the previous three years under the former owner and your projection for results over the next five years under your ownership. Do *not* be overly optimistic in projecting revenue and costs patterns or cash flow. Bankers make their living by sensing—and rejecting—unreasonable optimism.
- A best-case scenario should be written to illustrate how you *hope* to prosper. Write a worst-case scenario on how you would react if the economy or market conditions soured or major new competitors appeared on the scene.
- Describe any innovative journalistic or business tactics you will take to the new venture. Explain why you can run the paper better—more profitably—than its former owner.
- List consultants, advisers or, particularly, experienced employees available to help you get operations under way. Demonstrate you have backup.

Finally, remember this: Your banker will take a *businesslike* attitude toward your proposal. Your promises to practice the greatest weekly journalism ever seen will be important, of course. But the banker's bottom-line question will be whether you will run a profitable business and whether the bank will get its money back.

Also crucial: How much of the total consideration to seller will you offer in purchase price and how much in consultancy and noncompete covenant? To explain: You need assurance that once you buy the paper the owner will not reenter the market and compete against you. The owner knows the market, has personal contacts and could damage you. So you should offer payment over a number of years (try for 10) if the owner contractually agrees not to compete against you and, additionally, agrees to offer advice and assistance after you assume ownership.

Another important reason you should seek a noncompete covenant: payments under it are tax-deductible business expenses. This reduces considerably your cost of acquiring the paper. For the seller, a "noncompete" often is attractive because payments are received over a period of years and may be taxed at lower rates.

Caution: If too much of the total consideration is paid in noncompete, the Internal Revenue Service can rule that the covenant represents buyer-seller evasion of taxes and it can therefore impose higher taxes. Allocating no more than 29 percent of total consideration to noncompete is about right, but seek expert tax counsel on where exactly to peg your offer.

You also must decide how much to pay down. Sellers will decide based on their tax brackets. For buyers, of course, the smaller the down payment, the better.

Now, you have researched Dream Publishing and want to get your thinking straight on whether it is an attractive acquisition target.

1. Let's say you project that you can increase revenues 15 percent in the first year and 11 percent annually thereafter. The paper is in a growing market and its sales staff is poorly led; you can show the staff how to exploit sales potential better.

2. Let's say you project that you can reduce costs substantially in the first year because the owner—and his wife—are paying themselves handsomely and both drive company cars. You can eliminate those plus other high costs and serve as publisher at a $190,000 reduction in first-year costs. You think you can hold payroll increases to (worst-case scenario) 8 percent annually thereafter; newsprint and circulation costs will grow at 10 percent; and all other costs will increase 8 percent annually.

3. Capital expenditures will average $10,000 annually for your first five years, $20,000 for the next five (the press is in good shape and a new electronic editing system has been installed recently).

4. You will depreciate fixed assets straightline over 10 years.

5. The day you take over, you'll draw off $43,780 in cash and securities that the paper has in the bank.

6. Now, you're still worried about the commercial printing revenue. To be safe, discount 50 percent or $549,414 of it from the $2,809,268 in sales. Thus you come up with an "adjusted" figure of $2,259,854 for 1995 sales, and you will base your offer on that. Obviously, Dream Publishing and its market are not "hot." Let us say your research indicates that two times adjusted sales is correct. That yields an offer of $4,519,708 as total consideration.

Structure your offer this way: Of the total, 24 percent or $1,084,729 will be in noncompete; 14 percent or $151,862 to owner's wife because she was assistant publisher. Her noncompete and owner's $932,867 will be paid in equal annual installments over 10 years (no interest will be paid because a noncompete is for services rendered, not a note payable). With 24 percent of total consideration allocated to noncompetes, you must plan how to pay the remaining $3,434,979. Allocate 29 percent or $996,143 to down payment and pay the rest over 10 years in equal annual installments. Offer, say, 8 percent annual interest on the unpaid balances.

Now sit back and think. It is here, in my experience, that you may have convinced yourself the acquisition is a good deal and be emotionally committed to proceeding—and damn the cost. So, let your financial adviser calmly and objectively "run out" the projection to determine if the acquisition will be viable financially.

This involves projecting 10 years ahead with all the research and estimates made so far. Revenue and expense in years ahead, interest to be paid on any money borrowed for the purchase, payments to former owners, tax implications—all go into calculating how long to *payback*, or how many years it will take to recover acquisition costs and establish the paper's profitability.

No industrywide formula exists for what is an acceptable payback period. Some buyers require new acquisitions to "turn positive"—make contributions to profit—in two to three years; others, particularly private owners who need not justify deals to shareholders, plan to wait longer for payback. But let's assume payback for Dream Publishing works out at 6.3 years and that is acceptable. Now—but only now—are you ready to talk with the owner about money and terms.

HOW TO NEGOTIATE A DEAL

Acquisition lore has it that one buyer successfully negotiated a daily newspaper acquisition, from start to finish, in 30 minutes. Often, however, they take years. So plan your negotiations carefully.

Open Negotiations Cautiously

Here are guidelines for negotiating an acquisition:

Be patient. Newspapers are not widget factories to be bought and sold coldly. Many owners feel strong loyalty to their papers and communities. They want to know you and how you operate—how you will treat the paper. Before talking sale, give the owner time to become comfortable with you.

Before talking money and terms, determine if the owner is truly ready to sell. Some owners will lead you through costly and time-consuming discussions simply because they (a) love to negotiate and (b) want to determine their paper's market value.

Try to gain the owner's commitment to negotiate exclusively with you. The owner may take your offer to your competitor, who will bid up your price, but try for agreement that you won't be used that way. You don't want the owner revealing your negotiating strategy and pricing technique; your competitor would beat you with that knowledge if you met again on the acquisition circuit.

Open with an offer (a) high enough to capture the owner's attention but (b) low enough to give yourself upward negotiating room. Don't *ever* open with your "best" offer. Be prepared to prove, with your own balance sheet or banker's references, your ability to pay for the acquisition. The owner may demand security for unpaid notes, perhaps that you pledge back the newspaper stock if you default. He may ask for your *personal endorsement* of the notes. Beware: That means your personal assets—home, car—may be in the deal, along with your company's assets.

Present a package offer and require package acceptance. Don't agree, for example, on amount of down payment and leave open the interest rate on unpaid balances. You cannot agree to one without knowing your cost in the other.

In negotiations, each conversation, even over coffee, can be a serious probe into the other side's thinking. Listen carefully. A seemingly innocuous comment by the seller might signal where negotiations are headed. Be careful what you say. The seller is listening for signals, too, and your most offhand comment can go on the record.

Contract terms often are negotiated orally, almost informally, long before either side pushes forward a sheet of paper. So don't mention over coffee 10 percent interest on unpaid balances and expect to later write a contract offering 8 percent. That, simply put, is bad faith and can ruin your deal.

A formal *sales contract* will be signed at the *closing* when actual transfer of ownership takes place. It must be highly detailed to preclude any misunderstanding, and that makes it an unyielding document in your direct negotiations with seller. It's much better to lay before the seller a shorter yet precise and binding *offer to purchase.*

A Purchase Offer Checklist

The purchase offer is just that—your signed offer to buy the paper under certain terms and conditions. You can be committed once you present it to the seller, so your attorney must be consulted on its language. Let's outline a purchase offer.

1. State precisely what you offer to purchase—i.e., "100 percent of the stock of Dream Publishing, Inc., which publishes *The Dream Weekly News.*"
2. Definitively state the price—$3,434,979 (noncompetes are handled in a separate document) and how it will be paid (29 percent down with remainder paid in equal annual installments over 10 years). Notes on the unpaid amount will carry 8 percent simple (not compound) interest. Notes will be subordinated to any bank debt you already have. That means your bank gets paid before Dream Publishing does in a financial crunch. Your bank will insist on this; seller will argue against it. But subordination is the rule with most buyers.

3. State seller's responsibility for any undisclosed or unknown liabilities that arise later from conditions under seller's ownership. Specify that the cost of any such liabilities will be deducted from your future payments to seller.

4. Peg the entire deal, its term and conditions, to that balance sheet and profit and loss statement delivered to you earlier by the seller. Remember, a company's financial condition changes hourly. Nothing prevents the seller from drawing off that $43,780 in cash and securities after you get the balance sheet—unless you make seller warrant in this purchase offer that you are getting a company whose current financial condition is as good as or better than represented on the balance sheet. Include language committing the seller to deliver a company with current assets not less than—and current liabilities no greater (seller will press, of course, for upward adjustment of price if liabilities are lower or assets higher at closing).

5. Include language in which the seller warrants as true the facts about the newspaper delivered in negotiations. Seller should warrant accuracy of circulation figures; details of any union contracts, employment agreements or pending lawsuits; that all financial statements accurately and fairly represent the company's financial condition; and that the newspaper's equipment is in good operating condition and comes in the deal.

6. Language should assign to the seller any liabilities you aren't assuming. That should include all taxes prior to closing; any broker, legal or accounting fees incurred by the seller; and unpaid vacation pay or advertising discounts earned before closing.

7. Hold the seller to operating the paper normally between signing of purchase offer and closing. That is, seller should not rush back to the office and celebrate by giving the entire staff raises. You will have to pay those increases unless the agreement prohibits them.

8. Be sure the language requires all shareholders to sign. You may not get 100 percent of stock unless they do.

A Noncompete Checklist

Along with the seller's signed acceptance of your purchase offer, you must obtain signed agreement to the consultancy and noncompete covenant to be executed at closing. (With Dream Publishing, of course, we'll need noncompete agreements from both husband and wife.) The elements are as follows:

1. Define what the owner will *not* do. Don't exclude the owner simply from "newspaper publishing" in Dream Publishing's home county. The owner should agree "not to compete in, finance or support any advertising-related activity," not just publishing. Exclude the owner from competing in all counties contiguous to the home county or any other area you think appropriate.

2. Specify what the owner *will* do under the consultancy. That can include smoothing community and staff relations during transition to your ownership, meeting with advertisers or performing other tasks both of you agree would help ensure the newspaper's efficient, profitable operation.

3. Specify the payments you will make for services rendered. For Valley Publishing's owner, that will be $932,867 over 10 years or $93,286 annually. That's high, so assign real duties to the owner and make sure they are performed. Otherwise, the IRS might challenge the covenant as disguised purchase price and not a separate contract for services rendered.

4. Sometimes, the buyer retains the owner under an *employment contract* to continue as publisher. That contract would be separate, with consultancy/noncompete beginning on termination of employment. But that's academic for Dream Publishing's owner. He's going fishing.

Congratulations. Subject to closing and signing the actual sales agreement, you have bought a newspaper!

SUMMARY

If you want quick experience in all dimensions of management, weekly newspapering gives you best opportunities. A weekly manager "does it all." And, if you want to own a paper, weeklies offer your best chance for relatively low-cost entry into entrepreneurship. (But even the cheapest weeklies are expensive these days.)

Weeklies of free or paid circulation now number more than 7,400. Circulation is over 55.4 million. Weekly ad revenue is hard to calculate, but probably is $5 billion or more annually. Weeklies are the dominant ad medium in many small towns and strong competitors in large-city markets.

Two environments are best for a weekly newspaper: (a) affluent suburbs, where weeklies can offer in-depth coverage dailies cannot match, and (b) in groups owned by publishers who achieve economy of scale by publishing several newspapers from a single facility.

There is no "average" weekly newspaper, but studies by the Inland Press Association show many weeklies are profitable. To buy a weekly, be prepared to pay two times annual sales volume, or thereabouts.

Your preacquisition homework must include analysis of the target paper, its market and it competitors. Financial reports for at least the preceding three years must be studied and projections made on cost of acquisition and when the new property will "turn positive," or start producing profit. Your offer to purchase must be structured carefully to meet the seller's tax needs and deliver maximum after-tax dollars.

RECOMMENDED READING

Another look at *How to Read a Financial Report* by Merrill Lynch Pierce Fenner & Smith Inc., One Liberty Plaza, 165 Broadway, New York, N.Y. 10080, would be wise for any nonaccountant reader setting forth on the acquisition trail.

Acquisition developments (and publicly owned newspaper groups) are covered superbly by John Morton, analyst for Lynch, Jones & Ryan, 1037 Thirtieth St., N.W., Washington, D.C. 20007, through *Newspaper Newsletter.*

Weekly newspaper affairs are reported by *Publisher's Auxiliary.* Three trade groups specialize in weeklies: National Newspaper Association, 1627 K St., N.W., Suite 400, Washington, D.C. 20006–1790; Suburban Newspapers of America, 111 E. Wacker Drive, Ill. 60601; and Inland Press Association, Inc., 777 Busse Highway, Park Ridge, Ill. 60068.

Also, note D. Earl Newsom, ed., *The Newspaper* (Englewood Cliffs, N.J.: Prentice-Hall, 1981); and, by editors of the *Harvard Post, How to Produce a Small Newspaper* (Boston: Harvard Common Press, 1983). Both offer much to students of community newspapers.

NOTE

1. Survey results used with permission from Inland Press Association, Inc., 777 Busse Highway, Park Ridge, IL 60068.

NAME INDEX

SUBJECT INDEX